ATHLETI~~CS~~

EDITOR: RON PICKERING　　**COMPILER:** MEL WATMAN

QUEEN ANNE PRESS
LONDON

© Brickfield Publications 1975

Edited and designed for Queen Anne Press by Graeme Wright.
Photographs, unless otherwise credited, supplied by E. D. Lacey.

All rights reserved. No part of this publication may be reproduced, stored in a retrieval system, or transmitted in any form or by any means electrical, mechanical, photocopied, recorded or otherwise without the prior permission of the publisher.

Published by The Queen Anne Press Limited
12 Vandy Street, London EC2A 2EN

Filmset and printed in Great Britain by
Cox & Wyman Ltd, London, Fakenham and Reading

Cover pictures: Britain's European gold medallists. Front cover: Brendan Foster, his devastating burst still to come, leads an uncertain 5000 metres field, with silver medallist Lasse Viren (blue vest) tucked in close. Back cover: A relaxed Ian Thompson acknowledges the tumultuous reception that greeted him as he entered the stadium over one and a half minutes ahead of his nearest rival. Double gold medallist Alan Pascoe repeated his 400 metres hurdles success in the Commonwealth Games in Christchurch earlier in the year. Pascoe's second European gold came in the 4 × 400m relay (l-r) Alan Pascoe, Glen Cohen, David Jenkins, Bill Hartley.

Contents

Foreword from Birds Eye 5
Foreword from David Hemery 6
Review and acknowledgements 7

1974 IN RETROSPECT

Abbreviations 12
January 13
Highlights
February 15
British Indoor Championships, Women's National Cross-Country Championships, UK v Spain (indoors), UK v Netherlands (women), Highlights
March 23
National Cross-Country Championships, European Indoor Championships, International Cross-Country Championships, Highlights
April 32
Highlights
May 34
West Germany v UK walking match, WAAA Pentathlon and Relay Championships, Inter-Regional Championships, Highlights
June 41
AAA Decathlon, Romania v UK (women), AAA Marathon, UK v East Germany, American AAU Championships, Poland v UK v Canada, Highlights
July 55
East German Championships, USA v USSR, International Decathlon/ Pentathlon meeting, AAA Championships, WAAA Championships, USSR Championships, UK v Czechoslovakia (men), UK v Czechoslovakia v Netherlands (women), Sweden v UK, Highlights
August 75
AAA Junior/Youth Championships, BAAB International Meeting, Spain v UK v Portugal (juniors), Norway v UK v Benelux, British League Final, Highlights
September 86
European Championships, Coca-Cola International Meeting, UK v West Germany (juniors), Pye Cup Finals, UK v Finland, France v UK decathlon/ pentathlon, Highlights
October, November, December 109
Highlights
1974 English Schools Championships 111

Whither the Olympics 117
Register of UK Clubs 121
Specialist Clubs 185
African Genesis 186
The European Champions 191
Those Diabolical Steroids 197
Who's Who in the British Team 202
Records 227
World, European, Commonwealth, UK, and Junior
World and British Rankings 234
1974 and All-time
Learning from the Stars 267
Discus, Javelin, Shot
The European Cup 274
1975 European Cup 280
Draw and Form Chart

ATHLETICS 75

Directory of All-Weather Athletic
  Tracks in Great Britain   283
Official Bodies, Officers, and Addresses 286
SPECIAL FEATURES
Whither the Olympics – James Coote
African Genesis – Bruce Tulloh
Those Diabolical Steroids – Ron
  Pickering
The European Cup – Cliff Temple

Foreword from Birds Eye

Not everything has been cheerful in the world of business and economics since the publication of *Athletics 74*, but fortunately the gloom has not dampened the spirits or enthusiasm of our athletes. We witnessed excellent performances at home and abroad, especially from our bank of talented youngsters, including the glamorous Donna Murray and Lesley Kiernan, and the determined Steve Ovett.

On several occasions during the past year I have spoken out against the dismal johnnies who delight in spreading misery, and I have pointed out that an attitude of optimism and confidence is one way of putting some of the greatness back into Britain. What better examples than the efforts of athletes like Brendan Foster, Alan Pascoe, David Jenkins, Ian Thompson, Joyce Smith, and Andrea Lynch, all of whom performed so brilliantly and helped to attract big crowds back to our stadiums.

The examples set by our current crop of world-beaters will surely encourage other young people to become interested and to participate in sport. Without doubt, fresh air and exercise provide the perfect opportunity for the beneficial release of youthful energy.

No one has done more in getting this message across than Dr Roger Bannister, and this foreword would not be complete without a tribute to his work. He has contributed so much to British sport and his efforts have made people much more aware of the importance and benefits of recreation and leisure activities.

We at Birds Eye are proud to be associated with the encouragement of sport in general and of athletics in particular. I feel sure that this second Yearbook will help to stimulate wider interest and ultimately even higher standards.

Kenneth Webb

Chairman
Birds Eye Foods Limited

Foreword from David Hemery

I was fascinated and impressed with *Athletics 74* and have spent hours reading the detailed and comprehensive review of the athletics year just past. Each season and event is clearly presented and the pictures bring back vivid memories of the personalities. I told Ron Pickering that I found it the most engaging book since the *Guinness Book of Records* – so now I find myself writing the foreword for *Athletics 75*.

Athletics can be enjoyed at many different levels. We have all been excited by watching our greatest athletes winning medals at the latest European Championships. If you are one who has a feeling that you'd like to try athletics to see how far you can go, I urge you to join a club and start competing.

This book can be a valuable tool, especially for the newcomer – to the sport or to an area. Clubs have cooperated in providing a fine survey of their facilities, coaches, training time, and a contact for further information. This is a great start in this difficult area of communication. I urge the young athlete to find a club and, if possible, a coach who has specialist knowledge. If you would like to find a coach in your area, why not write to the British Amateur Athletic Board, 70 Brompton Road, London SW3 1EE, asking them to put you in touch with your nearest qualified coach or ex-international athlete. Both will almost always be willing to help, at least with some advice on basic training and technique in their speciality.

Athletics 75 includes some thought-provoking and interesting articles. As a reference book and as a fine record of each athletics year, it is a must for clubs, track nuts, competitors, and followers alike.

Well done to the producers – and thank you to the sponsors.

David Hemery

Pickering's Pot-Pourri

Any one year that includes both a Commonwealth Games and a European Championships has to be a bit special – it enriches the record books, makes for comparison, and keeps us all busy. I confess that my involvement with track and field is such that, when asked to reflect on the past year, I naturally remember the highlights. I've forgotten the drab and prefer not to be reminded of the ugly, if there was any.

I left Christchurch in a wave of euphoria, because the Commonwealth Games are so special and because New Zealand had organised them so well. Since, in my own role as a television commentator, I am invariably involved in the business of instant commitment without the luxury of time for reflection, I get enormous pleasure from returning home to read what the pressmen have had to say about the events; and in particular their follow-up pieces in retrospection. Surprisingly, commentators and pressmen are usually complementary to one another – if rarely complimentary – but by the time I had caught up with my wife's carefully preserved press cuttings I began to wonder if we had all been covering the same event. I've already confessed to being very protective about the Commonwealth Games, but did they really 'Explode into Track War' as claimed in the *Sunday Express*, and had, as John Jackson wrote in the *Sunday Mirror*, 'Black Power taken control of the Commonwealth Games?'

I gathered it was all about David Bedford's tussle with the Kenyans in the 10,000 metres, in which he was rather badly spiked: a race which David Herd in the *Evening Standard* saw as 'A savage race filled with hate and venom' and where 'Bedford's socks were soaking with blood where the Kenyans had spiked him during 25 laps'. I am not sure how many times per lap he was spiked, but certainly John Goodbody of the *Evening News* saw the '6 inch gashes in his sunburnt legs'. To be fair, we were all het up about the Kenyans' tactics, but the world record holder ran badly – sadly – got his longer legs tangled with Juma and Mose, and paid the penalty. I don't honestly think tribal war began all over again when John Davies and Evans Mogaka tangled in the steeplechase, and I do believe the Jury of Appeal came up with the right result.

Few people could have been more disappointed than I was that David Bedford didn't win, for I had tipped him to do so. I still believe that he will win a big one yet, especially if he can get his injury problems resolved.

When the Christchurch Games came to their glorious end at that marvellous closing ceremony, the Kenyans and the British athletes were as happily entwined as the rest, which is why the Commonwealth Games are unique in terms of atmosphere and ambience. Long may they remain so, and long may their standards continue to rise to produce such epic races, or rather runs, as Filbert Bayi's 1500 metres!

Of course, another reason we get so involved when a character like David Bedford races is because of his enormous personal rapport with his supporters, despite any unpredictable qualities. This year, however, the mantle of No. 1 crowd puller has been firmly worn by Brendan Foster. Who else could fill a stadium at Gateshead with ecstatic followers on the same day that Sunderland played Newcastle at Roker Park? These same supporters carried their banners 'Howay Big Bren' to Rome and were amply rewarded on each occasion. It is this charisma that earned him the title of BBC's TV Personality of the Year over even the impeccable records of Ian Thompson or triple gold medallist Alan Pascoe, each of whom has his own wide band of followers but on a more widespread basis.

Brendan's identity is with the North-East of England and it is total. There he has literally transformed interest in athletics and is a household name with an enormous following. Asked recently why he turned down a direct offer of £26,000 to turn professional, he said: 'Because of all the work I have done and because a lot of people in the North-East have the faith that I can win in Montreal.' That's a faith that spreads far beyond the North-East, and this coming season should provide some excellent pointers in 1976. One can only hope that, like David Bedford's, Brendan's early season set-back with back trouble will quickly be resolved.

Certainly 1974 was the year of the individual rather than of the team, for our British men's team did not win a single match and it was sad to see us going down to Poland, Czechoslovakia, Sweden, and Finland.

The three great individual gold medals in Rome came from athletes who had already had great personal success in Christchurch. While it must have helped to have been surrounded by good team spirit, their success was a measure of their individual qualities rather than a reflection on Britain's place in world athletic standings at the moment. Each did much to dispel the myths about peaking twice in the same year, which left little excuse for those who didn't find their form on the big occasion. But then perhaps they have learnt the secret of 'biorhythms', or was it the year of Pollen 'B'?

Few will deny that we have waited long enough for reliable testing procedures for anabolic steroids, and there still remains a good deal of doubt about their efficiency or validity, especially in terms of retro-active testing. Nevertheless, it is worth reminding everyone that the new legislation came into force on 1 January 1975. By the time this book leaves the publishers, we may well know what sort of attitudes the legislators will take regarding their use. Certainly, as a practice, it must be stopped, but will the tests be aimed at safeguarding the health of our athletes, and, therefore, will the tests be for *all* events and *all* age groups? Or will the centre of attention again be on the poor old shot-putters? Spare them a thought, for last year it was they who carried British athletics to the public for the first half of the season at least.

Geoffrey Capes, with Mike Winch in very close attendance, did us all proud. Geoff's European Indoor title, the first in a throwing event since Arthur Rowe's in

1958; his victory over Al Feuerbach; and his prodigious 70ft 1½in to reach sixth in the world's all-time list: all were monumental milestones in British athletics. For all those who wrote off the throwing events in Rome, and who feel that the record books are about to be put back a decade or more because of the new tests for steroids, I am certain that they are in for a shock and that their cynicism will be largely unfounded. Nothing will please me more than to see the throwers have a great season, tests and all.

Having said that, the throwing scene will never quite be the same without Howard and Rosemary Payne. It is very doubtful that their proliferation of athletic vests for Great Britain will ever be matched by a husband and wife team. Yet this was no graceful retirement in terms of slowing down, for both went out at their best. Howard in particular finally retired at 43 once he had achieved his lifelong ambition of reaching both 70 metres and 230ft. Is it too much to hope that after a lifetime of dedication they, too, may be appropriately rewarded.

The other significant piece of legislation that came in during the year was the IOC's Rule 26 concerning eligibility; which in effect means that an athlete may be fully maintained by his association but cannot take financial reward for material profit. This provides adequate cover for those much envied countries such as West Germany, Finland, Sweden, and Canada who provide annual grants to their athletes on a sliding scale of ability to cover all training costs and travel to competition.

The advantages to the athlete are obvious, but the advantage to the association is one which our own governing body might well envy, for in effect it forms a contract, between the athlete and the association, which in turn guarantees the athlete turning out for the most important fixtures of the year. This is why Finland came over in strength, yet there is no question that a full Great Britain team would have beaten them if all our best athletes had turned out. It was no excuse to say that we didn't run because the rooms were too crowded in Rome two weeks earlier, which was the reason given in one press report. No one can deny they were, but the whole business of getting the crowds back to athletics and providing the right competition for all our athletes has to be a balanced compromise between those 12-event spectaculars, with the one or two tolerated field events, and the full-scale internationals with all events against carefully chosen opposition. Preferably there should be at least three teams taking part, and the meeting could include a small number of high quality invitation races with larger numbers, or alternatively have three or four athletes per team in the more popular middle-distance races – and all well presented.

If 1974 was the year the crowds came back to British athletics, it must be remembered that there were extenuating circumstances. Everyone in Britain wanted to pay tribute to those who had competed so well in Rome, and to have them all together with a host of other stars from all over the world in a much publicised meeting would have been a guaranteed success in any year. Even so, the IAC/Coca-Cola Meeting was well organised and a great number of people worked extremely hard for their much deserved success. Similarly, the Highland Games in Edinburgh and the key events at

Cwmbran and Gateshead achieved much the same success because they were given the backing of the athletes and because everything possible was done to publicise the meetings.

We need a judicious mixture of the desirable and the very necessary, well presented and publicised, spread around the various hot-beds of athletic interest. In the coming year this could do much for our sport at grass roots level, as well as for the international scene. However, with the calendar of fixtures now being stretched to as many as 15 so-called major meetings, the recipe for success cannot all revolve around repetition races for our top six star names. This is a suicidal course, for they will never make Montreal and our triple and high jumpers will remain in obscurity for ever. Surely it is now a case of going back to the drawing board with all the interested parties present, with the individual requirements of these key athletes being as carefully monitored as the needs of the team as a whole. I am convinced there is a great British public out there waiting for first-class sporting entertainment in the safe convivial company that track and field can provide. Once we get that, we will have no shortage of sponsors and, who knows, we may even be able to establish our grants system for deserving athletes to meet travel and training costs. It is a heartening thought.

It is heartening, too, to think that Britain might field an international team which includes Brendan Foster, Ian Stewart, David Bedford, David Black, and Tony Simmons competing in the same match. Come to think of it, given most of them in England's team, we could win back the International Cross-Country title from Belgium, with the individual title going to Ian Stewart. What a delight it is to see him back, and by the time this comes off the press we shall know his intentions.

The year was not without its sad notes, for among the tragic losses of many old friends I already miss the serenity of Maureen Dyson, and I really did think that John Cooper was indestructible. Just to think of him now brings back memories of a great era that included Volgograd in 1963 and Tokio in 1964.

However, I look forward to the Russians coming this season to the European Cup semi-final, and the final later, in Nice, if we make it; to Britain's first seven-foot high jump, preferably by either Brian Burgess or Milton Palmer, who at 16 years of age will really put the thing in perspective; and to a further positive growth of the sport at club level.

Now that Red China have a foot in the door, I hope they find a way to open it, may Black Africa continue to emerge, and may the government of South Africa become sensitive to the difference between multi-national and multi-racial just as her athletes would wish.

One further wish is that Britain's undisputed club champions, Cardiff AAC, get their much needed track in the capital city of the Principality. My final word must be of thanks to all concerned with the publication of *Athletics 75*, particularly to the sponsors, and to Mel Watman, who once again has saved me from carrying a year's copies of *Athletics Weekly* half way round the world.

R.J.Pickering
January 1975

1974 in Retrospect

A calendar of the major meetings and championships
held during 1974

Compiled by Mel Watman

ATHLETICS 75

Abbreviations

Aus	Australia	Ken	Kenya
Aut	Austria	Les	Lesotho
Bah	Bahamas	Lux	Luxembourg
Bar	Barbados	Ma	Mali
Bel	Belgium	Mal	Malaysia
Ber	Bermuda	Mau	Mauritius
Bol	Bolivia	Mex	Mexico
Bot	Botswana	Mgy	Malagasy
Bra	Brazil	Mli	Mali
BrH	British Honduras	Mor	Morocco
Bul	Bulgaria	Mwi	Malawi
Bur	Burma	NI	Northern Ireland
Cam	Cameroons	Nig	Nigeria
Can	Canada	NK	North Korea
CAR	Central African Republic	Nor	Norway
Cey	Ceylon (Sri Lanka)	NZ	New Zealand
Cha	Chad	Pak	Pakistan
Cub	Cuba	Phi	Philippines
Cze	Czechoslovakia	Pol	Poland
Dah	Dahomey	Por	Portugal
Den	Denmark	Rom	Romania
Dom	Dominican Republic	SA	South Africa
EG	East Germany (GDR)	Sen	Senegal
Egy	Egypt	Sco	Scotland
Eir	Republic of Ireland	Sin	Singapore
Eng	England	SK	South Korea
Eth	Ethiopia	SL	Sierra Leone
Fij	Fiji	Som	Somalia
Fin	Finland	Sov	Soviet Union (USSR)
Fra	France	Spa	Spain
Gab	Gabon	Swe	Sweden
Gam	Gambia	Swi	Switzerland
GB	Great Britain	Syr	Syria
Gha	Ghana	Tai	Taiwan
Gre	Greece	Tan	Tanzania
Guy	Guyana	Tha	Thailand
Hon	Honduras	Tog	Togoland
Hkg	Hong Kong	Tri	Trinidad & Tobago
Hol	Netherlands	Tun	Tunisia
Hun	Hungary	Tur	Turkey
Ice	Iceland	Uga	Uganda
Ind	India	UK	United Kingdom
Irq	Iraq	Uru	Uruguay
Irn	Iran	USA	United States of America
Isr	Israel	Wal	Wales
Ita	Italy	WG	West Germany
IvC	Ivory Coast	Yug	Yugoslavia
Jam	Jamaica	Zai	Zaire (Belgian Congo)
Jap	Japan	Zam	Zambia

Right: *Jannette Roscoe takes over from Ruth Kennedy for the third leg of England's gold medal winning 4 × 400 metres relay at the 1974 Commonwealth Games.*

January

JANUARY HIGHLIGHTS

It was an important month for shot-putting. Geoff Capes set a Commonwealth record of 20.59 metres (67' 6¾") at Crystal Palace on 6 January, improving to 20.64 metres (67' 8¾") in the more congenial climate of Timaru, New Zealand, on 19 January. Capes' predecessor as Britain's top shot-putter, Jeff Teale, was banned from all further international competition – although he had retired anyway. The British Amateur Athletic Board took action after the 1970 Commonwealth silver medallist had stated in a newspaper interview that he used anabolic steroids during his international career. It was the first such disqualification on record. George Woods (USA) established a world indoor best of 21.30 metres (69' 10¾") at Portland on 26 January, but that was merely the prelude to much greater things.

The British Commonwealth Games were staged in Christchurch from 25 January to 2 February. Detailed results appeared in *Athletics 74★* but here is a checklist of winners and UK record breakers:

100m/200m: D. Quarrie (Jam) 10.38/20.73. *400m:* C. Asati (Ken) 46.04. *800m:* J. Kipkurgat (Ken) 1:43.9. *1500m:* F. Bayi (Tan) 3:32.2 (world record) ... 7 – B. Foster (Eng) 3:37.6 (UK record). *5000m:* 1 B. Jipcho (Ken) 13:14.4; 2 Foster 13:14.6 (UK record). *10,000m:* R. Tayler (NZ) 27:46.4. *Mar:* I. Thompson (Eng) 2:09:12 (European best). *3000m Steeplechase:* 1 Jipcho 8:20.8; 2 J. Davies (Wal) 8:24.8 (UK record). *110m Hurdles:* F. Kimaiyo (Ken) 13.69. *400m Hurdles:* A. Pascoe (Eng) 48.83. *High Jump:* G. Windeyer (Aus) 2.16m (7' 1"). *Pole Vault:* D. Baird (Aus) 5.05m (16' 6¾"). *Long Jump:* A. Lerwill (Eng) 7.94m (26' 0¾"). *Triple Jump:* J. Owusu (Gha) 16.50m (54' 1¾"). *Shot:* G. Capes (Eng) 20.74m (68' 0½") (Commonwealth & UK record). *Discus:* R. Tait (NZ) 63.08m (206' 11"). *Hammer:* I. Chipchase (Eng) 69.56m (228' 2"). *Javelin:* C. Clover (Eng) 84.92m (278' 7") (Commonwealth & UK record). *Decathlon:* M. Bull (NI) 7417. *20 Miles Walk:* J. Warhurst (Eng) 2:35:23. *4 × 100m Relay:* Australia 39.31. *4 × 400m Relay:* Kenya 3:04.4. (Women) *100m/200m:* R. Boyle (Aus) 11.27/22.50. *400m:* 1 Y. Saunders (Can) 51.67; 2 V. Bernard (Eng) 51.94 (UK record). *800m:* C. Rendina (Aus) 2:01.1. *1500m:* G. Reiser (Can) 4:07.8. *100m Hurdles:* J. Vernon (Eng) 13.45. *High Jump:* B. Lawton (Eng) 1.84m (6' 0½"). *Long Jump:* M. Oshikoya (Nig) 6.46m (21' 2½"). *Shot/Discus:* J. Haist (Can) 16.12m (52' 10¾") & 55.52m (182' 2"). *Javelin:* P. Rivers (Aus) 55.48m (182' 0"). *Pentathlon:* M. Peters (NI) 4455. *4 × 100m Relay:* Australia 43.51. *4 × 400m Relay:* England (S. Pettett, R. Kennedy, J. Roscoe, V. Bernard) 3:29.2.

The death occurred of Clare Love, née Barnes (39), Irish international hurdler, and Ivy Thorpe, née Walker (62), who set a British 100 yards record of 11.3 in 1930.

★ *Athletics 74*, published by Queen Anne Press, 12 Vandy Street, London EC2A 2EN, price £1.95.

*England's Commonwealth Games gold medallists included Ian Chipchase (**above**) in the hammer, and Judy Vernon (**right**) in the 100 metres hurdles. Back home in February, Judy twice set a national indoor best at Cosford for the 60 metres hurdles.*

February

8, 9 February

BRITISH INDOOR CHAMPIONSHIPS

The 1973 British Indoor Championships suffered from the decision of most of the country's leading athletes to miss the meeting in order to concentrate on their long-term build-up towards Commonwealth Games selection. The 1974 edition of these Philips sponsored championships at RAF Cosford was adversely affected, too, by Christchurch. Of the 42 Commonwealth Games representatives who had entered, only 15 actually turned out – which was hardly surprising since the championships were being staged just a few days after the athletes' return from the other side of the world.

Judy Vernon and Geoff Capes, though, were in such fine fettle following their gold medal successes in New Zealand that even the long flight home and the time and climatic adjustments necessary could not blunt their performances.

Judy sliced a fifth of a second from Mary Peters' national best of 8.5 for 60 metres hurdles in her heat, and mustered another 8.3 clocking in the final. Not that she was in a class of her own, for Blondelle Thompson served notice of the astounding improvement that was to follow outdoors by running Judy to a tenth of a second, while both Ann Wilson and Lynne Ilott tied the former UK figures of 8.5. Judy also displayed a good turn of speed on the flat, losing only narrowly to Sonia Lannaman in the 60 metres.

The consistency of Geoff Capes' putting was impressive – 20.28 metres (66′ 6½″) in the second round backed by three other 66ft-plus efforts – and yet even that paled into insignificance alongside the news from America. The previous night (8 February) at Inglewood, California, George Woods had attained the incredible distance of 22.02 metres (72′ 2¾″) which not only shattered his week-old indoor record of 21.45 metres (70′ 4½″) but also topped Al Feuerbach's absolute world record, made outdoors, of 21.82 metres (71′ 7″). Still, by domestic standards, the Cosford competition was quite notable for personal bests achieved by John Alderson and Peter Tancred. Other than the women's hurdles, the only event to produce a record was the 60 metres, where Don Halliday's time of 6.7 equalled the UK all-comers best.

Another of Scotland's representatives in Christchurch, Rosemary Wright, helped make up for her disappointment there by leading all the way in the 800 metres, reaching the half-distance in a swift 60.7 and winning by over 30 metres. Similar tactics were employed in the 1500 metres by Norine Braithwaite, with dramatic results. Norine, who had to drop out of the Christchurch 1500 metres final (she was running a temperature of 104), should not really have raced at Cosford because an infected tooth was causing her trouble. Run she did, though, zipping through 800 metres in 2:14.5 and 1000 metres in 2:51.6 before starting to fall victim to her depleted physical resources. She won the race, but her last 400 metres took all of 83.8 seconds and she finished at a walk before collapsing. It was a brave but ill-advised performance and little more was heard of Norine for the rest of the year.

MEN

60m: 1 D. Halliday 6.7 (*eq UK all-comers best*); 2 G. Edwards 6.8; 3 G. Vince 6.9; 4 D. Roberts 6.9; 5 R. Turkington 7.0; 6 A. Cornaby 7.1.

400m: 1 J. Aukett 47.9; 2 F. McSweeney (Eir) 48.3; 3 I. Saunders 49.0; 4 J. McMillan 49.5.
800m: 1 R. Weatherburn 1:52.8; 2 S. Trew 1:53.6; 3 T. Whitbread 1:54.9; 4 J. Glover 1:55.2; 5 A. Dyke 1:56.6; 6 D. Guest 1:57.9.
1500m: 1 C. Thomas 3:53.4; 2 W. Wilkinson 3:53.9; 3 M. Fromant 3:54.0; 4 J. Carroll 3:54.0; 5 P. Shaw 3:56.4; 6 S. Mitchell 3:56.8.
3000m: 1 R. Smedley 8:00.0; 2 D. Fowles 8:03.6; 3 R. McDonald 8:12.6; 4 D. Nicholl 8:15.2; 5 R. Milne 8:18.0; 6 S. Lawrence 8:21.8.
2000m Steeplechase: 1 I. Gilmour 5:34.6; 2 P. Griffiths 5:35.4; 3 R. Harris 5:40.0; 4 R. McAndrew 5:48.4; 5 M. Dixon 5:52.4; 6 A. Murray (Eir) 5:53.2.
60m Hurdles: 1 C. J. Kirkpatrick 8.0; 2 G. Gower 8.1; 3 P. Kelly 8.2; 4 R. Palmer 8.4; 5 M. Jackson 8.7. A. McKenzie scratched.
High Jump: 1 J. Fanning (Eir) 2.01m (6' 7"); 2 M. Butterfield 1.95m (6' 4¾"); 3 A. Hepburn 1.92m (6' 3½"); 4 C. Boreham 1.88m (6' 2"); 5 eq M. Shorten, L. Spencer, & C. Wilson 1.88m.
Pole Vault: 1 M. Bull 5.00m (16' 4¾"); 2 A. Williams 4.60m (15' 1¼"); 3 D. Lease 4.60m; 4 S. Chappell 4.40m (14' 5¼"); 5 K. Stock 4.20m (13' 9¼"); 6 T. Gardner 4.20m.
Long Jump: 1 P. Scott 7.33m (24' 0¾"); 2 P. Templeton 7.10m (23' 3½"); 3 S. Wright 7.04m (23' 1¼"); 4 P. Turkington 6.88m (22' 7"); 5 T. Collins 6.79m (22' 3½"); 6 S. White 6.74m (22' 1½").
Triple Jump: 1 P. Blackburn 15.54m (51' 0"); 2 M. Lardi (Swi) 15.51m (50' 10¾"); 3 D. Johnson 15.06m (49' 5"); 4 S. Power 14.89m (48' 10½"); 5 W. Nowak 14.77m (48' 5½"); 6 P. Clarke 14.44m (47' 4½").
Shot: 1 G. Capes 20.28m (66' 6½"); 2 M. Winch 19.14m (62' 9½"); 3 J. Alderson 17.64m (57' 10½"); 4 P. Tancred 17.24m (56' 6¾"); 5 S. Clark 16.10m (52' 10"); 6 J. Watts 15.34m (50' 4").

WOMEN

60m: 1 S. Lannaman 7.5; 2 J. Vernon 7.5; 3 S. Colyear 7.6; 4 S. Pengilley 7.7; 5 G. Spurgin 7.7; 6 L. Drysdale 7.8.
400m: 1 S. Colyear 57.2; 2 L. Taylor 57.3. C. Warden & P. Lloyd scratched.
800m: 1 R. Wright 2:07.2; 2 C. McMeekin 2:12.7; 3 G. Garbutt 2:13.6; 4 P. Reece 2:13.6; 5 C. Stenhouse 2:19.8; 6 D. Brooks 2:27.1.
1500m: 1 N. Braithwaite 4:37.4; 2 C. Curthoys 4:42.2; 3 C. Readdy 4:44.4; 4 A. Roblin 4:56.3; 5 A. Morris 5:02.7.
60m Hurdles: 1 J. Vernon 8.3 (*UK national best*); 2 B. Thompson 8.4; 3 A. Wilson 8.5; 4 L. Ilott 8.5; 5 B. Ruttledge 8.6; 6 J. Honour 9.0.
High Jump: 1 A. Wilson 1.75m (5' 8¾"); 2 C. Mathers 1.75m; 3 eq S. Wright, P. Dimmock, R. Few, & T. Dainton 1.70m (5' 7").
Long Jump: 1 M. Chitty 5.79m (19' 0"); 2 J. Honour 5.78m (18'11¾"); 3 S. Reeve 5.60m (18' 4½"); 4 J. Stokoe 5.45m (17' 10½"); 5 B. Ruttledge 5.44m (17' 10¼"); 6 P. Williams 5.40m (17' 8¾").
Shot: 1 J. Kerr 13.23m (43' 5"); 2 D. Howarth 13.10m (42' 11¾"); 3 E. Elliott 12.69m (41' 7¾"); 4 S. Reeve 12.52m (41' 1"); 5 E. Jackson 11.19m (36' 8½"); 6 J. Gray 10.66m (34' 11¾").

23 February
WOMEN'S NATIONAL CROSS-COUNTRY CHAMPIONSHIPS

Rita Ridley, the winner from 1969 to 1972, regained the title from Joyce Smith at Western Park, Leicester, in one of the closest championship races in years. The former Commonwealth 1500 metres champion dropped Joyce, unable to train for three weeks because of a knee injury, on the last of the four laps and held on to win by the narrow margin of three seconds. There was a lively scrap for second place between Joyce, her clubmate Carol Gould, and Ann Yeoman. It was Carol, a mother of two, who found the most speed at the finish and she pipped Joyce for runner-up honours. Ann, a clear second with 400 metres to go, had to settle for fourth position.

The victory was some consolation for Rita, who failed only by a stride to qualify for Christchurch and the chance to defend her title. The girl who beat her for that place in the trial race, Sheila Carey, placed 11th at Leicester. Joan Allison, second to Rita in the 1970 Games and second again in 1974, finished 8th.

SENIOR CHAMPIONSHIP (5400m)

1	R. Ridley	20:03	20	P. Winter	21:20	39	M. Sonner	22:06
2	C. Gould	20:06	21	S. Brown	21:20	40	A. Briscoe	22:07
3	J. Smith	20:07	22	M. Coomber	21:21	41	J. Savage	22:08
4	A. Yeoman	20:10	23	P. Gunstone	21:27	42	B. Price	22:13
5	C. Tranter	20:14	24	V. Howe	21:28	43	M. Taylor	22:15
6	G. Goodburn	20:20	25	R. Young	21:30	44	D. Davis	22:17
7	D. Foreman (Eir)	20:22	26	T. Bateman	21:31	45	P. Turner	22:19
8	J. Allison	20:30	27	G. Adams	21:32	46	B. Stone	22:20
9	C. Haskett	20:32	28	P. Yeoman	21:33	47	J. Poyner	22:21
10	P. Yule	20:37	29	L. Bosher	21:36	48	J. Asgill	22:24
11	S. Carey	20:42	30	E. Brennan	21:38	49	K. Davis	22:33
12	M. O'Boyle	20:50	31	M. Beacham	21:40	50	P. Davis	22:36
13	P. Fowler	20:52	32	C. Readdy	21:44	**Team Placings**		
14	K. Barnett	20:55	33	H. Matthews	21:45	1	Barnet AC	50pts
15	B. Cardy	21:00	34	M. Speedman	21:48	2	Cambridge Harriers	92pts
16	A. Barrass	21:02	35	A. Pursglove	21:54	3	Stretford AC	109pts
17	A. Blake	21:06	36	M. Ashcroft	—	4	Aldershot F & D	110pts
18	C. McLoughlin	21:15	37	T. Wild	22:02	5	Brighton & Hove	139pts
19	B. Majumdar	21:16	38	J. Haigh	22:04	6	City of Stoke AC	190pts

INTERMEDIATES (4000m)

1	A-M. Robinson	15:14
2	B. Schofield	15:16
3	C. Boxer	15:22
4	A. Cherry	15:23
5	J. Williamson	15:25
6	M. Leisk	15:28

Team Placings
1	Aldershot F & D	44pts
2	Sale Harriers	83pts
3	Havering AC	139pts

JUNIORS (2800m)

1	H. Hill	10:27
2	G. Dainty	10:39
3	A. Tunnicliffe	10:45
4	W. Smith	10:48
5	C. Brace	10:48
6	J. Whiteley	10:51

Team Placings
1	Pitreavie AC	77pts
2	Bromsgrove & R	133pts
3	Cannock AC	178pts

GIRLS (2400m)

1	J. Priest	8:11
2	S. Johnson	8:21
3	F. Nixon	8:29
4	E. Harris	8:33
5	J. Moody	8:35
6	S. Samy	8:36

Team Placings
1	Sale Harriers	60pts
2	Leicester Coritanian	106pts
3	Cannock AC	109pts

Right: *Rita Ridley, here winning her fourth successive National cross-country championship in 1972, regained her title at Western Park, Leicester, in 1974.*

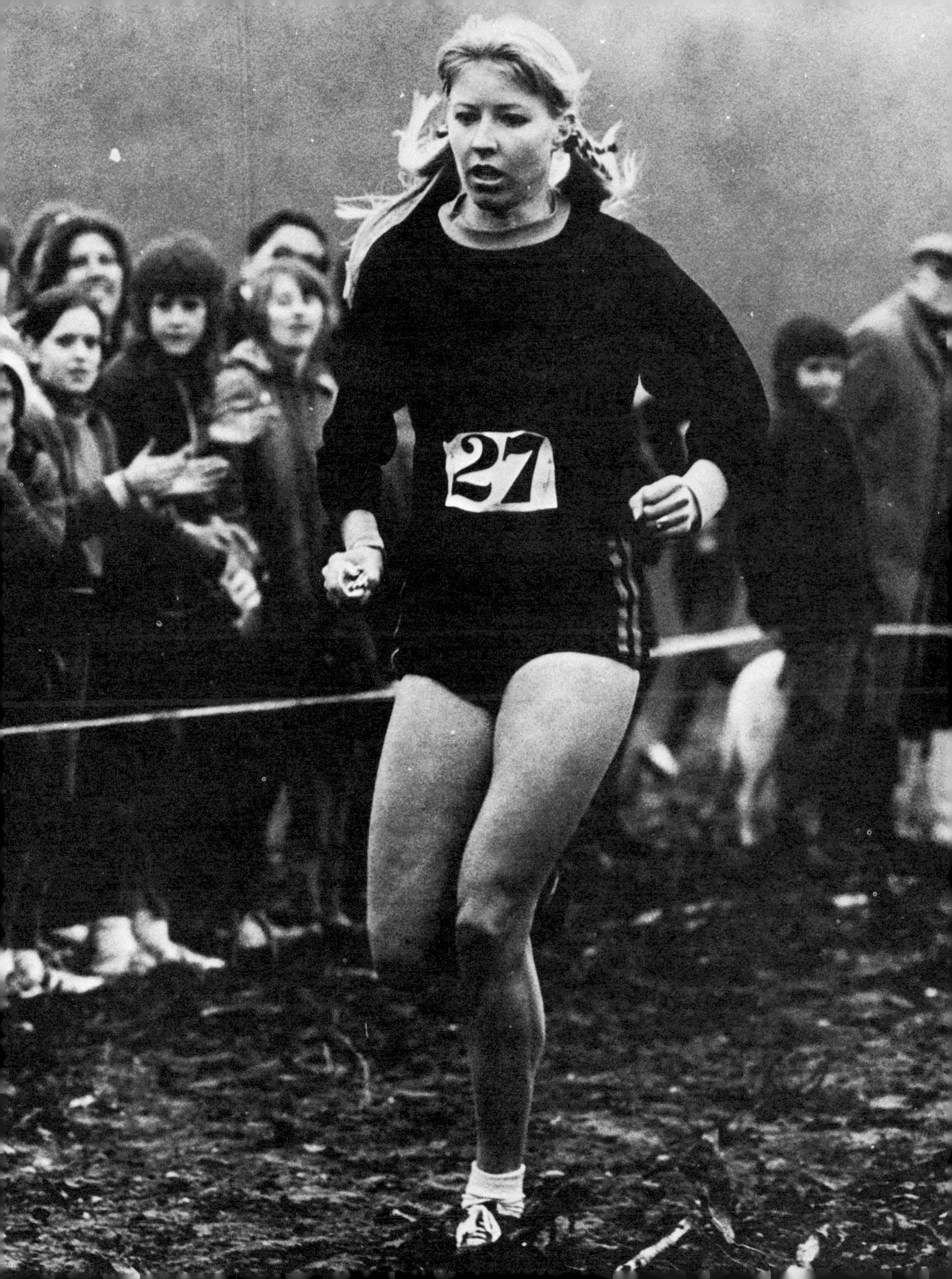
27

23 February
UK v SPAIN (MEN) – INDOORS
UK v NETHERLANDS (WOMEN)

The British men's team atoned for their unexpected defeat in Madrid the previous winter by slamming Spain 79–49 at RAF Cosford. The visitors' only successes came in the 3000 metres, high jump, and long jump. Star of the show was Geoff Capes who, by putting the shot 20.82 metres (68' 3¾"), became the first British athlete since Arthur Rowe over a decade earlier to establish a European 'record' in what may be termed a throwing event. Capes' opening heave exceeded Hartmut Briesenick's Continental indoor best and also was superior to the UK outdoor recorded he established in Christchurch. He followed up with two fouls, 20.08m (65' 10½"), 20.61m (67' 7½"), and 20.39m (66' 10¾").

The women's match against the Netherlands was even more one-sided, only the shot being won by the opposition. Judy Vernon maintained her sparkling form, reducing her 60 metres hurdles time by another tenth to 8.2 to equal an all-comers best held by none other than East Germany's Olympic champion, Annelie Ehrhardt. Other records came in the long jump where Ruth Martin-Jones produced the best ever indoor leap in Britain of 6.51 metres (21' 4¼"); in the 1500 metres where Mary Stewart celebrated her 18th birthday two days early with a runaway victory and UK junior best of 4:22.0; and in the 4 × 200 metres relay for which the British squad averaged 24.25 per leg.

MEN

60m: 1 D. Halliday (UK) 6.8; 2 L. Sanchez Paraiso (Spa) 6.8; 3 G. Edwards 6.9; 4 J. Sarrasqueta (Spa) 7.0.

400m: 1 J. Aukett (UK) 48.0; 2 J. Wilson (UK) 48.4; 3 A. Benito (Spa) 49.6; 4 L. Puertas (Spa) 49.9.

800m: 1 P. Lewis (UK) 1:50.0; 2 A. Fernandez (Spa) 1:50.8; 3 R. Weatherburn (UK) 1:51.2; 4 A. Ballbe (Spa) 1:52.2.

1500m: 1 R. Smedley (UK) 3:49.6; C. Thomas (UK) 3:51.3; 3 J. Martinez Bayo (Spa) 3:51.3; 4 J. Gordillo (Spa) 3:57.2.

3000m: 1 A. Burgos (Spa) 8:03.0; 2 R. Wilde (UK) 8:10.4; 3 D. Fowles (UK) 8:17.0; 4 J. Gonzales Amo (Spa) 8:17.2.

60m Hurdles: 1 C. Kirkpatrick (UK) 8.0; 2 G. Gower (UK) 8.1; 3 R. Cano (Spa) 8.3; 4 G. Calleja (Spa) 8.4.

4 × 200m: 1 UK 1:27.8 (D. Halliday, G. Vince, G. Cohen, J. Aukett); 2 Spain 1:28.9 (L. Sanchez Paraiso, A. Perez, F. Espinach, J. Sarrasqueta).

High Jump: 1 M. Perarnau (Spa) 2.06m (6' 9"); 2 D. Gonzales Berenguer (Spa) 2.00m (6' 6¾"); 3 C. Boreham (UK) 1.90m (6' 2¾"); 4 M. Butterfield (UK) 1.85m (6' 0¾").

Pole Vault: 1 M. Bull (UK) 5.05m (16' 6¾"); 2 B. Hooper (UK) 4.90m (16' 0¾"); 3 M. Consegal (Spa) 4.70m (15' 5"); E. Alonso (Spa) no height.

Long Jump: 1 R. Blanquer (Spa) 7.65m (25' 1¼"); 2 G. Hignett (UK) 7.58m (24' 10½"); 3 P. Scott (UK) 7.26m (23' 10"); 4 J. de Sola (Spa) 7.24m (23' 9").

Triple Jump: 1 P. Blackburn (UK) 15.73m (51' 7¼"); 2 A. Santamaria (Spa) 15.49m (50' 10"); 3 D. Johnson (UK) 15.45m (50' 8¼"); 4 R. Cid (Spa) 15.20m (49' 10½").

Shot: 1 G. Capes (UK) 20.82m (68' 3¾") (*European, UK national & UK all-comers best*); 2 M. Winch (UK) 19.59m (64' 3¼"); 3 M. Parajon (Spa) 15.95m (52' 4"); 4 B. Allende (Spa) 14.64m (48' 0½").

Match Result: UK 79, Spain 49.

WOMEN

60m: 1 A. Lynch (UK) 7.4; 2 S. Lannaman (UK) 7.4; 3 W. Schurink (Hol) 7.8; 4 E. van Lienen (Hol) 7.8.

400m: 1 R. Kennedy (UK) 55.7; 2 S. Colyear (UK) 56.9; 3 J. de Leeuw (Hol) 58.0; 4 T. Nieuwenhuizen (Hol) 58.1.

800m: 1 R. Wright (UK) 2:06.7; 2 W. Hillen (Hol) 2:08.9; 3 G. Dourass (UK) 2:11.3; 4 J. Kok (Hol) 2:12.1.

1500m: 1 M. Stewart (UK) 4:22.0; 2 J. van Gerwen (Hol) 4:31.2; 3 J. Lochhead (UK) 4:37.3; 4 G. van den Akker (Hol) 4:52.0.

60m Hurdles: 1 J. Vernon (UK) 8.2 (*UK national best, equals UK all-comers best*); 2 B. Thompson (UK) 8.4; 3 M. van Wissen (Hol) 8.4; 4 M. van Doorn (Hol) 8.8.

4 × 200m: 1 UK 1:37.0 (*UK all-comers & national best*) (A. Lynch 25.3, J. Vernon 24.1, W. Hill 24.2, S. Lannaman 23.4); 2 Netherlands 1:44.5 (W. Schurink, E. van Lienen, J. de Leeuw, M. van Doorn).

High Jump: 1 B. Lawton (UK) 1.79m (5′ 10½″); 2 A. Bouma (Hol) 1.79m; 3 A. Wilson (UK) 1.73m (5′ 8″); 4 M. van Laar (Hol) 1.73m.

Long Jump: 1 R. Martin-Jones (UK) 6.51m (21′ 4¼″) (*UK all-comers best*); 2 J. Honour (UK) 6.08m (19′ 11½″); 3 R. Koekoek (Hol) 5.86m (19′ 2¾″); 4 M. van Doorn (Hol) 5.84m (19′ 2″).

Shot: 1 E. Schalks (Hol) 14.59m (47′ 10½″); 2 B. Bedford (UK) 13.77m (45′ 2¼″); 3 R. Payne (UK) 13.53m (44′ 4¾″); 4 B. Bogers (Hol) 13.53m.

Match Result: UK 63, Netherlands 32.

FEBRUARY HIGHLIGHTS

The big news of the indoor season was the colossal shot-putting mark of 22.02 metres (72′ 2¾″) by the correspondingly huge George Woods – all 1.88 metres (6′ 2″) and 132kg (290 lb) of him – at Inglewood, California, on 8 February. It was the first 22-metre put in history, indoors or out. Woods, silver medallist in the last two Olympics, attributed his improvement to a new style that affords him both good speed and balance, allowing him to concentrate on other essentials of technique. Behind him, arch-rival Al Feuerbach, holder of the official world record (i.e. outdoor) of 21.82 metres (71′ 7″), made history too by becoming the first man to top 70 feet . . . and lose!

Neither Woods nor Feuerbach took part in the American AAU Indoor Championships in New York on 22 February, but the shot still produced a remarkable result when Terry Albritton, just turned 19 and with a previous best of 19.63 metres (64′ 5″), fired one out to 21.05 metres (69′ 0¾″)!

AAU winners: *60y:* H. Washington 6.0. *600y:* W. Williams 1:11.3. *1000y:* R. Wohlhuter 2:06.8. *Mile:* J. Walker (NZ) 4:01.6. *3 Miles:* R. Tayler (NZ) 13:08.6. *60y Hurdles:* T. Hill 6.9. *High Jump:* T. Woods 2.18m (7′ 2″). *Pole Vault:* V. Dias 5.38m (17′ 8″). *Long Jump:* J. Proctor 7.87m (25′ 10″). *Triple Jump:* M. Tiff 16.46m (54′ 0″). *Shot:* T. Albritton 21.05m (69′ 0¾″).

Many world indoor bests were registered during the month, among which were 6.4 for 60 metres by Vladimir Ostavnov (Sov), Dorel Cristudor (Rom), Zenon Nowosz (Pol), Valeriy Borzov (Sov), and Juris Silovs (Sov); 29.3 for 300 yards by Marshall Dill (USA); 45.9 for 400 metres by Alfons Brijdenbach (Bel); 3:55.0 for the mile by Tony Waldrop (USA); 13:05.2 for 3 miles and 13:30.8 for 5000 metres by Emiel Puttemans (Bel); and 6.8 for 55 metres hurdles by Rod Milburn (USA). Women's records included 7.08 for 60 metres by Irena Szewinska (Pol); 10.48 for 100 yards by Renate Stecher (EG); 1:18.4 for 600 yards by Yvonne Saunders

ATHLETICS 75

(Can); 2:01.8 for 800 metres and 2:02.3 for 880 yards by 15-year-old Mary Decker (USA); 4:12.2 for 1500 metres, 9:02.4 for 3000 metres and 9:39.4 for 2 miles by Francie Larrieu (USA); 7.9 for 60 metres hurdles by Grazyna Rabsztyn (Pol); 1.92m (6' 3½") for the high jump by Rita Kirst (EG); and 20.36m (66' 9¾") for the shot by Helena Fibingerova (Cze).

That 6.8 for 55 metres hurdles by Rod Milburn was his final race as an amateur. He, fellow Olympic champion Dave Wottle, and Commonwealth Games hero Ben Jipcho (Ken) were the three biggest names to join the International Track Association professional troupe. Best of the new 'pro' records were 6.7 for 60 yards hurdles – that's 5½ inches shorter than 55 metres – by Milburn and a pole vault of 5.53 metres (18' 1¾") by Steve Smith.

A breakthrough for women distance runners in the USA was achieved with the staging of the first official AAU marathon championship for them at San Mateo, California, on 9 February. The winner was Judy Ikenberry (31) in 2:55:17 . . . with 10-year-old Mary Etta Boytano filling fourth place in 3:01:15! Miki Gorman, the 'world record' holder at 2:46:36 in 1973, did not compete.

The death occurred of Fred Housden (81), an international high hurdler and pole vaulter of half a century ago who achieved his greatest fame as David Hemery's coach; Glenn Morris (61), the 1936 Olympic decathlon champion who later played Tarzan on the screen; Percy Reading (64), who covered a record 129 miles 749 yards in a 24-hour walk at White City in 1946; and Bert Healion (57) who was only inches away from the world record when he set an Irish hammer record of 58.80 metres (192' 11") in 1943.

Above: *Helena Fibingerova of Czechoslovakia set a world indoor best of 20.36 metres for the shot in February.* **Right:** *Scotland's Jim Brown, ninth in the National, finished a praiseworthy fourth in the International cross-country later in March.*

March

2 March

NATIONAL CROSS-COUNTRY CHAMPIONSHIPS

Dave Black's prospects looked bleak on the second of the three laps constituting the National 9 miles cross-country championship at Graves Park, Sheffield. Anxious to make up for the one blot on an otherwise astonishingly successful record – his downfall in the 1973 'National' when inexplicably he finished only 45th – the 21-year-old Midlander found himself in trouble again when he developed stitch and fell back to seventh place. 'I couldn't get going', he said. 'I thought I didn't have a dog's chance – like last year.'

Black did not panic. When the attack passed he gradually set about making up the 100 yards deficit. At the start of the last lap the leaders were Bernie Ford and Scottish champion Jim Brown, but Brown dropped back soon afterwards and Ford was joined by another Scot, Andy McKean. Meanwhile, Black's relentless pursuit continued: with a mile to go he had caught the leaders, and he proceeded to open up a winning gap of some 40 yards to complete one of the greatest finishing efforts in the race's history. Dave Bedford and Malcolm Thomas, the two previous champions, were not among the thousand starters, while Commonwealth marathon hero Ian Thompson reverted to his former anonymity by placing an unnoticed 162nd.

Neil Coupland of the Southampton club comes home to win the Junior title at the National cross-country championships.

NATIONAL CROSS-COUNTRY CHAMPIONSHIPS

SENIOR CHAMPIONSHIP (9 MILES)

1	D. Black	47:42	22	J. Wild	48:59	43	D. Nicholl	49:38
2	B. Ford	47:48	23	J. Eley	49:01	44	Graham Tuck	49:43
3	A. McKean	47:50	24	S. Kenyon	49:03	45	A. Holden	49:44
4	P. Standing	47:54	25	J. Temperton	49:05	46	C. Spedding	49:45
5	F. Briscoe	47:57	26	J. Myatt	49:07	47	R. Richardson	49:46
6	Grenville Tuck	48:01	27	D. Hopkins	49:09	48	J. Davies	49:47
7	R. Patterson	48:03	28	M. Baxter	49:10	49	F. Davies	49:48
8	M. Beevor	48:06	29	I. Gilmour	49:12	50	M. Freary	49:48
9	Jim Brown	48:06	30	D. Cannon	49:19			
10	M. Tagg	48:09	31	K. Angus	49:23			
11	R. Smedley	48:26	32	A. Bird	49:24	**Team Placings**		
12	A. Simmons	48:31	33	D. Fownes	49:24	1	Derby & County AC	337pts
13	A. Blinston	48:35	34	K. Darlow	49:25	2	Airedale & Spen Valley	376pts
14	P. Gilsenan	48:36	35	A. Spence	49:28	3	Hercules Wimbledon AC	419pts
15	J. Alder	48:38	36	T. Baker	49:30	4	Tipton Harriers	447pts
16	R. Wilde	48:39	37	A. Domleo	49:32	5	Bolton United Harriers	461pts
17	M. Turner	48:44	38	R. Treadwell	49:33	6	Gateshead Harriers	548pts
18	J. Roberts	48:47	39	J. Lane	49:36	7	Aldershot Farnham & D	570pts
19	R. Harrison	48:55	40	D. Coates	49:37	8	Manchester & District	663pts
20	G. Stevens	48:57	41	P. Adams	49:37	9	Edinburgh AC	743pts
21	D. Lem	48:58	42	W. Robinson	49:38	10	Birchfield Harriers	771pts

JUNIORS (6 MILES)

1	N. Coupland	33:11
2	D. Long	33:13
3	M. Kearns	33:23
4	G. Morgan	33:53
5	J. Odlin	34:00
6	R. Crabb	34:06
7	H. Elliott	34:10
8	N. Saunders	34:19
9	A. Barnett	34:23
10	K. Steere	34:26

Team Placings
1 City of Stoke AC 102pts
2 Birmingham University 139pts
3 City of Hull AC 164pts

YOUTHS (4 MILES)

1	M. Longthorn	21:18
2	R. Callan	21:21
3	I. Ray	21:32
4	K. Dumpleton	21:34
5	G. Forster	21:51
6	G. Rowsell	21:54
7	K. Harrison	21:55
8	A. Hitchen	21:57
9	S. Emson	21:58
10	G. Barr	22:01

Team Placings
1 Bristol AC 118pts
2 Springburn Harriers 178pts
3 City of Hull AC 209pts

9, 10 March
EUROPEAN INDOOR CHAMPIONSHIPS

Barrie Kelly, John Whetton, Lynn Davies, Alan Pascoe, Ian Stewart, Ricky Wilde, Marilyn Neufville, Margaret Beacham, Peter Stewart, Verona Bernard... all have won gold medals for Britain in the European Indoor Championships, and to that company can be added the name of Geoff Capes. His shot-putting triumph in Gothenburg was significant for several reasons. He displayed admirable competitive qualities; his winning put was a European indoor best and well in excess of his official UK outdoor record; and the victory was Britain's first in a European 'heavy' event championship since Arthur Rowe's outdoor success in 1958, also in Sweden.

There was a sensational start to the competition when East Germany's Heinz-Joachim Rothenburg opened with 20.87 metres (68' 5¾") to add 5cm (2") to Capes' European indoor best. Capes, although fortified by a warm-up toss thought to be over 71 feet, had to wait nervously for 10 minutes before it was his turn. 'That figure of 20.87 was sticking in my mind, and I was literally shaking', said Capes, 'but once I went through the glide it felt easy'. His was a stunning reply, for the 16lb ball thudded down at 20.95 metres (68' 8¾").

Rothenburg never came really close to that, but Capes always feared he might and was unable to relax until his opponent fouled his final attempt. Capes underlined his supremacy by reaching 20.90 metres (68' 7") in the second round, while his sixth and last try ('it went all wrong and slipped all ways as it left my fingers') still carried out to 20.77 metres (68' 1¾").

Britain's other great moment came in the women's 60 metres where Andrea Lynch – who had lost by merely four-hundredths of a second to Raelene Boyle in the Commonwealth Games 100 metres – held Renate Stecher to just one-hundredth. That's about four inches! Andrea gave an indication of her form by beating East Germany's double Olympic champion in the semi-final, clocking a UK best of 7.24. In spite of having been cautioned for one false start, Andrea made a lightning getaway in the final and was pipped only in the final stride or two. Andrea's time was another British best of 7.17 and behind her came two of the sprint world's most celebrated names: Irena Szewinska and Mona-Lisa Pursiainen.

No other Britons won medals, but Rosemary Wright (800 metres) and Judy Vernon (60 metres hurdles) placed fourth and set UK indoor bests; and Mary Stewart (whose brothers Ian and Peter are both former European indoor champions) improved upon her junior figures when finishing fifth in the 1500 metres, one place ahead of Olympic champion Lyudmila Bragina (Sov).

Overall, standards were the highest yet. World bests fell to Poland's Michal Joachimowski in the triple jump; the USSR's Nadyezhda Ilyina in a 400 metres semi-final (but she was beaten in the final); Bulgaria's Tonka Petrova in the 1500 metres; East Germany's Annelie Ehrhardt in a 60 metres hurdles semi-final (she had to scratch from the final); and Czechoslovakia's Helena Fibingerova in the shot. European bests were broken by Capes and by Poland's Elzbieta Katolik in the 800 metres. A casualty in the latter final was Lilyana Tomova (Bul), who had to drop out on the first lap with an injury that stopped

EUROPEAN INDOOR CHAMPIONSHIPS

her training for two months. She was to enjoy better luck in September, winning the European 800 metres title in the outstanding time of 1:58.1. Riitta Salin (Fin), a brilliant 400 metres winner in Rome in 50.14, made far less of an impact in Gothenburg: she was eliminated in the first round with a time of 54.76!

Geoff Capes – a European and UK best to win the European Indoor shot at Gothenburg.

MEN

60m: 1 V. Borzov (Sov) 6.58; **2** M. Kokot (EG) 6.63; **3** A. Kornelyuk (Sov) 6.66; **4** C. Garpenborg (Swe) 6.66; **5** J. Silovs (Sov) 6.68; **6** Z. Nowosz (Pol) 6.70; **7** L. Gresa (Hun) 6.71; **8** V. Papageorgopoulos (Gre) 6.73.

400m: 1 A. Brijdenbach (Bel) 46.60; **2** A. Scheibe (EG) 46.80; **3** G. Arnold (WG) 46.94; **4** F. Demarthon (Fra) 47.08.

800m: 1 L. Susanj (Yug) 1:48.1; **2** A. Zsinka (Hun) 1:48.5; **3** J. Plachy (Cze) 1:49.5; **4** R. Gysin (Swi) 1:50.7; **5** M. Skowronek (Pol) 1:51.3; **6** P. Meyer (Fra) 1:57.5.

ATHLETICS 75

1500m: 1 H. Szordykowski (Pol) 3:41.8; 2 T. Wessinghage (WG) 3:42.0; 3 W. Staszak (Pol) 3:43.5; 4 P. Lupan (Rom) 3:44.7; 5 F. Hagberg (Swe) 3:47.0; 6 A. Asgeirsson (Ice) 3:55.6.
3000m: 1 E. Puttemans (Bel) 7:48.6; 2 P. Thijs (Bel) 7:51.8; 3 P. Penkava (Cze) 7:51.8; 4 A. Kvalheim (Nor) 7:53.4; 5 R. Smedley (UK) 7:54.4; 6 J. Jansky (Cze) 7:55.0; 7 A. Burgos (Spa) 7:56.4; 8 J. Kondzior (Pol) 8:07.8.
60m Hurdles: 1 A. Moshiashvili (Sov) 7.66; 2 M. Wodzynski (Pol) 7.68; 3 F. Siebeck (EG) 7.75; 4 L. Wodzynski (Pol) 7.94; 5 G. Buttari (Ita) 8.01; 6 K. Clerselius (Swe) 8.05; 7 V. Myasnikov (Sov) 8.51; 8 G. Drut (Fra) walked in (7.87 heat).
High Jump: 1 K. Sapka (Sov) 2.22m (7' 3¼"); 2 I. Major (Hun) 2.20m (7' 2½"); 3 V. Maly (Cze) 2.20m; 4 J. Torring (Den) 2.17m (7' 1½"); 5 E. Del Forno (Ita) 2.17m; 6 V. Abramov (Sov) 2.17m; 7 R. Almen (Swe) 2.17m; 8 W. Boller (WG) 2.17m.
Pole Vault: 1 T. Slusarski (Pol) 5.35m (17' 6½"); 2 A. Kalliomaki (Fin) 5.30m (17' 4½"); 3 J. Lauris (Sov) 5.30m; 4 eq R. Kuretzky (WG) & W. Buciarski (Pol) 5.20m (17' 0¾"); 6 V. Ohl (WG) 5.20m; 7 Y. Tananika (Sov) 5.20m; 8 R. Dionisi (Ita) 5.10m (16' 8¾"). M. Bull (UK) 10th with 5.00m (16' 4¾").
Long Jump: 1 J-F. Bonheme (Fra) 8.17m (26' 9¾"); 2 H. Baumgartner (WG) 8.10m (26' 7"); 3 M. Klauss (EG) 8.03m (26' 4¼"); 4 V. Podluzhniy (Sov) 7.97m (26' 1¾"); 5 G. Cybulski (Pol) 7.86m (25' 9½"); 6 A. Lerwill (UK) 7.84m (25' 8¾"); 7 R. Blanquer (Spa) 7.69m (25' 2¾"); 8 F. Wartenberg (EG) 7.65m (25' 1¼").
Triple Jump: 1 M. Joachimowski (Pol) 17.03m (55' 10½") (*world best*); 2 M. Bariban (Sov) 16.88m (55' 4¾"); 3 B. Lamitie (Fra) 16.56m (54' 4"); 4 R. Garnys (Pol) 16.51m (54' 2"); 5 J. Drehmel (EG) 16.48m (54' 1"); 6 R. Kick (WG) 15.85m (52' 0"); 7 C. Valetudie (Fra) 15.71m (51' 6½"); 8 M. Perez (Spa) 15.68m (51' 5¼").
Shot: 1 G. Capes (UK) 20.95m (68' 8¾") (*European & UK best*); 2 H-J. Rothenburg (EG) 20.87m (68' 5¾"); 3 J. Brabec (Cze) 19.87m (65' 2¼"); 4 V. Stoev (Bul) 19.85m (65' 1½"); 5 A. Yarosh (Sov) 19.69m (64' 7¼"); 6 J. Vlk (Cze) 19.65m (64' 5¾"); 7 M. Winch (UK) 19.20m (63' 0"); 8 F. Schladen (WG) 18.84m (61' 9¾").
4×2 Laps Relay: 1 Sweden 3:04.6; 2 France 3:05.5.

WOMEN

60m: 1 R. Stecher (EG) 7.16; 2 A. Lynch (UK) 7.17 (*UK best*); 3 I. Szewinska (Pol) 7.20; 4 M-L. Pursiainen (Fin) 7.24; 5 L. Maslakova (Sov) 7.35; 6 L. Haglund (Swe) 7.35; 7 A. Richter (WG) 7.35; 8 S. Telliez (Fra) 7.37.
400m: 1 J. Pavlicic (Yug) 52.64; 2 N. Ilyina (Sov) 52.81 (52.44 s-f, *world best*); 3 W. Dietsch (EG) 52.84; 4 A. Handt (EG) 53.51.
800m: 1 E. Katolik (Pol) 2:02.4 (*European best*); 2 G. Ellenberger (WG) 2:02.5; 3 G. Hoffmeister (EG) 2:02.6; 4 R. Wright (UK) 2:05.2 (*UK best*); 5 V. Gerassimova (Sov) 2:10.8; L. Tomova (Bul) did not finish (2:05.3 heat).
1500m: 1 T. Petrova (Bul) 4:11.0 (*world best*); 2 K. Krebs (EG) 4:11.3; 3 T. Kazachkova (Sov) 4:14.5; 4 I. Silai (Rom) 4:17.1; 5 M. Stewart (UK) 4:19.0; 6 L. Bragina (Sov) 4:20.8; 7 U. Prasek (Pol) 4:21.3; 8 B. Sudicka (Cze) 4:21.5.
60m Hurdles: 1 eq A. Fiedler (EG) & G. Rabsztyn (Pol) 8.08; 3 M. Antenen (Swi) 8.19; 4 J. Vernon (UK) 8.25 (8.23 s-f, *eq UK best*); 5 T. Vorochobko (Sov) 8.26; 6 I. Bruzsenyak (Hun) 8.39; T. Nowak (Pol) fell (8.27 semi-final); A. Ehrhardt (EG) scratched (7.90 s-f, *eq world best*).
High Jump: 1 R. Witschas (EG) 1.90m (6' 2¾"); 2 M. Karbanova (Cze) 1.88m (6' 2"); 3 R. Kirst (EG) 1.88m; 4 C. Popescu (Rom) 1.86m (6' 1¼"); 5 T. Galka (Sov) 1.86m; 6 E. Mundinger (WG) 1.83m (6' 0"); 7 R. Ahlers (Hol) 1.83m; 8 eq A-E. Karlsson (Swe) & G. Ejstrup (Den) 1.80m (5' 10¾").
Long Jump: 1 M. Antenen (Swi) 6.69m (21' 11½"); 2 A. Schmalfeld (EG) 6.56m (21' 6½"); 3 V. Stefanescu (Rom) 6.39m (20' 11¾"); 4 J. Nygrynova (Cze) 6.38m (20' 11¼"); 5 V. Viscopoleanu (Rom) 6.32m (20' 9"); 6 R. Martin-Jones (UK) 6.30m (20' 8"); 7 N. Gavrilova (Sov) 6.28m (20' 7¼"); 8 M. Treinite (Sov) 6.28m.
Shot: 1 H. Fibingerova (Cze) 20.75m (68' 1") (*world best*); 2 N. Chizhova (Sov) 20.62m (67' 8"); 3 M. Adam (EG) 19.70m (64' 7¾"); 4 I. Khristova (Bul) 19.23m (63' 1¼"); 5 F. Melnik (Sov) 18.61m (61' 0¾"); 6 E. Stoyanova (Bul) 18.04m (59' 2¼"); 7 E. Krachevskaya (Sov) 18.02m (59' 1½"); 8 J. Bognar (Hun) 17.82m (58' 5¾").
4×2 Laps Relay: 1 Sweden 3:38.2; 2 Bulgaria 3:39.2.

16 March

INTERNATIONAL CROSS-COUNTRY CHAMPIONSHIPS

Even though lacking the services of their star, Emiel Puttemans, Belgium retained the international championship at Monza, near Milan. Belgium also supplied the individual winner in little known Erik De Beck (22), a cross-country specialist and protégé of Gaston Roelants whose best track times of 14:13 for 5000 and 29:45 for 10,000 metres were far inferior to those of the men he beat for the coveted title. Spain's Mariano Haro finished second for the third year running, with European marathon champion Karel Lismont of Belgium third. Little noticed in 12th place was Manfred Kuschmann (EG), the man destined to win the European 10,000 metres title in Rome.

Jim Brown (Scotland), the international junior champion of the previous year, was the highest placed UK runner in fourth place, while England's first scorer (7th) was surprising Ray Smedley, the Olympic 1500 metres representative. England, team champions for nine successive years prior to a disastrous showing in 1973 (5th), finished a close second to Belgium. England's humiliation this time came in the junior race, occupying 11th place ahead only of Northern Ireland and Kuwait. Led in by Rita Ridley, England retained the women's championship, individual honours going to Paola Pigni-Cacchi (Italy) ahead of Finland's Nina Holmen, the future European 3000 metres champion.

MEN'S SENIOR CHAMPIONSHIP (12km)

1 E. De Beck (Bel)	35:23.8	
2 M. Haro (Spa)	35:24.6	
3 K. Lismont (Bel)	35:26.6	
4 J. Brown (Sco)	35:29.2	
5 D. Uhlemann (WG)	35:30.4	
6 W. Scholz (EG)	35:31.8	
7 R. Smedley (Eng)	35:35.8	
8 N. Tijou (Fra)	35:36.4	
9 D. Black (Eng)	35:37.2	
10 F. Fava (Ita)	35:38.4	
11 B. Ford (Eng)	35:48.4	
12 M. Kuschmann (EG)	35:54.2	
13 M. Smet (Bel)	36:00.8	
14 G. Roelants (Bel)	36:03.2	
15 P. Paivarinta (Fin)	36:06.2	
16 Gren Tuck (Eng)	36:07.6	
17 P. Halle (Nor)	36:08.4	
18 T. Kantanen (Fin)	36:12.6	
19 A. Zaddem (Tun)	36:16.4	
20 L. Rault (Fra)	36:18.6	
21 L. Lauro (Ita)	36:24.0	
22 M. Karst (WG)	36:26.6	
23 E. Leddy (Eir)	36:27.0	
24 K. Leiteritz (EG)	36:28.8	
25 G. Umbach (EG)	36:29.8	
26 S. De La Parte (Spa)	36:30.8	
27 F. Grillaert (Bel)	36:32.6	
28 C. Solone (Ita)	36:34.0	
29 K. Boro (Nor)	36:34.6	
30 F. Briscoe (Eng)	36:35.4	
31 R. McDonald (Sco)		
32 A. Garderud (Swe)		
33 S. Nikkari (Fin)		
34 B. Wassenaar (Hol)		
35 H. Scharn (Hol)		
36 M. Beevor (Eng)		
37 R. Leibold (WG)		
38 P. Liardet (Fra)		
39 J. Prianon (Fra)		
40 M. Tagg (Eng)		
41 M. Bel Haoucine (Mor)		
42 M. Thomas (Wal)		
43 H. Jaddour (Mor)		
44 G. Frahmcke (WG)		
45 E. Gijselinck (Bel)		
46 A. McKean (Sco)		
47 C. Falconer (Sco)		
48 D. Walsh (Eir)		
49 R. Jourdan (Fra)		
50 A. Vaes (Bel)		

Team Placings

1 Belgium	103pts
2 England	109pts
3 France	215pts
4 West Germany	220pts
5 East Germany	226pts
6 Spain	269pts
7 Scotland	273pts
8 Italy	278pts
9 Finland	337pts
10 Morocco	363pts

MEN'S JUNIOR CHAMPIONSHIP (7km)

1	R. Kimball (USA)	21:30.8
2	V. Ortis (Ita)	21:33.0
3	J. Treacy (Eir)	21:42.4
4	D. Millonig (Aut)	21:48.0
5	M. Centrowitz (USA)	21:48.0
6	E. Roscoe (USA)	21:52.2
7	B. Zouhri (Mor)	21:54.2
8	M'Hamed Naoumi (Mor)	21:55.2
9	R. Schoofs (Bel)	21:56.4
10	P. Davey (USA)	21:58.2

Team Placings

1	USA	22pts
2	Morocco	58pts
3	Italy	90pts
4	Scotland	93pts
5	Eire	95pts
6	Belgium	102pts

WOMEN'S CHAMPIONSHIP (4km)

1	P. Cacchi (Ita)	12:42.0
2	N. Holmen (Fin)	12:47.6
3	R. Ridley (Eng)	12:54.0
4	A. Yeoman (Eng)	12:58.6
5	P. Vihonen (Fin)	13:02.0
6	B. Luswikowska (Pol)	13:03.2
7	J. Smith (Eng)	13:04.4
8	M. Stewart (Sco)	13:05.6
9	C. Valero (Spa)	13:13.4
10	M. Gargano (Ita)	13:14.8
11	J. Van Sentberghe (Bel)	13:18.6
12	C. Choate (USA)	13:20.8
13	S. Cruciata (Ita)	13:21.8
14	C. Gould (Eng)	13:23.8
15	C. Tranter (Eng)	13:24.2
16	S. Tyynela (Fin)	13:25.0
17	M. Molz (Bel)	13:28.8
18	J. Debrouwers (Fra)	13:29.8
19	M. Lucas (Spa)	13:30.2
20	C. Kofferschlager (WG)	13:31.0

Team Placings

1	England	28pts
2	Italy	50pts
3	Finland	61pts
4	Belgium	97pts
5	USA	98pts
6	Poland	98pts

MARCH HIGHLIGHTS

The USSR easily defeated an under-strength USA men's team, 89–72, in an indoor match in Moscow on 2 March. The Soviet women won 69–52. World bests were recorded in the 60 metres (6.4) by Cliff Outlin (USA) and Aleksandr Kornelyuk (Sov); 60 metres hurdles (7.3) by Tom Hill (USA); women's 60 metres (7.1) by Martha Watson (USA), Lyudmila Maslakova (Sov), and Nadyezhda Besfamilnaya (Sov); and women's shot (20.40 metres/66' 11¼") by Nadyezhda Chizhova (Sov), this last mark being broken later in the month at the European Indoor Championships.

It's not often the honorary secretary of a governing body in sport is young enough to be simultaneously a successful competitor, but Peter Marlow (32) – elected Race Walking Association hon sec six months earlier – emerged as national 10 miles walk champion at Whetstone, Leicester, on 16 March. Roger Mills, one of the favourites, finished ninth after having lost much ground early on when he had to stop to massage his cramped shins. Another contender, Olly Flynn, was disqualified when out in front at 7 miles.

Result: 1 P. Marlow 72:58; 2 R. Thorpe 73:32; 3 E. Taylor 73:42; 4 B. Adams 73:55; 5 J. Webb 74:04; 6 R. Wallwork 74:16; 7 A. Seddon 74:28; 8 M. Holmes 74:44; 9 R. Mills 75:03; 10 J. Lord 76:29.
Team: Belgrave Harriers.

Marlow collected another national title on 30 March, this time the AAA 10,000 metres walk championship at West London Stadium. Flynn was again disqualified, after battling for the lead throughout 16 laps.

Result: 1 P. Marlow 44:58.4; 2 B. Adams 45:51.0; 3 S. Lightman 46:30.0; 4 A. Seddon 46:55.2; 5 M. Holmes 47:08.2; 6 J. Lord 47:41.6; 7 R. Wallwork 48:19.4; 8 G. Biddulph 48:25.0; 9 A. Buchanan 48:40.0; 10 A. Smallwood 48:48.0.

Emiel Puttemans helped himself to world indoor bests of 12:59.0 for 3 miles and 13:24.6 for 5000 metres at Pantin (France) on 17 March. He was supposed to have represented Belgium in the International Cross-Country Championships that day and he offended the Belgian Athletics Federation even more when he did turn out for a cross-country race in Italy the following weekend: instead scoring a runaway win in the 'Five Mills' classic in 31:08.6 ahead of Frank Shorter (USA) 31:19.4 and Britain's Brendan Foster, 31:34.8. Puttemans was promptly banned from further foreign competition until mid-summer . . . and his year ended on a dismal note when he withdrew from the European Championships because of poor form.

Eight national indoor bests among the younger age groups were posted at Cosford on 22, 23 March in the appropriate AAA and WAAA Championships. The record setters were:

(men under 20) *800m:* W. Tarquini & A. Dyke 1:52.6; *Triple Jump:* A. Moore 14.77m (48' 5½"). (Youths) *800m:* M. Edwards 1:55.6. (Intermediate women) *400m:* A. Robertson 56.7; *60m Hurdles:* J. Long 8.7; *High Jump:* F. Stacey & J. Harrison 1.71m (5' 7¼"); *Long Jump:* J. Bowerman 5.80m (19' 0½"); *Shot:* J. Oakes 12.18m (39' 11½")

Janis Walsh (15) broke Sonia Lannaman's UK junior 60 metres best with 7.5 in an open race. Birchfield Harriers, with 43.4 in the men's 4 × 100 metres, and Wolverhampton & Bilston AC, with 4:26.0 in the men's medley and 47.7 in the women's 4 × 100 metres, captured the senior relay titles.

Sweden's Chris Garpenborg broke a 15-year-old European record when he ran 100 yards in 9.3 at Albuquerque, New Mexico, on 23 March.

John Cooper (33), Olympic 400 metres hurdles and 4 × 400 metres relay silver medallist in Tokyo, was among those killed in the world's worst air disaster near Paris. A successful and popular member of the British team from 1961 to 1969, he first broke the UK 400 metres hurdles record in 1963 and improved to 50.1 in the Olympics next year. Although his fastest 400 metres time on the flat was only 47.6, John was a relay runner of the highest class, timed at 45.6 for his leg in Tokyo.

Janis Walsh – promising much for the future.

April

APRIL HIGHLIGHTS

Ian Thompson, a marathon runner only since the previous October, made it three victories in three marathons by winning the Marathon to Athens race on 6 April in 2:13:50.2. The Boston Marathon on 15 April went to Irishman Neil Cusack in 2:13:39. Miki Gorman, 38-year-old Los Angeles housewife, finished in 2:47:11, second only to her world's best of 2:46:36.

Chris Garpenborg, a Swedish student in the USA, improved the European 100 yards record again, to 9.2, at Tucson (Arizona) on 6 April, and tied that mark at El Paso (Texas) on 20 April.

World junior records were established by Don Merrick (USA) with a 9.2 100 yards at Bradenton, Florida, on 6 April and Yuriy Sedykh (Sov) with a hammer throw of 70.86 metres (232′ 6″) at Alushta on 7 April.

Olympic 20 kilometres walk champion Peter Frenkel (EG) achieved world records for 2 hours (26,930 metres/16 miles 1289 yards) and 30 kilometres (2:14:21.2) in Berlin on 15 April.

Breaking four minutes for the *eighth* consecutive race since January, an unprecedented sequence, Tony Waldrop (USA) became the fifth fastest miler in history with 3:53.2 in Philadelphia on 27 April. Britain's Ray Smedley was third in a personal best of 3:57.7.

Brendan Foster recorded the astonishing time of 24:28 for his 5 miles 900 yards leg in the AAA National Road Relay at Sutton Coldfield on 27 April. That was 28 seconds faster than Dave Black and 32 seconds better than Bernie Ford, and it represented 26:38.4 pace for 6 miles!

Result: 1 Tipton Harriers 4:06:35; **2** Edinburgh Southern Harriers 4:07:06; **3** Cardiff AAC 4:07:15; **4** Gateshead Harriers 4:07:19; **5** Coventry Godiva Harriers 4:09:35; **6** Airedale & Spen Valley AC 4:09:50.

Howard Payne (UK) won the South African 'open' hammer championship at Pretoria on 27 April with 68.98 metres (226′ 4″), with European champion Uwe Beyer (WG) in third place. Payne, aged 43, had registered a personal best of 69.76 metres (228′ 10″) at Johannesburg the previous week.

Left: *Ian Thompson, here winning his fourth-ever marathon, at the European Championships, had made the Marathon to Athens in April his third successive victory.* **Above:** *Tony Waldrop (USA), seen winning the AAA 1500 metres in July, set an equally amazing sequence in April, running his eighth successive sub-four-minute mile since January.*

May

25 May
WEST GERMANY v UK WALKING MATCH

World records were smashed in both events of this track walking match in Hamburg. Olympic 50 kilometres champion Bernd Kannenberg set 20 kilometres figures of 1:24:45.0 and 41-year-old Gerhard Weidner became the oldest world recordbreaker in history when he covered 20 miles in 2:30:38.6.

Kannenberg picked up unofficial world bests at 15 kilometres (63:18.0), 10 miles (68:00.4) and one hour (14,241 metres/8 miles 1495 yards) on the way, and his feat of covering 50 laps at an average speed of over 8¾mph in cold and blustery conditions is acknowledged as probably the greatest in walking annals. He finished nearly four laps ahead of the first British representative, Roger Mills, and covered the 5000 metres segments in 21:15.0, 20:54.6, 21:08.4, and 21:27.0.

Weidner's record walk, although exceptional for an athlete of his age, was not quite in the same class. He passed the 20 kilometres point in 1:32:09.8, and his 5 miles splits were 37:00.6, 37:02.4, 37:36.6, and 38:59.0. British records, held by Paul Nihill, fell to Roy Thorpe (2:24:18.2 for 30 kilometres) and fast finishing John Warhurst (2:34:25.4 for the full 20 miles). The West Germans won the match by 26 points to 18.

20 KILOMETRES

1 B. Kannenberg (WG)	1:24:45.0*	(42:09.6 at 10km)
2 H. Mayr (WG)	1:30:59.4	(45:36.0 at 10km)
3 R. Mills (UK)	1:31:24.2	(45:24.0 at 10km)
4 O. Flynn (UK)	1:32:15.8	(45:25.0 at 10km)
5 P. Marlow (UK)	1:32:28.8	(45:28.0 at 10km)
6 A. Taylor (UK)	1:34:21.2	(46:38.4 at 10km)
7 M. Kolvenbach (WG)	1:34:21.4	(46:38.4 at 10km)
S. Richter (WG)	disqualified	(45:25.0 at 10km)

Points: WG 13, UK 9.

*World record

20 MILES

1 G. Weidner (WG)	2:30:38.6*	(1:14:03.0 at 10M)
2 H. Schubert (WG)	2:33:33.8	(1:16:23.0 at 10M)
3 J. Warhurst (UK)	2:34:25.4†	(1:17:18.0 at 10M)
4 R. Thorpe (UK)	2:35:44.0	(1:16:15.8 at 10M)
5 A. Seddon (UK)	2:37:35.4	(1:20:00.0 at 10M)
6 M. Holmes (UK)	2:42:01.4	(1:17:57.0 at 10M)
7 L. Frey (WG)	2:44:55.6	(1:18:04.0 at 10M)
8 H. Michalski (WG)	2:47:33.0	(1:18:51.2 at 10M)

Points: WG 13, UK 9.
Match Result: WG 26, UK 18.

*World record   †UK record

26, 27 May
WAAA PENTATHLON & RELAY CHAMPIONSHIPS

With Olympic and Commonwealth champion Mary Peters now retired, the way was clear for Ann Wilson to gain her second national pentathlon title. The contest at Crystal Palace was staged on one day (26 May) and Ann led from the first event, the 100 metres hurdles, onwards. Her final score of 4248 points proved to be her highest tally for the year. In terms of depth it was probably the best pentathlon yet in Britain, with eight girls, including teenagers Gillian Smith, javelin expert Tessa Sanderson, and Sue Mapstone, topping 3800 points.

Stretford AC scored an excellent double in the WAAA sprint relay championships next day. They set a formidable UK club record of 1:36.0 for 4 × 200 metres (24.0 per leg average) and were only a fifth of a second outside the 4 × 100 metres figures with 45.4.

In non-championship events, also held in

Left: *May saw Donna Murray quickly make a name for herself as a 400 metres runner when she clocked 53.5 in her first serious attempt.*

ATHLETICS 75

Commonwealth bronze medallist Ann Wilson won her second national pentathlon title with 4248 points.

conjunction with the men's inter-regional meeting, Andrea Lynch equalled (for the second time in a fortnight) the UK all-comers 100 metres record of 11.3, and Christine Warden, née Howell, set a British 400 metres hurdles record of 58.9. Donna Murray ran an immensely promising 53.5 in the first top-class 400 metres of her career.

PENTATHLON

1 A. Wilson 4248 pts (14.0; 11.72m (38' 5½"); 1.73m (5' 8"); 6.14m (20' 1¾"); 25.8).
2 G. Taylor 3993 pts (15.0; 10.95m (35' 11¼"); 1.65m (5' 5"); 5.52m (18' 1½"); 24.2).
3 S. Wright 3984 pts (14.8; 10.09m (33' 1¼"); 1.73m (5' 8"); 5.68m (18' 7¾"); 25.3).
4 J. Honour 3954 pts. **5** G. Smith 3911 pts. **6** P. Chapman 3895 pts. **7** T. Sanderson 3877 pts. **8** S. Mapstone 3850 pts.
9 B. Corbett 3697 pts. **10** B. Ruttledge 3687 pts.

4×100 METRES RELAY

1 Stretford 45.4; **2** Mitcham 46.0; **3** London Olympiades 46.9; **4** Birchfield 47.0; **5** Bristol 47.1; **6** Epsom & Ewell 48.6;
7 Wigmore 48.7; **8** Mitcham 'B' 48.8.

4×200 METRES RELAY

1 Stretford 1:36.0; **2** Mitcham 1:37.1; **3** London Olympiades 1:37.7; **4** Birchfield 1:40.0; **5** Bristol 1:40.8; **6** Mitcham 'B' 1:42.3; **7** Wigmore 1:42.4.

26, 27 May

INTER-REGIONAL CHAMPIONSHIPS

It didn't have much to do with the inter-regional framework, but the shot-putting clash between Geoff Capes and world record holder Al Feuerbach generated far and away the most interest in this meeting. The pair were in combat for the third time in four days. The American had won at Crystal Palace on 22 May, setting a UK all-comers mark of 21.12 metres (69′ 3½″) to counter Capes' new national record of 20.81 metres (68′ 3¼″); and again next day at Hanover, 21.25 metres (69′ 8¾″) to 20.38 metres (66′ 10½″).

It was a case of third time lucky for Capes, though. He pushed the shot out to 20.90 metres (68′ 7″), another UK record, and Feuerbach was unable to do better than 20.40 metres (66′ 11¼″). Capes therefore became the only man, other than George Woods (and he only twice), to have defeated Feuerbach in outdoor competition since the Munich Olympics. It was a disaster, however, for Britain's other international class shot-putter, Mike Winch. 'Winkle', as Capes calls him, has modelled himself on Feuerbach and was so inspired in his first competition (22 May) against his hero that he improved two whole feet with 20.43 metres (67′ 0¼″) – making 10 feet of progress in exactly two years – but on this second occasion he found himself so utterly drained that he was reduced to a mere 18.64 metres (61′ 2″).

Jim Aukett wins the 400 metres at the Inter-Regional Championships in a championship-best 46.6.

ATHLETICS 75

TEAM SCORES

1 Middlesex 70 pts; **2** Surrey 60 pts; **3** East Midlands 52 pts; **4** Lancashire 46 pts; **5** Staffordshire/Warwickshire 44 pts; **6 eq** Hampshire/Sussex, Kent 43 pts; **8** South Western Counties 41 pts; **9** Essex/Hertfordshire 36 pts; **10** Yorkshire 35 pts; **11** South Wales 32 pts; **12** North Eastern Counties 30 pts; **13** Cheshire/North Wales 22 pts; **14** Eastern Counties 21 pts; **15** Gloucestershire/Worcestershire/Herefordshire/Shropshire 13 pts; **16** Berkshire/Buckinghamshire/Oxfordshire/Northamptonshire 11 pts.

INDIVIDUAL PLACINGS

100m: 1 S. Green (Kent) 10.5; **2** B. Green (Lancs) 10.5; **3** G. Edwards (S. Wales) 10.6; **4** D. Cole (Middx) 10.6; **5** T. Bonsor (Staffs) 10.7; **6** D. Roberts (Ches) 10.8; **7** T. Collins (Essex) 10.8; **8** P. Lavender (Surrey) 11.0.

200m: 1 A. Bennett (Staffs) 21.3; **2** R. Kennedy (Glos) 21.9; **3** R. Griffiths (Essex) 22.0; **4** R. Kislingbury (Middx) 22.1; **5** K. Jackson (NE) 22.2; **6** S. White (Berks) 22.2; **7** H. Davies (SW) 22.6; **8** D. Artley (Yorks) 22.8.

400m: 1 J. Aukett (Staffs) 46.6; **2** S. Marlow (Essex) 46.7; **3** J. Wilson (Middx) 46.9; **4** I. Saunders (Ches) 47.5; **5** D. Laing (Surrey) 48.0; **6** M. Delaney (S. Wales) 48.0; **7** C. Campbell (Hants) 48.7; **8** M. Hatch (Lancs) 48.8.

800m: 1 P. Browne (Middx) 1:50.1; **2** A. Dyke (S. Wales) 1:50.7; **3** R. Weatherburn (NE) 1:51.3; **4** Peter Lewis (Staffs) 1:51.9; **5** P. Banning (Hants) 1:52.4; **6** J. Gerrard (Lancs) 1:52.6; **7** C. Van Rees (Essex) 1:52.7; **8** M. Fromant (Surrey) 1:53.3.

Mile: 1 D. Black (Staffs) 4:00.2; **2** C. Thomas (Surrey) 4:01.0; **3** D. Gibbon (NE) 4:01.3; **4** P. Ratcliffe (S. Wales) 4:02.3; **5** D. Nicholl (Yorks) 4:02.5; **6** J. Douglas (SW) 4:02.6; **7** M. Knowles (EM) 4:06.9.

5000m: 1 A. Weatherhead (Essex) 13:48.8; **2** J. Goater (Hants) 13:52.8; **3** F. Briscoe (Lancs) 13:54.6; **4** R. Newble (Kent) 13:59.0; **5** D. Slater (Yorks) 14:01.2; **6** J. Bednarski (SW) 14:06.4; **7** P. Gilsenan (Berks) 14:06.8; **8** D. Lem (EM) 14:11.6.

10,000m: 1 C. Stewart (Hants) 28:54.0; **2** K. Penny (Kent) 28:56.4; **3** Grenville Tuck (EC) 29:07.0; **4** S. Walker (Essex) 29:08.6; **5** D. Hopkins (S.Wales) 29:35.2; **6** P. Romaine (EM) 29:42.0; **7** K. Angus (Yorks) 29:49.6; **8** D. Collins (SW) 30:00.4.

3000m Steeplechase: 1 J. Bicourt (Surrey) 8:36.6; **2** D. Camp (NE) 8:38.8; **3** I. Gilmour (SW) 8:53.6; **4** C. Moxsom (Essex) 8:58.2; **5** R. Bean (EC) 9:05.0; **6** H. Richards (Middx) 9:07.0; **7** R. Cytlau (Glos) 9:10.0; **8** D. Long (Hants) 9:10.4.

110m Hurdles: 1 A. Pascoe (Hants) 14.2; **2** G. Gower (Kent) 14.5; **3** P. Kelly (Staffs) 14.8; **4** R. Gyles (S. Wales) 15.1; **5** R. Palmer (Berks) 15.3; **6** K. Purves (Middx) 15.3; **7** N. Gerrard (Ches) 15.3; **8** R. Davidson (NE) 15.3.

400m Hurdles: 1 A. James (Lancs) 52.5; **2** M. Whittingham (Surrey) 53.9; **3** M. Ollier (Ches) 54.1; **4** R. Parker (Hants) 54.2; **5** S. Hinchliffe (Middx) 56.4; **6** J. Dixon (SW) 56.8; **7** D. Corcos (Essex) 56.9; C. O'Neill (Glos) did not finish.

3000m Walk: 1 B. Adams (EM) 12:29.2; **2** P. Nihill (Surrey) 12:34.2; **3** S. Lightman (Middx) 12:55.2; **4** K. Carter (Kent) 12:57.6; **5** A. Taylor (Lancs) 13:14.0; **6** D. Stevens (Hants) 13:18.0; **7** A. Malone (Ches) 13:52.2; **8** D. Brewster (NE) 13:58.2.

10,000m Walk: 1 C. Lawton (Surrey) 46:07.8; **2** R. Wallwork (Lancs) 46:24.2; **3** S. Lightman (Middx) 46:58.0; **4** G. Toone (EM) 47:27.0; **5** C. Fogg (SW) 48:58.8; **6** A. Buchanan (Hants) 49:50.0; **7** R. Parkings (Kent) 50:49.2; **8** L. Mockett (Essex) 50:50.2.

High Jump: 1 M. Butterfield (Yorks) 2.00m (6' 6¾"); **2** M. Shorten (EC) 1.95m (6' 4¾"); **3** C. Wilson (EM) 1.95m; **4** G. Vose (Surrey) 1.95m; **5** D. Kidner (Middx) 1.95m; **6** R. Gyles (S. Wales) 1.95m; **7** A. Dainton (Essex) 1.95m; **8** A. Nursey (Kent) 1.90m (6' 2¾").

Pole Vault: 1 C. Carrigan (USA-guest) 5.20m (17' 0¾"); **2** B. Hooper (Surrey) 5.00m (16' 4¾"); **3** A. Williams (Kent) 4.70m (15' 5"); **4** D. Lease (S. Wales) 4.60m (15' 1"); **5** S. Chappell (Berks) 4.30m (14' 1¼"); **6** C. Kidd (Yorks) 4.20m (13' 9¼"); **7** T. Gardner (Essex) 4.10m (13' 5¼"); **8** R. Griffiths (Hants) 4.00m (13' 1¼").

Long Jump: 1 P. Scott (Yorks) 7.44m (24' 5"); **2** P. Blackburn (EM) 7.31m (23' 11¾"); **3** D. Cole (Middx) 7.30m (23' 11½"); **4** P. Templeton (SW) 7.26m (23' 10"); **5** S. Wright (Lancs) 7.20m (23' 7½"); **6** J. Morgan (Kent) 7.20m; **7** C. Wright (Glos) 7.02m (23' 0½"); **8** S. Atkins (Staffs) 6.88m (22' 7").

INTER-REGIONAL CHAMPIONSHIPS/MAY HIGHLIGHTS

Triple Jump: 1 P. Blackburn (EM) 15.62m (51' 3"); 2 R. Heward-Mills (SW) 15.52m (50' 11"); 3 A. Moore (Staffs) 15.39m (50' 6"); 4 G. Doerr (Surrey) 14.95m (49' 0¾"); 5 J. Phillips (Ches) 14.62m (47' 11¾"); 6 P. Davies (Middx) 14.53m (47' 8"); 7 P. Clarke (Essex) 14.42m (47' 3¾"); 8 P. Bevan (Glos) 14.42m.

Shot: 1 G. Capes (EM) 20.90m (68' 7")*; 2 A. Feuerbach (USA-guest) 20.40m (66' 11¼"); 3 M. Winch (Hants) 18.64m (61' 2"); 4 P. Tancred (Middx) 17.55m (57' 7"); 5 M. Wilkins (USA-guest) 17.22m (56' 6"); 6 W. Fuller (Surrey) 17.15m (56' 3¼"); 7 J. Alderson (Yorks) 16.64m (54' 7¼"); 8 R. Dale (Ches) 15.91m (52' 2½").
*Commonwealth & UK national record.

Discus: 1 M. Wilkins (USA-guest) 60.80m (199' 6"); 2 W. Tancred (EC) 60.36m (198' 0"); 3 P. Tancred (Middx) 57.96m (190' 2"); 4 J. Hillier (Kent) 56.06m (183' 11"); 5 M. Cushion (Surrey) 55.04m (180' 7"); 6 J. Watts (Yorks) 52.44m (172' 0"); 7 G. Dirkin (Lancs) 51.34m (168' 5"); 8 D. Roscoe (Ches) 49.88m (163' 8").

Hammer: 1 H. Payne (Staffs) 66.48m (218' 1"); 2 I. Chipchase (NE) 65.90m (216' 2"); 3 P. Dickenson (Middx) 63.42m (208' 1"); 4 J. Whitehead (EM) 58.90m (193' 3"); 5 E. Berry (SW) 57.78m (189' 7"); 6 C. Melluish (Surrey) 55.34m (181' 7"); 7 D. Bayes (Yorks) 53.12m (174' 3"); 8 K. Lasis (Hants) 53.00m (173' 11").

Javelin: 1 B. Roberts (SW) 73.94m (242' 7"); 2 R. Silvester (Middx) 73.90m (242' 5"); 3 D. Heath (Essex) 68.34m (224' 2"); 4 K. Holmes (Glos) 65.14m (213' 8"); 5 K. Taylor (Lancs) 64.62m (212' 0"); 6 A. Bosworth (EM) 60.10m (197' 2"); 7 H. Frobisher (Yorks) 59.82m (196' 3"); 8 C. Byerley (Hants) 58.28m (191' 2").

Abbreviations: (Berks) Berkshire/Buckinghamshire/Oxfordshire/Northamptonshire; (Ches) Cheshire/North Wales; (EC) Eastern Counties; (EM) East Midlands; (Glos) Gloucestershire/Worcestershire/Herefordshire/Shropshire; (Hants) Hampshire/Sussex; (NE) North Eastern Counties; (Staffs) Staffordshire/Warwickshire; (SW) South Western Counties.

MAY HIGHLIGHTS

Usually slow into his running, Ivory Crockett (USA) got away to what his coach described as 'the best start of his career' at Knoxville, Tennessee, on 11 May. The outcome was sprinting history: the first wind-free nine-second 100 yards – an average speed of 22.73 mph. The watches indicated 9.1, 9.0, 9.0, and 8.9 (thus officially 9.0). The oft-equalled world record had stood at 9.1 since Bob Hayes established it in 1962. A short (5' 8"), dynamic athlete who burst into prominence at 19 when he won the American 100 yards title in 1969, Crockett had a previous fastest of 9.2. Unimpressed was Olympic champion Valeriy Borzov: 'He is not consistent enough to be considered one of the great ones. He has run a fast time before, but always failed on the big occasion.'

Peter Frenkel's world walking records for 2 hours and 30 kilometres lasted only a few weeks: Bernd Kannenberg (WG) covered 27,153 metres (16 miles 1535 yards) and clocked 2:12:58 at Kassel on 11 May.

Olly Flynn, pulled out for lifting in the two previous national championships in 1974, maintained contact throughout in the Race Walking Association 20 kilometres at Sheffield on 11 May and won his first major title.

Result: 1 O. Flynn 92:06; 2 P. Marlow 92:32; 3 R. Mills 93:06; 4 A. Seddon 93:46; 5 M. Holmes 93:58; 6 J. Warhurst 94:21; 7 A. Taylor 94:40; 8 K. Carter 94:50; 9 J. Lord 95:07; 10 C. Lawton 95:48.
Team: Southend AC.

Aided by strong following winds, Andrea Lynch and Judy Vernon recorded extraordinary times in Lisbon on 18 May. Andrea was credited with 10.9 for 100 metres (+ 4.1m wind) to become only the fourth woman in the world to crack 11 seconds, and Judy was awarded 12.9 in the 100 metres hurdles (+ 6.1m wind).

Tony Waldrop (USA) stretched his four-minute mile sequence to nine with a 3:59.8 effort on 14 May, but there it stopped for he ran 4:05.0 in his next race.

New Zealander John Delamere long jumped 7.79 metres (25' 6¾") in Los Angeles on 18 May – an unexceptional result, only he was using the somersault style of jumping known as the 'flip'. It was the best distance yet recorded with this method, which the IAAF banned later in the summer.

Scotsman Alastair Wood (41), once Britain's fastest ever marathoner, won what was dubbed the 'World Veterans Championship' at Draveil (France) on 19 May in 2:30:06.

Faina Melnik (USSR) brought the women's world discus record very close to the magical 70-metre line (which she has crossed in training) in Prague on 27 May with a toss of 69.90 metres (229' 4"). John Powell (USA) topped the other world discus record with 69.48 metres (227' 11") in helpful gale-force conditions at Lancaster, California, on 19 May but won't get credit for it. The 'meeting', consisting solely of the discus event, was not officially sanctioned and it was left to the athletes to mark each other's throws. The 6' 7" tall Kent Gardenkrans (Sweden) broke the world junior record with 61.98 metres (203' 4") at Modesto, California, on 25 May.

Ben Jipcho (Kenya) ended his first season as a professional with a 3:56.6 indoor mile in New York on 29 May. It was his 18th victory in 20 races with the ITA troupe, taking his total prize money up to $16,700.

One of Britain's most talented young athletes, the walker Phil Embleton, died of leukemia aged 25. He distinguished himself in 1971 by defeating Paul Nihill for the national 10 miles title and placing sixth in the European 20 kilometres championship. The following year he established himself as an Olympic medal contender after setting a world's best 10,000 metres time of 41:55.6, but he had already contracted his fatal disease by the time he walked in Munich, where he finished 14th in the 20 kilometres. Fred Kelly (USA), 1912 Olympic 110 metres hurdles champion, died at the age of 82.

Above: *Olly Flynn kept his feet on the ground and won the RWA 20 kilometres title at Sheffield.*
Right: *Marianne Adam was just too much for the British girls in the UK–East Germany meet at Crystal Palace.*

June

8, 9 June

AAA DECATHLON CHAMPIONSHIPS

With Peter Gabbett and Barry King no longer competing, and with Mike Bull, Stewart McCallum, and Dave Kidner non-starters, the AAA decathlon championship at Aldersley, Wolverhampton, was lacking all the most successful British all-rounders of recent years. Consequently, only one man – Mike Corden (7035) – topped 7000 points, itself a mark far below top international standards.

Corden was fifth with 3406 points at the end of the first day but came through strongly during the second half. A personal best pole vault of 4.00 metres (13′ 1½″) carried him into third position and he took the lead after throwing the javelin 61.22 metres (200′ 10″), nearly 10 metres farther than anyone else. Corden, whose personal best score stood frustratingly at 6997, needed 4:33.3 in the 1500 metres to reach 7000 ... and he went on to run 4:28.0. Second and third placers Alan Drayton and Cliff 'Snowy' Brooks (the latter was the overnight leader with 3715 points) also ran up best-ever scores.

A close-fought junior championship saw John Howell, a discus specialist, defeat sprinter/jumper Roy Mitchell by 50 points after Mitchell had built up a massive first-day lead with 3504 points. Later in the year, Mitchell was to become Britain's youngest ever 7000-point decathlete.

MEN

1 M. Corden 7035 pts: 11.9; 6.46m (21′ 2½″); 12.32m (40′ 5″); 1.87m (6′ 1½″); 51.6; 16.3; 41.90m (137′ 5″); 4.00m (13′ 1½″); 61.22m (200′ 10″); 4:28.0.
2 A. Drayton 6786 pts: 11.3; 6.88m (22′ 7″); 12.04m (39′ 6″); 1.75m (5′ 8¾″); 51.0; 15.4; 36.78m (120′ 8″); 3.70m (12′ 1½″); 49.56m (162′ 7″); 4:47.9.
3 C. Brooks 6642 pts: 11.1; 6.80m (22′ 3¾″); 13.58m (44′ 6¾″); 1.84m (6′ 0½″); 51.5; 16.3; 34.80m (114′ 2″); 3.50m (11′ 5¾″); 43.70m (143′ 4″); 4:59.6.
4 N. Phipps 6599 pts; **5** C. Youngs 6567 pts; **6** R. Snow 6472 pts; **7** L. Spencer 6075 pts; **8** A. Shaw 6013 pts; **9** J. Crotty 5669 pts; **10** R. Hopkins 5537 pts.

JUNIORS

1 J. Howell 6073 pts; **2** R. Mitchell 6023 pts; **3** W. Dubose 5987 pts; **4** G. Richards 5581 pts; **5** M. Hay 5572 pts; **6** A. Nickson 5437 pts.

9 June

ROMANIA v UK v WEST GERMANY v ITALY (women)

The British women's team overwhelmed Italy, 93–40, but lost both to Romania (53–82) and West Germany (50–84) in a four-nations match in Bucharest. Only one of the 13 events on the programme was won by a British athlete: the 200 metres. Donna Murray, having gained in strength and confidence through her 400 metres running, dropped down to her first love with excellent results. She scored by two metres over Annegret Kroniger in a personal best of 23.3, and Sharon Colyear provided good support by finishing close behind the West Germans in fourth place.

Revelling in the warm conditions, the British sprinters and hurdlers acquitted themselves well. Judy Vernon equalled the UK 100 metres hurdles record of 13.2, with Blondelle Thompson registering her fastest legal time of 13.5; European junior champion Sonia Lannaman clocked a personal best 100 metres of 11.3 (just a tenth outside the national record), and Liz Barnes also ran faster than ever before with 53.9 for 400 metres.

But, even allowing for some of the British girls performing below their normal standard after completing an exhausting journey in the early hours of the day of the match, the weaknesses of the team were plain to see. The 800 and 1500 metres runners could finish only fifth and sixth, while in the field events the highest placings were a third (long jumper Ruth Martin-Jones) and a fourth (discus thrower Rosemary Payne).

The Romanians accounted for the outstanding performances of the meeting. Virginia Ioan (whose husband is a 2.17 metres/7′ 1½″ jumper) cleared 1.92 metres (6′ 3½″) to break the national (and, for a long time, world) record of 1.91 metres (6′ 3¼″) held by the legendary Iolanda Balas since 1961; Valeria Stefanescu won the hurdles in 12.9 and the long jump with 6.50 metres (21′ 4″); Argentina Menis threw the discus 65.52 metres (205′ 1″); and Mariana Suman made astonishing progress by running 400 metres in 51.9 and 800 metres in 2:03.9 as against 1973 bests of 54.3 and 2:07.8.

Sonia Lannaman ran a personal best 11.3 in the Bucharest meet, yet still placed third in the 100 metres behind two West German girls.

100m: 1 A. Richter (WG) 11.3; **2** I. Helten (WG) 11.3; **3** S. Lannaman (UK) 11.3; **4** H. Golden (UK) 11.5; **5** C. Molinari (Ita) 11.5; **6** L. Nappi (Ita) 11.6; **7** C. Enescu (Rom) 11.8; **8** C. Niculescu (Rom) 12.0.

200m: 1 D. Murray (UK) 23.3; **2** A. Kroniger (WG) 23.5; **3** C. Tackenberg (WG) 23.6; **4** S. Colyear (UK) 23.6; **5** L. Nappi (Ita) 23.8; **6** C. Molinari (Ita) 24.0; **7** M. Condovici (Rom) 24.3; **8** A. Stancu (Rom) 24.8.

400m: 1 R. Wilden (WG) 51.8; **2** M. Suman (Rom) 51.9; **3** J. Roscoe (UK) 53.6; **4** E. Barnes (UK) 53.9; **5** D. Jost (WG) 54.3; **6** D. Govoni (Ita) 55.4; **7** L. Leau (Rom) 55.5; **8** E. Rossi (Ita) 56.6.

800m: 1 M. Suman (Rom) 2:03.9; **2** G. Klein (WG) 2:05.0; **3** R. Fiza (Rom) 2:05.7; **4** M. Siegl (WG) 2:06.0; **5** L. Kiernan (UK) 2:06.2; **6** R. Wright (UK) 2:06.7; **7** A. Ramello (Ita) 2:08.0; **8** C. Mutschlechner (Ita) 2:10.5.

1500m: 1 N. Andrei (Rom) 4:14.6; **2** I. Silai (Rom) 4:16.3; **3** B. Kraus (WG) 4:17.5; **4** S. Schenk (WG) 4:20.8; **5** P. Yeoman (UK) 4:26.2; **6** M. Coomber (UK) 4:26.4; **7** Lovisolo (Ita) 4:28.7; **8** Leone (Ita) 4:35.6.

100m Hurdles: 1 V. Stefanescu (Rom) 12.9; **2** J. Vernon (UK) 13.2 (*equals UK record*); **3** M. Koschinski (WG) 13.2; **4** C. Enescu (Rom) 13.4; **5** B. Thompson (UK) 13.5; **6** A. Battaglia (Ita) 13.8; **7** A. Tonelli (Ita) 14.5.

High Jump: 1 V. Ioan (Rom) 1.92m (6' 3½"); **2** E. Teodorescu (Rom) 1.83m (6' 0"); **3** K. Wagner (WG) 1.83m; **4** U. Meyfarth (WG) 1.75m (5' 8¾"); **5** B. Lawton (UK) 1.75m; **6** S. Dettamanti (Ita) 1.75m; **7** S. Wright (UK) 1.70m (5' 7"); **8** M. Casadei (Ita) 1.65m (5' 5").

Long Jump: 1 V. Stefanescu (Rom) 6.50m (21' 4"); **2** A. Catineanu (Rom) 6.40m (21' 0"); **3** R. Martin-Jones (UK) 6.29m (20' 7¾"); **4** U. Hedicke (WG) 6.18m (20' 3½"); **5** E. Trocha (WG) 6.14m (20' 1¾"); **6** A. Wilson (UK) 6.00m (19' 8¼"); **7** M. Martinelli (Ita) 5.80m (19' 0½"); **8** M. Pozzo (Ita) 5.73m (18' 9¾").

Shot: 1 V. Cioltan (Rom) 18.02m (59' 1½"); **2** E. Wilms (WG) 16.52m (54' 2½"); **3** C. Petrucci (Ita) 15.93m (52' 3½"); **4** M. Loghin (Rom) 15.75m (51' 8¼"); **5** H. Jaxt (WG) 14.90m (48' 10¾"); **6** B. Bedford (UK) 14.32m (46' 11¾"); **7** R. Payne (UK) 13.53m (44' 4¾"); **8** I. Nistri (Ita) 13.52m (44' 4¼").

Discus: 1 A. Menis (Rom) 65.52m (205' 1"); **2** O. Catarama (Rom) 58.14m (190' 9"); **3** L. Westermann (WG) 58.06m (190' 6"); **4** R. Payne (UK) 53.94m (177' 0"); **5** B. Berendonk (WG) 52.68m (172' 10"); **6** R. Scaglia (Ita) 49.52m (162' 5"); **7** M. Ritchie (UK) 47.56m (156' 0"); **8** I. Nistri (Ita) 38.28m (125' 7").

Javelin: 1 A. Koloska (WG) 55.98m (183' 8"); **2** E. Zorgo (Rom) 55.80m (183' 1"); **3** I. Pecec (Rom) 54.88m (180' 1"); **4** C. Peters (WG) 54.84m (179' 11"); **5** T. Sanderson (UK) 51.44m (168' 9"); **6** P. Carter (UK) 47.22m (154' 11"); **7** G. Amici (Ita) 42.66m (139' 11"); **8** A. Arienti (Ita) 42.60m (139' 9").

4 × 100m Relay: 1 West Germany 44.1; **2** UK 45.4; **3** Italy 45.8; **4** Romania 46.1.

4 × 400m Relay: 1 Romania 3:36.0; **2** West Germany 3:36.1; **3** UK 3:37.4; Italy disqualified.

Match Result: Romania 75, West Germany 59; Romania 82, UK 53; Romania 83, Italy 50; West Germany 84, UK 50; West Germany 99, Italy 44; UK 93, Italy 40.

15 June

AAA MARATHON CHAMPIONSHIP

Not since the Dorando incident at the 1908 Olympics has a marathon disqualification provoked such a furore. The decision of referee Arthur Winter to rule out Bob Sercombe and Colin Kirkham for cutting corners unleashed a storm of protest that was still blowing through the correspondence columns of *Athletics Weekly* two months later.

Sercombe, who finished fourth, and Kirkham (eighth) were disqualified for refusing to obey the referee's instructions to stay on the left-hand side of the road while negotiating a right-hand bend at the 21 miles mark. Mr Winter's decision may, technically, have been a correct one – but it was an unprecedented action and unwarranted in that practically everybody in the race, including men who finished ahead of the 'guilty' pair, did precisely the

AAA MARATHON CHAMPIONSHIP

same at various points of the Windsor course.

The controversy occupied so much attention that excellent performances by the leading runners on a hot, sticky day went almost unnoticed. Akio Usami (Jap) led from the early stages to win by over three minutes from Bernie Plain, who thus clinched his place for the European Championships. As Commonwealth champion Ian Thompson had already been picked for Rome, and therefore excused this selection trial, the next Briton to finish would qualify for the third team spot. That runner was Bob Sercombe, which added another twist to the drama. Would the selectors overlook his claims in view of the disqualification? The answer was no, for it was judged that the incident in question had not materially affected his final position: 28 seconds ahead of the next man, Keith Angus.

1	A. Usami (Jap)	2:15:16
2	B. Plain	2:18:32
3	E. Lesse (EG)	2:18:44
4	R. Sercombe★	2:19:52
5	K. Angus	2:20:20
6	R. Hill	2:21:36
7	T. Johnston	2:21:42
8	C. Kirkham★	2:22:17
9	J. Norman	2:22:30
10	J. Alder	2:24:12
11	M. Critchley	2:24:22
12	E. Austin	2:24:30
13	R. Atkinson	2:25:30
14	M. Craven	2:26:07
15	M. Coleby	2:26:11
16	Y. Hamada (Jap)	2:26:21
17	S. Satoh (Jap)	2:26:29
18	G. Jansen (Hol)	2:26:40
19	D. Patterson	2:27:15
20	L. Umbach (EG)	2:27:29
21	G. Dugdale	2:28:23
22	J. Newsome	2:29:03
23	D. Pratt	2:30:04
24	D. Lee	2:30:31
25	L. Mann	2:31:05
★ Disqualified		

Japan's Akio Usami, 12th in the 1972 Olympic marathon, won the controversial 1974 AAA marathon convincingly.

19, 20 June

UK v EAST GERMANY

A number of excellent individual performances by home athletes tended to obscure the fact that, overall, the British men's and women's teams were outclassed by the East Germans at Crystal Palace in a match sponsored by Philips. The men, who had heroically held their opponents to 16 points in Leipzig the previous summer, this time succumbed by 41; while the British girls suffered their heaviest defeat at home in losing by 46 points. Nevertheless, the latter result was an improvement on Leipzig where the GDR steamrollered their way to a 56-point margin, winning every event.

Once again, the man of the hour was Geoff Capes. Having already in 1974 beaten one top East German, Heinz-Joachim Rothenburg, for the European indoor title, he proceeded to defeat another and even more formidable rival in Hartmut Briesenick, Europe's first (and, at that time, only) 70-foot exponent, a renowned competitor who was reigning European champion and the Olympic bronze medallist.

Briesenick took an early lead with 20.30 metres (66′ 7¼″); lost it to Capes who put 20.60 metres (67′ 7″) in the second round; and regained it with 20.74 metres (68′ 0½″) – his best mark of the year – on his fifth attempt. Briesenick made no secret of his delight, but his joy proved of short duration: Capes immediately replied with exactly 21 metres (68′ 10¾″) – a British record. The onus now was on Briesenick as he squared up for his final trial, but he fell short with 20.77 metres (68′ 1¾″). Mike Winch, dying to beat Capes just once, was frustrated yet again, but as consolation his own fifth round put of 20.18 metres (66′ 2½″) – the second longest of his career – shunted Rothenburg back into last place. Seven points for the British putters, four for the East Germans . . . that will long be remembered with satisfaction.

Unfortunately, that proved to be the only field events success of the match, and it was left to trackmen Steve Green (200 metres in a personal best of 21.1), David Jenkins (400 metres in 45.8), Tony Simmons (5000 metres in his fastest time of 13:28.8), and the 4×400 metres squad (3:03.9) to chalk up the only other victories on the men's side. There was a second UK record, albeit a most modest one by international standards, when Colin Boreham high jumped 2.11 metres (6′ 11″) . . . 33 years after that height was first achieved by Les Steers (USA)!

A more significant high jump mark came in the women's match when petite 19-year-old Val Harrison, just 1.64 metres (5′ 4½″) tall, flopped over 1.83 metres to become the world's shortest six-foot jumper. Only world record holder Yordanka Blagoyeva (Bul) had ever exceeded her own physical height by such a margin.

There were two British victories in the women's match and Jannette Roscoe, who had never previously won an international race, was involved in both. She pipped Angelika Handt in the final strides of the 400 metres, and helped the relay team to win in a sparkling 3:30.0. Donna Murray ran a superb anchor leg, taking over level with Ellen Streidt, passing her decisively in the finishing straight and clocking 51.3 for her stint. Andrea Lynch, running what she described as the strongest race of her life, held Renate Stecher to six-hundredths of a second in the 100 metres (11.44 to

11.50), and in a non-match event Joyce Smith set a UK 3000 metres record of 9:04.4.

Jannette Roscoe, involved in both British victories against the East German women, wins the 400 metres with Jutta Meier third and Liz Barnes fourth.

ATHLETICS 75

MEN

100m: 1 H-J. Zenk (EG) 10.8; 2 J. Pfennig (EG) 10.8; 3 S. Green (UK) 10.8; 4 L. Piggot (UK) 10.9.

200m: 1 S. Green (UK) 21.1; 2 H-J. Bombach (EG) 21.2; 3 A. Bennett (UK) 21.3; 4 E. Weise (EG) 21.8.

400m: 1 D. Jenkins (UK) 45.8; 2 A. Scheibe (EG) 46.1; 3 R. Schwara (EG) 46.7; 4 J. Aukett (UK) 46.9.

800m: 1 H-H. Ohlert (EG) 1:46.8; 2 D. Fromm (EG) 1:47.0; 3 D. McMeekin (UK) 1:47.2; 4 F. Clement (UK) 1:48.5.

1500m: 1 K-P. Justus (EG) 3:39.0; 2 H-H. Ohlert (EG) 3:41.4; 3 R. Smedley (UK) 3:41.9; 4 R. MacDonald (UK) 3:43.1.

5000m: 1 A. Simmons (UK) 13:28.8; 2 B. Ford (UK) 13:35.2; 3 W. Scholz (EG) 13:49.0; 4 J. Lautzschmann (EG) 13:57.6.

10,000m: 1 M. Kuschmann (EG) 28:10.0; 2 K-H. Leiteritz (EG) 28:33.0; 3 C. Stewart (UK) 29:01.8; 4 F. Briscoe (UK) 29:39.2.

3000m Steeplechase: 1 J. Straub (EG) 8:31.0; 2 W. Cierpinski (EG) 8:33.2; 3 D. Camp (UK) 8:34.4; 4 J. Davies (UK) 8:41.8.

110m Hurdles: 1 T. Munkelt (EG) 14.2; 2 C. Kirkpatrick (UK) 14.5; 3 D. Wilson (UK) 14.5; K. Fiedler (EG) did not finish.

400m Hurdles: 1 J. Laser (EG) 50.2; 2 W. Hartley (UK) 50.7; 3 J. Mayer (EG) 50.8; 4 C. O'Neill (UK) 51.6.

High Jump: 1 R. Beilschmidt (EG) 2.17m (7' 1½"); 2 C. Boreham (UK) 2.11m (6' 11") (*UK national record*); 3 S. Junge (EG) 2.06m (6' 9"); 4 A. Lerwill (UK) 2.06m.

Pole Vault: 1 W. Reinhardt (EG) 5.25m (17' 2¾"); 2 B. Hooper (UK) 5.00m (16' 4¾"); 3 M. Bull (UK) 4.70m (15' 5"); 4 U. Pubanz (EG) 4.60m (15' 1").

Long Jump: 1 M. Klauss (EG) 7.84m (25' 8¾") (& 7.84m); 2 A. Lerwill (UK) 7.84m (& 7.72m); 3 W. Lauterbach (EG) 7.69m (25' 2¾"); 4 G. Hignett (UK) 7.43m (24' 4½").

Triple Jump: 1 J. Drehmel (EG) 16.53m (54' 2¾"); 2 L. Gora (EG) 16.08m (52' 9¼"); 3 W. Clark (UK) 15.60m (51' 2¼"); 4 R. Heward-Mills (UK) 15.27m (50' 1¼").

Shot: 1 G. Capes (UK) 21.00m (68' 10¾") (*Commonwealth & UK national record*); 2 H. Briesenick (EG) 20.77m (68' 1¾"); 3 M. Winch (UK) 20.18m (66' 2½"); 4 H-J. Rothenburg (EG) 20.00m (65' 7½").

Discus: 1 G. Muller (EG) 61.58m (202' 0"); 2 H. Losch (EG) 61.44m (201' 7"); 3 W. Tancred (UK) 59.70m (195' 10"); 4 P. Tancred (UK) 54.48m (178' 9").

Hammer: 1 R. Theimer (EG) 72.40m (237' 6"); 2 K-H. Beilig (EG) 70.74m (232' 1"); 3 H. Payne (UK) 69.50m (228' 0"); 4 C. Black (UK) 59.02m (193' 8").

Javelin: 1 M. Ahlert (EG) 80.18m (263' 1"); 2 D. Travis (UK) 78.96m (259' 1"); 3 W. Hanisch (EG) 77.68m (254' 10"); 4 B. Roberts (UK) 72.26m (237' 1").

4 × 100m Relay: 1 East Germany (H-J. Zenk, J. Pfennig, H-J. Bombach, E. Weise) 39.7; 2 UK (L. Piggot, D. Halliday, I. Matthews, B. Green) 40.0.

4 × 400m Relay: 1 UK 3:03.9 (J. Wilson 46.8, S. Marlow 45.9, W. Hartley 46.1, D. Jenkins 45.1); 2 East Germany 3:04.0 (R. Kokot 47.2, J. Utikal 45.7, R. Schwara 46.2, A. Scheibe 44.9).

Match Result: East Germany 126, UK 85.

Non-Match Event
20km Walk: 1 S. Zschiegner (EG) 1:33:05.0; 2 O. Flynn (UK) 1:33:47.2; 3 P. Marlow (UK) 1:35:25.6; K-H. Stadtmuller (EG) did not finish.

WOMEN

100m: 1 R. Stecher (EG) 11.4; 2 A. Lynch (UK) 11.5; 3 P. Kandarr (EG) 11.9; S. Lannaman (UK) did not finish.

200m: 1 R. Stecher (EG) 23.2; 2 D. Murray (UK) 23.7; 3 D. Maletzki (EG) 24.1; 4 S. Colyear (UK) 24.3.

400m: 1 J. Roscoe (UK) 53.5; 2 A. Handt (EG) 53.6; 3 J. Meier (EG) 54.4; 4 E. Barnes (UK) 54.5.

48

UK V EAST GERMANY/AMERICAN AAU CHAMPIONSHIPS

800m: **1** M. Cierpinski (EG) 2:01.6; **2** A. Barkusky (EG) 2:05.2; **3** R. Wright (UK) 2:05.9; **4** L. Kiernan (UK) 2:06.2.

1500m: **1** G. Hoffmeister (EG) 4:09.6; **2** U. Klapeczynski (EG) 4:11.7; **3** M. Stewart (UK) 4:18.7; **4** C. Tranter (UK) 4:23.8.

100m Hurdles: **1** A. Ehrhardt (EG) 13.2; **2** A. Fiedler (EG) 13.6; **3** J. Vernon (UK) 13.7; **4** B. Thompson (UK) 13.9.

High Jump: **1** R. Witschas (EG) 1.89m (6' 2¼") (*UK all-comers record*); **2** R. Kirst (EG) 1.86m (6' 1¼"); **3** V. Harrison (UK) 1.83m (6' 0"); **4** B. Lawton (UK) 1.80m (5' 10¾").

Long Jump: **1** A. Schmalfeld (EG) 6.47m (21' 2¾"); **2** K. Albertus (EG) 6.38m (20' 11¼"); **3** R. Martin-Jones (UK) 6.32m (20' 9"); **4** A. Wilson (UK) 6.07m (19' 11").

Shot: **1** M. Adam (EG) 19.11m (62' 8½"); **2** M. Lange (EG) 18.89m (61' 11¾"); **3** B. Bedford (UK) 15.02m (49' 3½"); **4** J. Kerr (UK) 13.97m (45' 10").

Discus: **1** G. Hinzmann (EG) 61.98m (203' 4"); **2** S. Engel (EG) 60.00m (196' 10"); **3** R. Payne (UK) 55.44m (181' 11"); **4** M. Ritchie (UK) 47.98m (157' 5").

Javelin: **1** R. Fuchs (EG) 65.58m (215' 2"); **2** J. Todten (EG) 62.06m (203' 7"); **3** T. Sanderson (UK) 51.22m (168' 0"); **4** P. Carter (UK) 45.74m (150' 1").

4 × 100m Relay: **1** East Germany (P. Kandarr, R. Stecher, C. Heinich, D. Maletzki) 43.8; **2** UK (H. Golden, M. Williams, J. Vernon, A. Lynch) 44.5.

4 × 400m Relay: **1** UK 3:30.0 (C. Warden 54.4, J. Roscoe 52.6, V. Bernard 51.7, D. Murray 51.3); **2** East Germany 3:30.6 (G. Anton 55.0, J. Meier 52.2, A. Handt 51.6, E. Streidt 51.8).

Match Result: East Germany 90, UK 44.

Non-Match Event:
3000m: **1** J. Smith 9:04.4 (*Commonwealth & UK national record*); **2** A. Yeoman 9:21.2; **3** C. Gould 9:24.4.

21, 22 June
AMERICAN AAU CHAMPIONSHIPS

Ivory Crockett's reign as 'world's fastest human' lasted six weeks. He was deposed unceremoniously at Westwood, California, on 21 June when he trailed in seventh in the AAU 100 metres final (10.2), while up front 20-year-old Steve Williams had stopped the watches at 9.9, 9.9, and 10.0 to tie the world record of 9.9 first established by Jim Hines in 1968. The assisting breeze of 1.3 metres per second was well within the limit. Feeling twinges in his leg (he was just recovering from a thigh injury), Williams eased off in the last 15 yards when he knew the race was safely his . . . and that might have cost him a 9.8 clocking. Short of conditioning, Williams wound up only fourth in the 200 metres

Steve Williams.

next day, the title going to Jamaica's Don Quarrie who had, in the 100 metres, equalled the Commonwealth record of 10.0 in second place.

Rick Wohlhuter missed the world 800 metres record by a bare fifth of a second with 1:43.9, and another remarkable middle-distance run came in the 1500 metres with 19-year-old Tom Byers, merely a 4:18.3 miler in 1973, running New Zealander Rod Dixon to a couple of yards in 3:37.9 – the equivalent of close to 3:55 for a mile! 'I can't believe it', he gasped.

100m: **1** S. Williams 9.9 (*equals World record*); **2** D. Quarrie (Jam) 10.0 (*equals Commonwealth record*); **3** R. Jones 10.1; **4** S. Riddick 10.1; **5** M. Lutz 10.2; **6** D. Meriwether 10.2; **7** I. Crockett 10.2; **8** H. Williams 10.3.

200m: **1** D. Quarrie (Jam) 20.5; **2** J. Gilkes (Guy) 20.7; **3** R. Jones 20.7; **4** S. Williams 20.7; **5** J. Pettus 21.1; **6** M. McFarland 21.1; **7** L. Wilson 21.1; **8** M. Lutz 21.1.

400m: **1** M. Peoples 45.2; **2** D. Bond 45.6; **3** T. Erickson 45.7; **4** H. Frazier 46.0; **5** B. Brown 46.0; **6** C. Mills 46.2; **7** F. Sowerby (Antigua) 46.2; **8** S. Vinson 46.4.

800m: **1** R. Wohlhuter 1:43.9; **2** J. Walker (NZ) 1:45.3; **3** J. Robinson 1:45.7; **4** M. Robinson 1:46.0; **5** K. Francis 1:46.2; **6** B. Dyce (Jam) 1:46.2; **7** L. Paul 1:47.0; **8** R. Geter 1:54.0.

1500m: **1** R. Dixon (NZ) 3:37.5; **2** T. Byers 3:37.9; **3** J. Hartnett (Eir) 3:38.1; **4** M. Slack 3:38.5; **5** B. Fischer 3:38.6; **6** L. Hilton 3:39.1; **7** T. Fulton 3:40.4; **8** R. McAfee 3:41.5.

5000m: **1** R. Buerkle 13:33.4; **2** F. Shorter 13:34.6; **3** D. Kardong 13:35.6; **4** E. Castaneda 13:35.8; **5** M. Liquori 13:40.6; **6** D. Quax (NZ) 13:45.2; **7** S. Stageberg 13:47.6; **8** M. Peterson 13:52.4.

10,000m: **1** F. Shorter 28:16.0; **2** R. Buerkle 28:25.0; **3** G. Bjorklund 28:28.4; **4** C. Maguire 28:29.4; **5** G. Tuttle 28:35.2; **6** J. Anderson 28:49.0; **7** S. Eden 29:21.8; **8** G. Herold 29:30.6.

3000m Steeplechase: **1** J. Johnson 8:28.8; **2** D. Brown 8:28.8; **3** M. Manley 8:29.0; **4** E. Leddy (Eir) 8:35.2; **5** R. Addison 8:35.6; **6** D. Timm 8:36.4; **7** G. Innes 8:38.8; **8** J. Lucas 8:48.0.

110m Hurdles: **1** C. Foster 13.4; **2** T. Hill 13.5; **3** W. Davenport 13.5; **4** C. Rich 13.7; **5** C. Jackson 13.7; **6** J. Wilson 13.8; **7** L. Shipp 13.8; **8** G. Carty 13.9.

400m Hurdles: **1** J. Bolding 48.9; **2** R. Mann 49.5; **3** J. King 49.5; **4** M. Shine 49.9; **5** W. Williams 49.9; **6** R. Cassleman 50.2; **7** C. Stevenson 50.9; **8** J. Gailey 51.1.

High Jump: **1** D. Stones 2.21m (7' 3¼"); **2** R. Brown 2.19m (7' 2¼"); **3** M. Branch 2.19m; **4** R. Smith 2.13m (7' 0"); **5** M. Fleer 2.13m; **6** P. Matzdorf 2.13m; **7** M. Embree 2.13m; **8** D. Adama 2.13m.

Pole Vault: **1** D. Roberts 5.33m (17' 6"); **2** T. Porter 5.18m (17' 0"); **3** R. Carter 5.18m; **4** V. Dias 5.18m; **5** J. Taylor 5.03m (16' 6"); **6 eq** P. Aldrich, R. Pullard, & R. Slover 5.03m.

Long Jump: **1** B. Moore 8.07m (26' 5¾"); **2** A. Robinson 8.03m (26' 4¼"); **3** H. Jackson (Jam) 7.95m (26' 1¼"); **4** D. Seay 7.92m (26' 0"); **5** W. Rea 7.92m (25' 11¾"); **6** J. Herndon 7.77m (25' 6"); **7** C. Ehizuelen (Nig) 7.64m (25' 0¾"); **8** S. Whitley 7.62m (25' 0¼").

Triple Jump: **1** J. Craft 16.58m (54' 4¾"); **2** C. Ehizuelen (Nig) 16.45m (53' 11¾"); **3** J. Butts 16.34m (53' 7¼"); **4** T. Haynes 16.32m (53' 6½"); **5** M. Tiff 16.29m (53' 5¼"); **6** H. Jackson (Jam) 16.15m (53' 0"); **7** R. Dupree 16.15m; **8** K. McBryde 15.89m (52' 1½").

Shot: **1** A. Feuerbach 21.58m (70' 9¾"); **2** G. Woods 21.40m (70' 2½"); **3** J. Stuart 20.44m (67' 0¾"); **4** P. Shmock 20.06m (65' 9¾"); **5** D. LeDuc 20.03m (65' 8¾"); **6** S. Walker 19.82m (65' 0¼"); **7** R. Marks 19.35m (63' 5¾"); **8** D. Doupe 18.59m (61' 0").

Discus: **1** J. Powell 65.50m (214' 11"); **2** M. Wilkins 62.72m (205' 9"); **3** R. Drescher 60.86m (199' 8"); **4** M. Smith 59.54m (195' 4"); **5** L. Kennedy 57.88m (189' 11"); **6** J. McGoldrick 57.76m (189' 6"); **7** M. Louisiana 57.20m (187' 8"); **8** D. Tollefson 57.18m (187' 7").

Hammer: 1 S. De Autremont 69.04m (226′ 6″); 2 P. Farmer (Aus) 68.20m (223′ 9″); 3 T. Gage 67.60m (221′ 9″); 4 W. Shuff 66.62m (218′ 7″); 5 L. Hart 64.88m (212′ 10″); 6 P. Galle 63.20m (207′ 4″); 7 W. Diehl 62.54m (205′ 2″); 8 A. Bessette 62.08m (203′ 8″).

Javelin: 1 S. Colson 85.54m (280′ 8″); 2 F. Luke 84.84m (278′ 4″); 3 A. Hall 80.92m (265′ 6″); 4 W. Schmidt 79.74m (261′ 7″); 5 M. Sonsky 76.72m (251′ 8″); 6 D. Reiss 74.98m (246′ 0″); 7 R. Kouvolo 73.34m (240′ 7″); 8 G. Derwin 72.30m (237′ 2″).

Decathlon: (at Richmond, Va, 14, 15 June) 1 B. Jenner 8245; 2 J. Bennett 7913; 3 F. Samara 7852; 4 J. Warkentin 7837; 5 S. Gough 7786; 6 R. Wanamaker 7689; 7 R. Evans 7635; 8 M. Hill 7472.

29, 30 June

POLAND v UK v CANADA

Close matches are the norm when British and Polish men confront each other, and this latest clash in Warsaw was no exception. Britain led by three points after the first day, but it was Poland who finished ahead by just two points – leaving Britain still seeking her first win in this series.

Quite the most encouraging aspect of the match was that Britain's 12 successes (to Poland's nine) included all four throwing events. Howard Payne, who first competed against Poland way back in 1961, not only won the hammer but for good measure achieved his life's ambition of throwing 70 metres. In fact he reached 70.88 metres (232′ 6″), an astonishing achievement for a man of 43 in his 21st year of hammer twirling.

Four others won with personal bests: Ainsley Bennett in the 200 metres, 18-year-old Steve Ovett in the 800 metres, Bill Hartley in the 400 metres hurdles, and Alan Lerwill in the long jump. Charles Kirkpatrick didn't win, but he displayed remarkable improvement in the 110 metres hurdles, progressing from 14.1 to 13.7 to tie for third on the UK all-time list. As the results indicate, Warsaw lived up to its reputation as a paradise for sprinters and high hurdlers in search of fast times, and some of the performances should be treated with caution.

The girls also took advantage of the flattering conditions to set three UK records. Andrea Lynch ran 100 metres in 11.1 behind Irena Szewinska's Polish record of 10.9, Helen Golden clocked 23.0 for 200 metres in a non-match event, and both Judy Vernon and Blondelle Thompson (improving half a second) were credited with 13.0 in the 100 metres hurdles. Helen also equalled the former British record of 11.2 behind Andrea in the 100. Additionally, Christine Warden set national 400 metres hurdles figures of 58.0 in a non-scoring race and Tessa Sanderson improved her UK junior record to 53.70 metres (176′ 2″) in the javelin. Donna Murray continued her rise to the top as a 400 metres runner, clocking 52.2 and narrowly failing to catch Commonwealth champion Yvonne Saunders (Can).

MEN

100m: 1 Z. Nowosz (Pol) 10.2; 2 R. Martin (Can) 10.3; 3 D. Halliday (UK) 10.3; 4 M. Woronin (Pol) 10.3; 5 M. Nash (Can) 10.4; 6 S. Green (UK) 10.8.

200m: 1 A. Bennett (UK) 20.9; 2 R. Martin (Can) 21.0; 3 Z. Nowosz (Pol) 21.1; 4 S. Green (UK) 21.3; 5 G. Madry (Pol) 21.3; 6 A. Dukowski (Can) 21.4.

ATHLETICS 75

400m: 1 D. Jenkins (UK) 45.5; 2 M. Wasik (Pol) 46.7; 3 Z. Jaremski (Pol) 46.9; 4 H. Fraser (Can) 47.1; 5 S. Marlow (UK) 47.8; 6 G. Bogue (Can) 49.4.

800m: 1 S. Ovett (UK) 1:46.8; 2 D. McMeekin (UK) 1:47.2; 3 A. Kupczyk (Pol) 1:47.6; 4 K. Linkowski (Pol) 1:48.6; 5 R. Makolosky (Can) 1:48.9; 6 P. Richardson (Can) 1:50.9.

1500m: 1 P. Craig (Can) 3:39.9; 2 H. Szordykowski (Pol) 3:40.3; 3 R. Smedley (UK) 3:40.5; 4 P. Banning (UK) 3:41.4; 5 H. Wasilewski (Pol) 3:41.6; 6 P. Spir (Can) 3:46.8.

5000m: 1 A. Simmons (UK) 13:33.6; 2 G. McLaren (Can) 13:34.4; 3 B. Malinowski (Pol) 13:35.2; 4 E. Mleczko (Pol) 13:38.8; 5 B. Ford (UK) 13:43.0; 6 R. Munro (Can) 14:49.6.

10,000 metres: 1 H. Nogala (Pol) 28:30.2; 2 D. Shaughnessy (Can) 28:33.2; 3 B. Plain (UK) 28:46.0; 4 T. Howard (Can) 28:51.8; 5 Z. Pierzynka (Pol) 29:04.6; 6 John Brown (UK) 29:29.8.

3000m Steeplechase: 1 H. Lesiuk (Pol) 8:31.6; 2 J. Kondzior (Pol) 8:32.2; 3 J. Bicourt (UK) 8:32.6; 4 D. Camp (UK) 8:36.6; 5 D. Kerr (Can) 8:53.0; 6 G. Hutchinson (Can) 9:07.2.

110m Hurdles: 1 L. Wodzynski (Pol) 13.3; 2 M. Wodzynski (Pol) 13.4; 3 C. Kirkpatrick (UK) 13.7; 4 D. Wilson (UK) 13.9; 5 G. Neeland (Can) 14.4; 6 D. Taillon (Can) 14.4.

400m Hurdles: 1 W. Hartley (UK) 49.9; 2 T. Kulczycki (Pol) 50.3; 3 D. Jarvis (Can) 51.0; 4 S. Black (UK) 51.7; 5 W. Szlendek (Pol) 52.4; 6 H. Grange (Can) 55.3.

20km Walk: 1 J. Ornoch (Pol) 1:29:02.8; 2 R. Mills (UK) 1:34:12.6; 3 F. Sliwinski (Pol) 1:36:10.4; 4 B. Adams (UK) 1:41:16.6.

4×100m Relay: 1 UK (L. Piggot, D. Halliday, I. Matthews, C. Monk) 39.7; 2 Canada 39.8; Poland did not finish.

4×400m Relay: 1 UK (J. Wilson, J. Aukett, W. Hartley, D. Jenkins) 3:04.2; 2 Poland 3:05.4; 3 Canada 3:07.9.

High Jump: 1 D. Bauck (Can) 2.16m (7' 1"); 2 J. Wszola (Pol) 2.14m (7' 0¼"); 3 J. Wrzosek (Pol) 2.14m (7' 0¼"); 4 G. Joy (Can) 2.08m (6' 9¾"); 5 A. Lerwill (UK) 2.00m (6' 6¾"); 6 C. Boreham (UK) 1.95m (6' 4¾").

Pole Vault: 1 W. Buciarski (Pol) 5.15m (16' 10¾"); 2 B. Simpson (Can) 5.15m; 3 T. Slusarski (Pol) 5.15m; 4 B. Hooper (UK) 5.00m (16' 4¾"); 5 K. Wenman (Can) 4.90m (16' 0¾"); M. Bull (UK) no height (broken pole).

Long Jump: 1 A. Lerwill (UK) 7.98m (26' 2¼"); 2 S. Szudrowicz (Pol) 7.80m (25' 7¼"); 3 G. Hignett (UK) 7.63m (25' 0½"); 4 A. Kedzierski (Pol) 7.59m (24' 11"); 5 R. Cuttell (Can) 7.44m (24' 5"); 6 G. Bell (Can) 7.04m (23' 1¼").

Triple Jump: 1 M. Joachimowski (Pol) 16.67m (54' 8¼"); 2 R. Garnys (Pol) 16.52m (54' 2½"); 3 D. Johnson (UK) 15.80m (51' 10"); 4 W. Clark (UK) 15.75m (51' 8¼"); 5 G. Bell (Can) 15.45m (50' 8¼"); 6 D. Watt (Can) 15.43m (50' 7½").

Shot: 1 G. Capes (UK) 20.58m (67' 6¼"); 2 M. Winch (UK) 19.42m (63' 8¾"); 3 M. Breczynski (Pol) 18.62m (61' 1¼"); 4 E. Antczak (Pol) 18.47m (60' 7¼"); 5 B. Dologiewicz (Can) 18.42m (60' 5¼"); 6 B. Caulfield (Can) 18.18m (59' 7¾").

Discus: 1 W. Tancred (UK) 60.74m (199' 3"); 2 S. Wolodko (Pol) 59.70m (195' 10"); 3 Z. Gryzbon (Pol) 58.08m (190' 7"); 4 J. Hillier (UK) 56.04m (183' 10"); 5 A. Roost (Can) 55.38m (181' 8"); 6 B. Chambul (Can) 51.88m (170' 2").

Hammer: 1 H. Payne (UK) 70.88m (232' 6"); 2 S. Jaglinski (Pol) 69.02m (226' 5"); 3 C. Black (UK) 66.98m (219' 9"); 4 J. Rys (Pol) 65.70m (215' 7"); 5 B. Dolegiewicz (Can) 45.32m (148' 8"); 6 B. Chambul (Can) 30.66m (100' 7").

Javelin: 1 D. Travis (UK) 78.86m (258' 9"); 2 J. Kaczmarczyk (Pol) 77.16m (253' 2"); 3 B. Werner (Pol) 76.76m (251' 10"); 4 R. Dowswell (Can) 76.64m (251' 5"); 5 R. Silvester (UK) 74.98m (246' 0"); 6 P. Olsen (Can) 74.88m (245' 8").

Match Result: Poland 111, UK 109; UK 128, Canada 83; Poland 131, Canada 79.

Non-Match Event
200m: 1 C. Monk (UK) 20.7.

WOMEN

100m: 1 I. Szewinska (Pol) 10.9; 2 A. Lynch (UK) 11.1 (*UK national record*); 3 A. Szubert (Pol) 11.2; 4 H. Golden (UK) 11.2; 5 M. Bailey (Can) 11.3; 6 P. Loverock (Can) 11.5.

200m: 1 I. Szewinska (Pol) 22.4; **2** M. Bailey (Can) 23.1; **3** A. Szubert (Pol) 23.3; **4** A. Lynch (UK) 23.3; **5** D. Murray (UK) 23.4; **6** P. Loverock (Can) 24.3.

400m: 1 Y. Saunders (Can) 51.9; **2** D. Murray (UK) 52.2; **3** K. Kacperczyk (Pol) 52.4; **4** D. Piecyk (Pol) 53.7; **5** J. Roscoe (UK) 53.9; **6** B. Walsh (Can) 54.6.

800m: 1 E. Katolik (Pol) 2:02.2; **2** M. Crowley (Can) 2:03.9; **3** R. Wright (UK) 2:04.3; **4** J. Januchta (Pol) 2:04.3; **5** H. Tanner (UK) 2:07.9; **6** G. Reiser (Can) 2:09.0.

1500m: 1 C. Surdel (Pol) 4:15.3; **2** J. Smith (UK) 4:15.9; **3** T. Wright (Can) 4:17.3; **4** U. Prasek (Pol) 4:18.7; **5** M. Stewart (UK) 4:19.2; **6** A-M. Davis (Can) 4:22.4.

3000m: 1 T. Wright (Can) 9:08.0; **2** A. Yeoman (UK) 9:09.2; **3** R. Pentlinowska (Pol) 9:13.8; **4** A-M. Davis (Can) 9:29.0; **5** C. Gould (UK) 9:32.0; **6** D. Siemieniuk (Pol) 9:44.0.

100m Hurdles: 1 T. Nowak (Pol) 12.6; **2** J. Vernon (UK) 13.0 (*UK national record*); **3** B. Thompson (UK) 13.0 (*UK national record*); **4** S. Bradley (Can) 13.5; **5** B. Nowakowska (Pol) 13.6; **6** L. Damman (Can) 13.8.

High Jump: 1 B. Lawton (UK) 1.86m (6' 1¼"); **2** D. Brill (Can) 1.84m (6' 0½"); **3** V. Harrison (UK) 1.82m (5' 11½"); **4** L. Hanna (Can) 1.78m (5' 10"); **5** D. Holowinska (Pol) 1.75m (5' 8¾"); **6** J. Szmatloch (Pol) 1.70m (5' 7").

Long Jump: 1 B. Eisler (Can) 6.41m (21' 0½"); **2** A. Wilson (UK) 6.30m (20' 8"); **3** M. Sadalska (Pol) 6.28m (20' 7¼"); **4** R. Martin-Jones (UK) 6.26m (20' 6½"); **5** K. Pulczynski (Pol) 6.22m (20' 5"); **6** D. Jones (Can) 6.10m (20' 0¼").

Shot: 1 L. Chewinska (Pol) 18.13m (59' 5¾"); **2** J. Kalina (Pol) 16.56m (54' 4"); **3** D. Jones (Can) 14.44m (47' 4½"); **4** B. Bedford (UK) 14.40m (47' 3"); **5** J. Kerr (UK) 14.39m (47' 2½"); **6** J. Haist (Can) 14.09m (46' 2¾").

Discus: 1 D. Rosani (Pol) 53.94m (177' 0"); **2** J. Haist (Can) 53.48m (175' 5"); **3** R. Payne (UK) 53.08m (174' 2"); **4** C. Martin (Can) 50.24m (164' 10"); **5** D. Cymer (Pol) 48.18m (158' 1"); **6** J. Thompson (UK) 42.96m (140' 11").

Javelin: 1 D. Jaworska (Pol) 55.52m (182' 2"); **2** T. Sanderson (UK) 53.70m (176' 2"); **3** F. Flak (Pol) 51.80m (169' 11"); **4** S. Corbett (UK) 48.88m (160' 4"); **5** L. Beland (Can) 46.12m (151' 4"); **6** L. Kern (Can) 42.60m (139' 9").

4 × 100m Relay: 1 Poland 43.6; **2** UK (H. Golden, M. Williams, J. Vernon, A. Lynch) 44.3; **3** Canada 45.2.

4 × 400m Relay: 1 UK (E. Barnes, J. Roscoe, V. Bernard, D. Murray) 3:32.0; **2** Poland 3:32.2; **3** Canada 3:35.0.

Match Result: Poland 80, UK 66; UK 81, Canada 65; Poland 85, Canada 61.

Non-Match Events

200m: 1 H. Golden (UK) 23.0 (*UK national record*); **2** B. Bakulin (Pol) 23.2; **3** S. Colyear (UK) 23.3; **4** M. Williams (UK) 23.5.

400m: 1 R. Kennedy (UK) 53.5.

400m Hurdles: 1 C. Warden (UK) 58.0 (*Commonwealth & UK national record*); **2** S. Howell (UK) 59.5; **3** Zwolinska (Pol) 59.6.

JUNE HIGHLIGHTS

The European 110 metres hurdles record of 13.2, held since 1959 (when it constituted a world record) by Martin Lauer of West Germany, was equalled by Guy Drut (Fra) in Paris on 3 June. The following wind was, at 2 metres per second, the maximum allowable for record purposes. He tied the mark again (with a 1.9-metre wind) at Fontainebleau on 8 June. Another European record to be equalled was the steeplechase figure of 8:18.4, achieved by Michael Karst (W G) in Helsinki on 26 June. Miroslav Kodejs (Cze) set a European 440 yards hurdles record of 49.4 in Prague on 30 June, although intrinsically this was a full second inferior to David Hemery's 400 metres hurdles record.

Only a lack of foresight by officials prevented Rick Wohlhuter (USA) claiming two world records at Eugene, Oregon, on 8 June. Wohlhuter broke his own 880 yards record all right – with 1:44.1 – and he must have been inside the global 800 metres standard of 1:43.7 by Marcello Fiasconaro (Ita) en route. Unfortunately, no timekeepers were stationed at that point (five yards short of 880 yards). It is probable that Wohlhuter passed 800 metres in 1:43.4/1:43.5. He reached 440 yards in 51.0 and was alone on the second lap, winning by over 50 yards.

Ten years after winning her first Olympic gold medal, Irena Szewinska (Pol) embarked on the most brilliant phase to date of an already fabulously successful career. Early in the month she set national records of 11.0 for 100 metres and 22.3 for 200 metres; then in East Germany she twice beat Renate Stecher most convincingly: 11.2 to 11.3, against the wind, in Berlin on 12 June, and a world record of 22.0 as against Stecher's 22.5 in Potsdam next day. The wind in the 200 was a permissible 1.9 metres and the electrical time was 22.21, also the fastest on record. And that wasn't all, for in Warsaw on 22 June she ran the second 400 metres race of her life – and smashed the world record by 1.1 seconds with the breathtaking time of 49.9! The 51 and 50 sec barriers had been shattered at one stroke. Intermediate times were 11.8 at 100 metres, 22.9 at 200 (faster than the UK record!), and 35.7 at 300.

Roy Thorpe, the Commonwealth silver medallist, led practically throughout in the Race Walking Association national 20 miles championship, held in hot weather conditions at Redditch on 15 June.

Result: 1 R. Thorpe 2:39:47; **2** R. Dobson 2:42:45; **3** J. Warhurst 2:44:54; **4** B. Adams 2:48:30; **5** C. Fogg 2:48:45; **6** R. Middleton 2:49:41; **7** A. Seddon 2:50:03; **8** P. Hodkinson 2:50:44; **9** J. Nye 2:53:27; **10** P. Selby 2:53:27. **Team:** Southend AC.

A share in a world sprint record came Britain's way when Andrea Lynch clocked 7.2 for the rarely run 60 metres at Crystal Palace on 22 June. The aiding wind was 1.5 metres per second and Raelene Boyle (Aus) was second in 7.4. The same day, in Warsaw, Andrea's training companion Judy Vernon again equalled the UK 100 metres hurdles record of 13.2.

The world record for 440 yards of 52.2 was equalled by Debra Sapenter in the American Women's Championships at Bakersfield, California, on 29 June, but such a performance – worth 51.9 for 400 metres – hardly merits the distinction of an IAAF world record plaque. Irena Szewinska's 49.9 400 metres would have left the American some 15 metres behind.

A classic 1500 metres return match between Filbert Bayi (Tan) and his Christchurch runner-up John Walker (NZ) was staged in Helsinki on 27 June. Bayi hurtled through 400 in 52.9, 800 in 1:50.4, and 1200 in 2:50.4 before running out of steam in the closing stages. Walker, whose intermediate times were 57.5, 1:56.5, and 2:53.0, won in 3:33.4 with Bayi showing 3:37.0.

Right: *Giving vent to pent-up emotions: 16-year-old Lesley Kiernan bursts into tears as she breaks the tape to win the 800 metres final at the WAAA Championships in July. Two months later, and just 17, she was competing in Rome at the European Championships.*

July

3-6 July
EAST GERMAN CHAMPIONSHIPS

East Germans won 10 gold medals at the European Championships, but the star of their national championships at Leipzig two months earlier was a man who had to settle for the bronze award in Rome: hammer exponent Reinhard Theimer (26). During the qualifying round on 4 July he unleashed a throw of 76.60 metres (251' 4") to eclipse the world record held by West Germany's Walter Schmidt.

Other GDR records were set by Jurgen Straub (steeplechase), Klaus Schonberger (400 metres hurdles), Karl-Heinz Stadtmuller (20 kilometres walk) and Marianne Adam (women's shot). Shock result of the meeting was the defeat of world record holder Ruth Fuchs in the javelin – her first for three years.

MEN

100m: **1** M. Kokot 10.2; **2** J. Zenk 10.3; **3** H-J. Bombach 10.3; **4** M. Droese 10.3; **5** W. Lobe 10.4; **6** J. Pfeifer 10.4; **7** E. Weise 10.4; **8** E. Ray 10.4.

200m: **1** H-J. Bombach 20.5; **2** J. Zenk 20.6; **3** M. Droese 20.9; **4** S. Schenke 20.9; **5** J. Pfeifer 21.0; **6** A. Kuhne 21.1; **7** E. Ray 21.1; **8** E. Weise 21.2.

400m: **1** A. Scheibe 45.8; **2** J. Utikal 46.1; **3** B. Stops 46.2; **4** R. Kokot 46.2; **5** G. Pollakowski 46.5; **6** R. Schwara 46.5; **7** G. Arnold 46.7; **8** S. Lathan 47.0.

800m: **1** H-H. Ohlert 1:46.3; **2** G. Stolle 1:46.4; **3** D. Fromm 1:46.6; **4** E. Gohlke 1:47.0; **5** E. Muller 1:47.7; **6** V. Seifert 1:48.4; **7** D. Westkamper 1:49.0; **8** U. Schmidt 1:49.2.

1500m: **1** K-P. Justus 3:40.5; **2** B. Exner 3:40.6; **3** K-P. Weippert 3:40.6; **4** H. Stechemesser 3:42.0; **5** J. Hemmerling 3:43.3; **6** H. Lohmann 3:44.9; **7** H. Bartke 3:46.9; **8** B. Wagner 3:49.2.

5000m: **1** M. Kuschmann 13:27.6; **2** W. Scholz 13:35.0; **3** W. Cierpinski 13:39.4; **4** K-H. Leiteritz 13:46.6; **5** J. Lautzschmann 14:00.2; **6** S. Arndt 14:00.4; **7** H-H. Brautigam 14:10.8; **8** S. Bar 14:11.2.

10,000m: **1** M. Kuschmann 28:09.6; **2** K-H. Leiteritz 28:13.6; **3** J. Lautzschmann 28:24.2; **4** L. Obschonka 28:37.4; **5** E. Lesse 28:54.0; **6** M. Schroder 29:15.0; **7** J. Truppel 29:17.2; **8** H-H. Brautigam 29:29.2.

3000m Steeplechase: **1** J. Straub 8:30.0; **2** W. Cierpinski 8:32.6; **3** F. Baumgartl 8:44.6; **4** S. Nordwig 8:57.4; **5** U. Pischel 8:59.2; **6** H. Tannert 9:01.2; **7** S. Kutschbach 9:03.8; **8** G. Muller 9:05.6.

110m Hurdles: **1** F. Siebeck 13.6; **2** T. Munkelt 13.6; **3** K. Fiedler 13.6; **4** H-J. Gerhardt 14.2; **5** R. Bethge 14.2; **6** J. Wehnert 14.4; **7** S. Lanzendorf 14.6; **8** P. Fink 14.6.

400m Hurdles: **1** K. Schonberger 49.2; **2** J. Mayer 50.0; **3** S. Schwatke 50.4; **4** H. Jonas 51.1; **5** H-U. Ludwig 51.5; **6** U. Ludwig 52.3; **7** F. Ekelmann 53.5.

20km Walk: **1** K-H. Stadtmuller 1:25:13.0; **2** P. Frenkel 1:25:16.4; **3** L. Lipowski 1:27:18.2; **4** R. Berner 1:28:00.2 (*world junior record*); **5** H. Gauder 1:29:46.4; **6** S. Zschiegner 1:29:54.2; **7** R. Roder 1:30:17.0; **8** M. Kroel 1:30:41.0.

High Jump: **1** R. Beilschmidt 2.14m (7' 0¼"); **2** C. Dressler 2.11m (6' 11"); **3** S. Junge 2.11m (6' 11"); **4** D. Kazmierski 2.11m (6' 11"); **5** P. Hertel 2.11m (6' 11"); **6** E. Kirst 2.08m (6' 9¾"); **7** W. Heinrich 2.00m (6' 6¾"); **8** H. Schymiczek 2.00m (6' 6¾").

Pole Vault: **1** W. Reinhardt 5.00m (16' 4¾"); **2** M. Fruhauf 4.80m (15' 9"); **3** J. Bottcher 4.80m (15' 9"); **4** B. Neumann 4.80m (15' 9"); **5** A. Weber 4.80m (15' 9"); **6** P. Wienick 4.80m (15' 9"); **7** A. Berger 4.80m (15' 9"); **8** J. Krumpolt 4.60m (15' 1").

Long Jump: **1** M. Klauss 7.88m (25' 10¼"); **2** F. Wartenberg 7.85m (25' 9¼"); **3** W. Lauterbach 7.81m (25' 7½"); **4** H. Beck 7.64m (25' 0¾"); **5** L. Gawlik 7.46m (24' 5¾"); **6** H-D. Toboldt 7.41m (24' 3¾"); **7** S. Dahne 7.37m (24' 2¼"); **8** A. Hanel 7.33m (24' 0¾").

EAST GERMAN CHAMPIONSHIPS

Triple Jump: 1 J. Drehmel 16.35m (53' 7¾"); 2 K. Hufnagel 16.25m (53' 3¾"); 3 L. Gora 15.84m (51' 11¼"); 4 K-D. Mirow 15.33m (50' 3½"); 5 W. Lehmann 15.23m (49' 11¾"); 6 F. Schuster 15.06m (49' 5"); 7 H. Natzmer 14.86m (48' 9"); 8 W. Volks 14.38m (47' 2¼").

Shot: 1 H. Briesenick 20.29m (66' 7"); 2 U. Beyer 20.20m (66' 3¼") (*European junior record*); 3 P. Hlawatschke 19.66m (64' 6"); 4 H-P. Gies 19.38m (63' 7"); 5 N. Jahl 19.17m (62' 10¾"); 6 G. Lochmann 18.53m (60' 9½"); 7 M. Kaiser 18.52m (60' 9¼"); 8 J. Dressler 17.28m (56' 8½").

Discus: 1 G. Muller 60.60m (198' 10"); 2 H. Losch 59.84m (196' 4"); 3 S. Pachale 59.64m (195' 8"); 4 N. Thiede 59.36m (194' 9"); 5 K-D. Grube 54.58m (179' 1"); 6 L. Schlage 53.88m (176' 9"); 7 W. Warnemunde 53.06m (174' 1"); 8 H. Klink 50.98m (167' 3").

Hammer: 1 R. Theimer 73.62m (241' 6") In qualifying: 76.60m (251' 4") (*world record*); 2 J. Sachse 72.32m (237' 3"); 3 R. Engwicht 70.66m (231' 10"); 4 M. Seidel 70.22m (230' 4"); 5 H. Muller 68.38m (224' 4"); 6 K-H. Beilig 67.82m (222' 6"); 7 W. Skibba 67.22m (220' 6"); 8 J. Weiser 66.64m (218' 8").

Javelin: 1 M. Ahlert 80.62m (263' 4"); 2 D. Fuhrmann 77.46m (254' 1"); 3 M. Stolle 75.52m (247' 9"); 4 W. Hanisch 74.64m (244' 10"); 5 N. Kuske 73.66m (241' 8"); 6 D. Michel 73.14m (239' 11'); 7 W. Balster 72.30m (237' 2"); 8 D. Trensch 69.58m (228' 3").

WOMEN

100m: 1 R. Stecher 11.1; 2 C. Heinich 11.3; 3 B. Eckert 11.3; 4 D. Maletzki 11.3; 5 P. Kandarr 11.3; 6 R. Hoser 11.4; 7 K. Bodendorf 11.5; 8 R. Kupfer 11.6.

200m: 1 R. Stecher 22.6; 2 D. Maletzki 22.8; 3 P. Kandarr 22.9; 4 K. Bodendorf 22.9; 5 C. Heinich 23.0; 6 R. Hoser 23.2; 7 B. Steinhardt 23.6.

400m: 1 E. Streidt 51.5; 2 A. Handt 51.7; 3 B. Rohde 52.4; 4 G. Anton 52.5; 5 W. Dietsch 53.2; 6 J. Meier 53.9; 7 J. Morig 54.3; 8 C. Krause 55.3.

800m: 1 G. Hoffmeister 2:00.4; 2 W. Pohland 2:00.6; 3 M. Cierpinski 2:01.0; 4 E. Zinn 2:02.5; 5 A. Barkusky 2:03.6; 6 E. Fischer 2:03.6; 7 L. Cerveny 2:04.7; 8 C. Neumann 2:08.7.

1500m: 1 G. Hoffmeister 4:09.8; 2 U. Klapezynski 4:09.9; 3 K. Krebs 4:10.7; 4 W. Pohland 4:13.2; 5 C. Stoll 4:13.3; 6 D. Gluth 4:14.8; 7 I. Wagner 4:15 0; 8 S. Franke 4:17.3.

100m Hurdles: 1 A. Ehrhardt 12.8; 2 A. Fiedler 12.9; 3 G. Berend 13.1; 4 B. Eckert 13.2; 5 R. Walden 13.3; 6 B. Muller 13.8; 7 B. Schubert 14.0; 8 M. Filipiak 14.4.

High Jump: 1 R. Witschas 1.90m (6' 2¾"); 2 R. Kirst 1.84m (6' 0½"); 3 G. Krause 1.81m (5' 11¼"); 4 J. Krautwurst 1.75m (5' 8¾"); 5 K. Pfeifer 1.70m (5' 7"); 6 S. Krause 1.70m (5' 7"); 7 E. Planitzer 1.70m (5' 7"); 8 M. Messer 1.70m (5' 7").

Long Jump: 1 M. Voelzke 6.44m (21' 1½"); 2 A. Liebsch 6.31m (20' 8½"); 3 H. Anders 6.23m (20' 5¼"); 4 M. Olfert 6.20m (20' 4¼"); 5 S. Thon 6.15m (20' 2¼"); 6 K. Albertus 6.10m (20' 0½"); 7 E. Ahrendt 6.04m (19' 9¾"); 8 B. Seifert 6.01m (19' 8¾").

Shot: 1 M. Adam 20.61m (67' 7½"); 2 M. Lange 18.91m (62' 0½"); 3 B. Griessing 18.18m (59' 7¾"); 4 I. Schoknecht 17.90m (58' 8¾") (*world junior record*); 5 K. Schulze 17.79m (58' 4½"); 6 B. Loewe 17.74m (58' 2½"); 7 P. Gassmann 16.81m (55' 2"); 8 M. Droese 16.38m (53' 9").

Discus: 1 G. Hinzmann 62.72m (205' 9"); 2 B. Regel 61.64m (202' 3"); 3 A. Braun 59.30m (194' 7"); 4 K. Holdke 58.34m (191' 5"); 5 S. Engel 57.26m (187' 10"); 6 M. Kuhne 56.46m (185' 3"); 7 M. Droese 55.42m (181' 10"); 8 B. Sander 54.72m (179' 6").

Javelin: 1 J. Todten 64.34m (211' 1"); 2 R. Fuchs 61.18m (200' 9"); 3 U. Hommola 58.60m (192' 3"); 4 S. Kargel 55.62m (182' 6"); 5 A. Kopsch 54.40m (178' 6"); 6 M. Skudre 50.56m (165' 10"); 7 R. Stange 49.28m (161' 8"); 8 D. Jauche 47.72m (156' 7").

5, 6 July
USA v SOVIET UNION

The American men won for the ninth time in 12 matches against the Soviet Union, reversing the previous year's defeat, but the USSR women won their encounter so convincingly (for the 11th time) that it was the visitors who ran out ahead on aggregate at Durham, North Carolina. The two-day crowd of 65,000 saw two world records in the women's events: Lyudmila Bragina, having shown relatively indifferent form since her epic Olympic 1500 metres victory, shaved a fifth of a second off her own world record for 3000 metres with 8:52.8; and the Soviet sprint relay squad of Natalya Karnaukova, Lyudmila Maslakova, Marina Sidorova, and Nadyezhda Besfamilnaya set new figures of 44.15 for the practically extinct (outside USA) 4 × 110 yards event. The 4 × 100 metres record is worth a good second faster than that.

Two of the best American victories came in 800 metres races. Mary Decker, all of 15, produced an outdoor best of 2:02.3 to repeat her win of the previous year, and Rick Wohlhuter strung together laps of 52.5 and 51.5 for a super-fast 1:44.0.

MEN

100m: 1 R. Jones (US) 10.23; 2 S. Williams (US) 10.30; 3 A. Kornelyuk (Sov) 10.46; 4 J. Silovs (Sov) 10.57.

200m: 1 R. Jones (US) 20.81; 2 M. Lutz (US) 20.83; 3 V. Borzov (Sov) 20.84; 4 J. Silovs (Sov) 21.52.

400m: 1 D. Bond (US) 46.12; 2 M. Peoples (US) 46.28; 3 S. Kocher (Sov) 46.56; 4 V. Yurchenko (Sov) 47.41.

800m: 1 R. Wohlhuter (US) 1:44.0; 2 J. Robinson (US) 1:47.5; 3 P. Litovchenko (Sov) 1:48.9; 4 V. Ponomaryov (Sov) 1:49.0.

1500m: 1 V. Ponomaryov (Sov) 3:42.0; 2 V. Pantelei (Sov) 3:42.1; 3 T. Byers (US) 3:45.3; 4 M. Slack (US) 3:50.3.

5000m: 1 R. Buerkle (US) 13:26.2; 2 B. Kuznyetsov (Sov) 13:40.0; 3 M. Zhelobovskiy (Sov) 13:44.0; 4 D. Kardong (US) 13:54.6.

10,000m: 1 V. Zotov (Sov) 29:34.4; 2 C. Maguire (US) 29:36.4; 3 P. Andreyev (Sov) 29:37.8; 4 G. Tuttle (US) 29:53.8.

3000m Steeplechase: 1 J. Johnson (US) 8:33.4; 2 N. Mayorov (Sov) 8:39.4; 3 D. Brown (US) 8:44.6; S. Skripka (Sov) disqualified (8:30.2).

110m Hurdles: 1 T. Hill (US) 13.53; 2 C. Foster (US) 13.60; 3 A. Moshiashvili (Sov) 14.02; 4 Y. Mazepa (Sov) 14.14.

400m Hurdles: 1 Y. Gavrilenko (Sov) 49.63; 2 M. Shine (US) 49.83; 3 V. Savchenko (Sov) 50.86; 4 J. King (US) 51.60.

4 × 110y Relay: 1 USA 39.28; 2 Soviet Union 40.02.

4 × 440y Relay: 1 USA 3:05.0; 2 Soviet Union 3:07.4.

20km Walk: 1 N. Smaga (Sov) 1:37:26; 2 Y. Ivchenko (Sov) 1:37:26; 3 F. Godwin (US) 1:38:32; 4 J. Brown (US) 1:41:32.

High Jump: 1 R. Brown (US) 2.19m (7' 2¼"); 2 V. Abramov (Sov) 2.19m (7' 2¼"); 3 S. Budalov (Sov) 2.19m (7' 2¼"); 4 M. Branch (US) 2.16m (7' 1").

Pole Vault: 1 V. Trofimenko (Sov) 5.13m (16' 10"); 2 T. Porter (US) 4.98m (16' 4"); D. Roberts (US) and Y. Issakov (Sov) no height.

Long Jump: 1 V. Podluzhny (Sov) 8.05m (26' 5"); 2 A. Robinson (US) 8.03m (26' 4¼"); 3 B. Moore (US) 7.86m (25' 9½"); 4 V. Saneyev (Sov) 7.47m (24' 6").

Triple Jump: 1 V. Saneyev (Sov) 16.56m (54' 4"); 2 G. Byessonov (Sov) 16.32m (53' 6½"); 3 J. Craft (US) 15.76m (51' 8½"); 4 J. Butts 15.41m (50' 6¾").

Shot: 1 V. Voikin (Sov) 20.69m (67' 10¾"); 2 J. Stuart (US) 20.17m (66' 2¼"); 3 A. Yarosh (Sov) 20.03m (65' 8¾"); 4 P. Shmock (US) 19.60m (64' 3¾").

Discus: 1 M. Wilkins (US) 61.12m (200' 6"); 2 R. Drescher (US) 58.94m (193' 4"); 3 V. Zhurba (Sov) 55.60m (182' 5"); 4 V. Voikin (Sov) 49.66m (162' 11").
Hammer: 1 A. Spiridonov (Sov) 74.66m (244' 11"); 2 A. Bondarchuk (Sov) 73.02m (239' 7"); 3 S. DeAutremont (US) 67.08m (220' 1"); 4 T. Gage (US) 64.68m (212' 2").
Javelin: 1 S. Colson (US) 86.98m (285' 4"); 2 F. Luke (US) 82.74m (271' 5"); 3 J. Lusis (Sov) 81.66m (267' 11"); 4 J. Zirnis (Sov) 81.54m (267' 6").
Match Result: USA 117, Soviet Union 102.

WOMEN

100m: 1 R. Bowen (US) 11.62; 2 L. Maslakova (Sov) 11.65; 3 N. Besfamilnaya (Sov) 11.74; 4 M. Render (US) 11.78.
200m: 1 F. Sichting (US) 23.17; 2 M. Sidorova (Sov) 23.57; 3 R. McManus (US) 24.00; 4 N. Ilyina (Sov) 24.16.
400m: 1 D. Sapenter (US) 52.13; 2 N. Ilyina (Sov) 52.88; 3 I. Barkane (Sov) 53.45; 4 S. Choates (US) 54.30.
800m: 1 M. Decker (US) 2:02.3; 2 N. Sabaite (Sov) 2:02.7; 3 V. Gerassimova (Sov) 2:04.4; 4 R. Campbell (US) 2:04.4.
1500m: 1 T. Kazankina (Sov) 4:14.4; 2 T. Kazachkova (Sov) 4:18.2; 3 J. Brown (US) 4:26.7; 4 J. Graham (US) 4:30.1.
3000m: 1 L. Bragina (Sov) 8:52.8 (*world record*); 2 T. Pangelova (Sov) 9:13.4; 3 C. Choate (US) 9:39.8; 4 M. Harewicz (US) 9:45.4.
100m Hurdles: 1 N. Lebedyeva (Sov) 13.2; 2 M. Rallins (US) 13.2; 3 P. Johnson (US) 13.4; 4 L. Popovskaya (Sov) 13.6.
4 × 110y Relay: 1 Soviet Union 44.15 (*world record*); 2 USA 44.29.
4 × 440y Relay: 1 Soviet Union 3:34.3; 2 USA 3:36.3.
High Jump: 1 J. Huntley (US) 1.83m (6' 0"); 2 T. Schlachto (Sov) 1.80m (5' 11"); 3 T. Galka (Sov) 1.73m (5' 8"); 4 P. Spencer (US) 1.67m (5' 6").
Long Jump: 1 M. Watson (US) 6.50m (21' 4"); 2 W. White (US) 6.46m (21' 2½"); 3 M. Treinite (Sov) 6.32m (20' 9"); 4 O. Rukavishnikova (Sov) 6.16m (20' 2½").
Shot: 1 N. Chizhova (Sov) 21.22m (69' 7½"); 2 F. Melnik (Sov) 17.53m (57' 6¼"); 3 M. Seidler (US) 17.01m (55' 9¾"); 4 C. Reinhoudt (US) 14.62m (47' 11¾").
Discus: 1 F. Melnik (Sov) 66.32m (217' 7"); 2 T. Danilova (Sov) 57.88m (189' 11"); 3 M. Driscoll (US) 49.10m (161' 1"); 4 L. Langford (US) 48.08m (157' 9").
Javelin: 1 S. Babich (Sov) 59.76m (196' 1"); 2 K. Schmidt (US) 58.28m (191' 2"); 3 N. Marakina (Sov) 56.08m (184' 0"); 4 L. Cannon (US) 52.42m (172' 0").
Pentathlon: 1 L. Popovskaya (Sov) 4557; 2 O. Rukabishnikova (Sov) 4321; 3 M. McMillin (US) 3982; 4 M. King (US) 3934.
Match Result: Soviet Union 90, USA 67.   **Overall Match Result:** Soviet Union 192, USA 184.

6, 7 July

INTERNATIONAL DECATHLON & PENTATHLON

The Dutch won the men's decathlon against the UK, Denmark, and Spain, and the women's pentathlon against the UK and Denmark at Middlesbrough – both on a team and individual basis. Mike Corden, the AAA champion, languished in 15th and last place at the end of the first day's events but finished strongly to fill fifth position with a score close to 7000 points. Chris Youngs, substituting for Commonwealth champion Mike Bull, dropped from second to 12th on the second day but still recorded his highest ever score. There was a personal best, too, in the pentathlon by international high jumper Sue Wright.

ATHLETICS 75

DECATHLON

1 E. Schutter (Hol) 7253pts. 11.4; 7.24m (23' 9"); 12.01m (39' 5"); 1.93m (6' 4"); 49.5; 15.3; 38.36m (125' 10"); 4.30m (14' 1¼"); 40.94m (134' 4"); 4:29.9.
2 R. Cano (Spa) 7146pts. 11.4; 6.90m (22' 7¾"); 11.20m (36' 9"); 1.87m (6' 1½"); 50.8; 15.2; 36.78m (120' 8"); 4.10m (13' 5¼"); 56.38m (185' 0"); 4:31.1.
3 B. Ibsen (Den) 7036pts. 11.8; 6.97m (22' 10½"); 11.23m (36' 10¼"); 1.84m (6' 0½"); 51.5; 15.9; 39.12m (128' 4"); 3.80m (12' 5½"); 54.48m (178' 9"); 4:11.1.
4 E. Hansen (Den) 7005pts; **5** M. Corden (UK) 6969pts; **6** A. Drayton (UK) 6924pts; **7** J. de Noorlander (Hol) 6843pts;
8 A. Hasle (Den) 6837pts; **9** F. van der Ham (Hol) 6824pts; **10** N. Phipps (UK) 6712pts; **11** F. Schryders (Hol) 6707pts;
12 C. Youngs (UK) 6694pts; **13** J. Campos (Spa) 6444pts; **14** A. Ortiz (Spa) 6398pts.
Teams: **1** Netherlands 20,920pts; **2** Denmark 20,878pts; **3** UK 20,605pts; **4** Spain 19,988pts.

PENTATHLON

1 C. Jansen (Hol) 4306pts. 15.0; 12.56m (41' 2½"); 1.71m (5' 7¼"); 6.25m (20' 6¼"); 24.4.
2 A. Wilson (UK) 4189pts. 14.3; 10.49m (34' 5"); 1.75m (5' 8¾"); 6.25m (20' 6¼"); 25.6.
3 M. van Doorn (Hol) 4135pts. 14.6; 10.76m (35' 3¾"); 1.77m (5' 9¾"); 5.96m (19' 6¾"); 25.5.
4 S. Wright (UK) 4104pts; **5** G. Taylor (UK) 4021pts; **6** L. Janson (Den) 3797pts; **7** M. Hansen (Den) 3776pts;
8 L. Larsen (Den) 3520pts.
Teams: **1** Netherlands 8441pts; **2** UK 8293pts; **3** Denmark 7573pts.

Don Halliday (1) wins his 100 metres heat from Gareth Edwards (10) and Japan's Masahide Jinnu at the AAA Championships.

12, 13 July
NATIONWIDE BUILDING SOCIETY AAA CHAMPIONSHIPS

It has long been a controversial issue whether the AAA Championships, in effect Britain's national championships, should continue to be thrown open to the world. Those in favour of the traditional format argue that the presence of top-line stars from abroad enhances the meeting's crowd appeal and affords valuable international competition for Britain's leading athletes. Others feel that true national championships should be restricted to UK competitors only and that the influx of foreigners deprives many home athletes of the chance of reaching finals.

The 1974 championships added fuel to the fire. The appearance of a most distinguished American party, including world record holders Steve Williams, Dwight Stones, and Al Feuerbach, should have ensured a bumper attendance at Crystal Palace, but damp, cold weather kept Saturday's crowd down to a mere 7,000 – second lowest in living memory for these championships. The overseas contingent fared so well that only nine of the 19 titles at stake stayed at home; and British athletes had also to contend with such situations as having five foreigners among 10 runners in one heat of the 1500 metres and there being 11 visitors in the 29-strong 5000 metres field.

The Americans put up a formidable showing, claiming eight of the 11 events they contested. Particularly impressive were Steve Williams, whose seemingly effortless though gigantic strides carried him to a casual 100 metres victory in a wind-aided 10.16; Jim Bolding, who showed why he was ranked number one 400 metres hurdler in the world for 1974 by defeating sub-50sec

For Howard Payne, the 1974 AAA Championships were the last in a distinguished career.

performer Bill Hartley by a dozen metres in a UK all-comers record of 49.1; and Al Feuerbach, whose opening put of 21.37 metres (70′ 1½″), another all-comers record, ended Geoff Capes' hopes of victory – although the British athlete did well enough to hold world indoor record holder George Woods at bay.

The most eye-catching British victories came in the middle- and long-distance running department. Young Steve Ovett won the 800 metres à la Wottle (he was seventh with 200 metres to run); Brendan Foster tossed in a 59.2 eighth lap to break up the 5000 metres field; a short-of-training Dave Bedford ('hunted turned hunter') sat in for once and took the lead only in the last lap of the 10,000 metres; and John Davies crushed a good international steeplechase field in the second fastest time of his career. David Jenkins won his fourth consecutive 400 metres title, while Howard Payne was the highest placed UK hammer thrower for the 12th time since 1961.

100m: *Heat 1:* **1** S. Williams (USA) 10.6; **2** B. Green 10.8; **3** D. Roberts 10.8; **4** R. Turkington 11.1; **5** R. McStocker 11.2; **6** S. Matthews 11.2. *Heat 2:* **1** I. Matthews 10.9; **2** K. Roenn (Swe) 10.9; **3** M. Lutz (USA) 11.1; **4** G. Vince 11.1; **5** S. Bell 11.1; **6** D. Chapman 11.3. *Heat 3:* **1** D. Halliday 10.8; **2** G. Edwards 10.9; **3** M. Jinno (Jap) 11.0; **4** T. Collins 11.1; **5** B. Kelly 11.1. *Heat 4:* **1** L. Piggot 10.7; **2** S. Green 10.8; **3** T. Bonsor 10.9; **4** A. Cornaby 10.9; **5** P. Evans 11.2. *Semi 1:* **1** L. Piggot 10.6; **2** B. Green 10.6; **3** D. Roberts 10.6; **4** S. Green 10.7; **5** M. Lutz (USA) 10.7; **6** A. Cornaby 10.9; **7** T. Collins 11.0; **8** G. Vince 11.1. *Semi 2:* **1** S. Williams (USA) 10.3; **2** D. Halliday 10.5; **3** K. Roenn (Swe) 10.6; **4** I. Matthews 10.6; **5** M. Jinno (Jap) 10.6; **6** T. Bonsor 10.8; **7** R. Turkington 10.8; **8** G. Edwards 10.9. *FINAL:* **1** S. Williams (USA) 10.2 (10.16); **2** D. Halliday 10.4; **3** B. Green 10.5; **4** D. Roberts 10.5; **5** L. Piggot 10.5; **6** S. Green 10.5; **7** I. Matthews 10.7; **8** K. Roenn (Swe) 10.8.

200m: *Heat 1:* **1** M. Lutz (USA) 21.6; **2** A. Bennett 21.7; **3** I. Matthews 22.4; **4** G. Wood 22.4; **5** S. White 22.7; **6** R. Griffiths 23.0. *Heat 2:* **1** C. Monk 21.9; **2** S. Green 22.2; **3** T. Collins 22.3; **4** T. Rodwell 22.5; **5** G. Vince 23.6. *FINAL:* **1** M. Lutz (USA) 20.9; **2** C. Monk 21.0; **3** A. Bennett 21.0; **4** I. Matthews 21.4; **5** S. Green 21.4; **6** T. Collins 21.6; **7** G. Wood 22.0; **8** T. Rodwell 22.0.

400m: *Heat 1:* **1** D. Jenkins 47.0; **2** S. Marlow 47.6; **3** F. McSweeney (Eir) 47.8; **4** I. Saunders 47.9; **5** J. Caines 49.6; **6** S. McCallum 49.8; **7** R. Minting 50.2. *Heat 2:* **1** G. Cohen 47.5; **2** J. Wilson 47.6; **3** M. Delaney 47.8; **4** D. Laing 47.9; **5** R. Jenkins 48.0; **6** C. Jacks 49.3. *FINAL:* **1** D. Jenkins 46.1; **2** S. Marlow 47.2; **3** F. McSweeney (Eir) 47.3; **4** G. Cohen 47.4; **5** M. Delaney 47.7; **6** I. Saunders 47.9; **7** J. Wilson 48.0; **8** D. Laing 48.5.

800m: *Heat 1:* **1** M. Winzenried (USA) 1:48.1; **2** S. Ovett 1:48.4; **3** J. Greatrex 1:48.9; **4** A. Settle 1:49.4; **5** A. Roper 1:50.7; **6** J. McCarthy 1:51.5; **7** M. Bissell 1:51.7; **8** M. Fromant 1:54.8. *Heat 2:* **1** C. Campbell 1:47.9; **2** A. Carter 1:48.0; **3** B. Dyce (Jam) 1:48.3; **4** Phil Lewis 1:49.5; **5** N. Carroll (Eir) 1:50.2; **6** Peter Lewis 1:51.5; **7** E. Coffey 1:52.9; **8** T. Ishii (Jap) 1:53.7. *Heat 3:* **1** D. McMeekin 1:48.6; **2** P. Browne 1:48.9; **3** M. v. d. Heuvel (Hol) 1:49.2; **4** N. O'Shaughnessy (Eir) 1:49.4; **5** R. Anastasio (USA) 1:49.8; **6** A. Dyke 1:50.1; **7** R. Weatherburn 1:51.0; **8** J. Gerrard 1:53.4. *FINAL:* **1** S. Ovett 1:46.8; **2** A. Carter 1:47.0; **3** B. Dyce (Jam) 1:47.1; **4** M. Winzenried (USA) 1:47.2; **5** C. Campbell 1:47.8; **6** P. Browne 1:48.1; **7** D. McMeekin 1:49.1; **8** J. Greatrex 1:53.9.

1500m: *Heat 1:* **1** A. Waldrop (USA) 3:41.9; **2** F. Clement 3:41.9; **3** J. Douglas 3:42.3; **4** D. Gibbon 3:42.6; **5** T. Gregan (Eir) 3:42.8; **6** D. Wright 3:46.3; **7** D. Nicholl 3:47.1; **8** M. Downs 3:47.7; **9** T. Pribul 3:52.7; **10** P. Shaw 3:56.5. *Heat 2:* **1** R. Smedley 3:44.8; **2** P. Lawther 3:45.5; **3** G. Whittleston 3:46.0; **4** D. Quax (NZ) 3:48.9; **5** J. Cadman 3:49.1; **6** K. Humphries (Eir) 3:52.6; **7** G. Davis 3:53.3; **8** J. Carroll 3:58.1. *Heat 3:* **1** G. Crouch (Aus) 3:43.7; **2** E. Coghlan (Eir) 3:43.8; **3** S. Daggatt (USA) 3:44.0; **4** D. Moorcroft 3:44.5; **5** G. Robinson (NZ) 3:44.9; **6** C. Barber 3:46.9; **7** J. Theophilus 3:49.6; **8** R. Small 3:55.8; **9** N. Gates 3:57.9; **10** T. Ishii (Jap) 4:02.5. *FINAL:* **1** A. Waldrop (USA) 3:41.9; **2** G. Crouch (Aus) 3:42.2; **3** R. Smedley 3:42.8; **4** F. Clement 3:43.2; **5** D. Gibbon 3:43.8; **6** J. Douglas 3:43.9; **7** P. Lawther 3:45.0; **8** E. Coghlan (Eir) 3:45.0; **9** G. Whittleston 3:55.7.

5000m: **1** B. Foster 13:27.4; **2** J. Hermens (Hol) 13:35.2; **3** W. Meier (Swi) 13:38.4; **4** C. Stewart 13:38.4; **5** P. Geis (USA) 13:39.8; **6** M. Haro (Spa) 13:41.8; **7** R. Wilde 13:42.6; **8** A. Staynings 13:44.2; **9** L. Hilton (USA) 13:45.6; **10** R. Newble 13:45.8; **11** F. Briscoe 13:48.4; **12** D. Tibaduiza (Col) 13:48.6; **13** M. Kearns 13:55.8; **14** D. Slater 13:56.6; **15** T. Gregan (Eir) 13:57.6; **16** Jim Brown 13:58.6; **17** B. Cole 14:02.8; **18** P. Thys (Bel) 14:05.8; **19** A. Byrne 14:06.4; **20** H. Kita (Jap) 14:06.4; **21** B. Smith 14:09.0; **22** H. Starkey 14:09.6; **23** K. Ozawa (Jap) 14:14.0; **24** W. Domoney 14:16.6; **25** M. McLeod 14:28.4; **26** R. Holt 14:29.4; **27** A. Rushmer 14:31.0; **28** D. Fowles 14:34.6.

10,000m: **1** D. Bedford 28:14.8; **2** B. Ford 28:15.8; **3** A. Simmons 28:19.4; **4** Jim Brown 28:20.8; **5** G. Roelants (Bel) 28:24.8; **6** M. Baxter 28:30.2; **7** K. Penny 28:37.4; **8** John Brown 28:54.8; **9** P. Watson (NZ) 28:57.2; **10** Gren Tuck 28:57.8; **11** D. Black 28:59.2; **12** J. Wigley 28:59.6; **13** P. Standing 28:59.8; **14** S. Walker 29:11.8; **15** K. Ozawa (Jap) 29:16.6; **16** D. Tibaduiza (Col) 29:20.4; **17** M. Hattori (Jap) 29:39.4; **18** T. Johnston 29:40.4; **19** Graham Tuck 29:43.2; **20** S. Barr 29:53.8; **21** H. Kita (Jap) 30:02.6; **22** J. Alder 30:15.0; **23** M. Coleby 30:52.6.

3000m Steeplechase: *Heat 1:* **1** J. Davies 8.38.0; **2** C. Thomas 8:38.2; **3** T. Koyama (Jap) 8:38.4; **4** D. Coates 8:40.2; **5** S. Hollings 8:43.6; **6** A Weatherhead 8:50.6; **7** N. Jeffery 8:53.4; **8** R. Bean 8:56.4; **9** R. Cytlau 8:57.4; **10** R. Evans 9:07.8; **11** M. Barton 9:32.8. *Heat 2:* **1** H. Wehrli (Swi) 8:44.4; **2** J. Bicourt 8:44.8; **3** D. Camp 8:45.6; **4** D. Glans (Swe) 8:47.2; **5** I. Gilmour 8:47.2; **6** A. Holden 8:48.8; **7** V. Edigo (Spa) 8:50.6; **8** D. Long 9:02.8; **9** P. Waddington 9:27.2; **10** W. Robinson 9:33.2. *FINAL:* **1** J. Davies 8:26.8; **2** T. Koyama (Jap) 8:32.6; **3** D. Glans (Swe) 8:33.6; **4** J. Bicourt 8:36.6; **5** D. Camp 8:38.8; **6** S. Hollings 8:41.8; **7** V. Edigo (Spa) 8:42.2; **8** H. Wehrli (Swi) 8:44.2; **9** I. Gilmour 8:45.0; **10** A. Holden 8:45.0; **11** D. Coates 8:53.8; **12** C. Thomas 8:55.0; **13** A. Weatherhead 8:59.0.

110m Hurdles: *Heat 1:* **1** B. Price 14.6; **2** S. McCallum 14.9; **3** R. Palmer 14.9; **4** G. Shaw 15.1; **5** R. Davidson 15.1; **6** N. Gerrard 15.5; **7** A. James 15.6; **8** P. Mills (NZ) 15.6. *Heat 2:* **1** C. Kirkpatrick 14.7; **2** G. Gower 14.8; **3** A. Davis 15.1; **4** R. Gyles 15.1; **5** M. Kindon 15.1; **6** K. Purves 15.1; **7** M. Jackson 15.1; **8** A. Cronin 15.4. *FINAL:* **1** B. Price 13.9; **2** G. Gower 14.2; **3** C. Kirkpatrick 14.2; **4** S. McCallum 14.7; **5** R. Gyles 14.9; **6** R. Palmer 15.1; **7** A. Davis 15.2; **8** G. Shaw 15.2.

400m Hurdles: *Heat 1:* **1** J. Bolding (USA) 50.7; **2** C. O'Neill 51.3; **3** M. Whittingham 53.5; **4** U. Norman (Swe) 53.9; **5** P. Beattie 54.6; **6** D. West 55.2; **7** P. Mills (NZ) 57.2. *Heat 2:* **1** R. Steele (USA) 51.4; **2** S. James 52.4; **3** T. Crowe (Eir) 53.5; **4** W. Leyshon 54.0; **5** P. Hambley 54.1; **6** R. McIntosh (NZ) 55.7; **7** M. Ollier 57.1. *Heat 3:* **1** W. Hartley 51.2; **2** H. Hofer (Swi) 51.4; **3** S. Black 51.5; **4** N. Gregor 52.0; **5** S. Hinchliffe 55.2. *FINAL:* **1** J. Bolding (USA) 49.1 (*UK all-comers record*); **2** W. Hartley 50.6; **3** C. O'Neill 51.4; **4** R. Steele (USA) 51.5; **5** S. Black 51.7; **6** S. James 52.2; **7** H. Hofer (Swi) 52.4; **8** N. Gregor 52.7.

3000m Walk: **1** R. Mills 12:27.0; **2** P. Marlow 12:28.4; **3** B. Adams 12:40.2; **4** K. Carter 12:51.4; **5** C. Lawton 12:53.8; **6** A. Smallwood 12:56.8; **7** A. Seddon 13:02.2; **8** D. Stevens 13:19.0; **9** R. Parkins 13:34.4; **10** A. Banyard 13:39.2; **11** D. Hall 13:44.8; **12** D. Johnson 13:47.0; **13** D. Rosser 14:04.0; **14** R. Gardner 14:44.0.

High Jump: **1** D. Stones (USA) 2.14m (7′ 0¼″); **2** P. Matzdorf (USA) 2.14m (7′ 0¼″); **3** E. Eitel (WG) 2.11m (6′ 11″); **4** M. Jamrich (WG) 2.05m (6′ 8¾″); **5** R. Gyles 1.95m (6′ 4¾″); **6** M. Butterfield 1.95m (6′ 4¾″); **7** C. Boreham 1.95m (6′ 4¾″); **8** F. Keil (WG) 1.95m (6′ 4¾″); **9 eq** L. Hall and C. Schlag (WG) 1.90m (6′ 2¾″); **11** M. Shorten 1.90m (6′ 2¾″); **12** D. Coyle 1.90m (6′ 2¾″); **13** J. Fanning (Eir) 1.90m (6′ 2¾″); **14** A. Nursey 1.85m (6′ 0¾″); **15** H. Tretout 1.85m (6′ 0¾″).

Pole Vault: **1** C. Carrigan (USA) 5.10m (16′ 8¾″); **2** M. Tully (USA) 4.90m (16′ 0¾″); **3** R. Richards (USA) 4.90m (16′ 0¾″); **4** B. Hooper 4.80m (15′ 9″); **5** A. Williams 4.70m (15′ 5″); **6** D. Lease 4.45m (14′ 7¼″); **7** Jeff Fenge 4.30m (14′ 1¼″); **8** J. Gutteridge 4.15m (13′ 7¼″); **9** S. Clark 4.15m (13′ 7¼″); **10** N. Phipps 4.15m (13′ 7¼″).

Long Jump: **1** A. Lerwill 7.77m (25′ 6″); **2** G. Hignett 7.48m (24′ 6½″); **3** S. Atkins 7.30m (23′ 11½″); **4** P. Scott 7.30m (23′ 11½″); **5** R. Turkington 7.16m (23′ 6″); **6** W. Kirkpatrick 7.14m (23′ 5½″); **7** P. Templeton 7.13m (23′ 4¾″); **8** D. Porter 7.11m (23′ 4″); **9** S. Wright 7.03m (23′ 0¾″); **10** D. Cole 6.99m (22′ 11¼″); **11** G. Byham 6.93m (22′ 9″); **12** T. Paice 6.81m (22′ 4¼″); **13** P. Bevan 6.79m (22′ 3½″); **14 eq** S. White and K. Morrison 6.75m (22′ 1¾″); **16** D Shaw 6.65m (21′ 10″).

Triple Jump: **1** T. Inoue (Jap) 16.12m (52′ 10¾″); **2** W. Clark 15.78m (51′ 9¼″); **3** R. Johnson 15.40m (50′ 6¼″); **4** J. Vernon 15.36m (50′ 4¾″); **5** D. Johnson 15.33m (50′ 3½″); **6** M. Lardi (Swi) 15.18m (49′ 9¾″); **7** P. Knowles 15.03m (49′ 3¾″); **8** F. Attoh 14.84m (48′ 8¼″); **9** R. Heward-Mills 14.62m (47′ 11¾″); **10** J. Phillips 14.59m (47′ 10½″); **11** R. Edwards 14.47m (47′ 5¾″); **12** J. McLister 14.37m (47′ 1¾″); **13** S. Power (Eir) 14.35m (47′ 1″); **14** B. Camp 14.34m (47′ 0¾″).

ATHLETICS 75

Shot: 1 A. Feuerbach (USA) 21.37m (70' 1½") (*UK all-comers record*); **2** G. Capes 20.77m (68' 1¾"); **3** G. Woods (USA) 20.69m (67' 10¾"); **4** M. Winch 19.56m (64' 2¼"); **5** J. Alderson 17.52m (57' 5¾"); **6** R. Dale 16.01m (52' 6½"); **7** A. Satchwell 15.75m (51' 8¼"); **8** J. Watts 15.55m (51' 0¼").

Discus: 1 J. Powell (USA) 62.06m (203' 7"); **2** W. Tancred 60.02m (196' 11"); **3** J. Hillier 57.96m (190' 2"); **4** M. Cushion 53.76m (176' 4"); **5** G. Dirkin 53.08m (174' 2"); **6** P. Tancred 51.40m (168' 8"); **7** G. Tyler 49.88m (163' 8"); **8** A. Drzewiecki 49.50m (162' 5"); **9** D. Maloney 48.08m (157' 9"); **10** J. Watts 48.08m (157' 9"); **11** N. Griffin 47.54m (156' 0").

Hammer: 1 A. Barnard (SA) 70.62m (231' 8"); **2** H. Payne 67.50m (221' 5"); **3** B. Williams 67.26m (220' 8"); **4** P. Dickenson 65.86m (216' 1"); **5** I. Chipchase 65.84m (216' 0"); **6** C. Black 65.08m (213' 6"); **7** J. Whitehead 63.54m (208' 5"); **8** R. Marchant (SA) 61.42m (201' 6"); **9** E. Zablocki (Swe) 60.58m (198' 9"); **10** P. Aston 60.48m (198' 5"); **11** E. Berry 57.36m (188' 2"); **12** C. Melluish 56.64m (185' 2"); **13** B. Hartigan (Eir) 52.70m (172' 11"); **14** P. Conway (Eir) 50.38m (165' 3").

Javelin: 1 D. Travis 75.20m (246' 9"); **2** K. Sheppard 73.34m (240' 7"); **3** B. Roberts 71.94m (236' 0"); **4** W. Schmidt (USA) 69.52m (228' 1"); **5** C. Clover 68.48m (224' 8"); **6** D. Ottley 67.06m (220' 0"); **7** R. Silvester 67.00m (219' 10"); **8** B. Kennedy (Rho) 65.82m (215' 11"); **9** N. Aplin 63.22m (207' 5"); **10** P. Ostapowycz 58.84m (193' 0"); **11** D. Heath 57.80m (189' 7").

19, 20 July
WOMEN'S AAA CHAMPIONSHIPS

Only faulty pace judgment prevented Joyce Smith from breaking Lyudmila Bragina's newly established world 3000 metres record of 8:52.8 in her *heat* at the Birds Eye sponsored WAAA Championships at Crystal Palace. In the relaxed atmosphere of Friday evening's proceedings, Joyce set out to run 71 seconds per lap – an 8:52.5 schedule – but her first two circuits of 66.7 and 69.0 were too fast and she had to pay for her impetuosity later in the race. Passing 1500 metres in an extraordinary 4:22, Joyce had the world record slip from her grasp only in the last lap, which took her 71.6 sec. The final time of 8:55.6, smashing her own UK record of 9:04.4, ranked her second on the all-time list. In the final next afternoon Joyce was content to sit in and test her finishing speed. She flashed through the last lap this time in 63.6 to win in 9:07.2.

In addition to several championship bests, two other records were established. Raelene Boyle, winner of six Commonwealth gold medals, was as always highly motivated for the big occasion and, after losing nine short sprint races out of nine to Andrea Lynch since May, the Australian lass drove smoothly past her British friend and rival to register an all-comers 100 metres record of 11.2.

The rather less glamorous 3000 metres walk provided the other breakthrough, as tiny Marion Fawkes (she's less than 5 feet tall) brought her UK mark down to 14:33.6, only 8.6sec away from the world's best. The only other titles to remain in British custody were the 800 metres (a race marred when Mary Purcell and Maureen Crowley, the two favourites, fell at the final turn), 100 metres hurdles, high jump, and long jump.

100m: *Heat 1:* **1** A. Lynch 11.9; **2** C. Robinson (Can) 12.5; **3** S. Thomas 12.7; **4** R. Morris 12.8; **5** R. Everard 12.8; **6** J. Hoyte 12.8. *Heat 2:* **1** A. McClelland 12.2; **2** W. Hill 12.4; **3** D. Fitzgerald 12.5; **4** G. Spurgin 12.7; **5** S. McConachie 12.9; **6** P. Beauchamp 13.0. *Heat 3:* **1** R. Boyle (Aus) 12.0; **2** A. Wessels (SA) 12.1; **3** J. Pawsey 12.1; **4** E. Eddy 12.5; **5** V. Peat 12.6; **6** B. Goddard 12.7; **7** M. Collinson 13.1. *Heat 4:* **1** H. Golden 11.8; **2** L. Barratt 12.1; **3** L. Kellond (Can) 12.2; **4** K. Walker 12.2; **5** B. Martin 12.3; **6** L. Nash 12.6; **7** E. Mander 12.8. *Heat 5:* **1** D. Ramsden 11.9; **2** P. Collins (USA) 12.1; **3** D. Heath 12.2; **4** A. Neil 12.3; **5** W. Gerrard 12.5; **6** L. Boothe 12.6; **7** J. Wall 12.8. *Semi 1:* **1** A. Lynch

WAAA CHAMPIONSHIPS

11.9; **2** D. Ramsden 12.0; **3** A. Wessels (SA) 12.1; **4** L. Kellond (Can) 12.2; **5** K. Walker 12.3; **6** P. Collins (USA) 12.3; **7** A. McClelland 12.5; **8** S. Thomas 12.6. *Semi 2:* **1** R. Boyle (Aus) 11.7; **2** H. Golden 11.7; **3** L. Barratt 12.1; **4** J. Pawsey 12.2; **5** D. Heath 12.3; **6** W. Hill 12.4; **7** C. Robinson (Can) 12.5; **8** D. Fitzgerald 12.6. *FINAL:* **1** R. Boyle (Aus) 11.2 (11.23) (*UK all-comers record*); **2** A. Lynch 11.3 (11.27); **3** H. Golden 11.4; **4** D. Ramsden 11.7; **5** A. Wessels (SA) 11.7; **6** L. Barratt 11.8; **7** J. Pawsey 12.0.
200m: *Heat 1:* **1** H. Golden 24.2; **2** W. Hill 25.2; **3** A. Wessels (SA) 25.2; **4** L. Barratt 25.3; **5** W Gerrard 25.4; **6** S. McConachie 25.7. *Heat 2:* **1** M. Bailey (Can) 24.1; **2** G. Taylor 24.2; **3** D. Heath 24.7; **4** L. Cordy (USA) 24.9; **5** H. Oakes 25.0; **6** K. Walker 25.1; **7** B. Goddard 25.4. *Heat 3:* **1** R. Boyle (Aus) 23.9; **2** P. Loverock (Can) 24.5; **3** B. Martin 24.9; **4** A. McClelland 25.3; **5** J. Hoyte 25.6; **6** L. Biddles 25.8. *Heat 4:* **1** S. Colyear 24.3; **2** C. van Straaten (SA) 24.8; **3** J. Pawsey 24.9; **4** C. Robinson (Can) 25.0; **5** D. Fitzgerald 25.6. *Semi 1:* **1** M. Bailey (Can) 23.9; **2** H. Golden 24.4; **3** C. van Straaten (SA) 24.6; **4** D. Heath 24.9; **5** B. Martin 25.0; **6** K. Walker 25.1; **7** H. Oakes 25.2; *Semi 2:* **1** R. Boyle (Aus) 23.9; **2** G. Taylor 23.9; **3** S. Colyear 24.2; **4** P. Loverock (Can) 24.2; **5** W. Hill 24.6; **6** L. Cordy (USA) 24.6; **7** J. Pawsey 24.8; **8** C. Robinson (Can) 25.0. *FINAL:* **1** R. Boyle (Aus) 23.2; **2** H. Golden 23.6; **3** C. van Straaten (SA) 23.8; **4** P. Loverock (Can) 24.1; **5** S. Colyear 24.2; **6** G. Taylor 24.3; **7** W. Hill 24.6.
400m: *Heat 1:* **1** J. Roscoe 54.4; **2** A. Littlejohn 54.9; **3** L. Taylor 54.9; **4** A. Smyth 55.0; **5** B. Walsh (Can) 55.6; **6** D. Peake 57.6; **7** D. Churchill 61.0. *Heat 2:* **1** Y. Saunders (Can) 53.9; **2** C. Warden 54.2; **3** P. Lloyd 55.1; **4** P. O'Dwyer (Eir) 55.9; **5** H. Page 56.6; **6** E. McMeekin 57.8; **7** M. Russell 58.0; **8** N. Klarkowski 59.1. *Heat 3:* **1** D. Murray 54.1; **2** E. Barnes 54.6; **3** M. McGowan (Can) 55.4; **4** A. Halliday 55.8; **5** L. Forde (Bar) 56.8; **6** J. Spiers 57.0; **7** H. Grier 57.6; **8** T. Hollingsworth 58.8. *Heat 4:* **1** V. Bernard 53.0; **2** C. Toussaint (USA) 54.1; **3** A. Morrison (Eir) 54.7; **4** A. Mackie (Can) 54.8; **5** T. Doyle 56.8; **6** E. Brown 57.2; **7** R. Chettleburgh 58.5; **8** S. Reed 59.1. *Heat 5:* **1** R. Kennedy 54.7; **2** C. Walsh (Eir) 55.0; **3** B. Nichols (USA) 56.0; **4** A. Creamer 56.2; **5** S. Pettett 57.1; **6** C. McMeekin 58.1; **7** L. Greenwood 59.3; **8** S. Richardson 59.8. *Semi 1:* **1** J. Roscoe 53.8; **2** Y. Saunders (Can) 53.7; **3** C. Toussaint (USA) 53.9; **4** E. Barnes 54.0; **5** P. Lloyd 54.9; **6** A. Morrison (Eir) 55.6; **7** L. Taylor 55.6; **8** M. McGowan (Can) 55.9. *Semi 2:* **1** V. Bernard 53.5; **2** C. Walsh (Eir) 54.3; **3** C. Warden 54.6; **4** D. Murray 54.7; **5** R. Kennedy 54.9; **6** A. Mackie (Can) 55.6; **7** A. Littlejohn 55.7; **8** B. Nichols (USA) 56.4. *FINAL:* **1** Y. Saunders (Can) 51.9; **2** D. Murray 52.6; **3** V. Bernard 53.1; **4** J. Roscoe 53.5; **5** C. Warden 53.8; **6** C. Walsh (Eir) 53.9; **7** E. Barnes 54.0; **8** C. Toussaint (USA) 54.7.
800m: *Heat 1:* **1** M. Purcell (Eir) 2:09.9; **2** S. Howell 2:11.4; **3** P. Reece 2:12.9; **4** D. Davies 2:15.2; **5** A. Sullivan 2:16.2; **6** M. Sonner 2:17.3; **7** D. Coward 2:18.5; **8** D. Churchill 2:20.0. *Heat 2:* **1** R. Wright 2:11.3; **2** H. Tanner 2:11.7; **3** M. Speedman 2:12.3; **4** G. Dourass 2:12.6; **5** P. Bagley 2:13.6; **6** R. Ennis 2:15.5; **7** A. Lawson 2:20.0; **8** A. Disley 2.24.0. *Heat 3:* **1** M. Crowley (Can) 2:07.1; **2** L. Kiernan 2:08.4; **3** C. Stenhouse 2:11.5; **4** C. Hanson 2:12.1; **5** G. Garbutt 2:12.5; **6** G. Adams 2:13.4; **7** J. Kimber 2:14.3; **8** S. Odell 2:16.7. *Heat 4:* **1** L. Atkin 2:12.9; **2** M. Coomber 2:12.9; **3** S. Walters (SA) 2:13.7; **4** S. Smith 2:14.7; **5** J. Poynor 2:15.8; **6** A. Kirkham 2:16.7; **7** M. Sorbie 2:17.5; **8** J. Low 2:19.7. *Semi 1:* **1** L. Kiernan 2:08.0; **2** M. Purcell (Eir) 2:08.0; **3** S. Howell 2:09.7; **4** L. Atkin 2:10.3; **5** M. Speedman 2:12.5; **6** S. Walters (SA) 2:14.3; **7** G. Dourass 2:16.8; **8** G. Adams 2:22.1. *Semi 2:* **1** M. Crowley (Can) 2:08.1; **2** H. Tanner 2:08.2; **3** M. Coomber 2:08.3; **4** R. Wright 2:08.6; **5** C. Hanson 2:10.6; **6** P. Reece 2:10.8; **7** C. Stenhouse 2:12.9; **8** G. Garbutt 2:13.9. *FINAL:* **1** L. Kiernan 2:05.1; **2** M. Purcell (Eir) 2:09.8; **3** M. Coomber 2:10.1; **4** H. Tanner 2:10.2; **5** M. Crowley (Can) 2:10.2; **6** L. Atkin 2:11.8; **7** S. Howell 2:11.8.
1500m: *Heat 1:* **1** G. Reiser (Can) 4:17.6; **2** A-M. Davis (Can) 4:20.2; **3** C. Tranter 4:25.4; **4** J. Lochhead 4:26.4; **5** C. Curthoys 4:28.7; **6** M. Beacham 4:29.9; **7** B. Majumdar 4:38.0; **8** C. Roy 4:43.5; **9** C. Butler 4:43.9; **10** L. Cobden 4:47.0; **11** V. Cole 4:52.4; **12** C. Wilcox 5:18.6. *Heat 2:* **1** T. Wright (Can) 4:19.5; **2** G. Andersen (Nor) 4:19.9; **3** G. Goodburn 4:27.4; **4** P. Yule 4:28.7; **5** N. Braithwaite 4:30.2; **6** C. McLoughlin 4:30.5; **7** C. Hanson 4:32.3; **8** A. Roberts 4:39.9; **9** M. Chambers 4:41.9; **10** T. Bateman 4:44.9; **11** J. Asgill 4:45.4; **12** A. Briscoe 4:45.8; **13** A. Morris 4:56.2; **14** L. Abraham 4:59.7. *FINAL:* **1** G. Andersen (Nor) 4:10.0; **2** T. Wright (Can) 4:10.7; **3** G. Reiser (Can) 4:17.7; **4** A-M. Davis (Can) 4:19.3; **5** C. Tranter 4:23.2; **6** G. Goodburn 4:25.7; **7** P. Yule 4:30.0; **8** M. Beacham 4:30.4; **9** J. Lochhead 4:41.8.
3000m: *Heat 1:* **1** J. Smith 8:55.6 (*Commonwealth, UK all-comers & UK record*); **2** B. van Roy (Bel) 9:33.8; **3** C. Haskett 9:34.0; **4** P. Yeoman 9:37.0; **5** C. Readdy 9:40.6; **6** B. Price 10:09.6; **7** J. Haigh 10:18.8; **8** C. Simpson 10:30.0; **9** C. Bosher 10:34.0; **10** H. Mathews 10:39.0; **11** P. Jones 11:04.2. *Heat 2:* **1** C. Gould 9:32.4; **2** A. Yeoman 9:32.4; **3** D. Nagle (Eir) 9:33.6; **4** A. Blake 9:35.2; **5** R. Ridley 9:36.8; **6** M. Ashcroft 9:57.8; **7** V. Howe 10:09.2; **8** J. Rice 10:23.4; **9** M. Taylor 10:27.6; **10** B. Brown 10:53.0. *FINAL:* **1** J. Smith 9:07.2; **2** A. Yeoman 9:17.2; **3** P. Yeoman 9:23.8; **4** C. Gould 9:27.6; **5** B. van Roy (Bel) 9:31.6; **6** A. Blake 9:33.8; **7** C. Haskett 9:37.0; **8** C. Readdy 9:39.4; **9** D. Nagle (Eir) 9:42.2; **10** V. Howe 9:47.2; **11** M. Ashcroft 9:56.0.

ATHLETICS 75

100m Hurdles: *Heat 1:* **1** J. Vernon 13.6; **2** S. Bradley (Can) 13.9; **3** S. Mapstone 14.0; **4** P. Pryce 14.1; **5** L. Boothe 14.1; **6** J. Stokoe 15.5; **7** K. Booth 16.2. *Heat 2:* **1** B. Thompson 13.7; **2** E. Damman (Can) 14.1; **3** D. Stewart 14.3; **4** B. Ruttledge 14.4; **5** G. Smith 14.8; **6** A. Sutton 15.1. *Heat 3:* **1** L. Drysdale 13.8; **2** H. de Lange (SA) 14.3; **3** S. Holmstrom 14.5; **4** P. Chapman 14.6; **5** E. Eddy 15.0; **6** G. Howell 15.5. *Heat 4:* **1** M. Nimmo 13.6; **2** I. van Rensburg (SA) 13.6; **3** L. Ilott 13.9; **4** P. Collins (USA) 14.2; **5** S. Bousfield 14.6; **6** J. Long 14.6; **7** H. Alderton 14.8. *Semi 1:* **1** L. Drysdale 13.5; **2** J. Vernon 13.6; **3** L. Ilott 13.8; **4** I. van Rensburg (SA) 13.9; **5** E. Damman (Can) 14.1; **6** B. Ruttledge 14.2; **7** P. Pryce 14.3; **8** S. Holmstrom 14.4. *Semi 2:* **1** H. de Lange (SA) 13.6; **2** B. Thompson 13.6; **3** M. Nimmo 13.7; **4** P. Collins (USA) 14.1; **5** S. Mapstone 14.4; **6** P. Chapman 14.5; **7** S. Bradley (Can) 14.5; **8** D. Stewart 14.6. *FINAL:* **1** L. Drysdale 13.5 (13.45); **2** J. Vernon 13.5 (13.46); **3** B. Thompson 13.5 (13.50); **4** H. de Lange (SA) 13.7; **5** M. Nimmo 13.9; **6** I. van Rensburg (SA) 14.0; **7** L. Ilott 14.3; **8** P. Collins (USA) 14.3.

400m Hurdles: 1 H. de Lange (SA) 58.4; **2** L. Robinson 62.5; **3** J. Farry 62.7; **4** L. Davies 64.8; **5** D. Stewart 65.6; **6** M. Cope 66.6; **7** S. Davidson 66.7; **8** G. Howell 70.5.

3000m Walk: 1 M. Fawkes 14:33.6 (*UK best performance*); **2** B. Jenkins 15:07.4; **3** S. Wish 15:22.0; **4** P. Branson 15:48.4; **5** J. Farr 16:05.0; **6** J. Mulvenna 16:19.0; **7** S. de Giovanni 16:39.6; **8** M. Brown 16:56.0; **9** B. Francis 16:56.0.

High Jump: 1 V. Harrison 1.82m (5' 11½"); **2** D. Brill (Can) 1.82m (5' 11½"); **3** L. Hanna (Can) 1.79m (5' 10½"); **4** B. Lawton 1.79m (5' 10½"); **5** R. Watt 1.79m (5' 10½"); **6** G. Smith 1.73m (5' 8"); **7** S. Wright 1.73m (5' 8"); **8** C. Mathers 1.73m (5' 8"); **9** T. Dainton 1.73m (5' 8"); **10** A. Manley 1.73m (5' 8"). Other contestants: C. Gilbert (USA), D. Bird, R. Few, A. Tueit (Nor), D. Brown, F. Stacey and A. Mullins 1.70m (5' 7"); M. Daniels, B. Lewis and P. Dimmock 1.65m (5' 5"); I. McCormick, J. Crouchley and C. Bruce 1.60m (5' 3"); J. Walden 1.55m (5' 1"), B. Jones 1.50m (4' 11").

Long Jump: 1 R. Martin-Jones 6.26m (20' 6½"); **2** A. Wilson 6.19m (20' 3¾"); **3** B. Eisler (Can) 6.17m (20' 3"); **4** P. Williams 5.90m (19' 4¼"); **5** S. Mapstone 5.86m (19' 2¾"); **6** J. Jay 5.76m (18' 10¾"); **7** G. Taylor 5.65m (18' 6½"); **8** P. Chapman 5.63m (18' 5¾"). Non-qualifiers: B. McPherson 5.59m (18' 4¼"); S. Lewis 5.57m (18' 3¼"), E. Mullins 5.56m (18' 3"); N. Njoku 5.54m (18' 2¼"); G. Fitzgerald (USA) 5.51m (18' 1"); J. Wall 5.49m (18' 0¼"); J. Sanderson 5.49m (18' 0¼"); A. Neil 5.44m (17' 10¼"); S. Colyear 5.37m (17' 7½"); C. Earlington 5.37m (17' 7½"); J. Murray 5.21m (17' 1¼"); E. Butters 5.20m (17' 0¾"); J. Richardson 5.19m (17' 0½); S. Hayes 5.13m (16' 10"); V. Thompson 4.97m (16' 3¾").

Shot: 1 J. Haist (Can) 15.03m (49' 3¾"); **2** B. Bedford 14.65m (48' 0¾"); **3** J. Kerr 14.17m (46' 6"); **4** R. Payne 13.77m (45' 2¼"); **5** D. Howarth 12.96m (42' 6¼"); **6** E. Elliott 12.65m (41' 6"); **7** F. Cooney (Eir) 12.64m (41' 5¾"); **8** V. Head 12.55m (41' 2¼"). Non-qualifiers: V. Redford 12.28m (40' 3½"); J. Frampton 12.18m (39' 11½"); J. Beese 12.13m (39' 9¾"); G. Bird 11.93m (39' 1¾"); J. Thompson 11.86m (38' 11"); J. Wraith 11.49m (37' 8½"); N. Njoku 10.94m (35' 10¾"); L. King 10.93m (35' 10½"); S. Goddard 10.45m (34' 3½").

Discus: 1 J. Haist (Can) 56.38m (185' 0"); **2** R. Payne 51.70m (169' 7"); **3** C. Martin (Can) 50.94m (167' 1"); **4** M Ritchie 49.58m (162' 8"); **5** J. Thompson 47.74m (156' 7"); **6** J. Fielding 46.12m (151' 4"); **7** J. Elsmore 43.56m (142' 11"); **8** D. Swinyard 40.88m (134' 1"). Non-qualifiers: B. Bedford 44.76m (146' 10"); L. Mallin 44.22m (145' 1"); G. Bird 42.86m (140' 7"); J. Kerr 42.68m (140' 0"); V. Head 41.56m (136' 4"); J. Frampton 40.82m (133' 11"); J. Beese 40.22m (131' 11"); D. Prothero 39.00m (127' 11"); E. Andres (Swi) 38.38m (125' 11"); E. Bali 37.96m (124' 6"); L. King 37.64m (123' 6"); M. Dunne (Eir) 37.22m (122' 1"); V. Hindley 35.62m (116' 10"); J. Gray 35.02m (114' 11"); P. Littleworth 34.70m (113' 10").

Javelin: 1 E. Janko (Aut) 61.56m (202' 0"); **2** S. Corbett 51.98m (170' 6"); **3** T. Sanderson 51.18m (167' 11"); **4** A. Goodlad 48.34m (158' 7"); **5** P. Carter 48.26m (158' 4"); **6** A. Farquhar 46.72m (153' 3"); **7** A. King 42.06m (138' 0"); **8** L. Kern (Can) 42.04m (137' 11"). Non-qualifiers: S. Brodie 41.90m (137' 5"); Y. Fountain 40.42m (132' 7"); J. Williams 39.98m (131' 2"); C. Slater 39.86m (130' 9"); S. Spragg 38.44m (126' 1"); C. Waxler 38.32m (125' 9"); B. Richardson 38.26m (125' 6"); L. Hamilton 37.58m (123' 3"); L. Rice 36.54m (119' 10"); A. Davis 36.22m (118' 10").

23-26 July
SOVIET CHAMPIONSHIPS

Valeriy Borzov ('I'm far from my best shape') added to his bulging collection of titles with two more in the Soviet Championships at Moscow, winning narrowly yet authoritatively the 100 metres in 10.2 and the 200 metres in 21.0. Since 1969 he has won the 100 and 200 four times each in five attempts.

The most surprising result, in view of events to come, was the hammer throwing defeat of future European champion and world record holder Aleksey Spiridonov by Valentin Dmitrenko, who in Rome was to place no higher than fourth. Natalya Lebedyeva set a national record of 13.0 for the women's 100 metres hurdles.

MEN

100m: 1 V. Borzov 10.2; 2 A. Kornelyuk 10.3; 3 J. Silovs 10.3; 4 Aksinin 10.4; 5 Kravzov 10.4; 6 Atamas 10.5; 7 Svelichkiy 10.5; 8 Trussov 10.6.

200m: 1 V. Borzov 21.0; 2 A. Zhidkikh 21.1; 3 C. Rachmanov 21.4; 4 Lovezkiy 21.5; 5 Lebedyev 21.8; 6 Lyutarevich 21.8; 7 Korovin 21.9; 8 Panassov 22.0.

400m: 1 V. Nossenko 46.4; 2 V. Yurchenko 46.5; 3 V. Mikhailov 46.9; 4 Semyonov 47.0; 5 Taranov 47.4; 6 Zyganov 47.4; 7 Kosban 47.4; 8 Aliyev 47.6.

800m: 1 G. Chernishov 1:48.6; 2 P. Litovchenko 1:48.6; 3 Y. Chudyakov 1:49.2; 4 Ponomaryov 1:49.8; 5 Yakubovich 1:50.0; 6 Goncharov 1:50.2; 7 Krivopatko 1:50.8; 8 Chorochorin 1:51.1.

1500m: 1 P. Anissim 3:42.5; 2 V. Panteley 3:42.6; 3 Ulymov 3:42.7; 4 Volkov 3:42.7; 5 Abramov 3:42.8; 6 Nedbalyuk 3:42.9

5000m: 1 M. Zhelobovskiy 13:42.0; 2 M. Abdulin 13:42.4; 3 V. Kuznyetsov 13:42.8; 4 V. Satonskiy 13:43.0; 5 A. Ibraimov 13:43.8; 6 A. Storoshev 13:43.8; 7 V. Afonin 13:43.8; 8 L. Mosseyev 13:44.4.

10,000m: 1 V. Zotov 28:33.0; 2 N. Puklakov 28:33.8; 3 V. Merkushin 28:34.4; 4 S. Dshumanasarov 28:34.8; 5 M. Yarulin 28:38.6; 6 P. Andreyev 28:42.2; 7 V. Mochalov 28:45.0; 8 N. Sviridov 28:45.6.

3000m Steeplechase: 1 S. Skripka 8:26.6; 2 J. Grigas 8:27.4; 3 V. Lissovskiy 8:27.8; 4 N. Mayorov 8:30.6; 5 V. Filonov 8:31.8; 6 G. Vassilkov 8:32.0; 7 A. Velichko 8:36.4; 8 A. Beinarovich 8:37.2.

110m Hurdles: 1 V. Myasnikov 13.8; 2 E. Perevertsev 13.9; 3 A. Moshiashvili 14.0; 4 Kulebyakin 14.1; 5 Mazepa 14.1; 6 Balachnichev 14.3; 7 Sinitsin 14.5; 8 Nikitenko 14.6.

400m Hurdles: 1 Y. Gavrilenko 49.7; 2 A. Karasyov 50.2; 3 D. Stukalov 50.5; 4 Y. Fyodorov 50.6; 5 V. Mashkowski 50.9; 6 V. Savchenko 51.0; 7 Nagainik 51.4; 8 Krizstein 51.5.

High Jump: 1 K. Sapka 2.23m (7' 3¾"); 2 V. Abramov 2.21m (7' 3"); 3 V. Schkurichev 2.19m (7' 2¼"); 4 V. Bolshov 2.16m (7' 1"); 5 M. Shelnov 2.13m (6' 11¾"); 6 S. Senyukov 2.13m (6' 11¾"); 7 A. Moroz 2.13m (6' 11¾"); 8 V. Kozlov 2.13m (6' 11¾").

Pole Vault: 1 V. Kishkun 5.35m (17' 6½"); 2 Y. Issakov 5.30m (17' 4½"); 3 J. Lauris 5.30m (17' 4½"); 4 V. Boiko 5.20m (17' 0¾"); 5 Gusyev 5.00m (16' 4¾"); 6 eq Prokhorenko and Krylov 5.00m (16' 4¾"); 8 Babenkov 4.80m (15' 9").

Long Jump: 1 V. Podluzhniy 7.90m (25' 11"); 2 T. Lepik 7.81m (25' 7½"); 3 Y. Shubin 7.73m (25' 4½"); 4 Subkov 7.67m (25' 2"); 5 Yautakis 7.57m (24' 10"); 6 Vereskun 7.45m (24' 5½"); 7 Brossmann 7.43m (24' 4½"); 8 Shcherbina 7.32m (24' 0¼").

Triple Jump: 1 V. Saneyev 17.05m (55' 11¼"); 2 M. Segal 16.74m (54' 11¼"); 3 N. Sinichkin 16.55m (54' 3¾"); 4 G. Bessonov 16.45m (53' 11¾"); 5 V. Bor 16.31m (53' 6¼"); 6 S. Sidorenko 16.25m (53' 3¾"); 7 A. Piskulin 16.23m (53' 3"); 8 M. Bariban 16.21m (53' 2¼").

Shot: 1 A. Baryshnikov 20.32m (66' 8"); 2 V. Voikin 20.31m (66' 7¾"); 3 A. Yarosh 19.84m (65' 1¼"); 4 A. Nossenko 19.80m (64' 11½"); 5 R. Plunge 19.58m (64' 3"); 6 Y. Mironov 19.53m (64' 1"); 7 L. Smelash 19.11m (62' 8½"); 8 A. Aronov 18.99m (62' 3¾").

Discus: 1 V. Kuusemae 61.00m (200' 1"); 2 G. Gutov 59.86m (196' 5"); 3 V. Titov 59.20m (194' 3"); 4 V. Redkin 58.26m (191' 2"); 5 V. Pensikov 58.18m (190' 10"); 6 V. Lyakhov 58.10m (190' 7"); 7 Zhurba 57.36m (188' 2"); 8 Vichor 55.38m (181' 8").

Hammer: 1 V. Dmitrenko 75.52m (247' 9"); 2 A. Spiridonov 74.12m (243' 2"); 3 D. Pkhakadse 71.98m (236' 2"); 4 A. Bondarchuk 71.74m (235' 4"); 5 Y. Sedykh 70.16m (230' 2"); 6 A. Yakunin 69.34m (227' 6"); 7 A. Kozlov 69.12m (226' 9"); 8 V. Korolyov 68.64m (225' 2").

Javelin: 1 A. Makarov 83.70m (274' 7"); 2 N. Grebnyev 83.60m (274' 3"); 3 J. Lusis 82.88m (271' 11"); 4 V. Feldmanis 81.12m (266' 2"); 5 J. Zirnis 79.08m (259' 5"); 6 D. Sitnikov 78.62m (257' 11"); 7 A. Chupilko 78.02m (256' 0"); 8 Belan 76.56m (251' 2").

20km Walk: 1 V. Golubnichiy 1:28:21; 2 Y. Ivchenko 1:28:29; 3 V. Shaloshik 1:29:33; 4 Y. Lyungin 1:29:35; 5 N. Turintsev 1:29:40; 6 N. Polosov 1:29:49; 7 M. Alekseyev 1:29:57; 8 B. Barannikov 1:30:13.

WOMEN

100m: 1 M. Sidorova 11.4; 2 L. Maslakova 11.5; 3 T. Chernikova 11.6; 4 G. Mitrokhina 11.6; 5 Karnauchova 11.8; 6 Besfamilnaya 11.8; 7 Belova 11.9; 8 Basilina 11.9.

200m: 1 M. Sidorova 23.3; 2 T. Chernikova 23.7; 3 L. Maslakova 23.8; 4 M. Visla 23.9; 5 Ivanova 24.0; 6 Stepanova 24.0; 7 Belova 24.5; 8 Levshova 24.6.

400m: 1 N. Ilyina 52.5; 2 I. Klimovich 52.9; 3 L. Aksyonova 53.1; 4 I. Barkane 53.1; 5 L. Golovanova 53.4; 6 N. Sokolova 53.4; 7 L. Runzo 54.2; 8 Denissova 54.7.

800m: 1 N. Morgunova 2:01.6; 2 V. Gerassimova 2:01.7; 3 Y. Safina 2:02.3; 4 O. Vachruscheva 2:03.2; 5 S. Stuula 2:03.9; 6 S. Styrkina 2:04.5; 7 T. Yelisarova 2:05.5; 8 R. Ismailova 2:05.7.

1500m: 1 L. Bragina 4:09.8; 2 T. Pangelova 4:10.0; 3 S. Akhtyamova 4:14.0; 4 O. Dvirna 4:14.1; 5 T. Kazachkova 4:15.5; 6 A. Teslenko 4:15.8; 7 T. Gaistyan 4:17.8; 8 A. Krynina 4:20.0.

3000m: 1 L. Bragina 9:05.0; 2 I. Bondarchuk 9:11.8; 3 A. Daabolinya 9:13.6; 4 L. Korchagina 9:14.6; 5 G. Romanova 9:15.0; 6 N. Kossolapova 9:17.0; 7 G. Golovinskaya 9:18.2; 8 S. Ulmasova 9:18.6.

100m Hurdles: 1 N. Lebedyeva 13.0; 2 T. Anissimova 13.4; 3 N. Tkachenko 13.5; 4 S. Spassovchodskaya 13.5; 5 L. Kononova 13.6; 6 T. Kolesnikova 13.7; 7 L. Schurchal 13.8; 8 Siver 14.0.

High Jump: 1 T. Galka 1.82m (5' 11½"); 2 V. Akhramenko 1.82m (5' 11½"); 3 G. Filatova 1.79m (5' 10½"); 4 L. Kuselenkova 1.79m (5' 10½"); 5 T. Schlachto 1.79m (5' 10½"); 6 O. Bondaryenko 1.76m (5' 9¼"); 7 eq N. Kaseyeva, V. Avilova, T. Denissova and L. Schpakova 1.76m (5' 9¼").

Long Jump: 1 L. Alfeyeva 6.66m (21' 10¼"); 2 T. Timokhova 6.48m (21' 3¼"); 3 K. Lotova 6.47m (21' 2¾"); 4 S. Ivanova 6.33m (20' 9¼"); 5 A. Lomakina 6.12m (20' 1"); 6 Rukavishnikova 6.10m (20' 0¼"); 7 Gavrilova 6.09m (19' 11¾"); 8 Kaigorodova 6.06m (19' 10¾").

Shot: 1 N. Chizhova 21.14m (69' 4¼"); 2 S. Krachevskaya 19.00m (62' 4"); 3 F. Melnik 18.91m (62' 0½"); 4 A. Ivanova 18.78m (61' 7½"); 5 R. Taranda 18.43m (60' 5¾"); 6 Y. Korablyova 17.96m (58' 11¼"); 7 T. Bufetova 17.72m (58' 1¾"); 8 R. Makauskaite 17.40m (57' 1").

Discus: 1 F. Melnik 68.02m (223' 2"); 2 N. Sivoplyassova 57.22m (187' 9"); 3 N. Sergeyeva 57.20m (187' 8"); 4 N. Gorbachova 56.68m (185' 11"); 5 H. Parts 55.74m (182' 10"); 6 T. Danilova 55.52m (182' 2"); 7 T. Pastuchova 55.48m (182' 0"); 8 L. Khmelevskaya 55.42m (181' 10").

Javelin: 1 T. Shigalova 57.94m (190' 1"); 2 S. Babich 56.80m (186' 4"); 3 G. Slakomanova 56.66m (185' 11"); 4 N. Marakina 56.28m (184' 8"); 5 L. Makarova 56.00m (183' 9"); 6 V. Tikhonova 52.72m (172' 11"); 7 Gussarova 49.52m (162' 5"); 8 Ormanova 48.08m (157' 9").

26, 27 July
UK v CZECHOSLOVAKIA (men)
UK v CZECHOSLOVAKIA v NETHERLANDS (women)

The British team, overall, was in somewhat lacklustre mood for a Philips sponsored match staged in cheerless weather before a thin crowd at Edinburgh's Meadowbank Stadium. Although the men beat Czechoslovakia, it was only by the narrow margin of six points (as against 20 in the last encounter), and the women's match finished as a tie – a far cry from the British girls' crushing win the previous season. The Dutch, once among Europe's strongest teams, were involved in the women's affair but were hopelessly outclassed on this occasion.

The best performances came mainly from the Czechs. Olympic champion Ludvik Danek, showing no signs of decline at the age of 37, set a UK all-comers record in the discus of 66.44 metres (218′ 0″), and another top throws star, Helena Fibingerova, put the shot 20.75 metres (68′ 1″) to finish over 20 feet ahead of her closest British challenger! Eva Suranova long jumped the magnificent distance of 6.74 metres (22′ 1½″), albeit with wind assistance, and Jozefina Cerchlanova made quite a name for herself by equalling the Czech 800 metres record of 2:04.7, well clear of Lesley Kiernan, on the first day and scoring an even finer win in the 400 metres on the second, pipping Verona Bernard in another national record of 52.0.

Britain's outstanding winner was reliable Geoff Capes, whose *worst* of five valid puts thudded out at 20.45 metres (67′ 1¼″). Mike Winch ensured maximum points here as he overtook the redoubtable Jaroslav Brabec (whose personal best is 21.04 metres or 69′ 0½″) in the fifth round. Although looking a little sluggish – not surprisingly, as in a desperate attempt to make up for lost training time he had run 20 miles only the previous day – Brendan Foster kicked to victory over Frank Clement in the 1500 metres, his first since Christchurch. On the women's side, Helen Golden displayed superb form on her home track to dip under 23 seconds (22.97 electrically timed) for a wind-assisted 200 metres. Her winning margin was a good half-dozen metres.

MEN

100m: **1** D. Halliday (UK) 10.4; **2** B. Green (UK) 10.5; **3** J. Demec (Cze) 10.5; **4** J. Matousek (Cze) 10.6.

200m: **1** A. Bennett (UK) 20.9; **2** J. Matousek (Cze) 20.9; **3** C. Monk (UK) 20.9; **4** J. Kynos (Cze) 21.4.

400m: **1** M. Tulis (Cze) 47.3; **2** S. Marlow (UK) 47.6; **3** J. Wilson (UK) 47.7; **4** F. Stross (Cze) 48.3.

800m **1** S. Ovett (UK) 1:48.8; **2** A. Carter (UK) 1:49.2; **3** J. Plachy (Cze) 1:49.5; **4** L. Karsky (Cze) 1:50.1.

1500m: **1** B. Foster (UK) 3:41.2; **2** F. Clement (UK) 3:41.7; **3** I. Kovac (Cze) 3:41.7; **4** S. Polak (Cze) 3:42.6.

5000m: **1** P. Penkava (Cze) 14:08.6; **2** C. Stewart (UK) 14:10.0; **3** J. Goater (UK) 14:12.0; **4** P. Suchan (Cze) 14:22.8.

10,000m: **1** S. Hoffman (Cze) 28:28.4; **2** Jim Brown (UK) 28:28.4; **3** M. Baxter (UK) 28:28.6; **4** J. Jansky (Cze) 28:30.4.

3000m Steeplechase: **1** D. Camp (UK) 8:39.8; **2** D. Moravcik (Cze) 8:40.0; **3** J. Bicourt (UK) 8:40.8; **4** F. Bartos (Cze) 8:44.0.

110m Hurdles: **1** L. Nadenicek (Cze) 13.8; **2** B. Price (UK) 13.9; **3** G. Gower (UK) 14.2; **4** P. Cech (Cze) 15.5.

400m Hurdles: **1** M. Kodejs (Cze) 50.8; **2** I. Danis (Cze) 50.8; **3** W. Hartley (UK) 50.9; **4** S. Black (UK) 52.2.

ATHLETICS 75

High Jump: 1 V. Maly (Cze) 2.15m (7' 0½"); 2 R. Moravec (Cze) 2.15m (7' 0½"); 3 A. Lerwill (UK) 2.00m (6' 6¾");
4 C. Boreham (UK) 2.00m (6' 6¾").
Pole Vault: 1 B. Hooper (UK) 4.90m (16' 0¾"); 2 A. Williams (UK) 4.80m (15' 9"); 3 A. Hadinger (Cze) 4.70m (15' 5");
4 A. Stevak (Cze) 4.70m (15' 5'").
Long Jump: 1 P. Tolnay (Cze) 7.75m (25' 5¼"); 2 A. Lerwill (UK) 7.72m (25' 4"); 3 J. Broz (Cze) 7.61m (24' 11¾");
4 S. Atkins (UK) 7.05m (23' 1¾").
Triple Jump: 1 J. Vycichlo (Cze) 16.21m (53' 2¼"); 2 P. Sasin (Cze) 15.84m (51' 1¾"); 3 D. Johnson (UK) 15.62m
(51' 3"); 4 W. Clark (UK) 15.12m (49' 7¼").
Shot: 1 G. Capes (UK) 20.77m (68' 1¾"); 2 M. Winch (UK) 19.88m (65' 2¾"); 3 J. Brabec (Cze) 19.75m (64' 9¾");
4 J. Vlk (Cze) 19.37m (63' 6¾").
Discus: 1 L. Danek (Cze) 66.44m (218' 0") (*UK all-comers record*); 2 W. Tancred (UK) 62.44m (204' 10"); 3 J. Silhavy
(Cze) 61.64m (202' 3"); 4 J. Hillier (UK) 59.76m (196' 1").
Hammer: 1 J. Charvat (Cze) 70.16m (230' 2"); 2 H. Payne (UK) 69.06m (226' 7"); 3 J. Hajek (Cze) 68.74m (225' 6");
4 C. Black (UK) 68.12m (223' 6").
Javelin: 1 D. Travis (UK) 78.56m (257' 9"); 2 K. Sheppard (UK) 77.92m (255' 8"); 3 T. Babiak (Cze) 75.86m (248' 11");
4 J. Halva (Cze) 74.64m (244' 10").
4×100m Relay: 1 Czechoslovakia 40.0; UK (B. Green, C. Monk, L. Piggot, D. Halliday) (40.2) disqualified.
4×400m Relay: 1 UK (S. Marlow, A. Pascoe, W. Hartley, D. Jenkins) 3:08.6; 2 Czechoslovakia 3:09.0.
Match Result: UK 108; Czechoslovakia 102.
Invitation 100m: 1 L. Piggot (UK) 10.5; 2 M. Kralik (Cze) 10.7; 3 S. Atkins (UK) 10.8.

WOMEN

100m: 1 A. Lynch (UK) 11.3 (11.25); 2 H. Golden (UK) 11.5; 3 V. van Gool (Hol) 11.5; 4 E. Suranova (Cze) 11.6;
5 E. van Lienen (Hol) 11.9; 6 V. Knapova (Cze) 11.9.
200m: 1 H. Golden (UK) 23.0 (22.97); 2 S. Colyear (UK) 23.8; 3 W. van Gool (Hol) 23.9; 4 V. Knapova (Cze) 24.3;
5 E. van Lienen (Hol) 24.5; 6 J. Veverkova (Cze) 24.5.
400m: 1 J. Cerchlanova (Cze) 52.0; 2 V. Bernard (UK) 52.0; 3 T. Wunderink (Hol) 53.0; 4 J. Roscoe (UK) 53.9;
5 J. Hermanska (Cze) 54.8; 6 R. van Kruiswyk (Hol) 56.3.
800m: 1 J. Cerchlanova (Cze) 2:04.7; 2 L. Kiernan (UK) 2:06.6; 3 M. de Schipper (Hol) 2:07.8; 4 M. Coomber (UK)
2:08.6; 5 J. Hermanska (Cze) 2:09.8; 6 W. Hillen (Hol) 2:14.5.
1500m: 1 B. Sudicka (Cze) 4:24.3; 2 C. Tranter (UK) 4:25.2; 3 G. Goodburn (UK) 4:29.3; 4 H. Nerudova (Cze)
4:38.6; 5 J. van Gerwen (Hol) 4:44.5; 6 M. de Schipper (Hol) 4:52.0.
3000m: 1 N. Varcabova (Cze) 9:31.8; 2 C. Gould (UK) 9:32.6; 3 M. Privrelova (Cze) 9:41.2; 4 A. Blake (UK) 9:43.0.
100m Hurdles: 1 J. Vernon (UK) 13.4; 2 L. Drysdale (UK) 13.5; 3 J. Krchova (Cze) 14.0; 4 M. Schonauerova (Cze)
14.2; 5 M. van Wissen (Hol) 14.2; 6 M. van Doorn (Hol) 14.7.
High Jump: 1 M. Mracnova (Cze) 1.86m (6' 1¼"); 2 M. Hubnerova (Cze) 1.83m (6' 0"); 3 V. Harrison (UK) 1.75m
(5' 8¾"); 4 R. Watt (UK) 1.75m (5' 8¾"); 5 M. van Doorn (Hol) 1.75m (5' 8¾"); 6 M. Ackermans (Hol) 1.75m (5' 8¾").
Long Jump: 1 E. Suranova (Cze) 6.74m (22' 1¼"); 2 J. Nygrynova (Cze) 6.49m (21' 3½"); 3 C. Janssen (Hol) 6.40m
(21' 0"); 4 A. Wilson (UK) 6.26m (20' 6½"); 5 R. Martin-Jones (UK) 6.12m (20' 1"); 6 R. Koekoek (Hol) 6.01m (19' 8¾").
Shot: 1 H. Fibingerova (Cze) 20.75m (68' 1"); 2 L. Duchonova (Cze) 15.25m (50' 0½"); 3 B. Bedford (UK) 14.55m
(47' 9"); 4 J. Kerr (UK) 14.03m (46' 0½"); 5 E. Schalk (Hol) 13.82m (45' 4¼"); 6 R. Stalman (Hol) 13.79m (45' 3").
Discus: 1 H. Vyhnalova (Cze) 59.90m (196' 6"); 2 R. Payne (UK) 53.56m (175' 9"); 3 R. Stalman (Hol) 52.16m (171' 1");
4 J. Matysova (Cze) 51.96m (170' 6"); 5 M. Ritchie (UK) 51.44m (168' 9"); 6 E. Schalk (Hol) 40.78m (133' 9").
Javelin: 1 L. Kuys (Hol) 50.82m (166' 9"); 2 E. van Beusekom (Hol) 50.62m (166' 1"); 3 T. Sanderson (UK) 50.18m
(164' 7"); 4 J. Segetova (Cze) 49.46m (162' 3"); 5 S. Corbett (UK) 48.76m (160' 0"); 6 E. Kubanova (Cze) 45.72m (150' 0").

4 × 100m Relay: 1 UK (H. Golden, D. Ramsden, J. Vernon, A. Lynch) 45.1; **2** Netherlands 45.8; **3** Czechoslovakia 45.9.
4 × 400m Relay: 1 UK (C. Warden, J. Roscoe, V. Bernard, D. Murray) 3:32.6; **2** Czechoslovakia 3:38.9; **3** Netherlands 3:39.5.
Match Result: UK 73, Czechoslovakia 73; UK 87, Netherlands 48; Czechoslovakia 79, Netherlands 56.
Invitation 200m: 1 D. Murray (UK) 23.2; **2** R. Kennedy (UK) 23.9; **3** L. Barratt (UK) 24.0.

30, 31 July

SWEDEN v UK

Take Frank Clement for example. He ran the fastest race of his life, breaking Brendan Foster's UK 1500 metres record with 3:37.4 – and yet finished behind both his Swedish rivals. It reflected the match as a whole. The British men performed well enough, but the home athletes in Stockholm were all too often just that little better. Sweden won by five points, a dramatic change of fortunes from the previous year's encounter at Crystal Palace when Britain won by 29 points.

That 1500 metres provided the highlight of the men's match. It was a fast race throughout, for Clement and Ray Smedley had decided to set a swift pace in the hope of dropping the opposition, whom they later admitted they underrated. They kept to schedule with 58.2 at 400 metres, 1:56.9 at 800, and 2:55.5 at 1200, but the plan failed in so far as the Swedes simply tucked in behind and surged past in the closing stages. After a dour struggle along the finishing straight, Ulf Hogberg got home first in a national record of 3:36.6, one tenth ahead of steeplechase ace Anders Garderud. Nevertheless, the key to Sweden's match success was their supremacy in the field events, in which they built up a 51–34 advantage.

The British girls had an easy passage in their match, which featured a UK record by Donna Murray in the 400 metres, a UK junior record by Tessa Sanderson in the javelin, a Swedish record by Gunilla Lindh in the 800 metres (she having won the 1500 metres the night before in a personal best time), and a world's best in the 3000 metres walk by Margareta Simu. Donna, whose time electrically was 51.77, thus became British record holder in her first season of serious racing at the event.

MEN

100m: 1 C. Garpenborg (Swe) 10.5; **2** D. Halliday (UK) 10.7; **3** B. Green (UK) 10.7; **4** R. Trulsson (Swe) 10.8.
200m: 1 A. Bennett (UK) 21.0; **2** C. Monk (UK) 21.0; **3** T. Johansson (Swe) 21.1; **4** P-O. Sjoberg (Swe) 21.3.
400m: 1 D. Jenkins (UK) 45.6; **2** P-O. Sjoberg (Swe) 46.2; **3** M. Fredriksson (Swe) 46.3; **4** J. Wilson (UK) 47.5.
800m: 1 A. Carter (UK) 1:47.1; **2** D. McMeekin (UK) 1:47.2; **3** A. Svensson (Swe) 1:47.2; **4** B. Johansson (Swe) 1:49.2.
1500m: 1 U. Hogberg (Swe) 3:36.6; **2** A. Garderud (Swe) 3:36.7; **3** F. Clement (UK) 3:37.4 (*UK record*); **4** R. Smedley (UK) 3:39.6.
5000m: 1 D. Black (UK) 13:29.6; **2** B. Najde (Swe) 13:41.8; **3** B. Ford (UK) 13:42.4; **4** G. Holm (Swe) 14:18.2.
10,000m: 1 N. Karlsson (Swe) 28:45.2; **2** B. Plain (UK) 28:45.4; **3** G. Bengtsson (Swe) 28:46.6; **4** K. Penny (UK) 29:41.4.
3000m Steeplechase: 1 D. Glans (Swe) 8:24.0; **2** J. Davies (UK) 8:28.2; **3** S. Hollings (UK) 8:39.6; **4** K-E. Stahl (Swe) 8:49.2.

ATHLETICS 75

110m Hurdles: 1 B. Price (UK) 14.1; **2** K. Clerselius (Swe) 14.2; **3** C. J. Kirkpatrick (UK) 14.4; **4** B. Forssander (Swe) 14.6.
400m Hurdles: 1 A. Pascoe (UK) 50.2; **2** C. O'Neill (UK) 51.7; **3** K. Clerselius (Swe) 52.2; **4** G. Muller (Swe) 52.7.
High Jump: 1 I. Nyman (Swe) 2.18m (7' 1¾"); **2** R. Almen (Swe) 2.18m (7' 1¾"); **3** C. Boreham (UK) 2.00m (6' 6¾"); **4** M. Butterfield (UK) 2.00m (6' 6¾").
Pole Vault: 1 K. Isaksson (Swe) 5.25m (17' 2¾"); **2** I. Jernberg (Swe) 5.00m (16' 4¾"); M. Bull (UK) and B. Hooper (UK) failed at opening height.
Long Jump: 1 A. Lerwill (UK) 7.64m (25' 0¼"); **2** A. Fransson (Swe) 7.61m (24' 11¾"); **3** U. Jarfelt (Swe) 7.54m (24' 9"); **4** G. Hignett (UK) 7.44m (24' 5").
Triple Jump: 1 P-O. Smiding (Swe) 15.69m (51' 5¾"); **2** D. Johnson (UK) 15.61m (51' 2½"); **3** B-E. Oberg (Swe) 15.29m (50' 2"); **4** W. Clark (UK) 15.17m (49' 9¼").
Shot: 1 H. Hoglund (Swe) 20.17m (66' 2¼"); **2** M. Winch (UK) 19.67m (64' 6½"); **3** T. Carlsson (Swe) 18.92m (62' 1"); **4** W. Tancred (UK) 18.35m (60' 2½").
Discus: 1 W. Tancred (UK) 62.02m (203' 6"); **2** L. Haglund (Swe) 61.76m (202' 7"); **3** K. Gardenkrantz (Swe) 59.60m (195' 6"); **4** J. Hillier (UK) 57.92m (190' 0").
Hammer: 1 H. Payne (UK) 69.32m (227' 5"); **2** I. Chipchase (UK) 68.76m (225' 7"); **3** B. Holmstrom (Swe) 66.32m (217' 7"); **4** S. Blomqvist (Swe) 66.00m (216' 6").
Javelin: 1 L. Koski-Vahala (Swe) 84.60m (277' 7"); **2** J. Svensson (Swe) 79.30m (260' 2"); **3** D. Travis (UK) 76.74m (251' 9"); **4** C. Clover (UK) 76.36m (250' 6").
10,000m Walk: 1 H. Tenggren (Swe) 43:56.0; **2** S. Lightman (UK) 44:43.0; **3** C. Lawton (UK) 45:16.4; **4** T. Glans (Swe) 45:39.0.
4 × 100m Relay: 1 Sweden 39.9; **2** UK (B. Green, C. Monk, L. Piggot, D. Halliday) 40.1.
4 × 400m Relay: 1 UK (J. Wilson, G. Cohen, S. Marlow, D. Jenkins) 3:05.7; **2** Sweden 3:07.3.
Match Result: Sweden 107, UK 102.

WOMEN

100m: 1 A. Lynch (UK) 11.5; **2** L. Haglund (Swe) 11.6; **3** H. Golden (UK) 11.6; **4** A. Utterberg (Swe) 12.0.
200m: 1 H. Golden (UK) 23.4; **2** S. Colyear (UK) 24.2; **3** A. Utterberg (Swe) 24.4; **4** I. Nilsson (Swe) 24.5.
400m: 1 D. Murray (UK) 51.8 (*UK record*); **2** V. Bernard (UK) 52.2; **3** A. Larsson (Swe) 53.7; **4** L. Malmstrom (Swe) 55.4.
800m: 1 G. Lindh (Swe) 2:02.6; **2** R. Wright (UK) 2:06.0; **3** H. Tanner (UK) 2:08.7; **4** M. Fossberg (Swe) 2:10.2.
1500m: 1 G. Lindh (Swe) 4:09.9; **2** J. Smith (UK) 4:13.7; **3** C. Tranter (UK) 4:22.8; **4** K. Joenna (Swe) 4:34.4.
3000m: 1 E. Gustafsson (Swe) 9:12.2; **2** S. Larsson (Swe) 9:18.0; **3** P. Yeoman (UK) 9:19.8; **4** C. Gould (UK) 9:20.2.
100m Hurdles: 1 B. Thompson (UK) 13.6; **2** L. Drysdale (UK) 13.6; **3** T. Puskas (Swe) 14.6; **4** C. Sallstrom (Swe) 14.7.
High Jump: 1 A. Karlsson (Swe) 1.80m (5' 10¾"); **2** B. Lawton (UK) 1.77m (5' 9¾"); **3** R. Watt (UK) 1.74m (5' 8½"); **4** A. Tannander (Swe) 1.65m (5' 5").
Long Jump: 1 A. Wilson (UK) 6.20m (20' 4"); **2** R. Martin-Jones (UK) 6.16m (20' 2½"); **3** L. Wallin (Swe) 5.89m (19' 4"); T. Puskas (Swe) retired.
Shot: 1 I. Wehmonnen (Swe) 15.33m (50' 3½"); **2** B. Bedford (UK) 14.84m (48' 8¼"); **3** G. Johansson (Swe) 14.46m (47' 5¼"); **4** J. Kerr (UK) 14.16m (46' 5½").
Discus: 1 R. Payne (UK) 51.92m (170' 4"); **2** U. Buuts (Swe) 49.24m (161' 6"); **3** M. Ritchie (UK) 49.00m (169' 9"); **4** G. Johansson (Swe) 46.34m (152' 0").
Javelin: 1 T. Sanderson (UK) 54.10m (177' 6"); **2** S. Corbett (UK) 51.08m (167' 7"); **3** O. Westmann (Swe) 46.96m (154' 1"); **4** G. Andersson (Swe) 45.52m (149' 4").

3000m Walk: **1** M. Simu (Swe) 14:19.4 (*world best performance*); **2** B. Holmqvist (Swe) 14:26.0; **3** M. Fawkes (UK) 14:40.4; **4** B. Jenkins (UK) 15:16.4.

4 × 100m Relay: **1** UK (L. Barratt, D. Ramsden, H. Golden, A. Lynch) 45.2; **2** Sweden 46.0.

4 × 400m Relay: **1** UK (C. Warden. J. Roscoe, E. Barnes, D. Murray) 3:33.9; **2** Sweden 3:41.3.

Match Result: UK 86, Sweden 59.

JULY HIGHLIGHTS

Anders Garderud of Sweden reclaimed sole possession of the European 3000 metres steeplechase record with a time of 8:15.2 in Stockholm on 2 July. Other European records during the month were registered by Irena Szewinska of Poland with 22.8 for 220 yards in Athens on 10 July, and by Manfred Ommer of West Germany with 9.2 for 100 yards and 10.0 for 100 metres (equalling the records) at Leverkusen on 22 July.

The middle-distance star of the European circuit was not Filbert Bayi, who in any case had to cut short his tour after injuring himself in a fall during a 1500 metres race in Oslo, but New Zealander John Walker – the man who followed the Tanzanian home in the world record shattering 1500 metres at the Commonwealth Games. Having disposed of Bayi in Helsinki on 27 June (3:33.4 to 3:37.0), Walker produced another sizzling 1500 metres in Milan on 2 July (3:34.3), and two days later in Oslo made a startling debut over 3000 metres. He unleashed a 54.4 last lap to win in 7:40.6, for third place on the world all-time list. Walker kept up the pressure with further 1500 metres runs of 3:35.4 in Stockholm on 18 July and 3:35.7 in Turin on 24 July.

Krystyna Kacperczyk of Poland set a world's best of 56.51 for the women's 400 metres hurdles at Augsburg on 13 July. This performance, together with Lyudmila Bragina's 8:52.8 for 3000 metres, is to be listed by the IAAF as an inaugural world record.

Donna Murray, in between her 400 metres exploits, registered the fastest ever 200 metres time by a British girl of 22.9 at Bristol on 14 July, but the following wind of 2.4 metres per second prevented its being forwarded as a UK record.

Steve Ovett (18), the newly crowned AAA 800 metres champion, became Britain's youngest sub-four minute miler at Haringey on 17 July, combining quarters of 60.2, 61.1, 63.0, and 55.1 for a time of 3:59.4. Jim Ryun (USA) ran 3:59.0 at the age of 17 and 3:55.3 at 18.

Just as in August 1973, Bill Tancred managed to break the UK discus record on successive days. He reached 64.40 metres (211' 3") at Loughborough on 20 July, equalling the Commonwealth record, and progressed to 64.94 metres (213' 1") from the same circle next day.

Bob Dobson retained his RWA national 50 kilometres walk title at Hendon on 20 July. His time was a fast one for a hilly course that proved so trying that 36 of the 122 starters failed to finish.

Result: **1** R. Dobson 4:16:58; **2** J. Warhurst 4:18:58; **3** R. Thorpe 4:24:08; **4** A. Banyard 4:27:21; **5** B. Adams 4:31:51; **6** J. Nye 4:35:19; **7** K. Harding 4:37:59; **8** R. Middleton 4:38:30; **9** C. Fogg 4:39:03; **10** M. Holmes 4:40:08. **Team:** Sheffield United H.

Jim Bolding (USA) set world figures of 48.7 for 440 yards hurdles in Turin on 24 July, passing the 400 metres mark in 48.3. Earlier, in Milan on 2 July, he had posted an American 400 metres hurdles record of 48.1, second only to John Akii-

Bua (Uga) and equal to David Hemery (UK) on the all-time list. Fellow American Rick Wohlhuter, already a world record breaker for 880 yards, obliterated the world 1000 metres standard of 2:16.0 by South Africa's Danie Malan with the revolutionary time of 2:13.9 in Oslo on 30 July. His target had been 2:15. He went through 400 metres in 51.7 and 800 metres in 1:46.8.

Winners of titles at the WAAA Intermediate and Junior Championships, at Wolverhampton on 27 July, were:

(Intermediates) *100m:* A. McClelland 12.4. *200m:* E. Douglas 24.6. *400m:* K. Colebrook 55.5. *800m:* J. Lawrence 2:11.0. *1500m:* (held at Crystal Palace on 20 July) A. Tunnicliffe 4:33.6. *80m Hurdles:* S. Strong 12.1. *200m Hurdles:* F. Macauley 28.5. *High Jump:* V. Mullin 1.75m (5' 8¾"). *Long Jump:* J. Bowerman 5.83m (19' 1½"). *Shot:* J. Oakes 11.95m (39' 2½"). *Discus:* K. Mallard 39.38m (129' 2"). *Javelin:* J. King 44.80m (147' 0"). *2500m Walk:* S. Saunders 12:47.8. (Juniors) *100m:* J. Walsh 12.1. *200m:* S. Howells 24.9. *800m:* F. Nixon 2:15.2. *1500m:* S. Ludlam 4:39.7. *75m Hurdles:* J. Duffield 11.5. *High Jump:* V. Kelly 1.71m (5' 7¼"). *Long Jump:* M. Killoran 5.29m (17' 4¼"). *Shot:* M. Walton 11.26m (36' 11½"). *Discus:* F. Condon 33.60m (110' 3"). *Javelin:* C. Whitmore 34.70m (113' 10"). *2500m Walk:* E. Cox 12:53.2.

One of Britain's most distinguished walkers, Bert Cooper, died aged 64. He won the AAA 2 miles championship on seven consecutive occasions between 1932 and 1938, and he set world records of 12:38.2 for 3000 metres and 21:52.4 for 5000 metres in 1935. Olympic decathlon champion in 1932, Jim Bausch (USA), died at the age of 68.

Left: *Jim Bolding (USA) – world figures over the 'lows' at 440 yards and challenging Akii-Bua's 400 metres supremacy.*
Right: *Berwyn Price's fast, if erratic, high hurdling was a welcome points-winner for national champions Cardiff as they retained their title in August.*

August   CANTABRIAN

3, 4 August
AAA UNDER 20 CHAMPIONSHIPS

The incentive of selection for an international match in Madrid the following weekend helped several of Britain's leading young athletes overcome the gloomy, wet conditions at Crystal Palace in order to produce outstanding performances. Championship records by Roger Jenkins in the 400 metres, Milton Palmer in the high jump, Keith Stock in the pole vault, Aston Moore in the triple jump, and Simon Rodhouse in the discus assured them of their trip to the sunshine; while further meeting bests fell to the injury-prone Commonwealth javelin champion Charles Clover and to walker Jacky Lord.

Milton Palmer proved to be the most precocious performer on view. This tall, Jamaican-born schoolboy didn't quite match his earlier personal best of 2.02 metres (6' 7½"), but he fell only a centimetre (½") short and captured the title ahead of lads up to four years his senior. He didn't turn 16 until a month later! Milton, who has composed Mozart-influenced works for the wind section of the school orchestra and hopes one day to play the clarinet at the Royal Festival Hall, had never jumped higher than 1.66 metres (5' 5½") prior to switching from straddle to flop at the beginning of 1973. Now he is in a position to become Britain's first seven-footer.

JUNIORS

100m: 1 S. Green 10.6; 2 G. Edwards 10.6; 3 R. Meredith 10.7.
200m: 1 A. Harley 21.5; 2 L. Hoyte 21.6; 3 A. McMaster 21.7.
400m: 1 R. Jenkins 47.3; 2 C. Van Rees 48.3; 3 B. Jones 48.3.
800m: 1 A. Dyke 1:51.1; 2 A. Mottershead 1:52.0; 3 P. Chimes 1:52.5.
1500m: 1 P. Williams 3:53.7; 2 B. Moss 3:54.4; 3 S. Bolam 3:54.7.
3000m: (held at Crystal Palace, 13 July) 1 J. Treacy (Eir) 8:15.6; 2 B. Moss 8:16.4; 3 J. Odlin 8:18.4.
5000m: 1 W. Sheridan 14:29.0; 2 J. Odlin 14:31.8; 3 A. Armitage 14:37.8.
2000m Steeplechase: 1 J. Tierney 5:49.6; 2 D. Warren 5:56.8; 3 P. Caden 5:57.4.
110m Hurdles: 1 T. James 15.1; 2 M. Jackson 15.1; 3 N. Gerrard 15.3.
400m Hurdles: 1 P. Mills (NZ) 54.4; 2 S. Johnson 55.2; 3 W. Greaves 55.9.
10,000m Walk: 1 J. Lord 45:20.0; 2 D. Cotton 47:31.2; 3 M. Angrove 49:01.4.
High Jump: 1 M. Palmer 2.01m (6' 7"); 2 M. Shorten 1.98m (6' 6"); 3 G. Vose 1.95m (6' 4¾").
Pole Vault: 1 K. Stock 4.60m (15' 1"); 2 C. Boreham 4.50m (14' 9"); 3 W. Best 4.30m (14' 1¼").
Long Jump: 1 R. Mitchell 7.30m (23' 11½"); 2 T. Paice 7.10m (23' 3½"); 3 L. Hoyte 6.97m (22' 10½").
Triple Jump: 1 A. Moore 15.56m (51' 0¾"); 2 F. Attoh 15.21m (49' 11"); 3 G. Doerr 15.20m (49' 10½").
Shot: 1 S. Rodhouse 14.72m (48' 3½"); 2 I. Lindley 14.72m (48' 3½"); 3 R. Slaney 13.74m (45' 1").
Discus: 1 R. Slaney 48.46m (159' 0"); 2 P. Buxton 45.74m (150' 1"); 3 J. Howell 43.90m (144' 0").
Hammer: 1 J. Scott 55.78m (183' 0"); 2 M. Mileham 50.44m (165' 6"); 3 M. Petra 49.66m (162' 11").
Javelin: 1 C. Clover 75.50m (247' 8"); 2 D. Ottley 70.36m (230' 10"); 3 P. Yates 67.56m (221' 8").

AAA U-20 CHAMPIONSHIPS/BRITISH INTERNATIONAL GAMES

YOUTHS

100m: 1 D. Hill 10.9; 2 C. Beswick 11.1; 3 E. Tulloch 11.1.
200m: 1 E. Tulloch 22.1; 2 I. Cooper 22.3; 3 C. Beswick 22.5.
400m: 1 M. Francis 49.5; 2 D. Bluemink 50.1; 3 R. Bishop 50.6.
800m: 1 S. Caldwell 1:54.2; 2 G. Cook 1:54.4; 3 N. Brooks 1:56.0.
1500m: 1 M. Bateman 3:53.2; 2 S. Cahill 3:56.4; 3 P. Gower 3:57.0.
1500m Steeplechase: 1 S. Evans 4:18.1; 2 C. Sly 4:24.7; 3 S. McArthur 4:31.3.
100m Hurdles: 1 J. Longman 13.4; 2 I. Ratcliffe 13.5; 3 J. Holton 13.7.
2000m Walk: 1 M. Dunion 8:33.4; 2 G. Morris 8:38.6; 3 S. Tidey 8:55.8.
High Jump: 1 A. Brewster 1.90m (6' 2¾"); 2 B. Burgess 1.85m (6' 0¾"); 3 G. Murray 1.85m (6' 0¾").
Pole Vault: 1 L. Hennessy 3.90m (12' 9½"); 2 K. Latham 3.75m (12' 3½"); 3 N. McPhee 3.40m (11' 1¾").
Long Jump: 1 A. Earle 6.74m (22' 1½"); 2 A. Taylor 6.62m (21' 8¾"); 3 R. Hodges 6.56m (21' 6¼").
Triple Jump: 1 L. McGinley 13.85m (45' 5¼"); 2 P. Cartwright 13.26m (43' 6"); 3 L. Grayson 13.17m (43' 2½").
Shot: 1 G. Patience 15.94m (52' 3¾"); 2 S. Hughes 14.72m (48' 3½"); 3 M. Strzadala 14.30m (46' 11").
Discus: 1 J. Brice 44.62m (146' 5"); 2 G. Patience 44.14m (144' 10"); 3 D. Allen 43.64m (143' 2").
Hammer: 1 B. Riddles 56.00m (183' 9"); 2 R. Gibson 53.48m (175' 5"); 3 S. Watson 51.80m (169' 11").
Javelin: 1 L. Evans 60.12m (197' 3"); 2 I. Trimby 57.50m (188' 8"); 3 S. Morton 54.88m (180' 1").

10 August

BRITISH INTERNATIONAL GAMES

An important landmark in British field events history was reached at Crystal Palace when Geoff Capes graduated from potential 70-footer status to becoming a fully fledged member (only the sixth in the world) of the 'club'. How did it feel to unleash a put of 21.37 metres (70' 1½")? 'Halfway across the circle I thought it was going to go – and it went'. Capes added: 'Everything was right. I've been waiting all year for that feeling'.

The eagerly awaited Emsley Carr Mile, bringing together Brendan Foster, Frank Clement, Ray Smedley, Steve Ovett, and the American Len Hilton, failed to live up to expectations even if the first three finishers did comfortably better four minutes. Foster had made no secret of his wish to break the UK record (3:55.3) but,

Mike Winch.

suffering an understandable reaction the week after his momentous world record (see August highlights), he lacked the vital spark on this occasion and finished third behind Clement (under four minutes for the first time) and Smedley.

Another disappointment was the sight of Alan Pascoe having to pull up with hamstring trouble soon after the start of his 400 metres hurdles race against the world's number one, Jim Bolding (USA). But, happily, both he and Foster were restored to their greatest form in time for the main challenge: the European Championships.

MEN

100y: 1 D. Halliday 9.9; 2 D. Roberts 9.9; 3 B. Green 9.9; 4 S. Green 10.0; 5 L. Piggot 10.0; 6 R. Kennedy 10.1.

200m: 1 A. Bennett 21.6; 2 C. Monk 21.8; 3 S. Green 21.9; 4 L. Sarria (Spa) 21.9; 5 R. Kennedy 22.7; 6 T. Bonsor 22.7; 7 J. Martinez (Spa) 22.9.

400m: 1 G. Cohen 46.9; 2 I. Saunders 47.3; 3 D. Laing 47.6; 4 M. Delaney 47.7; 5 J. Lopez (Spa) 48.4.

800m: 1 D. McMeekin 1:47.7; 2 A. Settle 1:48.1; 3 P. Browne 1:48.3; 4 J. Greatrex 1:49.0; 5 A. Fernandez-Ortiz (Spa) 1:52.0; 6 C. Campbell 1:54.5; 7 C. van Daalen (Hol) 1:56.2.

Emsley Carr Mile: 1 F. Clement 3:57.4; 2 R. Smedley 3:58.0; 3 B. Foster 3:58.4; 4 L. Hilton (USA) 4:03.0; 5 S. Ovett 4:03.5; 6 D. Gibbon 4:03.9; 7 D. Moorcroft 4:11.5; 8 C. Barber 4:19.3.

5000m: 1 D. Black 13:39.2; 2 C. Stewart 13:39.6; 3 M. Baxter 13:40.4; 4 M. Haro (Spa) 13:41.8; 5 A. Weatherhead 13:48.0; 6 A. Simmons 13:49.6; 7 K. Penny 13:54.4; 8 F. Briscoe 13:57.2.

3000m Steeplechase: 1 D. Camp 8:32.2; 2 S. Hollings 8:34.2; 3 J. Bicourt 8:37.8; 4 A. Staynings 8:40.2; 5 A. Campos (Spa) 8:45.2; 6 C. Thomas 8:49.6; 7 D. Coates 8:50.6; 8 A. Holden 8:55.0.

400m Hurdles: 1 J. Bolding (USA) 50.1; 2 W. Hartley 51.1; 3 S. Black 51.2; 4 C. O'Neill 51.3; 5 A. James 52.4; 6 G. Weinhandl (Aut) 52.8; 7 F. Suarez (Spa) 53.5. A. Pascoe dnf.

4×100m Relay: 1 UK 'B' (D. Roberts, A. Lerwill, L. Piggot, S. Green) 39.8; 2 UK 'A' (B. Green, C. Monk, A. Bennett, D. Halliday) 39.8; 3 Spain 40.3.

Pole Vault: 1 M. Bull 5.20m (17' 0¾"); 2 B. Hooper 5.10m (16' 8¾").

Shot: 1 G. Capes 21.37m (70' 1½") (*equals UK all-comers record; new Commonwealth and UK record*); 2 M. Winch 19.87m (65' 2¼"); 3 J. Hillier 15.82m (51' 11").

Hammer: 1 I. Chipchase 70.76m (232' 2"); 2 H. Payne 68.74m (225' 6"); 3 B. Williams 68.62m (225' 1"); 4 C. Black 68.20m (223' 9"); 5 P. Dickenson 67.66m (222' 0"); 6 J. Whitehead 62.62m (205' 5").

Javelin: 1 B. Roberts 78.08m (256' 2"); 2 K. Sheppard 77.34m (253' 9"); 3 R. Silvester 75.98m (249' 3").

WOMEN

100m: 1 H. Golden 11.8; 2 C. Molinari (Ita) 11.9; 3 S. Lannaman 11.9; 4 D. Ramsden 12.0; 5 S. Colyear 12.1; 6 L. Barratt 12.2; 7 L. Gnecchi (Ita) 12.5.

200m: 1 H. Golden 24.0; 2 G. Taylor 24.1; 3 D. Heath 24.7.

400m: 1 D. Murray 52.2; 2 V. Bernard 52.8; 3 R. Kennedy 53.8; 4 W. Hill 54.1; 5 J. Roscoe 54.3; 6 E. Barnes 54.6; 7 C. Warden 55.2; 8 R. Wright 56.2.

1500m: 1 J. Smith 4:17.0; 2 A. Yeoman 4:18.5; 3 P. Yeoman 4:18.9; 4 C. Haskett 4:21.0; 5 J. Allison 4:23.4; 6 C. Gould 4:24.2; 7 G. Goodburn 4:28.5; 8 P. Yule 4:29.7.

100m Hurdles: 1 B. Thompson 13.7; 2 J. Vernon 13.7; 3 L. Drysdale 13.8; 4 M. Nimmo 14.0; 5 L. Ilott 14.1; 6 A. Wilson 14.3; 7 S. Holmstrom 14.4.

4×100m Relay: 1 UK (L. Barratt, D. Ramsden, H. Golden, S. Lannaman) 45.0; Italy (45.5) disqualified.

High Jump: 1 B. Lawton 1.86m (6' 1¼"); 2 V. Harrison 1.80m (5' 10¾"); 3 R. Watt 1.80m (5' 10¾"); 4 A. Wilson 1.75m (5' 8¾"); 5 S. Wright 1.75m (5' 8¾"); 6 C. Mathers 1.70m (5' 7"); 7 T. Dainton 1.70m (5' 7"); 8 R. Few 1.65m (5' 5").

SPAIN v UK v PORTUGAL (JUNIORS)

10 August

SPAIN v UK v PORTUGAL
(junior men)

The heat was on the British junior men's team in Madrid, and not only from the sun. The Spaniards put up a tremendous fight and it all hinged on the final event, the 4×400 metres relay. Britain won that and thus the match, but only by the slim margin of four points. Portugal were obliterated to the tune of 142–58.

Roger Jenkins upheld the family's good name in international competition by winning the 400 metres, dipping under 47 seconds for the first time: his mark of 46.8 equalled the all-important European qualifying standard. Another to stake a strong claim for Rome selection was Lesley Kiernan. After having missed the 800 metres standard of 2:05.0 by one and two tenths in earlier races, she struck out strongly in her race (the girls' events were not on a match basis), passing the bell in 60.2 and holding on stoutly to record 2:04.5.

MEN

100m: 1 M. Arnau (Spa) 10.5; 2 J. Carbonell (Spa) 10.6; 3 G. Edwards (UK) 10.7; 4 R. Meredith (UK) 10.8; 5 J. Silva (Por) 10.8; 6 A. Santos (Por) 10.9.

200m: 1 M. Arnau (Spa) 21.0; 2 J. Reverter (Spa) 21.4; 3 L. Hoyte (UK) 21.6; 4 A. Harley (UK) 21.8; 5 A. Santos (Por) 22.2; 6 J. Silva (Por) 22.4.

400m: 1 R. Jenkins (UK) 46.8; 2 C. Van Rees (UK) 47.9; 3 L. Puerta (Spa) 48.6; 4 A. Paez (Spa) 49.0; 5 A. Borges (Por) 50.5; 6 A. Ribeiro (Por) 50.7.

800m: 1 J. L. Egea (Spa) 1:49.9; 2 A. Dyke (UK) 1:50.2; 3 A. Mottershead (UK) 1:50.8; 4 M. Gomes (Por) 1:53.5; 5 L. Marimon (Spa) 1:54.1; 6 F. Marinho (Por) 1:56.4.

1500m: 1 P. Williams (UK) 3:50.0; 2 A. Atabia (Por) 3:50.3; 3 J. L. Gonzalez (Spa) 3:51.3; 4 M. Fernandez (Spa) 3:57.3; 5 R. Bolam (UK) 3:58.4; 6 J. Campos (Por) 4:10.5.

5000m: 1 W. Sheridan (UK) 14:41.8; 2 C. Alario (Spa) 14:44.3; 3 J. Odlin (UK) 14:47.2; 4 J. Sena (Por) 14:50.6; 5 I. Feijoo (Spa) 15:45.0; 6 J. Campos (Por) 16:22.6.

2000m Steeplechase: 1 M. Nunez (Spa) 5:47.8; 2 E. Guzman (Spa) 5:47.8; 3 D. Warren (UK) 5:55.4; 4 J. Tierney (UK) 5:56.8; 5 M. Paiva (Por) 5:57.0; 6 A. Ribeiro (Por) 6:01.6.

110m Hurdles: 1 J. Lloveras (Spa) 14.4; 2 A. James (UK) 15.0; 3 M. Jackson (UK) 15.0; 4 J. Moracho (Spa) 15.1; 5 A. Maruta (Por) 16.6; 6 N. Andrade (Por) 17.2.

400m Hurdles: 1 G. Tejeda (Spa) 54.2; 2 W. Greaves (UK) 54.4; 3 S. Johnson (UK) 55.0; 4 A. Maruta (Por) 57.2; 5 A. Horcajada (Spa) 60.0; 6 J. Tarre (Por) 60.2.

High Jump: 1 M. Perarnau (Spa) 2.06m (6' 9"); 2 F. Morrilas (Spa) 2.06m (6' 9"); 3 M. Shorten (UK) 2.00m (6' 6¾"); 4 M. Palmer (UK) 1.95m (6' 4¾"); 5 R. Vergamota (Por) 1.85m (6' 0¾"); 6 L. Leite (Por) 1.80m (5' 10¾").

Pole Vault: 1 J. Astola (Spa) 4.40m (14' 5¼"); 2 R. Oriol (Spa) 4.20m (13' 9¼"); 3 K. Stock (UK) 4.10m (13' 5¼"); 4 R. Vergamota (Por) 4.00m (13' 1½"); 5 M. Neves (Por) 3.80m (12' 5½"); C. Boreham (UK) no height.

Long Jump: 1 R. Mitchell (UK) 7.25m (23' 9½"); 2 S. Risco (Spa) 7.22m (23' 8¼"); 3 T. Paice (UK) 7.08m (23' 2¾"); 4 J. Infanta (Spa) 7.03m (23' 0¾"); 5 A. Rodriguez (Por) 6.73m (22' 1"); 6 M. Macedo (Por) 6.19m (20' 3¾").

Triple Jump: 1 F. Attoh (UK) 15.44m (50' 8"); 2 A. Moore (UK) 15.24m (50' 0"); 3 J. Infanta (Spa) 15.19m (49' 10"); 4 A. Solanas (Spa) 15.00m (49' 2½"); 5 C. Caciro (Por) 13.87m (45' 6¼"); 6 M. Neves (Por) 13.62m (44' 8¼").

Shot: 1 I. Lindley (UK) 14.77m (48' 5½"); 2 S. Rodhouse (UK) 14.54m (47' 8½"); 3 F. M. Correa (Spa) 14.51m (47' 7¼"); 4 E. Santo (Por) 12.97m (42' 6¾"); 5 F. Pujadas (Spa) 12.73m (41' 9¼"); 6 J. Alves (Por) 11.85m (38' 10½").

Discus: 1 R. Slaney (UK) 48.56m (159' 4"); 2 P. Buxton (UK) 45.26m (148' 6"); 3 C. Buron (Spa) 42.46m (139' 4"); 4 J. Hermida (Spa) 41.14m (135' 0"); 5 J. Esteves (Por) 40.96m (134' 4"); 6 E. Santo (Por) 35.90m (117' 9").

Hammer: **1** P. Scott (UK) 55.00m (180' 5"); **2** J. B. Gayoso (Spa) 49.20m (161' 5"); **3** R. Nuche (Spa) 48.80m (160' 1"); **4** M. Mileham (UK) 47.28m (155' 1"); **5** J. Onterelo (Por) 45.28m (148' 7"); **6** A. Alemida (Por) 42.06m (138' 0").

Javelin: **1** D. Ottley (UK) 71.84m (235' 8"); **2** P. Yates (UK) 67.10m (220' 2"); **3** M. Canavos (Spa) 62.78m (206' 0"); **4** M. Ferrer (Spa) 52.34m (171' 9"); **5** J. Alves (Por) 51.44m (168' 9"); **6** M. Pereira (Por) 48.34m (158' 7").

4 × 100m Relay: **1** Spain 40.6; **2** UK (G. Edwards, R. Meredith, A. Harley, L. Hoyte) 41.2; **3** Portugal 42.5.

4 × 400m Relay: **1** UK (B. Jones, P. Hoffmann, C. Van Rees, R. Jenkins) 3:11.4; **2** Spain 3:18.8; **3** Portugal 3:23.4.

Match Results: UK 102, Spain 98; UK 142, Portugal 58; Spain 139, Portugal 62.

Invitation 100m: A. McMaster (UK) 10.9. **200m:** A. McMaster 21.8.

WOMEN

100m: **1** J. Walsh (UK) 11.8; **2** E. C. Muniz (Spa) 12.1; **3** D. V. Jorba (Spa) 12.4.

400m: **1** J. Colebrook (UK) 55.3; **2** R. Colorado (Spa) 55.7; **3** J. S. Perez (Spa) 56.1.

800m: **1** L. Kiernan (UK) 2:04.5; **2** R. Orchandiano (Spa) 2:09.7; **3** M. Garay (Spa) 2:12.5.

1500m: **1** R. Morrish (UK) 4:31.0; **2** C. Hanson (UK) 4:34.5; **3** E. Escudero (Spa) 4:35.3.

100m Hurdles: **1** S. Mapstone (UK) 14.2; **2** M. J. Martinez (Spa) 15.0.

Long Jump: **1** S. Mapstone (UK) 6.04m (19' 9¾"); **2** J. S. Perez (Spa) 5.76m (18' 10¾").

20, 21 August

NORWAY v UK v BENELUX (men)

Roger Jenkins clinched his place in the team for Rome by lowering his personal best again, to 46.7, in the final tuning-up match against Norway and Benelux in Oslo. Jenkins finished about a dozen metres behind the outstanding young Belgian, Alfons Brijdenbach (credited with a 45.0sec 400 metres earlier in the season), but he succeeded in his primary task of beating Glen Cohen, his only rival for the vacant spot in the 400 metres team. John Bicourt in the steeplechase and Steve Black in the 400 metres hurdles were others to win last-minute selection, while javelin thrower Dave Travis and 800 metres star Andy Carter passed what amounted to fitness tests. Unhappily, Carter aggravated his previous injury in the process and was unable to run in Rome.

Among other personal best performances was a 20.8sec 200 metres victory by Ainsley Bennett, a vastly improved sprinter who had run no faster than 21.6 the previous season. Bennett also served notice of his great potential at 400 metres with a 46.7 split in the relay. An unusual but encouraging occurrence was the gaining of maximum points in three of the heavy events: shot (even without Geoff Capes), discus, and hammer.

100m: **1** C. Monk (UK) 10.5; **2** D. Roberts (UK) 10.5; **3** A. Garshol (Nor) 10.6; **4** L. Micha (Ben) 10.6; **5** O. Rost (Nor) 10.7; **6** B. de Jaeger (Ben) 11.4.

200m: **1** A. Bennett (UK) 20.8; **2** A. Brijdenbach (Ben) 20.9; **3** C. Monk (UK) 21.0; **4** R. Heerenveen (Ben) 21.4; **5** O. Rost (Nor) 21.6; **6** T. Bjelland (Nor) 22.3.

400m: **1** A. Brijdenbach (Ben) 45.2; **2** R. Jenkins (UK) 46.7; **3** T. van de Goolberg (Ben) 47.2; **4** G. Cohen (UK) 47.5; **5** O. Evensen (Nor) 47.7; **6** R. Tjore (Nor) 48.8.

800m: **1** A. Settle (UK) 1:47.7; **2** A. Carter (UK) 1:47.7; **3** J. van Wezer (Ben) 1:48.5; **4** S. Svensen (Nor) 1:48.8; **5** A. Galgerud (Nor) 1:51.1; **6** H. Schaarn (Ben) 1:53.3.

Above: *Getting in on the gold rush. With 80 metres to go in the 4 × 400m relay, David Jenkins closes up on Finland's Markku Kukkoahu and Britain are on their way to their second gold on a remarkable Sunday at the 11th European Championships.*
Right: *Britain's 18-year-old Steve Ovett chases Luciano Susanj in their 800 metres semi-final, which Ovett won. But the next day the blistering Yugoslav burnt off the field with half a lap to go; Ovett took the silver in 1:45.8, a European junior record.*

Above: *Women's discus champion Faina Melnik (Sov) flanked by silver medallist Argentina Menis (Rom), right, and bronze medallist Gabriele Hinzmann (EG).* **Left:** *Sprint queen of the Rome Championships: Irena Szewinska (Pol) vanquished Olympic champion Renate Stecher in both the 100 and 200.* **Below:** *Geoff Capes' bronze in the shot was a disappointment after superb performances earlier in the season.*
Opposite page. Right: *Andrea Lynch was at her brilliant best in the 100 metres to take the bronze in a high-class field.*
Far right: *Hungary's Ilona Bruzsenyak overcame run-up problems to clear 6.65 metres (21' 10") for gold.* **Below:** *So easy for Annelie Ehrhardt (EG) in her 100m hurdles semi as Chantel Rega (Fra) and Valeria Stefanescu (Rom) trail. In the final it was the same story: Ehrhardt by two metres.*

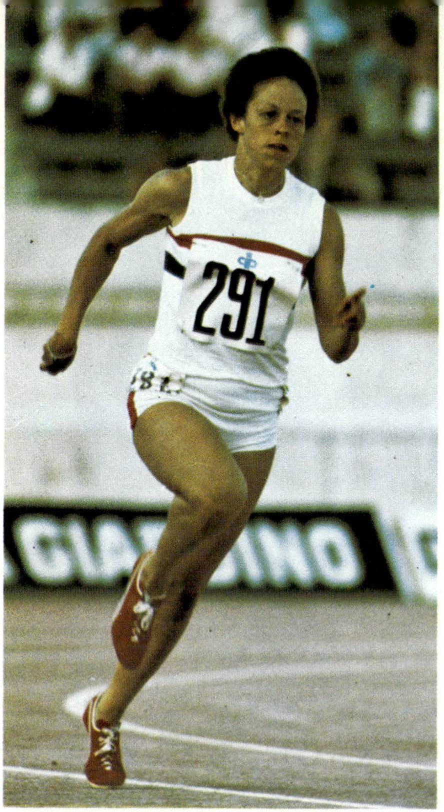
291

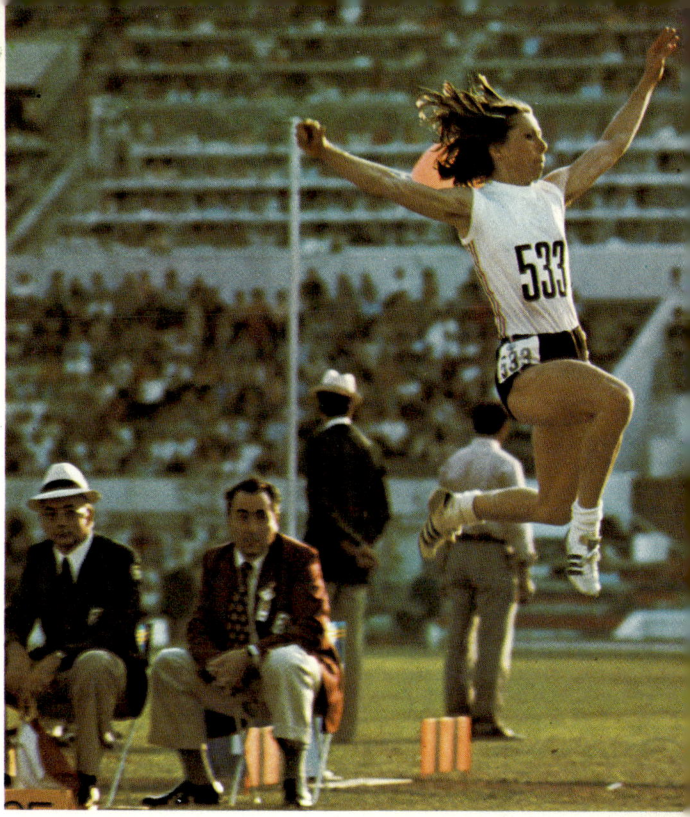
533

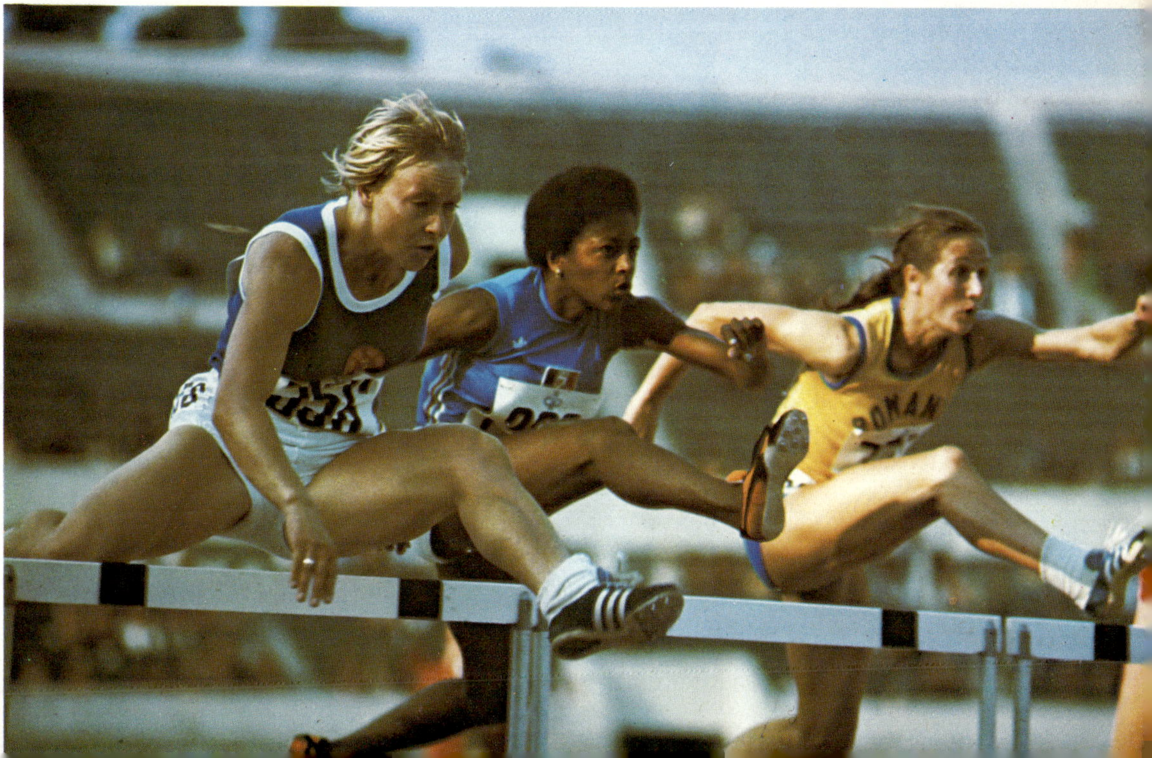

Above: *Hogberg (Swe) leads the 1500 metres field with silver medallist Hansen (Den) and bronze medallist Wessinghage (WG) challenging on the outside – and eventual winner Klaus-Peter Justus (EG) is not yet in the picture at this late stage!*
Below: *Roger Mills bravely staggers home to take fourth place in the 20km walk. Two months later, his perseverance was rewarded when the Russian Zhaloshik was disqualified and Mills awarded the bronze.*

NORWAY V UK V BENELUX (MEN)/BRITISH LEAGUE FINALS

1500m: 1 R. Smedley (UK) 3:42.0; 2 K. Kvalheim (Nor) 3:42.4; 3 H. Schaarn (Ben) 3:43.0; 4 L. Kaupang (Nor) 3:43.5; 5 E. van Mullen (Ben) 3:44.2; 6 D. Gibbon (UK) 3:44.8.

3000m: 1 L. Schots (Ben) 7:53.8; 2 J. Davies (UK) 7:54.0; 3 A. Kvalheim (Nor) 7:54.4; 4 D. Black (UK) 7:56.4; 5 M. Smets (Ben) 8:16.6; 6 P. Haga (Nor) 8:17.2.

5000m: 1 K. Boro (Nor) 13:30.4; 2 J. Hermens (Ben) 13:31.0; 3 P. Halle (Nor) 13:34.6; 4 B. Ford (UK) 13:35.8; 5 A. Staynings (UK) 13:39.0; 6 W. van Rentergem (Ben) 14:05.0.

10,000m: 1 K. Penny (UK) 28:59.0; 2 E. Rombaux (Ben) 28:59.2; 3 John Brown (UK) 29:00.6; 4 A. Risa (Nor) 29:00.8; 5 W. van Rentergem (Ben) 29:02.6; 6 A. Fornaess (Nor) 29:03.8.

3000m Steeplechase: 1 P. Thijs (Ben) 8:29.8; 2 J. Bicourt (UK) 8:31.0; 3 S. Hollings (UK) 8:34.8; 4 H. Leyens (Ben) 8:36.2; 5 A. Olsen (Nor) 8:37.2; 6 H. Knudsen (Nor) 9:02.6.

110m Hurdles: 1 B. Price (UK) 13.9; 2 C. J. Kirkpatrick (UK) 14.1; 3 H. Fimland (Nor) 14.2; 4 Y. Kirpach (Ben) 14.3; 5 A. Dahm (Nor) 14.7; 6 A. Friedenberg (Ben) 14.8.

400m Hurdles: 1 F. Nusse (Ben) 50.5; 2 S. Black (UK) 50.7; 3 C. O'Neill (UK) 50.9; 4 O. Grasbakken (Nor) 52.0; 5 J. Torgersen (Nor) 52.5; 6 W. van der Wijngarden (Ben) 52.8.

High Jump: 1 L. Falkum (Nor) 2.14m (7' 0¼"); 2 P. Vik (Nor) 2.12m (6' 11½"); 3 B. Brokken (Ben) 2.12m (6' 11½"); 4 P. de Preter (Ben) 2.03m (6' 8"); 5 M. Butterfield (UK) 2.03m (6' 8"); 6 A. Lerwill (UK) 1.85m (6' 0¾").

Pole Vault: 1 M. Bull (UK) 4.80m (15' 9"); 2 W. Sorteberg (Nor) 4.60m (15' 1"); 3 E. Dewil (Ben) 4.50m (14' 9"); 4 E. Schutter (Ben) 4.30m (14' 1¼"); 5 L. Skarstad (Nor) 4.30m (14' 1¼"); D. Lease (UK) no height.

Long Jump: 1 G. Hignett (UK) 7.60m (24' 11¼"); 2 J. Haugen (Nor) 7.55m (24' 9¼"); 3 A. Lerwill (UK) 7.48m (24' 6½"); 4 R. Sedoc (Ben) 7.48m (24' 6½"); 5 T. Haugland (Nor) 7.07m (23' 2¼"); 6 R. Desruelles (Ben) 6.95m (22' 9¾").

Triple Jump: 1 D. Johnson (UK) 15.76m (51' 8½"); 2 R. Sedoc (Ben) 15.71m (51' 6½"); 3 A. Moore (UK) 15.49m (50' 9¾"); 4 O. Moland (Nor) 14.86m (48' 9"); 5 A. van Hoorn (Ben) 14.74m (48' 4¼"); K. Flogstad (Nor) no result.

Shot: 1 M. Winch (UK) 19.63m (64' 4¾"); 2 W. Tancred (UK) 19.00m (62' 4"); 3 B. Bang Andersen (Nor) 18.62m (61' 1"); 4 L. Rise (Nor) 17.75m (58' 2¾"); 5 G. Schroeder (Ben) 17.60m (57' 9"); 6 A. Friedenberg (Ben) 11.94m (39' 2").

Discus: 1 W. Tancred (UK) 60.80m (199' 6"); 2 J. Hillier (UK) 57.88m (189' 11"); 3 T. Lislerud (Nor) 56.94m (186' 10"); 4 K. Hjeltnes (Nor) 56.06m (183' 11"); 5 G. Schroeder (Ben) 55.26m (181' 3"); 6 H. Zitsen (Ben) 53.40m (175' 2").

Hammer: 1 I. Chipchase (UK) 67.32m (220' 10"); 2 H. Payne (UK) 65.34m (214' 4"); 3 A. Busterud (Nor) 64.02m (210' 0"); 4 A. Lothe (Nor) 63.34m (207' 10"); 5 E. van der Bleecken (Ben) 58.52m (192' 0"); 6 J. Mortier (Ben) 49.28m (161' 8").

Javelin: 1 T. Thorslund (Nor) 78.58m (257' 10"); 2 D. Travis (UK) 77.14m (253' 1"); 3 H. Lorentzen (Nor) 76.44m (250' 9"); 4 B. Roberts (UK) 73.66m (241' 8"); 5 T. Duchateau (Ben) 66.30m (217' 6"); 6 L. Carlier (Ben) 60.86m (199' 8").

4 × 100m Relay: 1 UK (D. Roberts, C. Monk, A. Bennett, A. Lerwill) 40.1; 2 Norway 40.8; Benelux disqualified.

4 × 400m Relay: 1 UK (J. Wilson, A. Bennett, G. Cohen, R. Jenkins) 3:06.4; 2 Benelux 3:06.8; 3 Norway 3:31.2.

Match Result: UK 195, Norway 125½, Benelux 119½.

24 August

BRITISH LEAGUE FINALS

Despite a shaky start in the first of the four matches, when the club placed only third with 224 points, Cardiff AAC made it a hat-trick of British League titles. The Welshmen got steadily better as the season progressed: they won the second match with 260 points, the third with 277 points, and the final meeting – held at Cwmbran as there is no track of suitable standard in Cardiff itself – with a record total of 287 points. On that last occasion, Cardiff athletes placed in the first three in 32 of the 36 events

81

ATHLETICS 75

('A' and 'B' strings), proof indeed of the club's all-round strength.

Wolverhampton and Bilston AC, second in all four matches, gained runner-up honours – their best showing in the League – while 1970 and 1971 winners, Thames Valley Harriers, finished third. Birchfield Harriers, inaugural League champions in 1969, were relegated to division two.

FINAL LEAGUE TABLES 1974

Division One
1 Cardiff AAC 22
2 Wolverhampton & Bilston 20
3 Thames Valley Harriers 16
4 Edinburgh Southern 11
5 Birchfield Harriers 10
6 Sale Harriers 5
Relegated: Birchfield and Sale

Division Two
1 Borough of Enfield 20 (946 match points)
2 Hillingdon AC 20 (932½ match points)
3 Polytechnic Harriers 16
4 City of Stoke 14
5 Southampton & Eastleigh 9
6 Reading AC 5
Promoted: Enfield and Hillingdon
Relegated: Southampton and Reading

Division Three
1 Edinburgh AC 17
2 Woodford Green 16 (894 match points)
3 Luton United 16 (864½ match points)
4 Bristol AC 13½
5 Liverpool H & AC 12
6 Brighton & Hove 9½
Promoted: Edinburgh and Woodford Green
Relegated: Liverpool and Brighton

Division Four
1 Stretford AC 22
2 Swansea Harriers 19
3 Coventry Godiva 15
4 Croydon Harriers 14
5 Notts AC 10
6 Achilles Club 4
Promoted: Stretford and Swansea
Relegated: Notts and Achilles
New qualifiers: Metropolitan Police and Essex Beagles

DIVISION ONE RESULTS

11 May, at Meadowbank. **1** Thames Valley 244; **2** Wolverhampton & Bilston 226; **3** Cardiff 224; **4** Edinburgh Southern 202; **5** Birchfield 192; **6** Sale 164.
100m: D. Roberts (C) 10.6. **200m**: A. Bennett (B) 21.3. **400m**: J. Aukett (WB) 47.3. **800m**: P. Lewis (WB) 1:52.5. **1500m**: A. Settle (S) 3:48.8. **5000m**: B. Plain (C) 14:03.4. **3000m Steeplechase**: G. Bryan-Jones (ES) 8:56.8. **110m Hurdles**: P. Kelly (WB) 15.3. **400m Hurdles**: P. Kelly (WB) 54.3. **4 × 100m Relay**: Thames Valley 41.8. **4 × 400m Relay**: Wolverhampton & Bilston 3:14.1. **High Jump**: D. Kidner (TV) 1.85m (6′ 0¾″). **Pole Vault**: D. Lease (C) 4.50m (14′ 9″). **Long Jump**: D. Cole (TV) 7.14m (23′ 5¼″). **Triple Jump**: W. Clark (ES) 14.87m (48′ 9½″). **Shot**: W. Tancred (B) 17.55m (57′ 7″). **Discus**: W. Tancred (B) 59.22m (194′ 3″). **Hammer**: C. Black (ES) 65.90m (216′ 2″). **Javelin**: J. Ferrary (B) 60.78m (199′ 5″).

1 June, at Aldersley. **1** Cardiff 260; **2** Wolverhampton & Bilston 257; **3** Thames Valley 215; **4** Birchfield 210; **5** Edinburgh Southern 178; **6** Sale 139.
100m: I. Matthews (TV) 10.4. **200m**: A. Bennett (B) 21.8. **400m**: J. Aukett (WB) 47.7. **800m**: P. Lewis (WB) 1:52.4. **1500m**: R. Smedley (B) 3:47.5. **5000m**: M. Critchley (C) 14:17.4. **3000m Steeplechase**: G. Bryan-Jones (ES) 8:55.6. **110m Hurdles**: P. Kelly (WB) 15.4. **400m Hurdles**: W. Leyshon (C) 53.1. **4 × 100m Relay**: Thames Valley 41.8. **4 × 400m Relay**: Wolverhampton & Bilston 3:14.0. **High Jump**: R. Gyles (C) 1.93m (6′ 4″). **Pole Vault**: S. Chappell (TV) 4.20m (13′ 9¼″). **Long Jump**: D. Cole (TV) 7.38m (24′ 2½″). **Triple Jump**: W. Clark (ES) 15.43m (50′ 7½″). **Shot**: W. Tancred (B) 17.63m (57′ 10¼″). **Discus**: W. Tancred (B) 56.72m (186′ 1″). **Hammer**: C. Black (ES) 67.20m (220′ 6″). **Javelin**: P. Stewart (C) 63.42m (208′ 1″).

BRITISH LEAGUE FINALS

29 June, at West London. **1** Cardiff 277; **2** Wolverhampton & Bilston 257; **3** Thames Valley 195; **4** Edinburgh Southern 180; **5** Sale 178; **6** Birchfield 170.
100m: R. Kennedy (WB) 10.8. **200m:** I. Saunders (S) 22.0. **400m:** M. Delaney (C) 47.8. **800m:** A. Settle (S) 1:49.7.
1500m: P. Ratcliffe (C) 3:48.7. **5000m:** J. Davies (TV) 13:49.6. **3000m Steeplechase:** S. Hollings (S) 8:38.8.
110m Hurdles: B. Price (C) 14.6. **400m Hurdles:** S. James (WB) 52.6. **4 × 100m Relay:** Cardiff 42.4. **4 × 400m Relay:** Cardiff 3:17.4. **High Jump:** M. Butterfield (C) 2.03m (6' 8"). **Pole Vault:** S. Chappell (TV) 4.40m (14' 5¼").
Long Jump: S. Atkins (WB) 7.15m (23' 5½"). **Triple Jump:** A. Moore (B) 15.11m (49' 7"). **Shot:** J. Watts (WB) 15.58m (51' 1½"). **Discus:** J. Watts (WB) 52.22m (171' 4"). **Hammer:** J. Whitehead (B) 60.16m (197' 4"). **Javelin:** H. Wurzer (B) 62.70m (205' 8").

24 August, at Cwmbran. **1** Cardiff 287; **2** Wolverhampton & Bilston 256; **3** Birchfield 203; **4** Edinburgh Southern 195; **5** Thames Valley 164; **6** Sale 151.
100m: D. Halliday (WB) 10.6. **200m:** D. Roberts (C) 21.9. **400m:** G. Cohen (WB) 46.8. **800m:** R. Smedley (B) 1:51.8.
1500m: C. Thomas (TV) 3:48.7. **5000m:** R. Smedley (B) 14:14.8. **3000m Steeplechase:** S. Hollings (S) 8:35.0.
110m Hurdles: B. Price (C) 14.1. **400m Hurdles:** W Leyshon (C) 53.3. **4 × 100m Relay:** Wolverhampton & Bilston 40.9 (UK club best). **4 × 400m Relay:** Wolverhampton & Bilston 3:14.2. **High Jump:** M. Butterfield (C) 2.05m (6' 8¾").
Pole Vault: D. Lease (C) 4.30m (14' 1¼"). **Long Jump:** D. Cole (TV) 7.51m (24' 7¾"). **Triple Jump:** W. Clark (ES) 15.43m (50' 7½"). **Shot:** J. Watts (WB) 15.21m (49' 11"). **Discus:** J. Watts (WB) 53.66m (176' 0"). **Hammer:** H. Payne (B) 65.56m (215' 1"). **Javelin:** G. Brooks (C) 60.98m (200' 1").

DIVISION TWO RESULTS

11 May, at Aldersley. **1** Hillingdon 238; **2** Enfield 236; **3** Stoke 225; **4** Polytechnic 212; **5** Southampton & Eastleigh 195; **6** Reading 171.

1 June, at West London. **1** Hillingdon 247; **2** Enfield 243; **3** Polytechnic 214; **4** Stoke 191; **5** Southampton & Eastleigh 186; **6** Reading 179.

29 June, at Southampton. **1** Stoke 243; **2** Polytechnic 230; **3** Enfield 218; **4** Hillingdon 211½; **5** Southampton & Eastleigh 200½; **6** Reading 151.

24 August, at Chiswick. **1** Enfield 249; **2** Hillingdon 236; **3** Polytechnic 228; **4** Southampton & Eastleigh 184; **5** Reading 179; **6** Stoke 177.

Leading performances: 100m: A. Cornaby (R) 10.7. **200m:** T. Paice (E) 21.9. **400m:** C. Campbell (P) 48.5. **800m:** C. Campbell (P) 1:52.1 **1500m:** J. Brown (H) 3:54.4. **5000m:** M. Absolom (S) 14:24.4. **3000m Steeplechase:** G. Stevens (R) 9:06.4. **110m Hurdles:** G. Gower (H) 14.6. **400m Hurdles:** R. Parker (SE) 54.5. **4 × 100m Relay:** Polytechnic 42.8. **4 × 400m Relay:** Polytechnic 3:18.4. **High Jump:** M. Campbell (H) 1.95m (6' 4¾"). **Pole Vault:** C. Kidd (H) 4.45m (14' 7¼"). **Long Jump:** T. Paice (E) 7.41m (24' 3¾"). **Triple Jump:** C. Kidd (H) 15.22m (49' 11¼"). **Shot:** G. Capes (E) 19.57m (64' 2½"). **Discus:** J. Hillier (H) 55.94m (183' 6"). **Hammer:** P. Dickenson (H) 66.66m (218' 8"). **Javelin:** B. Taylor (E) 63.38m (207' 11").

DIVISION THREE RESULTS

11 May, at Luton. **1** Edinburgh AC 243; **2** Luton 231½; **3** Woodford Green 211; **4** Liverpool 194; **5** Bristol 190½; **6** Brighton & Hove 189.

1 June, at Meadowbank. **1** Edinburgh AC 251; **2** Liverpool 219; **3 eq** Bristol and Brighton & Hove 202; **5** Luton 194; **6** Woodford Green 192.

29 June, at Bristol. **1** Woodford Green 251; **2** Bristol 249; **3** Edinburgh AC 204; **4** Luton 196; **5** Liverpool 184; **6** Brighton & Hove 173.

24 August, at Brighton. **1** Luton 243; **2** Woodford Green 240; **3** Brighton & Hove 239½; **4** Bristol 199; **5** Liverpool 168; **6** Edinburgh AC 166½.

Leading performances: 100m: R. Griffiths (Lut), S. Brodie (E) and W. Hartley (Liv) 10.8. **200m:** S. Bell (E) 21.6. **400m:** W. Hartley (Liv) 47.4. **800m:** S. Ovett (BH) 1:53.7. **1500m:** S. Ovett (BH) 3:46.2. **5000m:** A. Simmons (Lut) 13:50.6. **3000m Steeplechase:** C. Moxsom (WG) 9:03.2. **110m Hurdles:** D. Wilson (E) 14.6. **400m Hurdles:** C. O'Neill (B) 52.4. **4 × 100m Relay:** Luton and Edinburgh 42.9. **4 × 400m Relay:** Edinburgh 3:19.4. **High Jump:** B. Burgess (E) 1.95m (6' 4¾"). **Pole Vault:** C. Boreham (Lut) 4.30m (14' 1¼"). **Long Jump:** P. Templeton (B) 7.25m (23' 9½"). **Triple Jump:** J. Bucknall (B) 14.77m (48' 5½"). **Shot:** M. Winch (BH) 19.60m (64' 3¾"). **Discus:** M. Cushion (WG) 55.84m (183' 2"). **Hammer:** P. Aston (WG) 62.10m (203' 9"). **Javelin:** K. Holmes (B) 72.48m (237' 9").

DIVISION FOUR RESULTS

11 May, at Stretford. **1** Stretford 249; **2** Swansea 221; **3** Croydon 210; **4** Notts 202; **5** Coventry Godiva 184; **6** Achilles 180.

1 June, at Swansea. **1** Swansea 262; **2** Coventry Godiva 253; **3** Stretford 226; **4** Notts 199; **5** Croydon 174; **6** Achilles 131.

29 June, at Croydon. **1** Stretford 279; **2** Croydon 236; **3** Coventry Godiva 224; **4** Swansea 207; **5** Notts 160; **6** Achilles 153.

24 August, at Nottingham. **1** Stretford 282; **2** Swansea 232; **3** Coventry Godiva 223½; **4** Croydon 190½; **5** Notts 182; **6** Achilles 133.

Leading performances: 100m: T. Bonsor (Cov) 10.6. **200m:** T. Bonsor (Cov) 21.9. **400m:** R. Benn (Cro) 48.1. **800m:** A. Dyke (Sw) 1:51.4. **1500m:** J. Theophilus (Sw) 3:50.4. **5000m:** S. Mitchell (N) 14:20.4. **3000m Steeplechase:** S. Baker (N) 9:14.6. **110m Hurdles:** A. Davis (Cov) 14.8. **400m Hurdles:** A. James (St) 52.4. **4 × 100m Relay:** Stretford 42.7. **4 × 400m Relay:** Croydon 3:19.0. **High Jump:** C. Richards (Sw) and C. Wilson (N) 1.90m (6' 2¾"). **Pole Vault:** K. Stock (Cro) 4.50m (14' 9"). **Long Jump:** G. Hignett (St) 7.13m (23' 4¾"). **Triple Jump:** A. Vincent (Cov) 14.81m (48' 7¼"). **Shot:** J. Corbett (St) 14.20m (46' 7¼"). **Discus:** G. Dirkin (St) 50.64m (166' 2"). **Hammer:** B. Williams (St) 63.16m (207' 3"). **Javelin:** P. Ostapowycz (St) 67.46m (221' 4").

AUGUST HIGHLIGHTS

If it's rare for an athlete to set a world record in his own home town, it must be unique for one to reach such dizzy heights of endeavour in a meeting he himself has dreamed up and helped organise. It happened to Brendan Foster, though, at Gateshead on 3 August. Running 3000 metres at a star-studded inauguration of the Tartan track, the metropolitan borough's newly appointed sports and recreation manager – with a full to overflowing crowd of over 10,000 hero worshippers to egg him on – placed Gateshead firmly on the athletics map by smashing Emiel Puttemans' world record. Foster's time of 7:35.2 took 2.4 seconds off the Belgian's figures and it ranks as one of the supreme track runs of all time. After following Mike Baxter's pace for 3½ laps, Foster was on his own for the remaining four circuits. Covering the fifth lap in a lung-searing 60 seconds flat, he reached 2000 metres in 5:04.0, less than a second slower than Dave Bedford's UK record for the distance! There was still a kilometre to go, but never for a stride did Foster falter as – seemingly carried around on a wave of sound from his ecstatic fans – he raced to the second world record of his career. His lap times were 60.0, 60.5, 62.2, 61.3, 60.0, 62.1, 59.9, and 29.2 for the final 200 metres. The first 1500 metres took 3:49.0, the second solo half 3:46.2.

Anders Garderud (Swe) broke his European record, and missed the world record held by Ben Jipcho (Ken) by a mere fifth of a second, with an 8:14.2 steeplechase in Helsinki on 1 August. He reached the halfway mark in 4:05.0, as against Jipcho's pace of 4:09.6. There was a spectacular mile race at this meeting: world 880 yards and 1000 metres record holder Rick Wohlhuter (USA) won in 3:54.4 ahead of Rod Dixon (NZ) 3:54.9, John Walker (NZ) 3:54.9, Mike Boit (Ken) 3:55.4, and Ulf Hogberg (Swe) 3:56.7. Wohlhuter covered the final 120 yards, from the 1500 metres mark, in a sizzling 13.9.

Marion Fawkes added another British record to her collection by walking 5000 metres in 25:02.0 at Warley on 4 August. Bob Dobson broke Don Thompson's 14-year-old UK record when he walked 50 kilometres in 4:11:22.0 in a track race in Paris on 10 August. He also beat the 30 miles record en route with 4:02:49.2.

Thames Valley Harriers (42.0 for 4 × 100 metres) and Bournemouth AC (3:20.8 for 4 × 400 metres) won AAA relay titles at Crystal Palace on 4 August.

Kent Gardenkrans (Swe) improved on his world junior discus record with 62.04 metres (203' 6") at Helsingborg on 11 August. Other world junior records were created in the women's events by Marianne Voelzke (EG) with a 6.77 metres (22' 2½") long jump in Berlin on 24 August, Ilona Schoknecht (EG) with a shot-put of 18.67 metres (61' 3") at Potsdam on 26 August, and Evelin Schlaak (EG) with a discus throw of 63.26 metres (207' 6"), also at Potsdam on 26 August.

David Jenkins equalled his UK 400 metres record of 45.2 in Zurich on 16 August, but he lost in a desperately close finish to European record holder Karl Honz (WG), who won in 45.14. Jenkins' electrical time was 45.16. Les Piggot tied the UK all-comers 100 metres record of 10.3 at the Edinburgh Highland Games on 17 August.

East German women equalled two world records in Berlin on 24 August. Rosi Witschas high jumped 1.94 metres (6' 4¼") and the 4 × 100 metres relay team of Doris Maletzki, Renate Stecher, Christina Heinich, and Barbel Eckert clocked 42.6. Another East German, Karin Krebs, set a world's best of 2:35.0 for the women's 1000 metres at Potsdam two days later.

Al Feuerbach (USA) put the shot 21.38 metres (70' 1¾") with his right hand and 15.67 metres (51' 5") with his left at Malmo on 24 August for the best ever two-handed aggregate. Using a spiral technique, in which he turns in the ring like a discus thrower, Aleksandr Baryshnikov (USSR) unexpectedly broke the European shot record with 21.70 metres (71' 2½") in Moscow on 25 August. Twelve days later, in the European Championships, he could muster only 20.13 metres (66' 0½") for fourth place.

Anders Garderud of Sweden.

September

2–8 September

EUROPEAN CHAMPIONSHIPS

The European Athletics Championships are acknowledged as second only in importance and quality to the Olympic Games themselves, and the week-long meeting in Rome was no exception. Indeed, the women's events were fully up to Olympic standard, with six of the winning performances superior to those in Munich and the remainder very close. Consequently, it was the women who stole the show in Rome's magnificent Stadio Olimpico.

Rosemarie Witschas brought the Championships to a climactic finale when she broke one of the most prestigious world records on the books by straddling over a bar placed at 1.95 metres (6' 4¾"). This added a centimetre to the mark she previously shared with Bulgaria's Yordanka Blagoyeva. Only 1.75 metres (5' 8¾") tall, Witschas thus jumped 20cm (8") above her own head, which is equal to Blagoyeva's record 'differential'. The stylish East German entered the competition at 1.70 metres (5' 7") and had no failures until the bar was raised to 1.93 metres (6' 4"). She cleared on the second attempt, to clinch victory, and then for good measure made 1.95 metres on the third try before failing at the extraordinary height of 1.97 metres (6' 5½"). What's more, Witschas – together with compatriot Rita Kirst and the Czech girl, Milada Karbanova – had to put up with some inexcusable behaviour by a large number of Italian fans during the vital stages of the competition. In a misguided attempt to boost the chances of Italy's competitor, Sara Simeoni, these 'sportsmen' produced a deafening chorus of whistling whenever one of her rivals prepared to jump.

There were two other world records in the women's programme: by javelin thrower Ruth Fuchs (EG) and by the East German sprint relay squad. Fuchs, an astonishingly consistent performer in an event notorious for its vicissitudes, opened up with what would, in any case, have been a winning throw of 62.36 metres (204' 7"), and then proceeded to put it all together in the second round – the spear landing no less than 67.22 metres (220' 6") away from the scratch line. It eclipsed her own record of 66.10 metres (216' 10"), and the title was hers with over five metres to spare.

Doris Maletzki, Renate Stecher, Christina Heinich, and Barbel Eckert teamed up to win the 4 × 100 metres in the fastest ever time of 42.51, and in the process they avenged East Germany's defeats by West Germany both at the previous European Championships and at the Munich Olympics. Further triumphs by Gunhild Hoffmeister in the 1500 metres (in the second fastest ever time), hurdler Annelie Ehrhardt, and the 4 × 400 metres squad ensured East Germany's continuing supremacy in the women's department. Altogether, 15 medals were gained, the same as in Helsinki three years earlier.

Despite all the East German successes, it was a Pole who claimed top individual honours. Irena Szewinska, greater than ever after 10 years in the highest world class, won her first European 100 metres crown, regained the 200 metres title she had previously won in 1966 (emphatically defeating Olympic champion Renate Stecher in both events), and helped Poland

For Rosi Witschas, the European Championships brought more than just a gold medal: the East German straddle exponent leapt 8 inches above her own height to set a new world record of 1.95 metres (6' 4¾").

to third place in the 4 × 100 metres relay. Yet her most brilliant performance was reserved for an event in which she did not gain a medal: the 4 × 400 metres relay. When Szewinska took over for the final leg, Poland were fifth and nearly 30 metres behind the leaders. At the finish, having overtaken West Germany's Rita Wilden, she was less than 10 metres behind the winner! Although she was away slowly, Szewinska soon worked up to an unprecedented pace, zipping through 200 metres in 22.9 and completing her lap in what would have been for anyone else the unbelievable time of 48.5! As it was, she had run 400 metres 1.4 seconds faster – with the slight advantage of a slow rolling start – than her own pending world record. Astonishing to reflect that until Szewinska's 49.9 earlier in the season, no woman had ever bettered 51 seconds off blocks, and yet now a time of around 49sec is beginning to look feasible.

Szewinska did not take part in the individual 400 metres, which saw three girls breaking 51sec. Riitta Salin's winning mark of 50.14, fastest ever on electrical timing, was probably the equal of Szewinska's hand-timed 49.9 and she too dipped under 50 seconds in the relay, with an anchor leg of 49.9. Finland finished second in that relay to add to the gold medals won by Salin and Nina Holmen (in the inaugural 3000 metres) and the bronze awards gained by Mona-Lisa Pursiainen (200 metres) and Pirkko Helenius (long jump). It represented a gigantic leap forward by a nation which, previously, had met with little success in major women's championships.

The once all-conquering Soviet women's team had to make do with three gold medals. Nadyezhda Chizhova and Faina Melnik, respectively the greatest shot and discus exponents in history, gained further honours to nobody's surprise, but Nadyezhda Tkachenko's pentathlon victory over world record holder Burglinde Pollak (EG) was considered an upset. The remaining golds went to Lilyana Tomova (Bul) in the 800 metres and to Ilona Bruzsenyak (Hun) in the long jump.

Like Western Europe's in general, the British women, taken overall, did not shine, although all credit to Andrea Lynch (100 metres) and Joyce Smith (3000 metres) for their bronze medals in the face of strong opposition.

The picture, from the British point of view, was encouragingly different in the men's events. No fewer than nine medals were obtained, four of them of the gold variety. Only the Soviet Union and East Germany fared better.

Britain's three individual champions were all men who had scaled the heights seven months earlier at the Commonwealth Games, proving that, with intelligent preparation, an athlete can reach more than one peak in a year. With their proven competitive ability and skilful application, Brendan Foster, Ian Thompson, and Alan Pascoe must rank high on anyone's list of Montreal Olympic gold medal contenders.

With world record holder Emiel Puttemans (Bel) a non-starter for the 5000 metres, Foster was a clear favourite – a fact acknowledged by the opposition who in effect were battling for second place. The hot, humid conditions were all against very fast running, but such was Foster's pace (he broke away with a 60.2 eighth lap) that although he took a leisurely 62.2 for his last lap (he was 80 metres ahead at the bell!) his final time of

13:17.2 was barely four seconds away from the world record. Thompson dominated his event, too. Racing and winning the fourth marathon of his 10-month career in that event, Thompson forced the pace from early in the proceedings and dropped his last two challengers after about 15 miles. His winning margin was over 1½ minutes. Alan Pascoe won his gold medal in the 400 metres hurdles by a tenth of a second, but it was enough as he held defending champion Jean-Claude Nallet (Fra) at bay over the last three hurdles and the run-in to the tape. Injuries and illness had made Pascoe a possible non-starter in Rome, and though he ran better than he expected to reach the final, he did not think he could run faster than 49.1 – and he wasn't sure whether that would suffice. In fact he clocked 48.82, a personal best, in the final, having been unable to break 50sec while preparing for Rome.

A second gold medal came Pascoe's way four days later when the British 4 × 400 metres squad scored an unanticipated victory over an admittedly injury-stricken West German team. Glen Cohen, on the first leg, produced the fastest time (46.7) of his career; hurdler Bill Hartley (45.8) brought his team up to third place; Pascoe (46.5) held the position; and David Jenkins, taking over nearly 10 metres behind Finland and France, ran with superb power and judgment to take the lead 50 metres from the end and hold off Karl Honz (WG), the man who had wrested his 400 metres title a few days earlier. Jenkins' time was a magnificent 44.3.

Joining Jenkins as silver medallists in individual events were Steve Ovett (800 metres) and Tony Simmons (10,000 metres). Ovett, whose athletic maturity belies his age (he's only 18), did incredibly well to take second place in a European junior record of 1:45.8, and yet he was displeased with his result. He was boxed in at the crucial moment when Yugoslavia's Luciano Susanj made his lightning strike for home with 200 metres to go, and Ovett could not forgive himself for having finished without running himself out.

Susanj's performance was hailed by many as the finest of the men's programme. During that final 200 metres he opened up a lead of nearly 15 metres, an enormous margin at this level of 800 metres racing, and his time of 1:44.1 was only four-tenths of a second outside the world record. Simmons, an 'infant prodigy' many years ago (in 1963 he set a world's best mile time, for a 14 year old, of 4:29.8), has only quite recently found himself as an international class distance runner on the track, and in the cauldron that was Rome he startled everyone, himself included, by failing by inches only to capture the European title. Running the last lap in under 55 seconds, Simmons made dramatic inroads into the lead of Manfred Kuschmann (EG) along the finishing straight and they were awarded the same time.

There was drama aplenty, too, in the 20 kilometres walk. In a harrowing scene, reminiscent of Dorando Pietri and Jim Peters, Britain's Roger Mills – in a state of collapse from heat exhaustion – weaved, lurched, and staggered towards the finishing line for a highly commendable fourth place. He deserved a medal for his courage in finishing . . . and so it came to pass when, two months later, third-placing Vladimir Shaloshik (Sov) was disqualified as a result of the drug test taken straight after the event. Thus, Mills was promoted to bronze medallist.

Britain's other bronze medal winner was shot-putter Geoff Capes. He was below his best with 20.21 metres (66' 3¾"), but so was everyone else in the field and Hartmut Briesenick (EG) was able to retain his title with a put of 20.50 metres (67' 3¼"), well short of his distance in 1971. The only other successful defence (other than by Chizhova, Melnik and the East German 4 × 400 squad in the women's events) came in the 100 metres, where Valeriy Borzov (Sov) made it three titles in a row despite being below his very best. He did not seek to retain his 200 metres championship which went, amid great excitement, to Italy's Pietro Mennea. Viktor Saneyev (Sov) in the triple jump and Christoph Hohne (EG) in the 50 kilometres walk won back titles they last gained in 1969; while Vladimir Golubnichiy (Sov) notched up his first European title in the city where, 14 years earlier, he had become Olympic champion for the first time!

That other seemingly indestructible Soviet star, javelin thrower Janis Lusis, finally ceded the European championship he has held continuously since 1962. He placed sixth as Hannu Siitonen (Fin) produced the world's longest throw for 1974: 89.58 metres (293' 11"). Other highlights included a gripping high jump contest in which Dr Jesper Torring (Den) won on the countback from 1971 champion Kestutis Sapka (Sov) with a leap of 2.25 metres (7' 4½"); one of the greatest steeplechase races of all time, won by Bronislaw Malinowski (Pol) in 8:15.0 after covering the second half of the race in around 4:02; an immaculate display of high hurdling by Guy Drut (Fra); and a very fine decathlon won by Ryszard Skowronek (Pol) in which Leonid Litvinenko (Sov) found his score of 8122 points insufficient for a medal.

The next European Championships will be staged in Prague in 1978.

MEN

100m: *Heats (first three and four fastest losers to semi-finals).* Heat 1: **1** V. Borzov (Sov) 10.49; **2** D. Chauvelot (Fra) 10.56; **3** Z. Nowosz (Pol) 10.64; **4** M. Droese (EG) 10.65; **5** L. Micha (Bel) 10.67; **6** J. Demec (Cze) 10.80; **7** L. Malin (Fin) 10.85. *Heat 2:* **1** P. Mennea (Ita) 10.46; **2** K. Ehl (WG) 10.54; **3** A. Kornelyuk (Sov) 10.63; **4** A. Swierczynski (Pol) 10.73; **5** H-J. Zenk (EG) 10.82; **6** E. Lepold (Hun) 10.97. *Heat 3:* **1** C. Garpenborg (Swe) 10.53; **2** K-D. Bieler (WG) 10.54; **3** R. Vilen (Fin) 10.57; **4** Y. Silov (Sov) 10.62; **5** J. Martinez (Spa) 10.82; **6** D. Halliday (UK) 10.86; **7** L. Korona (Hun) 10.95. *Heat 4:* **1** A. Rajamaki (Fin) 10.58; **2** V. Papageorgopoulos (Gre) 10.59; **3** M. Ommer (WG) 10.59; **4** S. Schenke (EG) 10.70; **5** L. Gresa (Hun) 10.74; **6** M. Woronin (Pol) 10.77; **7** H. Trulsson (Swe) 10.78; **8** L. Bohman (Cze) 10.92. *Semi-Finals (first four to final).* S-F 1: **1** V. Borzov (Sov) 10.39; **2** M. Ommer (WG) 10.42; **3** C. Garpenborg (Swe) 10.42; **4** A. Kornelyuk (Sov) 10.45; **5** K. Ehl (WG) 10.50; **6** R. Vilen (Fin) 10.52; **7** L. Micha (Bel) 10.55; **8** M. Droese (EG) 10.59. *S-F 2:* **1** D. Chauvelot (Fra) 10.28; **2** P. Mennea (Ita) 10.29; **3** Y. Silov (Sov) 10.36; **4** K-D. Bieler (WG) 10.44; **5** V. Papageorgopoulos (Gre) 10.44; **6** A. Rajamaki (Fin) 10.46; **7** Z. Nowosz (Pol) 10.61; **8** S. Schenke (EG) 10.69. *FINAL:* (−1.0m wind) **1** Valeriy Borzov (Sov) 10.27; **2** Pietro Mennea (Ita) 10.34; **3** Klaus-Dieter Bieler (WG) 10.35; **4** Yuriy Silov (Sov) 10.35; **5** Dominique Chauvelot (Fra) 10.35; **6** Manfred Ommer (WG) 10.36; **7** Christer Garpenborg (Swe) 10.39; **8** Aleksandr Kornelyuk (Sov) 10.43.

200m: *Heats (first three and fastest loser to semi-finals).* Heat 1: **1** B. Cherrier (Fra) 20.96; **2** L. Benedetti (Ita) 21.11; **3** R. Heerenveen (Hol) 21.24; **4** C. Monk (UK) 21.25; **5** J. Matousek (Cze) 21.36; **6** R. Tempel (WG) 21.51; **7** M. Bedynski (Pol) 21.53. *Heat 2:* **1** H-J. Bombach (EG) 21.04; **2** J. Arame (Fra) 21.09; **3** A. Bennett (UK) 21.13; **4** M. Woronin (Pol) 21.60. *Heat 3:* **1** M. Ommer (WG) 21.23; **2** P. Mennea (Ita) 21.24; **3** P. Muster (Swi) 21.41; **4** P. Petrov (Bul) 21.49; **5** I. Farkas (Hun) 22.06. *Heat 4:* **1** H-J. Zenk (EG) 21.30; **2** P. Leroux (Fra) 21.40; **3** S. Green (UK) 21.54; **4** L. Sarria (Spa) 21.54; **5** Z. Nowosz (Pol) 21.67; **6** M. Kralik (Cze) 21.67. *Heat 5:* **1** F-P. Hofmeister (WG) 21.03; **2** T. Johansson (Swe)

21.34; **3** A. Rajamaki (Fin) 21.48; **4** N. Oliosi (Ita) 21.54; **5** M. Arnau (Spa) 21.72; **6** J. Kynos (Cze) 22.38.
Semi-Finals (first four to final). S-F 1: **1** H-J. Bombach (EG) 20.81; **2** M. Ommer (WG) 20.92; **3** B. Cherrier (Fra) 20.94; **4** A. Rajamaki (Fin) 20.97; **5** L. Benedetti (Ita) 21.11; **6** P. Leroux (Fra) 21.22; **7** T. Johansson (Swe) 21.26; **8** C. Monk (UK) 21.32. *S-F 2:* **1** P. Mennea (Ita) 20.83; **2** F-P. Hofmeister (WG) 21.09; **3** J. Arame (Fra) 21.16; **4** A. Bennett (UK) 21.23; **5** R. Heerenveen (Hol) 21.44; **6** H-J. Zenk (EG) 21.46; **7** S. Green (UK) 21.52; **8** P. Muster (Swi).
FINAL: (−0.68m wind) **1** Pietro Mennea (Ita) 20.60; **2** Manfred Ommer (WG) 20.76; **3** Hans-Jurgen Bombach (EG) 20.83; **4** Joseph Arame (Fra) 20.87; **5** Franz-Peter Hofmeister (WG) 20.93; **6** Bruno Cherrier (Fra) 21.02; **7** Ainsley Bennett (UK) 21.29; A. Rajamaki (Fin) scratched.

400m: *Heats (first four and four fastest losers to semi-finals). Heat 1:* **1** H-R. Schloske (WG) 45.92; **2** A. Brijdenbach (Bel) 46.00; **3** F. Demarthon (Fra) 46.11; **4** A. Scheibe (EG) 46.38; **5** P-O. Sjoberg (Swe) 46.63; **6** R. Jenkins (UK) 46.78; **7** R. Siedlicki (Pol) 47.35. *Heat 2:* **1** B. Herrmann (WG) 46.30; **2** M. Kukkoaho (Fin) 46.38; **3** J. Utikal (EG) 46.44; **4** T.v.d. Goolberg (Hol) 46.46; **5** M. Cikic (Yug) 46.68; **6** M. Fredriksson (Swe) 47.01; **7** S. Marlow (UK) 48.71. *Heat 3:* **1** O. Karttunen (Fin) 46.50; **2** D. Jenkins (UK) 46.60; **3** E. Carlgren (Swe) 46.97; **4** K. Honz (WG) 46.98; **5** J. Alebic (Yug) 47.41; **6** P. Abetti (Ita) 47.80. *Semi-Finals (first four to final). S-F 1:* **1** K. Honz (WG) 46.24; **2** F. Demarthon (Fra) 46.28; **3** M. Kukkoaho (Fin) 46.29; **4** E. Carlgren (Swe) 46.51; **5** J. Utikal (EG) 46.62; **6** H-R. Schloske (WG) 46.64; **7** P-O. Sjoberg (Swe) 46.68; **8** R. Jenkins (UK) 47.30. *S-F 2:* **1** D. Jenkins (UK) 45.93; **2** O. Karttunen (Fin) 46.36; **3** M. Fredriksson (Swe) 46.39; **4** B. Herrmann (WG) 46.40; **5** A. Brijdenbach (Bel) 46.43; **6** M. Cikic (Yug) 47.04; **7** A. Scheibe (EG) 47.24; **8** T.v.d. Goolberg (Hol) 47.40.
FINAL: **1** Karl Honz (WG) 45.04 (*Championship record*); **2** David Jenkins (UK) 45.67; **3** Bernd Herrmann (WG) 45.78; **4** Markku Kukkoaho (Fin) 45.84; **5** Ossi Karttunen (Fin) 45.87; **6** Mikael Fredriksson (Swe) 46.12; **7** Erik Carlgren (Swe) 46.15; **8** Francis Demarthon (Fra) 46.90.

800m: *Heats (first three and four fastest losers to semi-finals). Heat 1:* **1** J.Van Wezer (Bel) 1:47.7; **2** G. Stolle (EG) 1:47.7; **3** M. Fiasconaro (Ita) 1:47.8; **4** H. Langenbach (WG) 1:47.9; **5** D. McMeekin (UK) 1:48.1; **6** A. Ballbe (Spa) 1:48.2; **7** G. Hasler (Liech) 1:50.2. *Heat 2:* **1** G. Ghipu (Rom) 1:46.9; **2** S. Ovett (UK) 1:47.0; **3** J. Plachy (Cze) 1:47.1; **4** V. Ponomaryov (Sov) 1:47.1; **5** F. Mamede (Por) 1:47.5; **6** A. Svensson (Swe) 1:47.5; **7** W. Wulbeck (WG) 1:47.6. *Heat 3:* **1** L. Susanj (Yug) 1:48.4; **2** D. Fromm (EG) 1:48.6; **3** M. Taskinen (Fin) 1:48.7; **4** S-E. Nielsen (Den) 1:48.9; **5** J. Sisovsky (Cze) 1:48.9; **6** S. Mermingis (Gre) 1:49.8; **7** S-J. Svendsen (Nor) 1:50.9. *Heat 4:* **1** H-H. Ohlert (EG) 1:49.7; **2** M. Philippe (Fra) 1:49.8; **3** J. Schmid (WG) 1:49.9; **4** P. Litovchenko (Sov) 1:50.0; **5** N. Onescu (Rom) 1:50.1; **6** J. Kayser (Lux) 1:54.2; A. Carter (UK) scratched. *Semi-Finals (first four to final). S-F 1:* **1** S. Ovett (UK) 1:47.1; **2** L. Susanj (Yug) 1:47.2; **3** G. Stolle (EG) 1:47.4; **4** W. Wulbeck (WG) 1:47.4; **5** M. Philippe (Fra) 1:47.5; **6** A. Svensson (Swe) 1:47.7; **7** J. Plachy (Cze) 1:47.9; **8** H-H. Ohlert (EG) 1:48.6. *S-F 2:* **1** V. Ponomaryov (Sov) 1:47.6; **2** M. Fiasconaro (Ita) 1:47.7; **3** D. Fromm (EG) 1:47.7; **4** M. Taskinen (Fin) 1:47.7; **5** G. Ghipu (Rom) 1:47.8; **6** J. Van Wezer (Bel) 1:48.0; **7** F. Mamede (Por) 1:48.5; **8** J. Schmid (WG) 1:48.6.
FINAL: **1** Luciano Susanj (Yug) 1:44.1 (*Championship record*); **2** Steve Ovett (UK) 1:45.8; **3** Markku Taskinen (Fin) 1:45.9; **4** Vladimir Ponomaryov (Sov) 1:46.0; **5** Gerhard Stolle (EG) 1:46.2; **6** Marcello Fiasconaro (Ita) 1:46.3; **7** Dieter Fromm (EG) 1:46.3; **8** Willi Wulbeck (WG) 1:46.3.

1500m: *Heats (first three and three fastest losers to final). Heat 1:* **1** U. Hogberg (Swe) 3:42.0; **2** H. Scharn (Hol) 3:42.5; **3** R. Gysin (Swi) 3:42.6; **4** K-P. Justus (EG) 3:42.8; **5** H. Szordykowski (Pol) 3:43.7; **6** I. Kovac (Cze) 3:44.7; **7** J. Hartnett (Eir) 3:46.6; **8** F. Mamede (Por) 3:47.1; **9** G. Larsen (Den) 3:47.7. *Heat 2:* **1** H. Wasilewski (Pol) 3:43.0; **2** T. Wessinghage (WG) 3:43.1; **3** G. Ekman (Swe) 3:43.2; **4** G. Ghipu (Rom) 3:43.4; **5** L. Zarcone (Ita) 3:44.4; **6** P. Anisim (Sov) 3:44.7; **7** F. Clement (UK) 3:45.0; **8** L-M. Kaupang (Nor) 3:47.0; G. Hasler (Liech) did not finish. *Heat 3:* **1** P-H. Wellmann (WG) 3:42.4; **2** V. Pantelei (Sov) 3:42.6; **3** M. Philippe (Fra) 3:42.7; **4** T. Hansen (Den) 3:43.1; **5** P. Vasala (Fin) 3:43.3; **6** G. Riga (Ita) 3:43.5; **7** R. Smedley (UK) 3:43.6; **8** D. Janczuk (Pol) 3:45.2; **9** N. Onescu (Rom) 3:46.7; **10** J. Charvetto (Gib) 3:55.4.
FINAL: **1** Klaus-Peter Justus (EG) 3:40.6; **2** Tom Hansen (Den) 3:40.8; **3** Thomas Wessinghage (WG) 3:41.1; **4** Haico Scharn (Hol) 3:41.3; **5** Vladimir Pantelei (Sov) 3:41.4; **6** Pekka Vasala (Fin) 3:41.5; **7** Paul-Heinz Wellmann (WG) 3:41.6; **8** Rolf Gysin (Swi) 3:41.8; **9** U. Hogberg (Swe) 3:42.3; **10** G. Ekman (Swe) 3:42.5; **11** H. Wasilewski (Pol) 3:42.7; **12** M. Philippe (Fra) 3:46.0.

5000m: *Heats (first four and three fastest losers to final). Heat 1:* **1** W. Polleunis (Bel) 13:38.6; **2** K. Boro (Nor) 13:38.6; **3** P. Penkava (Cze) 13:38.8; **4** M. Kuschmann (EG) 13:39.2; **5** D. Black (UK) 13:41.8; **6** F. Cerrada (Spa) 13:56.8; **7** W. Meier (Swi) 14:05.4; **8** M. Koussis (Gre) 14:07.0; A. Simoes (Por) did not finish. *Heat 2:* **1** P. Paivarinta (Fin) 13:56.6;

2 A. Kvalheim (Nor) 13:56.8; **3** S. Hoffman (Cze) 13:59.4; **4** V. Zatonski (Sov) 14:01.4; **5** H. Nogala (Pol) 14:07.0; **6** C. Stewart (UK) 14:17.2; **7** E. Coghlan (Eir) 14:29.6; L. Schots (Bel) did not finish. *Heat 3:* **1** B. Foster (UK) 13:37.0; **2** J. Hermens (Hol) 13:37.4; **3** K. Kvalheim (Nor) 13:37.8; **4** L. Viren (Fin) 13:38.2; **5** I. Floriou (Rom) 13:39.0; **6** P. Svet (Yug) 13:40.8; **7** K-P. Hildenbrand (WG) 13:41.4; **8** C. Cairoche (Fra) 13:59.6; E. Van Mullem (Bel) did not finish. *FINAL:* **1** Brendan Foster (UK) 13:17.2 *(Championship record);* **2** Manfred Kuschmann (EG) 13:24.0; **3** Lasse Viren (Fin) 13:24.6; **4** Jos Hermens (Hol) 13:25.6; **5** Ilie Floriou (Rom) 13:27.2; **6** Arne Kvalheim (Nor) 13:27.2; **7** Stanislav Hoffman (Cze) 13:29.0; **8** Klaus-Peter Hildenbrand (WG) 13:32.0; **9** V. Zatonski (Sov) 13:39.6; **10** P. Svet (Yug) 13:41.6; **11** K. Boro (Nor) 13:45.8; **12** P. Penkava (Cze) 14:00.6; **13** P. Paivarinta (Fin) 14:14.2; **14** K. Kvalheim (Nor) 14:19.0; **15** W. Polleunis (Bel) 14:23.2.

10,000m: **1** Manfred Kuschmann (EG) 28:25.8; **2** Tony Simmons (UK) 28:25.8; **3** Giuseppe Cindolo (Ita) 28:27.2; **4** Bronislaw Malinowski (Pol) 28:28.0; **5** Nikolay Puklakov (Sov) 28:29.2; **6** Knut Boro (Nor) 28:29.2; **7** Lasse Viren (Fin) 28:29.2; **8** Mariano Haro (Spa) 28:36.0; **9** D. Black (UK) 28:36.6; **10** B. Ford (UK) 28:37.4; **11** K. Lismont (Bel) 28:41.2; **12** P. Liardet (Fra) 28:42.8; **13** S. Hoffman (Cze) 28:44.4; **14** I. Floriou (Rom) 28:51.8; **15** H. Nogala (Pol) 29:04.8; **16** P. Suchan (Cze) 29:06.0; **17** A. Risa (Nor) 29:07.4; **18** P. Svet (Yug) 29:08.4; **19** P. Paivarinta (Fin) 29:21.6; **20** J. Jansky (Cze) 29:23.2; **21** K-H. Leiteritz (EG) 29:32.6; **22** J. Hermens (Hol) 29:41.0; **23** E. Legowski (Pol) 29:49.6; **24** M. Koussis (Gre) 29:54.6; F. Fava (Ita), M. Smet (Bel), D. Uhlemann (WG), C. Lopes (Por), P. Halle (Nor), V. Zotov (Sov), & W. Polleunis (Bel) did not finish.

Marathon: **1** Ian Thompson (UK) 2:13:18.8; **2** Eckhard Lesse (EG) 2:14:57.4; **3** Gaston Roelants (Bel) 2:16:29.6; **4** Bernie Plain (UK) 2:18:02.2; **5** Jose Reveyn (Bel) 2:19:36.4; **6** Ferenc Szekeres (Hun) 2:20:12.8; **7** Giuseppe Cindolo (Ita) 2:20:28.2; **8** Neil Cusack (Eir) 2:22:05.0; **9** P. Leiviska (Fin) 2:22:45.6; **10** Y. Laptev (Sov) 2:23:15.6; **11** P. Accaputo (Ita) 2:24:06.0; **12** D. McDaid (Eir) 2:25:07.8; **13** J. Jensen (Den) 2:26:54.2; **14** R. Sercombe (UK) 2:27:13.0; **15** J. Jansky (Cze) 2:27:40.4; **16** E. Legowski (Pol) 2:27:45.8; **17** V. Mladek (Cze) 2:30:16.8; **18** P. Suchan (Cze) 2:30:42.6; **19** R. Paukkonen (Fin) 2:31:11.2; **20** G. Mielke (WG) 2:32:21.6; **21** R. Chudecki (Pol) 2:34:15.0; **22** A. Strelezh (Sov) 2:34:55.2. Y. Velikorodnikh (Sov), K. Lismont (Bel), A. Fernandez (Spa), P. Helmer (Den), A. Galabov (Bul), T. Tsimingatos (Gre), F. Kolbeck (Fra), & A. Mangano (Ita) did not finish.

3000m Steeplechase: *Heats (first three and three fastest losers to final). Heat 1:* **1** F. Fava (Ita) 8:25.2; **2** M. Karst (WG) 8:26.4; **3** D. Glans (Swe) 8:28.0; **4** P. Thys (Bel) 8:34.2; **5** J-P. Villain (Fra) 8:45.0; **6** J. Bicourt (Fra) 8:52.4; **7** A. Risa (Nor) 8:58.8; K-A. Soeltoft (Den) did not finish. *Heat 2:* **1** B. Malinowski (Pol) 8:23.6 *(Championship record);* **2** T. Kantanen (Fin) 8:23.6; **3** F. Bartos (Cze) 8:32.0; **4** J. Davies (UK) 8:36.0; **5** S. Soernes (Nor) 8:44.2; **6** H. Leyens (Bel) 8:45.4; **7** P. Martin (Fra) 8:46.8; **8** E. Leddy (Eir) 9:04.6. *Heat 3:* **1** A. Garderud (Swe) 8:23.6 *(eq Championship record);* **2** G. Cefan (Rom) 8:25.8; **3** H. Wehrli (Swi) 8:26.0; **4** G. Frahmcke (WG) 8:26.8; **5** D. Moravcik (Cze) 8:28.0; **6** G. Buchheit (Fra) 8:31.0; **7** A. Campos (Spa) 8:38.2; **8** D. Camp (UK) 8:44.7. *FINAL:* **1** Bronislaw Malinowski (Pol) 8:15.0 *(Championship record);* **2** Anders Garderud (Swe) 8:15.4; **3** Michael Karst (WG) 8:18.0; **4** Franco Fava (Ita) 8:19.0; **5** Hans-Peter Wehrli (Swi) 8:26.2; **6** Gheorghe Cefan (Rom) 8:26.2; **7** Gerd Frahmcke (WG) 8:26.6; **8** Gerard Buchheit (Fra) 8:30.2; **9** D. Glans (Swe) 8:31.4; **10** D. Moravcik (Cze) 8:34.4; **11** T. Kantanen (Fin) 8:43.2; **12** F. Bartos (Cze) 8:49.6.

110m Hurdles: *Heats (first four and four fastest losers to semi-finals). Heat 1:* **1** G. Drut (Fra) 13.82; **2** F. Siebeck (EG) 13.93; **3** P. Sicinski (Pol) 13.99; **4** E. Sebestien (Rom) 14.14; **5** V. Hoferek (Cze) 14.25; **6** B. Price (UK) 14.28; **7** S. Catasta (Ita) 14.40; **8** G. Calleja (Spa) 14.54. *Heat 2:* **1** V. Myasnikov (Sov) 14.08; **2** L. Wodzynski (Pol) 14.13; **3** K. Fiedler (EG) 14.19; **4** M. Schumann (WG) 14.31; **5** L. Nadenicek (Cze) 14.34; **6** S. Liani (Ita) 14.43; **7** J. Lloveras (Spa) 14.60; **8** Y. Kirpach (Lux) 14.63. *Heat 3:* **1** M. Wodzynski (Pol) 13.84; **2** T. Munkelt (EG) 13.92; **3** E. Pereversev (Sov) 13.96; **4** G. Buttari (Ita) 13.98; **5** P. Cech (Cze) 14.06; **6** E. Vassiliou (Gre) 14.37; **7** C. Clerselius (Swe) 14.98. *Semi-Finals (first four to final). S-F 1:* **1** M. Wodzynski (Pol) 13.59; **2** G. Buttari (Ita) 13.64; **3** B. Price (UK) 13.78; **4** T. Munkelt (EG) 13.83; **5** E. Sebestien (Rom) 13.91; **6** P. Cech (Cze) 14.07; **7** V. Myasnikov (Sov) 14.19; **8** L. Nadenicek (Cze) 14.38. *S-F 2:* **1** G. Drut (Fra) 13.46; **2** F. Siebeck (EG) 13.46; **3** L. Wodzynski (Pol) 13.61; **4** K. Fiedler (EG) 13.64; **5** P. Sicinski (Pol) 13.77; **6** V. Hoferek (Cze) 13.89; **7** M. Schumann (WG) 14.04; **8** E. Pereversev (Sov) 14.21. *FINAL:* (+0.5m wind) **1** Guy Drut (Fra) 13.40 *(Championship record);* **2** Miroslaw Wodzynski (Pol) 13.67; **3** Leszek Wodzynski (Pol) 13.71; **4** Thomas Munkelt (EG) 13.72; **5** Giuseppe Buttari (Ita) 13.85; **6** Klaus Fiedler (EG) 13.96; **7** Berwyn Price (UK) 14.05; **8** Frank Siebeck (EG) 14.79.

400m Hurdles: *Heats (first three and four fastest losers to semi-finals). Heat 1:* **1** M. Kodejs (Cze) 50.31; **2** V. Savchenko (Sov) 50.36; **3** W. Hartley (UK) 50.42; **4** F. Aumas (Swi) 50.50; **5** Y. Bratanov (Bul) 51.02; **6** G. Parris (Gre) 51.44. *Heat 2:* **1** D.

EUROPEAN CHAMPIONSHIPS

Stukalov (Sov) 50.48; **2** J. Hewelt (Pol) 50.54; **3** K. Schonberger (EG) 50.60; **4** F. Nusse (Hol) 50.73; **5** J. Carvalho (Por) 51.32; **6** G. Ballati (Ita) 51.47. *Heat 3:* **1** J-C. Nallet (Fra) 50.16; **2** J. Mayer (EG) 50.88; **3** L. Danis (Cze) 51.09; **4** W. Reibert (WG) 51.18; **5** S. Black (UK) 51.19; **6** Y. Yordanov (Bul) 52.05; **7** G. Mueller (Swe) 52.72. *Heat 4:* **1** Y. Gavrilenko (Sov) 50.28; **2** R. Ziegler (WG) 50.35; **3** A. Pascoe (UK) 50.54; **4** S. Tziortzis (Gre) 50.65; **5** J. Struyk (Hol) 51.83.
Semi-Finals (first four to final). S-F 1: **1** D. Stukalov (Sov) 49.67; **2** A. Pascoe (UK) 49.77; **3** S. Tziortzis (Gre) 49.79; **4** R. Ziegler (WG) 49.87; **5** M. Kodejs (Cze) 49.93; **6** F. Aumas (Swi) 50.46; **7** Y. Bratanov (Bul) 50.66; **8** J. Mayer (EG) 50.71. *S-F 2:* **1** Y. Gavrilenko (Sov) 49.63; **2** J. Hewelt (Pol) 49.79; **3** J-C. Nallet (Fra) 49.79; **4** V. Savchenko (Sov) 49.88; **5** K. Schonberger (EG) 50.04; **6** W. Hartley (UK) 50.55; **7** F. Nusse (Hol) 51.14; **8** I. Danis (Cze) 53.28.
FINAL: **1** Alan Pascoe (UK) 48.82 (*Championship record*); **2** Jean-Claude Nallet (Fra) 48.94; **3** Yevgeniy Gavrilenko (Sov) 49.32; **4** Stavros Tziortzis (Gre) 49.71; **5** Dmitriy Stukalov (Sov) 49.98; **6** Viktor Savchenko (Sov) 50.01; **7** Jerzy Hewelt (Pol) 50.26; **8** Rolf Ziegler (WG) 50.49.

4 × 100 Metres Relay: *Heats (first four to final). Heat 1:* **1** Italy 39.27; **2** East Germany 39.33; **3** Poland 39.78; **4** Spain 40.01; **5** Sweden 40.11; **6** Finland 40.20; **7** Hungary 40.36. *Heat 2:* **1** France 39.24; **2** Soviet Union 39.55; **3** Bulgaria 39.95; **4** Czechoslovakia 40.00; **5** UK (D. Roberts, A. Lerwill, C. Monk, D. Halliday) 40.33; West Germany disqualified.
FINAL: **1** France (L. Sainte-Rose, J. Arame, B. Cherrier, D. Chauvelot) 38.69 (*Championship record*); **2** Italy (V. Guerini, N. Oliosi, L. Benedetti, P. Mennea) 38.88; **3** East Germany (M. Kokot, M. Droese, H-J. Bombach, S. Schenke) 38.99; **4** Soviet Union (A. Kornelyuk, A. Aksinin, Y. Silov, V. Borzov) 39.03; **5** Poland (A. Swierczynski, M. Bedynski, R. Madry, Z. Nowosz) 39.35; **6** Spain (J. Sanchez Paraiso, L. Sarria, J. Sarrasqueta, M. Arnau) 39.87; **7** Bulgaria (L. Zapryanov, P. Petrov, G. Gantchev, M. Doytchev) 39.91; **8** Czechoslovakia (J. Matousek, J. Demec, J. Kynos, L. Bohman) 39.92.

4 × 400 Metres Relay: *Heats (first three and two fastest losers to final). Heat 1:* **1** Finland 3:04.6; **2** UK 3:04.7; **3** France 3:05.3; **4** Netherlands 3:06.3; **5** Italy 3:08.5; **6** Yugoslavia 3:37.8. *Heat 2:* **1** Soviet Union 3:05.3; **2** Sweden 3:05.5; **3** East Germany 3:05.8; **4** West Germany 3:05.8; **5** Czechoslovakia 3:06.3.
FINAL: **1** UK (Glen Cohen, Bill Hartley, Alan Pascoe, David Jenkins) 3:03.3; **2** West Germany (R. Ziegler, H-R. Schloske, H. Kohler, K. Honz) 3:03.5; **3** Finland (S. Lonnquist, O. Karttunen, M. Taskinen, M. Kukkoaho) 3:03.6; **4** France (J-C. Nallet, R. Velasquez, J. Carette, F. Demarthon) 3:04.6; **5** East Germany (R. Kokot, B. Stops, J. Utikal, A. Scheibe) 3:05.0; **6** Netherlands (R. Heerenveen, R.v.d. Heuvel, F. Nusse, T.v.d. Goolberg) 3:06.3; **7** Sweden (P-O. Sjoberg, D. Grama, E. Carlgren, M. Fredriksson) 3:12.6; Soviet Union (V. Yurchenko, V. Nosenko, Y. Gavrilenko, S. Kocher) did not finish.

High Jump: *Qualifiers* (at 2.14m/7' 0¼"): R. Sainte-Rose (Fra), G. Moreau (Bel), I. Major (Hun), J. Torring (Den), R. Bergamo (Ita), V. Maly (Cze), D. Patronis (Gre), G. Ferrari (Ita), K. Sapka (Sov), V. Abramov (Sov), A. Pesonen (Fin), J. Wzsola (Pol), L-R. Falkum (Nor), B. Brokken (Bel). *Non-qualifiers:* E. Kelemen (Hun), R. Moravec (Cze), W. Boller (WG), L. Nyman (Swe), F. Bonnet (Fra), P. Szorad (Hun), V. Papadimitriou (Gre), S. Molotilov (Sov), P. De Preter (Bel) & G. Marqueta (Spa) 2.11m (6' 11"), E. Del Forno (Ita), R. Almen (Swe), M. Perarnau (Spa) & P. Poaniewa (Fra) 2.08m (6' 9¾"), D. Temin (Yug) & J. Wrzosek (Pol) 2.05m (6' 8¾").
FINAL: **1** Jesper Torring (Den) 2.25m (7' 4½") (*Championship record*) (2.10-1, 2.16-1, 2.19-1, 2.21-1, 2.23-1, 2.25-2, 2.27-fail); **2** Kestutis Sapka (Sov) 2.25m (7' 4½") (2.00-1, 2.05-1, 2.10-1, 2.13-1, 2.16-2, 2.19-2, 2.21-1, 2.23-1, 2.25-2, 2.27-fail); **3** Vladimir Maly (Cze) 2.19m (7' 2¼") (2.05-1, 2.10-2, 2.13-1, 2.16-2, 2.19-1, 2.21-fail); **4** Istvan Major (Hun) 2.19m (7' 2¼") (2.05-1, 2.10-2, 2.13-2, 2.16-2, 2.19-2, 2.21-fail); **5** Jacek Wszola (Pol) 2.19m (7' 2¼") (2.05-1, 2.10-2, 2.13-1, 2.16-3, 2.19-3, 2.21-fail); **6** Leif Roar Falkum (Nor) 2.16m (7' 1") (2.05-1, 2.10-1, 2.13-1, 2.16-1, 2.19-1, 2.21-fail); **7** Rodolfo Bergamo (Ita) 2.16m (7' 1") (2.05-1, 2.10-1, 2.13-2, 2.16-1, 2.19-fail); **8** Bruno Brokken (Bel) 2.13m (6' 11¾") (2.00-1, 2.05-3, 2.10-1, 2.13-1, 2.16-fail); **9** D. Patronis (Gre) 2.13m (6' 11¾"); **10 eq** A. Pesonen (Fin) & G. Ferrari (Ita) 2.10m (6' 10¾"); **12** V. Abramov (Sov) 2.10m (6' 10¾"); **13** R. Sainte-Rose (Fra) 2.10m (6' 10¾"); **14** G. Moreau (Bel) 2.00m (6' 6¾").

Pole Vault: **1** Vladimir Kishkun (Sov) 5.35m (17' 6½") (*eq Championship record*) (5.00-1, 5.20-3, 5.30-1, 5.35-2, 5.40-fail); **2** Wladyslaw Kozakiewicz (Pol) 5.35m (17' 6½") (5.00-1, 5.20-2, 5.30-2, 5.35-2, 5.40-fail); **3** Yuriy Isakov (Sov) 5.30m (17' 4½") (5.00-1, 5.20-1, 5.30-1, 5.35-fail); **4 eq** Antti Kalliomaki (Fin) (5.00-1, 5.20-2, 5.30-1, 5.40-fail) & Wojciech Buciarski (Pol) 5.30m (17' 4½") (5.00-1, 5.20-2, 5.30-1, 5.35-fail); **6** Kjell Isaksson (Swe) 5.30m (17' 4½") (5.00-1, 5.20-1, 5.30-3, 5.35-fail); **7 eq** Tadeusz Slusarski (Pol) & Janis Lauris (Sov) 5.20m (17' 0¾") (5.00-1, 5.20-1, 5.30-fail); **9** P. Abada (Fra) 5.10m (16' 8¾"); **10** B. Hooper (UK) 5.10m (16' 8¾"); **11** F. Tracanelli (Fra) 5.00m (16' 4¾"); **12** H. Busche (WG) 5.00m (16' 4¾"); **13** T. Tongas (Gre) 4.80m (15' 9"); **14** S. Fraquelli (Ita) 4.80m (15' 9"); M. Bull (UK) no height (failed 5.00m/16' 4¾").

Long Jump: *Qualifiers:* V. Podluzhny (Sov) 7.91m (25′ 11½″), J. Rousseau (Fra) 7.83m (25′ 8¼″), R. Bernhard (Swi) 7.77m (25′ 6″), H. Baumgartner (WG) 7.73m (25′ 4½″), T. Lepik (Sov), 7.72m (25′ 4″), E. Schubin (Sov) 7.72m (25′ 4″). W. Lauterbach (EG) 7.68m (25′ 2½″), M. Klauss (EG) 7.67m (25′ 2″), A. Lerwill (UK) 7.67m (25′ 2″), N. Stekic (Yug) 7.67m (25′ 2″), R. Blanquer (Spa) 7.66m (25′ 1¾″), F. Wartenberg (EG) 7.62m (25′ 0″). *Non-qualifiers:* D. Iordache (Rom) 7.58m (24′ 10½″), P-C. Molinaris (Ita) 7.53m (24′ 8½″), G. Zante (Fra) 7.51m (24′ 7¾″), G. Cybulski (Pol) 7.50m (24′ 7¼″), J. Busse (WG) 7.49m (24′ 7″), S. Szudrowicz (Pol) 7.48m (24′ 6½″), Z. Beta (Pol) 7.47m (24′ 6¼″), J-F. Bonheme (Fra) 7.43m (24′ 4½″), U. Jarfeldt (Swe) 7.41m (24′ 3¾″), U. Kowring (WG) 7.37m (24′ 2¼″).
FINAL: **1** Valeriy Podluzhny (Sov) 8.12m (26′ 7¾″) (8.12, 7.94, 7.88, —, 8.04, 8.10); **2** Nenad Stekic (Yug) 8.05m (26′ 5″) (7.94, 7.03, 7.70, 7.70, 7.96, 8.05); **3** Yevgeniy Schubin (Sov) 7.98m (26′ 2¼″) (7.98, —, 7.89, —, 7.85, —); **4** Hans Baumgartner (WG) 7.93m (26′ 0¼″) (—, —, 7.91, —, 7.93, —); **5** Rolf Bernhard (Swi) 7.91m (25′ 11½″) (7.80, 7.48, —, 7.91, 6.37, 7.17); **6** Wolfram Lauterbach (EG) 7.87m (25′ 10″) (7.78, 7.72, 5.88, —, —, 7.87); **7** Max Klauss (EG) 7.73m (25′ 4½″) (—, 7.73, 7.67, —, 7.73, pass); **8** Tonu Lepik (Sov) 7.73m (25′ 4½″) (7.36, 7.57, 7.73, —, 7.67, —); **9** A. Lerwill (UK) 7.68m (25′ 2½″); **10** J. Rousseau (Fra) 7.58m (24′ 10½″); **11** R. Blanquer (Spa) 7.38m (24′ 2½″); **12** F. Wartenberg (EG) 7.25m (23′ 9½″).

Triple Jump: 1 Viktor Saneyev (Sov) 17.23m (56′ 6½″) (—, 17.23, —, 16.86, 16.83, —); **2** Carol Corbu (Rom) 16.68m (54′ 8¾″) (16.44, 16.32, —, 16.40, —, 16.68); **3** Andrzej Sontag (Pol) 16.61m (54′ 6″) (16.13, 16.61, —, 16.32, 16.37, 16.30); **4** Jorg Drehmel (EG) 16.54m (54′ 3¼″) (16.54, 15.75, 16.23, 16.33, —, 16.05); **5** Michal Joachimowski (Pol) 16.53m (54′ 2¾″) (16.53, 13.88, 16.03, 16.43, 14.16, —); **6** Lothar Gora (EG) 16.42m (53′ 10½″) (—, 16.42, —, —, —, —); **7** Jiri Vycichlo (Cze) 16.37m (53′ 8½″) (16.17, —, 16.37, 16.18, —, —); **8** Nikolay Sinichkin (Sov) 16.17m (53′ 0¾″) (15.69, 15.47, 16.17, 16.17, 15.95, 15.78); **9** P. Kuukasjarvi (Fin) 16.12m (52′ 10¼″); **10** A. Kathiniotis (Gre) 15.99m (52′ 5½″); **11** R. Garnys (Pol) 15.97m (52′ 4¾″); **12** M. Segal (Sov) 15.89m (52′ 1¾″); **13** B. Lamitie (Fra) 15.83m (51′ 11¼″); **14** K. Flogstad (Nor) 15.07m (49′ 5½″); **15** E. Buzzelli (Ita) 12.84m (42′ 1½″).

Shot: *Qualifiers:* W. Komar (Pol) 20.00m (65′ 7½″), R. Reichenbach (WG) 19.61m (64′ 4″), U. Beyer (EG) 19.57m (64′ 2½″), R. Stahlberg (Fin) 19.48m (63′ 11″), H. Briesenick (EG) 19.37m (63′ 6¾″), G. Capes (UK) 19.37m (63′ 6¾″), O. Lindskjold (Den) 19.30m (63′ 4″), V. Stoev (Bul) 19.29m (63′ 3½″), M. Winch (UK) 19.29m (63′ 3½″), J. Brabec (Cze) 19.21m (63′ 0¼″), V. Voikin (Sov) 19.16m (62′ 10½″), A. Baryshnikov (Sov) 19.10m (62′ 8″), J. Vlk (Cze) 19.09m (62′ 7¾″). *Non-qualifiers:* N. Khristov (Bul) 18.59m (61′ 0″), M. Janousek (Cze) 18.56m (60′ 10¾″), H. Haldorsson (Ice) 18.28m (59′ 11¾″), A. Gropelli (Ita) 18.06m (59′ 3″), H. Hoglund (Swe) 17.99m (59′ 0¼″), J. Forst (WG) 17.74m (58′ 2½″), M. Breczewski (Pol) 17.49m (57′ 4¾″).
FINAL: **1** Hartmut Briesenick (EG) 20.50m (67′ 3¼″) (18.50, 20.26, 20.06, 19.92, 20.50, —); **2** Ralf Reichenbach (WG) 20.38m (66′ 10½″) (20.38, 19.27, 19.91, 19.39, 20.05, 19.80); **3** Geoff Capes (UK) 20.21m (66′ 3¾″) (19.62, 20.08, 20.31, 20.04, —, 20.21); **4** Aleksandr Baryshnikov (Sov) 20.13m (66′ 0½″) (—, 20.13, —, 20.01, —, 20.12); **5** Valeriy Voikin (Sov) 20.07m (65′ 10¼″) (20.05, —, 19.55, 20.07, —, —); **6** Wladyslaw Komar (Pol) 19.82m (65′ 0½″) (—, 19.73, 19.82, —, —, —); **7** Jaroslav Brabec (Cze) 19.73m (64′ 8¾″) (19.73, —, —, —, 19.38, —); **8** Udo Beyer (EG) 19.63m (64′ 5″) (19.44, —, 19.63, —, —, —); **9** V. Stoev (Bul) 19.62m (64′ 4½″); **10** J. Vlk (Cze) 19.42m (63′ 8¾″); **11** R. Stahlberg (Fin) 19.25m (63′ 2″); **12** M. Winch (UK) 18.89m (61′ 11¾″); **13** O. Lindskjold (Den) 18.84m (61′ 9¾″).

Discus: *Qualifiers:* L. Danek (Cze) 61.60m (202′ 1″), P. Kahma (Fin) 61.06m (200′ 4″), G. Fejer (Hun) 60.08m (197′ 1″), V. Velev (Bul) 59.50m (195′ 2″), V. Penzikov (Sov) 59.50m (195′ 2″), G. Muller (EG) 59.46m (195′ 1″), L. Gajdzinski (Pol) 59.42m (194′ 11″), A. De Vincentis (Ita) 59.04m (193′ 8″), W. Schmidt (EG) 58.90m (193′ 3″), H-D. Neu (WG) 58.80m (192′ 11″), R. Bruch (Swe) 58.40m (191′ 7″), S. Pachale (EG) 58.28m (191′ 2″), S. Simeon (Ita) 58.22m (191′ 0″), F. Tegla (Hun) 58.16m (190′ 10″), J. Tuomola (Fin) 58.00m (190′3″). *Non-qualifiers:* M. Tuokko (Fin) 57.82m (189′ 8″), V. Zhurba (Sov) 57.62m (189′ 0″), W. Tancred (UK) 57.36m (188′ 2″), J. Muranyi (Hun) 57.36m (188′ 2″), S. Wolodko (Pol) 57.24m (187′ 9″), J. Silhavy (Cze) 57.04m (187′ 2″), J. Hillier (UK) 55.58m (182′ 4″), N. Tsiaras (Gre) 55.58m (182′ 4″).
FINAL: **1** Pentti Kahma (Fin) 63.62m (208′ 9″) (58.50, —, 62.28, 59.70, 61.72, 63.62); **2** Ludvik Danek (Cze) 62.76m (205′ 11″) (60.40, 60.24, 62.00, 61.14, 62.76, 62.60); **3** Ricky Bruch (Swe) 62.00m (203′ 5″) (58.62, 50.50, —, 62.00, —, —); **4** Siegfried Pachale (EG) 61.20m (200′ 9″) (59.94, 60.24, 61.20, —, 59.20, —); **5** Velko Velev (Bul) 61.00m (200′ 1″) (61.00, —, —, 59.72, —, 60.42); **6** Viktor Penzikov (Sov) 60.86m (199′ 8″) (57.40, 59.68, 60.86, 59.66, 60.66, 59.62); **7** Armando De Vicentis (Ita) 59.68m (195′ 9″) (—, 57.78, 59.68, 57.50, 58.70, 58.68); **8** Wolfgang Schmidt (EG) 59.56m (195′ 5″) (59.56, —, 57.44, 59.06, 58.88, 58.52); **9** G. Fejer (Hun) 59.46m (195′ 1″); **10** F. Tegla (Hun) 59.46m (195′ 1″); **11** L. Gajdzinski (Pol) 58.88m (193′ 2″); **12** H-D. Neu (WG) 58.80m (192′ 11″); **13** G. Muller (EG) 58.32m (191′ 4″); **14** S. Simeon (Ita) 56.14m (184′ 2″); **15** J. Tuomola (Fin) 55.58m (182′ 4″).

EUROPEAN CHAMPIONSHIPS

Hammer: *Qualifiers:* A. Spiridonov (Sov) 72.36m (237' 5"), J. Sachse (EG) 72.32m (237' 3"), H. Kangas (Fin) 70.84m (232' 5"), R. Theimer (EG) 70.64m (231' 9"), M. Huning (WG) 70.10m (230' 0"), V. Dmitryenko (Sov) 69.76m (228' 10"), E. Klein (WG) 69.38m (227' 7"), I. Chipchase (UK) 69.28m (227' 3"), K-H. Beilig (EG) 69.14m (226' 10"), I. Encsi (Hun) 69.06m (226' 7"), C. Black (UK) 69.04m (226' 6"), U. Beyer (WG) 68.48m (224' 8"), S. Jaglinski (Pol) 68.46m (224' 7"). *Non-qualifiers:* P. Stiefenhofer (Swi) 67.76m (222' 4"), H. Payne (UK) 67.44m (221' 3"), A. Bondarchuk (Sov) 66.62m (218' 7"), P. Sternad (Aut) 66.44m (218' 0"), J. Charvat (Cze) 65.54m (215' 0"), F.De Boni (Ita) 65.12m (213' 8"), J. Accambray (Fra) 64.98m (213' 2"), J. Hajek (Cze) 64.80m (212' 7"), D. Mikolajczyk (Fra) 62.12m (203' 10").
FINAL: **1** Aleksey Spiridonov (Sov) 74.20m (243' 5") (74.14, 73.54, 69.52, —, 72.88, 74.20); **2** Jochen Sachse (EG) 74.00m (242' 9") (71.44, 70.42, 72.26, 73.28, 73.08, 74.00); **3** Reinhard Theimer (EG) 71.62m (235' 0") (70.18, 70.36, —, 71.62, 71.42, —); **4** Valentin Dmitryenko (Sov) 71.18m (233' 6") (70.16, —, 71.18, —, 70.50, —); **5** Uwe Beyer (WG) 71.04m (233' 1") (69.76, 67.62, —, 68.26, 67.14, 71.04); **6** Manfred Huning (WG) 70.58m (231' 7") (—, 68.66, 70.58, 68.88, —, —); **7** Heikki Kangas (Fin) 70.04m (229' 9") (67.26, 68.50, 70.04, 69.28, 66.54, 67.68); **8** Istvan Encsi (Hun) 68.50m (224' 9") (67.04, 68.50, 68.34, 68.50, 67.02, —); **9** E. Klein (WG) 68.48m (224' 8"); **10** I. Chipchase (UK) 68.44m (224' 6"); **11** K-H. Beilig (EG) 67.82m (222' 6"); **12** C. Black (UK) 65.54m (215' 0"); **13** S. Jaglinski (Pol) 65.52m (214' 11").

Javelin: *Qualifiers:* K. Wolfermann (WG) 82.64m (271' 1"), D. Travis (UK) 82.38 m (270' 3"), W. Hanisch (EG) 82.08m (269' 3"), L. Koski-Vahala (Swe) 81.80m (268' 4"), S. Leroy (Fra) 80.90m (265' 5"), M. Nemeth (Hun) 80.86m (265' 3"), M. Wessing (WG) 80.56m (264' 4"), T. Thorslund (Nor) 80.10m (262' 9"), H. Siitonen (Fin) 79.70m (261' 6"), N. Grebnyov (Sov) 79.48m (260' 9"), G. Erdelyi (Hun) 79.10m (259' 6"), J. Lusis (Sov) 78.44m (257' 4"), J. Jaakola (Fin) 78.40m (257' 3"), A. Aho (Fin) 78.38m (257' 2"). *Non-qualifiers:* A. Makarov (Sov) 77.92m (255' 8"), M. Milenski (Bul) 77.10m (252' 11"), R. Cramerotti (Ita) 73.54m (241' 3"), L. Tuita (Fra) 68.86m (225' 11"), B. Roberts (UK) 3 fouls.
FINAL: **1** Hannu Siitonen (Fin) 89.58m (293' 11") (84.72, 89.58, 82.48, —, —, pass); **2** Wolfgang Hanisch (EG) 85.46m (280' 8") (85.46, —, 81.22, —, —, pass); **3** Terje Thorslund (Nor) 83.68m (274' 6") (77.42, 75.76, 83.68, —, —, —); **4** Nikolay Grebnyov (Sov) 83.66m (274' 6") (83.66, 82.26, 76.52, —, 78.38, —); **5** Klaus Wolfermann (WG) 83.36m (273' 6") (83.36, 77.62, —, 78.02, —, —); **6** Janis Lusis (Sov) 83.06m (272' 6") (79.28, —, 80.94, 81.64, 80.84, 83.06); **7** Miklos Nemeth (Hun) 81.06m (265' 11") (70.82, 70.32, 81.06, 76.72, —, 67.04); **8** Lauri Koski-Vahala (Swe) 79.92m (262' 2") (76.80, 79.92, 74.70, 75.48, 77.00, 70.64); **9** A. Aho (Fin) 79.38m (260' 5"); **10** G. Erdelyi (Hun) 78.06m (256' 1"); **11** D. Travis (UK) 75.42m (247' 5"); **12** S. Leroy (Fra) 74.62m (244' 10"); **13** J. Jaakola (Fin) 73.32m (240' 7"); **14** M. Wessing (WG) 71.68m (235' 2").

Decathlon: **1** Ryszard Skowronek (Pol) 8207 (*Championship record*) (10.97, 7.49m, 13.10m, 1.95m, 47.90, 14.79, 43.26m, 5.10m, 64.14m, 4:30.9); **2** Yves Le Roy (Fra) 8146 (10.95, 7.72m, 13.37m, 1.98m, 48.41, 15.04, 46.66m, 4.65m, 61.42m, 4:35.5); **3** Guido Kratschmer (WG) 8132 (10.83, 7.60m, 13.56m, 2.01m, 48.44, 14.29, 42.10m, 4.20m, 63.58m, 4:31.0); **4** Leonid Litvinenko (Sov) 8122 (11.14, 7.01m, 14.60m, 1.89m, 48.76, 14.64, 45.20m, 4.40m, 65.10m, 4:09.7); **5** Ryszard Katus (Pol) 7920 (11.14, 7.38m, 14.47m, 1.92m, 49.62, 14.54, 43.06m, 4.40m, 64.22m, 4:41.0); **6** Phillip Andres (Swi) 7836 (11.08, 7.08m, 11.98m, 1.95m, 47.37, 15.30, 38.34m, 4.60m, 60.52m, 4:13.2); **7** Josef Zeilbauer (Aut) 7792 (11.19, 7.11m, 14.32m, 2.04m, 48.66, 14.82, 41.74m, 4.20m, 53.78m, 4:34.8); **8** Aleksandr Blinyayov (Sov) 7742 (11.46, 7.52m, 14.36m, 1.95m, 51.55, 15.63, 47.94m, 4.50m, 61.12m, 4:44.8); **9** E. Stroot (WG) 7704; **10** R. Ghesquiere (Bel) 7591; **11** E. Kozakiewicz (Pol) 7522; **12** J-P. Schoebel (Fra) 7486; **13** L. Pernica (Cze) 7456; **14** H. Kyosola (Fin) 7384; **15** R. Cano (Spa) 7024; **16** R. Lespagnard (Bel) 6937. Did not finish: H. Born (Swi), R. Backman (Swe), L. Hedmark (Swe), R. Zigert (Sov), M. Bettella (Ita), R. Pihl (Swe), S. Hallgrimsson (Ice), V. Bogdan (Rom).

20 Kilometres Walk: 1 Vladimir Golubnichiy (Sov) 1:29:30.0; **2** Bernd Kannenberg (WG) 1:29:38.2; **3** Roger Mills (UK) 1:32:33.8; **4** Armando Zambaldo (Ita) 1:33:04.8; **5** Jan Ornoch (Pol) 1:33:19.6; **6** Amos Seddon (UK) 1:34:17.6; **7** Sandro Bellucci (Ita) 1:34:52.4; **8** Hans Tenggren (Swe) 1:35:47.0; **9** V. Galusic (Yug) 1:36:32.2; **10** O. Hemmingsson (Swe) 1:37:07.6; **11** S. Zschiegner (EG) 1:37:45.0; **12** E. Semerdjoev (Bul) 1:39:42.4; **13** M. Vala (Cze) 1:39:50.8; **14** J-C. Decosse (Fra) 1:39:54.8; **15** Y. Ivchenko (Sov) 1:39:56.0. V. Visini (Ita), C. Karagiorgos (Gre), G. Lelievre (Fra) & P. Frenkel (EG) did not finish: K-H. Stadtmuller (EG) disqualified. Vladimir Shaloshik (Sov), who finished third in 1:31:48.0, was later disqualified after a dope test was found positive.

50 Kilometres Walk: 1 Christoph Hohne (EG) 3:59:05.6 (*Championship record*); **2** Otto Bartsch (Sov) 4:02:38.8; **3** Peter Selzer (EG) 4:04:28.4; **4** Vittorio Visini (Ita) 4:05:43.6; **5** Venyamin Soldatenko (Sov) 4:09:31.6; **6** Winfried Skotnicki (EG) 4:10:19.0; **7** Gerhard Weidner (WG) 4:10:52.4; **8** Heinrich Schubert (WG) 4:16:05.0; **9** B. Kannenberg (WG) 4:21:47.0; **10** D. Carpentieri (Ita) 4:22:42.6; **11** J. Warhurst (UK) 4:26:34.6; **12** R. Valore (Ita) 4:30:22.8; **13** D. Bjorkegren (Swe) 4:31:08.8; **14** R. Dobson (UK) 4:35:26.4; **15** S. Ingvarsson (Swe) 4:36:18.2. S. Bondarenko (Sov) & O. Andersson (Swe) disqualified; Y. Kamenov (Bul) & M. Bartos (Cze) did not finish.

WOMEN

100m: *Heats (first three and four fastest losers to semi-finals).* Heat 1: **1** R. Stecher (EG) 11.54; **2** S. Lannaman (UK) 11.76; **3** L. Haglund (Swe) 11.81; **4** W. van Gool (Hol) 11.95; **5** C. Molinari (Ita) 11.95; **6** B. Haest (Aut) 12.03. Heat 2: **1** I. Szewinska (Pol) 11.39; **2** L. Maslakova (Sov) 11.54; **3** B. Eckert (EG) 11.63; **4** E. Schittenhelm (WG) 11.75; **5** R. Bottiglieri (Ita) 12.08; **6** J. Szabo (Hun) 12.40. Heat 3: **1** M-L. Pursiainen (Fin) 11.31; **2** I. Helten (WG) 11.56; **3** H. Golden (UK) 11.67; **4** Z. Karoly (Hun) 12.22; **5** S. Telliez (Fra) 12.98. Heat 4: **1** A. Lynch (UK) 11.39; **2** A. Richter (WG) 11.41; **3** C. Heinich (EG) 11.58; **4** T. Tchernikova (Sov) 11.79; **5** D. Jedrejek (Pol) 11.92; **6** L. Nappi (Ita) 12.01.
Semi-Finals (first four to final). S-F 1: **1** M-L. Pursiainen (Fin) 11.34; **2** A. Richter (WG) 11.34; **3** R. Stecher (EG) 11.38; **4** C. Heinich (EG) 11.48; **5** S. Lannaman (UK) 11.53; **6** H. Golden (UK) 11.59; **7** T. Tchernikova (Sov) 11.75; **8** D. Jedrejek (Pol) 11.90. S-F 2: **1** I. Szewinska (Pol) 11.15 (*Championship record*); **2** L. Maslakova (Sov) 11.35; **3** B. Eckert (EG) 11.43; **4** A. Lynch (UK) 11.46; **5** E. Schittenhelm (WG) 11.49; **6** I. Helten (WG) 11.65; **7** W.van Gool (Hol) 11.70; **8** L. Haglund (Swe) 11.72.
FINAL: (−1.2m wind) **1** Irena Szewinska (Pol) 11.13 (*Championship record*); **2** Renate Stecher (EG) 11.23; **3** Andrea Lynch (UK) 11.28; **4** Lyudmila Maslakova (Sov) 11.36; **5** Annegret Richter (WG) 11.36; **6** Mona-Lisa Pursiainen (Fin) 11.42; **7** Barbel Eckert (EG) 11.46; **8** Christina Heinich (EG) 11.63.

200m: *Heats (first three and four fastest losers to semi-finals).* Heat 1: **1** M-L. Pursiainen (Fin) 23.13; **2** P. Kandarr (EG) 23.44; **3** C. Krause (WG) 23.51; **4** B. Bakulin (Pol) 23.56; **5** I. Szabo (Hun) 23.78. Heat 2: **1** R. Stecher (EG) 23.35; **2** M. Sidorova (Sov) 23.55; **3** A. Kroniger (WG) 23.55; **4** H. Golden (UK) 24.02; **5** L. Nappi (Ita) 24.22. Heat 3: **1** L. Maslakova (Sov) 23.45; **2** I. Szewinska (Pol) 23.87; **3** E. Possekel (WG) 24.08; **4** S. Colyear (UK) 24.14. Heat 4: **1** D. Maletzki (EG) 23.77; **2** W.van Gool (Hol) 23.84; **3** R. Wallez (Bel) 24.00; **4** A. Lynch (UK) 24.22. *Semi-Finals (first four to final).* S-F 1: **1** R. Stecher (EG) 23.01; **2** L. Maslakova (Sov) 23.35; **3** C. Krause (WG) 23.49; **4** H. Golden (UK) 23.54; **5** B. Bakulin (Pol) 23.81; **6** W.van Gool (Hol) 23.86; **7** D. Maletzki (EG) 24.07; **8** E. Possekel (WG) 24.29. S-F 2: **1** I. Szewinska (Pol) 22.88; **2** M-L. Pursiainen (Fin) 23.17; **3** A. Kroniger (WG) 23.29; **4** P. Kandarr (EG) 23.50; **5** I. Szabo (Hun) 23.97; **6** S. Colyear (UK) 23.98; **7** R. Wallez (Bel) 24.03; **8** M. Sidorova (Sov) 24.66.
FINAL: (−2.85m wind) **1** Irena Szewinska (Pol) 22.51 (*Championship record*); **2** Renate Stecher (EG) 22.68; **3** Mona-Lisa Pursiainen (Fin) 23.17; **4** Lyudmila Maslakova (Sov) 23.31; **5** Helen Golden (UK) 23.38; **6** Annegret Kroniger (WG) 23.38; **7** Christiane Krause (WG) 23.78; **8** Petra Kandarr (EG) 23.99.

400m: *Heats (first three and four fastest losers to semi-finals).* Heat 1: **1** N. Sokolova (Sov) 53.21; **2** J. Cerchlanova (Cze) 53.23; **3** D. Piecyk (Pol) 53.30; **4** D. Murray (UK) 53.49; **5** D. Forest (Fra) 55.35. Heat 2: **1** R. Salin (Fin) 51.88; **2** A. Handt (EG) 52.21; **3** K. Kacperczyk (Pol) 52.76; **4** J. Roscoe (UK) 53.28; **5** T. Wunderink (Hol) 53.30; **6** C. Walsh (Eir) 54.15. Heat 3: **1** E. Streidt (EG) 51.79; **2** R. Wilden (WG) 51.91; **3** K. Kafer (Aut) 52.20; **4** R. Wallez (Bel) 52.82; **5** I. Barkane (Sov) 53.01; **6** G. Nowaczyk (Pol) 53.34. Heat 4: **1** N. Ilyina (Sov) 52.30; **2** V. Bernard (UK) 52.46; **3** J. Pavlicic (Yug) 53.11; **4** P. Wilmi (Fin) 53.43; **5** K. Claus (WG) 54.26; **6** I. Arva (Hun) 54.90. *Semi-Finals (first four to final).* S-F 1: **1** E. Streidt (EG) 51.40 (*Championship record*); **2** R. Wilden (WG) 51.46; **3** N. Ilyina (Sov) 51.65; **4** J. Pavlicic (Yug) 51.87; **5** K. Kacperczyk (Pol) 52.07; **6** J. Roscoe (UK) 52.85; **7** R. Wallez (Bel) 53.02; **8** T. Wunderink (Hol) 53.46. S-F 2: **1** R. Salin (Fin) 51.46; **2** A. Handt (EG) 51.67; **3** K. Kafer (Aut) 52.14; **4** V. Bernard (UK) 52.18; **5** I. Barkane (Sov) 52.52; **6** D. Piecyk (Pol) 52.92; **7** J. Cerchlanova (Cze) 53.77; **8** N. Sokolova (Sov) 53.82.
FINAL: **1** Riitta Salin (Fin) 50.14 (*Championship record*); **2** Ellen Streidt (EG) 50.69; **3** Rita Wilden (WG) 50.88; **4** Nadyezhda Ilyina (Sov) 51.22; **5** Angelika Handt (EG) 51.24; **6** Karoline Kafer (Aut) 51.77; **7** Verona Bernard (UK) 52.61; **8** Jelica Pavlicic (Yug) 53.01.

800m: *Heats (first four and four fastest losers to semi-finals).* Heat 1: **1** M-F. Dubois (Fra) 2:01.2; **2** E. Katolik (Pol) 2:01.4; **3** M. Suman (Rom) 2:01.5; **4** N. Morgunova (Sov) 2:01.7; **5** M. Purcell (Eir) 2:02.8; **6** B. Jennes (Den) 2:09.2. Heat 2: **1** G. Hoffmeister (EG) 2:02.6; **2** G. Klein (WG) 2:02.7; **3** N. Sabaite (Sov) 2:02.9; **4** N. Schtereva (Bul) 2:03.2; **5** A-M. Van Nuffel (Bel) 2:03.6; **6** R. Wright (UK) 2:03.9. Heat 3: **1** L. Tomova (Bul) 2:02.1; **2** V. Gerasimova (Sov) 2:02.2; **3** W. Pohland (EG) 2:02.3; **4** G. Lindh (Swe) 2:02.3; **5** L. Kiernan (UK) 2:02.8; **6** J. Januchta (Pol) 2:04.7. *Semi-Finals (first four to final).* S-F 1: **1** M. Suman (Rom) 2:00.2; **2** M-F. Dubois (Fra) 2:00.3; **3** V. Gerasimova (Sov) 2:00.8; **4** G. Klein (WG) 2:01.5; **5** W. Pohland (EG) 2:01.9; **6** M. Purcell (Eir) 2:04.0; **7** N. Schtereva (Bul) 2:04.1; **8** R. Wright (UK) 2:04.9. S-F 2: **1** G. Hoffmeister (EG) 2:03.0; **2** E. Katolik (Pol) 2:03.1; **3** L. Tomova (Bul) 2:03.3; **4** N. Morgunova (Sov) 2:03.6; **5** A-M. Van Nuffel (Bel) 2:04.1; **6** L. Kiernan (UK) 2:05.4; N. Sabaite (Sov) & G. Lindh (Swe) scratched.
FINAL: **1** Lilyana Tomova (Bul) 1:58.1 (*Championship record*); **2** Gunhild Hoffmeister (EG) 1:58.8; **3** Mariana Suman

EUROPEAN CHAMPIONSHIPS

(Rom) 1:59.8; **4** Marie-Francoise Dubois (Fra) 1:59.9; **5** Valentina Gerasimova (Sov) 2:00.1; **6** Nina Morgunova (Sov) 2:00.8; **7** Elzbieta Katolik (Pol) 2:01.4; **8** Gisela Klein (WG) 2:01.5.

1500m: *Heats (first three and three fastest losers to final). Heat 1:* **1** G. Hoffmeister (EG) 4:11.7; **2** G. Dorio (Ita) 4:12.1; **3** T. Pangelova (Sov) 4:12.8; **4** N. Andrei (Rom) 4:14.1; **5** R. Tschavdarova (Bul) 4:15.1; **6** C. Surdel (Pol) 4:18.7; **7** W. Soerum (Nor) 4:19.3; **8** L. Olafsson (Den) 4:28.0; **9** S. Schenk (WG) 4:30.1. *Heat 2:* **1** T. Kazankina (Sov) 4:11.4; **2** L. Tomova (Bul) 4:11.5; **3** E. Wellmann (WG) 4:11.5; **4** G. Lindh (Swe) 4:11.5; **5** U. Klapezynski (EG) 4:11.7; **6** C. Valero (Spa) 4:13.0; **7** S. Castelein (Bel) 4:13.2; **8** N. Holmen (Fin) 4:14.6. *Heat 3:* **1** G. Andersen (Nor) 4:11.5; **2** J. Smith (UK) 4:12.0; **3** K. Krebs (EG) 4:13.2; **4** N. Schtereva (Bul) 4:14.7; **5** M. Purcell (Eir) 4:15.1; **6** L. Bragina (Sov) 4:17.8; **7** S. Cruciata (Ita) 4:22.6.
FINAL: **1** Gunhild Hoffmeister (EG) 4:02.3 (*Championship record*); **2** Lilyana Tomova (Bul) 4:05.0; **3** Grete Andersen (Nor) 4:05.2; **4** Tatyana Kazankina (Sov) 4:05.9; **5** Tamara Pangelova (Sov) 4:08.9; **6** Ulrike Klapezynski (EG) 4:10.5; **7** Carmen Valero (Spa) 4:11.6; **8** Joyce Smith (UK) 4:12.3; **9** G. Dorio (Ita) 4:12.7; **10** E. Wellmann (WG) 4:16.3; **11** G. Lindh (Swe) 4:17.5; K. Krebs (EG) scratched.

3000m: **1** Nina Holmen (Fin) 8:55.2; **2** Lyudmila Bragina (Sov) 8:56.2; **3** Joyce Smith (UK) 8:57.4; **4** Natalia Andrei (Rom) 8:59.0; **5** Paola Cacchi (Ita) 9:01.4; **6** Bronislawa Ludwichowska (Pol) 9:05.2; **7** Ann Yeoman (UK) 9:07.0; **8** Tamara Pangelova (Sov) 9:10.6; **9** I. Bondarchuk (Sov) 9:16.6; **10** R. Pentlinowska (Pol) 9:22.8; **11** E. Gustafsson (Swe) 9:24.2; **12** R. Tschavdarova (Bul) 9:31.0; **13** S. Castelein (Bel) 9:31.2; **14** M. Moser (Swi) 9:32.8; **15** C. Valero (Spa) 9:35.4; **16** U. Prasek (Pol) 9:48.4; G. Hodey (WG) did not finish.

100m Hurdles: *Heats (first four and four fastest losers to semi-finals). Heat 1:* **1** A. Ehrhardt (EG) 13.32; **2** J. Vernon (UK) 13.74; **3** M. Koschinski (WG) 13.84; **4** M. Hansen (Den) 14.12; **5** B. Nowakowska (Pol) 14.23; **6** A. Battaglia (Ita) 14.36. *Heat 2:* **1** A. Fiedler (EG) 13.48; **2** T. Anisimova (Sov) 13.54; **3** G. Rabsztyn (Pol) 13.71; **4** V. Stefanescu (Rom) 13.83; **5** L. Drysdale (UK) 13.97. *Heat 3:* **1** T. Nowak (Pol) 13.20; **2** N. Lebedyova (Sov) 13.52; **3** P. Sokolova (Bul) 13.65; **4** G. Berend (EG) 13.66; **5** C. Rega (Fra) 13.72; **6** B. Thompson (UK) 13.76. *Semi-Finals (first four to final).*
S-F 1: **1** A. Ehrhardt (EG) 13.03; **2** V. Stefanescu (Rom) 13.26; **3** N. Lebedyova (Sov) 13.34; **4** G. Rabsztyn (Pol) 13.48; **5** P. Sokolova (Bul) 13.60; **6** L. Drysdale (UK) 13.68; **7** C. Rega (Fra) 13.78; **8** B. Nowakowska (Pol) 13.95.
S-F 2: **1** T. Nowak (Pol) 13.18; **2** A. Fiedler (EG) 13.28; **3** T. Anisimova (Sov) 13.35; **4** G. Berend (EG) 13.51; **5** J. Vernon (UK) 13.65; **6** B. Thompson (UK) 13.72; **7** M. Koschinski (WG) 13.90; **8** M. Hansen (Den) 14.11.
FINAL: (+0.2m wind) **1** Annelie Ehrhardt (EG) 12.66 (*Championship record*); **2** Annerose Fiedler (EG) 12.89; **3** Teresa Nowak (Pol) 12.91; **4** Valeria Stefanescu (Rom) 13.04; **5** Gudrun Berend (EG) 13.14; **6** Tatyana Anisimova (Sov) 13.16; **7** Natalya Lebedyova (Sov) 13.19; **8** Grazyna Rabsztyn (Pol) 13.53.

4 × 100 Metres Relay: **1** East Germany (D. Maletzki, R. Stecher, C. Heinich, B. Eckert) 42.51 (*World record*); **2** West Germany (E. Schittenhelm, A. Kroniger, A. Richter, I. Helten) 42.75; **3** Poland (E. Dlugolecka, D. Jedrejek, B. Bakulin, I. Szewinska) 43.48; **4** UK (L. Barratt, D. Ramsden, H. Golden, A. Lynch) 43.94; **5** France (N. Goletto, C. Delachanal, N. Pani, S. Telliez) 44.18; **6** Hungary (Z. Karoly, J. Szabo, I. Szabo, I. Arva) 44.51; **7** Italy (M. Gnecchi, A. Carli, L. Nappi, C. Molinari) 44.56.

4 × 400 Metres Relay: **1** East Germany (W. Dietsch, B. Rohde, A. Handt, E. Streidt) 3:25.2 (*Championship record*); **2** Finland (M. Eklund, M-L. Pursiainen, P. Wilmi, R. Salin) 3:25.7; **3** Soviet Union (I. Klimovicha, N. Sokolova, I. Barkane, N. Ilyina) 3:26.1; **4** Poland (G. Nowaczyk, K. Kacperczyk, D. Piecyk, I. Szewinska) 3:26.4; **5** West Germany (D. Jost, E. Barth, H. Falck, R. Wilden) 3:27.9; **6** UK (R. Kennedy, J. Roscoe, V. Bernard, D. Murray) 3:29.6; **7** Romania (I. Slavic, A. Badescu, L. Diaconiuc, M. Suman) 3:20.8; **8** Czechoslovakia (E. Kovalcikova, J. Hermanska, E. Stefkova, J. Cerchlanova) 3:36.3.

High Jump: *Qualifiers* (at 1.80m/5′ 10¾″): M. Hubnerova (Cze), R. Witschas (EG), G. Filatova (Sov), U. Meyfarth (WG), M. Karbanova (Cze), A. Bouma (Hol), S. Simeoni (Ita), R. Kirst (EG), V. Ioan (Rom), M. Mracnova (Cze), B. Lawton (UK), K. Wagner (WG), M-C. Debourse (Fra), T. Galka (Sov), R. Watt (UK). *Non-qualifiers:* A. Tveit (Nor) 1.78m (5′ 10″), V. Harrison (UK) 1.78m (5′ 10″), G. Ejstrup (Den) 1.75m (5′ 8¾″), S. Valkanova (Bul) 1.75m (5′ 8¾″), A-E. Karlsson (Swe) 1.70m (5′ 7″).
FINAL: **1** Rosemarie Witschas (EG) 1.95m (6′ 4¾″) (*World record*) (1.70-1, 1.75-1, 1.80-1, 1.83-1, 1.86-1, 1.89-1, 1.91-1, 1.93-2, 1.95-3, 1.97-fail); **2** Milada Karbanova (Cze) 1.91m (6′ 3¼″) (1.75-1, 1.80-1, 1.83-1, 1.86-1, 1.89-1, 1.91-2, 1.93-fail); **3** Sara Simeoni (Ita) 1.89m (6′ 2¼″) (1.70-1, 1.75-1, 1.80-1, 1.83-1, 1.86-1, 1.89-1, 1.91-fail); **4** Rita Kirst (EG) 1.89m (6′ 2¼″) (1.70-1, 1.75-1, 1.80-1, 1.83-1, 1.86-2, 1.89-2, 1.91-fail); **5** Miloslava Hubnerova (Cze) 1.86m (6′ 1¼″) (1.70-1, 1.75-1, 1.80-2, 1.83-1, 1.86-2, 1.89-fail); **6** Galina Filatova (Sov) 1.86m (6′ 1¼″) (1.65-1, 1.70-1, 1.75-1, 1.80-1, 1.83-1,

1.86-3, 1.89-fail); **7** Ulrike Meyfarth (WG) 1.83m (6′ 0″) (1.70-1, 1.75-1, 1.80-1, 1.83-1, 1.86-fail); **8** Maria Mracnova (Cze) 1.83m (6′ 0″) (1.70-1, 1.75-1, 1.80-1, 1.83-2, 1.86-fail); **9** M-C. Debourse (Fra) 1.83m (6′ 0″); **10** A. Bouma (Hol) 1.83m (6′ 0″); **11** K. Wagner (WG) 1.83m (6′ 0″); **12** V. Ioan (Rom) 1.80m (5′ 10¾″); **13** T. Galka (Sov) 1.75m (5′ 8¾″); **14** R. Watt (UK) 1.70m (5′ 7″); **15** B. Lawton (UK) 1.70m (5′ 7″).

Long Jump: *Qualifiers:* P. Helenius (Fin) 6.57m (21′ 6¾″), I. Bruzsenyak (Hun) 6.51m (21′ 4¼″), V. Stefanescu (Rom) 6.49m (21′ 3½″), C. Janssen (Hol) 6.47m (21′ 2¾″), M. Voelzke (EG) 6.40m (21′ 0″), J. Nygrynova (Cze) 6.37m (20′ 10¾″), L. Alfeyova (Sov) 6.36m (20′ 10½″), A. Schmalfeld (EG) 6.35m (20′ 10″), I. Szabo (Hun) 6.35m (20′ 10″), E. Suranova (Cze) 6.33m (20′ 9¼″), K. Lotova (Sov) 6.32m (20′ 9″), T. Timockova (Sov) 6.32m (20′ 9″), M. Antenen (Swi) 6.30m (20′ 8″).
Non-qualifiers: M. Lambrou (Gre) 6.23m (20′ 5½″), I. Lusti (Swi) 6.13m (20′ 1½″), B. Wilkes (WG) 6.27m (20′ 7″), T. Rautanen (Fin) 6.27m (20′ 7″), D. Cantineanu (Rom) 6.18m (20′ 3½″).
FINAL: **1** Ilona Bruzsenyak (Hun) 6.65m (21′ 10″) (6.26, 6.25, 6.37, 6.43, 6.65, 6.41); **2** Eva Suranova (Cze) 6.60m (21′ 8″) (6.57, —, 6.60, 6.57, 6.50, —); **3** Pirkko Helenius (Fin) 6.59m (21′ 7½″) (6.59, —, —, 6.48, —, 6.49); **4** Angela Schmalfeld (EG) 6.56m (21′ 6¾″) (—, 6.32, 6.44, —, 6.56, —); **5** Marianne Voelzke (EG) 6.56m (21′ 6¾″) (—, 6.42, 6.56, —, —, 6.31); **6** Lidia Alfeyova (Sov) 6.54m (21′ 5½″) (6.43, 6.24, 6.36, 6.37, 6.54, 6.44); **7** Tatyana Timockova (Sov) 6.50m (21′ 4″) (5.69, 6.19, 6.50, —, 6.13, 6.37); **8** Meta Antenen (Swi) 6.33m (20′ 9¼″) (6.33, 6.32, 6.17, 6.03, 5.96, 6.08); **9** I. Szabo (Hun) 6.32m (20′ 9″); **10** K. Lotova (Sov) 6.29m (20′ 7¾″); **11** J. Nygrynova (Cze) 6.28m (20′ 7¼″); **12** V. Stefanescu (Rom) 6.25m (20′ 6¼″); C. Janssen (Hol) 3 fouls.

Shot: 1 Nadyezhda Chizhova (Sov) 20.78m (68′ 2¼″)(*Championship record*); (20.30, —, 20.78, 19.71, 20.19, —);
2 Marianne Adam (EG) 20.43m (67′ 0½″) (20.43, 20.18, 19.86, —, 20.09, 20.42); **3** Helena Fibingerova (Cze) 20.33m (66′ 8½″) (20.14, 20.16, —, —, 19.79, 20.33); **4** Ivanka Khristova (Bul) 19.17m (62′ 10¾″) (19.17, 19.04, —, —, 19.02, —); **5** Ludwika Chewinska (Pol) 18.98m (62′ 3¼″) (18.62, 18.76, 18.98, 18.57, 18.62, —); **6** Marita Lange (EG) 18.60m (61′ 0¼″) (18.31, 18.53, 18.60, —, 18.50, 18.43); **7** Elena Stoyanova (Bul) 18.48m (60′ 7¾″) (—, 18.39, 18.26, 18.08, —, 18.48); **8** Esfir Krachevskaya (Sov) 18.27m (59′ 11¼″) (17.39, 18.23, 18.19, —, 18.27, 18.05); **9** Y. Korablyova (Sov) 18.17m (59′ 7½″); **10** R. Bakhtschevanova (Bul) 17.97m (58′ 11½″); **11** C. Petrucci (Ita) 14.97m (49′ 1½″).

Discus: 1 Faina Melnik (Sov) 69.00m (226′ 4″) (*Championship record*) (69.00, 67.12, 68.18, 64.42, —, —);
2 Argentina Menis (Rom) 64.62m (212′ 0″) (59.24, 62.86, 60.46, 63.26, 64.62, 61.90); **3** Gabriele Hinzmann (EG) 62.50m (205′ 1″) (61.30, 60.48, 59.88, —, 62.50, —); **4** Maria Vergova (Bul) 61.92m (203′ 2″) (54.86, 60.98, 61.92, —, 61.20, 59.98); **5** Karin Holdke (EG) 58.92m (193′ 4″) (58.92, 55.88, 57.02, —, —, —); **6** Olimpia Catarama (Rom) 58.30m (191′ 3″) (56.68, 58.02, 58.30, 58.12, 55.14, 57.02); **7** Liesel Westermann (WG) 57.40m (188′ 4″) (53.74, 57.40, 57.36, —, 56.20, —); **8** Vassilka Stoeva (Bul) 57.12m (187′ 5″) (55.56, —, 57.12, 53.84, 55.72, 53.24); **9** H. Vyhnalova (Cze) 55.24m (181′ 3″); **10** S. Bojkova (Bul) 54.28m (178′ 1″); **11** R. Payne (UK) 49.16m (161′ 3″).

Javelin: *Qualifiers:* J. Todten (EG) 60.78m (199′ 5″), R. Fuchs (EG) 59.88m (196′ 5″), N. Urbancic (Yug) 59.72m (195′ 11″), L. Mollova (Bul) 57.70m (189′ 4″), D. Jaworska (Pol) 56.26m (184′ 7″), F. Kinder (Pol) 56.10m (184′ 1″), L. Pecec (Rom) 55.44m (181′ 11″), T. Zhigalova (Sov) 55.32m (181′ 6″), E. Janko (Aut) 55.10m (180′ 9″), A. Koloska (WG) 54.62m (179′ 2″), S. Kargel (EG) 54.02m (177′ 3″), E. Zorgo (Rom) 53.98m (177′ 1″). *Non-qualifiers:* T. Sanderson (UK) 53.28m (174′ 10″), S. Babich (Sov) 51.78m (169′ 10″), L. Kuys (Hol) 49.42m (162′ 2″), G. Amici (Ita) 48.72m (159′ 10″), M. Kucserka (Hun) 47.12m (154′ 7″), L. Wuyts (Bel) 45.54m (149′ 5″), E.Van Beuzekom (Hol) 39.44m (129′ 5″).
FINAL: **1** Ruth Fuchs (EG) 67.22m (220′ 6″) (*World record*) (62.36, 67.22, 60.20, —, 49.98, —); **2** Jacqueline Todten (EG) 62.10m (203′ 9″) (58.50, 54.38, 56.96, 59.14, 55.92, 62.10); **3** Natasa Urbancic (Yug) 61.66m (202′ 3″) (—, 59.26, 59.58, 58.12, 61.66, —); **4** Lutvjan Mollova (Bul) 60.80m (199′ 6″) (57.82, 58.00, 55.84, 60.06, —, 60.80); **5** Sabine Kargel (EG) 57.10m (187′ 4″) (57.10, 55.90, 53.86, —, —, 51.82); **6** Felicja Kinder (Pol) 57.02m (187′ 1″) (57.02, 54.26, 55.18, 54.20, 56.16, 53.88); **7** Tatyana Zhigalova (Sov) 56.64m (185′ 10″) (—, 56.64, —, 55.08, —, 50.80); **8** Ameli Koloska (WG) 56.36m (184′ 11″) (55.02, 53.86, 56.36, 53.72, —, 53.42); **9** E. Janko (Aut) 55.16m (181′ 0″); **10** E. Zorgo (Rom) 54.44m (178′ 7″); **11** D. Jaworska (Pol) 54.02m (177′ 3″); **12** I. Pecec (Rom) 52.18m (171′ 2″).

Pentathlon: 1 Nadyezhda Tkachenko (Sov) 4776 (13.39, 16.07m, 1.74m, 6.36m, 24.20); **2** Burglinde Pollak (EG) 4676 (13.36, 15.80m, 1.71m, 6.19m, 24.46); **3** Zoia Spasovkhovskaya (Sov) 4550 (13.27, 14.48m, 1.65m, 6.37m, 24.96); **4** Siegrun Thon (EG) 4548 (13.58, 12.68m, 1.71m, 6.35m, 23.97); **5** Lyudmila Popovskaya (Sov) 4548 (13.89, 14.87m, 1.74m, 6.08m, 24.60); **6** Ilona Bruzsenyak (Hun) 4399 (13.63, 11.52m, 1.71m, 6.45m, 24.98); **7** Margrit Olfert (EG) 4391 (13.57, 14.35m, 1.60m, 6.06m, 24.87); **8** Christel Voss (WG) 4384 (14.06, 13.76m, 1.80m, 5.85m, 25.58); **9** P. Sokolova (Bul) 4323; **10** D. Focic (Yug) 4289; **11** U. Jacob (WG) 4247; **12** M. Papp (Hun) 4207; **13** A. Wilson (UK) 4152; **14** C. Janssen (Hol) 4151; F. Picaut (Fra) & S. Yurukova (Bul) did not finish.

13 September

IAC/COCA-COLA FLOODLIT MEETING

Britain's successes in the European Championships, and particularly the three gold medals won on the final day (8 September), which went down very well indeed on television, sparked off colossal interest in the International Athletes' Club's Coca-Cola International Meeting. Some 18,000 fans packed the Crystal Palace with thousands of others milling around outside unable to get in. With the exception of Steve Ovett (on holiday in Italy), all of Britain's medallists in Rome were present – plus newly crowned champions, Jesper Torring (Den), Luciano Susanj (Yug), Karl Honz (WG), Bronislaw Malinowski (Pol), and Irena Szewinska (Pol); not to mention American world record holders Steve Williams, Dwight Stones, and Al Feuerbach.

High spots of a glittering night's sport included David Jenkins' 400 metres victory in 45.72 over the man who dethroned him in Rome, Karl Honz; Alan Pascoe's 49.29 400 metres hurdles, fastest ever at home by a British athlete; a UK steeplechase record of 8:22.6 by John Davies behind Malinowski; another devastating run by Brendan Foster with Ray Smedley excelling himself to take second place (American star, Steve Prefontaine, failed to finish this 2 miles race); a super-fast 400 metres by Mrs Szewinska (her time of 50.32 was the third quickest ever) with Donna Murray (51.85) rehabilitating herself after the Rome disappointment by beating Olympic and European medallist Rita Wilden (WG); and an extraordinary display of speed walking by Roger Mills whose mile time of 6:08.9 is a world's best.

MEN

400m: 1 D. Jenkins 45.7; **2** K. Honz (WG) 46.1; **3** A. Brijdenbach (Bel) 46.2; **4** G. Cohen 47.3; **5** E. Carlgren (Swe) 47.5; **6** J. Wilson 47.8; **7** M. Fiasconaro (Ita) 48.1; **8** S. Williams (USA) 49.0.

1000m: 1 T. Hansen (Den) 2:18.8; **2** L. Susanj (Yug) 2:19.1; **3** A. Settle 2:19.1; **4** E. Hoving (Hol) 2:20.5; **5** F. Clement 2:21.8; **6** C. Silei (Ken) 2:22.1; **7** P. Browne 2:22.5; **8** J. Van Wezer (Bel) 2:22.8.

2 Miles: 1 B. Foster 8:23.0; **2** R. Smedley 8:25.6; **3** J. Hermens (Hol) 8:25.6; **4** L. Viren (Fin) 8:25.8; **5** D. Black 8:27.2; **6** E.Van Mullen (Bel) 8:28.8; **7** C. Stewart 8:31.4; **8** B. Ford 8:35.8.

3000m Steeplechase: 1 B. Malinowski (Pol) 8:21.2 (*UK all-comers record*); **2** J. Davies 8:22.6 (*UK national record*); **3** F. Fava (Ita) 8:28.0; **4** J. Bicourt 8:31.2; **5** M. Manley (USA) 8:33.2; **6** E. Mogaka (Ken) 8:36.4; **7** K. Kvalheim (Nor) 8:45.8; **8** C. Thomas 8:49.8.

400m Hurdles: 1 A. Pascoe 49.3; **2** J. Hewelt (Pol) 50.3; **3** W. Hartley 50.4; **4** S. Black 51.4; **5** F. Kimaiyo (Ken) 51.5; **6** C. O'Neill 51.6; **7** B. Price 52.8.

Mile Walk: 1 R. Mills 6:08.9 (*World's best performance*); **2** G. Lelievre (Fra) 6:11.0; **3** B. Adams 6:20.8; **4** A. Seddon 6:32.0; **5** P. Marlow 6:35.3; **6** R. Dobson 6:41.6; **7** K. Carter 6:41.7; **8** A. Buchanan 6:44.7.

High Jump: 1 D. Stones (USA) 2.20m (7' 2½"); **2** J. Torring (Den) 2.15m (7' 0½"); **3** L. Falkum (Nor) 2.10m (6' 10¾"); **4** J. Hawkins (Can) 2.08m (6' 9¾"); **5** M. Butterfield 2.05m (6' 8¾"); **6** J. Fanning (Eir) 2.00m (6' 6¾").

Pole Vault: 1 W. Kozakiewicz (Pol) 5.30m (17' 4½"); **2** W. Buciarski (Pol) 5.20m (17' 0¾"); **3** D. Baird (Aus) 5.20m (17' 0¾"); **4** C. Carrigan (USA) 5.10m (16' 8¾"); **5** M. Bull 5.00m (16' 4¾"); **6** A. Williams 4.80m (15' 9"); **7** K. Stock 4.60m (15' 1").

Shot: 1 A. Feuerbach (USA) 20.96m (68' 9¼"); **2** R. Reichenbach (WG) 19.90m (65' 3½"); **3** G. Capes 19.67m (65' 6½"); **4** M. Winch 18.47m (60' 7¼").

ATHLETICS 75

WOMEN

100m: 1 A. Lynch 11.5; **2** R. Boyle (Aus) 11.7; **3** H. Golden 11.8; **4** D. Ramsden 11.8; **5** A. Neil 12.2.

400m: 1 I. Szewinska (Pol) 50.3 (*UK all-comers record*); **2** D. Murray 51.9; **3** R. Wilden (WG) 52.2; **4** V. Bernard 52.2; **5** J. Roscoe 53.2; **6** K. Kacperczyk (Pol) 53.3; **7** E. Barnes 54.0.

1000m: 1 L. Kiernan 2:40.3; **2** R. Wright 2:41.6; **3** J. Allison 2:42.5; **4** M. Coomber 2:43.5; **5** R. Tata (Ken) 2:43.9; **6** F. Larrieu (USA) 2:44.2; **7** P. Yeoman 2:45.8; **8** G. Goodburn 2:46.8.

100m Hurdles: 1 eq L. Drysdale & J. Vernon 13.7; **3** A. Wilson 14.2; **4** P. Chapman 14.2; **5** L. Boothe 14.4; **6** L. Ilott 14.6; **7** B. Ruttledge 14.8; **8** J. Long 14.8.

14 September

UK v WEST GERMANY (juniors)

Two Commonwealth Games gold medallists in javelin thrower Charles Clover and 400 metres runner Ruth Kennedy won their specialities in the Apollo-sponsored junior international at Warley, but that did not prevent West Germany winning both matches. Clover apart, Britain's only field event victor in the men's match was triple jumper Aston Moore (and there wasn't a single second placer in those eight events). But the girls did better, with discus thrower Lesley Mallin and javelin thrower Tessa Sanderson gaining top honours.

The other British winners were Roger Jenkins (400 metres), Paul Williams (1500 metres), John Tierney (steeplechase), Jacky Lord (walk), Sonia Lannaman (100 metres) and three of the four relay teams.

MEN

100m: 1 W. Bastians (WG) 10.8; **2** S. Green (UK) 10.8; **3** G. Edwards (UK) 11.0; **4** F. Heckel (WG) 11.1.

200m: 1 F. Grimminger (WG) 21.5; **2** R. Tempel (WG) 21.6; **3** L. Hoyte (UK) 22.0; **4** S. Hall (UK) 22.1.

400m: 1 R. Jenkins (UK) 47.2; **2** H. Schmid (WG) 48.3; **3** M. Clark (UK) 48.3; **4** G. Dubberman (WG) 48.4.

800m: 1 H. Hudak (WG) 1:54.5; **2** A. Mottershead (UK) 1:54.8; **3** M. Edwards (UK) 1:55.6; **4** P. Benz (WG) 1:57.8.

1500m: 1 P. Williams (UK) 3:49.8; **2** P. Lawther (UK) 3:49.9; **3** L. Friebe (WG) 3:51.1; **4** H. Schittenhelm (WG) 3:59.9.

3000m: 1 R. Manz (WG) 8:17.8; **2** U. Betz (WG) 8:24.6; **3** J. Odlin (UK) 8:29.4; **4** G. Harvey (UK) 8:45.6.

5000m: 1 K. Fleschen (WG) 14:08.6; **2** W. Sheridan (UK) 14:46.6; **3** R. Strieder (WG) 14:50.2; **4** A. Armitage (UK) 15:10.4.

2000m Steeplechase: 1 J. Tierney (UK) 5:47.8; **2** B. Schneider (WG) 5:50.6; **3** D. Warren (UK) 5:59.0; A. Ritter (WG) did not finish.

110m Hurdles: 1 K-J. Kerl (WG) 14.9; **2** N. Gerrard (UK) 15.2; **3** H-W. Schmitt (WG) 15.3; **4** M. Jackson (UK) 15.6.

400m Hurdles: 1 T. Loewe (WG) 53.8; **2** S. Johnson (UK) 54.4; **3** W. Greaves (UK) 54.8; **4** F. Mayr (WG) 55.3.

10,000m Walk: 1 J. Lord (UK) 46:18.2; **2** B. Lines (UK) 47:13.0; **3** K-H. Bruckmaier (WG) 49:07.6; **4** W. Werner (WG) 49:18.6.

High Jump: 1 J. Lichtenberg (WG) 2.04m (6' 8¼"); **2** O. Seehorsch (WG) 2.04m (6' 8¼"); **3** M. Palmer (UK) 1.95m (6' 4¾"); **4** M. Shorten (UK) 1.90m (6' 2¾").

Pole Vault: 1 J. Schulze (WG) 4.50m (14' 9"); **2** W. Reinbold (WG) 4.50m (14' 9"); **3** C. Boreham (UK) 4.40m (14' 5¼"). K. Stock (UK) failed at opening height – 4.20m.

Long Jump: 1 J. Verschl (WG) 7.60m (24' 11¼"); **2** D. Merz (WG) 7.44m (24' 5"); **3** R. Mitchell (UK) 7.38m (24' 2½"); **4** T. Paice (UK) 7.07m (23' 2½").

Triple Jump: 1 A. Moore (UK) 15.65m (51' 4¼"); 2 W. Walther (WG) 14.95m (49' 0¾"); 3 F. Attoh (UK) 14.91m (48' 11"); 4 K. Wittmann (WG) 14.52m (47' 7¾").

Shot: 1 U. Gelhausen (WG) 16.17m (53' 0¾"); 2 K. Hohmann (WG) 15.92m (52' 2¾"); 3 S. Rodhouse (UK) 15.11m (49' 7"); 4 I. Lindley (UK) 14.65m (48' 0¾").

Discus: 1 T. Berlep (WG) 48.00m (157' 6"); 2 U. Kaminski (WG) 45.86m (150' 5"); 3 J. Howell (UK) 45.38m (148' 11"); 4 R. Slaney (UK) 44.56m (146' 2").

Hammer: 1 K. Ploghaus (WG) 60.60m (198' 10"); 2 R. Klein (WG) 58.00m (190' 3"); 3 P. Scott (UK) 53.92m (176' 11"); 4 M. Mileham (UK) 50.30m (165' 0").

Javelin: 1 C. Clover (UK) 76.06m (249' 6"); 2 M. Rupprecht (WG) 70.12m (230' 1"); 3 D. Ottley (UK) 69.82m (229' 1"); 4 G. Baur (WG) 67.34m (220' 11").

4 × 100m Relay: 1 West Germany 40.8; 2 UK (G. Edwards, R. Meredith, L. Hoyte, S. Green) 41.1.

4 × 400m Relay: 1 UK (R. Benn, M. Clark, C. Van Rees, R. Jenkins) 3:14.1; 2 West Germany 3:14.6.
Match Result: West Germany 124, UK 97.

GIRLS

100m: 1 S. Lannaman (UK) 11.8; 2 U. Weichenthal (WG) 12.1; 3 J. Walsh (UK) 12.4; 4 B. Holzapfel (WG) 12.5.

200m: 1 C. Schniggendiller (WG) 24.4; 2 C. Steger (WG) 24.5; 3 E. Douglas (UK) 24.8; 4 A. McClelland (UK) 25.3.

400m: 1 R. Kennedy (UK) 53.8; 2 W. Hill (UK) 54.4; 3 B. Bruckner (WG) 57.2; 4 K. Schubert (WG) 59.1.

800m: 1 U. Fischer (WG) 2:09.4; 2 C. McMeekin (UK) 2:09.5; 3 K. Colebrook (UK) 2:10.8; 4 M. Siegl (WG) 2:10.8.

1500m: 1 B. Kraus (WG) 4:22.1; 2 M. Stewart (UK) 4:26.2; 3 R. Morrish (UK) 4:29.5; 4 B. Dzuibany (WG) 4:49.3.

100m Hurdles: 1 H. Xalter (WG) 14.8; 2 E. Eddy (UK) 15.1; 3 S. Mapstone (UK) 15.1; 4 M. Nissl (WG) 16.8.

High Jump: 1 A. Wolf (WG) 1.73m (5' 8"); 2 I. Scholz (WG) 1.73m (5' 8"); 3 F. Stacey (UK) 1.73m (5' 8"); 4 A. Gilson (UK) 1.65m (5' 5").

Long Jump: 1 C. Lemkamp (WG) 6.35m (20' 10"); 2 G. Hetzel (WG) 6.15m (20' 2¼"); 3 S. Mapstone (UK) 6.13m (20' 1¼"); 4 J. Bowerman (UK) 5.76m (18' 10¾").

Shot: 1 J. Weide (WG) 13.50m (44' 3½"); 2 S. Demuth (WG) 12.36m (40' 6¾"); 3 V. Head (UK) 11.92m (39' 1¼"); 4 J. Oakes (UK) 11.54m (37' 10¼").

Discus: 1 L. Mallin (UK) 45.34m (148' 9"); 2 K. Eilers (WG) 40.78m (133' 9"); 3 E. Klebert (WG) 40.06m (131' 5"); 4 K. Mallard (UK) 38.96m (127' 10").

Javelin: 1 T. Sanderson (UK) 52.50m (172' 3"); 2 S. Wosch (WG) 51.64m (169' 5"); 3 E. Holmschmidt (WG) 47.74m (156' 7"); 4 J. King (UK) 41.04m (134' 8").

4 × 100m Relay: 1 UK (J. Walsh, D. Heath, A. McClelland, S. Lannaman) 45.6; 2 West Germany 45.8.

4 × 400m Relay: 1 UK (K. Colebrook, A. Clarkson, W. Hill, R. Kennedy) 3:40.1; 2 West Germany 3:48.7.
Match Result: West Germany 71, UK 64.

20, 21 September

PYE GOLD CUP FINAL

Cardiff AAC underlined their position as Britain's foremost athletic club by winning the Pye Gold Cup at Crystal Palace. British League champions for the past three seasons, Cardiff did not enter for the inaugural cup competition in 1973, but this time they set about the task in their usual efficient fashion and toppled cup-holders Wolverhampton & Bilston AC by six points after a ding-dong struggle. The Welsh club supplied only three individual winners – Dave Roberts (100 metres), Berwyn Price (110 metres hurdles), and Mike Butterfield (high jump)

– but it was their all-round strength that won the day. Second place was gained in five events and third position in four events.

Among several worthy performances was a Scottish 400 metres hurdles record of 51.6 by Norm Gregor, followed only 1¾ hours later by a personal best 800 metres of 1:49.4; Berwyn Price's 14.0 high hurdles on a rainsoaked track; and a high jump contest which saw three athletes clear 2.03 metres (6' 8"), including 16-year-old Brian Burgess.

The first ever British Women's Club Cup, an important development, was carried off by Mitcham AC. Tessa Sanderson tied her UK junior javelin record of 54.10 metres (177' 6").

MEN

100m: 1 D. Roberts (C) 10.7; **2** R. Kennedy (W&B) 11.0; **3 eq** I. Saunders (Sale) & D. Cole (TVH) 11.1; **5** A. McMaster (EAC) 11.2; **6** G. Hignett (Stret) 11.2; **7** D. Hislop (ESH) 11.3; **8** A. Gillies (H) 11.3.

200m: 1 R. Jenkins (EAC) 21.6; **2** R. Kennedy (W&B) 21.9; **3** I. Saunders (Sale) 21.9; **4** G. Hignett (Stret) 21.9; **5** I. Matthews (TVH) 22.1; **6** A. Gillies (H) 22.4; **7** M. Delaney (C) 22.5; **8** D. Hislop (ESH) 22.7.

400m: 1 G. Cohen (W&B) 47.2; **2** I. Saunders (Sale) 47.4; **3** M. Delaney (C) 48.3; **4** P. Hoffmann (EAC) 48.8; **5** M. Francis (Stret) 49.6; **6** N. Wade (H) 50.0.

800m: 1 A. Settle (Sale) 1:48.4; **2** N. Gregor (EAC) 1:49.4; **3** A. Gibson (H) 1:50.2; **4** R. Weatherburn (ESH) 1:50.4; **5** M. Edwards (W&B) 1:51.1; **6** C. Cusick (Stret) 1:52.3; **7** R. Yarrow (C) 1:52.9.

1500m: 1 A. Settle (Sale) 3:47.2; **2** C. Thomas (TVH) 3:48.1; **3** R. Weatherburn (ESH) 3:49.1; **4** R. Knowles (EAC) 3:52.8; **5** John Brown (H) 3:52.9; **6** P. Ratcliffe (C) 3:54.3; **7** D. Guest (W&B) 3:57.3.

5000m: 1 eq J. Davies (TVH) & J. Dingwall (EAC) 14:13.8; **3** B. Plain (C) 14:16.6; **4** L. Reilly (Sale) 14:20.6; **5** T. Jeffries (W&B) 14:30.4; **6** N. Bailey (ESH) 14:53.2; **7** T. Parker (Stret) 14:57.0.

10,000m: 1 A. Moore (H) 29:20.6; **2** A. Hutton (ESH) 29:36.8; **3** S. Edmunds (Sale) 29:56.6; **4** M. Critchley (C) 30:14.4; **5** G. Dugdale (TVH) 30:53.8; **6** D. Gunstone (EAC) 31:06.0; **7** H. Elder (W&B) 31:21.6.

3000m Steeplechase: 1 J. Davies (TVH) 8:36.2; **2** I. Gilmour (W&B) 8:45.4; **3** R. McAndrew (C) 8:53.4; **4** P. Gaytor (Sale) 9:19.4; **5** N. Bailey (ESH) 9:20.6; **6** P. Griffiths (H) 9:29.6; **7** R. Morris (EAC) 9:38.4.

110m Hurdles: 1 B. Price (C) 14.0; **2** G. Gower (H) 14.7; **3** P. Kelly (W&B) 14.8; **4** S. McCallum (ESH) 15.2; **5** P. Hambley (Stret) 15.2.

400m Hurdles: 1 N. Gregor (EAC) 51.6; **2** A. James (Stret) 52.3; **3** S. McCallum (ESH) 52.7; **4** W. Leyshon (C) 52.8; **5** S. James (W&B) 53.8; **6** M. Ollier (S) 54.9; **7** I. Arnold (TVH) 55.5; **8** E. Shirley (Hill) 57.0.

High Jump: 1 M. Butterfield (C) 2.03m (6' 8"); **2** A. McKenzie (ESH) 2.03m (6' 8"); **3** B. Burgess (EAC) 2.03m (6' 8"); **4** M. Palmer (W&B) 2.00m (6' 6¾"); **5** T. Hoyte (TVH) 1.90m (6' 2¾"); **6** P. Hambley (Stret) 1.90m (6' 2¾"); **7** N. Edge (Sale) 1.85m (6' 0¾").

Pole Vault: 1 M. Bull (W&B) 4.80m (15' 9"); **2** D. Lease (C) 4.50m (14' 9"); **3** C. Kidd (Hill) 4.50m (14' 9"); **4** P. Goulding (TVH) 4.00m (13' 1½"); **5** R. Sinclair (ESH) 3.50m (11' 5¾").

Long Jump: 1 D. Cole (TVH) 7.32m (24' 0¼"); **2** G. Hignett (Stret) 7.28m (23' 10¾"); **3** S. Atkins (W&B) 7.15m (23' 5½"); **4** A. Wells (ESH) 6.87m (22' 6½"); **5** K. Morrison (EAC) 6.77m (22' 2½"); **6** R. Gyles (C) 6.73m (22' 1").

Triple Jump: 1 W. Clark (ESH) 15.36m (50' 4¾"); **2** S. Power (C) 15.05m (49' 4½"); **3** C. Kidd (Hill) 14.59m (47' 10½"); **4** P. Davies (TVH) 14.38m (47' 2¼"); **5** P. Walker (Sale) 14.35m (47' 1"); **6** M. Cannavan (W&B) 14.18m (46' 6¼"); **7** P. Hambley (Stret) 14.09m (46' 2¾"); **8** K. Morrison (EAC) 14.09m (46' 2¾").

Shot: 1 J. Watts (W&B) 15.16m (49' 9"); **2** H. Davidson (ESH) 15.01m (49' 3"); **3** J. Walters (C) 14.70m (48' 2¾"); **4** B. Williams (Stret) 14.45m (47' 5").

Discus: 1 J. Hillier (H) 53.72m (176' 3"); **2** G. Dirkin (Stret) 52.36m (171' 9"); **3** C. Black (ESH) 44.54m (146' 1"); **4** J. Walters (C) 43.52m (142' 9"); **5** S. Breen (TVH) 41.64m (136' 7").

PYE GOLD CUP FINAL

Hammer: 1 C. Black (ESH) 65.16m (213′ 9″); **2** P. Dickenson (H) 65.00m (213′ 3″); **3** W. Robertson (EAC) 52.58m (172′ 6″); **4** J. Watts (W&B) 52.16m (171′ 11″); **5** D. Bell (Sale) 48.94m (160′ 7″); **6** E. Lawlor (TVH) 46.58m (152′ 10″); **7** A. Davie (Card) 45.46m (149′ 2″); **8** G. Dirkin (Stret) 40.46m (132′ 9″).

Javelin: 1 P. Ostapowycz (Stret) 67.20m (220′ 6″); **2** G. Brooks (C) 58.94m (193′ 4″); **3** P. Ramsey (W&B) 58.00m (190′ 3″).

4 × 100m Relay: 1 Thames Valley Harriers 41.0; **2** Cardiff 41.5; **3** Wolverhampton & Bilston 41.6; **4** Edinburgh AC 41.9; **5** Stretford 42.0; **6** Sale 43.8; **7** Hillingdon 43.8. Edinburgh Southern Harriers disqualified.

4 × 400m Relay: 1 Edinburgh AC 3:12.5; **2** Cardiff 3:12.9; **3** Sale 3:15.0; **4** Wolverhampton & Bilston 3:16.2; **5** Stretford 3:16.6; **6** Thames Valley Harriers 3:20.1; **7** Edinburgh Southern Harriers 3:20.7; **8** Hillingdon 3:21.2.

Final Scores: 1 Cardiff 113; **2** Wolverhampton & Bilston 107; **3** Edinburgh AC 94; **4** Edinburgh Southern Harriers 94; **5** Thames Valley Harriers 89½; **6** Sale 86½; **7** Stretford 76; **8** Hillingdon 75.

WOMEN

100m: 1 A. Lynch (M) 11.6; **2** H. Golden (ESH) 11.8; **3** A. Neil (LOAC) 12.3; **4** S. Colyear (S) 12.3; **5** S. Thomas (Bir) 12.5; **6** V. Bernard (W&B) 12.5.

200m: 1 H. Golden (ESH) 23.3; **2** A. Lynch (M) 23.9; **3** V. Bernard (W&B) 24.3; **4** D. Heath (S) 24.6; **5** B. Martin (LOAC) 25.2; **6** E. Eddy (Bir) 25.4.

400m: 1 V. Bernard (W&B) 53.0; **2** J. Roscoe (S) 53.2; **3** A. Littlejohn (ESH) 54.6; **4** L. Taylor (Ex) 56.0; **5** C. Stenhouse (Bris) 56.8; **6** J. Pawsey (M) 56.8; **7** J. Honick (Bris) 57.3; **8** D. Fitzgerald (LOAC) 58.6.

800m: 1 R. Wright (W&B) 2:06.7; **2** A. Clarkson (ESH) 2:08.8; **3** M. Sonner (LOAC) 2:09.8; **4** C. Tranter (S) 2:10.2; **5** L. Taylor (Ex) 2:10.3; **6** G. Dourass (Bir) 2:13.7; **7** S. Smith (Bris) 2:14.2; **8** A. Briscoe (M) 2:25.5.

1500m: 1 R. Wright (W&B) 4:26.1; **2** R. Morrish (Ex) 4:28.4; **3** C. Tranter (S) 4:30.9; **4** A. Briscoe (M) 4:36.2; **5** S. Smith (Bris) 4:46.3; **6** B. Lyall (ESH) 4:48.6; **7** S. Hassan (Bir) 4:51.5; **8** M. Sonner (LOAC) 4:55.4.

3000m: 1 A. Briscoe (M) 10:00.4; **2** S. Hassan (Bir) 10:10.4; **3** S. Aris (Bris) 10:22.2; **4** J. Asgill (S) 10:22.2; **5** J. Rice (Ex) 10:49.2.

100m Hurdles: 1 J. Vernon (M) 13.8; **2** S. Colyear (S) 14.5; **3** B. Ruttledge (Bris) 15.2; **4** M. Wells (ESH) 15.3; **5** T. Sanderson (W&B) 15.9.

High Jump: 1 R. Watt (ESH) 1.60m (5′ 3″); **2** D. Cooper (Bris) 1.60m (5′ 3″); **3** J. Bowerman (M) 1.60m (5′ 3″); **4** K. Allinson (S) 1.55m (5′ 1″); **5** L. Haysman (LOAC) 1.55m (5′ 1″); **6** T. Sanderson (W&B) 1.55m (5′ 1″).

Long Jump: 1 R. Martin-Jones (Bir) 6.26m (20′ 6½″); **2** A. Neil (LOAC) 5.88m (19′ 3½″); **3** L. Boothe (M) 5.84m (19′ 2″); **4** P. Williams (S) 5.80m (19′ 0¼″); **5** J. Jay (Bris) 5.76m (18′ 10¾″); **6** S. Lewis (W&B) 5.65m (18′ 6¼″); **7** S. Brodie (ESH) 5.34m (17′ 6¼″).

Shot: 1 B. Bedford (M) 14.56m (47′ 9¼″); **2** M. Ritchie (ESH) 13.30m (43′ 7¾″); **3** S. Reeve (Bir) 11.89m (39′ 0¼″); **4** M. Pulman (LOAC) 11.71m (38′ 5″); **5** A. Jackson (S) 10.19m (33′ 5¼″).

Discus: 1 M. Ritchie (ESH) 49.52m (162′ 5″); **2** J. Kerr (M) 43.04m (141′ 2″); **3** M. Pulman (LOAC) 36.94m (121′ 2″); **4** M. Pasquetti (Bir) 36.44m (119′ 7″).

Javelin: 1 T. Sanderson (W&B) 54.10m (177′ 6″); **2** A. King (Bir) 44.12m (144′ 9″); **3** S. Brodie (ESH) 42.50m (139′ 5″); **4** K. Skuse (Bris) 41.06m (134′ 8″); **5** M. Greenslade (Ex) 36.62m (120′ 2″); **6** C. Tripp (LOAC) 34.84m (114′ 4″).

4 × 100m Relay: 1 Mitcham 45.1; **2** Stretford 45.4; **3** Edinburgh Southern Harriers 46.3; **4** Wolverhampton & Bilston 47.0; **5** London Olympiades 47.7; **6** Birchfield 47.8; **7** Bristol 48.9; **8** Exeter 49.1.

4 × 400m Relay: 1 Wolverhampton & Bilston 3:38.8; **2** Edinburgh Southern Harriers 3:39.3; **3** Stretford 3:45.5; **4** Mitcham 3:47.2; **5** Birchfield 3:51.8; **6** London Olympiades 4:01.4; **7** Exeter 4:02.1; **8** Bristol 4:03.7.

Finals Results: 1 Mitcham 87; **2** Edinburgh Southern 83; **3** Wolverhampton & Bilston 76; **4** Stretford 69; **5** Birchfield 58; **6** London Olympiades 54; **7** Bristol 50; **8** Exeter 40.

25, 26 September

UK v FINLAND

Dual international matches may, as critics claim, be an outdated concept, and certainly they no longer attract big crowds in Britain. Nevertheless they can still generate excitement when the teams are closely matched. This was the case at Crystal Palace for the season's finale when Finland beat Britain in the men's match by a single point... and the women's encounter ended in a tie! That latter result is an indication of how Finland's women athletes have progressed in 1974 (together with a recession in British standards), for in the only previous clash, in 1972, Britain won by 82 points to 53. On that occasion the little known Riitta Salin and Nina Holmen came last in their events, the 200 and 1500 metres respectively. This time, as brand new European champions, Salin won the 200 and 400 metres plus a victorious 50.9 relay anchor, and Holmen took the 3000 metres. Two years can make a lot of difference to an athlete's career.

Chasing Salin home in all three races was Donna Murray, who ended an eventful season in fine style with times of 23.6 (finishing ahead of Mona-Lisa Pursiainen and Helen Golden), 52.0 (only a fifth of a second outside her UK record), and a 51.8 relay leg. Another meritorious British performance in the chilly conditions came from the admirably consistent Tessa Sanderson (18), who improved her national junior record to 55.04 metres (180' 7") for second place on the UK all-time javelin list. Rosemary Payne, who with husband Howard was making a final international appearance, bowed out with a win in the discus.

On the men's side, David Jenkins was his usual tower of strength with a 200/400 metres double and a winning relay anchor. Star of the Finnish team was Pekka Paivarinta, who made up in no uncertain manner for his poor showing in the Rome 5000 and 10,000 metres. On the first night he won the 5000 by almost 10 seconds from Olympic champion Lasse Viren; on the second he uncorked a 57.6 last lap in a personal best of 28:18.4 for 10,000.

MEN

100m: 1 D. Roberts (UK) 10.7; 2 R. Vilen (Fin) 10.7; 3 B. Green (UK) 10.9; 4 R. Raty (Fin) 10.9.

200m: 1 D. Jenkins (UK) 21.2; 2 O. Karttunen (Fin) 21.3; 3 S. Green (UK) 21.6; 4 M. Juhola (Fin) 22.0.

400m: 1 D. Jenkins (UK) 46.2; 2 O. Karttunen (Fin) 47.0; 3 R. Jenkins (UK) 47.4; 4 S. Lonnqvist (Fin) 48.5.

800m: 1 A. Settle (UK) 1:49.3; 2 P. Browne (UK) 1:49.5; 3 J. Honkanen (Fin) 1:49.8; 4 H. Hamalainen (Fin) 1:52.5.

1500m: 1 P. Vasala (Fin) 3:43.1; 2 R. Smedley (UK) 3:46.2; 3 K. Lumiaho (Fin) 3:50.2; 4 P. Banning (UK) 3:58.1.

5000m: 1 P. Paivarinta (Fin) 13:43.4; 2 L. Viren (Fin) 13:53.2; 3 C. Stewart (UK) 13:53.4; 4 A. Simmons (UK) 14:14.2.

10,000m: 1 P. Paivarinta (Fin) 28:18.4; 2 Jim Brown (UK) 28:23.8; 3 Grenville Tuck (UK) 28:25.8; 4 R. Holmen (Fin) 28:48.2.

3000m Steeplechase: 1 T. Kantanen (Fin) 8:34.4; 2 J. Bicourt (UK) 8:41.2; 3 J. Davies (UK) 8:53.0; 4 M. Pulkkinen (Fin) 8:59.2.

110m Hurdles: 1 B. Price (UK) 14.1; 2 A. Pascoe (UK) 14.3; 3 R. Alanen (Fin) 14.9; 4 P. Pursiainen (Fin) 14.9.

400m Hurdles: 1 W. Hartley (UK) 50.9; 2 S. Black (UK) 51.7; 3 R. Koivu (Fin) 52.0; 4 R. Alanen (Fin) 55.1.

UK V FINLAND

High Jump: 1 H. Sundell (Fin) 2.10m (6' 10¾"); **2** A. Personen (Fin) 2.06m (6' 9"); **3** C. Boreham (UK) 1.85m (6' 0¾"). M. Palmer (UK) failed at opening height.

Pole Vault: 1 A. Kalliomaki (Fin) 5.20m (17' 0¾"); **2** M. Bull (UK) 5.20m (17' 0¾"); **3** B. Hooper (UK) 5.10 (16' 8¾"); **4** V. Aartolahti (Fin) 5.00m (16' 4¾").

Long Jump: 1 A. Lerwill (UK) 7.61m (24' 11¾"); **2** H. Mattila (Fin) 7.60m (24' 11¼"); **3** T. Taavitsainen (Fin) 7.39m (24' 3"); **4** G. Hignett (UK) 7.26m (23' 10").

Triple Jump: 1 P. Kuukasjarvi (Fin) 15.84m (51' 11¾"); **2** D. Johnson (UK) 15.52m (50' 11"); **3** A. Moore (UK) 15.21m (49' 11"); **4** J. Maki-Maunus (Fin) 15.17m (49' 9¼").

Shot: 1 R. Stahlberg (Fin) 19.96m (65' 6"); **2** M. Winch (UK) 18.98m (62' 3½"); **3** M. Yrjola (Fin) 18.66m (61' 2¾"); **4** W. Tancred (UK) 18.46m (60' 6¾").

Discus: 1 P. Kahma (Fin) 59.80m (196' 2"); **2** J. Rinne (Fin) 58.24m (191' 1"); **3** W. Tancred (UK) 56.84m (186' 6"); **4** J. Hillier (UK) 54.68m (179' 5").

Hammer: 1 H. Kangas (Fin) 69.70m (228' 8"); **2** I. Chipchase (UK) 69.46m (227' 11"); **3** R. Miettinen (Fin) 69.34m (227' 6"); **4** H. Payne (UK) 68.78m (225' 8").

Javelin: 1 H. Siitonen (Fin) 84.56m (277' 5"); **2** S. Hovinen (Fin) 82.86m (271' 10"); **3** D. Travis (UK) 79.02m (259' 3"); **4** K. Sheppard (UK) 76.68m (251' 7").

4 × 100m Relay: 1 UK (D. Roberts, A. Lerwill, B. Cole, B. Green) 41.3; Finland disqualified.

4 × 400m Relay: 1 UK (R. Jenkins, W. Hartley, A. Pascoe, D. Jenkins) 3:06.7; **2** Finland 3:06.9.

Match Result: Finland 105, UK 104.

WOMEN

100m: 1 M-L. Pursiainen (Fin) 11.5; **2** S. Lannaman (UK) 11.5; **3** H. Golden (UK) 11.9; **4** U. Lax (Fin) 12.4.

200m: 1 R. Salin (Fin) 23.5; **2** D. Murray (UK) 23.6; **3** M-L. Pursiainen (Fin) 23.7; **4** H. Golden (UK) 24.0.

400m: 1 R. Salin (Fin) 51.5; **2** D. Murray (UK) 52.0; **3** R. Kennedy (UK) 53.5; **4** P. Wilmi (Fin) 53.9.

800m: 1 R. Wright (UK) 2:06.1; **2** M. Coomber (UK) 2:07.1; **3** S. Haapakoski (Fin) 2:11.3; **4** P. Vihonen (Fin) 2:11.8.

1500m: 1 S. Tyynela (Fin) 4:21.2; **2** P. Yeoman (UK) 4:23.3; **3** R. Wright (UK) 4:24.7; **4** A. Wirkberg (Fin) 4:33.9.

3000m: 1 N. Holmen (Fin) 9:12.4; **2** J. Smith (UK) 9:18.0; **3** A. Yeoman (UK) 9:23.8; **4** S. Tyynela (Fin) 9:36.8.

100m Hurdles: 1 L. Drysdale (UK) 13.9; **2** U. Lempiainen (Fin) 14.2; **3** M. Nimmo (UK) 14.6; **4** P. Taimisto (Fin) 15.0.

High Jump: 1 B. Lawton (UK) 1.80m (5' 10¾"); **2** R. Watt (UK) 1.75m (5' 8¾"); **3 eq** E. Kelo (Fin) & S. Sundqvist (Fin) 1.70m (5' 7").

Long Jump: 1 P. Helenius (Fin) 6.16m (20' 2½"); **2** R. Martin-Jones (UK) 6.09m (19' 11¾"); **3** T. Rautanen (Fin) 5.88m (19' 3½"); **4** A. Wilson (UK) 5.80m (19' 0½").

Shot: 1 C. Barck (Fin) 15.84m (51' 11¾"); **2** R. Metso (Fin) 15.71m (51' 6½"); **3** B. Bedford (UK) 15.09m (49' 6¼"); **4** J. Kerr (UK) 14.07m (46' 2").

Discus: 1 R. Payne (UK) 52.56m (172' 5"); **2** M. Ritchie (UK) 51.36m (168' 6"); **3** R. Metso (Fin) 50.98m (167' 3"); **4** S. Riihela (Fin) 50.80m (166' 8").

Javelin: 1 A. Mustakallio (Fin) 55.54m (182' 3"); **2** T. Sanderson (UK) 55.04m (180' 7"); **3** P. Kumpulainen (Fin) 54.60m (179' 1"); **4** A. Goodlad (UK) 46.58m (152' 10").

4 × 100m Relay: 1 UK (S. Colyear, L. Barratt, H. Golden, S. Lannaman) 45.0; **2** Finland 46.1.

4 × 400m Relay: 1 Finland 3:32.3; **2** UK (W. Hill, E. Barnes, R. Kennedy, D. Murray) 3:33.3.

Match Result: UK 73, Finland 73.

28, 29 September

FRANCE v UK DECATHLON/PENTATHLON

Yves Le Roy, the European silver medallist, led the French team to a crushing victory over Britain's decathletes at Stade Colombes, Paris, with a national record score of 8229 points, second highest in the world for 1974. There were encouraging personal best scores, though, for Alan Drayton and Roy Mitchell – over 7000 for the first time. Mitchell's score was a UK junior record – and he set lifetime bests in every event bar two, the discus and pole vault! Sue Wright won the pentathlon with her highest ever score, including personal bests in the hurdles, long jump, and 200 metres.

DECATHLON

1 Y. Le Roy (Fra) 8229pts: 10.9; 7.44m (24′ 5″); 14.59m (47′ 10½″); 1.96m (6′ 5″); 48.4; 14.7; 46.50m (152′ 7″); 4.70m (15′ 5″); 64.66m (212′ 2″); 4:41.9.

2 P. Bobin (Fra) 7636; **3** J-P. Schoebel (Fra) 7451; **4** M. Le Rouge (Fra) 7396; **5** A. Drayton (UK) 7127; **6** R. Mitchell (UK) 7088; **7** M. Pradet (Fra) 6972; **8** E. Sveinsson (Ice) 6884; **9** D. Millepied (Fra) 6852; **10** M. Corden (UK) 6801; **11** C. Youngs (UK) 6676; **12** K. Fredriksen (Ice) 6619; **13** V. Vilhjamason (Ice) 6428; **14** H. Johanneson (Ice) 6349; **15** N. Phipps (UK) 6319; **16** R. Snow (UK) 5881.

Teams: 1 France 30,712pts; **2** UK 27,692pts; **3** Iceland 26,280 pts.

JUNIORS

1 G. Delaune (Fra) 6642; **2** G. Loigerot (Fra) 6534; **3** J-C. Rheder (Fra) 6395; **4** W. Dubose (UK) 6192; **5** P. Sellier (Fra) 6159; **6** M. Hay (UK) 5927; **7** G. Richards (UK) 5381; J. Howell (UK) did not finish.

Teams: 1 France 19,571pts; **2** UK 17,500pts.

PENTATHLON

1 S. Wright (UK) 4192pts: 14.1; 9.67m (31′ 8¾″); 1.72m (5′ 7¾″); 6.18m (20′ 3½″); 24.7.

2 F. Picaut (Fra) 4108; **3** S. Mapstone (UK) 3999; **4** P. Chapman (UK) 3914; **5** G. Borfiga (Fra) 3871; **6** V. Dumon (Fra) 3825.

Teams: 1 UK 12,105pts; **2** France 11,814pts.

SEPTEMBER HIGHLIGHTS

British marathon international, John Newsome, completed an iron-man double by winning the South London Harriers' 30 miles road race in 2:46.49 on 7 September and the Road Runners Club's London to Brighton 52¾ miles run in 5:16.07 only 22 days later. In an extraordinarily close finish to such a long race, Newsome crossed the line in Brighton just six seconds ahead of Cavin Woodward.

There were two performances of top world class in the 7th Asian Games, at Teheran (Iran) from 9 to 15 September: a 2.21 metres (7′ 3″) high jump by the host nation's Teymour Ghiassi, and an Asian long jump record of 8.07 metres (26′ 5¾″) by T. C. Yohannan of India. China returned to the international fold, their athletes winning 21 medals to rank second to Japan (32).

SEPTEMBER HIGHLIGHTS

Winners: Men: *100m/200m:* A. Ratanapol (Thai) 10.42/21.09; *400m:* W. Wimaladase (Sri Lanka) 46.21; *800m:* Sri Ram Singh (Ind) 1:47.6; *1500m:* M. Younis (Pak) 3:49.3; *5000m:* Shivnath Singh (Ind) 14:20.6; *10,000m:* Y. Hamada (Jap) 30:50.0; *3000m Steeplechase:* T. Koyama (Jap) 8:58.0; *110m Hurdles:* Tsui Lin (Chi) 14.26; *400m Hurdles:* T.F. Al-Saffar (Iraq) 51.69; *4×100m Relay:* Thailand 40.14; *4×400m Relay:* Sri Lanka 3:07.4; *High Jump:* T. Ghiassi (Iran) 2.21m (7′ 3″); *Pole Vault:* Y. Kigawa (Jap) 5.00m (16′ 4¾″); *Long Jump:* T.C. Yohannan (Ind) 8.07m (26′ 5¾″); *Triple Jump:* T. Inoue (Jap) 16.45m (53′ 11¾″); *Shot/Discus:* D-A. Keshmiri (Iran) 18.04m (59′ 2¼″) & 56.82m (186′ 5″); *Hammer:* S. Murofushi (Jap) 66.54m (218′ 4″); *Javelin:* T. Yamada (Jap) 76.12m (249′ 9″); *Decathlon:* V. S. Chuhan (Ind) 7375.
Women: *100m/200m/100m Hurdles:* E. Rot (Isr) 11.90/23.79/13.31; *400m:* Chee Swee Lee (Sin) 55.08; *800m:* N. Kawano (Jap) 2:08.1; *1500m:* Sun Mei-hua (Chi) 4:28.7; *Relays:* Japan 46.62/3:43.5; *High Jump:* O. Abramovich (Isr) 1.78m (5′ 10″); *Long Jump:* Hsiao Chieh-ping (Chi) 6.31m (20′ 8½″); *Shot:* Ok Ja Paik (SK) 16.28m (53′ 5″); *Discus:* Kao Yu-kuei (Chi) 51.84m (170′ 1″); *Javelin:* Chou Mao-chia (Chi) 53.06m (174′ 1″); *Pentathlon:* K. Shimizu (Jap) 3890.

Newly crowned European hammer champion, Aleksey Spiridonov (Sov), achieved another great success four days after his victory in Rome by breaking the world record with 76.66 metres (251′ 6″) in Munich on 11 September. At the same meeting, on the following day, Andrea Lynch defeated world record holder Renate Stecher (EG) over 100 metres, 11.29 to 11.38. The Olympic champion lost two metres at the start and was able to catch up only half that margin.

Ilona Schoknecht (EG) again improved the world junior shot record in Berlin on 15 September; she reached 19.23 metres (63′ 1¼″). The senior world record fell to Helena Fibingerova, the Czech girl who placed third in Rome, with 21.57 metres (70′ 9¼″) at Gottwaldov on 21 September. The record came in the first round and she attained 21.37 metres (70′ 1½″) two puts later.

Lilyana Tomova powers past Gunhild Hoffmeister for the European 800 metres title and record.

Alfons Brijdenbach (Bel), whose elimination from his 400 metres semi-final was one of the big shocks of the European Championships, bounced back with a European 300 metres best of 32.2 at Bad Durrheim (WG) on 22 September, ahead of Karl Honz (WG) and David Jenkins (UK), the gold and silver medallists in Rome.

Marion Fawkes, the individual winner in 25:01, led England to victory in an international 5000 metres walking race at Rouen on 22 September. England scored 37 points to defeat Sweden (35), France (28), Switzerland (11), and Spain (10).

Edinburgh Athletic Club broke all known records when their 10-man team, running one mile each at a time, covered 297 miles 1145 yards in 24 hours of continuous running at Meadowbank Stadium, Edinburgh, on 28, 29 September. Their average was 4:50.9 per mile.

Ray Middleton (38), a British international since 1961, broke one of the oldest records on the books when he walked 53 miles 352 yards (85,618m) in the Accolade 8 hours track event at Haringey on 29 September. Ken Harding and John Lees also broke the previous record of 51 miles 1042 yards (83,029m) set in 1935 by Harold Whitlock. Middleton lapped the track 214 times!

The IAAF banned the somersault style of long jumping known as the 'flip', which they considered dangerous and not within the spirit of long jumping. The technique, evolved by American coach Tom Ecker, calls for the jumper to take advantage of the natural forward rotation created at take-off by performing a forward somersault in the air, landing in much the same manner as in conventional long jumping. The longest distance

Belgium's Alfons Brijdenbach.

achieved with the style is 7.79 metres (25′ 6¾″) by New Zealander John Delamere.

Maureen Dyson, who as 19-year-old Maureen Gardner failed only by inches to win the Olympic 80 metres hurdles title at Wembley in 1948, died after a long illness at the age of 45. The wife of former AAA chief national coach Geoff Dyson, Maureen gained another silver medal behind Holland's Fanny Blankers-Koen at the 1950 European Championships. Her best time was 11.2, plus a wind-assisted 11.1.

OCTOBER HIGHLIGHTS

In a thrilling finish, Keith Angus (UK) won the Kosice marathon in Czechoslovakia on 6 October in a personal best time of 2:20:09. He entered the stadium 30 metres behind Joachim Truppel (EG) but outsprinted him to win by a similar margin.

Allan Seatory, German resident but British qualified, became the second UK discus thrower (after Bill Tancred) to exceed 200 feet. He recorded 61.00 metres (200′ 1″) at Bremerhaven on 6 October.

Result of the AAA National Six-Stage Road Relay at Wimbledon on 19 October:

1 Liverpool Harriers 1:44:08; **2** Invicta AC 1:44:50; **3** Cardiff AAC 1:45:04; **4** Sheffield United H 1:45:40; **5** Tipton H 1:45:48; **6** City of Stoke AC 1:46:05. Fastest lap (3¾ miles) times were 16:51 by Dave Black, 16:52 by Keith Penny, and 17:00 by Kevin Steere.

Two remarkable long jumping performances were achieved at an international meeting in Rio from 25 to 27 October. Nedo Stekic (Yug), the European silver medallist, came close to the European record with a leap of 8.24 metres (27′ 0½″), while the indestructible Willye White (USA) – Olympic silver medallist at Melbourne in 1956 when she was 17 – defeated an all-star field with 6.50 metres (21′ 4″).

Nineteen-year-old French girl, Chantal Langlace, established a world's best marathon time of 2:46:24 at Neuf Brisach (Fra) on 27 October in a race won by Welshman Dic Evans in 2:18:33. The previous day, at Essen, Christa Vahlensieck, née Kofferschlager, of West Germany had been timed in 2:42:38 – but the course was found to be 745 metres (some three minutes) short.

One of the most colourful competitors of the 1950s, José Telles da Conceicao of Brazil, who was Olympic high jump bronze medallist in 1952 and a 200 metres finalist four years later (he had run 100 metres in 10.2), was shot dead in Rio. He was 43.

NOVEMBER HIGHLIGHTS

Mick Mulloy, from the Republic of Ireland, led throughout to break the world's best time for 30 miles held by Jeff Julian (NZ) with 2:47:34. Running at Walton-on-Thames on 2 November he completed the track run in 2:44:47. Don Ritchie, runner-up in 2:49:38, became only the fourth man ever to better 2 hours 50 minutes.

European medallist Joyce Smith anchored Barnet & District AC to victory in the Women's National Road Relay Championship at Derby on 9 November.

Result: 1 Barnet & District 30:17; **2** Feltham 30:44; **3** Stretford 31:05; **4** Birchfield 32:07; **5** Aldershot Farnham & District 32:12; **6** Airedale & Spen Valley 32:50. *Fastest laps:* J. Smith 9:49, P. Yeoman 10:05, C. Tranter 10:09. **Intermediate Relay: 1** Pitreavie 24:10; **2** City of Stoke 24:30; **3** Aldershot Farnham & District 24:37. *Fastest lap:* A. Tunnicliffe 7:42. **Junior Relay: 1** Pitreavie 19:35; **2** Derby Ladies 19:37; **3** Aldershot Farnham & District 19:59. *Fastest lap:* R. Smeeth 6:25. **Minors Relay: 1** Aldershot Farnham & District 20:38; **2** Sale 21:03; **3** Bromsgrove 21:06. *Fastest lap:* A. Edwards 6:37.

Nick Rose, a British student at the University of Western Kentucky, won the American National Collegiate cross-country title in 29:22 at Bloomington, Indiana, on 25 November. He beat John Ngeno (Ken), who went on to win the American AAU championship a few days later, by a margin of 15 seconds.

Former European and Commonwealth champion Ron Hill (UK) finished seven minutes ahead of the closest of over 600 rivals in the Maryland marathon at Baltimore on 30 November. He clocked 2:17:23 in freezing conditions.

DECEMBER HIGHLIGHTS

Chantal Langlace's women's marathon record, reported in October highlights, was eclipsed on 1 December when Jacki Hansen, a 26-year-old American who runs 100 miles a week in training, was timed at 2:43:54.6 at Culver City, California. She finished 34th in a race won by Mario Cuezas of Mexico in 2:18:08.8.

Marion Fawkes, the dominant figure in British women's race walking, was a very comfortable winner of the National Road Walk Championship at Quinton on 7 December.

Result: **1** M. Fawkes 27:25; **2** P. Branson 28:14; **3** V. Lovell 28:41; **4** C. Coleman 28:55; **5** S. Booth 29:00; **6** S. Saunders 29:29; **7** K. Hill 29:42; **8** S. De Giovanni 29:59; **9** E. Smith 30:26; **10** S. Wish 30:32. **Team:** Harborne.

Olympic champion Frank Shorter (USA) notched up yet another international marathon triumph on 8 December as he won the Fukuoka classic in Japan for the fourth year running. His time was a fast 2:11:31.2 and he was followed in by Eckhard Lesse (EG) 2:12:02.4, Pekka Paivarinta (Fin) 2:13:09.0, Terry Manners (NZ) 2:13:11.2, and Britain's globe-trotting Chris Stewart, who clocked 2:13:11.8 as against 2:28:45 in his only previous marathon attempt.

Another of Britain's distance running Stewarts, Ian Stewart, made a successful return to international racing after turning his attentions to cycling. The former European and Commonwealth 5000 metres champion won a 4½ miles event at Gateshead on 14 December against one of the finest international fields ever assembled for a British cross-country race.

Result: **1** I. Stewart (UK) 23:21; **2** K. Boro (Nor) 23:23; **3** D. Black (UK) 23:35; **4** B. Foster (UK) 23:37; **5** M. Baxter (UK) 23:46; **6** Grenville Tuck (UK) 23:49.

The first world's best performance of the new indoor season fell to Britain's Verona Bernard at Cosford on 14 December. She clipped half a second off the 600 metres mark held by Waltraud Dietsch (EG) when recording 1:29.0. Andrea Lynch equalled her UK indoor 60 metres best of 7.2.

Rune Almen (Swe) set a world's best of 1.80 metres (5' 10¾") for the standing high jump at Orebro on 8 December. His best conventional leap is 2.23 metres (7' 3¾").

1974 English Schools Championships

Some 1800 competitors took part in the English Schools Championships at Shrewsbury on 12, 13 July. The cross-country championships were staged at Cheltenham on 2 March (girls) and Brighton on 23 March (boys), and the walking championships at Redditch on 11 May.

SENIOR BOYS

100m: 1 A. Gillies (Bucks) 11.2; **2** G. Moore (Yks) 11.3; **3** B. White (Sy) 11.4; **4** N. Sheffrin (Herts) 11.4; **5** J. Jakenfelds (Mx) 11.5; **6** L. Goucoul (Glos) 11.5.
200m: 1 P. Lavender (Sy) 22.2; **2** R. Sanderson (Camb) 22.6; **3** A. Bell (Yks) 22.7; **4** M. Mannell (Herts) 23.0; **5** N. Schoolcraft (Worcs) 23.0; **6** A. Gregory (Cumb) 23.2.
400m: 1 B. Jones (Lancs) 48.2 (*Championship best*); **2** C. Van Rees (Ex) 49.2; **3** R. Ashton (Corn) 49.4; **4** A. Cearns (Ex) 49.5; **5** B. Davey (Sy) 50.3; **6** P. Bray (Corn) 50.5.
800m: 1 M. Naldrett (Ches) 1:53.8; **2** J. Goodacre (Notts) 1:54.7; **3** M. Wilson (Som) 1:55.2; **4** P. Jerrum (Kt) 1:55.5; **5** C. Bewick (Dur) 1:55.9; **6** G. Parsons (Glos) 1:56.3.
1500m: 1 S. Emson (Stffs) 3:52.2; **2** R. Callan (Leics) 3:53.7; **3** P. Williams (Kt) 3:55.7; **4** M. Prince (Yks) 3:59.1; **5** P. Gaytor (Lancs) 4:01.4; **6** T. Butt (Herts) 4:02.8.
5000m: 1 M. Gratton (Kt) 14:52.4; **2** M. Deegan (Lancs) 14:59.6; **3** K. Dumpleton (Herts) 15:08.4; **4** M. Plant (Ches) 15:10.8; **5** C. Tidmarsh (W'morland) 15:12.6; **6** B. Dawkins (Hants) 15:13.0.
2000m Steeplechase: 1 D. Warren (Sy) 5:57.0; **2** S. Anning (Dev) 6:02.8; **3** V. LeGrand (Glos) 6:04.8; **4** D. Purcell (Sy) 6:07.0; **5** P. Gaden (Dev) 6:08.6; **6** L. George (Lancs) 6:08.6.
110m Hurdles: 1 M. Hatton (Berks) 15.3; **2** R. Parkinson (Mx) 15.4; **3** R. Honey (Ex) 15.4; **4** M. Kyle-Millward (Kt) 15.5; **5** K. Cheong (Lon) 15.5; **6** J. Roberts (Stffs) fell (15.0 heat).
400m Hurdles: 1 R. Harris (Hants) 55.2; **2** N. Chislett (Som) 55.4; **3** C. Lynch (Kt) 55.4; **4** E. Shirley (Mx) 56.2; **5** T. Birtles (Ches) 56.3; **6** C. Shaw (Leics) 57.4.
4 × 100m Relay: 1 Essex 44.5; **2** Buckinghamshire 45.1; **3** Middlesex 45.1; **4** Cumberland 45.1; Yorkshire disqualified (44.0 heat).
High Jump: 1 A. Dainton (Ex) 1.97m (6' 5½"); **2** G. Vose (Sy) 1.94m (6' 4¼"); **3** C. Meade (Sy) 1.94m (6' 4¼"); **4 eq:** R. Berry (Herts) and W. Innes (Ches) 1.89m (6' 2¼"); **6** B. Gorman (Som) 1.84m (6' 0½").
Pole Vault: 1 C. Boreham (Herts) 4.20m (13' 9¼"); **2** K. Homer (Stffs) 3.66m (12' 0"); **3** A. Baker (Stffs) 3.66m (12' 0"); **4** E. Woloczyn (Bucks) 3.58m (11' 9"); **5** S. Skill (Notts) 3.39m (11' 1½").
Long Jump: 1 D. Bryan (Lincs) 6.86m (22' 6¼"); **2** S. Pegler (Ches) 6.63m (21' 9"); **3** H. McLean (Ex) 6.51m (21' 4¼"); **4** T. Wade (Lon) 6.51m (21' 4¼"); **5** W. O'Brien (Wks) 6.51m (21' 4¼"); **6** S. Poulton (Ex) 6.46m (21' 2½").
Triple Jump: 1 G. Doerr (Sy) 14.77m (48' 5½"); **2** J. Ritchie (Worcs) 14.03m (46' 0½"); **3** C. Carden (Kt) 13.89m (45' 7"); **4** J. Davis (Ex) 13.88m (45' 6¼"); **5** S. Ashdown (Beds) 13.80m (45' 3½"); **6** N. Thrower (Dur) 13.78m (45' 2½").
Shot: 1 I. Lindley (Yks) 15.63m (51' 3½"); **2** M. Eyres (Ex) 14.43m (47' 4¼"); **3** V. Cuss (Som) 13.66m (44' 9¾"); **4** P. Myers (Dev) 13.41m (44' 0"). Only four competitors.

ATHLETICS 75

Discus: **1** C. Burns (Ex) 45.76m (150′ 1″); **2** R. Wheway (Som) 44.18m (144′ 11″); **3** P. Collins (Kt) 41.38m (135′ 9″); **4** N. Scragg (Kt) 41.34m (135′ 7″); **5** T. Rupar (Lancs) 39.10m (128′ 3″); **6** R. Hammond (Ches) 37.88m (124′ 3″).
Hammer: **1** E. Lawlor (Lon) 51.44m (168′ 9″); **2** M. Fenton (Suff) 49.30m (161′ 9″); **3** C. Preston (Ches) 48.22m (158′ 2″); **4** T. Minns (Camb) 45.50m (149′ 3″); **5** B. Reed (Ches) 45.30m (148′ 7″); **6** J. Thompson (Sx) 42.64m (139′ 11″).
Javelin: **1** P. Yates (Dev) 65.34m (214′ 4″); **2** C. Taylor (Mx) 58.90m (193′ 3″); **3** N. Wade (Lon) 58.44m (191′ 9″); **4** G. Brooks (Som) 58.18m (190′ 10″); **5** S. Ladds (Lincs) 56.98m (186′ 11″); **6** J. Trower (Sx) 52.34m (171′ 9″).
Winning County: Essex.
Cross-Country: **1** K. Dumpleton (Herts) 24:42; **2** M. Longthorn (Yks) 24:54; **3** I. Ray (Wilts) 24:55; **4** K. Steere (Norf) 25:11; **5** S. Emson (Stffs) 25:14; **6** P. Gayter (Lancs) 25:16. *Team:* Yorkshire.
10,000m Walk: **1** P. Dodd (Wks) 49:12; **2** D. Brewster (Cumb) 50:29; **3** M. Angrove (Wks) 51:36; **4** J. Mersh (Som) 51:48; **5** M. Bennett (Mx) 52:18; **6** I. Slatter (Sy) 52:53. *Team:* Warwickshire.

INTERMEDIATE BOYS

100m: **1** D. Hill (Mx) 11.0; **2** G. Ladlow (Ex) 11.3; **3** D. Bunce (Dur) 11.3; **4** D. Baptist (Lon) 11.3; **5** S. Burgen (Sy) 11.4; **6** I. Cooper (Hants) 11.4.
200m: **1** D. Henry (Wks) 22.9; **2** C. Beswick (Notts) 22.9; **3** S. Mynard (Leics) 22.9; **4** F. Thompson (Sx) 23.0; **5** M. Marsh (Wilts) 23.2; **6** M. Kinsey (Ches) 23.2.
400m: **1** M. Francis (Lancs) 49.8; **2** D. Bluemink (Yks) 49.9; **3** S. Moriarty (Sy) 51.0; **4** J. Lay (Ex) 51.0; **5** G. Whittock (Som) 51.3; **6** K. Duddy (N'land) 51.5.
800m: **1** M. Edwards (Stffs) 1:55.3; **2** G. Cook (Stffs) 1:55.6; **3** S. Greaves (Herts) 1:57.2; **4** S. Caldwell (Lancs) 1:57.6; **5** D. Arnold (Berks) 1:58.2; **6** C. Pascoe (Ex) 1:58.8.
1500m: **1** M. Bateman (Lancs) 3:58.4; **2** G. Power (Leics) 3:59.6; **3** M. Rose (Wks) 4:01.1; **4** N. Leach (Sx) 4:01.9; **5** S. Gilbey (Lon) 4:03.2; **6** P. Boswell (Ches) 4:05.5.
3000m: **1** N. Lees (Dby) 8:37.2; **2** N. Martin (Hants) 8:39.0; **3** G. Jackson (Sx) 8:40.8; **4** S. Cahill (Yks) 8:41.4; **5** N. Holliday (Ches) 8:51.6; **6** R. Swann (Hants) 8:51.8.
100m Hurdles: **1** M. Holtom (Stffs) 13.6; **2** J. Longman (Hants) 13.6; **3** S. Adams (Mx) 13.9; **4** I. Ratcliffe (Stffs) 13.9; **5** C. Hayes (Glos) 14.2; **6** P. Darrell (Mx) 14.2.
1500m Steeplechase: **1** J. Crowley (Yks) 4:20.6 (*Championship best*); **2** C. Sly (Mx) 4:22.3; **3** A. Howden (Yks) 4:25.4; **4** M. Boulton (Wks) 4:30.0; **5** J. Wilson (Sy) 4:31.9; **6** P. Sladen (Glos) 4:36.9.
4 × 100m Relay: **1** Middlesex 44.2; **2** London 44.5; **3** Hampshire 44.7; **4** Warwickshire 44.7; **5** Berkshire 45.2; **6** Lancashire 45.5.
High Jump: **1** M. Palmer (Wks) 1.94m (6′ 4¼″) (*Championship best*); **2** I. Murray (Camb) 1.84m (6′ 0½″); **3** M. Jones (Herts) 1.79m (5′ 10½″); **4** S. Parsons (Sy) 1.79m (5′ 10½″); **5** N. Duffin (Lancs) 1.79m (5′ 10½″); **6** P. Rose (Bucks) 1.79m (5′ 10½″).
Pole Vault: **1** R. Goodall (Ches) 4.00m (13′ 1½″) (*Championship best*); **2** K. Fenner (Herts) 3.70m (12′ 1½″); **3** N. McPhee (Herts) 3.62m (11′ 10½″); **4** T. Sigel (Som) 3.54m (11′ 7¼″); **5** J. Anderson (Kt) 3.54m (11′ 7¼″); **6** G. Bird (Lon) 3.46m (11′ 4¼″).
Long Jump: **1** H. Charterton (Berks) 6.59m (21′ 7½″); **2** A. Taylor (Lancs) 6.53m (21′ 5¼″); **3** T. Morgan (Stffs) 6.47m (21′ 2¾″); **4** A. Earle (Wks) 6.35m (20′ 10″); **5** G. Oakes (Lon) 6.35m (20′ 10″); **6** V. Brambley (Lon) 6.28m (20′ 7¼″).
Triple Jump: **1** K. Connor (Bucks) 14.25m (46′ 9″) (*Championship best*); **2** L. McGinley (Ches) 13.94m (45′ 9″); **3** D. Golley (Lancs) 13.53m (44′ 4¾″); **4** P. Cartwright (Sy) 13.27m (43′ 6½″); **5** J. Torpey (Sy) 13.15m (43′ 1¾″); **6** N. Bingham (Notts) 13.01m (42′ 8¼″).
Shot: **1** G. Whaley (Dby) 15.11m (49′ 7″); **2** M. Strzadala (Mx) 14.94m (49′ 0¼″); **3** N. Jeavons (Stffs) 14.64m (48′ 0½″); **4** S. Hughes (Yks) 14.62m (47′ 11¾″); **5** G. Van Bellew (Yks) 14.24m (46′ 8¾″); **6** M. Charge (Herts) 14.13m (46′ 4¼″).

1974 ENGLISH SCHOOLS CHAMPIONSHIPS

Discus: 1 P. Armstrong (Yks) 45.58m (149′ 6″); **2** O. Davis (Mx) 44.54m (146′ 1″); **3** P. Allen (Yks) 43.64m (143′ 2″); **4** A. Daum (Dor) 43.52m (142′ 9″); **5** R. Humphries (Worcs) 41.72m (136′ 10″); **6** T. Barker (Herts) 40.26m (132′ 1″).
Hammer: 1 A. Sparkes (Ches) 50.70m (166′ 4″); **2** S. Watson (N'land) 49.76m (163′ 3″); **3** J. Huizar (Norf) 48.88m (160′ 4″); **4** N. Akhtar (Mx) 48.26m (158′ 4″); **5** S. Munn (Ex) 45.24m (148′ 5″); **6** S. Sage (Sy) 43.20m (141′ 9″).
Javelin: 1 T. Smith (Mx) 61.80m (202′ 9″); **2** L. Evans (Lancs) 60.50m (198′ 6″); **3** C. Harbage (Yks) 56.48m (185′ 4″); **4** S. Morton (Stffs) 56.28m (184′ 8″); **5** S. Ward (Kt) 52.92m (173′ 7″); **6** T. Trimble (Ex) 49.66m (162′ 11″).
Winning County: Middlesex.
Cross-Country: 1 M. Bateman (Lancs); **2** S. Kendal (Stffs); **3** M. Howarth (Hants); **4** G. Jackson (Sx); **5** G. Hill (Glos); **6** N. Martin (Hants). *Team:* Gloucestershire.
5000m Walk: 1 M. Dunion (Ex) 23:31; **2** G. Morris (Sx) 23:59; **3** J. Mullarkey (Shrop) 24:17; **4** J. Dunsford (Mx) 24:18; **5** K. Underhill (Glos) 24:27; **6** J. Cunliffe (Wks) 24:36. *Team:* Warwickshire.

JUNIOR BOYS

100m: 1 B. Ford (Leics) 11.5; **2** D. Sissons (Dur) 11.7; **3** N. Douglas (Lon) 11.7; **4** R. Webley (Mx) 11.9; **5** D. Pike (Hunts) 11.9; **6** M. Bond (Lon) 11.9.
200m: 1 M. Garmston (Stffs) 23.5; **2** M. McFarland (Lon) 23.7; **3** D. Mote (Sy) 23.8; **4** P. Sharples (Som) 24.1; **5** J. Marsden (Norf) 24.2; **6** T. Smith (Lincs) 24.4.
400m: 1 D. Wishart (Lon) 53.7; **2** S. Banasiewicz (Mx) 54.3; **3** S. Hoffmann (Norf) 55.0; **4** S. Talbot (Kt) 55.2; **5** A. Richards (Wilts) 55.2; **6** S. Houlton (Yks) 60.0.
800m: 1 G. James (Lon) 2:05.5; **2** D. Rose (Yks) 2:06.5; **3** G. McBean (Dur) 2:07.5; **4** G. France (Ches) 2:08.0; **5** C. Rands (Lincs) 2:08.7; **6** K. Roberts (Hants) 2:08.7.
1500m: 1 R. Slater (Leics) 4:15.5; **2** J. Mayhew (Mx) 4:17.3; **3** R. Wood (Herts) 4:17.3; **4** N. Young (Kt) 4:18.6; **5** D. Morris (Sy) 4:18.6; **6** A. Martin (Dur) 4:23.5.
80m Hurdles: 1 C. Amos (Glos) 11.8; **2** M. Effiong (Mx) 12.0; **3** M. Robinson (Som) 12.0; **4** D. Knight (Dur) 12.1; **5** P. Wibberley (Lancs) 12.2; **6** I. Fenn-Tye (Ex) 12.2.
4×100m Relay: 1 London 45.9; **2** Middlesex 46.6; **3** Durham 46.7; **4** Hertfordshire 47.1; Staffordshire & Warwickshire disqualified.
High Jump: 1 M. Watts (Glos) 1.76m (5′ 9¼″); **2** D. Smiths (Beds) 1.76m (5′ 9¼″); **3** A. Udo (Mx) 1.73m (5′ 8″); **4** H. Jones (Oxon) 1.70m (5′ 7″); **5** A. Pearce (Dor) 1.70m (5′ 7″); **6** B. Long (Sy) 1.70m (5′ 7″).
Pole Vault: 1 M. Barnes (Som) 2.98m (9′ 9¼″); **2** J. Currie (Lon) 2.98m (9′ 9¼″); **3** G. Henry (Lon) 2.83m (9′ 3¼″); **4** A. Jackson (Herts) 2.83m (9′ 3¼″); **5** R. Linton (Lon) 2.60m (8′ 6¼″).
Long Jump: 1 M. Igwe (Mx) 6.10m (20′ 0¼″); **2** J. Jameson (Dur) 6.09m (19′ 11¾″); **3** P. Boys (Herts) 5.95m (19′ 6¼″); **4** I. Blomquist (Leics) 5.77m (18′ 11¼″); **5** S. Eckett (Som) 5.71m (18′ 8¾″); **6** D. Batchelor (Sy) 5.68m (18′ 7¾″).
Triple Jump: 1 W. Armstrong (N'land) 12.88m (42′ 3¼″); **2** L. Dexter (Hants) 12.41m (40′ 8¾″); **3** M. LeBreton (Dor) 12.23m (40′ 1½″); **4** M. Evans (Ches) 12.22m (40′ 1¼″); **5** A. Clarke (Dev) 12.22m (40′ 1¼″); **6** S. Knight (Wks) 12.11m (39′ 8¾″).
Shot: 1 A. Husk (Ex) 15.72m (51′ 7″); **2** I. Jackson (Wks) 13.78m (45′ 2½″); **3** C. Watts (Glos) 13.68m (44′ 10¾″); **4** J. Connor (Dur) 13.35m (43′ 9¾″); **5** N. Morris (Dev) 12.84m (42′ 1½″); **6** N. Staffieri (Glos) 12.82m (42′ 0¾″).
Discus: 1 C. Cotterill (Stffs) 40.56m (133′ 1″); **2** P. Major (Oxon) 40.00m (131′ 3″); **3** R. Bielski (Leics) 39.04m (128′ 1″); **4** I. McIntosh (Stffs) 36.14m (118′ 7″); **5** D. Stanton (Berks) 34.60m (113′ 6″); **6** I. Coleman (Dby) 34.22m (112′ 3″).
Hammer: 1 L. Alsop (Camb) 48.42m (158′ 10″); **2** K. McNab (Bucks) 47.32m (155′ 3″); **3** P. Garner (Stffs) 46.62m (152′ 11″); **4** C. Hackley (Stffs) 46.52m (112′ 7″); **5** C. Thorley (Bucks) 41.74m (136′ 11″); **6** J. Chapman (Dev) 39.94m (131′ 0″).

113

ATHLETICS 75

Javelin: 1 E. Walters (Dby) 53.04m (174' 0"); 2 J. Briden (Sy) 50.56m (165' 10"); 3 C. Hall (Lincs) 48.34m (158' 7"); 4 S. Wright (Dur) 47.60m (156' 2"); 5 C. Johnson (Lancs) 45.84m (150' 5"); 6 J. Mitchell (Yks) 44.74m (146' 9").

Winning County: London.

Cross-Country: 1 C. White (Kent) 13:55; 2 R. Peagood (Yks) 13:59; 3 R. Slater (Leics) 14:06; 4 S. Cahill (Yks) 14:12; 5 S. Farmer (Wks) 14:18; 6 M. Brown (Dur) 14:25. *Team:* London.

3000m Walk: 1 N. Oldnall (Worcs) 14:49; 2 C. Pope (Sx) 14:56; 3 K. Kelly (Wks) 15:00; 4 P. Carrol (Wks) 15:29; 5 I. Wainwright (Wks) 15:36; 6 A. Harman (Sx) 15:53. *Team:* Warwickshire.

SENIOR GIRLS

100m: 1 L. Nash (Som) 12.4; 2 S. Thomas (Wks) 12.5; 3 G. Spurgin (Stffs) 12.6; 4 R. Everard (Suff) 12.6; 5 C. Young (Lancs) 12.8; 6 E. Mansfield (Ches) 12.9.

200m: 1 D. Heath (Ches) 24.3; 2 R. Kennedy (Notts) 24.6; 3 W. Hill (Lancs) 24.8; 4 H. Oakes (Kt) 24.8; 5 M. Sutcliffe (Lancs) 25.3; 6 B. Goddard (Berks) 25.8.

400m: 1 T. Doyle (Ches) 56.7; 2 S. Pettett (Kt) 58.3; 3 G. Williams (Yks) 59.0; 4 S. Reed (Kt) 59.5; 5 L. Greenwood (Leics) 59.6; 6 B. Jackson (Hants) 60.4.

800m: 1 G. Garbett (Yks) 2:14.3; 2 C. Stenhouse (Glos) 2:17.0; 3 R. Duddle (Leics) 2:18.7; 4 S. Pearce (Sy) 2:18.9; 5 J. Fowle (Dev) 2:21.7.

1500m: 1 S. Hines (Ex) 4:38.7 (*Championship best*); 2 B. Schofield (Ches) 4:39.7; 3 C. Butler (Lon) 4:41.4; 4 J. Asgill (Ches) 4:43.4; 5 A. Pursglove (Glos) 4:43.6; 6 P. Davies (Stffs) 4:48.0.

100m Hurdles: 1 S. Holmstrom (Dur) 13.7 (*Championship best*); 2 B. Rutledge (Som) 14.5; 3 G. Smith (Yks) 14.9; 4 E. Eddy (Wks) 14.9; 5 L. Hunt (Sy) 15.1; 6 H. Alderton (Ex) 15.2.

4 × 100m Relay: 1 Kent 48.7; 2 Cheshire 49.0; 3 Lancashire 49.7; 4 Somerset 49.8; 5 Leicestershire 50.3; 6 Staffordshire 50.4.

High Jump: 1 D. Bird (Berks) 1.69m (5' 6½"); 2 C. Mathers (Mx) 1.69m (5' 6½"); 3 K. Allison (Lancs) 1.66m (5' 5¼"); 4 M. Giscombe (Notts) 1.66m (5' 5¼"); **5eq** A. Manley (Sy) & M. Daniels (Berks) 1.63m (5' 4¼").

Long Jump: 1 S. Mapstone (Ex) 5.81m (19' 0¾"); 2 E. Mullins (Dor) 5.65m (18' 6½"); 3 C. Earlington (Mx) 5.59m (18' 4"); 4 S. Lewis (Stffs) 5.47m (17' 11¼"); 5 T. Gandy (Ches) 5.43m (17' 9¾"); 6 C. Pears (N'land) 5.40m (17' 8½").

Shot: 1 D. Howarth (Lancs) 12.60m (41' 4¼"); 2 J. Wraith (Hants) 12.11m (39' 8¾"); 3 A. Jackson (Lancs) 10.94m (35' 10¾"); 4 V. Maw (Yks) 10.87m (35' 8"); 5 B. Wadeson (Leics) 10.74m (35' 3"); 6 J. Britton (Hants) 10.50m (34' 5½").

Discus: 1 L. Mallin (Dev) 43.58m (143' 0"); 2 V. Hindley (Stffs) 34.94m (114' 7"); 3 J. Pickering (Ches) 34.22m (112' 3"); 4 K. Zoepfel (Shrop) 33.60m (110' 3"); 5 E. Jordan (Lon) 31.50m (103' 4"); 6 S. Elsby (Leics) 28.86m (94' 8").

Javelin: 1 S. James (Som) 43.52m (142' 9"); 2 S. O'Toole (Wks) 41.32m (135' 7"); 3 J. Williams (Stffs) 41.10m (134' 10"); 4 J. Barnes (Sy) 40.04m (131' 4"); 5 L. Rice (Sy) 40.00m (131' 3"); 6 B. Richardson (Dur) 38.36m (125' 10").

Winning County: Cheshire.

Cross-Country: 1 B. Schofield (Ches); 2 C. House (Lincs); 3 A. Pursglove (Glos); 4 R. Young (Lancs); 5 S. Hines (Ex); 6 C. Boxer (Hants). *Team:* Lancashire.

5000m Walk: 1 S. De Giovanni (Sy) 28:43; 2 L. Hodgson (Cumb) 30:33; 3 K. Braznell (Stffs) 31:26 *Team:* Cumberland.

INTERMEDIATE GIRLS

100m: 1 W. Clarke (Lon) 12.2 (11.8sf (*eq championship best*)); 2 H. Barnett (Lon) 12.3; 3 L. Gillespie (Yks) 12.6; 4 C. Mooney (Norf) 12.6; 5 M. Ascroft (Wks) 12.7; 6 H. Hunte (Mx) 12.7 (12.0 sf).

200m: 1 A. McClelland (Ches) 24.8; 2 J. Bowerman (Sy) 24.9; 3 A. Lyne (Mx) 25.3; 4 H. Gray (Glos) 25.3; 5 A. Baldock (Kt) 25.3; 6 K. Palmer (Lancs) 25.7.

1974 ENGLISH SCHOOLS CHAMPIONSHIPS

400m: 1 J. Prictoe (Lincs) 57.8; **2** S. Brooks (Sy) 58.3; **3** D. Bain (Sx) 58.9; **4** P. Howell (Hants) 59.1; **5** D. Lucy (Sy) 59.2; **6** A. Goldswain (Bucks) 59.3.

800m: 1 J. Colebrook (Lincs) 2:11.7; **2** J. Rout (Mx) 2:14.6; **3** M. Cobden (Lon) 2:15.2; **4** M. Joyce (Sx) 2:15.5; **5** L. Pamment (Kt) 2:15.5; **6** J. Lawrence (Lancs) 2:15.7.

1500m: 1 A-M. Robinson (Ches) 4:35.8 (*Championship best*); **2** H. Fielon (Hants) 4:38.4; **3** S. Holmes (Lancs) 4:38.5; **4** A. Tunnicliffe (Stffs) 4:44.0; **5** J. Schusler (Dur) 4:51.4; **6** J. Barrass (Hants) 4:53.3.

80m Hurdles: 1 S. Strong (Ches) 11.6; **2** L. Ilderton (Stffs) 11.8; **3** K. Evans (Lancs) 12.0; **4** K. Harrison (Ches) 12.0; **5** F. McKnight (Ches) 12.1; **6** C. Bosah (Yks) 12.1.

4×100m Relay: 1 London 48.2; **2** Cheshire 48.8; **3** Lancashire 49.3; **4** Surrey 49.3; **5** Lincolnshire 49.4; **6** Somerset 49.4.

High Jump: 1 V. Mullin (Lancs) 1.72m (5′ 7¾″) (*Championship best*); **2** A. Gilson (Dor) 1.67m (5′ 5¾″); **3** G. Hitchen (Lancs) 1.64m (5′ 4½″); **4** D. Cooper (Som) 1.64m (5′ 4½″); **5** J. Sulik (Oxon) 1.64m (5′ 4½″); **6** J. Harrison (Leics) 1.58m (5′ 2¼″).

Long Jump: 1 C. Hill (Dur) 5.54m (18′ 2¼″); **2** D. Gray (Norf) 5.35m (17′ 6¾″); **3** K. Murray (Sy) 5.33m (17′ 6″); **4** S. Nairn (Mx) 5.25m (17′ 2¾″); **5** J. Binns (Mx) 5.23m (17′ 2″); **6** B. Clarke (Lon) 5.22m (17′ 1½″).

Shot: 1 J. Oakes (Kt) 12.01m (39′ 5″); **2** E. Service (Mx) 11.30m (37′ 1″); **3** B. Sapsed (Herts) 10.76m (35′ 3¾″); **4** L. Newton (Berks) 10.73m (35′ 2½″); **5** Y. Stewart (Worcs) 10.38m (34′ 0¾″); **6** J. Cox (Stffs) 10.10m (33′ 1¾″).

Discus: 1 V. Watson (Ches) 40.04m (131′ 4″); **2** K. Mallard (Leics) 38.18m (125′ 3″); **3** D. English (Notts) 36.58m (120′ 0″); **4** L. Smith (Dor) 35.86m (117′ 8″); **5** E. Robottam (Stffs) 35.40m (116′ 2″); **6** M. Maxwell (Berks) 35.32m (115′ 10″).

Javelin: 1 J. King (Sy) 42.56m (139′ 7″); **2** M. Mendham (Ex) 40.14m (131′ 8″); **3** G. Grey (Stffs) 39.04m (128′ 1″); **4** P. Inskip (Stffs) 36.38m (119′ 4″); **5** S. Hallam (Leics) 36.02m (118′ 2″); **6** M. Stanley (Yks) 33.74m (110′ 8″).

Winning County: Cheshire.

Cross-Country: 1 H. Hill (Stffs); **2** M. Joyce (Sx); **3** A-M Robinson (Ches); **4** L. Ward (Wks); **5** J. Williamson (Ches); **6** A. Tunnicliffe (Stffs). *Team:* Yorkshire.

3000m Walk: 1 S. Saunders (Wks) 14:57, **2** P. Branson (Wks) 15:06; **3** S. Wish (Wks) 15:15; **4** K. Hill (Worcs) 16:08; **5** E. Smith (Worcs) 16:18; **6** K. Pitts (Wks) 16:29. *Team:* Warwickshire.

JUNIOR GIRLS

100m: 1 S. Dickson (Dur) 12.8; **2** C. Croal (Dev) 12.9; **3** J. Davies (Dev) 13.0; **4** T. Wright (Ex) 13.0; **5** J. Butler (Ex) 13.0; **6** K. Duncan (Dur) 13.0.

200m: 1 J. Walsh (Sy) 24.4; **2** S. Howells (Wks) 24.9 (24.2 ht *Championship best*); **3** J. McGregor (Dur) 25.4; **4** B. Gauntlet (Herts) 25.4; **5** L. Burnett (Shrop) 26.1; **6** K. Sait (Hants) 26.6.

800m: 1 S. Parker (Ches) 2:13.5; **2** V. Weston (Lincs) 2:16.6; **3** J. White (Sy) 2:19.1; **4** P. Quow (Beds) 2:19.6; **5** C. Venner (Dev) 2:20.1; **6** S. Murray (Dev) 2:21.1.

1500m: 1 S. Ludlam (Hants) 4:41.4 (*Championship best*); **2** R. Smeeth (Sy) 4:44.5; **3** C. Brace (Herts) 4:45.3; **4** J. Moody (Yks) 4:47.8; **5** B. Madigan (Berks) 4:48.2; **6** S. Samy (Berks) 4:48.7.

75m Hurdles: 1 J. Duffield (Mx) 11.2; **2** N. Prenergast (Mx) 11.6; **3** D. Mathews (Sy) 11.6; **4** C. Hardacre (Lancs) 11.7; **5** B. Inman (Yks) 11.7; **6** B. Chilleystone (Norf) 11.9.

4×100m Relay: 1 Warwickshire 49.6; **2** Surrey 49.9; **3** Hertfordshire 50.3; **4** Hampshire 50.7; **5** Essex 51.1; Yorkshire disqualified.

High Jump: 1 V. Kelly (Stffs) 1.62m (5′ 3¾″); **2** D. Grant (Leics) 1.59m (5′ 2½″); **3** E. Wren (Herts) 1.59m (5′ 2½″); **4** Y. Peart (Oxon) 1.59m (5′ 2½″); **5** K. Smallwood (Hants) 1.59m (5′ 2½″); **6** R. Lambert (Ches) 1.56m (5′ 1¼″).

Long Jump: 1 L. Pears (N'land) 5.36m (17′ 7″); **2** J. Frank-Lynch (Sy) 5.33m (17′ 6″); **3** D. Wightman (Som) 5.25m (17′ 2¾″); **4** C. Stone (Mx) 5.25m (17′ 2¾″); **5** M. Clarke (Dur) 5.14m (16′ 10½″); **6** F. West (Lon) 5.12m (16′ 9¾″).

ATHLETICS 75

Shot: 1 Y. Ritchie (Lancs) 11.89m (39′ 0¼″); **2** M. Hancock (Herts) 11.04m (36′ 2¾″); **3** C. Dyer (Hants) 10.84m (35′ 6¾″); **4** A. Magson (Lancs) 10.67m (35′ 0¼″); **5** S. Condon (Berks) 10.47m (34′ 4¼″); **6** C. Williams (Dev) 10.42m (34′ 2¼″).
Discus: 1 F. Condon (Berks) 34.86m (114′ 4″); **2** D. Sturman (Ex) 31.46m (103′ 2″); **3** K. Spoul (Ex) 30.18m (99′ 0″); **4** J. Stokes (Worcs) 28.28m (92′ 9″); **5** J. Hunt (Wks) 27.40m (89′ 11″); **6** J. Minns (Berks) 27.24m (89′ 4″).
Javelin: 1 S. Metcalfe (Dur) 35.72m (117′ 2″); **2** C. Whitmore (Ex) 34.08m (111′ 10″); **3** J. Walker (Lincs) 33.80m (110′ 11″); **4** S. Walsh (Lancs) 33.76m (110′ 9″); **5** J. Skinner (Wks) 33.30m (109′ 3″); **6** Y. Gregory (Wks) 33.02m (108′ 4″).
Winning County: Surrey.
Cross-Country: 1 C. Bruce (Herts); **2** H. Donovan (Lancs); **3** D. Cresswell (Wks); **4** R. Smeeth (Sy); **5** F. Oldershaw (Dby); **6** D. Watson (Dby). *Team:* Surrey.
Overall Winners: Lancashire.
2500m Walk: 1 M. De Giovanni (Sy) 12:56; **2** E. Cox (Wks) 13:10; **3** J. Williams (Worcs) 13:27; **4** D. Ilderton (Stffs) 13:29; **5** J. Braznell (Worcs) 13:54; **6** E. Swannell (Mx) 13:57. *Team:* Warwickshire.
Overall Winners: Cumberland.
Overall Winners (track and field): Middlesex.

For Janis Walsh, the 1974 Junior Girls 200 metres title must surely be just one of many to come from what promises to be a most exciting career.

Whither the Olympics

James Coote *The Daily Telegraph*

The junketing and lobbying of the International Olympic Committee's 75th session in Vienna last October remains merely a faint memory to the 74 IOC members, 21 presidents and secretaries of international sports federations, and the countless others who attended the meeting. But underneath all the fraternisation and bonhomie of that meeting remains an underlying worry: whether the IOC will be proved correct in their controversial decision to award the 1980 Olympic Games to Moscow, the first time these will have gone to Eastern Europe. There is also serious concern over the method needed to cope with that giant red dragon, the Peoples' Republic of China, emerging with ever increasing zest from its sporting isolation.

The China question, to the delight of Peking, is becoming so complicated as to be almost unfathomable. Obviously only one national Olympic committee can represent a country, which is why in the 1960s there was a struggle over the nomenclature of East and West Germany and North and South Korea. Each claimed to represent the entire geographical area which was obviously two separate political entities. This was resolved in Germany's case by the recognition as separate states of the German Federal Republic (West Germany) and the German Democratic Republic (East Germany); in Korea's by Korea (South Korea) and the Democratic Peoples' Republic of Korea (North Korea). Unfortunately, the same system cannot be applied to China, whose current IOC membership is held by the Republic of China, Nationalist China, Taiwan, or Formosa (depending on your attitude). This came about because, when Peking (the Peoples' Republic) withdrew from the IOC movement over 20 years ago, their vote was taken over by Taiwan, the Republic of China. Now Red China wish to return to Olympic competition, which they see as a necessary and useful non-belligerent field for propaganda, just as, in their own way, have East Germany, Kenya, and even France.

But the only way Red China can receive the vote is by persuading Taiwan to cease maintaining that they are the representatives of mainland Chinese – an impossibility as neither Mao Tse-tung nor Chiang Kai-shek recognises the existence of the other. The alternative is to squeeze Taiwan gradually out of the international arena, and this has been increasingly achieved these past 18 months by a combination of none-too-subtle pressure and intense diplomatic activity.

Gradually, Taiwan's affiliation with the international federations is being eroded, and once they are recognised by fewer than five (which could be by the time you read this article) Peking would automatically become members of the IOC; without having to force Lord Killanin and his members to choose between throwing out Taiwan, to the inclusion of China (which they would never do), or to exclude the nation with the largest population of the world – 732,000,000 – for the sake of an off-shore island which, admittedly, has won two Olympic medals but which, by comparison, has one-fiftieth of the population (15 million). The ethics of China's action are highly questionable, as is their attitude towards political opponents. Their behaviour in last year's Asian Games in Tehran by refusing to allow their sportsmen and women to compete 'face to face' against Israeli fencers and tennis players while allowing them to challenge athletes and swimmers simply because they race alongside shows the absurdity of the entire situation.

This ever increasing tendency to boycott political opponents should now be halted as both the International Olympic Committee and the international federations have issued statements deploring such behaviour. It is interesting to note that even the mighty Soviet Union were subjected to such political boycotting – by an Albanian in the recent world wrestling championships in Katowice, Poland. The IOC and the international federations have warned – and I have clear understanding that they will carry out these threats – they will disqualify and/or suspend any individual, team, or, in an extreme case, the entire representation of the country.

Thus one could see a competitor being penalised unless it was clear he was a political pawn of his national Olympic committee and national federation. Initial action would probably be a warning followed by suspension. This strong lead will be unpopular, but it could at least prevent sport from being increasingly a negative battlefield on which the winner could be only an Austrian, Swede, or Swiss; i.e. only 'non-committed countries'. This might also help Israel, whose competitors are gradually being squeezed out of tournaments by Asian federations and forced to seek affiliation from the less politically extreme European associations.

I hasten to emphasise that there is no suggestion that the Russians support political boycotts on the sports field, especially now that their one intention is to host the 1980 Olympic Games in the best possible way. Just as they shot the first man into space and will always be remembered for this record, so the target now is to 'normalise' themselves in the eyes of the world by producing the greatest, best organised, most trouble-free Games. They dare not lose face, which is why, on the one hand, they are over-sensitive to criticism, on the other are pouring all resources, including a bottomless financial budget, into the organising of 'Moscow 1980'. They know that nobody fully accepts the validity of their guarantees, so a memorable Olympics is more important now than it was when they first applied unsuccessfully in Amsterdam in 1970.

For more than a year now I have been dealing with the question of Moscow's desire – backed by the entire weight of the Praesidium – to gain the Olympics; first as a reporter on the spot when the Russians were criticised for refusing to allow Jews to watch the Israeli basketball team, and then as a journalist attacked on more than one occasion by the Russian press for my views. I have discussed Moscow's case and its attitude towards staging an Olympics with countless Russians from Sergei Pavlov, chairman of the Soviet Committee for Physical Culture and Sport, down.

While few of us can seriously applaud the political climate and attitude towards, say, abstract artists and non-existent freedom of speech, one *must* try to look at Moscow's case on strictly sporting merits. Forget, if possible, that the Soviet Union's medals are the product of a state system in which the successful sportsman is rewarded well with social privileges commensurate to his performance in the stadium; forget everything connected with the Soviet Union except for one point. In the sporting field, regardless of cost, Moscow will do their best to stage the greatest Olympics; the finest stadia, incorporating the most modern technological devices; they will build and rebuild anything and everything that is needed – airports, roads, hotels. But then, everyone is asking, what about those peripheral problems that form such an integral part of the Olympics: travel, entertainment, fraternisation with the locals, news coverage, relaxation for athletes, all of which are normally taken for granted? These are the areas where the problems will arise.

During the World Student Games in September 1973, many competitors complained bitterly of monotonously poor food, lack of opportunity for relaxation, a security system that made it almost impossible to travel from one part of the lodgings to another and meet fellow sportsmen, erratic transport, and lack of communications with the sports' organisers.

But what really baffles many observers is how the Soviet Union, with its never-failingly rigid bureaucratic system, which makes any request out of the norm a matter for state intervention, can truly hope to put all this aside just for three weeks or so. Whatever happens, all are agreed the Socialist Republic will never be the same again as the inhabitants of Moscow mingle with up to three million tourists and 50,000 cars – mostly from countries whose inhabitants, they have been told, are downtrodden by cruel leadership. How could the Praesidium really explain away an *Athletics Weekly* party with its colourful group of 'oppressed' workers gaily making whoopee in Red Square. Do Kosygin and Brezhnev really know what's going to hit them?

But seriously, while the IOC have obtained, from the Moscow organising committee and the government, guaranteed freedom of access for all accredited sports press, this does not apply either to tourists or even non-sporting press. The Russians will still be able to refuse entry to those they feel could be anti – and there will be nothing the IOC can do about it. True, the Moscow organisers have said they will try to ensure that visas can be obtained at the borders, but let me give you an example of how impossibly rigid they are, and how potentially troublesome.

An IOC member from West Germany, Bertold Beitz, who is managing director of the vast Krupps industrial concern, took his luxury yacht, *Germania VI*, with a large crew and some journalists to the waters of Tallin to inspect the yachting facilities offered by the Moscow organising committee. Due to a typical bureaucratic error, the Customs had not been told about the trip and Herr Beitz was forced to empty his pockets, open his wallet, and show all his papers as the yacht was searched from stem to stern for possible contraband. Obviously the error was later rectified and Herr Beitz given the full VIP treatment. But, as he said, 'When it happens to Bertold Beitz, an IOC member who, moreover, is well known to the Russians for many trips to Moscow for discussions over industrial cooperation, can you imagine what will happen to Mr Nobody? I have been acquainted with the Russians for 41 years and I know how long they take to change. Six years is a very small time indeed. I cannot see them changing sufficiently in that time to carry out all their guarantees. For instance, when the Moscow delegation came to present their case to the IOC on 23 October, one of their members wore a red shirt. I thought I was not seeing right. If it had been me, I would have thrown the chap out.'

True, Herr Beitz is an outspoken critic of the Moscow selection and was one of the members who voted in favour of Los Angeles, but what he says must be taken extremely seriously. He is a tough negotiator in charge of one of the biggest industrial complexes in the world, and if *he* has problems, what hope is there for us insignificant individuals?

What many people do not realise is that everything in Russia, unless you have VIP status, is a long, weary, time-consuming process – from booking in at your hotel to changing money (always a long queue, with one rude cashier; the second cashier filling interminable pages of figures) to eating in a restaurant. And don't forget that as the rouble is tied to an artificial rate (about 1.6 to the pound) everything works out viciously expensive. The blackmarket of up to 10 roubles to the pound gives a more realistic value, but of course that is illegal and should never be attempted.

To recall all these echoes of the past and problems of the present is *not* to be a 'hackneyed lackey of the capitalist press', but I am genuinely concerned about these Games, for what happens in 1980 will affect the future of the Olympics. There is a great possibility, for instance, that the 1984 Games could go to Tehran. Iran's attitude in the Asian Games, coupled with Moscow's behaviour in 1980, will set the seal on whether the IOC can control countries who refuse to allow political rivals to participate in sport; on whether there is any future hope at all of sport being practised in the sporting arenas of the world – or indeed whether the Olympics can survive beyond the 1980s. It should be recalled that in the ancient Olympics, two always warring nations, Athens and Sparta, never failed to make peace for the period of a Games – and they, politically, were even further apart than Washington, Peking, and Moscow. Food for thought.

The Clubs

A register of clubs in the United Kingdom
Southern, Midlands, Northern, Scotland, Wales, Northern Ireland

ATHLETICS 75

SOUTHERN AREA

*Questionnaire not returned, information based on entry in *Athletics 74*
†Insufficient information received

Club with Principal Track used, Secretaries, and nearest Public Transport

	Aldershot Farnham & District AC	Andover & District AC	Banbury Harriers AC	Barnet & District AC	Basildon AC
	Aldershot Military Stadium, Queens Avenue	Club Hut, London Road	George Napier School	Bethune Park Track, Beaconsfield Rd, N11	Gloucester Park, Cranes Farm Road
	Buses: 2, 3c, 4, 73, 76, 83, 86 Station: Aldershot	Buses: † Station: Andover junction	Buses: † Station: Banbury	Buses: 34, 221, 251. Station: Arnos Grove, New Southgate and Copthall Stadium (Station: Hendon Central)	Buses: † Station: Laindon
	Men: J. W. Lofts, 46 Perring Avenue, Farnborough, Hants GU14 9DB	Mrs P. A. Smith, 35 Wood Park, Ludgershall, Andover, Hants	Mrs J. Bateman, 60 Thornhill, Chacombe, Banbury	D. Burrage, 14 Burlington Rise, E. Barnet, Herts	Mrs N. Smith, 100 Sparrows Herne, Basildon, Essex
	Tel: Camberley 39118	Tel: Ludgershall 635	Tel: Banbury 710549	Tel: 01 368 5544	Tel: Basildon 21507
	Women: J. Horsburgh, 56 Kingsway, Aldershot, Hants				
	Tel: Aldershot 23006				
Men	■	■	■	■	■
Women	■				
Juniors	■			■	
League		■	■	■	■
All-Weather Track	■				
All-Weather Runways	■			■	■
Landing Beds	■	■		■	■
Floodlit Training	■	■	■	■	■
Indoor Training	■	■		■	■
Weight Training	■	■		■	■
Coaches	Sprints M Distance Throws	Sprints M Distance Jumps Throws	†	Sprints M Distance Throws	Sprints M Distance Jumps Throws
Active Membership	160	95	40	100	185
Training Sessions	Tues Eve Thurs Eve Sun am	Mon–Thurs Eves Sun am	Tues Eve (winter) Thurs Eve	Mon pm Tues pm Sun am	Mon Eve Wed Eve Thurs Eve Sun am
Junior Subscription	£1	£1	50p	£2	75p
Senior Subscription	£1·50	£2	£1·50	£4	£2

REGISTER OF CLUBS

Club					Events	Members	Training	Fees	Subs
Basingstoke AC Vyne School Buses: † Station: Basingstoke I.S. Byett, 21 Bardwell Close, Basingstoke, Hants RG 22606. Tel: Basingstoke 28401	■ ■ ■				M Distance	75	Tues pm Thurs pm	25p	£1
Bedford & County AC Newnham Track, Barkers Lane, Bedford Buses: 104, 105 Station: Bedford (Midland Road) F.E. Wooding, 54 Carlisle Road, Bedford Tel: Bedford 64928	■ ■ ■ ■				Sprints M Distance Jumps	150	Tues Eve Thurs Eve Sun am	80p	£1·50
***Belgrave Harriers** Belgrave Hall Buses: † Station: † P.B. Hilliar, 22 Allington Drive, Tonbridge, Kent Tel: 073 22 64168	■ ■				Sprints M Distance Jumps Throws	350	Tues Eve Thurs Eve Sat pm Sun am	£1·50	£3
Bexhill AC The Sports Centre, Little Common Road, Bexhill (Meeting Place) Buses: † Station: Bexhill Central S.G. Matthews, c/o The Sports Centre	■ ■				Sprints M Distance Jumps Throws	40	Every pm Sun am	65p	£1·35
Biggleswade AC Fairfield Recreation Ground Buses: † Station: Biggleswade D. Ball, 16 Saffron Road, Biggleswade, Bedfordshire SG18 8DJ Tel: Biggleswade 313137 xt63	■				Sprints M Distance	30	Tues Eve Thurs Eve Sat pm	25p	50p
Blackheath Harriers Ladywell, Croydon, Crystal Palace Buses: † Station: Hayes (Kent), Crystal Palace I.F. Smith, 4 Christchurch Road, Dartford, Kent DA1 3DH Winter HQ: 56 Bourne Way, Hayes, Kent	■				Sprints M Distance Jumps Throws	150	*Crystal Palace* Tues pm Thurs pm *Hayes* Wed pm Sat pm Sun am	£1·50	£3

123

ATHLETICS 75

SOUTHERN AREA

*Questionnaire not returned, information based on entry in *Athletics 74*
†Insufficient information received

Club with Principal Track used, Secretaries, and nearest Public Transport

	Bognor Regis AC	Boreham Wood AC	Borough of Enfield Harriers	Bournemouth AC	Bracknell AC Sports Centre
Senior Subscription	£1	£1·25	£2·50	£1 (ladies) / £2 (men)	£2
Junior Subscription	50p	30p	50p	25p / 50p / 90p	£1
Training Sessions	Mon Eve, Thurs Eve, Sun am	Mon Eve, Wed Eve, Sun am	Mon–Thurs Eves, Sun am	Mon–Fri Eves, Sat am (women only), Sun am	Tues Eve, Thurs Eve, Sun am
Active Membership	47	68	300	150	100
Coaches	Sprints, M Distance, Jumps, Throws	Sprints, M Distance, Jumps, Throws	Sprints, M Distance, Jumps, Throws	Sprints, M Distance, Jumps, Throws	Sprints, M Distance, Jumps, Throws
Weight Training	■	■	■		■
Indoor Training	■	■	■	■	
Floodlit Training				■	
Landing Beds	■	■		■	■
All-Weather Runways			■	■	■
All-Weather Track			Due 1975		
League	■		■	■	
Juniors	■		■	■	
Women	■	■	■	■	
Men	■	■	■	■	■

Bognor Regis AC
Hawthorn Road Recreation Ground
Buses: † Station: Bognor Regis
R.D. Wardale, 28 Dorset Road, Bognor Regis
Tel: Bognor 25871 (school)

Boreham Wood AC
Metropolitan Police Cadets Training Sports Centre
Buses: 107, 306, 292 Station: Elstree & Boreham Wood
Miss P.A. Poole, 30 Burghley Avenue, Boreham Wood, Herts
Tel: 01-953 4631

Borough of Enfield Harriers
Enfield Playing Fields, Donkey Lane
Buses: 135, 310 Station: Enfield
G.E. Sewell, 38 Sittingbourne Avenue, Enfield, Middx
Tel: 01-360 1064 (home) 01-363 9798 (club)

Bournemouth AC
Kings Park Athletic Centre, Boscombe
Buses: To Kings Park Station: Bournemouth Central
Men: C.G.A. Paulding, 550 Holdenhurst Road, Bournemouth
Tel: Bournemouth 33794
Women: Miss V.A. Trevett, 20 Loewy Cres, Parkstone, Poole, Dorset BH12 4PQ
Tel: Castle Hill 3003

Bracknell AC Sports Centre
Buses: 53, 56, 75 Station, Bracknell
C.J. Hickey, 31 Farm Close, Bracknell, Berks
Tel: Bracknell 28124

124

REGISTER OF CLUBS

Club	Events	Members	Training	Fees
Brighton & Hove AC Withdean Sports Arena Station: Preston Park, Brighton Buses: 5, 5B, 15, 110, 112 R.A. Hook, 42 Florence Road, Brighton Tel: Brighton 505767	Sprints ■ M Distance ■ Jumps ■ Throws ■	400	Tues pm Thurs pm Sun am	£1.50 £3
Cambridge & Coleridge AC University AC Track, Milton Road Buses: † Station: Cambridge C.E. Booth, 34 Quarry Lane, Swaffham Bulbeck, Cambridge CB5 0LU Tel: Cambridge 811178	Sprints ■ M Distance ■ Throws ■	150	Mon–Thurs Eves.	75p £3
Cambridge Harriers HQ Glenhurst Avenue, Bexley, Kent Buses: 89, 401, 467 Station: Bexley Charlton Park Track, SE7 Buses: 53, 54, 75 Station: Charlton *Men*: H.C. Rogers, 292 Bexley Lane, Sidcup, Kent Tel: 01-300 7875 *Women*: W. Meyer, 77 Kellaway Road, SE3 8PN Tel: 01-856 4152	Sprints ■ M Distance ■ Throws ■ At Sutcliffe Park	600	Tues Eve Wed Eve Thurs Eve Sat pm Sun am	(ladies) £1.50 (men) £2
Chelmsford AC Melbourne Park Stadium Buses: † Station: Chelmsford S.T. Marlow, 95 Woodland Avenue, Shenfield, Essex. Tel: 0277 215425	Sprints ■ M Distance ■ Jumps ■ Throws ■	180	Mon–Thurs pm Sun am	£1.25 £2
Colchester AC Winter HQ, Wilson Marriage School Summer Track: Garrison Track Buses: † Station: Colchester N.G. Palmer, 6 Fairhaven Ave, West Mersea, Essex CO5 8EZ. Tel: West Mersea 3482	Sprints ■ M Distance ■ Jumps ■ Throws ■	60	Mon Eve Tues Eve Thurs Eve	75p £2
Crawley AC Sports Centre, Haslett Avenue Buses: † Station: Three Bridges or Crawley Mrs B. Trussell, 5 Oxford Road, Tilgate, Crawley. Tel: Crawley 25199	Sprints ■ M Distance ■ Jumps ■ Throws ■	200	Mon Eve Wed Eve Fri Eve Sun am	50p + training fee 5p	£2 + training fee 10p

125

ATHLETICS 75

SOUTHERN AREA

*Questionnaire not returned, information based on entry in *Athletics 74*
†Insufficient information received

Club with Principal Track used, Secretaries, and nearest Public Transport

	Croydon Harriers	Dartford Harriers	Didcot AC	Diss AC	Dorking St Pauls AC	Duchy of Cornwall Olympiads
Senior Subscription	£1·25 £3	£2·50	£1	25p	£2	25p
Junior Subscription	£1	£1	50p	15p	50p £1	10p
Training Sessions	Tues pm Wed pm Thurs pm Sun am	Tues pm Thurs pm Sun am	Tues Eve Thurs Eve	Tues Eve Thurs Eve	Mon Eve Thurs Eve	Mon–Thurs pm
Active Membership	300	100	25	70	†	16
Coaches	Sprints M Distance Jumps Throws	Sprints M Distance Jumps	Sprints M Distance Throws	Sprints M Distance Jumps Throws	None	M Distance
Weight Training	■			■		
Indoor Training	■			■		
Floodlit Training	■					
Landing Beds						
All-Weather Runways	■					
All-Weather Track						
League	■	■	■	■	■	
Juniors	■	■	■	■	■	
Women	■					
Men	■	■	■	■	■	

Croydon Harriers
Croydon Arena, Albert Road, S. Norwood SE25 Station: Norwood Junction
Buses: 12, 197
M.A. Fleet, 101 Blenheim Gardens, Wallington, Surrey

Dartford Harriers
Central Park, Dartford   Station: Dartford
Buses: †
G.W. Hodder, 18 Bracondale Avenue, Northfleet
Tel: Southfleet 2455

Didcot AC
Youth Centre, Park Road   Station: Didcot
Buses: 112
F.C. Myers, Ridgewood Grange, Upton
Nr Didcot OX11 9JL. Tel: Blewbury 756

Diss AC
Diss Grammar School   Station: Diss
Buses: †
R.A. Wright, 'Kenmor', 17 The Close, Roydon,
Diss, Norfolk IP22 3RE. Tel: Diss 3601

Dorking St Pauls AC
Pixham Lane Sports Ground
Buses: 414, 470   Station: Dorking North
D. Powell, 67 Leslie Road, Dorking, Surrey
Tel: Dorking 5834

Duchy of Cornwall Olympiads
Heamoor CS School (Penzance)
and Toleus CS School (Redruth)
Buses: †   Station: Penzance & Redruth
M.A. Rowling, 'Chyreene', 39 Tregea Beacon,
Camborne. Tel: B. Pemberthy, Camborne 3301

126

REGISTER OF CLUBS

Club				Number	Days	Fees	
Ealing & Southall AC Pikes Bridge Track Buses: 105, 120 Station: Southall A.J. Helling, 16 Gateway Close, Northwood, Middx	■	■ ■ ■		†	80	Tues Eve Thurs Eve Sun am	£1·50 £2
Ealing Olympic Ladies AC Drayton Green W13 0JE Winter HQ: Eilleen Wilkinson School, Queens Drive W3 Buses: E.1 Station: † G.A. Wood, 11 Drayton Green, W13 0JE	■	■		M Distance	30	Tues Eve Fri Eve Sun am	50p £1
Eastbourne Rovers AC Princes Park, Oval Buses: Archery Station: Eastbourne Miss J. Long, 543 Seaside, Eastbourne, Sussex Tel: Eastbourne 28562 (H) 51192 (office)	■	■ ■	■	Throws	60	Tues Eve Wed Eve (winter) Thurs Eve Sun am	25p £1 50p
East Kent AC Training at Canterbury, Herne Bay & Whitstable Buses: † Stations: Canterbury, Herne Bay & Whitstable R.F.R. Clark, 66 Bournemouth Drive, Herne Bay, Kent CT6 8HH Tel: 022 73 62553	■	■		Sprints M Distance Jumps Throws	90	Tues Eve Wed Eve Thurs Eve Sun am	50p £1·25
Epsom & Ewell Harriers King George V Playing Fields, Ewell Buses: 418, 468 Station: West Ewell K.D. Vaughan, 51 Sunnymede Ave, West Ewell, Surrey. Tel: 01-393 5519	■	■ ■	■	Sprints M Distance Jumps Throws	418	Tues pm Wed pm Thurs pm Sun am	£1 £3 £1·50
Erith & District AC Erith Stadium, South Road Buses: 480, 99, 122A Station: Erith D. Wilkins, 48 The Pantiles, Bexleyheath, Kent Tel: Erith 36502	■	■ ■		Sprints M Distance Throws	†	Tues pm Thurs pm (summer only) Sun am	£1·25 £2·50 £2
Essex Beagles AC Mayesbrook Park, Lodge Avenue, Dagenham Buses: 87, 162, 62, 63 Station: Upney D. Cremin, 433 Lodge Avenue, Dagenham, Essex Tel: D. Green 01-550 8835 xt 343 (office)	■	■ ■	■	Sprints M Distance Jumps Throws	280	Tues Eve Thurs Eve Sun am	70p £2·50 £1·25

127

ATHLETICS 75

	Essex Ladies AC	Eton Manor AC	Exeter Harriers	*Exmouth AC	Faversham C & AC	Feltham AC
Senior Subscription	£1·50	£2·10	£1·50	£1	10p	£2·50
Junior Subscription	55p	£1	30p	50p	10p	£1
Training Sessions	Tues Eve Thurs Eve	Tues Eve Thurs Eve Sat pm Sun pm	Tues Eve Thurs Eve Sun am	Mon Eve Tues Eve Thurs Eve Sun am	Thurs Eve Sun am	Tues Eve Thurs Eve Sun am
Active Membership	80	86	130	†	15	†
Coaches	Sprints M Distance Jumps Throws	Sprints M Distance Jumps Throws	Sprints M Distance Jumps Throws	Sprints M Distance	Sprints M Distance Jumps	Sprints M Distance Jumps Throws
Weight Training		■	■			■
Indoor Training			■		■	
Floodlit Training	■		■	■		■
Landing Beds	■		■		■	■
All-Weather Runways	■		Pole Vault only			
All-Weather Track						
League	■	■	■			■
Juniors				■	■	■
Women	■		■			■
Men	■	■	■	■	■	■

SOUTHERN AREA

*Questionnaire not returned, information based on entry in *Athletics 74*
†Insufficient information received

Club with Principal Track used, Secretaries, and nearest Public Transport

Essex Ladies AC
Ashton Playing Fields, Woodford
Buses: 235 Station: South Woodford
J. King, 11 Field Close, Chingford E4

Eton Manor AC
Ive Farm, Villiers Close, E10
Buses: 58 Station: Leyton
L. Golding, 58 Love Lane, Woodford Bridge, Essex

Exeter Harriers
Clifton Hill Track
Buses: G, J Station: Exeter Central & St. Davids
Miss J. Phillips, 7 Jesmond Rd, Exeter EX1 2DG
Tel: 0392 59040 (H) 0392 74761 (school)

*Exmouth AC
Imperial Road
Mrs A. Greenwood, 21 Granary Lane, Budleigh Salterton, Devon
Tel: Budleigh Salterton 2290

Faversham C & AC
Queen Elizabeths School
Buses: † Station: Faversham
G.C. Ely, 19 Court St, Faversham, Kent ME13 7AT
Tel: Faversham 2206 (day) 3435 (evenings)

Feltham AC
The Arena, Shakespeare Avenue
Buses: 90B, 116, 117, 285 Station: Feltham
C.L. Milton, 20 Seaton Drive, Ashford, Middx
Tel: Ashford 58851

REGISTER OF CLUBS

Club									
Fleet & Crookham AC Peter Driver Sports Ground, Crookham Buses: 12, 83, 9, 73 Station: Fleet Mrs M. Kitching Ormonde, Avenue Road, Fleet, Aldershot, Hants Tel: Fleet 3032	■	■				Sprints M Distance Jumps Throws	70	Tues Eve Sun am	50p	£1·30
Folkestone AC Summer: Shorncliffe Camp Track Winter: Folkestone Sports Centre, Radnor Park Avenue Buses: † Station: Folkestone Central A.K. French, 18 Bathurst, Folkestone, Kent Tel: Folkestone 56330	■	■				Sprints M Distance	42	Tues Eve Thurs Eve Sun am	50p	£1
*Golden Vale AC St Josephs Parish Hall Buses: † Station: † D. Barry, 30 Bedford Road, W. Ealing, W13			■			M Distance	30	Weekday Eves Sat am/pm Sun am	50p	£1
Great Yarmouth & District AC Wellesley Road Recreation Ground Buses: † Station: Vauxhall B.D. Jarvis, 328 Beccles Rd, Gorleston-on-Sea Tel: Great Yarmouth 63966	■	■		■		Sprints M Distance Jumps Throws	80	Tues Eve Thurs Eve Sun am	50p	£1
Guernsey Island AC Osmond Priaulx Memorial Field, Footes Lane Buses: † Station: None O. Le Vallée, Janstars, Emrais Lane, Catel Guernsey Tel: 0481 55160				■	1975	M Distance	20	Tues Eve Sun am	50p	£2
Guildford & Godalming AC Bannister Running Track, Guildford Buses: † Station: Guildford L.G. Hobbs, 3 Woodlands Road, Guildford, Surrey. Tel: Guildford 4055	■	■		■		Sprints M Distance Jumps Throws	100	Tues Eve Thurs Eve Sun am	50p	£2
*Hadleigh Olympiads John H. Burrows Recreation Ground Buses: † Station: † C. Powell, 60 Smallgains Ave, Canvey Island, Essex Tel: Canvey Island 4222	■	■		■		Sprints M Distance Jumps Throws	120	Tues Eve Thurs Eve Sun am	75p	£1·50

129

SOUTHERN AREA

*Questionnaire not returned, information based on entry in *Athletics 74*
†Insufficient information received

Club with Principal Track used, Secretaries, and nearest Public Transport

	Haringey & Southgate AC	Harlow AC	*Haslemere Border AC	Hastings AC	Havering AC	Hayes – Phoenix Ladies AC
Senior Subscription	£5	£1·50 £2·50	£3	£1	£3	£1
Junior Subscription	£2	£1·50	50p £1 £1·50	50p	£1 £2	50p
Training Sessions	Tues pm Thurs pm Sun am	Mon Eve Thurs Eve Sun am	Tues Eve Wed Eve Thurs Eve Sat am/pm Sun am/pm	Tues Eve Wed Eve Thurs Eve Sun am	Mon Eve Wed Eve Sun am	Tues pm Thurs pm Sun am
Active Membership	270	100	40	45	250	30
Coaches	Sprints M Distance Jumps Throws	Sprints M Distance Jumps Throws	Sprints M Distance Jumps Throws	Sprints M Distance Jumps Throws	Sprints M Distance Jumps Throws	Sprints M Distance Jumps Throws
Weight Training	■	■	■	■	■	■
Indoor Training	■	■	■	■		
Floodlit Training	Sub includes free use of centre facilities	■		■	■	■
Landing Beds		■		■	■	■
All-Weather Runways	■	■			■	■
All-Weather Track	■		110m		■	
League	■	■	■	■	■	■
Juniors	■	■		■	■	■
Women	■	■		■	■	■
Men	■	■	■	■	■	

Haringey & Southgate AC
New River Sports Centre, White Hart Lane N22
Buses: W3   Station: Wood Green
F. Thomas, 10 St Georges Rd, Palmers Green N13
Tel: 01-886 1744

Harlow AC
Harlow Sports Centre
Buses: 724, 720, 718   Station: Harlow Town
D.W.E. Patey, 5 High Street, Stanstead Abbotts, Herts SG12 8AA

***Haslemere Border AC**
Woolmer High School
Buses: †   Station: †
P. Fillingham, 15 Weyland Close, Liphook

Hastings AC
William Parker Stadium, Parkstone Road
Buses: 74   Station: Hastings
B. Griffin, 22 Githa Road, Hastings
Tel: Hastings 431236

Havering AC
Hornchurch Stadium, Bridge Ave, Upminster
Buses: †   Station: Upminster Bridge
D.A. Howell, 74b Station Lane, Hornchurch, Essex RM12 6NA. Tel: Hornchurch 44265

Hayes – Phoenix Ladies AC
Hayes Stadium, Judge Heath Lane
Buses: †   Station: †
Miss P.E. Gaze, 33 Maricas Ave, Harrow HA3 6JA
Tel: 01-863 3961

REGISTER OF CLUBS

Club	Events	No.	Training Times	Fees
*Haywards Heath Harriers Buses: † Station: † Mrs D. Thomas, 33 Penn Crescent, Haywards Heath, Sussex	†	40	Tues Eve Sun am	25p / 50p
Hercules Wimbledon AC Wimbledon Park Track Buses: 77A Station: Wimbledon Park Mrs M. Payce-Drury, 60 Tranmere Road SW18 3QJ	Sprints M Distance Jumps Throws	280	Tues pm Thurs pm Sat am Sun am	50p / £2
Herne Hill Harriers Crystal Palace and (summer: Tooting Bec, winter: Brockwell Park) Buses: † Station: Crystal Palace, Tooting Bec & Herne Hill (BP) L. Fitton, 185 Rosendale Ave, W. Dulwich SE21 8LW Tel: 01-761 0583 (H) 01-222 8020 (office)	Sprints M Distance Jumps Throws	410	Tues Eve Thurs Eve Sun am	£1 / £2
Hertford AC Simon Balle School Buses: 310, 393, 724, 715, 395, 390, 350, 384, 331, 327, 351 Station: Hertford East or Hertford North R. Norman, Brook House, 16 London Road, Ware, Herts Tel: Ware 5506	M Distance Jumps Throws	46	Wed Eve Sun am	75p–£1 / £1·50
Highgate Harriers Parliament Hill Track Buses: 63, 214 Station: Gospel Oak F.S. Cuthbert, 37 The Meadway, Cuffley, Potters Bar, Herts Tel: Cuffley 2695	Sprints M Distance Jumps	150/200	Tues Eve Wed Eve Thurs Eve Sun am	£1 / £2
Hillingdon AC Hayes Stadium, Judge Heath Lane Buses: 98A, 204 Station: Hayes L.J. Cressy, 21 Boundary Road, Eastcote, Pinner, Middlesex Tel: 01-868 9978 Miss C.A. Jackson, 2 Juniper Close, Rickmansworth, Herts. Tel: Rickmansworth 76881 (ladies section)	Sprints M Distance Jumps Throws	300	Tues Eve Thurs Eve Sun am	£1 / £2 / £3

ATHLETICS 75

SOUTHERN AREA

*Questionnaire not returned, information based on entry in *Athletics 74*
†Insufficient information received

Club with Principal Track used, Secretaries, and nearest Public Transport

		Horsham Blue Star Harriers	Huntingdon AC	Ilford AC	Invicta AC	Ipswich Harriers
Senior Subscription		£1	£2	£2	£2	£1 (women) £2 (men)
Junior Subscription		50p	50p	75p £1·25	(15-18) 75p (18-21) £1·25	(U 15) 30p
Training Sessions		Mon Eve Tues Eve Wed Eve	Tues Eve Wed Eve Thurs Eve	Mon Eve Tues Eve Wed Eve Thurs Eve Sat pm Sun am	Tues Eve Thurs Eve Sun am	Tues Eve Wed Eve Thurs Eve Sun am
Active Membership		70	50	200	50	150
Coaches		Sprints M Distance Jumps Throws	Sprints M Distance Jumps Throws	Sprints M Distance Jumps Throws	Sprints M Distance Jumps Throws	Sprints M Distance Jumps Throws
Weight Training		■	■	■	■	■
Indoor Training		■	■			■
Floodlit Training			■	■		■
Landing Beds			■			■
All-Weather Runways						
All-Weather Track			■			
League		■		■	■	■
Juniors		■	■	■		■
Women				■		■
Men		■	■	■	■	■

Horsham Blue Star Harriers
Christ's Hospital School
Buses: † Station: Christ's Hospital
J. W. Linfield, Wyndham, Henfield Road,
Cowfold, Horsham, Sussex
Tel: Cowfold 545

Huntingdon AC
St Ivo Sports Complex
Buses: † Station: Huntingdon
L. Joyce, Manor Farm, Wistow, Huntingdon,
Cambs PE17 2QB
Tel: Warboys 689

Ilford AC
Cricklefield Sports Ground
Buses: 721, 86, 25 Station: Seven Kings
A.P. Tiffin, 287 Hornchurch Rd, Hornchurch,
Essex. Tel: Hornchurch 47366

Invicta AC
Upton School, Broadstairs
Buses: † Station: Broadstairs
Miss A.M. Christian, 9 Lenham Gardens,
Garlinge, Margate, Kent
Tel: Thanet 31601

Ipswich Harriers
Alderman Road Recreation Ground
Buses: † Station: Ipswich
A. Milton, Bramford Lodge, Bramford, Ipswich,
Suffolk IP8 4AZ

REGISTER OF CLUBS

Club							Events	Members	Training	Fee	Sub
Kent AC Ladywell Recreation Ground, Lewisham Buses: 36, 47, 54, 75, 141, 185 Station: Ladywell P.R. Yates, 18 Claremont Crescent, Crayford, Kent Tel: Crayford 25860	■	■	■	■			Sprints M Distance	75	Tues Eve Thurs Eve Sun am	75p	£3
London AC Hurlingham Stadium Buses: † Station: Putney Bridge T.H. Mendez, 1 Little Orchard, Woodham, Weybridge, Surrey. Tel: Byfleet 41866	■	■	■	■			Sprints M Distance Jumps Throws	60	Tues Eve Wed Eve Sun am	75p	£2
London Irish AC West London Stadium, Ducane Road Buses: 7, 72, 220 Station: East Acton (central line) J. Dorgan, 391 Harlesden Road, London NW10 Tel: 01-459 2368	■	■	■	■			Sprints M Distance Jumps Throws	65	Tues pm Thurs Eve Sun am	50p	£1
London Olympiades AC West London Stadium Buses: 7, 72 Station: East Acton H. Reynolds, 7 Monks Park Gdns, Wembley, Middx. Tel: 01-902 7537	■	■	■	■			Sprints M Distance Jumps Throws	50	Tues Eve Thurs Eve Sun am	50p	£1
Loughton AC Railways Sports Club, Highland Avenue Buses: 20A, 254 Station: Loughton B.R. Edwards, 'Woodcroft', Whitakers Way, Loughton, Essex. Tel: 01-508 2578	■				■	■	Sprints M Distance Jumps Throws	25	Tues Eve Sat pm	35p	£2
***Lowestoft AC** Buses: † Station: † B.R. Boardley, 191 St Peter's Street, Lowestoft, Suffolk Tel: Lowestoft 63591		■	■				Sprints Jumps	60	Mon Eve Wed Eve Sun am	25p	£1
Luton United AC Stockwood Park Buses: † Station: Luton A.W. Thorpe, 19 Hollybush Lane, Harpenden, Herts AL5 4AS Tel: Harpenden 61403	■	■	■				Sprints M Distance Throws	200	Mon Eve Wed Eve Sun am/pm	(U 16) 75p (16-18) £1·25 (18-20) £1·75	£2·50

133

ATHLETICS 75

	Maidenhead AC	Medway AC	Middlesex Ladies AC	Mitcham AC	*Newbury AC
Senior Subscription	£2	£2·50	£1·50	£2·50	£1·50
Junior Subscription		(U 18) £1 (18–21) £2	£1	£1·50	50p
Training Sessions	Tues Eve Thurs Eve	Mon Eve Thurs Eve Sun am	Mon Eve Tues Eve Wed Eve Thurs Eve Sat pm (winter) Sun am	Mon Eve Tues Eve Thurs Eve Sun am	Thurs Eve Sun am
Active Membership	80	209	250	100	60
Coaches	†	Sprints M Distance Jumps Throws	Sprints M Distance Jumps Throws	Sprints M Distance Jumps Throws	
Weight Training		■	■	■	■
Indoor Training		■	■		■
Floodlit Training			■		
Landing Beds	■	■	■		
All-Weather Runways			■		
All-Weather Track					
League		■		■	■
Juniors	■	■		■	■
Women	■	■	■	■	■
Men	■	■	■	■	■

SOUTHERN AREA

*Questionnaire not returned, information based on entry in *Athletics 74*
†Insufficient information received

Club with Principal Track used, Secretaries, and nearest Public Transport

Maidenhead AC
Braywick Playing Fields
Buses: † Station: Maidenhead
S. Wight, 1 Pendeen, Cannon Lane, Maidenhead, Berks
Tel: Littlewick Green 2348

Medway AC
Garrison Stadium, Gillingham
Buses: † Station: Gillingham
L. Smith, 5 The Shades, Knights Place, Strood, Kent ME2 2UD
Tel: Medway 70224 (home) 01-686 8710 (office)

Middlesex Ladies AC
Vale Farm Track, Sudbury & Bannister Stadium, Harrow
Buses: 245, 182 Station: N. Wembley, Sudbury Town, Hatch End for Harrow
Miss E. Matthews, 91 Abbotts Drive, North Wembley, Middlesex HA0 3SB
Tel: 01-904 7875

Mitcham AC
Tweedale Road, Carshalton
Buses: 157, 80, 80A Station: St Heliers or Morden (tube)
J. McKenna, 4 Almond Ave, Carshalton, Surrey
Tel: 01-647 3462

*Newbury AC
Girls County Grammar School
Buses: † Station: †
Miss P.B. Killbery, 8 Beverley Close, Thatcham, Newbury, Berks
Tel: Newbury 5306

134

REGISTER OF CLUBS

Club	Sprints	M Distance	Jumps	Throws	(events/members)	Training times	Fees
Newham AC Terence McMillan Stadium, Plaistow Buses: 262 Station: Plaistow D. Royle, 70 West Road, Stratford, London E15 Tel: 01-472 4849	■			■ (Sprints, Throws)	60	Mon Eve Wed Eve Thurs Eve Sun am	50p £1·25
Norfolk Olympiads Lakenham Playing Fields, Norwich Buses: † Station: Norwich E.C. Comber, 14 Stratford Cse, Norwich Nor 68C Tel: Norwich 24421	■	■		■ (Sprints, M Distance, Jumps, Throws)	120	Tues Eve Wed Eve Fri Eve (winter)	50p £1
***North Dorset AC** Christy's School, Shaftesbury Buses: † Station: † Miss B. Adams, P.E. Dept, Christy's School, Christy's Lane, Shaftesbury, Dorset Tel: Shaftesbury 2329	■		■	■ (Sprints, Jumps, Throws)		Tues Eve Wed Eve	50p £1
North London AC Finsbury Park Buses: † Station: Manor House D.J. Blackmore, 8 Beeston Way, Feltham, Middx Tel: 01-890 9584	■	■	■	■ (Sprints, M Distance, Jumps, Throws)	50+	Mon Eve Tues Eve Wed Eve Thurs Eve Fri Eve Sat pm Sun am	£1 £2
Oxford City AC Iffley Road Track Buses: † Station: Oxford S.A. Handscombe, Blue Haze, Stanville Road, Cumnorhill, Oxford Tel: Cumnor 2725		■	■	■ (M Distance, Jumps, Throws)	100	Tues Eve Thurs Eve	50p £2 £6
Oxford Ladies' AC Horspath Road Sports Ground Buses: 10 Station: Oxford Miss E.M. Little, 21 Ashlong Road, Headington, Oxford Tel: Oxford 63480	■	■		■ (Sprints, M Distance, Throws)	70	Tues Eve Thurs Eve	30p 75p

135

SOUTHERN AREA

*Questionnaire not returned, information based on entry in *Athletics 74*
†Insufficient information received

Club with Principal Track used, Secretaries, and nearest Public Transport

	Parkside AC	Peterborough AC	City of Plymouth AC	Polytechnic Harriers	*Poole AC
Senior Subscription	£1·25	£2	£1	£4·30	£2
Junior Subscription	75p	50p	50p	£1	£1
Training Sessions	Mon pm, Tues pm, Wed pm, Thurs pm, Sun am	Tues Eve, Thurs pm, Sun am	Tues Eve, Thurs Eve	Mon pm, Wed pm, Thurs pm, Sun am	Mon Eve, Tues Eve, Thurs Eve, Sun am/pm
Active Membership	35	†	200	†	15
Coaches	Sprints, M Distance, Jumps, Throws	Sprints, M Distance, Jumps, Throws	Sprints, M Distance, Jumps, Throws	Sprints, M Distance, Jumps, Throws	M Distance
Weight Training	■	■	■	■	■
Indoor Training		■	■	■	■
Floodlit Training		■			
Landing Beds	■	■		■	
All-Weather Runways		■		■	
All-Weather Track					
League		■	■	■	■
Juniors	■	■	■	■	
Women	■	■		■	
Men		■	■	■	■

Parkside AC
Bannister Stadium, Uxbridge Road
Buses: † Station: Hatch End
Mrs S. Parker, 145 The Ridgeway, North Harrow, Middlesex
Tel: 01-866 4588

Peterborough AC
Embankment Track, Bishops Road
Buses: † Station: Peterborough North
F.D. Slater, 9 Gladstone St, Peterborough PE1 2BE

City of Plymouth AC
The Brickfields
Buses: † Station: Plymouth North End
R. Harris, 18 Amados Dve, Plympton, Plymouth
Tel: Plymouth 39764

Polytechnic Harriers
Chiswick Stadium
Buses: E10 Station: Chiswick
R. Frith, 9 Holmes Rd, Strawberry Hill, Twickenham, Middlesex
Tel: 01-892 2826 (home) 01-891 1688 (bus)

***Poole AC**
Poole Sports Centre
Buses: † Station: †
Mrs S. Neville, 33 Pearce Avenue, Parkstone, Poole, Dorset

Club	Events	Members	Training	Fees
Portsmouth AC Alexandra Park Buses: 19, 20 Station: Portsmouth & Southsea A. Gibb, 8 Magdalen Court, 355 London Road, Portsmouth PO2 9HH Tel: Portsmouth 64574	Sprints M Distance Jumps Throws	100	Tues pm Thurs pm Sun am	(colts) 25p (youth) 50p (junior) £1 £2
Portsmouth Atalanta AC Alexndra Park Buses: † Station: Fratton Mrs V. Tubb, 46 Oliver Rd, Southsea, Hants	Sprints M Distance Jumps Throws	100	Mon pm/Eve Tues pm/Eve Thurs pm/Eve Sun am	30p 65p
***Queens Park Harriers** Vale Farm Sports Centre, Wembley Buses: † Station: † F. Petit, 39 Stedham Chambers, Coptie St, London W1 Tel: 01-636 5505	Sprints M Distance	150	Tues Eve Thurs Eve Sun am	40p (U 15) 75p (U 18) £1 (U 21) £1·50
Radley Ladies AC Radley College Buses: 8A from Oxford Station: Oxford, Didcot or Radley (occasional) Mrs O.D. Cameron, 19 Chaunterell Way, Abingdon, Oxfordshire	Sprints M Distance Jumps	40	Mon Eve Wed Eve Sun pm	80p (intermediate) £1 £1·25
Reading AC Palmer Park Buses: 16, 17 Station: Reading General L.C. Masters, 75 Hemdean Road, Caversham, Reading, Berks Tel: Reading 471120 Mrs S. Bacon, Holly View, 29 Heath Hill Road, Crowthorne, Berks Tel: Crowthorne 6264 (ladies section)	Sprints M Distance High Jump Javelin	200	Tues Eve Wed Eve Thurs Eve Sun pm	£1 (U 16) £2 (16-18) £3
Redhill & Reigate AC Battlebridge Track Buses: 414, 405 Station: Redhill D.C Ruddle, 49 Monson Road, Redhill RH1 2EU	Sprints M Distance Jumps Throws	130	Mon Eve Tues Eve Thurs Eve Sun am	£2 £3

ATHLETICS 75

SOUTHERN AREA

*Questionnaire not returned, information based on entry in *Athletics 74*
†Insufficient information received

Club with Principal Track used, Secretaries, and nearest Public Transport

	Ryde Harriers	Salisbury & District AC	Selsonia Ladies AC	Shaftesbury Harriers	Solent AC
Senior Subscription	£2.50	£2	£1.50	£3	£1
Junior Subscription	75p	£1.25	£1	75p (U 15) £1 (U 17) £1.50 (U 19)	50p
Training Sessions	Mon Eve Tues Eve Wed Eve Thurs Eve Fri Eve Sun am	Tues Eve Wed Eve Thurs Eve	Tues Eve Thurs Eve Sun am	Tues Eve Thurs Eve Sun am	Tues Eve Thurs Eve Sat pm
Active Membership	50	40	40	250	93
Coaches	Sprints M Distance Jumps Throws	M Distance Throws	Sprints M Distance Jumps Throws	Sprints M Distance Jumps Throws	Sprints M Distance Jumps Throws
Weight Training	■	■	■	■	
Indoor Training	■		■		■
Floodlit Training			■	■	
Landing Beds			■	■	
All-Weather Runways			■		
All-Weather Track	■				
League		■			
Juniors	■	■	■		■
Women	■	■	■		■
Men	■	■	■	■	■

Ryde Harriers
19 High Street, Oakfield
Buses: 6B, 16 Station: St John's Ryde
The Club Secretary, Ryde Harriers & Supporters Club, 19 High Street, Oakfield, Ryde, Isle of Wight

Salisbury & District AC
St Joseph's School, Laverstock
Buses: † Station: Salisbury
H. Fulford, 50 Gurnays Mead, West Wellow, Romsey, Hants
Tel: West Wellow 22124

Selsonia Ladies AC
Tooting Bec Track
Buses: 49 Station: Tooting Bec
Mr M.A. Patterson, 4 Dingley Lane, Drewstead Road, Streatham SW16 1AY
Tel: 01-769 2554

Shaftesbury Harriers
Copthall Stadium, Hendon
Buses: 113, 125, 240 Station: Hendon Central
B. Smith, 2A Ash Tree Road, Watford, Herts
Tel: Watford 34054

Solent AC
Cowes, Freshwater & Newport Area
Buses: † Station: †
A.R. Mellor, MBE, Lamb Cottage, Newtown, Newport, Isle of Wight
Tel: Calbourne 250

REGISTER OF CLUBS

Club	Location / Contact	Events	Members	Training	Fees
Southampton & Eastleigh AC	(1) Test Track, Porlock Road, Redbridge; (2) Sports Centre; (3) Deanery School, Marsh Lane; (4) Bishopstoke Recreation, Eastleigh. Buses: (1) 5, 9; (2) 4, 5, 6, 2; (3) 1, 3, 7, 9, 11, 13; (4) None. Stations: (1) Redbridge; (2) Southampton; (3) Southampton; (4) Eastleigh. A.F. Cropp, B.Sc., 8 Donnington Grove, Highfield, Southampton SO2 1RW. Tel: Southampton 556945	Sprints ■ / M Distance ■ / Jumps ■ / Throws ■	224	Tues Eve / Thurs Eve / Sun am	£1·50 (U 15) / £2·50 / £3·50
Southend-on-Sea AC	Southchurch Park. Buses: † Station: Southend East. P.A. Grumbridge, 19 Hermitage Road, Westcliff-on-Sea, Essex SS0 7NQ. Tel: Southend 41590	Sprints ■ / M Distance ■ / Jumps ■ / Throws ■	150	Tues Eve / Thurs Eve / Sun am	£1 / £2
South London Harriers AC	Tooting Common. Buses: 49, 249 Station: Tooting Bec. W.D. Thomas, 14 St Barnabas Road, Mitcham, Surrey CR4 2DU. Tel: 01-648 3603	M Distance ■ / Throws ■	150	Tues Eve / Thurs Eve / Sun am	50p (U 18) / £1 (U 20) / £2·25
Spartan Ladies AC	Wimbledon Common, Twickenham Track & Hurlingham Track. Buses: † Station: †. Miss M. Hartman, MBE, 70 Brompton Road, London SW3. Tel: 01-584 6876	Sprints ■ / M Distance ■ / Jumps ■ / Throws ■	30	Tues pm / Thurs pm / Sun am	50p / £1
Stevenage & N. Herts AC	Ridlins Wood Track, Stevenage. Buses: 800 Station: Stevenage. R.I.M Purkis, 25 Stonycroft, Stevenage, Herts SG1 3TW. Tel: Stevenage 50767. Mrs R.P. Osborne, 50 Cromwell Road, Stevenage, Herts. Tel: Stevenage 53896 (ladies section)	Sprints ■ / M Distance ■ / Jumps ■ / Throws ■	180	Tues Eve / Thurs Eve / Sun am	65p (boys) / £1·20 (youths) / £1·75 (junior) / £2·50

ATHLETICS 75

SOUTHERN AREA

*Questionnaire not returned, information based on entry in *Athletics 74*
†Insufficient information received

Club with Principal Track used, Secretaries, and nearest Public Transport

	Steyning AC	Surrey AC	Surrey Beagles AC*	Sutton & Cheam Harriers	Swindon AC
Senior Subscription	53p	£2·50	£1·50	£3	£1·25
Junior Subscription	25p	£1 (U 16) £1·75 (U 19)	75p	£1	25p (U 16) 75p (16–18)
Training Sessions	Tues pm Thurs pm Sun am/pm	Tues Eve Thurs Eve Sun am	Tues Eve Thurs Eve	Mon Eve Wed Eve Sun am	Tues Eve Wed Eve
Active Membership	30	200	120	70	60
Coaches	†	Sprints M Distance Jumps Throws	Jumps	Sprints M Distance Jumps Throws	Sprints M Distance
Weight Training		■	■	■	
Indoor Training		■	■	■	■
Floodlit Training					
Landing Beds		■		■	
All-Weather Runways		■			
All-Weather Track					
League		■	■	■	■
Juniors	■	■	■	■	
Women		■	■	■	■
Men	■	■	■	■	■

Steyning AC
Charlton Street
Buses: 80, 80A Station: Shoreham-by-Sea
D.J. Stevens, 26 Breach Close, Steyning,
Sussex BN4 3RZ
Tel: Steyning 814422

Surrey AC
Norbiton Sports Centre
Buses: 131, 285 Station: Norbiton
G.R.V. Davis, 135 Thetford Road, New
Malden, Surrey
Tel: 01-949 4684
S.C. Belton, 75 St Philips Avenue,
Worcester Park, Surrey
Tel: 01-337 8607 (ladies section)

*Surrey Beagles AC
Caterham Guards Depot
Buses: † Station: †
R.J. Teece, 24 Macauley Road, Caterham,
Surrey. Tel: Caterham 47416

Sutton & Cheam Harriers
Borough Sports Ground
Buses: 408, 470, 213, 725 Station: West Sutton
D. Bennett, 27 Lavender Close, Carshalton,
Surrey
Tel: 01-647 1877 (home) 01-643 3355 xt 487 (bus)

Swindon AC
Walcot School, Frobisher Drive
Buses: † Station: Swindon
W.A. Townsend, 280 Cricklade Road,
Swindon, Wilts SN2 6AY
Tel: Swindon 4559

REGISTER OF CLUBS

Club													
Taunton & West Somerset AC Somerset College of Art & Technology Buses: † Station: Taunton Mrs C. Brice, The Elms, Norton Fitzwarren Nr Taunton, Somerset Tel: Taunton 82866	■	■			■	■	Sprints M Distance Jumps Throws	80	Wed pm (winter) Thurs pm (summer) Sat pm (winter)	40p	£2
Thames Valley Harriers West London Stadium Buses: 72 Station: East Acton or White City P.J. Vivian, 4 Catherine's Close, West Drayton, Middlesex UB7 7PB A.C. Bentall (assistant secretary) Tel: Uxbridge 38870	■	■	■	■	■	■	Sprints M Distance Jumps Throws	200	Tues pm Thurs pm Sun am	50p (U 17) £1 (17–19 + students)	£2·50
Thurrock Harriers King George's Sports Ground Buses: † Station: Grays P.G. Orpin, 'Reduit', 24 King Edward Road, Stanford-le-Hope, Essex Tel: Stanford-le-Hope 6050	■	■	■	■		■	Sprints M Distance Jumps Throws	200	Mon Eve Tues Eve Wed Eve Thurs Eve Sat am/pm Sun am	50p	£1·50
Tiverton Harriers AC Bolham Road Buses: † Station: Tiverton Junction P.F. Main, 66 Temple Crescent, Tiverton, Devon Tel: Tiverton 4803					■		Sprints M Distance	45	Tues Eve Thurs Eve Sun am	50p	£1
Tonbridge AC Swanmead Buses: 7, 98 Station: Tonbridge Mrs V.M. Searle, Gulvac, Castle Hill, Brenchley, Tonbridge TN12 7BG Tel: Brenchley 2436	■	■	■	■	■	■	No qualified coaching	200	Tues Eve Thurs Eve Sun am	75p	£2
Torbay AC Torre Valley North Buses: 12, 30 Station: Torquay A.A. Sanders, 'Rozel', 11 Green Park Road, Paignton TQ3 1AH Tel: Torquay 22211 (bus)	■	■			■	■	Sprints M Distance Jumps Throws	270	Tues Eve Thurs Eve	50p (U 13)	£1

141

ATHLETICS 75

SOUTHERN AREA

*Questionnaire not returned, information based on entry in *Athletics 74*
†Insufficient information received

Club with Principal Track used, Secretaries, and nearest Public Transport

		Trowbridge & District AC — Sports Hall, Frome Road, Buses: † Station: † I.S. Farr, 24 Victoria Gardens, Trowbridge, Wilts Tel: Trowbridge 5605	*Twickenham AC — Craneford Way Stadium Buses: † Station: † T. Brooks, 214 High Road, Chiswick, London W4	Uxbridge & District Ladies AC — Uxbridge Track, Park Road Buses: 223 Station: Uxbridge A.C. Low, 60 Swakeleys Road, Ickenham, Uxbridge, Middx UB10 8BD Tel: Ruislip 38741	Vale of Aylesbury AC — Edinburgh Playing Fields Buses: † Station: Aylesbury A. Hepworth, 12 Vale Road, Aylesbury, Bucks HP20 1JA Tel: Aylesbury 84808	Verlea AC — Gosling Stadium, Welwyn Garden City Buses: † Station: Welwyn Garden City or St Albans Mrs P. Cantien, 2 Bull Stag Green, Hatfield, Herts Tel: Hatfield 66619
Senior Subscription		£1·10	£1·50	£2	50p to £3	£4
Junior Subscription		60p	75p	£1	£1·50 Depending on age	£1 (9-11) £1·50 (11-15) £2·50 (15-18)
Training Sessions		Tues Eve Thurs Eve Sun am	Tues Eve Thurs Eve Sun am	Mon Eve (winter) Tues Eve Wed Eve (winter) Thurs Eve Sun am	Tues Eve Thurs Eve	Tues Eve Wed Eve Thurs Eve Sat am Sun am/pm
Active Membership		40	85	80	150	300
Coaches		†	Sprints M Distance Jumps Throws	Sprints M Distance Jumps Throws Walks	†	Sprints M Distance Jumps Throws
Weight Training			■	■	■	■
Indoor Training				■	■	
Floodlit Training				■		
Landing Beds				■	■	■
All-Weather Runways						
All-Weather Track						
League		■	■		■	■
Juniors		■	■			
Women		■	■			
Men		■	■	■	■	

REGISTER OF CLUBS

Club					
Victoria Park Harriers Victoria Park Track, Hackney Buses: 6, 236, 30, S2 Station: † M.T. Carr, Flat 5, 52 Highbury Hill, London N5 Tel: 01-638 9427 (bus)	■ ■ ■	Sprints M Distance Jumps Throws	120	Mon Eve Tues Eve Wed Eve Thurs Eve Sun am/pm	£2	£3
Walthamstow AC Wadham Lodge Sports Ground Buses: 69, 38, W21 Station: Walthamstow Central B.W. Hart, 23 St James Street, London E17 Tel: 01-520 4548	■ ■ ■ ■	M Distance Throws	50	Tues Eve Thurs Eve	25p	£2
Walton AC Stompond Lane Sports Ground Buses: 218, 219 Station: Walton-on-Thames J.F. Harding, 15 Woodside Avenue, Walton-on-Thames Tel: Walton-on-Thames 27393	■ ■ ■	†	60	Tues Eve Thurs Eve Sun am	£1	£3
Watford Harriers Woodside Stadium Buses: 719, 347 Station: Watford Junction K. Morton, 17 Kendale, Hemel Hempstead, Herts Tel: 0442 3976	■ ■ ■ ■	Sprints M Distance Jumps Throws	120	Tues pm Thurs pm Sun am	£1	£3
West Cornwall AC Carn Brea Track, Pool, Nr Redruth Buses: † Station: Camborne/Redruth K.E.E. Naylor, 59 Pendrea Park, Camborne, TR14 8PF Cornwall Tel: Camborne 4005	■ ■ ■	Sprints M Distance Jumps	35	Tues Eve Thurs Eve	50p	£1·50
West Norfolk AC Norfolk College of Arts & Technology King's Lynn Buses: † Station: King's Lynn J.R. Humphreys, 376 Wootton Road, King's Lynn, Norfolk Tel: King's Lynn 672279	■ ■ ■	Sprints M Distance Jumps	60	Tues Eve Thurs Eve Sun am	50p	£1·50

143

ATHLETICS 75

SOUTHERN AREA

*Questionnaire not returned, information based on entry in *Athletics 74*
†Insufficient information received

Club with Principal Track used, Secretaries, and nearest Public Transport

	West Suffolk AC	Weymouth St Pauls Harriers & AC	Wigmore Ladies AC	Windsor, Slough & Eton AC	Woking AC
Senior Subscription	£1	£1	£1	£2	£2
Junior Subscription	25p	50p	50p	50p	£1
Training Sessions	Tues Eve, Thurs Eve	Tues Eve, Thurs Eve	Tues Eve, Thurs Eve, Sun am	Tues Eve, Thurs Eve, Sun am	Tues Eve, Thurs Eve, Sun am
Active Membership	50	50	40/50	330	60
Coaches	Sprints, M Distance, Jumps, Throws	†	Sprints, M Distance, Jumps, Throws	Sprints, M Distance, Jumps, Throws	Sprints, M Distance, Jumps, Throws
Weight Training			■	■	■
Indoor Training	■		■	■	■
Floodlit Training			■		■
Landing Beds	■	■	■	■	■
All-Weather Runways			■	■	
All-Weather Track			■	■	
League	■	■	■	■	■
Juniors	■	■	■	■	
Women	■	■	■	■	
Men	■	■		■	■

West Suffolk AC
Haverhill Sports Centre
Buses: † Station: Audley End
Mrs K. Lloyd, Weathercock Farm,
Barnardiston, Haverhill, Suffolk
Tel: Hundon 291

Weymouth St Pauls Harriers & AC
Athletic Centre, Knightsdale Road
Buses: † Station: Weymouth
R.J. Porter, 29 Comet Close,
Littlesea Rise, Weymouth

Wigmore Ladies AC
Crystal Palace Sports Centre
Buses: 227 Station: Crystal Palace
Mrs D. Reed, 16 Pickhurst Green,
Hayes, Bromley, Kent BR2 7QT
Tel: 01-462 1148

Windsor, Slough & Eton AC
Vansittart Road
Buses: 441, 417, 460, 353, 335, 704 Station:
Windsor & Eton or Riverside W & E
D. Daly, 11 Carter Close, Windsor
Tel: Windsor 51847

Woking AC
Sheerwater Track
Buses: † Station: Woking
E. Davidson, Hindlee, Lane End Drive,
Knaphill, Surrey

REGISTER OF CLUBS

Club	Facilities	Track (m)	Training	Fees
Wolverton AC Radcliffe School Buses: † Station: Wolverton A.R. Green, 13 Church Street, New Bradwell, Wolverton, Milton Keynes Tel: Wolverton 313315 (M. Callow – Chairman)	■ ■ ■	†	No qualified coach	Tues Eve Thurs Eve (summer)	50p £1
Women's Veterans' AC Mrs H. Rider, 1 Malthouse Lane, Shorne, Gravesend, Kent Tel: Shorne 2402		12			£1
Woodford Green AC Ashton Playing Fields Buses: 275, 10 Station: Woodford K. Hopson, 51 Kimberley Road, Chingford, London E4	■ ■ ■ ■ ■ ■ ■ ■	150	Sprints M Distance Jumps Throws	Mon Eve Tues Eve Wed Eve Thurs Eve Sat pm Sun am	£1 £1·50 £3
Worthing & District Harriers West Park, Worthing Buses: 31 Station: Durrington-on-Sea Mrs P. Leeves, 20 Falmer Close, Goring-by-Sea, Sussex Tel: Worthing 45837	■ ■ ■ ■ ■	175	Sprints M Distance Jumps Throws	Tues Eve Thurs Eve	50p £1·50
Wycombe Phoenix Harriers & AC Club House, Keep Hill Road Buses: † Station: High Wycombe R. Buzzard, 'Stoneways', 29 Chapmans Lane, Flackwell Heath, Bucks Tel: Bourne End 21804	■ ■ ■ ■ ■	200	Sprints M Distance Jumps Throws	Tues Eve Thurs Eve Sun am	20p £1·50 £1·50 to join
Yeovil Olympiads AC Yeovil Recreation Centre Buses: 264 Station: Yeovil Junction N. Chislett, 305 St Michaels Avenue, Yeovil, Somerset BA21 4ND Tel: Yeovil 22143	■ ■ ■	100	Sprints M Distance Jumps Throws	Mon Eve Thurs Eve	50p £1·50 (U 16) 75p (U 20 & still a student)

145

ATHLETICS 75

	Airedale & Spen Valley AC	Altrincham & District AC	Ashington Joint Welfare AC	Bankfield House AC	*Barrow AC
Senior Subscription	£1	£2	£3	10p (per session)	50p
Junior Subscription	60p	75p	Nil	5p (per session)	25p
Training Sessions	Mon Eve Tues Eve Wed Eve Thurs Eve Sat am/pm Sun pm	Tues Eve Thurs Eve Sun am	Mon am/pm Wed am/pm Fri am/pm Sun am/pm	Mon Eve Wed Eve	Tues Eve Thurs Eve Sun am
Active Membership	120	50	20	25	100
Coaches	Sprints M Distance	Sprints M Distance Jumps Throws	†	Sprints M Distance Jumps Throws	Sprints M Distance Jumps Throws
Weight Training		■			■
Indoor Training					■
Floodlit Training	■	■			
Landing Beds	■			■	
All-Weather Runways	■	■			
All-Weather Track	■				
League	■	■			■
Juniors	■	■	■		
Women	■	■	■		
Men	■	■	■	■	■

NORTHERN AREA

*Questionnaire not returned, information based on entry in *Athletics 74*
†Insufficient information received

Club with Principal Track used, Secretaries, and nearest Public Transport

Airedale & Spen Valley AC
Horsfall Playing Fields, Bradford
Spenborough Stadium, Cleckheaton
Buses: 77   Station: Bradford Exchange
K. Duckworth, 70 Marsh St, Bradford BD5 9PB
Tel: Bradford 29761

Altrincham & District AC
Grove Lane Athletic Track
Buses: 271, 280   Station: Altrincham
H.K. Roberts, 50 Cliftonville Drive, Swinton, Lancs

Ashington Joint Welfare AC
Hirst Welfare, Alexandra Road
Buses: †   Station: †
T. Douglas, 4 Rosalind Street, Ashington, Northumberland
Tel: Ashington 813011

Bankfield House AC
Heron Eccles Ground, Abbotshey Avenue, Liverpool 18
Buses: 86, 87   Station: Mossley Hill
Sec: Bankfield House, Banks Rd, Liverpool 19
Tel: 051 427 5796

***Barrow AC**
Risedale County Secondary School
Buses: †   Station: †
C.H. Wood, 8 Birchfields, Barrow-in-Furness, Lancs LA13 0JL

146

REGISTER OF CLUBS

Club								
*Billingham Synthonia AC Belasis Avenue Buses: † Station: † Dr I.J. Thompson, 1 Fernie Road, Hunters Hill, Guisborough, Yorks. Tel: Guisborough 2096	■ ■ ■	M Distance	23	Tues Eve Thurs Eve Sun am	50p	£1
Bingley Harriers & AC Bingley Beckfoot Grammar School Buses: † Station: Bingley M.J. Ebbage, 10 Hazel Beck, Bingley, Yorks BD16 1LZ. Tel: Bingley 5340	■ ■ ■ ■	Sprints M Distance Jumps Throws	100	Tues Eve Thurs Eve Sat pm	25p 50p	£2
Blackburn Harriers & AC Witton Park Athletics Arena Buses: † Station: Blackburn G. Kirby, 115 Revidge Road, Blackburn, Lancs BB2 6EE Tel: Blackburn 663 557 or 54664 (school)	■ ■ ■ ■ ■	Sprints M Distance Jumps Throws	200	Mon Eve Tues Eve Thurs Eve Sun am	80p	£1·50
Blackpool & Fylde AC Stanley Park Athletic Arena, Blackpool Buses: To North Railway Station Station: Blackpool North T.H. Brooks, 16 Manor Rd, Wrea Green, Preston PR4 2PB. Tel: Kirkham 2659	■ ■ ■ ■	Sprints M Distance	100	Tues Eve Thurs Eve Sun am	75p £1	£1·25 £1·50
Blaydon Harriers & AC Blaydon Comprehensive School Buses: Northern Station: Newcastle-upon-Tyne E.W. Garrett, 16 Knoll Rise, Dunston, Gateshead, Tyne & Wear NE11 9QQ. Tel: 0632-604943	■ ■ ■	Sprints M Distance Jumps Throws	60	Tues Eve Thurs Eve Sun am	1974 15p	1974 50p
Blyth AC 11th Avenue Field Buses: † Station: Newcastle J. Sharp, 20 Newsham Road, Blyth, Northumberland	■ ■ ■	Sprints M Distance Throws	50	Mon pm Tues pm Wed pm Thurs pm Sun am	50p	£1
Bolton United Harriers & AC Leverhulme Park Buses: † Station: Thynne Street, Bolton A.R. Elsby, 51 Tong Road, Little Lever, Nr Bolton, Lancs	■ ■ ■ ■	Sprints M Distance Jumps	150	Tues Eve Thurs Eve Sun am	25p 50p	£1·50

147

NORTHERN AREA

*Questionnaire not returned, information based on entry in Athletics 74
†Insufficient information received

Club with Principal Track used, Secretaries, and nearest Public Transport

	Senior Subscription	Junior Subscription	Training Sessions	Active Membership	Coaches	Weight Training	Indoor Training	Floodlit Training	Landing Beds	All-Weather Runways	All-Weather Track	League	Juniors	Women	Men
Border Harriers & AC Sheepmount Track, Carlisle Buses: † Station: Carlisle P.A. Nash, 87 Petteril St, Carlisle CA1 2AW Tel: Carlisle 26795	£1.50	50p	Mon pm Tues pm Thurs pm Sun am	†	Sprints M Distance Jumps Throws	■	■		■			■		■	■
***Boston AC** Boston Grammar School Buses: † Station: † R.W. Anderson, Boston Grammar School, Lincs Tel: Boston 2839	From 50p	From 10p	Tues Eve Thurs Eve	55	Sprints M Distance Jumps Throws				■			■			■
Burnley AC Barden Track, Barden Lane, Burnley Buses: † Station: Burnley Central R. Fisher, 21 Lee Street, Burnley, Lancs BB10 1NJ	£1.50	75p	Tues pm Thurs pm Sun am	50	†		■	■				■		■	■
Burn Road Harriers Grayfields Buses: † Station: Hartlepool 1974 Sec: G.W. Hurst, 7 Parkwood Avenue, Ighten Manor, Burnley, Lancs	50p	25p	Tues pm Thurs pm Sun am	50	Sprints M Distance Jumps Throws							■			■
Bury AC Market Street Track Buses: † Station: Bury W.M. Farnorth, 30 Lowercroft Rd, Bury, Lancs Tel: 061 764 3547	75p	25p	Tues Eve Thurs Eve Sun am	200	Sprints M Distance Jumps Throws		Ladies only		■			■		■	■
Clayton-Le-Moors Harriers Venues change Buses: ⎱ Venues change Station: ⎰ J.K. Windle, 2 Langholme Close, Carr Hall, Barrowford, Nelson, Lancs BB9 6DH	£1	50p	Tues Eve (May–Sept) Sat pm (Oct–Apr)	†	†							■			

REGISTER OF CLUBS

Club	Facilities		Events	Capacity	Times	Fees	
Darlington Harriers Longfield Road Stadium Buses: 1, 1A Station: Darlington M. Frazer, 11 Heslop Drive, Darlington, Co Durham Tel: Darlington 4822	■ ■ ■	HJ	Sprints M Distance Jumps	50	Tues Eve Thurs Eve Sun am	50p	£2
Derby & County AC Derby Municipal Sports Ground Buses: † Station: Derby Midland J.K. Bullock, 13 Mill Close, Newton Solney, Burton-upon-Trent Tel: Repton 2521	■ ■ ■ ■		Sprints M Distance Jumps Throws	†	Wed Eve Sun am	£1	£2·50
***Dorothy Hyman Track Club** Dorothy Hyman Sports Centre, Barnsley Buses: † Station: † Miss J.M. Sanderson, 5 Beaumont Street, Hoyland Common, Nr Barnsley	■ ■ ■ ■ ■ ■ ■		Sprints	100	Mon Eve Tues Eve Wed Eve Sat pm Sun pm	50p	£1
Durham City Harriers Framwellgate Moor Comprehensive School Buses: † Station: Durham J. McMahon, 28 Burnigill, Meadowfield, Co Durham	■ ■ ■		Sprints M Distance	40	Mon Eve Thurs Eve Sun am	£1	£1·50
East Cheshire Harriers & AC Richmond St, Ashton-under-Lyne Buses: † Station: Guide-Bride J. Murphy, 6 Warley Grove, Dukinfield, Cheshire	■ ■		Sprints	60	Tues pm Wed pm Thurs pm Sat pm Sun am	£1·50	£2·50
East Hull Harriers Pavilion, The Paddock, Nr Sutton Golf Course Buses: 56, 55C Station: Paragon J. Crawford, Lang Toft Villa, Beck Lane, Keyingham, Nr Hull. Tel: Key 2629	■		M Distance	†	Mon Eve Tues Eve Sat pm	40p	£1
Elswick Harriers Cowgate School, Cyprus Ave, Newcastle-upon-Tyne Buses: Cowgate Station: Newcastle Central R. Tinkler, 27 Waldridge Road, Chester-le-Street, Co Durham DH2 3AF	■ ■		Sprints M Distance	50	Tues Eve Thurs Eve	12½p 50p	£1·50

149

ATHLETICS 75

NORTHERN AREA

*Questionnaire not returned, information based on entry in *Athletics 74*
†Insufficient information received

Club with Principal Track used, Secretaries, and nearest Public Transport

	Fallowfield Club	Farnworth & District AC	Furness Track & Field Club	Gateshead Harriers & AC	Goole & District Harriers & AC
Senior Subscription	£1·50	37½p	£1·50	£2	80p
Junior Subscription	75p £1	12½p	50p	£1	20p 40p
Training Sessions	No set times	Tues Eve Thurs Eve Sun am	Mon pm Thurs pm Sun am	Tues Eve Thurs Eve Sun am	Mon Eve Wed Eve
Active Membership	45	20	150	100	†
Coaches	Sprints M Distance	Sprints M Distance	Sprints M Distance Jumps Throws	Sprints M Distance Jumps Throws	Sprints M Distance Jumps Throws
Weight Training		■	■	■	■
Indoor Training			■		
Floodlit Training		■	■	■	■
Landing Beds		■	■	■	■
All-Weather Runways	■		■		
All-Weather Track			■		
League		■	■	■	■
Juniors	■	■	■	■	■
Women	■	■	■	■	■
Men	■	■	■	■	■

Fallowfield Club
Fallowfield Stadium
Buses: † Station: Piccadilly, Manchester
N. Grattage, The Stadium, Whitworth Lane, Fallowfield, Manchester M14 6HH
Tel: 061 224 1378

Farnworth & District AC
Harper Green Road, Farnworth
Buses: 73, 675 Station: Bolton
W. Jackson, 21 Mossfield Rd, Kearsley, Bolton
Tel: Farnworth 78760

Furness Track & Field Club
West Shore School
Buses: West Shore Station: Barrow Central
R. Hewson, 2 Cumbria View, Walney Island, Barrow-in-Furness, Cumbria
Tel: Barrow 20351 xt46 (office)

Gateshead Harriers & AC
Gateshead Sports Stadium
Buses: Gateshead–Sunderland Route
Station: Newcastle Central
W. Anderson, 243 Rawling Road, Gateshead 8, Tyne & Wear
Tel: Gateshead 773630

Goole & District Harriers & AC
Victoria Pleasure Grounds, Marcus Street
Buses: † Station: Goole
C. Glasby, 60 Jefferson Street, Goole

150

REGISTER OF CLUBS

Club								Events	Members	Training	Fees
Gosforth Harriers & AC Broadway West Sports Ground Buses: † Station: South Gosforth D.F. Mullen, 19 Bowes Street, Newcastle-upon-Tyne NE3 1SJ Tel: Gosforth 841386	■					■		Sprints M Distance	75	Tues Eve Thurs Eve	25p	50p
Grimsby Harriers & AC King George V Stadium, Weelsby Road Buses: † Station: Grimsby, Cleethorpes Mrs B. Jones, 22 Springfield Road, Scartho, Grimsby, South Humberside	■					■		Sprints M Distance Jumps Throws	210	Mon Eve Wed Eve Sat pm Sun am	From 50p	£2
Halifax Harriers AC Spring Hall Mansion, Huddersfield Rd, Halifax Buses: 37, 42, 43, 55 Station: Halifax E.J. Williams, 20 Westfield Ave, Lightcliffe, Halifax HX3 8AP Tel: Halifax (0422) 23887	■		■					Sprints M Distance	50	Tues Eve Thurs Eve Sun am	50p £1	£1·50
Hallamshire Harriers & AC Hillsborough Park Sports Arena Buses: 81, 82, 83 Station: Sheffield T. Biggins, 19 Ulley Rd, Sheffield S13 8BD Tel: Sheffield 395929	■			LJ		■		Sprints M Distance Jumps Throws	100	Tues Eve Thurs Eve Sat pm Sun am	50p £1	£1·50
***Harrogate AC** Almsford Close Sports Ground Buses: † Station: † J.H. Hooper, 1 Kendal Rd, Harrogate, Yorks Tel: Harrogate 87337	■					■		M Distance	†	Tues Eve Sun am	50p	75p
Heaton Harriers Benfield Rd School, Newcastle-upon-Tyne 6 Buses: Service 1 Station: Walker Gate P. Coulson, 4 Preston Ave, North Shields, Northumberland	■					■		M Distance	30	Tues Eve Thurs Eve Sun am	50p	£1·50
***Holmfirth Harriers AC** New Mill Road, Brockholes Buses: † Station: † M.A. Booth, 12 Far End Lane, Honley, Huddersfield HD7 2NS Tel: Huddersfield 61766	■				■				84	Mon Eve Tues Eve Thurs Eve Sat pm Sun am	50p	75p

151

ATHLETICS 75

NORTHERN AREA

*Questionnaire not returned, information based on entry in *Athletica 74*
†Insufficient information received

Club with Principal Track used, Secretaries, and nearest Public Transport

Club	Senior Subscription	Junior Subscription	Training Sessions	Active Membership	Coaches	Weight Training	Indoor Training	Floodlit Training	Landing Beds	All-Weather Runways	All-Weather Track	League	Juniors	Women	Men
*Holbeach AC Castle Field Sports Centre Station: † R.E.S. Clay, 82 Spalding Road, Holbeach, Lincs PE12 7HH	50p	30p 40p	Tues Eve Thurs Eve Sun Eve	75	Sprints M Distance Jumps Throws	■			■	○		■	■	■	■
Houghton Harriers Bernard Gilpin School, Houghton-Le-Spring Buses: † Station: † J. Lauderdale, 47 Windsor Crescent, Houghton-Le-Spring, Tyne & Wear	£1	50p	Mon pm Wed pm Sun am	55	Sprints M Distance		■					■	■	■	■
Hull, City of, AC Costello Playing Fields, Anlaby Park Rd, North Buses: 63, 73 Station: Hull G. Norman, 5 Spinney Walk, Kingston upon Hull HU4 6XG. Tel: Hull 507012	£1·50	50p	Tues Eve Thurs Eve Sat pm Sun am	180	M Distance Jumps Throws	■	■	■	■			■	■	■	■
Hull Spartan AC Ald. Kneeshaw Recreation Centre Buses: 58 Station: Paragon E. Taylor, 455 Marfleet Lane, Hull Tel: Hull 73429	£1·75	75p £1	Mon Eve Tues Eve Wed Eve Thurs Eve Sun am	230	Sprints M Distance Jumps Throws	■	■	■	■			■			■
Jarrow & Hebburn AC Monkton Sports Ground Buses: † Station: Jarrow R. Charlton, 71 Hill Park Rd, Hill Park Estate, Jarrow, Tyne & Wear. Tel: Jarrow 898718	50p	25p	Tues pm Wed pm Thurs pm Sun am	30	Sprints M Distance Throws								■		■
*Kellingley (Knottingley) AC Kellingley Social Centre Buses: † Station: † R. Ellis, 64 Downland Crescent, Womersley Road, Knottingley	25p	12p	Mon pm Wed pm Fri pm Sun am	25	Sprints M Distance Jumps Throws	■						■	■		■

152

REGISTER OF CLUBS

Kendal AAC Longlands Girls/Boys School Buses: to Kendal Station: Kendal Mrs Tidmarsh, 33 Oak Tree, Kendal Tel: Kendal 23899	■ ■ ■		Sprints M Distance Throws	220	Tues Eve Thurs Eve	35p (U 15) 63p (U 19)	£1·25
Keswick AC Dog & Gun Inn Buses: Keswick Station: Penrith R.T. Brewster, 17 The Hawthorns, Keswick, Cumbria Tel: Keswick 73127	■ ■		M Distance	19	Thurs Eve	From 15p	£1
***Kirkby AC** Whitefield Drive Track Buses: † Station: † J. Stott, PO Box 17, Civic Buildings, Civic Centre, Kirkby, Liverpool L32 1TX	■ ■ ■ ■ ■		Sprints M Distance Jumps Throws	50	Tues Eve Wed Eve Thurs Eve Sun am	Nil	Nil
Lakeland AC Millom School Buses: † Station: Millom G.K. Thompson, 23 Pannatt Hill, Millom, Cumbria LA18 5DB	■ ■ ■		Sprints M Distance Jumps Throws	50	Mon Eve Tues Eve Wed Eve Thurs Eve	25p	£1
Lancaster & Morecambe AC College of Further Education, Morecambe Rd, Lancaster Buses: National Station: Damside Street, Lancaster & Euston Road, Morecambe A.W. Bibby, 8 Lonsdale Place, Lancaster LA1 4BX Tel: Lancaster 69329	■ ■ ■		Sprints M Distance Jumps Throws	80	Tues Eve Thurs Eve Sun am	37½p	£1
Leeds City AC Municipal Track, Temple Newsam Buses: 22 Station: Leeds D.M. Stark, 28 Baronscourt, Leeds LS15 7AP	■ ■		Sprints M Distance Jumps	140	Tues Eve Thurs Eve Sun am	£1	£2
Lincoln City & Colleges AC City Sports Centre & Ravendale Sports Ground Buses: † Station: St Marks M.J. Polkinghorne, The Limes, Jerusalem Rd, Skellingthorpe, Lincoln Tel: Lincoln 64124	■ ■		Sprints M Distance Jumps Throws	100	Tues Eve Thurs Eve Sat pm Sun am	65p	£2·50

153

ATHLETICS 75

NORTHERN AREA

*Questionnaire not returned, information based on entry in *Athletics 74*
†Insufficient information received

Club with Principal Track used, Secretaries, and nearest Public Transport

	Lincoln Wellington AC	*Liverpool Boundary Harriers	Liverpool Harriers & AC	Liverpool Pembroke AC	Longwood Harriers AC
Senior Subscription	1974 £1·50	£1	£2·50	£2	£1·50
Junior Subscription	1974 25p	50p	50p	£1	50p
Training Sessions	Tues Eve, Thurs Eve, Sun am	Wed Eve, Sun am	Mon pm, Wed pm, Thurs pm, Sun am	Tues Eve, Thurs Eve, Sun am	Tues Eve, Thurs Eve
Active Membership	†	12	200	100	167
Coaches	M Distance, Jumps, Throws		Sprints, M Distance, Jumps, Throws	Sprints, M Distance, Jumps, Throws	Sprints, M Distance, Jumps, Throws
Weight Training	■		■	■	
Indoor Training	■		■	■	■
Floodlit Training			■	■	
Landing Beds	■		■	■	
All-Weather Runways			■	■	
All-Weather Track			■	■	
League	■		■	■	■
Juniors	■	■	■	■	
Women	■		■	■	■
Men	■	■	■	■	■

Lincoln Wellington AC
Lindum Sports Club, Wragby Rd, Lincoln
Buses: Town Services
Station: Lincoln Central or St Marks
G.G. Nicholson, 15 Chelmer Close, N. Hykeham,
Tel: Lincoln 62378

*Liverpool Boundary Harriers
Buses: † Station: †
D. Dalton, 12 Grimshaw Green Lane, Parbold,
Nr Wigan, Lancashire WN7 BB

Liverpool Harriers & AC
Liverpool University Track, Mather Avenue,
Liverpool 18 (winter – Kirkby Stadium)
Buses: 86, 87 Station: Mossley Hill
T.J. O'Mahoney, 12 Kirkmore Rd, L'pool L18 4QN
Tel: J.C. Rice 051 722 2026

Liverpool Pembroke AC
Kirkby Stadium
Buses: 92, 93, 500 Station: Kirkby
J. Bradshaw, 13 Whitehall Ave, Appley Bridge,
Nr Wigan
Tel: Appley Bridge 3309

Longwood Harriers AC
Leeds Road Athletic Arena
Buses: 40, 41, Bradley Station: Huddersfield
J.G. Beckett, 32 Ingfield Ave, Dalton, Huddersfield
Tel: Huddersfield 28690

REGISTER OF CLUBS

Club				Events	Members	Training	Fees
Manchester AC William Scholes Playing Fields, Fallowfield, Manchester 19 Buses: † Station: Gatley W.G. Smith, 21 Almond Tree Road, Cheadle Hulme, Cheadle, Cheshire SK8 6HW Tel: 061 485 7764	■	■	■	Sprints M Distance Jumps Throws	150	Mon Eve Tues Eve Wed Eve Thurs Eve Sun Eve	50p £1·50
Manchester & District Harriers & AC Mellands Playing Fields, Manchester 18 Buses: 210 Station: Levenshulme W. Cooper, 6 Norfolk Cres, Failsworth, Manchester Tel: 061-681 8688	■		■	Sprints M Distance	40	Wed Eve Sun am	£1·50 £2
Manx AC Ballakermeen School, Douglas, Isle of Man B. Whitehead, 2 Marine View Close, Onchan, Isle of Man Tel: 0624 22314	■	■		Sprints M Distance Jumps	80	(summer) Mon Eve Thurs Eve (winter) Tues Eve	50p £1
Mid Cheshire AC Mid Cheshire College of Further Education, Hartford Campus Buses: Sandiway, Chester Station: Hartford & Greebank G.R. Harvey, 83 Hodge Lane, Hartford, Northwich, Cheshire CW8 3AG Tel: Northwich 77013	■	■		Sprints M Distance Jumps Throws	20	Tues pm Thurs pm Sat pm Sun am	25p 50p
Middlesbrough & Cleveland Harriers Clairville Stadium Buses: 263, 275 Station: Middlesbrough C.G. Vaux, 1 The Ridge, Saltburn-by-the-Sea, Cleveland TS12 1JQ. Tel: Saltburn 2701 (home) M'brough 44788 (office)	■	■	■	Sprints M Distance Jumps Throws	100	Weekday Eves Sun am	50p £1·50 £1
***Morpeth Harriers & AC** Grange House Field Buses: † Station: † E. Slaughter, 136 Alexandria Road, Ashington, Northumberland NE63 1AZ Tel: Ashington 814399	■			Sprints M Distance	60	Mon Eve Thurs Eve Sat pm Sun am	50p £1·50

155

ATHLETICS 75

NORTHERN AREA

*Questionnaire not returned, information based on entry in *Athletics 74*
†Insufficient information received

Club with Principal Track used, Secretaries, and nearest Public Transport

Club	Senior Subscription	Junior Subscription	Training Sessions	Active Membership	Coaches	Weight Training	Indoor Training	Floodlit Training	Landing Beds	All-Weather Runways	All-Weather Track	League	Juniors	Women	Men
North East Field Events Club (Second claim club only) Miss D.J. Swinyard, 72 Roseberry Avenue, North Shields, Tyne & Wear Tel: 089 45 75308	£1	50p		20	Throws	■	■	■					■	■	■
Northern Veterans AC N. Ashcroft, 16 Davids Avenue, Gt Sankey, Warrington WA5 1LN Tel: Penketh 5858	50p			400										Over 35 years	Over 40 years
Oldham & Royton Harriers & AC Westwood Park Track, Chadderton, Oldham (summer) Hillside Ave, Royton, Lancs (winter) Buses: 405 Station: Mumps, Oldham F. Hodson, 34 Alva Road, Oldham, Lancs Tel: 061 633 5381	£1	50p	Mon pm Thurs pm	53	Sprints M Distance	■		■	■			■	■	■	■
Pilkington Harriers & AC Ruskin Drive, St Helens Buses: † Station: St Helens E. Lawrence, 79 Moss Bank Rd, St Helens, Merseyside. Tel: St Helens 26202	£2	£1	Weekday Eves Sun am	60	Sprints M Distance Jumps Throws	■			■			■	■	■	■
Preston AC London Road Track Buses: † Station: † B. Duckworth, 'Ness Holt', 39 Regent Drive, Fulwood, Preston PR2 3JB	£1	25p 50p	Mon Eve Wed Eve	20	†							■	■		■
Preston Harriers & AC London Road Track Buses: Frenchwood Station: Preston N.D. Swindlehurst, 38 Glendale Crescent, Lostock Hall, Preston PR5 5YA, Lancs	£1·50	50p	Tues Eve Thurs Eve Sun am	30	Sprints Jumps Throws	■						■			■

156

REGISTER OF CLUBS

Club	Facilities	Events	Size	Training	Fees
Pudsey & Bramley AC Priesthorpe School, Pudsey Buses: 9, 72 Station: New Pudsey A. Baker, 37 Gainsborough Ave, Adel, Leeds LS16 7PQ. Tel: Leeds 671132	■ ■ ■ ■	M Distance	25	Tues Eve Thurs Eve Sun am	50p £1
Riddings Youth Centre AC Willoughby Road Buses: † Station: Scunthorpe J. Redhead, c/o Riddings Youth Centre Willoughby Road, Ashby, Scunthorpe Tel: Scunthorpe 3160	■ ■ ■ ■ ■	Sprints M Distance Jumps Throws	50	Mon Eve Wed Eve	3p (per night) Nil
Ripon AC No home ground Buses, Station, No home ground Mrs A. Grangle, 19 Oak Road, Ripon	■ ■ ■ ■	No qualified coaches	165	Mon Eve Wed Eve Thurs Eve Sun am	25p 50p (women) 50p £1 (men)
Rochdale Harriers & AC Springfield Park Buses: † Station: Castleton T. Smyth, 3 Barnes Meadows, Littleborough, Lancs Tel: 0706 78098	■	†	15	Mon pm Sat pm Sun am	25p 75p
Rossendale AC Marl Pits Sports Centre, Newchurch Road, Rawtenstall Buses: † Station: Rawtenstall Mrs K. Rawinson, 26 Inkerman St, Bacup, Lancs Tel: Bacup 5722	■ ■	*Ladies only* Sprints M Distance Jumps Throws	80	Tues Eve Thurs Eve Sun am	50p £1·50 £1
Rotherham Harriers & AC Herringthorpe Stadium Buses: Local Station: Rotherham R.G. Rowbotham, 68 Wickersley Road, Rotherham S60 3PP. Tel: Rotherham 2675	■ ■ ■ ■	Sprints M Distance Javelin	100	Mon pm Wed pm	15p 50p
Sale Harriers Crossford Bridge Buses: Manchester to Sale or Altrincham route Station: Dane Road, Sale H. Wilson, 3 Marley Drive, Sale, Cheshire	■ ■ ■ ■	Sprints M Distance Jumps Throws	350	Mon Eve Wed Eve Thurs Eve Sat pm Sun am	75p £2

157

ATHLETICS 75

NORTHERN AREA

*Questionnaire not returned, information based on entry in *Athletics 74*
†Insufficient information received

Club with Principal Track used, Secretaries, and nearest Public Transport

	Salford Harriers & AC	Salford Metropolitan AC	Saltwell Harriers	*Scunthorpe Harriers & AC	Sefton Harriers
Senior Subscription	£1·50	£1·25 +50p (training fee)	£1	£1	£3
Junior Subscription	50p	50p +25p (training fee)	50p	25p 40p	£2
Training Sessions	Tues Eve Thurs Eve Sun pm	Mon Eve Thurs Eve Sun am	Tues pm Thurs pm Sat am Sun am	Tues Eve Thurs Eve Fri Eve	Mon Eve Tues Eve Wed Eve Thurs Eve Sat pm
Active Membership	50	100	40	64	35
Coaches	M Distance	Sprints M Distance Jumps Throws	Sprints M Distance	Sprints M Distance	Sprints M Distance Jumps Throws
Weight Training		■		■	
Indoor Training				■	
Floodlit Training		■			
Landing Beds		■	■		
All-Weather Runways		■			
All-Weather Track		■	■		
League	■	■		■	
Juniors	■	■	■	■	■
Women		■			
Men	■	■	■	■	■

Salford Harriers & AC
Boggart Hole, Clough
Buses: 166 Station: Crumpsall
G. Doggett, 9 Athlone Ave, Moston, Manchester 10
Tel: 061 681 8533

Salford Metropolitan AC
Cleavely Track, Winton
Buses: 64, 66, 9, 15 Station: †
H.S. Brown, 8 Beechfield Road, Swinton, Manchester M27 1RE
Tel: 061 794 3844

Saltwell Harriers
Gateshead Youth Stadium
Buses: † Station: †
P. McDaid, 1 Bentinck Place, Newcastle-upon-Tyne NE4 6XN
Tel: Newcastle 35891

***Scunthorpe Harriers & AC**
Quibbell Park
Buses: † Station: †
G. Fowler, 15 Humber Cres, Scunthorpe, Lincs

Sefton Harriers
Crawfords Sports Ground
West Derby Village Hall (winter)
Buses: † Station: †
S.G. O'Keeffe, 84 Hilary Ave, Huyton, Liverpool L14 6US

REGISTER OF CLUBS

Club										Events	Members	Training	Fees
Sheffield City AC Hillsborough Park Arena Buses: 82, 83, 2 Station: Sheffield Midland R. Furness, 48 Lowedges Rd, Sheffield S8 7LB Tel: J. Sherwood, Sheffield 344011	■	■	■	■			■	■	■	Sprints M Distance Jumps Throws	120	Mon Eve Tues Eve Wed Eve Thurs Eve Sun am Sun pm	20p 50p £1
Sheffield United Harriers & AC Hillsborough Park & Westfield School Buses: † Station: Sheffield Midland G. Kirby, 4 Garth Way, Dronfield Tel: Dronfield 414484	■	■	■	■			■	■	■	†	100	Tues pm Thurs pm Sat pm Sun am	50p £2
Southern AC Castle Rushen High School, Castletown B. Doughty, Seaview Cottage, Port St Mary, Isle of Man	■				■		■		■	Sprints M Distance	30	Thurs Eve	25p 50p
***Southport AC** Isle of Wight Playing Fields R.J. Bishop, 24 Knowle Avenue, Ainsdale, Southport PR8 2PB					■		■		■	Jumps Throws	50	Tues Eve Thurs Eve Sun am	35p 75p £1
South Shields Harriers & AC Gypsies Green Stadium Buses: South Shields Station: South Shields J. Russell, 24 Windsor Drive, Cleadon, Nr Sunderland, Tyne & Wear SR6 7SY	■					■	■		■	Sprints M Distance Jumps Throws	60	Tues Eve Wed Eve Thurs Eve Sun am	15p £1
Spenborough & District AC Spenborough Athletic Stadium, Cleckheaton Buses: Cleckheaton Station: Dewsbury G.T. Fensom, 7 The Orchards, Church Lane, Gomersal, Cleckheaton BD19 4QJ	■	■					■	■	■	Sprints M Distance Jumps Throws	146	Mon Eve Tues Eve Wed Eve Thurs Eve Sun am/pm	25p+ £1·75 (track fee)	50p+ £2·75 (track fee)
***Stanley AC** Kings Head Playing Fields Buses: † Station: † A.B. Peveller, 27 Orwell Gardens, Stanley, Co Durham		■			■		■		■	M Distance	25	Tues Eve Thurs Eve Sun am	12½p 25p

159

ATHLETICS 75

	Stockport Harriers & AC	Stretford AC	Sunderland Harriers	Sutton (St Helens) Harriers & AC	*Swinton Sports & AC
Senior Subscription	£1·50	£1·50	£2	£2·50	£1·25
Junior Subscription	75p	15p	To G.Boys Club	75p	50p
Training Sessions	Tues Eve Thurs Eve (summer) Sat pm Sun am	Tues pm Thurs pm Sun am	Tues pm Thurs pm Sun am	Mon–Thurs Eves Sat Eve Sun am	Mon Eve Wed Eve Sun am
Active Membership	57	250	60	80	†
Coaches	Sprints M Distance Jumps	Sprints M Distance Jumps Throws	M Distance	Sprints M Distance Jumps Throws	†
Weight Training	■	■		■	
Indoor Training	■	■			
Floodlit Training		■			
Landing Beds	■	■			
All-Weather Runways		■		probable by April	
All-Weather Track					
League		■	■	■	■
Juniors	■	■	■	■	■
Women	■	■		■	■
Men	■	■	■	■	■

NORTHERN AREA

*Questionnaire not returned, information based on entry in *Athletics 74*
†Insufficient information received

Club with Principal Track used, Secretaries, and nearest Public Transport

Stockport Harriers & AC
Woodbank Stadium
Buses: †   Station: Stockport
G. Gluyas, 98 Charlestown Road East, Woodsmoor, Stockport, Cheshire
Tel: 061 483 2346

Stretford AC
Longford Park
Buses: 262   Station: Stretford
W. Murphy, 30 Gaydon Road, Sale, Cheshire
Tel: 061 969 4894

Sunderland Harriers
Thorney Close Track (Meet: Grindon Boys Club)
Buses: Grindon   Station: Sunderland
K. Carr, 55 Hanarden Crescent, Sunderland
Tel: Sunderland 60098

Sutton (St Helens) Harriers & AC
Chester Lane, Marshalls Cross
Buses: 23   Station: St Helens Junction
R. Adams, 91 Sandringham Drive, St Helens, Merseyside
Tel: Marshalls Cross 812498

*Swinton Sports & AC
Barton Road Sports Ground
Buses: †   Station: †
H.S. Brown, 8 Beechfield Road, Swinton, Manchester M27 1RE
Tel: 061 794 3844

160

REGISTER OF CLUBS

Club						
Thorne Rural District AC Welfare Grounds, Stainforth, Doncaster Buses: † Station: Stainforth/Hatfield G. Turner, 14 Kings Close, Hatfield, Doncaster Tel: 0302 841156	■ ■ ■ ■ ■ ■	Sprints M Distance Jumps	50	Tues Eve Thurs Eve Sun am	40p	75p
Wakefield Harriers & AC Thornes House School, Thornes Park Buses: 20,32,63,64 Station: Wakefield (Westgate) J.V. Newsome, 42 Upper Lane, Netherton, Wakefield, W. Yorks WF4 4NQ Tel: Horbury 4727	■ ■ ■ ■ ■	Sprints M Distance	100	Tues Eve Thurs Eve	50p £1	£2
*****Wallasey AC** St Georges Playing Fields Buses: † Station: † P. Holmes, 23 Kirket Lane, Higher Bebington, Wirral, Cheshire	■ ■ ■ ■ ■	Sprints M Distance Jumps Throws	120	Mon–Thurs Eves Sat pm Sun am	£1·50	£3
*****Wallsend Harriers & AC** Wallsend Sports Centre Buses: † Station: † W. Bell, Wallsend Sports Centre, Brigges Main, Wallsend, Northumberland Tel: Wallsend 626479	■ ■ ■ ■	Sprints M Distance	20	Mon–Thurs Eves Sun am	27p	£1·10
*****Warrington AC** Victoria Park Buses: † Station: † E. Whittaker, 52 Denbury Avenue, Grappenhall, Warrington	■ ■ ■ ■ ■	Sprints M Distance Jumps Throws	270	Mon Eve Wed Eve Sun am	25p	£1
*****Wigan & District Harriers & AC** Woodhouse Lane Stadium Buses: † Station: † W. Cockram, 31 Pepper Lane, Standish, Wigan	■ ■ ■ ■	Sprints M Distance Jumps Throws	49	Mon Eve Wed Eve Sat am	50p	£1
Winsford AC Wharton Sports Complex Buses: † Station: Winsford T.D. Finnigan, 39 Pulford Road, Grange Estate, Winsford, Cheshire	■ ■ ■ ■	Sprints M Distance Throws	50	Tues Eve Thurs Eve Sun am	30p	£1·50

ATHLETICS 75

	Wirral AC	York Harriers & AC	Yorkshire Race Walking Club	Berry Hill Mansfield AC
Senior Subscription	£2		50p	£1
Junior Subscription	50p £1		50p	30p
Training Sessions	Weekday Eves / Sat pm / Sun am		Mon Eve / Thurs Eve / Sun am	Tues Eve / Thurs Eve / Sun am
Active Membership	120		25	35
Coaches	Sprints / M Distance		†	Sprints / M Distance / Jumps / Throws
Weight Training	■			■
Indoor Training	■			■
Floodlit Training	■			
Landing Beds				
All-Weather Runways				
All-Weather Track				
League	■			■
Juniors	■		■	■
Women	■			■
Men	■			■

NORTHERN AREA

*Questionnaire not returned, information based on entry in *Athletics 74*
†Insufficient information received

Club with Principal Track used, Secretaries, and nearest Public Transport

*Wirral AC
Holmside Lane Ground
Buses: † Station: †
P.F. Humphreys, 32 Berry Drive, Great Sutton,
Wirral, Cheshire L66 4LT
Tel: 051 339 5651

York Harriers & AC
No Track
Buses: † Station: York
W. M. Denham, 26 Windmill Rise, Poppleton Rd
York YO2 4TX
Tel: York 798088

Club not functioning at present

Yorkshire Race Walking Club
HQ Sedbergh Boys Club, Huddersfield Rd,
Odsal
Buses: 63, 64 Station: Bradford
G. Dowling, 103 Fairbank Road, Bradford,
W. Yorks BD8 9JT
Tel: 0274 46083

MIDLANDS AREA

*Berry Hill Mansfield AC
CISWO Ground, Berry Hill
Buses: † Station: †
B. Banton, 190 Leeming Lane North,
Mansfield Woodhouse, Notts

162

REGISTER OF CLUBS

Club	Events	Members	Training	Fees
Birchfield Harriers (Ladies) Alexander Stadium, Perry Barr, Birmingham Buses: 33, 90, 91 Station: Perry Barr Miss N. Blaine, 5 Goodrest Croft, Yardley Wood, Birmingham 14 Tel: 021-474 3739 (ladies section) Mens section: †	Sprints ■ M Distance ■ Jumps ■ Throws ■	70	Tues Eve Thurs Eve Sun pm	50p	£2
Bridgnorth AC Oldbury Wells School Track & Bridgnorth Sports Centre Buses: † Station: Bridgnorth P. Meredith, 18 Bridge Road, Alveley, Salop Tel: Quatt 686	M Distance ■ Jumps ■	20	Tues Eve Thurs Eve	25p	50p
Bristol AC Whitchurch Sports Centre Buses: 11, 37 Station: Bristol Temple Meads A.E. Clark, 283 Redcatch Road, Knowle, Bristol BS3 5DA. Tel: Bristol 770165	Sprints ■ M Distance ■ Jumps ■ Throws ■	380	Mon Eve Tues Eve Wed Eve Thurs Eve Sun am	£1 (U 15) £2 (15-18) (family)	£3 £2
Bromsgrove & Redditch AC Abbey Stadium, Birmingham Road, Redditch Buses: 147 from Birmingham Station: Redditch Mrs R.D. Brownlie, 108 Stourbridge Road, Bromsgrove, Worcs B61 0AN (ladies section)	Sprints ■ M Distance ■ Jumps ■	120	Tues Eve Thurs Eve Sun am	25p (U 15) 50p (15-18) £1 (18-21) 50p (students)	£1·50
Burton AC Dovecliff Grammar School, St Mary's Drive Buses: † Station: Burton-on-Trent I.E. Smith, 18 St Andrew's Drive, Burton-on-Trent, Staffs DE13 0LG Tel: Burton 3082	Sprints ■ M Distance ■ Jumps ■	50	Mon Eve Wed Eve Sun am	50p	£1·50
Cannock Chase AC Cannock Festival Stadium N.J. Bailey, 15 Chaseley Avenue, Cannock, Staffs. Tel: Cannock 4624	Sprints ■ M Distance ■ Jumps ■ Throws ■	230	Mon– Thurs Eve Sun am	50p	£1
***Cheltenham & County Harriers** King George V Playing Fields D. Hobby, 8 Cleeve Rise, Newent, Glos	M Distance ■	45	Mon– Thurs Eves Sun am	75p	£1·50

163

ATHLETICS 75

		City of Stoke AC	Coventry Godiva Harriers	Daventry AC	Derby Ladies AC
Senior Subscription		£2	£1·50	75p	£1
Junior Subscription		50p	50p	25p	25p
Training Sessions		Mon Eve Tues Eve Wed Eve Thurs Eve Sun am	Tues Eve Thurs Eve Sun am	Tues pm Thurs pm Sun am	Tues Eve (spring & summer) Wed Eve (winter only) Thurs Eve (spring & summer) Sun am
Active Membership		200+	80 L	40	40
Coaches		Sprints M Distance Jumps Throws	Sprints M Distance Jumps Throws	Sprints M Distance Jumps Throws	Sprints M Distance Jumps Throws
Weight Training		■	■		
Indoor Training		■	■	■	
Floodlit Training		■		■	
Landing Beds		■	■	■	
All-Weather Runways					
All-Weather Track					
League		■	■	■	■
Juniors		■			
Women		■	■		
Men		■	■	■	

MIDLANDS AREA

*Questionnaire not returned, information based on entry in *Athletics 74*
†Insufficient information received

Club with Principal Track used, Secretaries, and nearest Public Transport

City of Stoke AC
Cobridge Stadium, Stoke-on-Trent
Buses: † Station: Stoke
T.C.B. Spencer, 10 Cambridge Drive, Clayton, Newcastle, Staffs ST5 3DD
Tel: Newcastle 616468
Mrs A. Johnson, 191 Middlewich Street, Crewe, Cheshire CW1 4DN
Tel: Crewe 584290 (ladies section)

Coventry Godiva Harriers
The Butts Stadium, Albany Road
Buses: † Station: Coventry
Mrs A. Smith, The Cottage, Upper Fulbrook, Nr Stratford-on-Avon
Tel: Snitterfield 374 (ladies section)

Daventry AC
Daventry School Sports Field
Buses: † Station: Daventry
R. Fenn, 21 St Augustin Way, Daventry, Northants
Tel: Northampton 56546 (work)

Derby Ladies AC
Derby Municipal Stadium, Moor Lane,
Osmanton Park Rd, Allenton, Derby
Buses, 31, 60 Station: Derby Midland
Mrs E. Dunphy, 6 Cobthorne Drive, Allestree, Derby DE3 2SY
Tel: Derby 50139

REGISTER OF CLUBS

Club	Events	Members	Training	Fees	Subs
Dudley & Stourbridge Harriers The Dell, Pensnett Road, Brierley Hill Buses: 137, 138 Station: Stourbridge Town R.G. Mulgrue, Wyddrington, The Vale, Church Road, Birmingham B15 3SU Tel: 021-454 6318	Sprints ■ M Distance ■ Jumps ■ Throws ■	100	Tues Eve Thurs Eve Sun am	40p	£2·50
Dursley & District AC Dursley Recreation Ground Buses: † Station: † L.E. Cooper, The Old Golden Heart, Pittcourt, North Nibley, Nr Dursley, Glos Tel: Wotton-Under-Edge 2181 (bus)	No registered ■ coaches	45	Tues pm Thurs pm	25p	£1
Gloucester AC Black Bridge, Podsmead Road Buses: 504, 507 Station: Gloucester T. Haines, 48 The Triangle, Gloucester GL2 0NG	Sprints ■ M Distance ■ Jumps ■ Throws ■	400	Mon Eve Tues Eve Wed Eve Thurs Eve Sun am	60p	£2
Halesowen AC Manor Abbey Sports Ground Buses: 137, 138 Station: Hagley A.E. Hey, 8 Tall Trees Drive, Pedmore, Stourbridge Tel: 72-76294	M Distance ■ Jumps (ladies) ■ Throws (ladies) ■	100	Mon Eve Tues Eve Wed Eve Sat pm Sun am	nil (U 15) 54p (15–18) £1·66	£3·24
Hereford & County AC Hereford Racecourse Buses: † Station: Hereford H.L. Samuels, The Barton, Abbeydore, Hereford Tel: Wormbridge 267	† ■	40	Tues Eve Thurs Eve Sun am	25p	£1
Holloway Polytechnic AC Birmingham Polytechnic Buses: 61, 62, 63 Station: New Street L.W. Lewis, Birmingham Polytechnic, Bristol Rd, South, Northfield, Birmingham B31 2AJ	Sprints ■ M Distance ■ Walking ■	14	Tues Eve Wed Eve Thurs Eve Sun am	5p (weekly)	5p (weekly)

ATHLETICS 75

MIDLANDS AREA

*Questionnaire not returned, information based on entry in *Athletics 74*
†Insufficient information received

Club with Principal Track used, Secretaries, and nearest Public Transport

	Kettering Town Harriers	Leamington Cycling & AC	Leicester Coritanian AC	Lozells Harriers
Senior Subscription	£1	£1	£2	£1
Junior Subscription	50p	25p (U 15) / 50p (U 18)	50p – £1 (depending on age)	50p / 15p (girls)
Training Sessions	Mon Eve / Tues Eve (winter) / Wed Eve / Sat pm / Sun am	Mon Eve / Tues Eve / Wed Eve / Thurs Eve / Fri Eve / Sun am (Oct/Mar – Tues, Thurs, Sun only)	Track always open / Club night Tuesday	Tues Eve / Thurs Eve / Sat pm / Sun am
Active Membership	50	75	180	150 / 50 L
Coaches	Sprints / M Distance / Jumps / Throws	Sprints / M Distance / Jumps / Throws	Sprints / M Distance / Jumps / Throws	Sprints / M Distance / Throws
Weight Training	■	■	■	■
Indoor Training			■	
Floodlit Training			■	■
Landing Beds		■	■	
All-Weather Runways			■	
All-Weather Track			■	
League	■		■	
Juniors	■	■		
Women	■		■	
Men	■	■	■	■

Kettering Town Harriers
Wickstead Park
Buses: † Station: Kettering
R. Davis, 36 Gotch Rd, Barton Seagrave, Kettering, Northants
Tel: Burton Latimer 3704

Leamington Cycling & AC
Edmonscote Road, Leamington Spa
Buses: † Station: Leamington Spa
C. Woodward, 24 Box Close, Whitnash, Leamington Spa, Warwickshire CV31 2QD

Leicester Coritanian AC
Saffron Lane Stadium
Buses: 5, 6, 8, 25, 88, 54 and Outer Circle
Station: Leicester (London Road)
R. H. Float, 31 Half Moon Cres, Oadby, Leicester
Tel: Oadby 2196

Lozells Harriers
Salford Sports Stadium
Buses: 64, 65, 66, 67, 40 Station: Aston
K. Firth, 23 Abbotts Road, Erdington, Birmingham B24 8HE
Tel: 021-382 2214
Miss L. Tunney, 36/4 Riddfield Rd, Firs Estate, Birmingham B36 8NU
Tel: 021-749 2141 (ladies section)

166

REGISTER OF CLUBS

Club	Facilities	Members	Training	Fees
Newark AC Grove Sports Centre, Balderton Buses: † Station: Newark P. Reed, 13 Gaitskell Way, Balderton, Newark, Notts	Sprints Jumps ⎫ limited Throws ⎭	50	Mon Eve Thurs Eve	75p	£1·50
*Northampton Phoenix AC British Timken Track Buses: † Station: † D.P. Willmott, 18 Garrick Road, Northampton NN1 5ND Tel: Northampton 33581	Sprints M Distance Jumps (No throwing facilities)	40	Mon Eve Tues Eve Wed Eve Thurs Eve Sun am	50p (U 15)
Notts AC (Ladies) Harvey Haddon Stadium, Bilborough Park Buses: † Station: Nottingham L.C. Wall, 19 Longacre, Woodthorpe, Notts Tel: Notts 53056 (bus) Notts 260563 (home) R. Picksley, 106 Ingram Road, Bulwell, Nottingham NG6 9GO Mens section: †	Sprints M Distance Jumps Throws	120	Tues Eve Thurs Eve Sun am	75p (U 16) £1·25 (16–18)	£2
Nottingham City Harriers & AC Wollaton Park I. Gibson, 49 Bridgford Rd, West Bridgford, Nottingham Tel: Nottingham 869717	Sprints M Distance Jumps	75	Tues Eve Thurs Eve Sat pm	50p
Nuneaton Harriers Pingles Athletic Track Buses: 765 Station: Trent Valley B.J. Ewington, 16 Hemsworth Drive, Bulkington, Nuneaton CV12 9PE	M Distance		Tues Eve Wed Eve Thurs Eve Sun am	50p	£1·50
Royal Sutton Coldfield AC Wyndley Leisure Centre R.C. Smedley, 41 Jerrard Drive, Sutton Coldfield, West Midlands B75 7TR	Sprints M Distance Throws	80	Tues pm Thurs pm Sun am	†	†
Rugby & District AC Rugby Sports Centre, Thornfield Buses: Many Station: Rugby Midland D.R. Ellis, Four Winds, Street Ashton, Nr Stretton-under-Fosse, Nr Rugby, Warwickshire Tel: Rugby 832688	Sprints M Distance Jumps (all unqualified)	120	Tues pm Wed pm Thurs pm Sun am	£1·50	£3

167

ATHLETICS 75

		*Shrewsbury & District AC	Solihull AC	Sparkhill Harriers	Stafford AC	Stourport AC	Sutton-in-Ashfield Harriers & AC
Senior Subscription		£2	†	£1	£1	£1·25	£1·50
Junior Subscription		25p	†	25p	50p	50p	75p
Training Sessions		Mon Eve Tues Eve Wed Eve	Tues Thurs Sun am	Tues Eve Wed Eve Thurs Eve Sat pm Sun am	Mon pm Wed pm Sun am	Tues Eve Thurs Eve (summer) Sun am (summer & winter)	Mon Eve Tues Eve Wed Eve Thurs Eve Sun am
Active Membership		55	†	140	†	60	75
Coaches		Sprints M Distance Jumps Throws	Sprints M Distance Jumps Throws	Sprints M Distance Jumps Throws	†	Sprints M Distance Jumps Throws	M Distance Jumps Throws
Weight Training		■		■			■
Indoor Training		■		■			
Floodlit Training							
Landing Beds		■	■	■			■
All-Weather Runways			■				
All-Weather Track							
League		■	■			■	■
Juniors		■	■			■	
Women		■	■			■	
Men		■	■	■		■	■

MIDLANDS AREA

*Questionnaire not returned, information based on entry in *Athletics 74*
†Insufficient information received

Club with Principal Track used, Secretaries, and nearest Public Transport

*Shrewsbury & District AC
Shrewsbury Technical College
Buses: †   Station: †
J. O'Leary, 11 Stretton Close, Telford,
Salop TF7 4LS

Solihull AC
Athletics & Youth Centre, Tudor Grange Park
Buses: †   Station: Solihull
F. H. Kirby, Solihull Athletics & Youth Centre,
Tudor Grange Park, Blossomfield Rd, Solihull
Tel: 021-705 4474

Sparkhill Harriers
188 Stratford Road, Shirley, Solihull
Buses: 150, 154   Station: Shirley
A.C. Hill, Sparkhill Harriers, Rear 188 Stratford
Road, Shirley, Solihull

Stafford AC
Rowley Park
Buses: †   Station: Stafford
D.J. Cowley, 6 Riverway, Stafford ST16 3TH

Stourport AC
Walshes Meadow
Buses: †   Station: Kidderminster
Mrs J. Barbour, 120 Bewdley Rd,
Stourport-on-Severn, Worcs DY13 8XH

Sutton-in-Ashfield Harriers & AC
Sutton Track, Mansfield Road
Buses: †   Station: Nottingham
J.W. Knight, 19 Winster Avenue, Ravensead,
Notts. Tel: Bidworth 4520

168

REGISTER OF CLUBS

Club	Facilities	Members	Training Times	Visitors	Fees
Tamworth AC — Woodhouse Sports Centre, Highfield Road, Tamworth. Buses: † Station: † P. Sarsen, 23 Cromwell Rd, Coton Green, Tamworth, Staffs. Tel: Tamworth 52216	Sprints, M Distance, Jumps, Throws (Restricted)	50	Thurs Eve, Sun am	50p	£1·50
Tipton Harriers — Gospel Oak Stadium. Buses: 245 Station: Owen Street. T.A. Talbot, 100 Aston Street, Toll-End, Tipton, West Midlands DY4 0JD. Tel: 021-557 4501 (home) 021-556 3579 (stadium)	Sprints, M Distance, Jumps, Throws (At Warley)	120	Stadium open from 8.00am to 10.30pm daily	50p (U 18) £1·50 (18-21)	£2
Warley AC — Hadley Stadium, Waterloo Rd, Smethwick. Buses: B82, 220 Station: Rolfe St, Smethwick. D. Pritchard, 59 Cemetery Road, Smethwick, Warley, West Midlands B67 6BD. Tel: 021-558 5100	Sprints, M Distance, Jumps, Throws	59	Mon Eve, Wed Eve, Thurs Eve, Sun am	50p	£1
West Bromwich Harriers — Heath Lane. Buses: 8, 9, 10, 11, 54 Station: Old Church. J. Buckby, 26 Hall Green Rd, West Bromwich. Tel: 021-588 2539	M Distance (Harriers only)	12	Mon Eve, Tues Eve, Wed Eve, Thurs Eve, Sat pm, Sun am	Nil	Nil
Westbury Harriers — Whitchurch Track, Bristol. Buses: 11 Station: Temple Meads. D. Burborough, 23 Westbrook Road, Brislington, Bristol BS4 5EE. Tel: 711737	Sprints, M Distance, Jumps, Throws	150	Mon Eve, Tues Eve, Thurs Eve, Sun am	50p	£1 (ladies) £2 (men)
Wolverhampton & Bilston AC — Aldersley Stadium. Buses: 34 Station: Wolverhampton High Level. K.J. Evans, 17 Edward Street, Wolverhampton WV1 1QR. Tel: Wolverhampton 771842	Sprints, M Distance, Jumps, Throws	500	Mon/Tues/Wed/Thurs Eves, Fri Eve, Sat pm, Sun am	50p	£1·50

169

ATHLETICS 75

	Worcester AC	Aberdeen AC	Airdrie Harriers AC	*Ayr Seaforth AC	Ayrshire AC
Senior Subscription	£1 (ladies) £1·50 (men)	£1·50	£1	£1·50	£1
Junior Subscription	25p	75p	75p	50p	£1
Training Sessions	Mon Eve Tues Eve Wed Eve Thurs Eve Sun am	Mon pm Wed pm	Mon Eve Tues Eve Wed Eve Thurs Eve Sun pm	Tues Eve Thurs Eve Sun am	Tues Eve Thurs Eve Sun pm
Active Membership	100	85	38	20	120
Coaches	None	None	Sprints M Distance Jumps Throws	Sprints	Sprints M Distance Jumps Throws
Weight Training	■		■	■	■
Indoor Training	■		■		
Floodlit Training					
Landing Beds		■			
All-Weather Runways		■			
All-Weather Track					
League	■	■	■	■	■
Juniors	■	■	■		■
Women	■	■			■
Men	■	■	■	■	■

MIDLANDS AREA

*Questionnaire not returned, information based on entry in *Athletics 74*
†Insufficient information received
Club with Principal Track used, Secretaries, and nearest Public Transport

Worcester AC
Nunnery Wood School
Buses: W1   Station: Shrub Hill, Worcester
J. Marshall, 14 Bilford Avenue, Worcester
Tel: Worcester 51898

SCOTLAND

Aberdeen AC
Linksfield Stadium
Buses: 1, 2   Station: Joint Station
Mrs J.L. Wood, 4 Cairnaquheen Gardens,
Aberdeen AB2 4HJ

Airdrie Harriers AC
Rawyards Park
Buses: †   Station: Airdrie
N. Taylor, 8 Woodburn Avenue, Airdrie ML6 9ED

*Ayr Seaforth AC
Dampark Stadium
D.N. Brackenridge, 53 Sycamore Crescent, Ayr
Tel: Ayr 67039

Ayrshire AC
Dam Park Stadium, also at Kilmarnock, Irvine
and Garnock
Buses: †   Station: Ayr
W.H. Parker, 22 Elder Ave, Beith, Ayrshire

REGISTER OF CLUBS

Club					
*Beith Harriers AC Gateside Road Buses: † Station: † W.H. Parker, 22 Elder Avenue, Beith, Ayrshire	■ ■ ■		M Distance	30	Wed Eve Thurs Eve Sat pm Sun pm	75p 25p	£1·50
Bellahouston Harriers AC Nethercraig Sports Ground, Glasgow Buses: 50, 26, 49 Station: Corkerhill B.A. Goodwin, 490 Tollcross Road, Glasgow G31 4XX. Tel: 041-556 4803	■ ■ ■ ■		Sprints M Distance Jumps Throws	160	Tues Eve Thurs Eve Sat pm Sun pm	£1	£2
Bute Shinty & Athletic Club The Meadows, Rothesay J. Duncan, 11 Barone Road, Rothesay, Isle of Bute, PA20 9HH Tel: Rothesay 3094	■ ■		Sprints M Distance Jumps Throws	30/40	Mon Eve Wed Eve Sun pm	25p	50p
Caithness AC Thurso Technical College Buses: † Station: Wemyss Bay then Ferry to Rothesay A.J. Gunn, 12 Scaraben Court, Thurso, Caithness Tel: Thurso 2981	■ ■	■	Sprints M Distance Jumps Throws	102	Mon am Tues pm Wed pm Thurs pm Fri pm Sat am Sun am	25p	£1
Cambuslang Harriers Dalton School and Cambuslang Rugby Club, Burnside Buses: 70, 71, 72, 73, 74, 75, 76, 77, 79 Station: Burnside – Blue Train, Cambuslang – Diesel D.W. Yuill, 5 Stanhope Drive, Burnside, Glasgow G73 5AQ. Tel: 041-647 7846	■ ■ ■		M Distance	60	Mon pm Tues pm Wed pm Thurs pm Sat pm Sun am	25p	£1
Clydesdale Harriers Whitecrook Track Buses: Numerous Station: Clydebank J. Sweeney, 11 Southend Road, Clydebank Tel: 041-388 2148	■ ■		Sprints M Distance Jumps Throws		Tues Eve Thurs Eve Sat pm Sun pm	75p	£1·25
Cupar & District AC Wetlands Playing Field Buses: † Station: Cupar J.L. Hendry, 'Kildene', Westfield Rd, Cupar, Fife Tel: Cupar 3456	■ ■		Sprints M Distance Jumps Throws	100	Tues Eve Thurs Eve Sun pm	75p	£1·50

171

ATHLETICS 75

SCOTLAND

*Questionnaire not returned, information based on entry in *Athletics 74*
†Insufficient information received

Club with Principal Track used, Secretaries, and nearest Public Transport

	Dumbarton AC Brock Baths Buses: † Station: † J. Walker, 2 First Avenue, Dumbarton	**Dundee Hawkhill Harriers** Caird Park Stadium Buses: 31, 33 Station: Tay Bridge, Dundee A.T. Barrie, 44 Albany Terrace, Dundee DD3 6HS Tel: 0382 23392	**East Coast Track Club** 31 Fishers Road, Port Seton Buses: 129 from Edinburgh Station: Prestonpans I. Stewart, 31 Fishers Rd, Port Seton, East Lothian Tel: Port Seton 812131	**East Kilbride AC** Murray Athletic Pavilion Buses: 77, 181 Station: East Kilbride A.H. Partridge, 13 Denholm Green, East Kilbride G75 0HR Tel: East Kilbride 38773	**East Lothian AC** Public School, Prestonpans Buses: 29 Station: Waverley, Edinburgh M.S. Moodie Jnr, 28D North Grange Avenue, Prestonpans, East Lothian
Senior Subscription	50p	£1·50 / £2·50	£1	£1·05	£1
Junior Subscription	25p	£1·50	50p	50p	75p
Training Sessions	†	Tues Eve / Thurs Eve / Sat pm / Sun pm	Mon Eve / Tues Eve / Wed Eve / Thurs Eve / Sun pm	Mon Eve / Thurs Eve / Sat pm / Sun pm	Mon Eve / Tues Eve / Wed Eve / Thurs Eve / Fri Eve / Sat am / Sun am/pm
Active Membership	20	60/70	6	50	40/50
Coaches	†	Sprints / M Distance / Jumps / Throws	Sprints / M Distance	M Distance	Sprints / M Distance / Jumps / Throws
Weight Training		■		■	■
Indoor Training	■	■	■	■	■
Floodlit Training					
Landing Beds		■		■	
All-Weather Runways		■			
All-Weather Track					
League	■	■		■	■
Juniors	■	■			■
Women		■			■
Men	■	■	■	■	■

REGISTER OF CLUBS

Club	Facilities	Events	Capacity	Times	Fees (members/non)
Edinburgh AC Meadowbank Stadium Buses: † Station: Waverley, Edinburgh N. Donachie, 41 Muirwood Crescent, Currie, Midlothian Tel: 031-449 2786	■ ■ ■ ■ ■ ■ ■ ■	Sprints M Distance Jumps Throws	350	Every day but coaches only available in evenings except Sat/Sun (all day)	75p / £2
Edinburgh Southern Harriers Fernieside and Meadowbank Stadium Buses: 33 Station: Waverley, Edinburgh I. Ross, 37 Dundas Street, Edinburgh EH3 6QQ Tel: 031-556 7971 (day) 031-332 2100 (night) Mrs P.M.F. Sinclair, 5 Bangholm Terrace, Edinburgh EH3 5QN Tel: 031-552 4428 (ladies section)	■ ■ ■ ■ ■ ■ ■ ■	Sprints M Distance Jumps Throws	150 L 200 M	(ladies) Mon/Tues Wed/Thurs Eves Sat pm Sun am (men) Tues Eve Thurs Eve Sat pm	£1 / £1 £1·50 / £3
Elgin AC Morriston Playing Field Buses: † Station: Elgin Mrs M.A. Cooke, 'Ommaroo', James Street, Lossiemouth IU31 6QZ	■ ■	Sprints M Distance Jumps Throws	12	Tues Eve Thurs Eve	25p / 50p
Falkirk Victoria Harriers The Hut – Thornhill Road Buses: Local service Station: Grahamston D. Wilson, 46 Castleton Cres, Grangemouth Tel: Grangemouth 6751	■ ■ ■	M Distance	30	Tues Eve Thurs Eve Sat pm Sun pm	50p / £1·25
*****Garscube Harriers AC** Maxwell Avenue, Bearsden Buses: † Station: † D. Simpson, 59 Lammerton Road, Kildrum, Cumbernauld, Dunbartonshire Tel: Cumbernauld 24608	■ ■ ■	Sprints M Distance	150	Tues Eve Thurs Eve Sat am/pm Sun pm	50p / £1
Greenock Wellpark Harriers 207 Old Inverkip Road Buses: † Station: Ravenscraig H. Docherty, 28 Mearns Street, Greenock	■ ■	Sprints M Distance	20	Tues Eve Thurs Eve Sat pm Sun pm	£1 / £2

173

ATHLETICS 75

SCOTLAND

*Questionnaire not returned, information based on entry in *Athletics 74*
†Insufficient information received

Club with Principal Track used, Secretaries, and nearest Public Transport

Club	Senior Subscription	Junior Subscription	Training Sessions	Active Membership	Coaches	Weight Training	Indoor Training	Floodlit Training	Landing Beds	All-Weather Runways	All-Weather Track	League	Juniors	Women	Men
Inverness Harriers AC Bught Park Buses: † Station: Inverness E.J. Roodhouse, 28 Ashie Rd, Inverness IV2 4EN Tel: Inverness 33179	£1·50	75p	Tues Eve Thurs Eve Sat am Sun am	100	Sprints									■	■
Kinlochleven AC Island Park Buses: † Station: Fort William A.B. Robertson, 6 Callart Road, Kinlochleven, Argyll Tel: Kinlochleven 240	50p	25p	†	25	Sprints M Distance Jumps Throws		■				■		■	■	■
Law & District AC Loch Park Stadium, Carluke Buses: † Station: Carluke R. Gallacher, 72 Caneluk Avenue, Carluke ML8	£1·50	20p 50p	Tues Eve Wed Eve Thurs Eve Sun pm	180	Sprints M Distance	■						■	■	■	■
Lewisvale Spartans Pinkie Playing Fields, Musselburgh Buses: † Station: Waverley, Edinburgh Mr Edgar, 6 Galt Avenue, Musselburgh Tel: 031-665 5398	£1	75p	Mon pm Tues pm Thurs pm	30	Sprints Jumps Throws	■						■	■	■	■
Livingston & District AC St Andrews School, Howdon Buses: 27, 35, 200, 201 Station: Midcalder Mrs D. Johnson, 3 Carlyle Court, Almond South, Livingston, West Lothian Tel: Livingston 31675	£1·25	25p	Wed Eve Sun pm	60	Sprints M Distance Throws	■								■	■
Lochaber AC Town Park, Fort William A.P. Maclean, 54 Carn Dearg Road, Fort William PH33 6QD	£1	25p	Tues pm Thurs pm Sun pm	40	M Distance	■							■	■	■

REGISTER OF CLUBS

Maryhill Harriers Caldercuilt Road Buses: 61 Station: Charing Cross, Glasgow T. Harrison, 9 Kirkoswald Drive, Clydebank G81 2HA Tel: 041-952 1694	■	■		M Distance	16	Tues Eve Thurs Eve Sat pm	75p	£1·25
Maryhill Ladies AC. Scotstoun Showgrounds and Bellahouston Sports Centre Buses: various Station: † Mrs M. Brown, 193 Sandy Road, Renfrew Tel: 041-886 3700	■ ■ ■ ■	■	■	Sprints M Distance Jumps Throws	80	Mon Eve Wed Eve Fri Eve Sun am/pm	£1·50 £2·50 (inter- mediate)	£3·50
***Monkland Harriers** Buses: † Station: † W. Drysdale, Ukintyre Wynd, Carluke, Lanarkshire ML8 5RW Tel: Carluke 3448 (home) or 041 557 4400	■	■			35	Mon Eve Tues Eve Wed Eve Thurs Eve Sat pm Sun pm	10p	65p
Paisley Harriers Leedhill, Paisley Buses: † Station: Paisley Gilmour Street D. Parker, 9 Waverley Gardens, Elderslie, Johnstone, Renfrewshire Tel: Johnstone 24928	■ ■	■		Sprints M Distance Jumps Throws	60	Mon–Thurs pm Sat pm Sun am/pm	75p	£1
Penicuik Harriers Penicuik High School Buses: † Station: Edinburgh G. McEwan, 1B West Cairn Crescent, Penicuik EH26 0AW Midlothian Tel: Penicuik 75503		■	■	Sprints M Distance	40	Mon Eve Thurs Eve	40p 80p	£1·20
Perth Strathay Harriers Bells Sports Stadium Buses: † Station: Perth S. Leitch, 5 Orchard Place, Perth PH2 0HS Tel: Perth 31016	■ ■	■		Sprints M Distance Jumps Throws	70	Tues Eve Thurs Eve Sat pm	£1	£1·50

175

ATHLETICS 75

		Pitreavie AC	Polbeath Harriers & AC	Ross-shire AC	St Andrews AC	Shettleston Harriers AC
Senior Subscription		£1·50	25p	£1·50	£1	£1·50
Junior Subscription		50p	25p	75p	50p	75p
Training Sessions		Tues Eve Wed Eve Thurs Eve Sun am/pm	Mon Eve Tues Eve Thurs Eve Sun pm	Sun pm	Mon Eve (summer) Tues Eve (winter) Wed Eve (summer)	Mon pm Tues Eve Wed Eve Thurs Eve Sun pm
Active Membership		175	30	6	100	50
Coaches		Sprints M Distance Jumps Throws	Sprints M Distance	†	Sprints M Distance Jumps Throws	Sprints M Distance Jumps Throws
Weight Training		■	■		■	■
Indoor Training		■	■		Winter only	■
Floodlit Training						
Landing Beds		■	■		■	
All-Weather Runways		■				■
All-Weather Track		■				
League		■	■		■	■
Juniors		■	■	■	■	■
Women		■	■	■		
Men		■	■	■	■	■

SCOTLAND

*Questionnaire not returned, information based on entry in *Athletics 74*
†Insufficient information received

Club with Principal Track used, Secretaries, and nearest Public Transport

Pitreavie AC
Pitreavie Playing Fields, Dunfermline
Buses: † Station: Dunfermline or Inverkeithing
G. McDonald, 46 Brucefield Avenue, Dunfermline, Fife

Polbeath Harriers & AC
West Calder High School
Buses: † Station: West Calder
A. Haggerty, 14 Langside Crescent, Polbeath, West Calder

Ross-shire AC
Buses: † Station: †
D.J. MacDonald, 186 Kirkside, Alness, Ross-shire
Tel: 2222

St Andrews AC
Station Park, St Andrews
Buses: † Station: Leuchars Junction
Mrs E. Gunstone, 11 Lawhead Road East, St Andrews, Fife KY16 9ND

Shettleston Harriers AC
Barrachnie Playing Fields
Buses: 62 Station: Garrowhill
W. Clark, 28 Kyle Drive, Giffnock, Renfrewshire
Tel: 041 633 0202

176

REGISTER OF CLUBS

Club							
Shettleston Harriers Ladies AC Garrowhill Cricket Club Buses: 3 Station: Garrowhill Miss K. Daly, 6 Elgin Place, Coatbridge, Lanarkshire Tel: 041 202 7542	■ ■ ■		Sprints M Distance	20	Tues pm Thurs pm Sun pm	25p	50p
Springburn Harriers Huntershill Sports Centre, Glasgow Buses: † Station: † D. McFarlane, 355 Ashgill Road, Glasgow G22 7HN	■ ■ ■		Sprints M Distance Jumps Throws	150	Tues pm Thurs pm Sat pm Sun am	£1	£1
Stirling AC Williamfield Buses: many Station: Stirling J.H. Murray, 75 Cedar Avenue, Polmaise, Stirling FK8 2PJ Tel: Stirling 61017	■ ■ ■	■ ■	Sprints M Distance Jumps Throws	30	Mon Eve (summer) Tues Eve (winter) Thurs Eve Sat pm	25p 50p 75p	£1
*Stranraer Harriers London Road Playing Fields Buses: † Station: † A.J. Robertson, 54 Hanover Street, Stranraer DG9 7RP	■ ■	■		63	Tues Eve Fri Eve	20p	30p
Strathclyde Ladies AC Milton Community Centre Buses: † Station: Dumbarton J. Munro, 3 Eastfield Place, Dumbarton	■ ■	■	Sprints M Distance Jumps Throws	45	Tues Eve Thurs Eve Sun pm	£1	£1
Tayside AC Carnoustie High School Buses: † Station: Carnoustie J.L. Ewing, 43 Hill Street, Monifieth, Angus DD5 4DH Tel: Monifieth 3945	■ ■	■	Sprints M Distance	25	Wed Eve Sun pm	50p	£1·50
Teviotdale Harriers Bath Street, Hawick Buses: † Station: Carlisle (44 miles) A.J. Samuel, 33 High Street, Hawick, Roxburghshire Tel: Hawick 3485	■ ■	■	†	62	Every Eve Children Tues & Thurs	25p	£1

ATHLETICS 75

SCOTLAND

Questionnaire not returned, information based on entry in Athletics 74
†Insufficient information received

Club with Principal Track used, Secretaries, and nearest Public Transport

	Vale of Leven AC	Victoria Park AC	Western AC	West of Scotland Harriers
Senior Subscription	50p	£1·12½	75p	£1
Junior Subscription	25p	30p / 75p	75p	60p
Training Sessions	Tues Eve / Thurs Eve / Sat pm	Tues Eve / Thurs Eve / Sat am/pm / Sun am/pm	Tues Eve (k) / Wed Eve (h) / Thurs Eve (k)	Tues Eve / Sat pm
Active Membership	80/100	100	50	40
Coaches	None	Sprints / M Distance / Jumps / Throws	Sprints / M Distance / Jumps / Throws	Sprints / M Distance
Weight Training		■	■	
Indoor Training			■	
Floodlit Training		■		
Landing Beds		■		
All-Weather Runways		■	■	
All-Weather Track				
League	■	■		■
Juniors	■	■		
Women	■	■		
Men	■	■		■

Vale of Leven AC
Vale of Leven Academy
Buses: 132, 133, 136 Station: Alexandria
J. Gardner, 50 Lomond Crescent,
Alexandria, Dumbartonshire G83 0RL
Tel: Alexandria 52687

Victoria Park AC
Scotstoun Showgrounds
Buses: 10, 10A Station: Jordanhill
J. Wallace Crawford, 24 Belsyde Avenue,
Glasgow G15 6AR
Tel: 041-944 6145 (home) 041-221 8167 (bus)

Western AC
Knightswood Sec School
& Huntershill Sports Ground
Buses: 58, 6, 45 Station: Anniesland-Bishopbriggs
Miss A. Lloyd, 2 Adamswell Terrace,
Moodiesburn, Chryston, Glasgow G69 0HA

West of Scotland Harriers
Stanalane Track
Buses: 57, 38 Station: Patterton
D.J. Wyper, 601 Clarkston Road, Glasgow
G44 3QD
Tel: 041 637 5460

WALES

	Aberdare Valley AC
Senior Subscription	£2
Junior Subscription	£1
Training Sessions	Mon–Fri Eves / Sun am/pm
Active Membership	40
Coaches	Sprints / M Distance / Jumps
Weight Training	■
Indoor Training	■
Floodlit Training	
Landing Beds	■
All-Weather Runways	
All-Weather Track	
League	■
Juniors	■
Women	
Men	■

Aberdare Valley AC
Michael Sobell Sports Centre, Aberdare
Buses: † Station: Abercynon
C. Daley, 12 Plane St, Rhydyfelin
Pontypridd, Mid Glamorgan

178

REGISTER OF CLUBS

Club	Facilities	Members	Training	Fees
*Abertillery Achilles AC The Park, Abertillery T.G. Legge, 58 Carlyle Street, Abertillery, Monmouthshire NP3 1UF Tel: Abertillery 2141 (office)	■ ■ ■ ■ (Sprints, M Distance, Throws)	30	Tues Eve Wed Eve Thurs Eve Sun am	Nil / Nil
Bargoed AC Buses: † Station: Bargoed W. Morgan, 14 Hillside Park, Bargoed, Glamorgan CF8 8NL	Club not functioning at present			
BP Llandarcy AC BP Refinery (Llandarcy) Ltd Buses: Neath/Swansea route Station: Neath B. Jones, Rock House, 27 School Road, Jersey Marine, Neath SA10 6JE Tel: Skewen 2590	■ ■ ■ ■ (Sprints, M Distance, Jumps)	90	Mon Eve Wed Eve	Nil / Nil
Brecon AC Brecon High School Buses: † Station: † L. Davies, Highmead, 10 Cradoc Road, Brecon Powys LD3 9LG Tel: Brecon 3323	■ ■ ■ ■ (M Distance) — Juniors only	30	Mon Eve Wed pm, Eve	50p / £1
Cardiff AC Maindy Stadium, North Road Buses: † Station: Cardiff Central Dr W.A.L. Evans, Winterbourne, Greenway Close, Llandough, Penarth, S. Glamorgan Tel: Penarth 708102	■ ■ ■ ■ ■ ■ (Sprints, M Distance, Jumps, Throws)	1000	Mon Eve Thurs Eve Fri Eve (U 11)	50p / £2
Carmarthen & District Harriers AC Ystrad Towy, Johnston Buses: All Carmarthen Station: Carmarthen W.D. Morgan, 9 Priory Close, Carmarthen Tel: Carmarthen 6622	■ ■ ■ ■ (Sprints, M Distance, Jumps, Throws)	†	Mon pm Thurs pm	50p / £1

179

ATHLETICS 75

		*Cleddaw AC	Cwmbran Olympiad AC	Gilwern Harriers	Newport Harriers AC	Pontypool AC
Senior Subscription		£1	£1	50p	£1	†
Junior Subscription		25p	†	25p	50p	75p
Training Sessions		Mon Eve Wed Eve	Mon Eve Thurs Eve Sun am	Mon Eve Tues Eve Wed Eve Thurs Eve Fri Eve Sun am	Tue Eve Thurs Eve Sat pm Sun am	Tues Eve Wed Eve Thurs Eve
Active Membership		150	†	30	150	70
Coaches		Sprints M Distance Jumps Throws	Sprints M Distance Jumps Throws	†	Sprints M Distance Throws	†
Weight Training		■	■		■	■
Indoor Training		■	■			■
Floodlit Training					■	
Landing Beds		■	■			
All-Weather Runways		■	■			
All-Weather Track		■	■			
League			■	■	■	■
Juniors		■	■	■	■	■
Women		■	■	■	■	■
Men		■	■	■	■	■

WALES

*Questionnaire not returned, information based on entry in *Athletics 74*
†Insufficient information received

Club with Principal Track used, Secretaries, and nearest Public Transport

*Cleddaw AC
Haverfordwest County School
T.B. Rees, 17 South Court,
Haverfordwest, Pembrokeshire

Cwmbran Olympiad AC
Cwmbran Sports Stadium
Buses: 125   Station: Newport
G. Matthiudis, 12 Ellwood Path, St Dials,
Cwmbran, Gwent NP4 4RD
Tel: Cwmbran 4295

Gilwern Harriers
Brynmawr Comp School
Buses: †   Station: †
H. Walbyof, 19 King Edward Road,
Brynmawr, Gwent

Newport Harriers AC
Glebelands Stadium, Bank St
Buses: 4A, 2, 7   Station: Newport
I.T. Adams, 5 Camelot Court, Caerleon,
Newport, Gwent NP6 1AD
Tel: Caerleon 421380

Pontypool AC
Pontypool Park
Buses: Pontypool Town Hall
Station: Pontypool Road
D. Counsell, 84 Sunnybank Road,
Griffithstown, Pontypool, Gwent NP4 5LM
Tel: Pontypool 55974

180

REGISTER OF CLUBS

Club	Events	Members	Times	Fees
Rhondda AC Winter: Rhondda College of Further Education Summer: Blaenclydach Track Buses: Tonypandy Station: Llwynypia D.A.R. Evans, 111 Brithwennydd Road, Trealaw, Tonypandy, Glamorgan CF40 2UG Tel: Pentre 2096	■ Sprints ■ M Distance ■ Jumps Throws	75	Tues Eve Thurs Eve Sat am Sun am	13p £1
Swansea Harriers AC University College Track, Sketty Lane Buses: † Station: Swansea J.H. Collins, Harrier Haunt, 40 Twyni-Teg, Killay, Swansea SA2 7NS Tel: Llanelli 2244 (business)	■ Sprints ■ M Distance Jumps ■ Throws	200	Mon Eve Wed Eve (winter) Thurs Eve (summer) Sun am	50p £1
Swansea Valley AC Ystradgynlais Rugby Field Buses: † Station: Swansea M. Cullen, 7 Graigfelen, Clydach, Swansea	■ Sprints ■ M Distance ■ Jumps ■ Throws	25	Weekday Evenings Sun pm	Nil Nil

NORTHERN IRELAND

Club	Events	Members	Times	Fees
Achilles AC Upper Malone Playing Fields Buses: 71, 72 Station: Great Victoria Street C. Linden, 118 Ladybrook Park, Belfast 11 Tel: Belfast 614689	■ Sprints ■ M Distance Access to Jumps ■ Throws	122	Mon Eve Tues Eve Sat pm Sun pm	£1·50 £3
Albert Foundry AC Paisley Park, Belfast Buses: † Station † R.J. Melville, 6 Westway Park, Belfast 13 Tel: Belfast 7746991 The facilities of this Club are temporarily unavailable	■ Sprints ■ M Distance Access to Jumps Throws			£2
Albertville Harriers Scouts Hall, Bray Street, Belfast Buses: † Station: † J.A. McCormick, 58 Bray Street, Belfast 13	■ M Distance	20	Thurs pm Sat pm	10p (per week) 20p (per week)

181

ATHLETICS 75

NORTHERN IRELAND

*Questionnaire not returned, information based on entry in *Athletics 74*
†Insufficient information received

Club with Principal Track used, Secretaries, and nearest Public Transport

	Annadale Striders	Ballydrain Harriers & AC	Ballymena AC	Bangor AC	Belfast Ladies AC	Craigavon AC
Senior Subscription	£3	£2	£1	£9.10	£2	£2
Junior Subscription	£2	£1	50p	£6.50	£1	£1
Training Sessions	†	Tues Eve, Thurs Eve, Sat pm	Mon Eve, Tues Eve, Thurs Eve, Sat pm, Sun occasionally	Tues Eve, Thurs Eve	Mon pm, Thurs pm, Sat pm, Sun occasionally	Tues Eve, Thurs Eve, Sat pm
Active Membership	65	20	330	18	50	15
Coaches	Sprints, M Distance	M Distance, Throws	Sprints, M Distance, Jumps, Throws	†	Sprints, M Distance, Jumps, Throws	None
Weight Training	■	■	■		■	■
Indoor Training	■	■	■		■	■
Floodlit Training						
Landing Beds		■	■		■	■
All-Weather Runways		■	■		■	
All-Weather Track		■	■		■	
League	■	■		■		■
Juniors		■	■		■	
Women			■	■	■	
Men	■	■	■	■		■

Annadale Striders
J. Connolly, 7 Ravenhill Avenue, Belfast BT6 8LD
Tel: Belfast 55659

Ballydrain Harriers & AC
Ballydrain Old School, Comber
Buses: † Station: Comber
S. Murray, 33 Linley Drive, Comber, Co Down

Ballymena AC
Ballymena Academy Sports Grounds
Buses: † Station: Ballymena
Mr & Mrs S. Kyle, 'Tir-Na-Nog',
38 Old Galgorm Road, Ballymena, Co Antrim
Tel: 0266 6471 (home) 0266 2424 (office)

Bangor AC
Uprichard Park
Buses: † Station: Bangor
R. W. Edwards, 1 Monea Close, Bangor, Co Down

Belfast Ladies AC
Buses: † Station: †
Mrs M. Cowdy, 4 The Square,
Hillsborough, Co Down
Tel: Hillsborough 682455

Craigavon AC
Brownstown Park, Portadown
Buses: † Station: Portadown, Craigavon
P. Tortolani, 15 Clanbrassil Drive,
Portadown, Craigavon, Co Armagh
Tel: Portadown 35645

REGISTER OF CLUBS

Club									
	£2	£2	£5	†	£1 (5p per week)	£2	£1		
	50p	£1	£3		50p	Nil	£1	50p	
	Tues Eve, Thurs Eve	Tues pm, Thurs pm	Mon-Fri Eve, Sat am, Sun am	Mon pm	Sun am	Tues Eve, Thurs Eve	Tues pm, Wed pm, Thurs pm, Sun pm		
	20	40	34	15	20	50	165		
	None	M Distance	Sprints, M Distance	Sprints, M Distance, Throws	Sprints, M Distance	Sprints, M Distance, Jumps, Throws	Sprints, M Distance, Jumps, Throws		
	■	■	■	■		■	■		
	■	■	■	■		■			
						Partial	■		
		■							
		■			■				
	■	■			■	■	■		
	■	■			■	■			
	○	■	■		■	■	■		

Duncairn Harriers
158A Cavehill Road, Belfast
Buses: † Station: York Road, Belfast
A.R. Jenkins, 29 Islandmagee Road,
Whitehead, Carrickfergus, Co Antrim BT38 9NE

East Antrim Harriers
Ballyclare High School
Buses: † Station: †
K. McAdam, 51 Ballymena Rd, Doagh,
Ballyclare, Co Antrim BT39 0QR

Enniskillen Canoeing & AC
Buses: † Station: †
Miss G. Allan, 16 Belmore Street, Enniskillen,
Co Fermanagh

Limavady AC
Technical College, Limavady
Buses: † Station: Limavady Junction
W.S. Maxwell, 51 Scroggy Road, Limavady
Tel: Limavady 2701 (home) Limavady 2334 (bus)

Seapark AC
Seapark, Carrick
Buses: Kilroot Station: Troopers Lane
A.E. Sewell, 90 Moyard Gardens, Green
Island, Co Antrim
Tel: Whiteabbey 66175

Shorts AC
Aircraft Park, Holywood Road, Belfast
Buses: Red 25 and 21, Blue 1 Station †
S. Beattie, 16 Gilnahirk Walk, Belfast BT5 7DS
Tel: Belfast 657615

Sparta AC
St Columbs College, Buncrana Road
Buses: † Station: †
P.L. Devine, 105 Marlborough Road, Derry
Tel: 2212

183

NORTHERN IRELAND

*Questionnaire not returned, information based on entry in *Athletics 74*
†Insufficient information received

Club with Principal Track used, Secretaries, and nearest Public Transport

		Trench House AC St Joseph's College Buses: Falls Road Station: Gt Northern, Belfast P. Cassidy, 15 Shancoole Park, Upper Cavehill, Belfast 14 Tel: Belfast 778951	Willowfield Temperance Harriers McMahon Memorial Hall Buses: Bloomfield Station † E. Campbell, 9 Dixon Park, Bangor, Co Down BT19 2AY Tel: Bangor 63061
Senior Subscription		Nil	£5
Junior Subscription		Nil	£2·50
Training Sessions		Mon am/pm Tues am/pm Wed pm Thurs am/pm Fri am/pm Sun available	Tues Eve Thurs Eve Sat pm
Active Membership		20/30	30
Coaches		Sprints M Distance Jumps	Sprints M Distance
Weight Training		■	■
Indoor Training		■	
Floodlit Training			
Landing Beds		■	
All-Weather Runways		■	
All-Weather Track		■	
League			■
Juniors		■	■
Women			
Men		■	■

Specialist Clubs

These clubs have been formed by athletes and coaches with the purpose of furthering interest in and the practice of the event concerned. They work in close association with the UK Coaching Scheme. The honorary officers whose names and addresses are given below welcome enquiries regarding club activities and membership.

Barrier Club *(Steeplechase)*
C. Elliott, 325 Streatham High Road, London SW15. Tel: 01-764 9889 (business).

British Milers Club *(800m–1500m)*
H. Wilson, 15 Hillside, Welwyn Garden City, Hertfordshire. Tel: Welwyn Garden 23555 (home); Watford 34793 (business).

British Race Walkers' Club
C.W. Fogg, PE Department, Metropolitan Police Training School, Aerodrome Road, London NW9. Tel: 01-205 5641.

British Sprint Club
J. Bailey, 120 Meadow Lane, Coalville, Leicestershire. Tel: Coalville 4198 (home).

Hammer Circle
C. Melluish, 39 Criffel Avenue, London SW2.

High Jumpers' Club of Great Britain
R. J. Murray, 11 New Farm Avenue, Bromley, Kent. Tel: 01-460 7548 (home).

Javelin Club
K.J Brookman, Rectory Farm House, Howe Street, Great Waltham, Nr Chelmsford, Essex. Tel: Little Waltham 714 (home); Braintree 934 (business).

Kangaroo Club *(Long and Triple Jump)*
D.J. Hayward, 'Woodlands', The Common, Bomere Heath, Shrewsbury, Shropshire. Tel: Bomere Heath 617 (home).

National Union of Track Statisticians
A. Huxtable, 78 Toynbee Road, London SW20. Tel: 01-542 7412 (home).

Pole Vaulters' Association
A.T. Neuff, 103 Crescent Drive, Petts Wood, Kent.

Road Runner's Club
P. Goodsell, 10 Honeywood Road, Colchester, Essex. Tel: Colchester 74637 (home).

Shot and Discus Circle
W. Sage, 53 Hatch Gardens, Padworth, Surrey. Tel: Burgh Heath 55980 (home).

Southern Counties Veterans AAA
F.S. Cuthbert, 37 The Meadway, Cuffley, Potters Bar, Hertfordshire.
Tel: 01-284 2695.

Specialist Clubs Committee
This committee consists of nominated representatives from most of the constituent clubs.
Hon. Secretary: M.D. Terry, 5 Grange Close, Heston, Middlesex. Tel: 01-571 3697 (home); 01-937 5400 ext 63 (business).

African Genesis
BRUCE TULLOH

The tide of African athletics continues to rise. First it was the Ethiopians, then the Kenyans and Tunisians, and now we have stars from all over the continent. The season before Olympic year is the time when one looks out for potential Olympic medallists, and for the first time we have to realise that the Games can no longer be regarded as a struggle between the United States and Europe, with occasional interventions from 'Down Under'. The African presence is going to make itself felt all the way through the track events, and in a few of the field events too. The tide rises in all directions – top class performances in more events; more countries producing class athletes; and greater depth in the leading countries.

Let us look at what is happening. I last reviewed the state of the sport in Africa in early 1973, not long after Munich and just before the All-African Games in Lagos. The Munich Games were the best ever for Africa – nine medals were collected, three of them gold, yet only two years later, without the stimulus of an Olympics, African records have been broken in 28 of the 38 standard events.

With the famous Ravelomanantsoa moving to the professional ranks, there is not at present any African sprinter who is really in world class. Adama Fall of Senegal was given a time of 9.9sec for 100 metres on one occasion, but his best valid mark is 10.3. This puts him in the same bracket as his compatriot Barka Sy (10.2) and the Nigerian Olakunle (10.3). The Ghanaians have a number of men around the 10.4 mark, but unless Karikari fulfils his youthful promise it is likely that the French-speaking countries will provide the next sprint star.

In the 400 metres we have tremendous richness of talent, for the one-lap event is one that African runners love. I have seen teams of untrained schoolboys average 51–52 seconds a man in relay events. Though Charles Asati, gold medallist in Edinburgh, Munich (relay), and Christchurch, is almost certainly past his best and Julius Sang is unlikely to improve further, the East Africans have many more coming along. The most promising of the bunch at present is Stephen Chepkwony, who set an African all-comers record of 45.5 in Nairobi last summer, ahead of Francis Mosyoki (45.7) and Asati. But Tanzania and Uganda both provided medallists (Kamanya and Ayoo) in Christchurch, and Nigeria, Ghana, Ethiopia, and Morocco all have men who have run 46.5 or better.

The vital step for any nation in sport is when they realise they are as good as the rest, when they go into competition expecting to win rather than lose. The 'superiority complex' established by the Kenyan middle-distance men certainly helped Filbert Bayi to the top, and it stamped a pattern on all the distance events from 800 metres upwards in Christchurch, reaching its epitome in the running of Bayi and

Jipcho. A significant race, but one that went largely unnoticed in Britain last summer, was the 800 metres in Zurich when Mike Boit beat Susanj. The Yugoslav champion was outstanding in Rome, but he was well beaten in Zurich – 1:44.2 to 1:44.7. Though this result may be discounted in relation to the European Championships, it is relevant to the Olympics.

The African runners now know they can beat the *wazungu* (white men). Bayi, Boit, and Kipkurgat should continue to improve, while such as Omwanza and Nyambui are waiting in the wings. From further north, Guettaya of Tunisia and Ebba of Ethiopia, both under 3:40 for 1500 last season, show there are many more to come.

In the longer distances, the main question is who will replace Keino, Jipcho, and Temu. Of course, that remarkable competitor Mohamed Gammoudi continues to produce good times, and his younger brother has now appeared on the scene. The Ethiopians, as distinct from Kenya and Tanzania, must have some good men, but the 1974 season saw little of them. The East Africans, on the other hand, took full advantage of the meetings in Scandinavia last summer and gained a lot of valuable experience. The most impressive of all, to my mind, was young John Ngeno, who ran away from Richard Juma (27:57 in Christchurch) to win the Helsinki Games 10,000 metres in 28:05.6 and was able to beat Frank Shorter a week later in Stockholm, in 28:11. When one remembers that Shorter is not only the Olympic marathon champion but also the American record holder for 10,000 metres, with 27:51.4, it appears that Kenya has a tremendous prospect. Nor should one forget his compatriots Kimeto and Kiingi, internationals while still at school.

Concluding the men's running events, it is obvious that the challenge in the barrier events is going to be strong, with such men as Kimaiyo, Koskei, and Mogaka of Kenya; the Senegalese had two men under 14 seconds for the high hurdles last season and in the low hurdles there is the looming threat of Akii-Bua and his 20-odd brothers! One should not leave without remarking on Mabuza's feat in Christchurch. This unknown marathon man (17th in Munich) came within seconds of Abebe Bikila's African marathon record and in doing so brought his country, Swaziland, into athletic reckoning for the first time.

In the field events, of course, Africa lags far behind and is likely to remain so. The increasing sophistication and cost of equipment, apart from the need for specialist coaching, create a gap between the richer and the poorer countries. The only exceptions to this are long and triple jumping. In the latter event the Ghanaians dominated the Commonwealth Games, with Owusu getting the gold, and since then a new name has emerged – Charlton Ehizuelen. This young Nigerian, now being coached in the United States, reached 16.82m last season, only one centimetre behind the wind-assisted jump that gave Mansour Dia (Senegal) sixth place in Munich. With competition from the Ghanaians and the Senegalese, both nations having men well over 16 metres, Ehizuelen is likely to be the first African over 17 metres this year.

In the long jump, Owusu's 8.06m in Munich, plus an 8.09m in May last year, still stand supreme, but a number of his fellow West Africans are within striking distance – Ehizuelen and Okoro of Nigeria, both over 7.80m, Diedhiou of Senegal

(7.72m), and Kingsley Adams of Ghana, whose 7.92m in 1973 plus a 7.97m last season make him the prime challenger.

When one considers the women's events, one finds promise rather than achievement, but there has been remarkable progress. Alice Annum has been joined by Modupe Oshikoya as an athlete of real world class, and both girls added to their Commonwealth Games honours by gaining medals in the American AAU championships last summer. In theory, the performance of Sabina Chebichi in Christchurch, when she set African records of 2:02.6 for 800 metres and 4:18.6 for 1500, should lead to fantastic things, since she was only 14 at the time. That 1500 metres record has since fallen to Rose Tata, who ran 4:16.7 in Italy last September. However, I hesitate to prophesy too much, for the Kenyan record in bringing on their female athletes has so far not been outstanding.

This point of bringing on young athletes is the vital one for African athletics. The school system will always throw up promising athletes, but how to bridge the gap between promise and world class? The efforts made by the Nigerians last year point the way.

In 1973 Nigeria held the African Games, after a lapse of eight years. Last August they took another significant step, with the holding of the Ghana-Nigeria Sports Festival in Lagos. Stars of the meeting were Annum and Oshikoya; the Nigerian girl won golds in the high jump, long jump, and hurdles, while the Ghanaian won the two sprints and anchored her relay squad to an African record of 44.7 in Lagos and later to 44.4 in Christchurch. What was equally significant was the fact that the full range of events was held, with 13 African Games records being surpassed, 11 of them by

Modupe Oshikoya – incredible natural all-round talent to unfold at Montreal.

women. Best of these was the 53.6sec 400 metres by Grace Bakari (Gha), which puts her within reach of Judith Ayaa's record. Other performances, such as a 4:33 1500 metres and a 43.98m throw in the women's discus, may not sound much by world standards, but they are stepping stones.

The men, strangely enough, were less impressive in Lagos, possibly because many of them were resting after a strenuous season in the United States. It was significant, however, that Ehizuelen beat Owusu in the triple (16.15m), Kingsley Adams won the long jump (7.89); while the high hurdler, Aboyade-Cole, a 13.8 man, was well beaten by another Nigerian, Godwin Obasogie.

There is no doubt that the efforts of the Nigerians will produce results. As well as their international meeting, a rare event, they have organised coaching courses, American-staffed, for several West and Central African countries, and put the recruitment of Nigerians by American colleges on an official basis. Other countries would benefit from their example.

There is one giant blank in this pattern of the sport in Africa. That blank is where South Africa should fit in. Nobody would dispute that South Africa has some magnificent athletes, many of whom would walk away with All-Africa titles and be contenders for Olympic medals. There are the sprinters Greef and van Heerden (20.6sec 200m), the middle-distance stars Malan (1:44 800m) and van Zijl (3:37 1500m) and distance men Bonzet and Mamabula (13:31 and 13:41 respectively for 5000m). In the throws the talent is equally impressive, with van Reenen's 68-metre discus throw, Barnard over 70 metres in the hammer, and two men over 80 metres with the javelin. In the women's events, Claudie van Straaten has run 52.2 for 400 metres, much faster than any other girl on African soil.

Because of the boycott on South Africa, these athletes cannot compete. There is no doubt that from a purely athletic point of view a great deal would be gained by competition between 'black' and 'white' Africa, but unfortunately it is not that simple. The sporting boycott is just one aspect of the constant diplomatic pressure put on South Africa from outside. We must remember that this boycott would be useless if South Africa were not a democracy. As it is, there is always the possibility that the pressure will lead to internal changes and true integration in all aspects of life. If South Africa were to give equal rights to all races, then the IAAF and the IOC would welcome them back. Until that time South Africa will be, as China has been for so long, an outsider. Though I for one do not sympathise with the government, I do have sympathy for the individual athletes.

ATHLETICS 75

Tanzania's phenomenal Filbert Bayi eclipses New Zealanders John Walker (2nd) and Rod Dixon (4th) – as well as fellow African Ben Jipcho (3rd) in more ways than one – at the end of perhaps the most outstanding piece of middle-distance front-running yet seen. Bayi's time, in winning this Commonwealth Games 1500 metres at Christchurch, was a world record 3:32.2.

The European Champions

VALERIY BORZOV (Sov)
(100 metres – 10.27)
In terms of gold medals he is the most successful sprinter in history: European 100 metres champion in 1969, 1971, and 1974, and 200 metres titlist in 1971; Olympic 100 and 200 metres winner in 1972. That's not all: he was the European junior 100 and 200 metres champion in 1968 and he picked up further gold medals at the European Indoor Championships in 1970, 1971, 1972, and 1974. An unparalleled competitor, he has yet to set an outdoor world record – 'my ultimate dream as a trackman'.
Born Kakhova, 20.10.1949; *Height:* 1.82m (5' 11½"), *Weight:* 82kg (181lb). *Best marks:* 100m – 10.0 (European record), 200m – 20.0 (European record), 400m – 47.6.

PIETRO MENNEA (Ita)
(200 metres – 20.60)
Became the first Italian sprinter since Livio Berruti's Olympic 200 metres triumph in the same stadium 14 years earlier to capture a major international title – and was, for the partisan home crowd in Rome, the great hero of the Championships. Has made steady progress as a competitor: 6th in the 1971 European Championships, 3rd in the 1972 Olympics, and now champion of Europe. Although more effective in the longer sprint he has been a co-holder of the European 100 metres record since 1972 and was second to Borzov in Rome.
Born Barletta, 28.6.1952; *Height:* 1.77m (5' 9¾"), *Weight:* 67kg (148lb). *Best marks:* 100m – 10.0 (European record), 200m – 20.2.

KARL HONZ (WG)
(400 metres – 45.04)
It was not until the autumn of 1971 that he began training specifically for 400 metres . . . and within a matter of months he was European record holder, with a sparkling 44.7 in the West German Championships. Was a strong medal contender at the Munich Olympics but finished only 7th. Worse, in the 4 × 400 metres relay he 'died' after running the first 200 in 20.1, fading from first to fourth in the final straight. He badly needed to make amends by winning the European title, which he did with ease.
Born Bankholzen, 28.1.1951; *Height:* 1.88m (6' 2"), *Weight:* 84kg (185lb). *Best marks:* 100m – 10.4, 200m – 20.6, 400m – 44.7 (European record).

LUCIANO SUSANJ (Yug)
(800 metres – 1:44.1)
Early bad luck (injury forced him to withdraw from the 1971 European Championships and 1972 Olympics) was overcome when he won European indoor titles at 400 metres (1973) and 800 metres (1974); and a series of fast runs established him as firm favourite for the 800 in Rome. There he emerged as one of the most impressive of all the champions, accelerating at 600 metres with unprecedented power and effect to score by one of the widest margins in championship history. His time of 1:44.1 was the fastest ever by a European-born runner.
Born Rijeka, 10.11.1948; *Height:* 1.85m (6' 0¾"), *Weight:* 73kg (161lb). *Best marks:* 100m – 10.6, 200m – 21.1, 400m – 45.9, 800m – 1:44.1, 1500m – 3:45.2.

KLAUS-PETER JUSTUS (EG)
(1500 metres – 3:40.6)
First made his mark as a 15-year-old at cross-country by winning the final of the GDR youth event which in 1967 attracted an original nationwide entry of over a million runners. He became European junior 1500 metres champion in 1970 but stagnated around the 3:39 mark from 1972 onwards. In Rome he was only ninth with 200 metres to run, but then came to life with a pulsating finishing burst which, in his own words, 'was unbelievable'.
Born Rudolstadt, 1.7.1951; *Height:* 1.73m (5' 8"), *Weight:* 61kg (134lb). *Best marks:* 800m – 1:47.5, 1500m – 3:39.0, 5000m – 13:52.4, 3000m steeplechase – 8:52.4.

BRENDAN FOSTER (UK)
(5000 metres – 13:17.2)
Few athletes can point to such a consistently inspired big-time record: at 1500 metres he set personal bests in the 1970 Commonwealth Games (finishing third), 1971

European Championships (third), and 1972 Olympics (fifth); while at the 1974 Commonwealth he produced two lifetime bests – both UK records – when finishing a close second to Ben Jipcho (Ken) in the 5000 and seventh in the world record 1500. Himself world record holder at 3000 metres and 2 miles, he was in his greatest form at Rome, making light of the oppressive humidity to triumph by a huge margin.

Born Hebburn, 12.1.1948; *Height:* 1.79m (5′ 10½″), *Weight:* 66kg (147lb). *Best marks:* 800m – 1:51.1, 1500m – 3:37.6, mile – 3:55.9, 3000m – 7:35.2 (world record), 2 miles – 8:13.8 (world record), 5000m – 13:14.6.

MANFRED KUSCHMANN (EG)
(10,000 metres – 28:25.8)

A distant runner-up to Foster in the 5000 (but still setting a national record), Kuschmann had enjoyed his own moment of glory six days earlier when he narrowly held off Tony Simmons (UK) for the 10,000 metres title. He had lost contact with the leading bunch at 7000 metres but came back strongly, dashed into the lead at the bell, and covered the last lap in 55.4. In the tradition of compatriot Jurgen Haase, European champion in 1966 and 1969, he combines the speed of a good 1500 metres runner with the stamina of a marathoner.

Born Coswig, 25.7.1950; *Height:* 1.75m (5′ 8¾″), *Weight:* 62kg (137lb). *Best marks:* 1500m – 3:43.0, 3000m – 7:48.8, 5000m – 13:24.0, 10,000m – 28:09.6, Marathon – 2:23.08.

IAN THOMPSON (UK)
(Marathon – 2:13:18.2)

What a marathon record: run four, won four . . . and all in the space of 10 months! Any possible doubts raised when he made the swiftest marathon debut of all-time (2:12:40) in the AAA championship in October 1973 were swept away when he produced an even greater performance in the Commonwealth Games three months later. He came home two minutes ahead in 2:09:12, a European best time and the fastest ever recorded in any championship event. Further victories followed in Athens in April (2:13:50) and in Rome. In 1975 he will attempt to make his mark on the track at 10,000 metres.

Born Birkenhead, 16.10.1949; *Height:* 1.69m (5′ 6½″), *Weight:* 60kg (131lb). *Best marks:* 1500m – 3:51.0, 5000m – 14:05.4, 10,000m – 30:10.0, Marathon – 2:09:12 (European best).

BRONISLAW MALINOWSKI (Pol)
(3000m steeplechase – 8:15.0)

Three of the winners at the first official European Junior Championships, staged in 1970, went on to gain full-fledged victories in Rome: Klaus-Peter Justus, long jumper Valeriy Podluzhny . . . and Bronislaw Malinowski. Like Anders Garderud (Swe), the favourite he beat for the gold medal, he is a flat runner of the very highest calibre, as his list of best marks bears out. Strong as well as fast, he covered the second half in Rome in about 4:02! He is half-British, his mother coming from Scotland.

Born Nowe, 4.6.1951; *Height:* 1.81m (5′ 11¼″), *Weight:* 65kg (143lb). *Best marks:* 1500m – 3:39.3, 3000m – 7:42.4, 2 miles – 8:17.8, 5000m – 13:28.0, 10,000m – 28:25.2, 3000m steeplechase – 8:15.0.

GUY DRUT (Fra)
(110m hurdles – 13.40)

Guy Drut, who also has British ancestry on his mother's side, has been filling for some seasons the role previously played by Michel Jazy (who, curiously, was born in the same mining town) of France's athletic superstar. His career has been one of ups and downs, which may be appropriate for a hurdler, and his clearcut win in Rome compensated for his acute disappointment at the previous Championships in 1971 when he crashed out of his heat. He was Olympic silver medallist in 1972.

Born Oignies, 6.12.1950; *Height:* 1.88m (6′ 2″), *Weight:* 73kg (161lb). *Best marks:* 110m hurdles – 13.2 (European record) and 13.1w, Pole vault – 5.20m (17′ 0¾″), Decathlon – 7565.

ALAN PASCOE (UK)
(400m hurdles – 48.82)

As a high hurdler, Alan Pascoe won European gold (indoors, 1969), silver (1971), and bronze (1969) medals – as well as picking up an Olympic 4 × 400 metres relay silver in 1972. But it is only since he moved up to 400 metres hurdles that his career has really taken off. He established himself as Europe's number one in 1973, captured the Commonwealth title in 48.8, and – almost unbelievably in view of injury and illness which bedevilled him to within a few days of the Championships – he repeated that time to triumph in Rome. He struck gold in the relay, too.

Born Portsmouth, 11.10.1947; *Height:* 1.85m (6′ 1″), *Weight:* 74kg (164lb). *Best marks:* 100m – 10.6w, 200m – 20.9, 400m – 46.8, 110m hurdles – 13.7, 400m hurdles – 48.8.

JESPER TORRING (Den)
(High jump – 2.25m/7′ 4½″)

Until 1974 Dr Torring was known as a talented all-rounder, equally at home running 400 metres, hurdling, high jumping, pole vaulting, or long jumping. He then decided to specialise in one event, the high jump . . . with spectacular results. In the course of one competition in

May he raised his personal best of 2.16m (7' 1") in four instalments up to 2.23m (7' 3¾"). He went even higher in Rome, flopping over 2.25m (7' 4½") – which is 39cm (15¼") above his own head.

Born Randers, 27.9.1947; *Height*: 1.86m (6' 1¼"), *Weight*: 72kg (159lb). *Best marks*: 400m – 47.6, 110m hurdles – 13.7, High jump – 2.25m (7' 4½"), Pole vault – 4.80m (15' 9"), Long jump – 7.80m (25' 7¼"), Decathlon – 7304.

VLADIMIR KISHKUN (Sov)
(Pole vault – 5.35m/17' 6½")

Every European Championships meeting throws up at least one surprising winner, and Vladimir Kishkun certainly qualifies for that description. True, he had vaulted 5.36m (17' 7") indoors and won the Soviet title with 5.35m (17' 6½"), but he was largely an unknown quantity, for he had not competed internationally before. In Rome he cleared 5.20m (17' 0¾") only at the third attempt, boldly passed up the next height of 5.30m (17' 4½"), and made 5.35m at the second try. He improved to 5.40m (17' 8½") soon after the Championships.

Born Leningrad, 5.11.1951; *Height*: 1.87m (6' 1¼"), *Weight*: 76kg (168lb). *Best mark*: Pole vault – 5.40m (17' 8½").

VALERIY PODLUZHNY (Sov)
(Long jump – 8.12m/26' 7¾")

When the great Soviet long jumper Igor Ter-Ovanesyan (former world record holder and three times European champion) retired after the 1972 Olympics, he nominated his young compatriot Valeriy Podluzhny as the man most likely to succeed him. Podluzhny, European junior champion for both the long jump and triple jump in 1970, has justified that confidence. He scored two big victories in 1973 – at the World Student Games and the European Cup final – and led from his opening jump in Rome.

Born Donyetsk, 22.8.1952; *Height*: 1.77m (5' 9¾"), *Weight*: 69kg (152lb). *Best marks*: 100m – 10.5, Long jump – 8.17m (26' 9¾") and 8.20m (26' 11")w, Triple jump – 16.29m (53' 5½").

VIKTOR SANEYEV (Sov)
(Triple jump – 17.23m/56' 6½")

There are few athletes one can designate, without reservation, as the 'greatest of all-time' in a specific event, but Viktor Saneyev surely merits that accolade. He is the nonpareil of triple jumping. Just consider his competitive record: 1968 – 1st Olympics, 1969 – 1st European, 1971 – 2nd European, 1972 – 1st Olympics, 1974 – 1st European. He has held the world record (except for a 14-month period) ever since the 1968 Olympics. His winning margin in Rome of 55cm (1' 9¾") was the widest at this level of competition for 20 years.

Born Sukhumi, 3.10.1945; *Height*: 1.88m (6' 2"), *Weight*: 78kg (172lb). *Best marks*: 100m – 10.5, Long jump – 7.90m (25' 11"), Triple jump – 17.44m (57' 2¾") (world record).

HARTMUT BRIESENICK (EG)
(Shot – 20.50m/67' 3¼")

Along with Valeriy Borzov in the 100 metres, Hartmut Briesenick was the only man in Rome to retain a title won three years earlier in Helsinki. His winning put on this occasion was far below the 21.08m (69' 2") he achieved in taking his first gold medal, but it enabled him to overtake Ralf Reichenbach (WG), the leader until the fifth round. He was European junior champion in 1968, became the first European to reach 21 metres (in 1971) and 70 feet (in 1972), and was Olympic bronze medallist in Munich.

Born Luckenwalde, 17.3.1949; *Height*: 1.91m (6' 3¼"), *Weight*: 116kg (256lb). *Best marks*: Shot – 21.67m (71' 1¼"), Discus – 57.56m (188' 10").

PENTTI KAHMA (Fin)
(Discus – 63.62m/208' 9")

As befits the brother of Markus Kahma, who placed fourth in the 1958 European decathlon championship, Pentti was himself a fair all-rounder before his weight rose to its present level. In 1969, the year he first bettered the discus thrower's twin landmarks of 60 metres and 200 feet, he long jumped 7.21m (23' 8"). He has steadily matured into one of the most consistent, as well as longest, throwers in the world and during 1974 carried the Finnish record out to 66.52m (218' 3").

Born Alavieska, 3.12.1943; *Height*: 1.88m (6' 2"), *Weight*: 110kg (243lb). *Best marks*: Long jump – 7.21m (23' 8"), Shot – 17.98m (59' 0"), Discus – 66.52m (218' 3"), Decathlon – 6551.

ALEKSEY SPIRIDONOV (Sov)
(Hammer – 74.20m/243' 5")

This tall, young Soviet hammer prospect was beginning to look like an eternal runner-up: second in the 1970 European Junior Championships, second in the 1973 World Student Games, second in the 1974 USSR Championships. Even his performances were stagnating: a best of 74.54m (244' 7") in 1972, 74.08m (243' 0") in 1973, 74.66m (244' 11") in 1974. Suddenly, everything changed. In Rome he led from start to finish and just four days later he broke the world record – using four turns as is his style – with 76.66m (251' 6").

Born Leningrad, 20.11.1951; *Height*: 1.92m (6' 3½"), *Weight*: 118kg (260lb). *Best mark*: Hammer – 76.66m (251' 6") (world record).

HANNU SIITONEN (Fin)
(Javelin – 89.58m/293′ 11″)
It is no exaggeration to claim that an era ended when Hannu Siitonen won in Rome with the longest throw in the world for the year. The dethroned champion, Janis Lusis (Sov), had won the European crown in 1971 . . . in 1969 . . . in 1966 . . . and in 1962! Siitonen became Finland's first European javelin champion since 1950 and it was a just reward for several seasons of outstandingly consistent results of around the 290 feet (88.40m) mark. He had not previously won a medal in Olympic or European competition.

Born Parikkala, 18.3.1949; *Height:* 1.83m (6′ 0″), *Weight:* 84kg (185lb). *Best mark:* Javelin – 93.90m (308′ 1″).

RYSZARD SKOWRONEK (Pol)
(Decathlon – 8207 pts)
Like Luciano Susanj's, Ryszard Skowronek's previous excursions into the Olympic and European arena were unhappy experiences. He was injured in the very first event in Helsinki; while in Munich he was forced to retire after seven events. He encountered no problems in Rome. A comfortable third after the first day's events, he moved into second place with a personal best pole vault of 5.10m (16′ 8¾″) and took the lead in the penultimate event, the javelin. His final score was a Polish record by one point.

Born Jeleniej Gora, 1.5.1949; *Height:* 1.83m (6′ 0″), *Weight:* 83kg (183lb). *Best mark:* Decathlon – 8207.

VLADIMIR GOLUBNICHIY (Sov)
(20 kilometres walk – 1 : 29 : 30.0)
No other walker can match the accomplishments of Vladimir Golubnichiy. Over a 19-year period, he has set world records and never placed worse than third in seven Olympic and European 20 kilometre races. He was Olympic champion in 1960 and 1968, silver medallist in 1972, and bronze medal winner in 1964, but as injury kept him out of the 1969 and 1971 Championships he had not previously managed to win a European title. At the age of 38 he put that right in Rome – 14 years after his Olympic triumph in that city.

Born Sumi, 2.6.1936; *Height:* 1.80m (5′ 10¾″), *Weight:* 75kg (165lb). *Best mark:* 20km walk – 1 : 26 : 55.

CHRISTOPH HOHNE (EG)
(50 kilometres walk – 3 : 59 : 05.6)
Christoph Hohne's record in the longer walk has also been consistently brilliant. During his 19 seasons of competition he has accumulated an Olympic title (1968), two European victories (1969 and 1974), and a second place (1971). He has also helped East Germany win the Lugano Cup (the IAAF's walking team competition) four successive times between 1965 and 1973, finishing first individually on three of those occasions.

Born Borsdorf, 12.2.1941; *Height:* 1.71m (5′ 7¼″), *Weight:* 62kg (137lb). *Best marks:* 50km walk – 3 : 52 : 53, 100km walk – 9 : 15 : 57.

WOMEN

IRENA SZEWINSKA (Pol)
(100 metres – 11.13, 200 metres – 22.51)
Even before 1974 Irena Szewinska was rated among the all-time greats. Her accomplishments included Olympic gold medals at 200 metres (1968) and sprint relay (1964), silver medals at 200 metres and long jump (1964), and bronze awards for 100 (1968) and 200 metres (1972); plus a hat-trick of European titles in 1966 and various world records. By the time the season was over Irena could fairly claim to be the greatest of them all. She demolished Olympic champion Renate Stecher (EG) in both the Rome sprints, set phenomenal world records of 22.0 for 200 and 49.9 for 400 metres . . . and was timed at 48.5 for a 400 metres relay leg, which is probably the most outstanding single performance in women's athletics history.

Born Leningrad, 24.5.1946; *Height:* 1.76m (5′ 9¼″), *Weight:* 64kg (141lb). *Best marks:* 100m – 10.9, 200m – 22.0 (world record), 400m – 49.9 (world record), 80m hurdles – 10.8, High jump – 1.68m (5′ 6″), Long jump – 6.67m (21′ 10¾″), Pentathlon – 4705 (old tables).

RIITTA SALIN (Fin)
(400 metres – 50.14)
As a result of training seriously for the first time the previous winter, sensational progress was made during 1974 by Riitta Salin. From a best mark of 53.9 for 400 metres in 1973, which was barely of international class, she pushed forward to 50.5 – second only to Szewinska's epoch-making 49.9 – a month before Rome. At the Championships she ran a finely controlled race to record 50.14, the fastest ever electrical clocking and equal in stature to Szewinska's hand time. Her husband, Ari, is Finnish 400 metres hurdles record holder.

Born Helsinki, 16.10.1950; *Height:* 1.73m (5′ 8″), *Weight:* 58kg (128lb). *Best marks:* 200m – 22.8, 400m – 50.1.

LILYANA TOMOVA (Bul)
(800 metres – 1 : 58.1)
After seriously injuring herself during the European Indoor Championships, Lilyana Tomova was off training for

THE EUROPEAN CHAMPIONS

Nearly there: Rosi Witschas, already European champion, setting a world record 1.95m at Rome

two months, and her whole summer season looked to be in jeopardy. However, she made a resoundingly well-timed comeback, and though beaten at the Balkan Games a month before Rome, she managed to lower her personal best 800 metres time to 1:59.1; and in the race that counted she produced a powerful finish to win in 1:58.1, the second fastest performance on record. She later gained a silver medal in the 1500 metres, in her first season at the event.

Born Plovdiv, 9.8.1946; *Height:* 1.68m (5' 6"), *Weight* 61kg (134lb). *Best marks:* 400m – 52.0, 800m – 1:58.1, 1500m – 4:05.0.

GUNHILD HOFFMEISTER (EG)
(1500 metres – 4:02.4)
Few could have begrudged the 30-year-old East German MP her first major international title. For years she had almost, but not quite, reached the topmost rung . . . second in the 1971 European 1500 metres after tripping over in the 800 metres final; third in the 800 and second in the 1500 at the 1972 Olympics; second to Tomova in the 800 earlier in the Rome proceedings. This time Hoffmeister, a deputy of the GDR's People's Chamber as well as being a PE teacher and mother of a seven-year-old daughter, won decisively in 4:02.3, the second fastest ever.

Born Forst, 6.7.1944; *Height:* 1.72m (5' 7¾"), *Weight:* 56kg (123lb). *Best marks:* 400m – 53.9, 800m – 1:58.8, 1500m – 4:02.3.

NINA HOLMEN (Fin)
(3000 metres – 8;55.2)
Finland's male long-distance runners have built up a tradition second to none since Hannes Kolehmainen's Olympic successes of 1912. Now, over 60 years later, Finnish women have taken their first step. Nina Holmen, in only her third season at the event, became the inaugural European 3000 metres champion – and in so doing became the first Finn to place higher than sixth in a European women's track final (Riitta Salin was to win a second gold medal two days later). Nina's winning time ranks her second on the world all-time list.

Born Ahtavalla, 29.9.1951; *Height:* 1.66m (5' 5¼"), *Weight:* 51kg (112lb). *Best marks:* 1500m – 4:11.6, 3000m – 8:55.2.

ANNELIE EHRHARDT (EG)
(100m hurdles – 12.66)
The last time Annelie Ehrhardt lost a hurdles race of importance was at the previous European Championships, in Helsinki in 1971. Her conqueror then was compatriot Karin Balzer, acknowledged at the time as the greatest of all hurdlers. During the ensuing three seasons Ehrhardt has surpassed even Balzer's achievements and stands unchallenged in her chosen event. Olympic champion, world record holder, and three times European indoor titlist, she performed in Rome with customary panache to

195

register a mark that, on electrical timing, was only 0.07sec slower than her world's best.

Born Ohrsleben, 18.6.1950; *Height:* 1.66m (5′ 5¼″), *Weight:* 58kg (128lb). *Best marks:* 100m – 11.3, 100m hurdles – 12.3 (world record), 200m hurdles – 25.8 (European record), Long jump – 6.15m (20′ 2¼″).

ROSEMARIE WITSCHAS (EG)
(High jump – 1.95m/6′ 4¾″)
In the age of the Fosbury Flop, Rosi Witschas struck a blow for supporters of the straddle style by not only winning the European title but breaking the world record into the bargain. Hers was probably the greatest of all the Rome performances, for she had to contend not just with the cream of the continent's jumpers but also with many thousands of Italian fans who, in support of Sara Simeoni (who placed third), tried to distract the East German during her attempts. The record height was 20cm (8″) above her own head, equalling the best differential on record.

Born Lohsa, 4.4.1952; *Height:* 1.75m (5′ 8¾″), *Weight:* 59kg (130lb). *Best mark:* High jump – 1.95m (6′ 4¾″) (world record).

ILONA BRUZSENYAK (Hun)
(Long jump – 6.65m/21′ 10″)
The Hungarian all-rounder made an inauspicious start to the proceedings. She made a hash of her run-up in the qualifying round and only went through on her third and final jump. For four rounds of the final she could not equal the distance she covered when qualifying, and as the fifth round opened she was back in sixth place. Suddenly, it all clicked: she hit the board smack on and sailed out to her best ever wind-free mark. She later filled sixth place in the pentathlon.

Born Pecsmegyer, 14.9.1950; *Height:* 1.65m (5′ 5″), *Weight:* 58kg (128lb). *Best marks:* 100m hurdles – 13.1, Long jump – 6.83m (22′ 5″) w and 6.65m (21′ 10″), Pentathlon – 4617.

NADYEZHDA CHIZHOVA (Sov)
(Shot – 20.78m/68′ 2¼″)
With Helena Fibingerova, the Czech who was to break the world record shortly afterwards, failing to pose the severe challenge anticipated, the way was clear for Nadya Chizhova to make further athletics history. Overtaking East Germany's Marianne Adam in the third round, she notched up her fourth consecutive European title, a feat previously accomplished only by her javelin throwing colleague, Janis Lusis. It was her fifth major gold medal, for she is the reigning Olympic champion and has not lost an important contest outdoors since the 1968 Olympics.

Born Usolie-Sibirkskoye, 29.9.1945; *Height:* 1.73m (5′ 8″), *Weight:* 95kg (209lb). *Best mark:* Shot – 21.45m (70′ 4½″).

FAINA MELNIK (Sov)
(Discus – 69.00m/226′ 4″)
Unquestionably the greatest female discus thrower in history, and possibly the strongest woman in the world (her weight training sessions are legendary, and she has been seen to throw the men's discus around 170 feet). Yet there was a time when Faina Melnik was told she had no prospects in sport! She was 20 and applying to enrol at a physical culture institute. Six years later, in 1971, she won the European title with a world record throw and has been dominant ever since, capturing the 1972 Olympic crown and constantly improving her world record.

Born Bakoto, 9.7.1945; *Height:* 1.72m (5′ 7¾″), *Weight:* 88kg (194lb). *Best marks:* Shot – 19.39m (63′ 7½″), Discus – 69.90m (229′ 4″) (world record).

RUTH FUCHS (EG)
(Javelin – 67.22m/220′ 6″)
What a big-time performer Ruth Fuchs has shown herself to be! The ultimate test of an athlete's skill and nerve is at an event like the Olympic Games or European Championships, and each time she has been so tested Ruth has summoned up an extra-special performance. She won the Olympic title in Munich with an outstanding throw, broke the world record with her first throw of 66.10m (216′ 10″) in the 1973 European Cup final, and smashed even those remarkable figures in Rome with her second cast of 67.22m (220′ 6″).

Born Egeln, 14.12.1946; *Height:* 1.69m (5′ 6½″), *Weight:* 65kg (143lb). *Best marks:* Long jump – 5.88m (19′ 3½″), Javelin – 67.22m (220′ 6″) (world record).

NADYEZHDA TKACHENKO (Sov)
(Pentathlon – 4776)
Though she is not outstandingly brilliant in any one event, in terms of all-round ability there has been only a handful of athletes who could compare with her for consistently high level results in all five pentathlon events. Nadyezhda Tkachenko's previous placings in major pentathlons were 9th in the 1972 Olympics, winner at the 1973 World Student Games, and second in the European Cup later the same season. In Rome she unexpectedly defeated world record holder Burglinde Pollak (EG), taking the lead in the second event and winning by exactly 100 points.

Born Kiev, 19.9.1948; *Height:* 1.66m (5′ 5¼″), *Weight:* 57kg (126lb). *Best performances:* 100m hurdles – 13.2, High jump – 1.78m (5′ 10″), Long jump – 6.56m (21′ 6¼″), Shot – 16.07m (52′ 8¼″), Pentathlon – 4776.

Those Diabolical Steroids

Ron Pickering

'To declare that sport during the present century has become a cultural phenomenon of enormous magnitude and complexity is an affirmation of the obvious', says Loy. 'Sport is fast becoming a social institution permeating education, economics, art, politics, law, mass communications, and international diplomacy. Its scope is awesome with nearly everyone becoming involved in some way if only vicariously.'

At the Munich Olympic Games there were 10,169 athletes from 123 countries commanding the interest of 1000 million spectators around the world, which produces a ratio of 100,000 spectators to every athlete. Despite the public's commitment to sport, as a social phenomenon it has received little serious study. For physical educationalists and coaches like myself, sport provides a medium for pursuing educational goals, but for almost everyone else it serves quite a different purpose. Therefore, any controversial issues, such as those that offend our so-called normal standards of moral behaviour, will be judged in a variety of ways by all concerned.

Few would deny that the Olympic athlete obtains a peak attainment of human expression in his sport and is therefore better qualified in that sphere than he may possibly be in any other. However, we can only wonder whether we are not placing a greater premium on the athlete as both an entertainer and as an example of our own society's very subjective standard for ethical and moral behaviour than ever before. Numerically the champion represents the merest tip of the iceberg in terms of participation, but his or her impact as the shop window for the sport is enormous. It may be an unwelcome burden for those who merely want to run, jump, or throw better than anyone else.

It is, therefore, not surprising that the widespread and still growing use of anabolic steroid drugs has aroused a great deal of controversial and emotive thought. Not that there is anything new about doping and sport, for it is as old as sport itself, but in the past it has largely been involved with professional sport, especially where betting was involved, and rarely with track and field with its roots seemingly so entrenched in the essence of fair play. It is obvious, too, that there is something insidious about the possible effects of these drugs when taken in large doses and especially when taken by women. As far as the popular press are concerned, it is all about changing women into men and men into freaks.

Anabolic steroids are synthesised male sex hormones that are androgenic by nature, meaning they produce masculine characteristics such as hirsuteness, deepening of the voice, and acne. Their anabolic effect is to enhance muscle growth by aiding protein synthesis, probably through the retention of body fluids – all of which is useful to the thrower in gaining weight so that he can apply more effective force to his implement over the greatest possible range and act as a more formidable counter-weight to the reaction of the release of the implement. Since the mechanical rules that govern efficient throwing techniques for women are identical to those for men, it is not difficult to see why their aspirations and temptations match those of their male colleagues, especially as their efforts in international athletic matches have always been dwarfed in more ways than one by their Eastern European counterparts.

It might be a mute point of argument, but it is important to remember that while everyone is now claiming that those who take steroids are cheats, what motivated most in the first place was an anxiety to compete on level terms with their foreign opposition, rather than to gain any unfair advantage. It is also worth mentioning that their use was never an attempt at any short cut to success, but merely a means to train harder.

In the first place steroids were used as a dietary supplement in much the same way as wheat germ oil, and apart from their use on horses, it was the bodybuilding fraternity who made the greatest use of them to develop muscular bulk without fat. Since the weightmen of athletics often used the same gymnasia for weightlifting, their adoption of them was almost inevitable, and this gradually grew as the knowledge and benefits of their use spread throughout the middle 1960s. It's worth remembering, however, that the Spanish Davis Cup player, Andrés Gimeno, was accused of having had massive doses of testosterone (natural sex hormone) before his game against Billy Knight back in 1961, well before any athlete's name was linked to their use and long before a famous racehorse was reported to be capable of producing more than 100 times the normal amount of testosterone naturally!

Their liberal use in the United States was made all the easier by their availability from many drug stores without prescription, and from the athletes' close association with physicians and pharmacists who were busy trying to adopt a policy of acceptable 'sports pharmaceuticals', often for their own financial gain. One typical American attitude was summed up by an eminent American physician, Allan J. Ryan, who said: 'Looked at from the purely professional viewpoint, every safe way to gaining an advantage over your opponent is ethical provided it conforms to the rules upon which you have jointly agreed. Judged from the observations of many years, even unsafe practices and those which skirt or ignore the rules may also be tolerated provided that it is understood that everyone else is doing it.' Since many see sport as a kind of international cold war, it was not difficult for them to convince themselves that the Eastern Bloc were light years ahead on drugs usage, if only because they have the best developed association of sport and medicine in the world. A sad irony!

Remember, too, that throughout the sixties there was no legislation against anabolic steroids, and it actually took until 1 January 1975 to come into effect. This despite the protestations from many of us since the early 1960s that their use was becoming widespread, that there were possible dangerous side effects, and that the empirical evidence as to their effectiveness was overwhelming.

Our own British Association of Sport and Medicine had condemned the use of hormones in their policy statement on doping, published as early as 1964. But a special medical advisory panel set up by the British Amateur Athletic Board in 1967 declared: 'There is as yet no evidence that a properly controlled experiment has ever been carried out to assess the effects of these drugs on muscle power. Their use as an ergogenic aid must therefore be considered "not proven". This is not a case of reactionary conservatism refusing to recognise progress; it is rather a case of seeking to find scientific truth in a morass of pseudo-scientific and hysterical mumbo-jumbo.'

At about the same time, in West Germany, a study group headed by Dr Reindell came to another conclusion: 'Hormones, to a limited extent those of the suprarenal glandular variety and, to a far greater extent, male sexual hormones, rate as some of the most widely used drugs. The effect of the former kind, though a subject of controversy, is minimal; that of sexual hormones, however, (in particular in the case of testosterone) can under certain circumstances produce considerable damage.'

In that period of more than a decade between the knowledge of their use and the lack of serious research, it was inevitable that their use would grow without reliable testing techniques, and this time lapse was tantamount to condoning their use rather than absolute condemnation.

In practical terms, more was being discovered by the athletes who used them than the doctors who devised their effectiveness. They discovered a feeling of well being, a capacity to recover quickly from severe bouts of training, and that their effect varied with the body types of users in much the same way as any slimming diet. Tall, skinny high jumpers and hurdlers could use them with impunity without making any real weight gains, but with much the same training benefits. Soon they were being used by athletes in almost every event and by many other sportsmen and women. In a survey conducted by L. Jay Silvester at the Munich Olympic Games of athletes in all events up to 5000 metres, 68 per cent of athletes questioned admitted to taking anabolic steroids at some time. Massive overdoses came about on the simple assumption that more would produce better and quicker results.

If one could possibly disregard the now accepted serious side effects, the moral implications of taking steroids were regarded in much the same way as the present cult of middle-distance runners using Pollen 'B' or Pollitabs, or even the growing use of vitamin injections to improve training conditions. I doubt whether it can be argued that these current practices make our sport fair for all, and I know of no monitoring of any long-term side effects of these so-called natural substances. Anabolic steroids are synthetically produced and therefore legislated against, but the curious anomaly is that they are a substitute for natural testosterone, which is not banned, though the Germans claim it is dangerous and athletes know it is just as effective.

We are now in the strange world of ethics and morality, which so often are a matter of personal choice for the individual, but must inevitably be based on the standards existing in his own sporting environment. At national level, these attitudes can vary from the politically motivated ideology, where the cost of winning is unimportant, to the 'holier than thou' stand, which claims that *we* have a special place in world standards of morality so it is important that we make the first sacrifices of our athletes.

Athletes, coaches, doctors, and legislators must examine their own consciences and declare where they stand and why. Having been in the vanguard of those diametrically opposed to the use of anabolic steroids for improved athletic performance, I feel it is time to reiterate my own viewpoint and attempt to rationalise, if only in part, my reasons and state those personal conclusions drawn from my own close association with a very large number of international athletes. In brief these are:

1. Large intakes of anabolic steroids (i.e. up to 100mg per day have been reported) coupled with high protein diets and a heavy programme of strength training produce both an increase in weight and measurable strength levels. These are far more marked in meso-endomorphic builds than the linear or ectomorphic. Similar weight and strength gains can be made without anabolic steroids but again primarily in heavily built athletes and over a longer period of time. To use straightforward weight gain as an indication of whether an athlete has taken steroids is totally illogical and cannot be used as a monitoring method. (NB: Mike Lindsay, one of our greatest competitive shot-putters, who was so opposed to their use that he retired from the sport in protest, had a bodyweight that fluctuated by 35lb below his competitive bodyweight.)

2. The same massive intakes over a long period can and have caused serious side effects, including liver damage and possible cancer, but they are rarely reported because of the guilt of involvement. This feed-back of information is critically needed and must be known to some coaches and physicians.

3. The more serious side effects are likely in women and young athletes, and if the recently introduced testing procedures are an attempt to safeguard the health of the athlete, it is in these areas that testing should be concentrated; i.e. junior international sides of both sexes as well as spot checks on senior internationals.

4. The well known 'placebo' effect has been responsible for much of the psychological addiction to such drugs; i.e. since many athletes believe they work, they do. Once these psychological barriers are overcome, performances will rise to overtake those levels reached with the aid of steroids.

5. 'Scare' tactics regarding their use and on the testing procedures will be totally ineffective in the same way as they failed with the 'social' drugs. What is needed is far greater dissemination of information, particularly from the medical profession to the athletes themselves as well as to coaches and administrators.

6. Physicians and pharmacists handle these substances with astonishing liberality and must share the responsibility for their widespread use. I know of no coach who can buy them without a medical prescription.

7. No costs should be spared to develop effective tests which include natural testosterone and which are retroactive. Once developed they must be universally

adopted and be accepted by visiting international teams, as well as home based athletes, in *all* events, for men and women.

The net cost of a perfect testing system carried out democratically may mean a real slowing down or partial halt for the record books, which is of little significance. Even this might be overcome or accelerated if a number of well known, highly talented and dedicated athletes, backed by coaches, were voluntarily monitored at monthly intervals and could match or better the performance of others whose trust has to be by word of mouth. A Utopian notion maybe, but then I believe that if our sport is to flourish at grass roots level, coaches should have one foot in the education camp and the other in public relations, rather than one in biomechanics and the other in exercise physiology. The former is an ethical base, the latter mere tools of the trade.

I do not believe that anabolic steroids have affected performance standards more than any other factor – technological improvement (or pollution) in events like pole vault, and wind in the case of javelin and discus, are of far greater significance and might be just as worthy of legislation. Nor do I believe that steroids are our most serious health hazard – the incidence of Achilles tendon trouble and other stress injuries due to a lack of qualitative or quantative work as a rational basis for training are far more prevalent.

What saddens me in an age when we should be worried about the world-wide democratization of our sport could be summed up by the recent cynical quotation in *Track and Field News*:

'As the weight trained, steroid stuffed, drug stimulated pole vaulter said as he sped down the synthetic runway, planted his glass fibre pole in the fibre-glass vault box, inched over the magnesium crossbar and fell onto his back into the £1000 foam rubber landing bed . . . "What a great natural athlete I am!"'

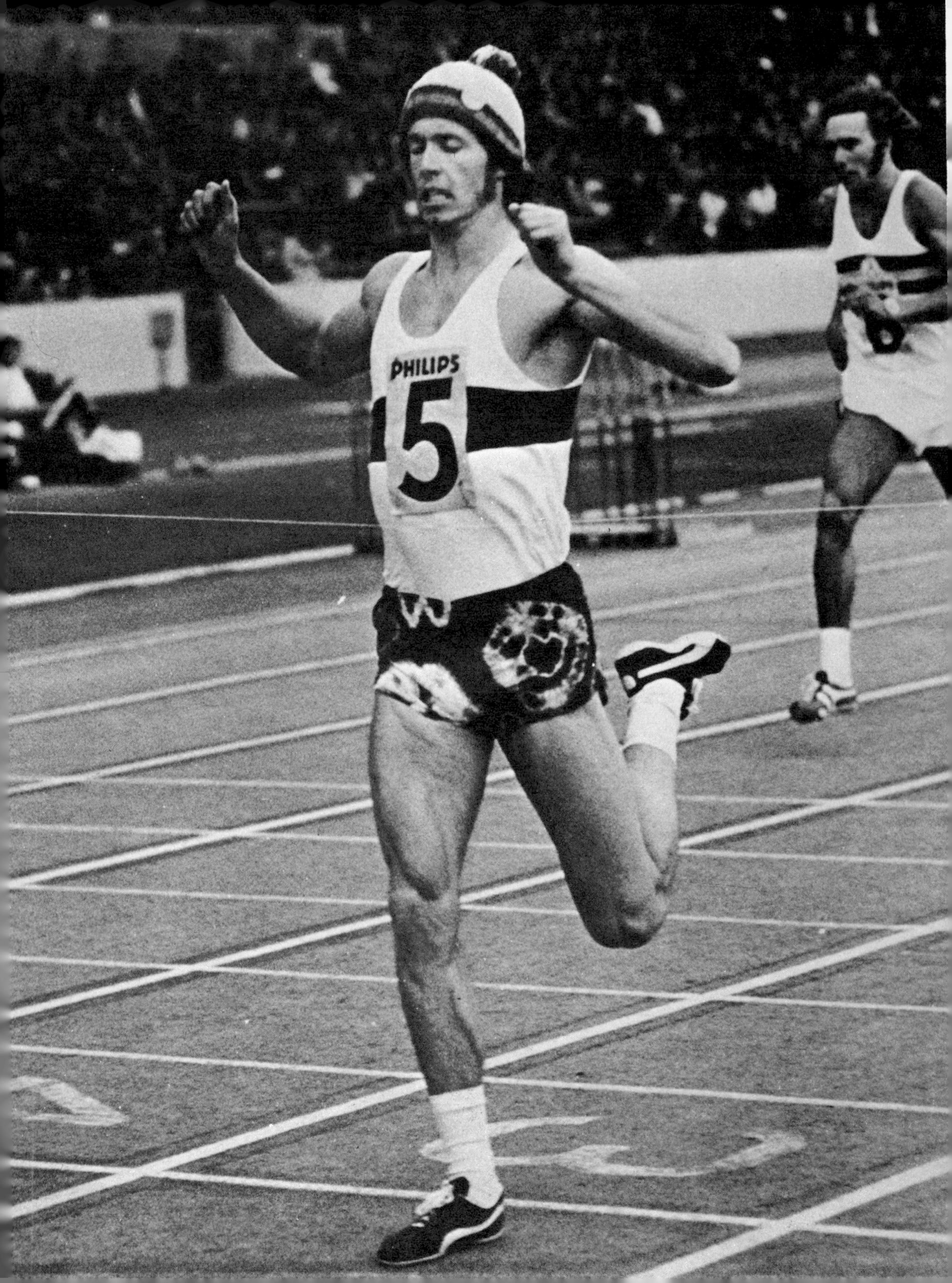
PHILIPS
5

Who's Who in the British Team

Brief biographical and career details of the 160 men and women who represented the UK senior team, indoors or out, during 1974. The information provided includes athletes' personal best performances in a variety of events, positions in major international championships (when placed in the first eight in Olympic, European, or Commonwealth Games; first three in relays) and year-by-year progression in their most significant events. Abbreviations: i = indoor performance; w = wind assisted performance.

BRIAN ADAMS
Leicester WC. *Born* Leicester, 13.3.1949; *Height*: 1.83m (6' 0"), *Weight*: 70kg (154lb); Teacher. *Best performances*: 3000m walk – 12:28.0, 20km walk – 1:33:26, 50km walk – 4:31:51. *Annual progression at 50km walk*: 1973 – 4:32:39; 1974 – 4:31:51.

STEWART ATKINS
Wolverhampton & Bilston AC. *Born* Lennoxtown (Scotland), 15.11.1951; *Height*: 1.83m (6' 0"), *Weight*: 76kg (168lb); Student. *Best performances*: 100m – 10.7w, High Jump – 1.90m (6' 2¾"), Long jump – 7.61m (24' 11¾")w & 7.85m (24' 10¼"). *Annual progression at long jump*: 1967 – 5.76m (18' 11"); 1968 – 6.39m (20' 11¼"); 1969 – 6.88m (22' 7"); 1970 – 7.30m (23' 11½")w; 1971 – 7.60m (24' 11¼")w; 1972 – 7.61m (24' 11¾")w; 1973 – 7.58m (24' 10½"); 1974 – 7.47m (24' 6¼").

JIM AUKETT
Wolverhampton & Bilston AC. *Born* Eastbourne, 15.4.1949; *Height*: 1.78m (5' 10"), *Weight*: 66kg (146lb); Dental surgeon. *Best performances*: 100m – 10.7w, 200m – 21.5w, 400m – 46.6, 800m – 1:52.4. *Annual progression at 400m*: 1966 – 52.4; 1967 – 51.1; 1968 – 51.0; 1969 – 48.2; 1970 – 47.2; 1971 – 47.5; 1972 – 48.6; 1973 – 46.7; 1974 – 46.6.

PHIL BANNING
Andover AC. *Born* Andover, 10.10.1950; Student. *Best performances*: 800m – 1:50.9, 1500m – 3:39.9, Mile – 4:00.4, 5000m – 14:06.4. *Annual progression at 1500m* (★ mile time less 18sec): 1967 – 4:00.1★; 1968 – 3:55.4; 1969 – 3:45.2; 1970 – 3:42.4★; 1971 – 3:41.2; 1972 – 3:43.3; 1973 – 3:39.9; 1974 – 3:41.4.

LIZ BARNES
Cambridge H. *Born* Woolwich, 3.8.1951; *Height*: 1.64m (5' 4½"), *Weight*: 54kg (120lb); Clerk. *Best performances*: 100m – 12.0w, 200m – 24.0w, 400m – 53.9, 800m – 2:10.0. *Annual progression at 400m*: 1967 – 60.4; 1968 – —; 1969 – 56.9; 1970 – —; 1971 – —; 1972 – —; 1973 – —; 1974 – 53.9.

LINDA BARRATT
Dorothy Hyman TC. *Born* Hemsworth (Yorks), 18.1.1952; *Height*: 1.65m (5' 5"), *Weight*: 54kg (119lb); Teacher. *Best performances*: 100m – 11.5, 200m – 23.9w. *Annual progression at 100m* (★ 100 yards time plus 1.0sec): 1965 – 12.7★; 1966 – 12.4★; 1967 – 12.2★; 1968 – 12.2★; 1969 – —; 1970 – 11.9; 1971 – 11.9w; 1972 – 11.6w; 1973 – 11.9; 1974 – 11.5.

MIKE BAXTER
Leeds City AC. *Born* Leeds, 28.5.1945; *Height*: 1.79m (5' 10½"), *Weight*: 66kg (147lb); Sales representative. *Best performances*: 1500m – 3:46.2, 5000m – 13:35.2, 10,000m – 28:16.0, 3000m steeplechase – 9:03.4. *Annual progression at 5000m* (★ 3 miles time plus 28sec) & *10,000m* (★ 6 miles time plus 60sec): 1962 – 15:40.0★, —; 1963 – 15:17.0★, —; 1964 – 15:04.0★, —; 1965 – 14:41.0★, —; 1966 – 14:23.6★, —; 1967 – 14:09.4★, 30:39.0★; 1968 – 13:57.0★, —; 1969 – 13:46.6, —; 1970 – 13:35.2, 30:10.4; 1971 – 13:39.6, 29:26.8; 1972 – 13:49.2, —; 1973 – 13:53.8, —; 1974 – 13:40.4, 28:16.0.

Left: *Jim Aukett was a colourful 400 metres winner for the AAA against Borough Road Colleges in May.*

BRENDA BEDFORD (née Sawyer)
Mitcham AC. *Born* London, 4.9.1937; *Height:* 1.78m (5' 10"), *Weight:* 86kg (189lb); Secretary. *Best performances:* Shot – 16.15m (53' 0"), Discus – 50.58m (165' 11"). *Championships:* 1966 Commonwealth – 6th shot & discus; 1970 Commonwealth – 5th shot, 6th discus; 1974 Commonwealth – 6th shot. *Annual progression at shot:* 1957 – 10.81m (35' 5½"); 1958 – 10.71m (35' 1½"); 1959 – 11.89m (39' 0"); 1960 – 11.73m (38' 5¾"); 1961 – 11.94m (39' 2"); 1962 – 12.88m (42' 3¼"); 1963 – 13.47m (44' 2¼"); 1964 – 13.42m (44' 0¼"); 1965 – 13.87m (45' 6¼"); 1966 – 14.67m (48' 1¾"); 1967 – 15.58m (51' 1½"); 1968 – 15.65m (51' 4¼"); 1969 – 15.30m (50' 2¼"); 1970 – 15.29m (50' 2"); 1971 – 14.93m (48' 11¾"); 1972 – 15.21m (49' 11"); 1973 – 16.15m (53' 0"); 1974 – 15.40m (50' 6¼").

AINSLEY BENNETT
Birchfield H. *Born* Jamaica, 22.7.1954; *Height:* 1.66m (5' 5½"); Purchasing clerk. *Best performances:* 100m – 10.5w, 200m – 20.6w & 20.8, 400m – 47.0. *Championships:* 1974 European – 7th 200m. *Annual progression at 200m:* 1973 – 21.6; 1974 – 20.6w.

VERONA BERNARD (now Mrs Elder)
Wolverhampton & Bilston AC. *Born* Wolverhampton, 5.4.1953; *Height:* 1.70m (5' 7"), *Weight:* 62kg (138lb); Laboratory assistant. *Best performances:* 100m – 11.7, 200m – 23.5, 400m – 51.9. *Championships:* 1973 European Indoor – 1st 400m; 1974 Commonwealth – 2nd 400m, 1st 4 × 400m; 1974 European – 7th 400m. *Annual progression at 400m:* 1969 – 57.7; 1970 – 57.1i; 1971 – 54.3; 1972 – 52.9; 1973 – 52.1; 1974 – 51.9.

JOHN BICOURT
Belgrave H. *Born* London, 25.10.1945; *Height:* 1.76m (5' 9½"), *Weight:* 68kg (150lb); Teacher. *Best performances:* 3000m – 8:01.8, 5000m – 13:57.6, 3000m steeplechase – 8:26.6. *Championships:* 1974 Commonwealth – 4th 3000mSC. *Annual progression:* 1965 – 9:28.4; 1966 – 9:09.6; 1967 – 8:57.6; 1968 – 8:51.2; 1969 – 8:50.2; 1970 – 8:46.8; 1971 – 8:46.0; 1972 – 8:34.8; 1973 – 8:26.6; 1974 – 8:29.6.

CHRIS BLACK
Edinburgh Southern H. *Born* Edinburgh, 1.1.1950; *Height:* 1.88m (6' 2"), *Weight:* 101kg (224lb); Draughtsman. *Best performances:* Discus – 48.70m (159' 9"), Hammer – 69.48m (227' 11"). *Championships:* 1974 Commonwealth – 6th hammer. *Annual progression:* 1967 – 41.04m (134' 8");

1968 – 50.22m (164' 9"); 1969 – 54.68m (179' 5"); 1970 – 57.36m (188' 2"); 1971 – 60.00m (196' 10"); 1972 – 66.42m (217' 11"); 1973 – 64.80m (212' 7"); 1974 – 69.48m (227' 11").

DAVE BLACK
Small Heath H. *Born* Tamworth (Staffs), 2.10.1952; *Height:* 1.80m (5' 11"), *Weight:* 65kg (144lb); Security officer. *Best performances:* Mile – 4:00.2, 3000m – 7:46.6, 5000m – 13:23.6, 10,000m – 27:48.6. *Championships:* 1974 Commonwealth – 3rd 5000m, 2nd 10,000m. *Annual progression at 5000m & 10,000m:* 1970 – 14:26.8, —; 1971 – 13:37.4, —; 1972 – 13:28.0, —; 1973 – 13:24.6, 27:55.6; 1974 – 13:23.6, 27:48.6.

STEVE BLACK
Essex Beagles. *Born* Woodford (Essex), 10.8.1949; *Height:* 1.80m (5' 11"), *Weight:* 73kg (161lb); Student. *Best performances:* 400m – 48.2, 400m hurdles – 50.7. *Annual progression at 400m hurdles:* 1968 – 53.0; 1969 – 53.1; 1970 – 52.4; 1971 – 51.1; 1972 – 51.2; 1973 – 50.9; 1974 – 50.7.

Right: *Dave Black wins the Inter-Regional mile.*
Far right: *Verona Bernard.* **Below:** *Chris Black.*
Below right: *Colin Boreham sets a new UK high jump record.*

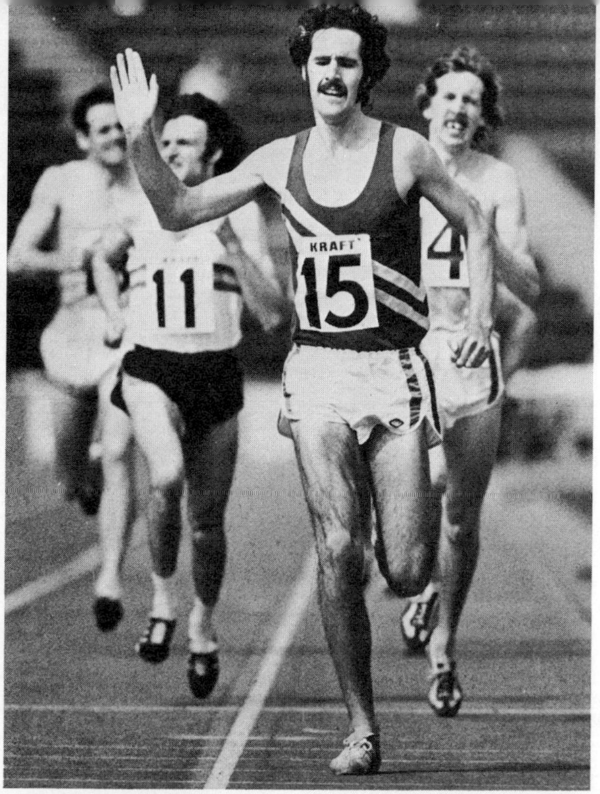
KRAFT
15
11
4

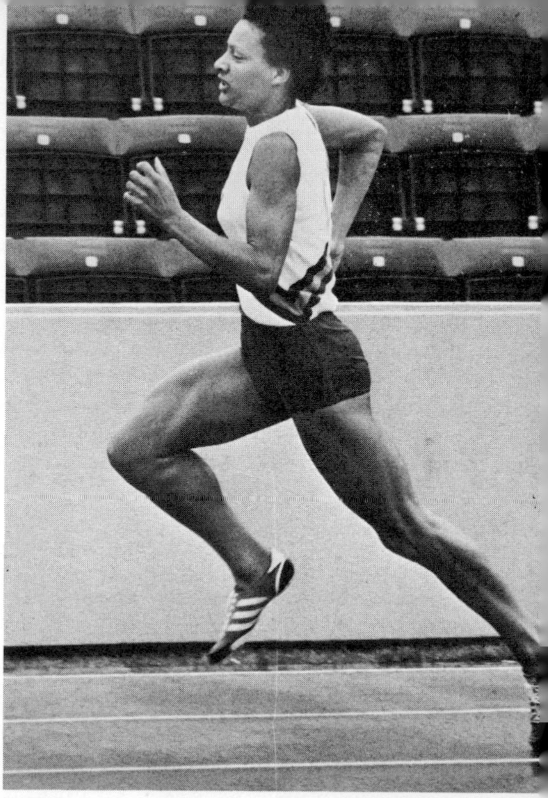

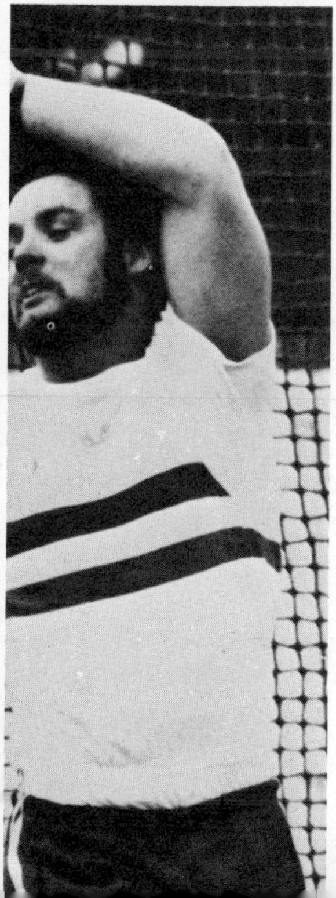

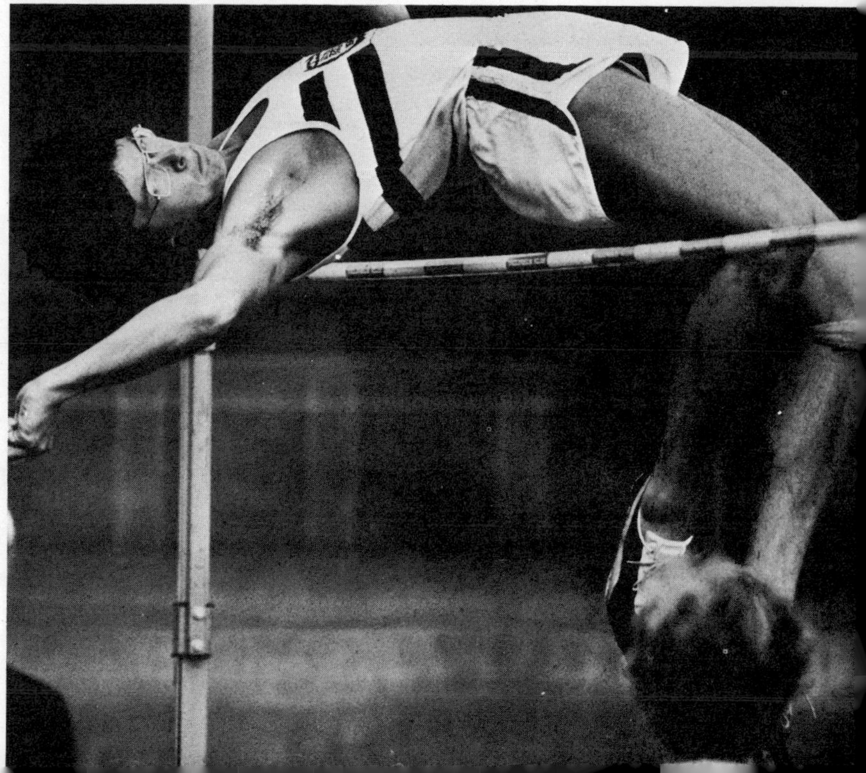

PETER BLACKBURN
Leicester Coritanian AC. *Born* 5.3.1950. *Best performances*: 100m – 10.7, Long jump – 7.44m (24' 5"), Triple jump – 15.77m (51' 9"), Javelin – 60.00m (196' 10"). *Annual progression at triple jump*: 1970 – 14.26m (46' 9¼")w; 1971 – 15.02m (49' 3½")w; 1972 – 15.62m (51' 3"); 1973 – 15.77m (51' 9"); 1974 – 15.73m (51' 7¼")i.

ALISON BLAKE
Aldershot F & D AC. *Born* 9.6.1948. *Best performance*: 3000m – 9:33.8. *Annual progression*: 1972 – 10:48.8; 1973 – 9:49.4; 1974 – 9:33.8.

COLIN BOREHAM
Bournemouth AC. *Born* Luton, 26.3.1954; *Height*: 1.88m (6' 2"), *Weight*: 76kg (168lb); Student. *Best performance*: High jump – 2.11m (6' 11") (UK record). *Annual progression*: 1969 – 1.52m (5' 0"); 1970 – 1.78m (5' 10"); 1971 – 2.00m (6' 6¾"); 1972 – 2.01m (6' 7"); 1973 – 2.03m (6' 8"); 1974 – 2.11m (6' 11").

FRANK BRISCOE
Hercules Wimbledon AC. *Born* Leigh (Lancs), 6.8.1947; *Height*: 1.80m (5' 11"), *Weight*: 65kg (144lb); Mathematician. *Best performances*: 880y – 1:52.5, Mile – 4:01.5, 5000m – 13:48.2, 10,000m – 28:41.2. *Annual progression at 5000m* (★ 3 miles time plus 28sec) & *10,000m*: 1966 – 14:45.4★, —; 1967 – 14:21.4★, —; 1968 – —; —; 1969 – 13:57.6, 29:23.8; 1970 – 14:08.2, 30:28.6; 1971 – 14:03.2, —; 1972 – —, —; 1973 – 14:09.6, —; 1974 – 13:48.2, 28:41.2.

JIM BROWN
Monkland H. *Born* Lanark (Scotland), 13.9.1952; *Height*: 1.70m (5' 7"), *Weight*: 58kg (128lb); Student. *Best performances*: 5000m – 13:51.2, 10,000m – 28:20.8. *Annual progression at 5000m & 10,000m*: 1971 – 14:03.4, —; 1972 – 13:59.8, 28:57.8; 1973 – 14:27.0, —; 1974 – 13:51.2, 28:20.8.

JOHN BROWN
Hillingdon AC. *Born* Rickmansworth (Herts), 8.12.1945; *Height*: 1.75m (5' 9"), *Weight*: 59kg (131lb); Gardener. *Best performances*: 1500m – 3:48.4, 5000m – 13:54.2, 10,000m – 28:43.0. *Annual progression at 10,000m* (★ 6 miles time plus 60sec): 1968 – 29:59.0★; 1969 – 29:57.0; 1970 – 29:51.6; 1971 – —; 1972 – —; 1973 – 29:18.2; 1974 – 28:43.0.

PETE BROWNE
Queens Park H. *Born* London, 3.2.1949; *Height*: 1.76m (5' 9½"), *Weight*: 66kg (145lb); Trainee accountant. *Best performances*: 400m – 48.0, 800m – 1:46.2, 1500m – 3:46.6, 400m hurdles – 55.1. *Championships*: 1971 European – 5th 800m. *Annual progression*: 1965 – 2:10.5; 1966 – 2:06.3; 1967 – 1:55.5; 1968 – 1:51.7; 1969 – 1:48.1; 1970 – 1:48.1; 1971 – 1:47.0; 1972 – 1:47.7; 1973 – 1:46.2; 1974 – 1:47.8.

MIKE BULL
Wolverhampton & Bilston AC. *Born* Belfast, 11.9.1946; *Height*: 1.84m (6' 0½"), *Weight*: 79kg (175lb); Lecturer. *Best performances*: 100m – 10.7, 400m – 49.2, 110m hurdles – 15.3, High jump – 1.88m (6' 2"), Pole vault – 5.25m (17' 2¾") (UK record), Long jump – 7.31m (23' 11¾"), Shot – 14.17m (46' 6"), Decathlon – 7417. *Championships*: 1966 Commonwealth – 2nd PV; 1969 European – 7th PV; 1970 Commonwealth – 1st PV; 1974 Commonwealth – 2nd PV, 1st decathlon. *Annual progression at pole vault*: 1963 – 3.60m (11' 9¾"); 1964 – 4.06m (13' 4"); 1965 – 4.34m (14' 3"); 1966 – 4.72m (15' 6"); 1967 – 4.80m (15' 9"); 1968 – 5.06m (16' 7½"); 1969 – 5.05m (16' 6¾"); 1970 – 5.10m (16' 8¼"); 1971 – 5.05m (16' 6¾"); 1972 – 5.21m (17' 1"); 1973 – 5.25m (17' 2¾"); 1974 – 5.20m (17' 0¾").

WHO'S WHO IN THE BRITISH TEAM

Above: *Mike Butterfield.*
Left: *Pete Browne (2) and Andy Carter (4).*
Right: *Frank Clement.*

MIKE BUTTERFIELD
Cardiff AAC. *Born* Staincliff (Yorks), 4.5.1953; *Height:* 1.94m (6' 4½"), *Weight:* 73kg (162lb); RAF electronic technician. *Best performances:* 110m hurdles – 15.1w, High jump – 2.06m (6' 9"). *Annual progression at high jump:* 1972 – 1.83m (6' 0"); 1973 – 2.06m (6' 9"); 1974 – 2.05m (6' 8¾").

DAVE CAMP
Morpeth H. *Born* Ilkeston (Derbyshire), 13.10.1946; *Height:* 1.75m (5' 9"), *Weight:* 60kg (131lb); Engineering manager. *Best performances:* 3000m – 8:09.0, 5000m – 14:12.0, 3000m steeplechase – 8:32.2. *Annual progression:* 1966 – 9:22.6; 1967 – 9:14.6; 1968 – 8:59.6; 1969 – 9:09.6; 1970 – 8:46.6; 1971 – 8:40.6; 1972 – 8:46.2; 1973 – 8:43.2; 1974 – 8:32.2.

GEOFF CAPES
Borough of Enfield H. *Born* Holbeach (Lincs), 23.8.1949; *Height:* 1.97m (6' 5½"), *Weight:* 136kg (300lb); Policeman. *Best performances:* Shot – 21.37m (70' 1½") (UK record), Discus – 58.34m (191' 5"), Javelin – 60.56m (198' 8"). *Championships:* 1970 Commonwealth – 4th shot; 1974 Commonwealth – 1st shot, 5th discus; 1974 European Indoor – 1st shot; 1974 European – 3rd shot. *Annual progression at shot:* 1966 – 14.91m (48' 11¼")i; 1967 – 16.09m (52' 9¾"); 1968 – 17.26m (56' 7¾")i; 1969 – 17.47m (57' 4"); 1970 – 17.73m (58' 2"); 1971 – 19.48m (63' 11"); 1972 – 20.18m (66' 2½"); 1973 – 20.47m (67' 2"); 1974 – 21.37m (70' 1½").

ANDY CARTER
Stretford AC. *Born* Exeter, 29.1.1949; *Height:* 1.83m (6' 0"), *Weight:* 72kg (159lb); Accountant. *Best performances:* 400m – 48.0, 800m – 1:45.1 (UK record), 1500m – 3:42.3, Mile – 3:59.3. *Championships:* 1971 European – 3rd 800m; 1972 Olympics – 6th 800m; 1973 European Cup final – 1st 800m; 1974 Commonwealth – 5th 800, 2nd 4 × 400m. *Annual progression at 800m:* 1967 – 1:56.1; 1968 – 1:50.3; 1969 – 1:46.8; 1970 – 1:47.2; 1971 – 1:46.2; 1972 – 1:46.5; 1973 – 1:45.1; 1974 – 1:45.6.

PRU CARTER (née French)
Havering AC. *Born* Hornchurch (Essex), 4.5.1950; *Height:* 1.61m (5' 3½"), *Weight:* 60kg (133lb); Teacher. *Best performance:* Javelin – 51.50m (168' 11"). *Championships:* 1974 Commonwealth – 4th. *Annual progression:* 1966 – 36.36m (119' 4"); 1967 – 42.18m (138' 5"); 1968 – 48.32m (158' 6"); 1969 – 47.72m (156' 7"); 1970 – 40.70m (133' 6"); 1971 – 47.60m (156' 2"); 1972 – 51.50m (168' 11"); 1973 – 51.12m (167' 8"); 1974 – 50.00m (164' 0").

PAT CHAPMAN (née Mawer) (now Mrs McNab)
Middlesex LAC. *Born* 25.2.1943. *Best performances:* 100m hurdles – 14.0, High jump – 1.65m (5' 5"), Long jump – 5.94m (19' 6"), Pentathlon – 4022. *Annual progression at pentathlon* (★old scoring tables): 1965 – 3883★; 1966 – 4123★; 1967 – —; 1968 – 4156★; 1969 – —; 1970 – 4162★; 1971 – 4230★ (3666); 1972 – 3567; 1973 – 3595; 1974 – 4022.

207

ATHLETICS 75

IAN CHIPCHASE
North Shields Poly Club. *Born* Hebburn (Co Durham), 26.2.1952; *Height:* 1.76m (5' 9½"), *Weight:* 101kg (224lb); Student. *Best performance:* Hammer – 71.00m (232' 11"). *Championships:* 1970 European Junior – 8th; 1974 Commonwealth – 1st. *Annual progression:* 1969 – 55.46m (181' 11"); 1970 – 59.14m (194' 0"); 1971 – 64.14m (210' 5"); 1972 – 62.80m (206' 0"); 1973 – 70.28m (230' 7"); 1974 – 71.00m (232' 11").

WILLIE CLARK
Edinburgh Southern H. *Born* Dundee, 3.5.1950; *Height:* 1.85m (6' 1"), *Weight:* 76kg (168lb); Merchant banker. *Best performances:* Long jump – 7.30m (23' 11½")w, Triple jump – 15.78m (51' 9¼"). *Annual progression at triple jump:* 1969 – 14.02m (46' 0")w; 1970 – 14.20m (46' 7")w; 1971 – 14.46m (47' 5¼"); 1972 – 14.92m (48' 11½"); 1973 – 15.68m (51' 5½"); 1974 – 15.78m (51' 9¼").

FRANK CLEMENT
Bellahouston H. *Born* Glasgow, 26.4.1952; *Height:* 1.80m (5' 11"), *Weight:* 66kg (145lb); Student. *Best performances:* 800m – 1:46.0, 1500m – 3:37.4 (UK record), Mile – 3:57.4, 5000m – 14:07.8, 3000m steeplechase – 9:27.0. *Championships:* 1973 World Student Games – 1st 1500m; 1973 European Cup final – 1st 1500m. *Annual progression at 800m and 1500m:* 1969 – —, 4:02.0; 1970 – 1:55.5, 3:51.7; 1971 – 1:52.7, 3:48.0, 1972 – 1:51.6, 3:44.4; 1973 – 1:46.0, 3:38.5; 1974 – 1:48.4, 3:37.4.

CHARLES CLOVER
Ipswich H. *Born* Ipswich, 13.5.1955; *Height:* 1.90m (6' 3"), *Weight:* 95kg (210lb); Packer. *Best performance:* Javelin – 84.92m (278' 7") (UK record & world junior best). *Championships:* 1973 European Junior – 4th; 1974 Commonwealth – 1st. *Annual progression:* 1971 – 60.36m (198' 0")★; 1972 – 77.58m (254' 6"); 1973 – 77.68m (254' 10"); 1974 – 84.92m (278' 7").
★700gm

GLEN COHEN
Wolverhampton & Bilston AC. *Born* 22.4.1954; *Best performances:* 200m – 21.7, 400m – 46.8. *Championships:* 1973 European Junior – 4th 400m, 3rd 4 × 400m; 1974 European – 1st 4 × 400. *Annual progression at 400m:* 1972 – 48.8; 1973 – 47.0; 1974 – 46.8.

A British International Games victory for Glen Cohen.

208

WHO'S WHO IN THE BRITISH TEAM

DEREK COLE
Thames Valley H. *Born* London, 10.6.1951; *Height:* 1.79m (5' 10½"); *Weight:* 80kg (176lb); Technician. *Best performances:* 100m – 10.4, 200m – 21.5, Long jump – 7.70m (25' 3¼")w & 7.46m (24' 5¾"), Triple jump – 14.19m (46' 6¾"). *Annual progression at long jump:* 1968 – 6.94m (22' 9¼"); 1969 – 6.81m (22' 4¼"); 1970 – 7.06m (23' 2")w; 1971 – 7.45m (24' 5¼"); 1972 – 7.70m (25' 3¼")w; 1973 – 7.46m (24' 5¾"); 1974 – 7.58m (24' 10½")w.

SHARON COLYEAR
Stretford AC. *Born* Manchester, 22.4.1955; *Height:* 1.69m (5' 6½"), *Weight:* 59kg (130lb); Bank clerk. *Best performances:* 100m – 11.5w, 200m – 23.3, 400m – 55.4, 100m hurdles – 14.2, 200m hurdles – 26.7 (UK record). *Annual progression at 200m:* 1969 – 25.2; 1970 – 24.7; 1971 – 23.8; 1972 – —; 1973 – 24.5; 1974 – 23.3.

MARGARET COOMBER (née MacSherry)
Cambridge H. *Born* Dartford, 13.5.1950; *Height:* 1.71m (5' 7½"), *Weight:* 57kg (127lb); Copy typist. *Best performances:* 400m – 55.3, 800m – 2:02.0, 1500m – 4:22.4. *Championships:* 1970 Commonwealth – 7th 1500m. *Annual progression at 800m and 1500m* (★ mile time less 20 sec): 1965 – 2:18.0, —; 1966 – 2:15.9, —; 1967 – 2:15.5, 4:45.9★; 1968 – 2:13.4, 4:36.6; 1969 – 2:08.0, 4:28.5; 1970 – 2:09.4, 4:22.4; 1971 – 2:06.1, 4:37.8; 1972 – 2:03.0, 4:31.5; 1973 – 2:02.0, 4:26.4; 1974 – 2:05.9, 4:24.5.

SHARON CORBETT
Solihull AC. *Born* Birmingham, 24.6.1953; *Height:* 1.78m (5' 10"), *Weight:* 70kg (154lb); Civil Servant. *Best performance:* Javelin – 53.88m (176' 9"). *Championships:* 1974 Commonwealth – 3rd. *Annual progression:* 1967 – 27.54m (90' 4"); 1968 – 34.26m (112' 5"); 1969 – 41.22m (135' 3"); 1970 – 40.32m (132' 3"); 1971 – 46.34m (152' 0"); 1972 – 48.00m (157' 6"); 1973 – 53.88m (176' 9"); 1974 – 51.98m (170' 6").

MIKE CORDEN
Longwood H. *Born* 15.4.1948. *Best performances:* 110m hurdles – 15.5, 400m hurdles – 55.4, High jump – 1.89m (6' 2¼"), Pole vault – 4.10m (13' 5½"), Shot – 13.27m (43' 6½"), Discus – 42.30m (138' 9"), Javelin – 63.16m (207' 3"), Decathlon – 7035. *Annual progression at decathlon:* 1968 – 5603; 1969 – —; 1970 – 6230; 1971 – 6195; 1972 – 6675; 1973 – 6997; 1974 – 7035.

Donna Murray, Sharon Colyear, and Helen Golden.

JOHN DAVIES
Thames Valley H. *Born* Rhondda (Wales), 20.11.1952; *Height:* 1.70m (5' 7"), *Weight:* 54kg (119lb); Operations planning clerk. *Best performances:* Mile – 4:05.0, 3000m – 7:54.0, 5000m – 13:49.6, 10,000m – 29:09.4, 3000m steeplechase – 8:22.6 (UK record). *Championships:* 1974 Commonwealth – 2nd 3000mSC. *Annual progression:* 1969 – 9:21.6; 1970 – 9:07.0; 1971 – 8:56.0; 1972 – 9:05.8; 1973 – 8:28.0; 1974 – 8:22.6.

BOB DOBSON
Basildon AC. *Born* London, 4.11.1942; *Height:* 1.78m (5' 10"), *Weight:* 70kg (154lb); Government service. *Best performances:* 3000m walk – 12:40.4, 20km walk – 1:30:02, 50km walk – 4:11:22 (UK best). *Championships:* 1970 Commonwealth – 4th 20M walk. *Annual progression at 50km walk:* 1969 – 4:37:03; 1970 – 4:20:22; 1971 – 4:17:44; 1972 – 4:25:36; 1973 – 4:14:29; 1974 – 4:11:22.

GLORIA DOURASS
Birchfield H. *Born* Birmingham, 13.11.1944; *Height:* 1.74m (5′ 8½″), *Weight:* 56kg (123lb); Secretary. *Best performances:* 100y – 11.0, 220y – 24.6, 400m – 54.6, 800m – 2:06.0, 1500m – 4:33.3 (indoor). *Championships:* 1966 Commonwealth – 8th 440y; 1970 Commonwealth – 4th 800m. *Annual progression at 800m:* 1966 – 2:17.2i; 1967 – 2:17.7; 1968 – —; 1969 – 2:12.6; 1970 – 2:06.4; 1971 – 2:06.0; 1972 – 2:07.3; 1973 – 2:06.5; 1974 – 2:06.2.

ALAN DRAYTON
Southampton & Eastleigh AC. *Born* Eastleigh, 29.9.1951; *Height:* 1.90m (6′ 3″), *Weight:* 84kg (186lb); Local government officer. *Best performances:* 110m hurdles – 14.9, High jump – 1.88m (6′ 2″), Pole vault – 4.25m (13′ 11½″), Long jump – 7.16m (23′ 6″), Triple jump – 14.69m (48′ 2½″), Decathlon – 7127. *Annual progression at decathlon:* 1971 – 5941; 1972 – 6139; 1973 – 6489; 1974 – 7127.

LORNA DRYSDALE
Solihull AC. *Born* Jamaica, 12.11.1954; *Height:* 1.65m (5′ 5″), *Weight:* 56kg (124lb); Shorthand typist. *Best performances:* 200m – 24.1w, 100m hurdles – 13.5. *Annual progression at 100m hurdles:* 1971 – 14.6w; 1972 – 14.2; 1973 – 14.0; 1974 – 13.5.

GARETH EDWARDS
Newport H. *Born* South Wales, 24.3.1955; *Height:* 1.80m (5′ 11″), *Weight:* 85kg (187lb); Milkman. *Best performances:* 100m – 10.4w & 10.6. *Championships:* 1973 European Junior – 8th. *Annual progression:* 1971 – 11.0w; 1972 – 10.8; 1973 – 10.6; 1974 – 10.4w.

VERONA ELDER (see Verona Bernard)

MARION FAWKES (née Adamson)
North Shields Poly AC. *Born* North Shields, 3.12.1948; *Height:* 1.51m (4′ 11½″), *Weight:* 43kg (95lb); Civil servant. *Best performances:* 3000m walk – 14:33.6 (UK best), 5000m walk – 24:59.2 (UK best). *Annual progression:* 1970 – 14:30.4 (2500m); 1971 – 13:46.2 (2500m); 1972 – 13:21.4 (2500m); 1973 – 15:04.6 (3000m), 26:05.0 (5000m); 1974 – 14:33.6 (3000m), 24:59.2 (5000m).

OLLY FLYNN
Basildon AC. *Born* Ipswich, 30.6.1950; *Height:* 1.90m (6′ 3″), *Weight:* 77kg (170lb); Clerk. *Best performances:* 3000m walk – 12:37.4, 20km walk – 1:29:26. *Annual progression at 20km walk:* 1971 – 1:36:35; 1972 – 1:33:32; 1973 – 1:33:34; 1974 – 1:29:26.

WHO'S WHO IN THE BRITISH TEAM

BERNIE FORD
Aldershot Farnham & District AC. *Born* Woking, 3.8.1952; *Height:* 1.78m (5' 10"), *Weight:* 63kg (140lb); Civil servant. *Best performances:* 1500m – 3:46.6, 5000m – 13:35.4, 10,000m – 28:10.0. *Annual progression at 5000m and 10,000m:* 1969 – 15:10.4; 1970 – 14:33.8; 1971 – 14:15.0; 1972 – 13:48.2, 28:47.0; 1973 – 13.51.0, 28:10.0; 1974 – 13:35.4, 28:15.8.

BRENDAN FOSTER
Gateshead H. *Born* Hebburn (Co Durham), 12.1.1948; *Height:* 1.79m (5' 10½"), *Weight:* 66kg (147lb); Recreational manager. *Best performances:* 800m – 1:51.1, 1500m – 3:37.6, Mile – 3:55.9, 3000m – 7:35.2 (world record), 2 Miles – 8:13.8 (world record), 5000m – 13:14.6 (UK record). *Championships:* 1970 Commonwealth – 3rd 1500m; 1971 European – 3rd 1500m; 1972 Olympics – 5th 1500m; 1973 European Cup final – 1st 5000m; 1974 Commonwealth – 7th 1500m, 2nd 5000m; 1974 European – 1st 5000m. *Annual progression at 1500m* (* mile time less 18sec) *and 5000m:* 1966 – 3:57.8*; 1967 – 3:49.4*; 1968 – —; 1969 – 3:47.1; 1970 – 3:40.6; 1971 – 3:39.2, 14:36.0; 1972 – 3:38.2, —; 1973 – 3:38.5, 13:24.8; 1974 – 3:37.6, 13:14.6.

DENNIS FOWLES
Cardiff AAC. *Born* 8.4.1951. *Best performance:* 3000m – 8:03.6i. *Annual progression:* 1973 – 8:12.2; 1974 – 8:03.6i.

DAVE GIBBON
Elswick H. *Born* Newcastle, 20.12.1952; *Height:* 1.78m (5' 10"), *Weight:* 63kg (140lb); Employment officer. *Best performances:* 800m – 1:53.0m, 1500m – 3:42.6, Mile – 4:01.3. *Annual progression at 1500m* (* mile time less 18 sec): 1969 – 3:56.8; 1970 – 3:59.8; 1971 – 3:55.4; 1972 – 3:49.4; 1973 – 3:43.8*; 1974 – 3:42.6.

JULIAN GOATER
Shaftesbury H. *Born* Southampton, 12.1.1953; *Height:* 1.83m (6' 0"), *Weight:* 63kg (140lb); Student. *Best performances:* 1500m – 3:43.5, 5000m – 13:38.8, 10,000m – 29:08.8. *Annual progression at 5000m:* 1970 – 14:33.8; 1971 – —; 1972 – 13:44.6; 1973 – 13:38.8; 1974 – 13:52.8.

HELEN GOLDEN
Edinburgh Southern H. *Born* Edinburgh, 16.5.1953; *Height:* 1.65m (5' 5"), *Weight:* 52kg (115lb); Clerk. *Best performances:* 100m – 11.2, 200m – 23.0 (UK record), 400m – 55.6. *Championships:* 1970 Commonwealth – 5th 100m, 4th 200m; 1970 European Junior – 3rd 100m, 1st 200m; 1974 European – 5th 200m. *Annual progression at 100m* (*100 yards time plus 1.0 sec) *and 200m:* 1966 – 12.9*, —; 1967 – 12.2*, —; 1968 – 12.0*w, 24.9w; 1969 – 11.6w, 23.8w; 1970 – 11.3w, 23.4w; 1971 – 11.8, 23.8; 1972 – 11.4w, 23.6; 1973 – 11.5w, 23.1; 1974 – 11.2, 23.0.

GLYNIS GOODBURN (now Mrs Penny)
Cambridge H. *Born* Eltham, 28.1.1951; *Height:* 1.65m (5' 5"), *Weight:* 51kg (112lb); Dental nurse. *Best performances:* 800m – 2:10.9, 1500m – 4:25.7. *Annual progression at 1500m* (* mile time less 20 sec): 1968 – 5:15.7*; 1969 – 4:54.5; 1970 – 4:39.6; 1971 – 4:40.9; 1972 – 4:43.6; 1973 – 4:26.0; 1974 – 4:25.7.

ANNE GOODLAD
Rotherham H. *Born* Conisbrough (Yorks), 28.5.1955; *Height:* 1.73m (5' 8"), *Weight:* 70kg (154lb). *Best performances:* Shot – 12.76m (41' 10½"), Javelin – 52.10m (170' 11"). *Annual progression at Javelin:* 1969 – 35.56m (116' 8"); 1970 – 38.70m (126' 11"); 1971 – 41.72m (136' 10"); 1972 – 46.70m (153' 2"); 1973 – 52.10m (170' 11"); 1974 – 49.78m (163' 4").

CAROL GOULD (née Firth)
Barnet & District AC. *Born* Shipley (Yorks), 10.7.1944; *Height:* 1.78m (5' 10"), *Weight:* 64kg (141lb); Housewife. *Best performances:* 800m – 2:11.0, 1500m – 4:24.2, 3000m – 9:20.2. *Annual progression at 3000m:* 1968 – 10:06.4; 1969 – —; 1970 – 10:24.0; 1971 – 10:15.0; 1972 – —; 1973 – 9:44.2; 1974 – 9:20.2.

GRAHAM GOWER
Hillingdon AC. *Born* Gravesend, 25.5.1947; *Height:* 1.83m (6' 0"), *Weight:* 68kg (150lb); Teacher. *Best performances:* 100y – 10.0, 110m hurdles – 14.1. *Annual progression at 110m hurdles:* 1965 – 15.4; 1966 – 14.6; 1967 – 14.3w; 1968 – 14.5; 1969 – 14.6; 1970 – 14.3; 1971 – 14.2; 1972 – 14.1; 1973 – 14.1w; 1974 – 14.2w.

BRIAN GREEN
Pilkington H. *Born* Ormskirk (Lancs), 15.5.1941; *Height:* 1.67m (5' 5¾"), *Weight:* 70kg (154lb); Technologist. *Best performances:* 100m – 10.1 (UK record), 200m – 20.7. *Championships:* 1970 Commonwealth – 3rd 4 × 100m. *Annual progression at 100m* (*100 yards time plus 0.9 sec): 1963 – 10.9; 1964 – 10.8*; 1965 – 10.7*w; 1966 – 10.6*w; 1967 – 10.8*; 1968 – 10.6*w; 1969 – 10.5w; 1970 – 10.4; 1971 – 10.4; 1972 – 10.1; 1973 – 10.4; 1974 – 10.5.

The rapidly improving Lorna Drysdale in winning form against Finland in September.

211

STEVE GREEN
Kent AC. *Born* London, 13.10.1955; *Height:* 1.75m (5′ 9″), *Weight:* 71kg (157lb). *Best performances:* 100m – 10.4w and 10.5, 200m – 21.0w and 21.1, 400m – 49.7. *Annual progression at 100m and 200m:* 1971 – 11.0w, —; 1972 – 10.6w, 21.5; 1973 – 10.4w, 21.0w; 1974 – 10.4w, 21.1.

DON HALLIDAY
Wolverhampton & Bilston AC. *Born* Perth (Scotland), 16.5.1947; *Height:* 1.74m (5′ 8½″), *Weight:* 65kg (143lb); RAF technician. *Best performances:* 100m – 10.3, 200m – 20.8. *Annual progression at 100m* (*100 yards time plus 0.9 sec): 1964 – 11.0*; 1965 – —; 1966 – 11.0*; 1967 – 10.7; 1968 – 10.7*; 1969 – 10.3w; 1970 – 10.3w; 1971 – 10.4; 1972 – 10.3; 1973 – 10.3; 1974 – 10.3.

VAL HARRISON
Liverpool H & AC. *Born* Liverpool, 30.10.1954; *Height:* 1.64m (5′ 4½″), *Weight:* 54kg (119lb); Student. *Best performance:* High jump – 1.83m (6′ 0″). *Championships:* 1970 Commonwealth – 5th. *Annual progression:* 1972 – 1.69m (5′ 6½″); 1973 – 1.79m (5′ 10½″); 1974 – 1.83m (6′ 0″).

BILL HARTLEY
Liverpool H & AC. *Born* Liverpool, 27.6.1950; *Height:* 1.88m (6′ 2″), *Weight:* 81kg (180lb); Horticulturist. *Best performances:* 100m – 10.8, 200m – 21.7, 400m – 47.1, 400m hurdles – 49.9. *Championships:* 1974 Commonwealth – 6th 400m hurdles, 2nd 4 × 400m; 1974 European – 1st 4 × 400m. *Annual progression at 400m hurdles:* 1968 – 54.3; 1969 – 52.9; 1970 – 52.7; 1971 – 52.0; 1972 – 52.1; 1973 – 50.5; 1974 – 49.9.

RODNEY HEWARD-MILLS
Leicester Coritanian AC. *Born* Newcastle, 28.8.1952; *Height:* 1.89m (6′ 2½″), *Weight:* 80kg (177lb); Student. *Best performances:* Long jump – 7.05m (23′ 1¾″), Triple jump – 15.77m (51′ 9″). *Annual progression at triple jump:* 1969 – 14.10m (46′ 3″); 1970 – 14.83m (48′ 8″); 1971 – 15.47m (50′ 9¼″); 1972 – 15.77m (51′ 9″); 1973 – 15.66m (51′ 4½″); 1974 – 15.59m (51′ 1¾″).

GEOFF HIGNETT
Stretford AC. *Born* Burscough (Lancs), 5.10.1950; *Height:* 1.89m (6′ 2½″), *Weight:* 81kg (178lb); Student. *Best performances:* 100m – 10.8, 200m – 21.9, Long jump – 7.79m (25′ 6¾″). *Championships:* 1970 Commonwealth – 7th long jump. *Annual progression:* 1965 – 5.89m (19′ 4″); 1966 – 6.42m (21′ 0¾″); 1967 – 6.67m (21′ 10½″); 1968 – 7.32m (24′ 0¼″); 1969 – 7.39m (24′ 3″); 1970 – 7.76m (25′ 5½″); 1971 – 7.79m (25′ 6¾″); 1972 – 7.67m (25′ 2″); 1973 – 7.71m (25′ 3½″)w; 1974 – 7.63m (25′ 0½″).

WENDY HILL
Bury AC. *Born* Manchester, 15.2.1956; *Height:* 1.68m (5′ 6″), *Weight:* 59kg (130lb); Student. *Best performances:* 100m – 11.7, 200m – 23.8, 400m – 54.1. *Championships:* 1973 European Junior – 8th 200m. *Annual progression at 100m and 200m:* 1970 – 12.8, —; 1971 – 11.9w, 25.4; 1972 – 11.8w, 24.4; 1973 – 11.7, 23.9w; 1974 – 11.7w, 23.8.

JOHN HILLIER
Hillingdon AC. *Born* London, 29.12.1944; *Height:* 1.99m (6′ 6¼″), *Weight:* 112kg (248lb); Teacher. *Best performances:* Shot – 16.49m (54′ 1¼″), Discus – 59.76m (196′ 1″). *Championships:* 1974 Commonwealth – 3rd discus. *Annual progression:* 1963 – 44.98m (147′ 7″); 1964 – 45.62m (149′ 8″); 1965 – 47.62m (156′ 3″); 1966 – 51.48m (168′ 11″); 1967 – 53.20m (174′ 6″); 1968 – 51.04m (167′ 5″); 1969 – 52.26m (171′ 5″); 1970 – 53.54m (175′ 8″); 1971 – 50.40m (165′ 4″); 1972 – 56.10m (184′ 1″); 1973 – 58.76m (192′ 9″); 1974 – 59.76m (196′ 1″).

HILARY HOLLICK (see Hilary Tanner)

STEVE HOLLINGS
Sale H. *Born* Wakefield (Yorks), 23.11.1946; *Height:* 1.68m (5′ 6″), *Weight:* 51kg (112lb); University lecturer. *Best performances:* 3000m – 8:02.6, 5000m – 14:05.8, 3000m steeplechase – 8:27.8. *Championships:* 1974 Commonwealth – 7th 3000m SC. *Annual progression:* 1966 – 9:19.2; 1967 – 9:39.0; 1968 – 9:40.2; 1969 – 9:08.4; 1970 – 9:22.6; 1971 – 8:45.8; 1972 – 8:31.2; 1973 – 8:27.8; 1974 – 8:34.2.

MIKE HOLMES
Yorkshire WC. *Born* Shipley (Yorks), 26.8.1951; *Height:* 1.78m (5′ 10″), *Weight:* 72kg (160lb); Engineering machine worker. *Best performances:* 3000m walk – 12:41.0, 20km walk – 1:33:58, 50km walk – 4:19:45. *Annual progression at 50km walk:* 1973 – 4:19:45; 1974 – 4:40:08.

WHO'S WHO IN THE BRITISH TEAM

JANET HONOUR (née Oldall)
Woking AC. *Born* London, 1.9.1950; *Height*: 1.70m (5' 7"), *Weight*: 60kg (132lb); Secretary. *Best performances*: 200m – 24.5w, 100m hurdles – 13.8w, High jump – 1.70m (5' 7"), Long jump – 6.09m (19' 11¾")i, Shot – 11.48m (37' 8"), Pentathlon – 4161. *Championships*: 1970 Commonwealth – 6th equal high jump. *Annual progression at pentathlon*: (★ old scoring tables): 1966 – 3909★; 1967 – 3965★; 1968 – 3983★; 1969 – 4097★; 1970 – 4410★; 1971 – 4633★ (4057); 1972 – 4161; 1973 – 4046; 1974 – 4043.

BRIAN HOOPER
Woking AC. *Born* Woking, 18.5.1953; *Height*: 1.74m (5' 8½"), *Weight*: 66kg (147lb); Student. *Best performance*: Pole vault – 5.20m (17' 0¾"). *Championships*: 1974 Commonwealth – 3rd. *Annual progression*: 1966 – 2.13m (7' 0"); 1967 – 2.59m (8' 6"); 1968 – 3.24m (10' 7½"); 1969 – 3.57m (11' 8½"); 1970 – 4.27m (13' 11¼")i; 1971 – 4.81m (15' 9¼"); 1972 – 5.10m (16' 8¾); 1973 – 5.16m (16' 11"); 1974 – 5.20m (17' 0¾").

BETTY JENKINS (née Franklin)
Birchfield H. *Born* Birmingham, 13.1.1938; *Height*: 1.71m (5' 7½"), *Weight*: 66kg (147lb); Wages clerk. *Best performances*: 3000m walk – 14:59.4, 5000m walk – 25:09.2. *Annual progression*: 1969 – 12:53.4 (2500m); 1970 – 13:04.0 (2500m); 1971 – 15:27.0 (3000m); 1972 – 15:24.2, 25:09.2 (5000m); 1973 – 14:59.4, 25:38.0; 1974 – 15:06.8, 26:57.8.

DAVID JENKINS
Heriot Watt AC. *Born* Point à Pierre (Trinidad), 25.5.1952; *Height*: 1.93m (6' 4"), *Weight*: 82kg (180lb). *Best performances*: 100m – 10.1, 200m – 20.3 (UK record), 400m – 45.2 (UK record), 400m Hurdles – 53.0. *Championships*: 1971 European – 1st 400m; 1972 Olympics – 2nd 4 × 400m; 1974 Commonwealth – 4th 400m; 1974 European – 2nd 400m, 1st 4 × 400m. *Annual progression at 200m and 400m*: 1967 – —, 53.4; 1968 – 22.4, 48.7; 1969 – 22.1, 46.5; 1970 – 21.1, 46.9; 1971 – 20.6, 45.5; 1972 – 20.3, 45.3; 1973 – 20.7, 45.2; 1974 – 20.5, 45.2.

ROGER JENKINS
Edinburgh AC. *Born* Liverpool, 30.9.1955; *Height*: 1.89m (6' 2½"), *Weight*: 76kg (168lb); Student. *Best performances*: 100m – 10.8, 200m – 21.3w and 21.5, 400m – 46.7. *Championships*: 1973 European Junior – 5th 400m, 3rd 4 × 400m. *Annual progression at 400m*: 1971 – 53.3; 1972 – —; 1973 – 46.1; 1974 – 46.7.

DAVE JOHNSON
Hallamshire H. *Born* Skirlaugh (Yorks), 18.5.1953; *Height*: 1.87m (6' 1½"), *Weight*: 81kg (180lb); Newsagent. *Best performances*: Long jump – 7.26m (23' 10")w, Triple jump – 15.80m (51' 10"). *Annual progression at triple jump*: 1967 – 12.04m (39' 6"); 1968 – 13.66m (44' 10"); 1969 – 13.66m (44' 10"); 1970 – 14.12m (46' 4"); 1971 – 15.12m (49' 7¼"); 1972 – 15.80m (51' 10"); 1973 – 15.29m (50' 2")i; 1974 – 15.80m (51' 10")w.

RUTH KENNEDY
Notts AC. *Born* Nottingham, 13.1.1957; *Height*: 1.66m (5' 5½"), *Weight*: 54kg (119lb); Student. *Best performances*: 200m – 23.7, 400m – 53.5. *Championships*: 1973 European Junior – 2nd 4 × 400m; 1974 Commonwealth – 1st 4 × 400m. *Annual progression at 400m*: 1972 – 56.8; 1973 – 54.6; 1974 – 53.5.

Ruth Kennedy.

Left: *Bernie Ford, second in the 5000 metres against the East Germans.* **Above:** *Steve Green (8) and Gareth Edwards.* **Below:** *Val Harrison – Britain's third woman 6-foot high jumper.* **Right:** *Roger Jenkins – a fraternal challenge.* **Far right:** *Brian Hooper enjoyed his best-ever season in 1974.*

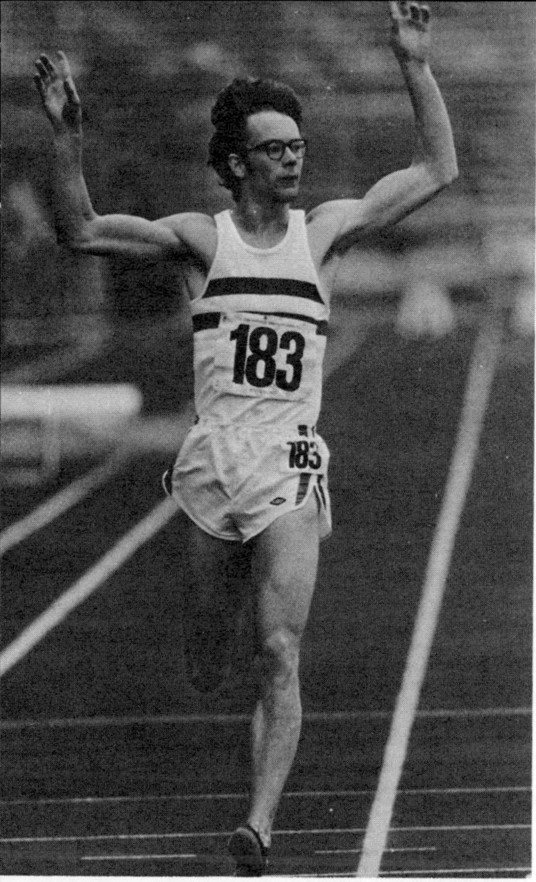
183
183

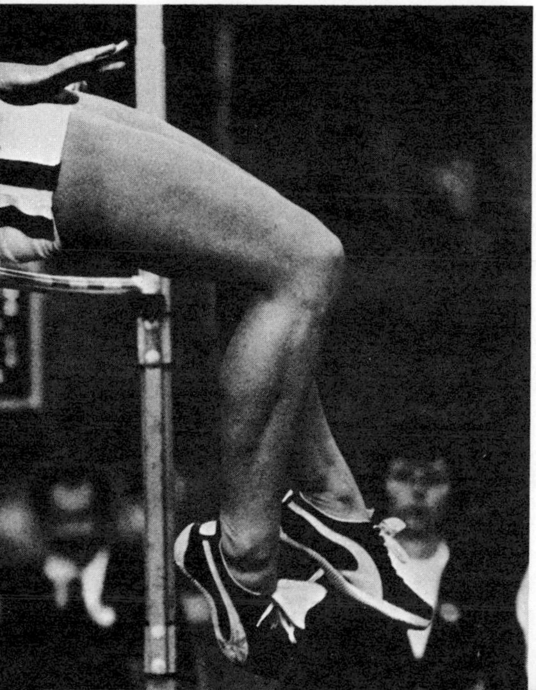

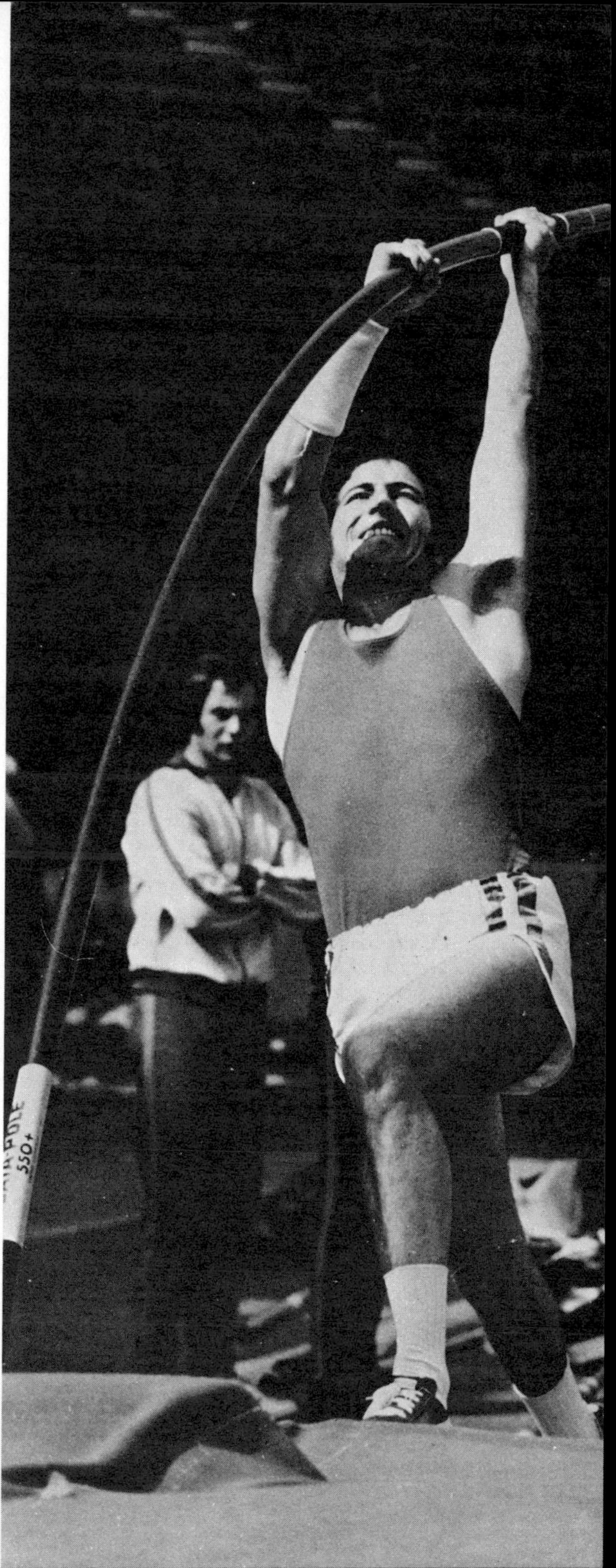
550+

JANIS KERR (née Quick)
Mitcham AC. *Born* London, 29.4.1946; *Height:* 1.84m (6' 0½"), *Weight:* 87kg (192lb); Railway clerk. *Best performances:* Shot – 14.70m (48' 2¾"), Discus – 47.18m (154' 9"). *Annual progression at shot:* 1962 – 11.63m (38' 2"); 1963 – 11.35m (37' 3"); 1964 – 11.55m (37' 10¾"); 1965 – 12.38m (40' 7½"); 1966 – 12.83m (42' 1"); 1967 – 12.77m (41' 11"); 1968 – 13.33m (43' 9"); 1969 – 13.37m (43' 10½"); 1970 – 13.76m (45' 1¾"); 1971 – 13.79m (45' 3"); 1972 – 14.10m (46' 3¼"); 1973 – 14.32m (46' 11¾"); 1974 – 14.70m (48' 2¾").

LESLEY KIERNAN
Havering AC. *Born* London, 9.8.1957; *Height:* 1.65m (5' 5"), *Weight:* 52kg (114lb); Receptionist. *Best performances:* 400m – 56.5, 800m – 2:02.8, 1500m – 4:24.8. *Championships:* 1973 European Junior – 2nd 800m. *Annual progression:* 1969 – 2:36.4; 1970 – 2:18.6; 1971 – 2:10.1; 1972 – 2:13.0; 1973 – 2:03.7; 1974 – 2:02.8.

CHARLES ('C.J.') KIRKPATRICK
Ballymena AC. *Born* Ballymena (N. Ireland), 9.6.1950; *Height:* 1.75m (5' 9"), *Weight:* 66kg (147lb); Medical student. *Best performances:* 100m – 10.6, 110m hurdles – 13.7, 400m hurdles – 53.3. *Championships:* 1974 Commonwealth – 5th 110m hurdles. *Annual progression:* 1968 – 15.5; 1969 – 15.0; 1970 – 14.6w; 1971 – 14.4; 1972 – 14.6w; 1973 – 14.1; 1974 – 13.7.

SONIA LANNAMAN
Solihull AC. *Born* Birmingham, 24.3.1956; *Height:* 1.62m (5' 4"), *Weight:* 52kg (114lb); Audio typist. *Best performances:* 100m – 11.3, 200m – 23.7w and 23.8. *Championships:* 1973 European Junior – 1st 100m, 3rd 4 × 100m; 1974 Commonwealth – 2nd 4 × 100m. *Annual progression at 100m* (★ 100y time plus 1.0sec): 1968 – 12.1★; 1969 – 11.9; 1970 – 11.8w; 1971 – 11.7w; 1972 – 11.4w; 1973 – 11.4; 1974 – 11.3.

BARBARA LAWTON (née Inkpen)
Aldershot Farnham & District AC. *Born* Farnham (Surrey), 28.10.1949; *Height:* 1.82m (5' 11½"), *Weight:* 72kg (159lb); Civil servant. *Best performances:* High jump – 1.87m (6' 1½") (UK record), Long jump – 6.33m (20' 9¼")w. *Championships:* (all High jump) 1969 European – 8th; 1971 European – 2nd equal; 1972 Olympics – 4th; 1974 Commonwealth – 1st. *Annual progression:* 1964 – 1.55m (5' 1"); 1965 – 1.62m (5' 4"); 1966 – 1.66m (5' 5½"); 1967 – 1.72m (5' 8")i; 1968 – 1.75m (5' 9"); 1969 – 1.78m (5' 10"); 1970 – 1.79m (5' 10½"); 1971 – 1.85m (6' 0¾"); 1972 – 1.86m (6' 1¼"); 1973 – 1.87m (6' 1½"); 1974 – 1.86m (6' 1¼").

CARL LAWTON
Belgrave H. *Born* Shaftesbury (Dorset), 20.1.1948; *Height:* 1.92m (6' 3½"), *Weight:* 76kg (168lb); Structural engineer. *Best performances:* 3000m walk – 12:53.8, 20km walk – 1:32:01, 50km walk – 4:19:00. *Annual progression at 50km walk:* 1971 – 4:19:00; 1972 – 4:37:34; 1973 – 4:36:08; 1974 – 4:31:44.

DAVE LEASE
Cardiff AAC. *Born* 26.3.1945; *Height:* 1.75m (5' 9"), *Weight:* 70kg (154lb); Teacher. *Best performances:* Pole vault – 4.80m (15' 9") (indoor), Javelin – 59.72m (195' 11"). *Championships:* 1970 Commonwealth – 8th PV. *Annual progression:* 1966 – 3.35m (11' 0"); 1967 – —; 1968 – 4.27m (14' 0")i; 1969 – 4.60m (15' 1¼")i; 1970 – 4.58m (15' 0½"); 1971 – 4.65m (15' 3"); 1972 – 4.80m (15' 9")i; 1973 – 4.70m (15' 5"); 1974 – 4.70m (15' 5").

ALAN LERWILL
Queens Park H. *Born* Portsmouth, 15.11.1946; *Height:* 1.88m (6' 2¼"), *Weight:* 82kg (182lb); Teacher. *Best performances:* 100m – 10.8, High jump – 2.10m (6' 10¾"), Long jump – 8.15m (26' 9")w and 7.98m (26' 2¼"), Triple jump – 16.21m (53' 2¼")w and 16.10m (52' 10"), 400m hurdles – 55.0, Decathlon – 6263. *Championships:* (all long jump) 1970 Commonwealth – 3rd; 1972 Olympics – 7th; 1974 Commonwealth – 1st. *Annual progression at high jump and long jump:* 1966 – 1.80m (5' 11"), 7.33m (24' 0¾"); 1967 – —, 7.53m (24' 8½"); 1968 – —, 7.69m (25' 2¾")w; 1969 – —, 7.69m (25' 2¾")w; 1970 – 1.85m (6' 1"), 7.94m (26' 0¾")w; 1971 – 2.04m (6' 8¼"), 8.12m (26' 7¾")w; 1972 – 2.00m (6' 6¾"), 8.15m (26' 9")w; 1973 – 2.10m (6' 10¾"), 7.95m (26' 1")w; 1974 – 2.06m (6' 9¼"), 7.98m (26' 2¼").

PHIL LEWIS
Wolverhampton & Bilston AC. *Born* Dublin, 10.11.1949; *Height:* 1.78m (5' 10"), *Weight:* 71kg (156lb); Teacher. *Best performances:* 400m – 48.8, 800m – 1:46.3, 1500m – 3:49.2. *Championships:* 1971 European Indoor – 2nd 800m; 1974 Commonwealth – 8th 800m. *Annual progression:* 1964 – 2:05.4; 1965 – 2:00.4; 1966 – 1:59.3; 1967 – 1:55.6; 1968 – 1:52.7; 1969 – 1:47.1; 1970 – 1:47.4; 1971 – 1:47.6; 1972 – 1:48.6; 1973 – 1:47.6; 1974 – 1:46.3.

WHO'S WHO IN THE BRITISH TEAM

SHAUN LIGHTMAN
Metropolitan WC. *Born* Hounslow (Middx), 15.4.1943; *Height:* 1.71m (5' 7½"), *Weight:* 70kg (154lb); Teacher. *Best performances:* 3000m walk – 12:47.4, 20km walk – 1:31:10, 50km walk – 4:15:13. *Championships:* 1970 Commonwealth – 7th 20 miles walk. *Annual progression at 50km walk:* 1964 – 4:56:10; 1965 – 5:00:36; 1966 – 4:53:15; 1967 – 4:26:56; 1968 – 4:22:23; 1969 – 4:24:58; 1970 – —; 1971 – —; 1972 – 4:26:36; 1973 – 4:15:13; 1974 – 4:47:00.

JEAN LOCHHEAD
Airedale & Spen Valley AC. *Born* Huddersfield, 24.12.1946; *Height:* 1.68m (5' 6"), *Weight:* 54kg (119lb); Self-employed. *Best performances:* 800m – 2:08.4, 1500m – 4:18.6, 3000m – 9:38.8. *Annual progression at 1500m* (★ mile time less 20sec): 1967 – 5:15.2★; 1968 – —; 1969 – 4:59.6; 1970 – 4:42.2; 1971 – 4:35.0; 1972 – 4:18.6; 1973 – 4:21.0; 1974 – 4:26.4.

ANDREA LYNCH
Mitcham AC. *Born* Barbados, 24.11.1952; *Height:* 1.57m (5' 2"), *Weight:* 52kg (114lb); Bank clerk. *Best performances:* 60m – 7.2 (world record), 100m – 10.9w and 11.1 (UK record), 200m – 23.1w and 23.2. *Championships:* 1970 European Junior – 2nd 100m; 1974 Commonwealth – 2nd 100m, 2nd 4 × 100m; 1974 European Indoor – 2nd 60m; 1974 European – 3rd 100m. *Annual progression at 100m and 200m:* 1969 – 12.0, 25.0w; 1970 – 11.8, 24.5; 1971 – 11.7w, 24.0w; 1972 – 11.4, 23.6; 1973 – 11.2, 23.8; 1974 – 10.9w, 23.1w.

RON MACDONALD
Monkland H. *Born* Coatbridge (Scotland), 7.11.1952; *Height:* 1.83m (6' 0"), *Weight:* 68kg (150lb); Student. *Best performances:* 800m – 1:52.6, 1500m – 3:43.0, Mile – 4:02.2, 3000m – 7:55.4, 5000m – 14:24.6. *Annual progression at 1500m* (★ mile time less 18sec): 1969 – 4:01.4; 1970 – 3:50.5; 1971 – 3:46.0★; 1972 – 3:43.0; 1973 – 3:44.5★; 1974 – 3:43.1.

DAVE McMEEKIN
Victoria Park AAC. *Born* Glasgow, 10.2.1953; *Height:* 1.75m (5' 9"), *Weight:* 58kg (128lb); Student. *Best performances:* 400m – 48.9, 800m – 1:46.8, 1500m – 3:43.1. *Annual progression at 800m:* 1968 – 1:58.3; 1969 – 1:56.3; 1970 – 1:52.5; 1971 – 1:51.5; 1972 – 1:48.5; 1973 – 1:47.4; 1974 – 1:46.8.

PAT McNAB (see Pat Chapman)

Dave McMeekin wins the BIG 800 metres.

SUE MAPSTONE
Harlow AC. *Born* London, 16.12.1956; *Height:* 1.69m (5' 6¾"), *Weight:* 60kg (133lb); Student. *Best performances:* 200m – 24.5, 100m hurdles – 14.0, High jump – 1.70m (5' 7")i, Long jump – 6.15m (20' 2¼")w, Shot – 10.91m (35' 9½"), Pentathlon – 4112. *Championships:* 1973 European Junior – 2nd pentathlon; 1974 Commonwealth – 7th pentathlon. *Annual progression* (★ pentathlon with 80m hurdles): 1970 – 3289 (Junior); 1971 – 3437★; 1972 – 3725★; 1973 – 4105; 1974 – 4112.

217

PETER MARLOW
Southend AC. *Born* London, 20.4.1941; *Height:* 1.73m (5' 8"), *Weight:* 65kg (144lb); Clerk. *Best performances:* 3000m walk – 12:23.0, 20km walk – 1:29:49. *Annual progression at 20km walk:* 1966 – 1:39:26; 1967 – —; 1968 – —; 1969 – —; 1970 – —; 1971 – —; 1972 – 1:33:50; 1973 – 1:31:59; 1974 – 1:29:49.

STEVE MARLOW
Chelmsford AC. *Born* London, 21.11.1953; *Height:* 1.85m (6' 1"), *Weight:* 80kg (175lb); Stockbroker's clerk. *Best performances:* 200m – 21.8w, 400m – 46.7. *Annual progression at 400m:* 1970 – 49.7; 1971 – 49.4; 1972 – 48.2; 1973 – 47.5; 1974 – 46.7.

RUTH MARTIN-JONES
Birchfield H. *Born* Criccieth (Wales), 28.1.1947; *Height:* 1.75m (5' 9"), *Weight:* 63kg (140lb); Travel organiser/teacher/translator. *Best performances:* 200m – 24.5, 100m hurdles – 14.4, High jump – 1.70m (5' 7"), Long jump – 6.54m (21' 5½")w and 6.51m (21' 4¼")i, Shot – 11.54m (37' 10½"), Pentathlon – 4294. *Championships:* 1970 Commonwealth – 6th pentathlon; 1974 Commonwealth – 3rd long jump. *Annual progression at long jump:* 1967 – 5.81m (19' 0¾"); 1968 – 5.60m (18' 4½"); 1969 – 5.82m (19' 1¼"); 1970 – 6.14m (20' 1¾"); 1971 – 6.41m (21' 0½")i; 1972 – 6.54m (21' 5½")w; 1973 – 6.38m (20' 11¼"); 1974 – 6.51m (21' 4¼")i.

IAN MATTHEWS
Thames Valley H. *Born* Plymouth, 11.4.1948; *Height:* 1.80m (5' 11"), *Weight:* 70kg (154lb); Accountant. *Best performances:* 100m – 10.4, 200m – 20.9w and 21.0. *Annual progression at 100m and 200m:* 1968 – 11.0, 22.2; 1969 – 10.7, 21.7; 1970 – 10.8, 21.6; 1971 – 10.6w, 21.4; 1972 – 10.4, 20.9w; 1973 – 10.4w, 21.1; 1974 – 10.4w, 21.2w.

ROGER MILLS
Ilford AC. *Born* Romford, 11.2.1948; *Height:* 1.82m (5' 11¾"), *Weight:* 74kg (164lb); Print buyer. *Best performances:* Mile walk – 6:08.9 (world best), 3000m walk – 12:08.2, 20km walk – 1:29:04. *Championships:* 1974 European – 3rd 20km walk. *Annual progression:* 1968 – 1:40:13; 1969 – 1:32:35; 1970 – 1:32:17; 1971 – 1:35:39; 1972 – 1:30:10; 1973 – 1:30:05; 1974 – 1:29:04.

ROY MITCHELL
Royal Navy AC. *Born* 1.1.1955. *Best performances:* 100m – 10.9, 110m hurdles – 15.0w, High jump – 2.02m (6' 7½"), Long jump – 7.39m (24' 3")w, Decathlon – 7088. *Annual progression at decathlon:* 1973 – 6183; 1974 – 7088.

CHRIS MONK
Leicester Coritanian AC. *Born* Isleworth (Middx), 29.9.1951; *Height:* 1.78m (5' 10"), *Weight:* 63kg (140lb); Teacher. *Best performances:* 100m – 10.4, 200m – 20.7. *Championships:* 1973 European Cup final – 1st 200m; 1974 Commonwealth – 6th 200m. *Annual progression:* 1969 – 22.3; 1970 – 21.6; 1971 – 21.4; 1972 – 21.5w; 1973 – 20.7; 1974 – 20.7w.

ASTON MOORE
Birchfield H. *Born* Jamaica, 8.2.1956; *Height:* 1.80m (5' 11"), *Weight:* 76kg (168lb); Sheet metal worker. *Best performance:* Triple jump – 15.65m (51' 4¼"). *Annual progression:* 1972 – 13.91m (45' 7¾"); 1973 – 14.71m (48' 3¼")w; 1974 – 15.65m (51' 4¼").

DONNA MURRAY
Southampton AAC. *Born* Southampton, 1.5.1955; *Height:* 1.70m (5' 7"), *Weight:* 57kg (127lb); Boutique manageress. *Best performances:* 100m – 11.5w and 11.6, 200m – 22.9w and 23.3, 400m – 51.8 (UK record). *Annual progression at 200m and 400m:* 1970 – 24.7, —; 1971 – 24.5w, 59.7; 1972 – 23.5, —; 1973 – 23.7, 56.9; 1974 – 22.9w, 51.8.

MYRA NIMMO
Maryhill Ladies AC. *Born* Edinburgh, 5.1.1954; *Height:* 1.65m (5' 5"), *Weight:* 57kg (126lb); Student. *Best performances:* 100m – 11.9, 200m – 24.5w, 100m hurdles – 13.5w, Long jump – 6.43m (21' 1¼"), Pentathlon – 3817. *Championships:* 1974 Commonwealth – 4th Long jump. *Annual progression:* 1970 – 5.83m (19' 1½")w; 1971 – 5.60m (18' 4½"); 1972 – —; 1973 – 6.43m (21' 1¼"); 1974 – 6.34m (20' 9¾").

COLIN O'NEILL
Bristol AC. *Born* Bristol, 14.8.1948; *Height:* 1.82m (5' 11¾"), *Weight:* 72kg (160lb); Technician. *Best performances:* 100y – 9.9, 200m – 21.7, 400m – 48.0, 400m hurdles – 50.6, Long jump – 7.20m (23' 7½"), Triple jump – 14.15m (46' 5"). *Championships:* 1974

WHO'S WHO IN THE BRITISH TEAM

Commonwealth – 8th 400m hurdles. *Annual progression:* 1967 – 53.4; 1968 – 54.9; 1969 – —; 1970 – 53.6; 1971 – 52.3; 1972 – 52.0; 1973 – 51.7; 1974 – 50.6.

STEVE OVETT
Brighton & Hove AC. *Born* Brighton, 9.10.1955; *Height:* 1.83m (6′ 0″), *Weight:* 70kg (154lb); Student. *Best performances:* 400m – 47.5, 800m – 1:45.8, Mile – 3:59.4. *Championships:* 1973 European Junior – 1st 800m; 1974 European – 2nd 800m. *Annual progression:* 1970 – 2:00.0; 1971 – 1:55.3; 1972 – 1:52.5; 1973 – 1:47.3; 1974 – 1:45.8.

MILTON PALMER
Wolverhampton & Bilston AC. *Born* Kingston (Jamaica), 9.9.1958; *Height:* 1.88m (6′ 2″), *Weight:* 73kg (161lb); Student. *Best performance:* High jump – 2.02m (6′ 7½″). *Annual progression:* 1969 – 1.24m (4′ 1″); 1970 – 1.39m (4′ 7″); 1971 – 1.47m (4′ 10″); 1972 – 1.66m (5′ 5½″); 1973 – 1.83m (6′ 0″); 1974 – 2.02m (6′ 7½″).

Milton Palmer.

ALAN PASCOE
Polytechnic H. *Born* Portsmouth, 11.10.1947; *Height:* 1.85m (6′ 1″), *Weight:* 74kg (164lb); Lecturer. *Best performances:* 100m – 10.6w, 200m – 20.9, 400m – 46.8, 110m hurdles – 13.7, 400m hurdles – 48.8. *Championships:* 1969 European Indoor – 1st 50m hurdles; 1969 European – 3rd 110m hurdles; 1971 European – 2nd 110m hurdles; 1972 Olympics – 2nd 4 × 400m; 1973 European Cup final – 1st 400m hurdles; 1974 Commonwealth – 1st 400m hurdles, 2nd 4 × 400m; 1974 European – 1st 400m hurdles, 1st 4 × 400m. *Annual progression at 110m and 400m hurdles:* 1965 – 15.6, —; 1966 – 14.4, —; 1967 – 13.9, 53.6; 1968 – 13.9, —; 1969 – 13.7, 54.2; 1970 – 13.8w, 52.4; 1971 – 13.7, 50.9; 1972 – 13.7, —; 1973 – 13.8, 49.5; 1974 – 14.1, 48.8.

HOWARD PAYNE
Birchfield H. *Born* Benoni (S. Africa), 17.4.1931; *Height:* 1.85m (6′ 1″), *Weight:* 105kg (231lb); University Lecturer. *Best performance:* Hammer – 70.88m (232′ 6″). *Championships:* 1958 Commonwealth – 4th; 1962 Commonwealth – 1st; 1966 Commonwealth – 1st; 1969 European – 8th; 1970 Commonwealth – 1st; 1974 Commonwealth – 2nd. *Annual progression:* 1954 – 26.82m (88′ 0″); 1955 – 41.34m (135′ 8″); 1956 – 48.12m (157′ 11″); 1957 – 54.20m (177′ 10″); 1958 – 58.28m (191′ 2″); 1959 – 57.38m (188′ 3″); 1960 – 61.34m (201′ 3″); 1961 – 62.56m (205′ 3″); 1962 – 63.64m (208′ 10″); 1963 – 63.18m (207′ 4″); 1964 – 63.10m (207′ 0″); 1965 – 61.18m (200′ 9″); 1966 – 63.18m (207′ 4″); 1967 – 62.40m (204′ 9″); 1968 – 68.06m (223′ 3″); 1969 – 67.64m (221′ 11″); 1970 – 69.24m (227′ 2″); 1971 – 68.20m (223′ 9″); 1972 – 67.80m (222′ 5″); 1973 – 69.42m (227′ 9″); 1974 – 70.88m (232′ 6″).

ROSEMARY PAYNE (née Charters)
Lozells H. *Born* Kelso (Scotland), 19.5.1933; *Height:* 1.74m (5′ 8½″), *Weight:* 77kg (171lb); College lecturer. *Best performances:* Shot – 14.67m (48′ 1¾″), Discus – 58.02m (190′ 4″) (UK record). *Championships:* (all discus) 1966 Commonwealth – 4th; 1970 Commonwealth – 1st; 1974 Commonwealth – 2nd and 7th Shot. *Annual progression at discus:* 1958 – 36.54m (119′ 11″); 1959 – 37.10m (121′ 8″); 1960 – —; 1961 – 34.72m (113′ 11″); 1962 – 40.86m (134′ 0″); 1963 – 44.64m (146′ 5″); 1964 – 48.24m (158′ 3″); 1965 – 50.66m (166′ 3″); 1966 – 50.92m (167′ 1″); 1967 – 50.72m (166′ 5″); 1968 – 48.70m (159′ 9″); 1969 – 52.22m (171′ 4″); 1970 – 55.04m (180′ 7″); 1971 – 54.78m (179′ 9″); 1972 – 58.02m (190′ 4″); 1973 – 56.40m (185′ 0″); 1974 – 55.44m (181′ 11″).

GLYNIS PENNY (see Glynis Goodburn)

KEITH PENNY
Cambridge H. *Born* 29.1.1950. *Best performances:* 1500m – 3:49.7, 3000m – 7:59.0, 5000m – 13:52.2, 10,000m – 28:37.4. *Annual progression at 10,000m:* 1972 – 29:27.6; 1973 – 29:03.4; 1974 – 28:37.4.

NICK PHIPPS
Woking AC. *Born* Newhaw (Surrey), 8.4.1952; *Height:* 1.85m (6′ 1″), *Weight:* 88kg (195lb); Car salesman. *Best performances:* High jump – 1.83m (6′ 0″), Pole vault – 4.50m (14′ 9¼″), Shot – 13.87m (45′ 6¼″), Discus – 41.56m (136′ 4″), Javelin – 56.58m (185′ 7″), Decathlon – 6892. *Annual progression at decathlon:* 1970 – 5440; 1971 – 6479; 1972 – 6670; 1973 – 6892; 1974 – 6712.

LES PIGGOT
Garscube H. *Born* Glasgow, 12.5.1942; *Height:* 1.80m (5′ 11″), *Weight:* 71kg (156lb); Sales director. *Best performances:* 100m – 10.2w and 10.3, 200m – 21.3. *Championships:* 1970 Commonwealth – 8th 100m; 1974 Commonwealth – 7th 100m. *Annual progression at 100m* (★ 100y time plus 0.9sec): 1962 – 11.2★; 1963 – 11.0★; 1964 – 10.8★; 1965 – 10.7★; 1966 – 10.7; 1967 – 10.6; 1968 – 10.6; 1969 – 10.6w; 1970 – 10.3w; 1971 – 10.5; 1972 – 10.2w; 1973 – 10.5; 1974 – 10.3.

BERNIE PLAIN
Cardiff AAC. *Born* Cardiff, 3.12.1946; *Height:* 1.74m (5′ 8½″), *Weight:* 58kg (129lb); Recreation officer. *Best performances:* 1500m – 3:48.8, 5000m – 13:38.6, 10,000m – 28:20.6, Marathon – 2:14:56. *Championships:* 1974 Commonwealth – 7th marathon; 1974 European – 4th marathon. *Annual progression at 10,000m and marathon:* 1969 – 29:41.0, —; 1970 – 28:51.8, —; 1971 – 29:22.6, 2:19:49; 1972 – 28:41.6, 2:16:18; 1973 – 28:20.6, 2:21:01; 1974 – 28:40.8, 2:14:56.

BERWYN PRICE
Cardiff AAC. *Born* Tredegar (Wales), 15.8.1951; *Height:* 1.90m (6′ 3″), *Weight:* 79kg (174lb); Recreation supervisor. *Best performances:* 100m – 10.8, 110m hurdles – 13.5 (UK record), 400m hurdles – 52.8. *Championships:* (all 110m hurdles) 1970 European Junior – 1st; 1973 World Student Games – 1st; 1974 Commonwealth – 2nd; 1974 European – 7th. *Annual progression:* 1968 – 15.6 (39″); 1969 – 15.1; 1970 – 14.1; 1971 – 13.9; 1972 – 13.7w; 1973 – 13.5; 1974 – 13.8.

DENISE RAMSDEN
Dorothy Hyman TC. *Born* Wakefield (Yorks), 11.2.1952; *Height:* 1.60m (5′ 3″), *Weight:* 52kg (115lb); Secretary. *Best performances:* 100m – 11.5w and 11.6; 200m – 24.4. *Championships:* 1969 European – 3rd 4 × 100m. *Annual progression at 100m* (★ 100y time plus 1.0sec): 1964 – 12.9★w; 1965 – 12.3★w; 1966 – 12.4★; 1967 – 11.4★w; 1968 – 11.6; 1969 – 11.5w; 1970 – 11.9; 1971 – 11.7w; 1972 – 11.7w; 1973 – 12.2; 1974 – 11.6.

MARGARET RITCHIE
Edinburgh Southern H. *Born* Kirkcaldy (Scotland), 6.7.1952; *Height:* 1.78m (5′ 10″), *Weight:* 81kg (180lb); Teacher. *Best performances:* Shot – 13.30m (43′ 7¾″). Discus – 52.18m (171′ 2″). *Championships:* 1974 Commonwealth – 6th discus. *Annual progression:* 1971 – 36.60m (120′ 1″); 1972 – 43.38m (142′ 4″); 1973 – 50.54m (165′ 10″); 1974 – 52.18m (171′ 2″).

BRIAN ROBERTS
Haringey & Southgate AC. *Born* Plymouth, 14.10.1946; *Height:* 1.83m (6′ 0¼″), *Weight:* 91kg (200lb); Teacher. *Best performance:* Javelin – 79.48m (260′ 9″). *Championships:* 1974 Commonwealth – 5th. *Annual progression:* 1966 – 57.86m (189′ 10″); 1967 – 63.36m (207′ 10″); 1968 – 65.82m (215′ 11″); 1969 – 63.26m (207′ 6″); 1970 – 65.58m (215′ 2″); 1971 – 74.30m (243′ 9″); 1972 – 76.38m (250′ 7″); 1973 – 76.58m (251′ 3″); 1974 – 79.48m (260′ 9″).

DAVID ROBERTS
Cardiff AAC. *Born* Bangor (Wales), 5.6.1949. *Best performances:* 100m – 10.5, 200m – 21.7. *Annual progression at 100m* (★ 100y time plus 0.9sec): 1966 – 10.8★; 1967 – 10.9★; 1968 – 11.0★; 1969 – —; 1970 – 10.7w; 1971 – 10.6w; 1972 – —; 1973 – 10.5w; 1974 – 10.5.

JANNETTE ROSCOE (née Champion)
Stretford AC. *Born* Tunbridge Wells, 10.6.1946; *Height:* 1.69m (5′ 6½″), *Weight:* 56kg (124lb); Lecturer. *Best performances:* 100m – 11.5w and 11.6, 200m – 23.7, 400m – 52.9, 800m – 2:12.3. *Championships:* 1970 Commonwealth – 4th 400m; 1974 Commonwealth – 4th 400m, 1st 4 × 400m. *Annual progression at 400m:* 1968 – 57.3; 1969 – 55.3; 1970 – 54.2; 1971 – 53.9; 1972 – 53.0; 1973 – 53.8; 1974 – 52.9.

THERESA SANDERSON
Wolverhampton & Bilston AC. *Born* Jamaica, 14.3.1956;

WHO'S WHO IN THE BRITISH TEAM

Height: 1.68m (5' 6"), *Weight:* 58kg (129lb); Shorthand typist. *Best performances:* 400m – 57.3, 100m hurdles – 14.9, High jump – 1.69m (5' 6¼"), Javelin – 54.10m (177' 6"), Pentathlon – 3877. *Championships:* 1974 Commonwealth – 5th javelin. *Annual progression:* 1970 – 31.86m (104' 6"); 1971 – 42.02m (137' 10"); 1972 – 43.06m (141' 3"); 1973 – 51.34m (168' 5"); 1974 – 54.10m (177' 6").

PHIL SCOTT
Bristol AC. *Born* Rotherham (Yorks), 22.8.1948; *Height:* 1.83m (6' 0"), *Weight:* 73kg (161lb); Teacher. *Best performances:* 100y – 9.9, Long jump – 7.74m (25' 4¾")i. *Annual progression at long jump:* 1967 – 6.82m (22' 4¾"); 1968 – 7.19m (23' 7")i; 1969 – 7.56m (24' 9¾"); 1970 – 7.32m (24' 0¼")i; 1971 – 6.94m (22' 9¼")i; 1972 – 7.22m (23' 8¼")w; 1973 – 7.74m (25' 4¾")i; 1974 – 7.47m (24' 6¼").

AMOS SEDDON
Borough of Enfield H. *Born* Leek (Staffs), 22.1.1941; *Height:* 1.76m (5' 9½"), *Weight:* 77kg (171lb); Policeman. *Best performances:* 3000m walk – 12:48.4, 20km walk – 1:28:50. *Championships:* 1974 European – 6th 20km walk. *Annual progression:* 1971 – 1:34:49; 1972 – 1:34:32; 1973 – 1:30:29; 1974 – 1:28:50.

BOB SERCOMBE
Newport H. *Born* Newport (Wales), 29.4.1950; *Height:* 1.73m (5' 8"), *Weight:* 59kg (130lb); Trainee accountant. *Best performances:* Marathon – 2:19:04. *Annual progression:* 1973 – 2:19:04; 1974 – 2:19:52.

TONY SETTLE
Sale H. *Born* Sale, 9.12.1953; *Height:* 1.80m (5' 11"), *Weight:* 62kg (136lb); Student teacher. *Best performances:* 800m – 1:47.7, 1500m – 3:46.9, Mile – 4:03.7. *Annual progression at 800m:* 1969 – 1:57.0; 1970 – 1:54.6; 1971 – 1:50.7; 1972 – 1:49.2; 1973 – 1:48.2; 1974 – 1:47.7.

KEVIN SHEPPARD
Walton AC. *Born* London, 9.6.1948; *Height:* 1.85m (6' 1"), *Weight:* 89kg (196lb); Student. *Best performance:* Javelin – 80.20m (263' 1"). *Annual progression:* 1967 – 65.56m (215' 1"); 1968 – 66.62m (218' 7"); 1969 – 67.84m (222' 7"); 1970 – 58.86m (193' 1"); 1971 – 68.74m (225' 6"); 1972 – 74.72m (245' 2"); 1973 – 74.78m (245' 4"); 1974 – 80.20m (263' 1").

RON SILVESTER
Haringey & Southgate AC. *Born* 9.1.1950. *Best performance:* Javelin – 75.98m (249' 3"). *Annual progression:* 1967 – 53.12m (174' 3"); 1968 – 60.56m (198' 8"); 1969 – 61.80m (202' 9"); 1970 – 66.02m (216' 7"); 1971 – 67.52m (221' 6"); 1972 – 67.86m (222' 8"); 1973 – 71.04m (233' 1"); 1974 – 75.98m (249' 3").

TONY SIMMONS
Luton United H. *Born* Maesteg (Wales), 6.10.1948; *Height:* 1.70m (5' 7"), *Weight:* 57kg (126lb); Paint technician. *Best performances:* 800m – 1:52.0, Mile – 4:03.1, 5000m – 13:28.8, 10,000m – 28:01.6, Marathon – 2:23:56, 3000m steeplechase – 8:55.0. *Championships:* 1974 Commonwealth – 7th 10,000m; 1974 European – 2nd 10,000m. *Annual progression at 5000m* (* 3 miles time plus 28sec) *and 10,000m* (* 6 miles time plus 60sec): 1965 – —, 31:18.4*; 1966 – 14:57.2*, 31:14.0*; 1967 – 14:15.8*, 30:11.8*; 1968 – 14:35.2*, —; 1969 – 14:03.2, 29:20.6; 1970 – 14:18.0, 29:28.0; 1971 – 14:20.0, —; 1972 – 13:40.2, 28:34.6; 1973 – 13:38.2, 28:01.6; 1974 – 13:28.8, 28:19.4.

RAY SMEDLEY
Birchfield H. *Born* Sutton Coldfield, 3.9.1951; *Height:* 1.83m (6' 0"), *Weight:* 70kg (155lb); Student. *Best performances:* 800m – 1:50.6, 1500m – 3:38.5, Mile –

3:57.7, 2 miles – 8:25.6, 5000m – 14:04.2. *Annual progression at 1500m* (★ mile time less 18sec): 1966 – 4:28.0★; 1967 – 4:05.8★; 1968 – 4:00.4★; 1969 – 3:45.8; 1970 – 3:53.0; 1971 – 3:45.0; 1972 – 3:38.5; 1973 – 3:42.8i; 1974 – 3:39.6.

JOYCE SMITH (née Byatt)
Barnet & District AC. *Born* London, 26.10.1937; *Height*: 1.69m (5′ 6½″), *Weight*: 54kg (119lb); Part-time clerk *Best performances*: 800m – 2:08.8, 1500m – 4:09.4, 3000m – 8:55.6 (UK record). *Championships*: 1974 European – 8th 1500m, 3rd 3000m. *Annual progression at 1500m* (★ mile time less 20sec) *and 3000m*: 1956 – 5:00.0★; 1959 – 4:36.6; 1960 – 4:41.1★; 1961 – 5:06.5★; 1965 – 4:31.5★; 1966 – 4:35.2★; 1967 – 4:44.8★; 1968 – —, 10:30.0; 1969 – 4:27.0, —; 1970 – 4:29.2, 9:52.2; 1971 – 4:25.2, 9:23.4; 1972 – 4:09.4, 9:05.8; 1973 – 4:15.1, 9:08.0; 1974 – 4:12.0, 8:55.6.

ROY SNOW
Harlow AC. *Born* 30.1.1948. *Best performances*: 400m hurdles – 56.6, High jump – 1.91m (6′ 3¼″), Long jump – 7.35m (24′ 1½″), Decathlon – 6472. *Annual progression at decathlon*: 1969 – 5926; 1970 – 6075; 1971 – —; 1972 – —; 1973 – 6149; 1974 – 6472.

TONY STAYNINGS
Bristol AC. *Born* 21.7.1953. *Best performances*: Mile relay leg – 4:00.8, 5000m – 13:39.0, 6 miles – 28:27.8, 3000m steeplechase – 8:45.8. *Annual progression at 5000m*: 1970 – 15:19.0; 1971 – 14:28.0; 1972 – 14:06.0; 1973 – 14:19.8; 1974 – 13:39.0.

CHRIS STEWART
Bournemouth AC. *Born* Bournemouth, 4.9.1946; *Height*: 1.75m (5′ 9″), *Weight*: 57kg (125lb); Philatelist. *Best performances*: 880y – 1:52.0, Mile – 4:00.5, 5000m – 13:38.4, 10,000m – 28:27.0, Marathon – 2:13:11.8. *Annual progression at 5000m* (★ 3 miles time plus 28sec) *and 10,000m*: 1964 – 14:54.4★, —; 1965 – 14:39.2★, 30:26.0; 1966 – —, —; 1967 – 13:48.8★, —; 1968 – 14:04.6, 29:06.0; 1969 – 13:57.4, —; 1970 – 13:49.6, —; 1971 – 13:52.2, —; 1972 – 13:44.2, —; 1973 – 13:44.6, 28:27.0; 1974 – 13:38.4, 28:54.0.

MARY STEWART
Birchfield H. *Born* Birmingham, 25.2.1956; *Height*: 1.65m (5′ 5″), *Weight*: 53kg (118lb). *Best performances*: 800m – 2:10.8, 1500m – 4:14.7. *Championships*: 1973 European Junior – 5th 1500m; 1974 Commonwealth – 4th 1500m. *Annual progression*: 1970 – 4:38.0; 1971 – 4:35.5; 1972 – 4:27.8; 1973 – 4:18.5; 1974 – 4:14.7.

WHO'S WHO IN THE BRITISH TEAM

BILL TANCRED
Birchfield H. *Born* Quetta (India), 6.8.1942; *Height:* 1.93m (6' 4"), *Weight:* 114kg (252lb); Lecturer. *Best performances:* Shot – 19.43m (63' 9"), Discus – 64.94m (213' 1") (UK record), Hammer – 57.10m (187' 4"), Javelin – 63.06m (206' 10"), Decathlon – 6015. *Championships:* 1966 Commonwealth – 8th shot; 1970 Commonwealth – 3rd discus; 1974 Commonwealth – 4th shot, 2nd discus. *Annual progression at discus:* 1961 – 42.48m (139' 5"); 1962 – 42.22m (138' 6"); 1963 – 47.88m (157' 1"); 1964 – 52.08m (170' 10"); 1965 – 51.82m (170' 0"); 1966 – 55.72m (182' 10"); 1967 – 54.96m (180' 4"); 1968 – 57.26m (187' 10"); 1969 – 57.76m (189' 6"); 1970 – 56.68m (185' 11"); 1971 – 58.00m (190' 3"); 1972 – 61.94m (203' 2"); 1973 – 63.98m (209' 11"); 1974 – 64.94m (213' 1").

PETER TANCRED
Queens Park H. *Born* Quetta (India), 20.10.1949; *Height:* 1.90m (6' 3"), *Weight:* 106kg (234lb); Student. *Best performances:* Shot – 18.35m (60' 2½"), Discus – 60.16m (197' 4"), Hammer – 53.50m (175' 6"). *Annual progression at discus:* 1966 – 44.54m (146' 2"); 1967 – 45.84m (150' 5"); 1968 – 53.62m (175' 11"); 1969 – 57.56m (188' 10"); 1970 – 54.02m (177' 3"); 1971 – 51.94m (170' 5"); 1972 – 56.44m (185' 2"); 1973 – 58.04m (190' 5"); 1974 – 60.16m (197' 4").

HILARY TANNER
Kent AC. *Born* Sidcup (Kent), 10.8.1951; *Height:* 1.60m (5' 3"), *Weight:* 48kg (106lb); Teacher. *Best performances:* 400m – 58.5, 800m – 2:06.9, 1500m – 4:31.1. *Annual progression at 800m:* 1971 – 2:16.2; 1972 – 2:15.7; 1973 – 2:06.9; 1974 – 2:07.5.

GLADYS TAYLOR
Essex Ladies AC. *Born* Jamaica, 5.3.1953; *Height:* 1.78m (5' 10"), *Weight:* 63kg (140lb); Audio typist. *Best performances:* 100m – 11.9, 200m – 23.9, 400m – 55.8, 100m hurdles – 14.3, High jump – 1.66m (5' 5¼"), Long jump – 5.95m (19' 6¼"), Shot – 11.11m (36' 5½"), Pentathlon – 4088. *Annual progression at pentathlon* (★ old tables): 1969 – 3871★; 1970 – 3989★; 1971 – 4265★ (3710); 1972 – —; 1973 – 4088; 1974 – 4021.

TONY TAYLOR
Blackburn H. *Born* 3.6.1947. *Best performances:* 3000m walk – 12:45.6, 20km walk – 1:33:18. *Annual progression at 20km walk:* 1970 – 1:34:13; 1971 – 1:33:52; 1972 – —; 1973 – —; 1974 – 1:33:18.

CLIVE THOMAS
Thames Valley H. *Born* Bridgend (Wales), 27.3.1947; *Height:* 1.85m (6' 1"), *Weight:* 65kg (144lb); Teacher. *Best performances:* 800m – 1:51.2, 1500m – 3:43.6, Mile – 4:01.0, 5000m – 14:10.6, 3000m steeplechase – 8:38.2. *Annual progression at 1500m* (★ mile time less 18sec): 1970 – 3:48.5; 1971 – 3:46.9; 1972 – 3:47.9; 1973 – 3:44.2★; 1974 – 3:43.6.

BLONDELLE THOMPSON
Birchfield H. *Born* St Kitts (West Indies), 5.9.1953; *Height:* 1.68m (5' 6"), *Weight:* 59kg (130lb); Video display operator. *Best performances:* 100m – 11.8w and 11.9, 200m – 24.3, 100m hurdles – 13.0 (UK record). *Annual progression at 100m hurdles:* 1970 – 14.6; 1971 – 14.6w; 1972 – 14.3; 1973 – 14.0; 1974 – 13.0.

IAN THOMPSON
Luton United H. *Born* Birkenhead, 16.10.1949; *Height:* 1.69m (5' 6½"), *Weight:* 60kg (131lb); Salesman. *Best performances:* 1500m – 3:51.0, 5000m – 14:05.4, 10,000m – 30:10.0, Marathon – 2:09.12 (European best). *Championships:* 1974 Commonwealth – 1st marathon; 1974 European – 1st marathon. *Annual progression:* 1973 – 2:12:40; 1974 – 2:09:12.

JANET THOMPSON
Bracknell AC. *Born* Woking (Surrey), 21.2.1954; *Height:* 1.85m (6' 1"), *Weight:* 84kg (185lb); Student. *Best performances:* Shot – 12.97m (42' 6¾"), Discus – 49.94m (163' 10"). *Annual progression at discus:* 1968 – 33.40m (109' 7"); 1969 – 35.96m (118' 0"); 1970 – 42.32m (138' 10"); 1971 – 45.64m (149' 9"); 1972 – 44.72m (146' 9"); 1973 – 48.28m (158' 5"); 1974 – 49.94m (163' 10").

ROY THORPE
Sheffield United H. *Born* York, 18.5.1934; *Height:* 1.73m (5' 8"), *Weight:* 60kg (132lb); Transport driver. *Best performances:* 20km walk – 1:30:16, 50km walk – 4:24:08. *Championships:* 1974 Commonwealth – 2nd 20 miles walk. *Annual progression at 50km walk:* 1966 – 4:59:35; 1967 – 4:56:40; 1968 – 5:06:39; 1969 – 4:42:39; 1970 – —; 1971 – 4:40:46; 1972 – 4:30:42; 1973 – 4:25:42; 1974 – 4:24:08.

CHRISTINE TRANTER
Stretford AC. *Born* Manchester, 30.3.1955; *Height:* 1.60m (5' 3"), *Weight:* 55kg (122lb); Student. *Best performances:*

400m – 58.5, 800m – 2:09.0, 1500m – 4:22.8. *Annual progression at 1500m:* 1970 – 4:45.9; 1971 – 4:52.5; 1972 – —; 1973 – 4:25.2; 1974 – 4:22.8.

DAVE TRAVIS

Surrey AC. *Born* Twickenham (Middx), 9.9.1945; *Height:* 1.83m (6' 0"), *Weight:* 86kg (190lb); Teacher. *Best performances:* 100m – 10.9w, 110m hurdles – 15.7, Pole vault – 3.60m (11' 9¼"), Triple jump – 14.15m (46' 5"), Javelin – 83.44m (273' 9"), Decathlon – 7067. *Championships:* (all javelin) 1966 Commonwealth – 6th; 1970 Commonwealth – 1st; 1974 Commonwealth – 2nd. *Annual progression:* 1961 – 52.58m (172' 6"); 1962 – 58.56m (192' 2"); 1963 – 64.64m (212' 1"); 1964 – 70.68m (231' 11"); 1965 – 76.44m (250' 10"); 1966 – 73.48m (241' 1"); 1967 – 76.98m (252' 7"); 1968 – 79.24m (260' 0"); 1969 – 81.68m (268' 0"); 1970 – 83.44m (273' 9"); 1971 – 81.76m (268' 3"); 1972 – 80.70m (264' 9"); 1973 – 81.06m (265' 11"); 1974 – 82.38m (270' 3").

GRENVILLE TUCK

Cambridge & Coleridge AC. *Born* Cambridge, 22.11.1950; *Height:* 1.73m (5' 8"), *Weight:* 54kg (119lb); Sports shop assistant. *Best performances:* 3000m – 7:58.4, 5000m – 13:56.8, 10,000m – 28:25.8, Marathon – 2:26:41. *Annual progression at 10,000m* (* 6 miles time plus 60sec): 1969 – 32:42.6*; 1970 – —; 1971 – 28:53.0; 1972 – 29:04.4; 1973 – 28:43.4; 1974 – 28:25.8.

JUDY VERNON (née Toeneboehn)

Mitcham AC. *Born* St Louis (USA), 25.9.1945; *Height:* 1.69m (5' 6½"), *Weight:* 59kg (130lb); Teacher. *Best performances:* 100m – 11.8, 200m – 23.6, 400m – 55.0, 100m hurdles – 12.9w and 13.0 (UK record), 400m hurdles – 59.9, High jump – 1.64m (5' 4½"), Long jump – 6.18m (20' 3½"), Shot – 11.34m (37' 2½"), Pentathlon – 4079. *Championships:* 1974 Commonwealth – 1st 100m hurdles, 2nd 4 × 100m. *Annual progression at 100m hurdles:* 1969 – 14.8; 1970 – 14.0; 1971 – 14.2; 1972 – 13.2; 1973 – 13.3; 1974 – 12.9w.

Bill Tancred, here setting a new British discus mark in 1972, has been adding inches to the record ever since.

WHO'S WHO IN THE BRITISH TEAM

GARY VINCE
Cardiff AAC. *Born* 22.9.1949. *Best performances:* 100m –
10.4w and 10.5, 200m – 21.5. *Annual progression at 100m:*
1969 – 10.7; 1970 – 10.6w; 1971 – 10.6w; 1972 – 10.6w;
1973 – 10.4w; 1974 – 10.6w.

CHRISTINE WARDEN (née Howell)
City of Hull AC. *Born* Cottingham (Yorks), 26.12.1950;
Height: 1.69m (5' 6½"), *Weight:* 58kg (128lb); Bank clerk.
Best performances: 200m – 24.7, 400m – 53.8, 400m hurdles –
58.0 (UK record). *Annual progression at 400m and 400m
hurdles:* 1967 – 58.9; 1968 – 57.3; 1969 – 56.8; 1970 – 55.0;
1971 – 55.1, —; 1972 – 55.7, —; 1973 – 55.6, 60.3;
1974 – 53.8, 58.0.

JOHN WARHURST
Sheffield United H. *Born* Sheffield, 1.10.1944; *Height:*
1.68m (5' 6"), *Weight:* 57kg (126lb); Nurseryman. *Best
performances:* 20km walk – 1:29:37, 50km walk – 4:12:37.
Championships: 1974 Commonwealth – 1st 20 miles walk.
Annual progression at 50km walk: 1969 – 4:28:58; 1970 –
4:26:44; 1971 – 4:28:36; 1972 – 4:12:37; 1973 – —;
1974 – 4:18:58.

RUTH WATT
Edinburgh Southern H. *Born* Hawick (Scotland),
16.11.1949; *Height:* 1.69m (5' 6½"), *Weight:* 54kg (119lb);
Teacher. *Best performance:* High jump – 1.80m (5' 10¾").
Championships: 1974 Commonwealth – 4th. *Annual
progression:* 1965 – 1.55m (5' 1"); 1966 – 1.57m (5' 2");
1967 – 1.64m (5' 4½"); 1968 – 1.57m (5' 2"); 1969 – 1.60m
(5' 3"); 1970 – 1.58m (5' 2¼"); 1971 – 1.73m (5' 8"); 1972 –
1.71m (5' 7¼"); 1973 – 1.77m (5' 9¾"); 1974 – 1.80m
(5' 10¾").

RAY WEATHERBURN
Edinburgh Southern H. *Born* 30.4.1949; Teacher. *Best
performances:* 800m – 1:50.4, 1500m – 3:45.2. *Annual
progression at 800m:* 1972 – 1:53.5; 1973 – 1:51.7; 1974 –
1:50.4.

RICKY WILDE
Manchester & District H. *Born* Ashton-under-Lyne
(Lancs), 13.10.1945; *Height:* 1.84m (6' 0½"), *Weight:* 63kg
(140lb); Draughtsman. *Best performances:* 800m – 1:52.5,
Mile – 4:01.5, 3000m – 7:47.0i, 5000m – 13:30.8, 10,000m
– 29:12.8, Marathon – 2:20:50. *Championships:* 1970

Ruth Watt.

European Indoor – 1st 3000m. *Annual progression at 5000m*
(★ 3 miles time plus 28sec): 1964 – 15:58.0★; 1965 – —;
1966 – 15:23.0★; 1967 – 14:23.6★; 1968 – 13:44.0; 1969 –
13:45.4; 1970 – —; 1971 – 14:07.8; 1972 – 13:30.8;
1973 – —; 1974 – 13:42.6.

ALLAN WILLIAMS
Cambridge H. *Born* London, 30.5.1953; *Height:* 1.75m
(5' 9"), *Weight:* 72kg (160lb); Student. *Best performance:*
Pole vault – 4.90m (16' 1"). *Annual progression:* 1969 –
3.37m (11' 0¾"); 1970 – 3.81m (12' 6"); 1971 – 4.42m
(14' 6")i; 1972 – 4.60m (15' 1"); 1973 – 4.75m (15' 7");
1974 – 4.90m (16' 1").

MARGARET WILLIAMS (née Critchley)
Bristol AC. *Born* Bristol, 4.4.1949; *Height:* 1.60m (5' 3"),
Weight: 51kg (112lb); Bank clerk. *Best performances:*
100m – 11.3w and 11.6, 200m – 23.1w and 23.2, 400m –
54.7. *Championships:* 1970 Commonwealth – 3rd 200m,
2nd 4×100m. *Annual progression at 200m:* 1963 – 26.7;
1964 – 25.7; 1965 – 25.3; 1966 – 24.7; 1967 – 23.9;
1968 – —; 1969 – 23.9; 1970 – 23.1w; 1971 – 23.7; 1972 –
23.3w; 1973 – —; 1974 – 23.1w.

ANN WILSON
Southend AC. *Born* Rochford (Essex), 29.9.1949; *Height:*
1.70m (5' 7"), *Weight:* 58kg (128lb); Bank clerk. *Best
performances:* 200m – 24.4, 100m hurdles – 13.2w and 13.3,
High jump – 1.77m (5' 9¾"), Long jump – 6.57m
(21' 6¾")w and 6.55m (21' 6"), Shot – 11.75m (38' 6¾"),

225

Pentathlon – 4433. *Championships:* 1966 Commonwealth – 6th 80m hurdles, 7th high jump; 1970 Commonwealth – 2nd high jump, 2nd long jump, 2nd pentathlon; 1974 Commonwealth – 7th high jump, 3rd pentathlon. *Annual progression at long jump and pentathlon* (★ old tables): 1963 – 5.03m (16′ 6½″), —; 1964 – 5.74m (18′ 10″)w, —; 1965 – 5.97m (19′ 7″), 4302★; 1966 – 6.22m (20′ 5″), 4676★; 1967 – 6.26m (20′ 6½″), 4605★; 1968 – 6.41m (21′ 0¼″)w, 4841★; 1969 – 6.18m (20′ 3¾″), 4614★; 1970 – 6.57m (21′ 6¾″)w, 5037★ (4426); 1971 – 6.50m (21′ 4″)w, 4298; 1972 – 6.53m (21′ 5¼″)w, 4433; 1973 – 6.12m (20′ 1″)i, 4011; 1974 – 6.30m (20′ 8″)w, 4248.

DAVE WILSON
Edinburgh AC. *Born* Edinburgh, 7.9.1951; *Height:* 1.90m (6′ 3″), *Weight:* 81kg (178lb); Student. *Best performances:* 110m hurdles – 13.9, High jump – 2.05m (6′ 8¾″), Decathlon – 6731. *Championships:* 1970 Commonwealth – 7th high jump. *Annual progression at 110m hurdles:* 1969 – 15.0w; 1970 – 14.6w; 1971 – 14.2; 1972 – 14.0; 1973 – 14.3w; 1974 – 13.9.

JOHN WILSON
Queens Park H. *Born* London, 11.10.1948; *Height:* 1.79m (5′ 10½″), *Weight:* 68kg (150lb); Teacher. *Best performances:* 100m – 10.6w, 200m – 21.3, 400m – 46.3. *Championships:* 1974 Commonwealth – 2nd 4 × 400m. *Annual progression at 400m:* 1965 – 49.2; 1966 – 48.1; 1967 – 48.0; 1968 – 47.1; 1969 – 47.7; 1970 – 47.6; 1971 – 47.1; 1972 – 47.5; 1973 – 46.3; 1974 – 46.9.

MIKE WINCH
Brighton & Hove AC. *Born* Que-Que (Rhodesia), 20.7.1948; *Height:* 1.82m (5′ 11½″), *Weight:* 105kg (231lb); Teacher. *Best performances:* Shot – 20.43m (67′ 0½″), Discus – 57.42m (188′ 5″). *Championships:* 1974 Commonwealth – 2nd shot. *Annual progression:* 1965 – 13.41m (44′ 0″); 1966 – 14.25m (46′ 9″); 1967 – 14.82m (48′ 7½″); 1968 – 14.59m (47′ 10½″); 1969 – 15.01m (49′ 3″); 1970 – 15.90m (52′ 2″); 1971 – 17.06m (55′ 11½″); 1972 – 18.66m (61′ 2¾″)i; 1973 – 19.82m (65′ 0½″)i; 1974 – 20.43m (67′ 0½″).

ROSEMARY WRIGHT (née Stirling)
Wolverhampton & Bilston AC. *Born* Timaru (New Zealand), 11.12.1947; *Height:* 1.57m (5′ 2″), *Weight:* 52kg (114lb); Teacher. *Best performances:* 200m – 24.7, 400m – 53.2, 800m – 2:00.2 (UK record), 1500m – 4:24.7.

Championships: 1966 Commonwealth – 4th 440y, 4th 880y; 1969 European Indoor – 3rd 400m; 1969 European – 8th 400m, 1st 4 × 400m; 1970 Commonwealth – 1st 800m; 1971 European Indoor – 3rd 800m; 1971 European – 3rd 800m; 1972 Olympics – 7th 800m. *Annual progression at 800m and 1500m* (★mile time less 20sec): 1962 – 2:34.2; 1963 – 2:26.2; 1964 – 2:14.7; 1965 – 2:13.1; 1966 – 2:04.6, 5:03.0★; 1967 – 2:09.8; 1968 – 2:06.6; 1969 – 2:05.1; 1970 – 2:04.2; 1971 – 2:02.1; 1972 – 2:00.2; 1973 – 2:03.9, 4:34.3i; 1974 – 2:03.9, 4:24.7.

SUE WRIGHT
Essex Ladies AC. *Born* Epping (Essex), 22.1.1950; *Height:* 1.80m (5′ 11″), *Weight:* 70kg (154lb); Secretary. *Best performances:* 200m – 24.7, 100m hurdles – 14.1, High jump – 1.80m (5′ 10¾″), Long jump – 6.18m (20′ 3½″), Pentathlon – 4192. *Annual progression at high jump and pentathlon* (★old tables): 1964 – 1.50m (4′ 11″); 1965 – 1.57m (5′ 2″); 1966 – 1.52m (5′ 0″); 1967 – —; 1968 – 1.58m (5′ 2¼″), 3918★; 1969 – 1.61m (5′ 3¼″); 1970 – 1.70m (5′ 7″); 1971 – 1.75m (5′ 8¾″)i; 1972 – 1.76m (5′ 9¼″); 1973 – 1.76m (5′ 9¼″); 1974 – 1.80m (5′ 10¾″), 4192.

ANN YEOMAN
Feltham AC. *Born* Isleworth (Middx), 30.3.1952; *Height:* 1.66m (5′ 5½″), *Weight:* 49kg (108lb); Clerk/typist. *Best performances:* 1500m – 4:18.5, 3000m – 9:07.0. *Championships:* 1974 European – 7th 3000m. *Annual progression:* 1972 – 9:30.8; 1973 – 9:29.2; 1974 – 9:07.0.

PAULA YEOMAN
Feltham AC. *Born* Isleworth (Middx), 30.3.1952; *Height:* 1.68m (5′ 6″), *Weight:* 54kg (120lb); Clerk/typist. *Best performances:* 800m – 2:09.9, 1500m – 4:19.0, 3000m – 9:19.8. *Annual progression at 1500m:* 1969 – 4:42.1; 1970 – 4:43.1; 1971 – 4:28.2; 1972 – 4:30.7; 1973 – 4:31.8; 1974 – 4:19.0.

CHRIS YOUNGS
Worthing AC. *Born* Shoreham (Sussex), 8.7.1952; *Height:* 1.93m (6′ 4″), *Weight:* 95kg (210lb); Student. *Best performances:* 110m hurdles – 15.3w, High jump – 1.93m (6′ 4″), Decathlon – 6694. *Annual progression at decathlon:* 1971 – 5405; 1972 – —; 1973 – —; 1974 – 6694.

Records

(W) World; (E) European; (C) Commonwealth; (UK) United Kingdom; (EJ) European Junior; (J) UK Junior.

MEN

100 METRES

(W) 9.9	Jim Hines (USA); 1968
	Ronnie Ray Smith (USA); 1968
	Charlie Greene (USA); 1968
	Eddie Hart (USA); 1972
	Rey Robinson (USA); 1972
	Steve Williams (USA); 1974
(E) 10.0	Armin Hary (WG); 1960
	Roger Bambuck (Fra); 1968
	Vladislav Sapeya (Sov); 1968
	Valeriy Borzov (Sov); 1969
	Gerd Metz (WG); 1970
	Manfred Kokot (EG); 1971
	Vasilios Papageorgopoulos (Gre); 1972
	Pietro Mennea (Ita); 1972
	Raimo Vilen (Fin); 1972
	Aleksandr Kornelyuk (Sov); 1973
	Michael Droese (EG); 1973
	Hans-Jurgen Bombach (EG); 1973
	Siegfried Schenke (EG); 1973
	Manfred Ommer (WG); 1974
(C) 10.0	Harry Jerome (Can); 1960
	Lennox Miller (Jam); 1968
	Don Quarrie (Jam); 1974
(UK) 10.1	Brian Green; 1972
(EJ) 10.1	Aleksandr Kornelyuk (Sov); 1969
	Franz-Peter Hofmeister (WG); 1970
	Hans-Joachim Zenk (EG); 1971
(J) 10.3	Peter Radford; 1958

100 YARDS

(W) 9.0	Ivory Crockett (USA); 1974
(E) 9.2	Chris Garpenborg (Swe); 1974
	Manfred Ommer (WG); 1974
(C) 9.1	Harry Jerome (Can); 1966
(UK) 9.4	Peter Radford; 1960

200 METRES

(W) 19.8	Tommie Smith (USA); 1968
	Don Quarrie (Jam); 1971
(E) 20.0	Valeriy Borzov (Sov); 1972
(C) 19.8	Don Quarrie (Jam); 1971
(UK) 20.3	David Jenkins; 1972
(EJ) 20.4	Jorg Pfeifer (EG); 1971
(J) 20.7	Ralph Banthorpe; 1968
	David Jenkins; 1971

220 YARDS

(W) 20.0	Tommie Smith (USA); 1966
(E) 20.5	Peter Radford (UK); 1960
(C) 20.2	Carl Lawson (Jam); 1973
	Don Quarrie (Jam); 1973

400 METRES

(W) 43.8	Lee Evans (USA); 1968
(E) 44.7	Karl Honz (WG); 1972
(C) 44.9	Julius Sang (Ken); 1972
(UK) 45.2	David Jenkins; 1973–74
(EJ) 45.5	David Jenkins (UK); 1971

440 YARDS

(W) 44.5	John Smith (USA); 1971
(E) 45.9	Robbie Brightwell (UK); 1962
(C) 45.2	Wendell Mottley (Tri); 1966

800 METRES

(W, E) 1:43.7	Marcello Fiasconaro (Ita); 1973
(C) 1:43.9	John Kipkurgat (Ken); 1974
(UK) 1:45.1	Andy Carter; 1973
(EJ) 1:45.8	Steve Ovett (UK); 1974

ATHLETICS 75

880 YARDS

(W) 1:44.1   Rick Wohlhuter (USA); 1974
(E) 1:46.7   Jozef Plachy (Cze); 1970
(C) 1:45.1   Peter Snell (NZ); 1962
(UK) 1:47.2   Chris Carter; 1968

1000 METRES

(W) 2:13.9   Rick Wohlhuter (USA); 1974
(E) 2:16.2   Jurgen May (EG); 1965
               Franz-Josef Kemper (WG); 1966
(C) 2:16.4   Mike Boit (Ken); 1973
(UK) 2:18.2   John Boulter; 1969

1500 METRES

(W, C) 3:32.2   Filbert Bayi (Tan); 1974
(E) 3:34.0   Jean Wadoux (Fra); 1970
(UK) 3:37.4   Frank Clement; 1974
(EJ) 3:39.0   Gheorghe Ghipu (Rom); 1973
(J) 3:43.1   Paul Lawther; 1974

MILE

(W) 3:51.1   Jim Ryun (USA); 1967
(E) 3:53.6   Michel Jazy (Fra); 1965
(C) 3:52.0   Ben Jipcho (Ken); 1973
(UK) 3:55.3   Peter Stewart; 1972
(J) 3:59.4   Steve Ovett; 1974

2000 METRES

(W, E) 4:56.2   Michel Jazy (Fra); 1966
(C) 5:03.2   Dave Bedford (UK); 1972

3000 METRES

(W, E, C) 7:35.2   Brendan Foster (UK); 1974
(EJ) 8:00.8   Dave Black (UK); 1971

2 MILES

(W, E, C) 8:13.8   Brendan Foster (UK); 1973

3 MILES

(W, E) 12:47.8   Emiel Puttemans (Bel); 1972
(C) 12:50.4   Ron Clarke (Aus); 1966
(UK) 12:58.2   Dave Bedford; 1971

5000 METRES

(W, E) 13:13.0   Emiel Puttemans (Bel); 1972
(C) 13:14.4   Ben Jipcho (Ken); 1974
(UK) 13:14.6   Brendan Foster; 1974
(EJ) 13:37.4   Dave Black (UK); 1971

6 MILES

(W, C) 26:47.0   Ron Clarke (Aus); 1965
(E) 26:51.6   Dave Bedford (UK); 1971

10,000 METRES

(W, E, C) 27:30.8   Dave Bedford (UK); 1973

10 MILES

(W, E) 46:04.2   Willy Polleunis (Bel); 1972
(C) 46:37.4   Jerome Drayton (Can); 1970
(UK) 46:44.0   Ron Hill; 1968

20,000 METRES

(W, E) 57:44.4   Gaston Roelants (Bel); 1972
(C) 58:39.0   Ron Hill (UK); 1968

1 HOUR

(W, E) 20,784m   Gaston Roelants (Bel); 1972
(C) 20,472m   Ron Hill (UK); 1968

15 MILES

(W, E) 1:12:22.6   Seppo Nikkari (Fin); 1973
(C) 1:12:48.2   Ron Hill (UK); 1965

25,000 METRES

(W, E) 1:14:55.6   Seppo Nikkari (Fin); 1973
(C) 1:15:22.6   Ron Hill (UK); 1965

30,000 METRES

(W, E, C) 1:31:30.4 Jim Alder (UK); 1970

MARATHON (Best Performances)

(W, C) 2:08:34   Derek Clayton (Aus); 1969
(E) 2:09:12   Ian Thompson (UK); 1974

2000 METRES STEEPLECHASE

(EJ) 5:28.2　　Frank Baumgartl (EG); 1973
(J) 5:41.4　　　David Long; 1973

3000 METRES STEEPLECHASE

(W, C) 8:14.0　Ben Jipcho (Ken); 1973
(E) 8:14.2　　　Anders Garderud (Swe); 1974
(UK) 8:22.6　　John Davies; 1974

120 YARDS HURDLES

(W) 13.0　　Rod Milburn (USA); 1971–73
(E) 13.2　　Martin Lauer (WG); 1959
　　　　　　Guy Drut (Fra); 1974
(C) 13.4　　Danny Smith (Bah); 1974
(UK) 13.5　　Berwyn Price; 1973

110 METRES HURDLES

(W) 13.1　　Rod Milburn (USA); 1973
(E) 13.2　　Martin Lauer (WG); 1959
　　　　　　Guy Drut (Fra); 1974
(C) 13.5　　Berwyn Price (UK); 1973

200 METRES HURDLES

(W) 22.5　　Martin Lauer (WG); 1959
　　　　　　Glenn Davis (USA); 1960
(E) 22.5　　Martin Lauer (WG); 1959
(C) 22.7　　Jim McCann (Aus); 1966
(UK) 23.0　　Alan Pascoe; 1969

400 METRES HURDLES

(W, C) 47.8　John Akii-Bua (Uga); 1972
(E) 48.1　　David Hemery (UK); 1968
(EJ) 50.1　　Jerzy Pietrzyk (Pol); 1973
(J) 51.1　　Andy Todd; 1967

440 YARDS HURDLES

(W) 48.7　　Jim Bolding (USA); 1974
(E) 49.4　　Miroslav Kodejs (Cze); 1974
(C) 49.7　　Gert Potgieter (SA); 1958
(UK) 50.2　　David Hemery; 1968

HIGH JUMP

(W) 2.30m　　Dwight Stones (USA); 1973
(E) 2.28m　　Valeriy Brumel (Sov); 1963
(C) 2.24m　　John Beers (Can); 1973
(UK) 2.11m　　Colin Boreham; 1974
(EJ) 2.25m　　Valeriy Brumel (Sov); 1961
(J) 2.05m　　David Wilson; 1970
　　　　　　　David Livesey; 1970

POLE VAULT

(W) 5.63m　　Bob Seagren (USA); 1972
(E) 5.55m　　Kjell Isaksson (Swe); 1972
(C) 5.34m　　Kirk Bryde (Can); 1972
(UK) 5.25m　　Mike Bull; 1973
(EJ) 5.40m　　Francois Tracanelli (Fra); 1970
(J) 5.10m　　Brian Hooper; 1972

LONG JUMP

(W) 8.90m　　Bob Beamon (USA); 1968
(E) 8.35m　　Igor Ter-Ovanesyan (Sov); 1967
　　　　　　　Josef Schwarz (WG); 1970
(C) 8.23m　　Lynn Davies (UK); 1968
(EJ) 7.96m　　Gerard Ugolini (Fra); 1968
　　　　　　　Grzegorz Cybulski (Pol); 1970
(J) 7.45m　　Angus McKenzie; 1972

TRIPLE JUMP

(W, E) 17.44m　Viktor Saneyev (Sov); 1972
(C) 17.02m　　Phil May (Aus); 1968
(UK) 16.46m　　Fred Alsop; 1964
(EJ) 16.47m　　Sergey Chaplygin (Sov); 1974
(J) 15.80m　　David Johnson; 1972

SHOT

(W) 21.82m　　Al Feuerbach (USA); 1973
(E) 21.70m　　Aleksandr Baryshnikov (Sov); 1974
(C) 21.37m　　Geoff Capes (UK); 1974
(EJ) 20.20m　　Udo Beyer (EG); 1974
(J) 16.80m　　Geoff Capes; 1968

DISCUS

(W) 68.40m　　Jay Silvester (USA); 1968
　　　　　　　Ricky Bruch (Swe); 1972
(E) 68.40m　　Ricky Bruch (Swe); 1972
(C) 64.94m　　Bill Tancred (UK); 1974
(EJ) 62.04m　　Kent Gardenkrans (Swe); 1974
(J) 51.10m　　Mike Lindsay; 1957

HAMMER

(W, E) 76.66m   Aleksey Spiridonov (Sov); 1974
(C) 71.26m   Barry Williams (UK); 1973
(EJ) 70.86m   Yuriy Sedykh (Sov); 1974
(J) 64.14m   Ian Chipchase; 1971

JAVELIN

(W, E) 94.08m   Klaus Wolfermann (WG); 1973
(C) 84.92m   Charles Clover (UK); 1974
(EJ) 84.92m   Charles Clover (UK); 1974

DECATHLON

(W, E) 8454   Nikolay Avilov (Sov); 1972
(C) 7903   Peter Gabbett (UK); 1971
(EJ) 7842   Josef Zeilbauer (Aut); 1971
(J) 7088   Roy Mitchell; 1974

4 × 100 METRES RELAY

(W) 38.2   United States; 1968–72
(E) 38.4   France; 1968
(C) 38.3   Jamaica; 1968
(UK) 39.3   National Team; 1968
(EJ) 39.5   East Germany; 1973
(J) 40.8   National Team; 1968

4 × 110 YARDS RELAY

(W) 38.6   Univ. of S. California; 1967
(E) 40.0   United Kingdom; 1963
(C) 39.8   Ghana; 1966

4 × 200 METRES RELAY

(W, E) 1:21.5   Italy; 1972
(C) 1:22.5   Trinidad and Tobago; 1972
(UK) 1:24.1   National Team; 1971

4 × 220 YARDS RELAY

(W) 1:21.5   Texas A and M University; 1970

4 × 400 METRES RELAY

(W) 2:56.1   United States; 1968
(E) 3:00.5   West Germany; 1968
                Poland; 1968
                United Kingdom; 1972
(C) 2:59.6   Kenya; 1968
(EJ) 3:06.8   East Germany; 1973
(J) 3:07.3   National Team; 1973

4 × 440 YARDS RELAY

(W, C) 3:02.8   Trinidad and Tobago; 1966
(E) 3:06.5   England; 1966

4 × 800 METRES RELAY

(W, E) 7:08.6   West Germany; 1966
(C) 7:11.6   Kenya; 1970
(UK) 7:17.4   National Team; 1970

4 × 880 YARDS RELAY

(W) 7:10.4   Univ. of Chicago TC; 1973
(E) 7:14.6   West Germany; 1968
(C) 7:11.6   Kenya; 1970
(UK) 7:17.4   National Team; 1970

4 × 1500 METRES RELAY

(W, C) 14:40.4 New Zealand; 1973
(E) 14:49.0   France; 1965
(UK) 15:06.6   National Team; 1971

4 × MILE RELAY

(W, C) 16:02.8 New Zealand; 1972
(E) 16:09.6   West Germany; 1969
(UK) 16:24.8   Northern Counties; 1961

3000 METRES WALK

(C) 11:51.2   Paul Nihill (UK) 1971
(J) 12:42.0   Barry Lines; 1974

2 MILES WALK

(C) 13:02.4   Stan Vickers (UK); 1960

5 MILES WALK

(C) 34:21.2   Ken Matthews (UK); 1959

10,000 METRES WALK

(C) 41:55.6   Phil Embleton (UK); 1971
(EJ) 42:39.0   Karl-Heinz Stadtmuller; (EG) 1971
(J) 45:20.0   Jacky Lord; 1974

7 MILES WALK

(C) 48:22.2   Ken Matthews (UK); 1964

RECORDS

ONE HOUR WALK

(C) 13,960m   Phil Embleton (UK); 1972

10 MILES WALK

(C) 1:09:40.6   Ken Matthews (UK); 1964

20,000 METRES WALK

(W, E) 1:24:45.0   Bernd Kannenberg (WG); 1974
(C) 1:28:45.8   Ken Matthews (UK); 1964

2 HOURS WALK

(W, E) 27,154m   Bernd Kannenberg (WG); 1974
(C) 26,118m   Ted Allsopp (Aus); 1956
(UK) 26,037m   Ron Wallwork; 1971

30,000 METRES WALK

(W, E) 2:12:58.0   Bernd Kannenberg (WG); 1974
(C) 2:24:18.2   Roy Thorpe (UK); 1974

20 MILES WALK

(W, E) 2:30:38.6   Gerhard Weidner (WG); 1974
(C) 2:34:25.4   John Warhurst (UK); 1974

30 MILES WALK

(W, E) 3:51:48.6   Gerhard Weidner (WG); 1973
(C) 4:02:49.2   Bob Dobson (UK); 1974

50 KILOMETRES WALK

(W, E) 4:00:27.2   Gerhard Weidner (WG); 1973
(C) 4:11:22.0   Bob Dobson (UK); 1974

WOMEN

60 METRES

(W) 7.2   Betty Cuthbert (Aus); 1960
         Irina Bochkaryova (Sov); 1960
         Andrea Lynch (UK); 1974
(E) 7.2   Irina Bochkaryova (Sov); 1960
         Andrea Lynch (UK); 1974
(C) 7.2   Betty Cuthbert (Aus); 1960
         Andrea Lynch (UK); 1974

100 YARDS

(W) 10.0   Chi Cheng (Tai); 1970
(E) 10.6   Heather Young (UK); 1958
         Dorothy Hyman (UK); 1962–64
         Mary Rand (UK); 1964
         Daphne Arden (UK); 1964
(C) 10.3   Marlene Willard (Aus); 1958

100 METRES

(W, E) 10.8   Renate Stecher (EG); 1973
(C) 11.1   Raelene Boyle (Aus); 1968–71
         Alice Annum (Gha); 1971
         Andrea Lynch (UK); 1974
(EJ) 11.2   Monika Meyer (EG); 1971
(J) 11.3   Sonia Lannaman; 1974

200 METRES

(W, E) 22.0   Irena Szewinska (Pol); 1974
(C) 22.5   Raelene Boyle (Aus); 1972–74
(UK) 23.0   Helen Golden; 1974
(EJ) 22.9   Barbel Eckert (EG); 1973
(J) 23.5   Donna Murray; 1972

220 YARDS

(W) 22.6   Chi Cheng (Tai); 1970
(E) 22.8   Irena Szewinska (Pol); 1974
(C) 22.9   Margaret Burvill (Aus); 1964
(UK) 23.6   Daphne Arden; 1964

400 METRES

(W, E) 49.9   Irena Szewinska (Pol); 1974
(C) 51.0   Marilyn Neufville (Jam); 1970
(UK) 51.8   Donna Murray; 1974
(EJ) 52.1   Brigitte Rohde (EG); 1972
(J) 52.3   Marilyn Neufville; 1970

ATHLETICS 75

440 YARDS

(W) 52.2	Kathy Hammond (USA); 1972
	Debra Sapenter (USA); 1974
(E) 53.7	Maria Itkina (Sov); 1959
(C) 52.4	Judy Pollock (Aus); 1965
(UK) 54.1	Deirdre Watkinson; 1966

800 METRES

(W, E) 1:57.5	Svetla Zlateva (Bul); 1973
(C) 2:00.2	Rosemary Stirling (UK); 1972
	Abigail Hoffman (Can); 1972
(EJ) 2:02.7	Barbara Wieck (EG); 1969
(J) 2:02.8	Lesley Kiernan; 1974

880 YARDS

(W, C) 2:02.0	Dixie Willis (Aus); 1962
	Judy Pollock (Aus); 1967
(E) 2:03.0	Vera Nikolic (Yug); 1967
(UK) 2:04.2	Anne Smith; 1966

1500 METRES

(W, E) 4:01.4	Lyudmila Bragina (Sov); 1972
(C) 4:04.8	Sheila Carey (UK); 1972
(EJ) 4:07.5	Inger Knutsson (Swe); 1973
(J) 4:14.7	Mary Stewart; 1974

MILE

(W, E) 4:29.5	Paola Cacchi (Ita); 1973
(C) 4:34.9	Glenda Reiser (Can); 1973
(UK) 4:36.2	Joan Allison; 1973

3000 METRES

(W, E) 8:52.8	Lyudmila Bragina (Sov); 1974
(C) 8:55.6	Joyce Smith (UK); 1974

100 METRES HURDLES

(W, E) 12.3	Annelie Ehrhardt (EG); 1973
(C) 12.5	Pam Ryan (Aus); 1972
(UK) 13.0	Judy Vernon; 1974
	Blondelle Thompson; 1974
(EJ) 13.1	Barbel Eckert (EG); 1973
(J) 13.7	Chris Perera; 1967

Rosemary Payne went out of athletics in 1974 while she was still at the top: leading British discus thrower and still Commonwealth and UK record holder.

RECORDS

400 METRES HURDLES

(W, E) 56.5   Krystyna Kacperczyk (Pol); 1974
(C) 58.0   Christine Warden (UK); 1974

HIGH JUMP

(W, E) 1.95m   Rosemarie Witschas (EG); 1974
(C) 1.88m   Debbie Brill (Can); 1975
(EJ) 1.92m   Ulrike Meyfarth (WG); 1972
(J) 1.80m   Carol Mathers; 1973

LONG JUMP

(W, E) 6.84m   Heide Rosendahl (WG); 1970
(C) 6.76m   Mary Rand (UK); 1964
(EJ) 6.77m   Marianne Voelzke (EG); 1974
(J) 6.39m   Moira Walls; 1970

SHOT

(W, E) 21.57m   Helena Fibingerova (Cze); 1974
(C) 17.26m   Val Young (NZ); 1964
(UK) 16.31m   Mary Peters; 1966
(EJ) 19.23m   Ilona Schoknecht (EG); 1974
(J) 14.03m   Jenny Bloss; 1968

DISCUS

(W, E) 69.90m   Faina Melnik (Sov); 1974
(C) 58.02m   Rosemary Payne (UK); 1972
(EJ) 63.26m   Evelin Schlaak (EG); 1974
(J) 48.82m   Lesley Mallin; 1974

JAVELIN

(W, E) 67.22m   Ruth Fuchs (EG); 1974
(C) 62.24m   Petra Rivers (Aus); 1972
(UK) 55.60m   Sue Platt; 1968
(EJ) 62.54m   Jacqueline Todten (EG); 1972
(J) 55.04m   Tessa Sanderson; 1974

PENTATHLON

(W, E) 4932   Burglinde Pollak (EG); 1973
(C) 4801   Mary Peters (UK); 1972
(EJ) 4538   Barbel Muller (EG); 1974
(J) 4141   Sue Scott; 1969

4 × 110 YARDS RELAY

(W, E) 44.2   Soviet Union; 1974
(C) 45.0   United Kingdom; 1968

4 × 200 METRES RELAY

(W, E, C) 1:33.8   United Kingdom; 1968

4 × 220 YARDS RELAY

(W, C) 1:35.8   Australia; 1969
(E) 1:36.0   East Germany; 1958

4 × 400 METRES RELAY

(W, E) 3:23.0   East Germany; 1972
(C) 3:28.7   United Kingdom; 1972
(EJ) 3:34.4   East Germany; 1973
(J) 3:37.0   National Team; 1973

4 × 440 YARDS RELAY

(W) 3:33.9   United States; 1972
(E) 3:34.3   Soviet Union; 1974

4 × 800 METRES RELAY

(W, E) 8:08.6   Bulgaria; 1973
(C) 8:23.8   United Kingdom; 1971

MILE WALK

(UK) 7:36.2   Judy Farr; 1965

3000 METRES WALK

(UK) 14:33.6   Marion Fawkes; 1974

5000 METRES WALK

(UK) 24:59.2   Marion Fawkes; 1974

4 × 100 METRES RELAY

(W, E) 42.5   East Germany; 1974
(C) 43.4   Australia; 1968
(UK) 43.7   National Team; 1968–72
(EJ) 44.4   East Germany; 1973
(J) 45.4   National Team; 1973

World and British Rankings
Compiled for *Athletics 75* by the National Union of Track Statisticians

1974 World List

MEN   w = wind assisted.   i = indoor mark

100 METRES
(y = 100 yards time)

9.0y	Ivory Crockett (USA)
9.9	Steve Williams (USA)
10.0	Don Quarrie (Jam)
10.0	Silvio Leonard (Cub)
10.0	Manfred Ommer (WG)
9.2y	Chris Brathwaite (Tri)
9.2y	Marshall Dill (USA)
9.2y	Chris Garpenborg (Swe)
9.2y	Reggie Jones (USA)
9.2y	Donald Merrick (USA)
9.2y	Rey Robinson (USA)
10.1	Steve Riddick (USA)
10.1	Juris Silovs (Sov)
10.1	Marv Nash (Can)
9.3y	20 men

200 METRES
(*220 yards time less 0.1)

20.1*	Don Quarrie (Jam)
20.2	Silvio Leonard (Cub)
20.2	Hans-Joachim Zenk (EG)
20.2	Steve Williams (USA)
20.3*	John Carlos (USA-pro)
20.4*	Larry Burton (USA)
20.4*	James Gilkes (Guy)
20.4*	Charles Joseph (Tri)
20.4	Jorg Pfeiffer (EG)
20.4	Pietro Mennea (Ita)
20.5*	Dale Connolly (USA)
20.5*	Clancy Edwards (USA)
20.5*	Larry Brown (USA)
20.5	Hans-Jurgen Bombach (EG)
20.5	Franz-Peter Hofmeister (WG)
20.5	Antti Rajamaki (Fin)
20.5*	Willie Smith (USA)
20.5	Aleksandr Zhidkikh (Sov)
20.6	16 men

400 METRES
(*440 yards time less 0.3)

44.7	Alberto Juantorena (Cub)
44.9*	Larence Jones (USA)
44.9*	Darwin Bond (USA)
45.0	Fons Brydenbach (Bel)
45.0	Karl Honz (WG)
45.1	Bernd Herrmann (WG)
45.2	Warren Edmonson (USA-pro)
45.2	Maurice Peoples (USA)
45.2	David Jenkins (UK)
45.3	Jim Bolding (USA)
45.4*	Evis Jennings (USA)
45.5*	Benny Brown (USA)
45.5	Terry Erickson (USA)
45.5*	Larry James (USA-pro)
45.5*	Charles Oliver (USA)
45.5*	Maxie Parks (USA)
45.5	Markku Kukkoaho (Fin)
45.6	Josip Alebic (Yug)
45.6*	Julius Sang (Ken)
45.6	Horst-Rudiger Schloske (WG)

800 METRES
(*880 yards time less 0.7)

1:43.4*	Rick Wohlhuter (USA)
1:43.9	John Kipkurgat (Ken)
1:44.1	Luciano Susanj (Yug)
1:44.2	Mike Boit (Ken)
1:44.9	John Walker (NZ)
1:45.3	Filbert Bayi (Tan)
1:45.4	Danie Malan (SA)
1:45.6	Andy Carter (UK)
1:45.7	James Robinson (USA)
1:45.8	Steven Ovett (UK)
1:45.9	Markku Taskinen (Fin)
1:45.9	Gheorghe Ghipu (Rom)
1:46.0	Daniel Omwanza (Ken)
1:46.0	Robert Ouko (Ken)

234

800 metres (cont)
1:46.0	Mark Robinson (USA)
1:46.0	Vladimir Ponomaryov (Sov)
1:46.0	Dieter Fromm (EG)
1:46.1	Marcello Fiasconaro (Ita)
1:46.2	Byron Dyce (Jam)
1:46.2	Keith Francis (USA)
1:46.2	Gerhard Stolle (EG)

1500 METRES
3:32.2	Filbert Bayi (Tan)
3:32.5	John Walker (NZ)
3:33.2	Ben Jipcho (Ken)
3:33.9	Rod Dixon (NZ)
3:34.2	Graham Crouch (Aus)
3:36.4	Len Hilton (USA)
3:36.6	Ulf Hogberg (Swe)
3:36.7	Anders Garderud (Swe)
3:36.8	Mike Boit (Ken)
3:36.9	Tom Hansen (Den)
3:37.2	Fanie Van Zijl (SA)
3:37.3	Danie Malan (SA)
3:37.4	Frank Clement (UK)
3:37.5	Tom Byers (USA)
3:37.6	Brendan Foster (UK)
3:37.7	Luigi Zarcone (Ita)
3:37.9	Marcelle Philippe (Fra)
3:38.0	Francesco Arese (Ita)
3:38.1	John Hartnett (Eir)
3:38.5	Mike Slack (USA)

1 MILE
3:53.2	Tony Waldrop (USA)
3:54.1	Filbert Bayi (Tan)
3:54.4	Rick Wohlhuter (USA)
3:54.5	Ulf Hogberg (Swe)
3:54.9	Rod Dixon (NZ)
3:54.9	John Walker (NZ)
3:55.0	Denis Fikes (USA)
3:55.4	Mike Boit (Ken)
3:55.6	Graham Crouch (Aus)
3:56.2	Knut Kvalheim (Nor)
3:56.3	John Hartnett (Eir)
3:56.4	Paul Cummings (USA)
3:56.4	Howell Michael (USA)
3:56.6	Ben Jipcho (Ken-pro)
3:56.6	Marty Liquori (USA)
3:56.7	Len Hilton (USA)
3:56.8	Peter Fuller (Aus)
3:56.9	Rolf Gysin (Swi)

1974 WORLD RANKINGS

1 mile (cont)
3:57.1	Pekka Vasala (Fin)
3:57.2	Fanie Van Zijl (SA)
3:57.2	Wilson Waigwa (Ken)

5000 METRES
(*3 miles time plus 28.0)
13:14.4	Ben Jipcho (Ken)
13:14.6	Brendan Foster (UK)
13:19.4*	Steve Prefontaine (USA) (& 13:22.2)
13:20.0*	Frank Shorter (USA)
13:20.4	Knut Kvalheim (Nor)
13:23.4	Dick Buerkle (USA)
13:23.6	Dave Black (UK)
13:23.6	Paul Geis (USA)
13:24.0	Manfred Kuschmann (EG)
13:24.4	Dick Quax (NZ)
13:24.6	Emiel Puttemans (Bel)
13:24.6	Lasse Viren (Fin)
13:25.2	Anders Garderud (Swe)
13:25.6	Knut Boro (Nor)
13:25.6*	Don Kardong (USA)
13:26.4	Arne Kvalheim (Nor)
13:27.2	Jos Hermens (Hol)
13:27.2	Ilie Floriou (Rom)
13:27.6	Per Halle (Nor)
13:28.0	Bronislaw Malinowski (Pol)

10,000 METRES
(*6 miles time plus 60.0)
27:43.6	Steve Prefontaine (USA)
27:46.4	Dick Tayler (NZ)
27:48.6	Dave Black (UK)
27:57.0	Richard Juma (Ken)
28:05.6	John Ngeno (Ken)
28:09.6*	Frank Shorter (USA) (& 28:11.2)
28:09.6	Manfred Kuschmann (EG)
28:13.6	Karl-Heinz Leiteritz (EG)
28:14.6	Knut Boro (Nor)
28:14.8	Dave Bedford (UK)
28:14.8	Dan Shaughnessy (Can)
28:15.8	Bernie Ford (UK)
28:16.0	Mike Baxter (UK)
28:16.2	Ewald Bonzet (SA)
28:17.2	Ian Stewart (UK)
28:18.0	Bill Scott (Aus)
28:18.2	Mark Smet (Bel)
28:18.4	Pekka Paivarinta (Fin)
28:19.4	Tony Simmons (UK)
28:20.8	Jim Brown (UK)
28:20.8	Wolfgang Kruger (WG)

ATHLETICS 75

MARATHON

2:09:12.0	Ian Thompson (UK)
2:11:13.0	Karel Lismont (Bel)
2:11:18.6	Jack Foster (NZ)
2:11:31.2	Frank Shorter (USA)
2:12:02.4	Eckhard Lesse (EG)
2:12:10.6	Pekka Paivarinta (Fin)
2:12:54.4	Richard Mabuza (Swaz)
2:12:58.6	Terry Manners (Aus)
2:13:04.2	Yasunori Hamada (Jap)
2:13:11.8	Chris Stewart (UK)
2:13:34.0	Akio Usami (Jap)
2:13:39.0	Neil Cusack (Eir)
2:13:40.0	Makoto Hattori (Jap)
2:13:47.0	Ferdie Le Grange (SA)
2:14:04.0	John Farrington (Aus)
2:14:15.4	Don Macgregor (UK)
2:14:21.0	Noriyasu Mizukami (Jap)
2:14:25.0	Tom Fleming (USA)
2:14:27.0	Ichiro Mihara (Jap)
2:14:33.8	Tom Howard (Can)

3000 METRES STEEPLECHASE

8:14.2	Anders Garderud (Swe)
8:15.0	Bronislaw Malinowski (Pol)
8:18.0	Michael Karst (WG)
8:19.0	Franco Fava (Ita)
8:19.6	Tapio Kantanen (Fin)
8:20.8	Ben Jipcho (Ken)
8:21.6	Takaharu Koyama (Jap)
8:22.6	John Davies (UK)
8:23.2	Doug Brown (USA)
8:24.0	Dan Glans (Swe)
8:24.6	Gerard Buchheit (Fra)
8:25.2	Knut Kvalheim (Nor)
8:25.8	Gheorghe Cefan (Rom)
8:26.0	Hans-Peter Wehrli (Swi)
8:26.0	Gerd Frahmcke (WG)
8:26.6	Sergey Skripka (Sov)
8:27.4	Jonas Grigas (Sov)
8:27.4	Evans Mogaka (Ken)
8:27.4	Sverre Sornes (Nor)
8:27.8	Vladimir Lisovskiy (Sov)

110 METRES HURDLES
(y = 120 yards mark)

13.2	Guy Drut (Fra)
13.3	Alejandro Casanas (Cub)
13.3	Leszek Wodzynski (Pol)
13.3	Miroslaw Wodzynski (Pol)
13.3	Charles Foster (USA)

110 metres Hurdles (cont)

13.3	Frank Siebeck (EG)
13.3y	Charles Rich (USA)
13.4	Thomas Hill (USA)
13.4y	Larry Shipp (USA)
13.4y	Danny Smith (Bah)
13.5	Ervin Sebestyen (Rom)
13.5	Petr Cech (Cze)
13.5	Willie Davenport (USA)
13.5	Klaus Fiedler (EG)
13.5	Thomas Munkelt (EG)
13.5y	Greg Coleman (USA)
13.5y	Robert Martin (USA)
13.5y	Efren Gipson (USA)
13.5y	Ricky Stubbs (USA)
13.5y	Tommy Lee White (USA)

400 METRES HURDLES
(*440 yards time less 0.3)

48.1	Jim Bolding (USA)
48.8	Alan Pascoe (UK)
48.9	Jean-Claude Nallet (Fra)
49.0	Ralph Mann (USA)
49.1	Miroslav Kodejs (Cze)
49.2	Klaus Schoenberger (EG)
49.3	Bruce Field (Aus)
49.3	William Koskei (Ken)
49.3	Yevgeniy Gavrilenko (Sov)
49.5	James King (USA)
49.6	Fatwell Kimaiyo (Ken)
49.6	John Akii Bua (Uga)
49.7	Mike Shine (USA)
49.7	Viktor Savchenko (Sov)
49.7	Stavros Tsiortzis (Gre)
49.7*	Ivan Danis (Cze)
49.8	Rolf Ziegler (WG)
49.9*	Bruce Collins (USA)
49.9	William Hartley (UK)
49.9*	Wes Williams (USA)
49.9	Francois Aumas (Swi)
49.9	Valeriy Moshkovskiy (Sov)

HIGH JUMP

2.28m	(7' 5¾")	Dwight Stones (USA)
2.25m	(7' 4½")	Jesper Torring (Den)
2.25m	(7' 4½")	Kestutis Sapka (Sov)
2.24m	(7' 4¼")	Vladimir Abramov (Sov)
2.23m	(7' 3¾")i	Sergey Budalov (Sov)
2.23m	(7' 3¾")	Imants Karlsons (Sov)
2.23m	(7' 3¾")	Rune Almen (Swe)
2.22m	(7' 3½")i	Tom Woods (USA) (& 2.21)
2.22m	(7' 3½")	Vladimir Maly (Cze)

High Jump (cont)

2.21m (7′ 3¼″)i	Bill Jankunis (USA)
2.21m (7′ 3″)	Mike Fleer (USA)
2.21m (7′ 3″)i	Enzo Dal Forno (Ita)
2.21m (7′ 3″)i	Valentin Gavrilov (Sov)
2.21m (7′ 3″)	Rory Kotinek (USA)
2.21m (7′ 3″)	Stanislav Molotilov (Sov)
2.21m (7′ 3″)	John Radetich (USA-pro)
2.21m (7′ 3″)	Sergey Senyukov (Sov)
2.21m (7′ 3″)	Paul Underwood (USA)
2.21m (7′ 3″)	Teymour Ghiassi (Iran)
2.21m (7′ 3″)i	Endre Kelemen (Hun)
2.21m (7′ 3″)i	Vello Lumi (Sov)

POLE VAULT

5.59m (18′ 4″)	Steve Smith (USA-pro)
5.48m (18′ 0¼″)	Bob Seagren (USA-pro)
5.42m (17′ 9½″)	Tadeusz Slusarski (Pol)
5.40m (17′ 8½″)i	Renato Dionisi (Ita)
5.40m (17′ 8½″)	Wojciech Buciarski (Pol)
5.40m (17′ 8½″)	Casey Carrigan (USA)
5.40m (17′ 8½″)	Kjell Isaksson (Swe)
5.40m (17′ 8½″)	Vladimir Kishkun (Sov)
5.40m (17′ 8½″)	Yuriy Isakov (Sov)
5.38m (17′ 8″)i	Vic Dias (USA) (& 5.34)
5.38m (17′ 8″)i	Buddy Williamson (USA-pro)
5.38m (17′ 7¾″)	Wladyslaw Kozakiewicz (Pol)
5.37m (17′ 7¼″)i	Vladimir Trofimyenko (Sov)
5.36m (17′ 7″)i	Sergey Krivozub (Sov)
5.36m (17′ 7″)	Bob Slover (USA)
5.35m (17′ 6½″)i	Antti Kalliomaki (Fin) (& 5.30)
5.33m (17′ 6″)	Roland Carter (USA)
5.33m (17′ 6″)	Dave Roberts (USA)
5.33m (17′ 6″)i	Francois Tracanelli (Fra)
5.33m (17′ 5¾″)	Reinhard Kuretzky (WG)

LONG JUMP

8.30m (27′ 2¾″)	Arnie Robinson (USA)
8.24m (27′ 0½″)	Nenad Stekic (Yug)
8.20m (26′ 10¾″)	Bouncy Moore (USA)
8.17m (26′ 9¾″)i	Jean-Francois Bonheme (Fra) (& 8.00)
8.17m (26′ 9¾″)	Valeriy Podluzhniy (Sov)
8.15m (26′ 9″)	Grzegorz Cybulski (Pol)
8.14m (26′ 8½″)	Tommy Haynes (USA)
8.11m (26′ 7½″)	Jerry Herndon (USA)
8.10m (26′ 7″)i	Hans Baumgartner (WG) (& 8.00)
8.09m (26′ 6¾″)	Jerry Proctor (USA)
8.09m (26′ 6½″)	Josh Owusu (Gha)
8.07m (26′ 5¾″)	T.C. Yohannen (Ind)
8.03m (26′ 4¼″)i	Max Klauss (EG) (& 7.96)
8.02m (26′ 3¾″)i	Henry Hines (USA-pro)

Long Jump (cont)

8.01m (26′ 3½″)i	Frank Wartenberg (EG)
7.98m (26′ 2¼″)	Alan Lerwill (UK)
7.98m (26′ 2¼″)	Jacques Rousseau (Fra)
7.98m (26′ 2¼″)	Yevgeniy Schubin (Sov)
7.97m (26′ 2″)	Anthony Carter (USA)
7.97m (26′ 1¾″)	Kingsley Adams (Gha)
7.97m (26′ 1¾″)	Aleksey Perevyerzyev (Sov)

TRIPLE JUMP

17.23m (56′ 6½″)	Viktor Saneyev (Sov)
17.06m (55′ 11¾″)	Jorg Drehmel (EG)
17.03m (55′ 10½″)i	Michal Joachimowski (Pol) (& 16.89)
16.88m (55′ 4½″)i	Mikhail Bariban (Sov) (& 16.61)
16.83m (55′ 2½″)	Pedro Perez (Cub)
16.83m (55′ 2½″)	Nikolay Sinichkin (Sov)
16.82m (55′ 2¼″)	Charlton Ehizuelen (Nig)
16.77m (55′ 0¼″)	Milan Spasojevic (Yug)
16.76m (54′ 11¾″)	Clarence Taylor (USA)
16.74m (54′ 11¼″)	Mikhail Syegal (Sov)
16.74m (54′ 11¼″)	Stanislav Penyayev (Sov)
16.71m (54′ 10″)i	Milan Tiff (USA) (& 16.62)
16.68m (54′ 8¾″)	Mohinder Singh Gill (Ind)
16.68m (54′ 8¾″)	Carol Corbu (Rom)
16.68m (54′ 8¾″)	Juri Vycichlo (Cze)
16.64m (54′ 7¼″)	Anatoliy Piskulin (Sov)
16.63m (54′ 6¾″)	Sergey Sidorenko (Sov)
16.63m (54′ 6¾″)	Andrzej Sonntag (Pol)
16.63m (54′ 6¾″)i	Tommy Haynes (USA)
16.56m (54′ 4″)i	Bernard Lamitie (Fra)

SHOT

22.02m (72′ 2¾″)i	George Woods (USA) (& 21.42)
21.70m (71′ 2½″)	Aleksandr Barishnikov (Sov)
21.60m (70′ 10½″)	Al Feuerbach (USA)
21.42m (70′ 3½″)i	Fred DeBernardi (USA-pro) (& 21.41)
21.37m (70′ 1½″)	Geoff Capes (UK)
21.37m (70′ 1¼″)i	Randy Matson (USA-pro) (& 20.72)
21.35m (70′ 0½″)	Ron Semkiw (USA)
21.26m (69′ 9″)	Reijo Stahlberg (Fin)
21.19m (69′ 6¼″)	Wladyslaw Komar (Pol)
21.12m (69′ 3½″)	Brian Oldfield (USA-pro)
21.05m (69′ 0¾″)i	Terry Albritton (USA) (& 20.38)
20.91m (68′ 7¼″)	Heinz-Joachim Rothenburg (EG)
20.88m (68′ 6″)i	Karl Salb (USA-pro) (& 20.73)
20.86m (68′ 5¼″)	Hans-Peter Gies (EG)
20.80m (68′ 3″)	Ralf Reichenbach (WG)
20.77m (68′ 1¾″)	Hartmut Briesenick (EG)
20.69m (67′ 10¾″)	Valeriy Voikin (Sov)
20.66m (67′ 9½″)	Hans Hoglund (Swe)
20.53m (67′ 4½″)	Jesse Stuart (USA)
20.48m (67′ 2¼″)	Jaromir Vlk (Cze)

DISCUS

68.16m (223' 7")	Ricky Bruch (Swe)
68.08m (223' 4")	John Powell (USA)
68.04m (223' 3")	John Van Reenan (SA)
67.18m (220' 5")	Ludvik Danek (Cze)
66.52m (218' 3")	Pentti Kahma (Fin)
65.64m (215' 4")	Siegfried Pachale (EG)
65.22m (214' 0")	Viktor Penzikov (Sov)
65.14m (213' 8")	Mac Wilkins (USA)
64.94m (213' 1")	Gunnar Muller (EG)
64.94m (213' 0")	Bill Tancred (UK)
64.40m (211' 3")	Markku Tuokko (Fin)
64.32m (211' 0")	Erlendur Valdimarsson (Ice)
64.26m (210' 10")	Hein-Direck Neu (WG)
64.10m (210' 4")	Wolfgang Schmidt (EG)
64.02m (210' 0")	Ferenc Tegla (Hun)
63.88m (209' 7")	Hartmut Losch (EG)
63.78m (209' 3")	Velko Velev (Bul)
63.60m (208' 8")	Larry Kennedy (USA)
63.08m (206' 11")	Robin Tait (NZ)
62.90m (206' 4")	Dick Drescher (USA)

HAMMER

76.66m (251' 6")	Aleksey Spiridonov (Sov)
76.60m (251' 4")	Reinhard Theimer (EG)
75.52m (247' 9")	Valentin Dmitryenko (Sov)
74.44m (244' 3")	Dzhumbyer Pkhakadze (Sov)
74.42m (244' 2")	Jochen Sachse (EG)
73.80m (242' 1")	Vasiliy Khmelyevskiy (Sov)
73.70m (241' 9")	Klaus Dieter Beilig (EG)
73.44m (240' 11")	Edwin Klein (WG)
73.36m (240' 8")	Manfred Hüning (WG)
73.10m (239' 10")	Anatoliy Bondarchuk (Sov)
72.56m (238' 1")	Manfred Seidel (EG)
72.14m (236' 8")	Josef Hajek (Cze)
72.10m (236' 6")	Viktor Korolyov (Sov)
71.92m (235' 11")	Aleksandr Kozlov (Sov)
71.76m (235' 5")	Adam Barnard (SA)
71.74m (235' 4")	Heikki Kangas (Fin)
71.60m (234' 11")	Ivan Kunowski (Sov)
71.54m (234' 8")	Jaroslav Charvat (Cze)
71.50m (234' 7")	Mikhail Rusanovskiy (Sov)
71.36m (234' 1")	Hans-Martin Lotz (WG)

JAVELIN

89.58m (293' 11")	Hannu Siitonen (Fin)
88.26m (289' 6")	Klaus Wolfermann (WG)
87.44m (286' 10")	Miklos Nemeth (Hun)
86.96m (285' 4")	Sam Colson (USA)
86.70m (284' 5")	Aleksandr Makarov (Sov)
86.28m (283' 1")	Nikolay Grebnyev (Sov)
86.24m (282' 11")	Jorma Jaakola (Fin)
86.24m (282' 11")	Seppo Hovinen (Fin)
85.88m (281' 9")	Aimo Aho (Fin)
85.88m (281' 9")	Lauri Koski-Vahala (Swe)
85.82m (281' 6")	Janis Zirnis (Sov)
85.46m (280' 4")	Wolfgang Hanisch (EG)
85.34m (280' 0")	Vilnis Feldmanis (Sov)
85.26m (279' 8")	Pekka Lappalainen (Fin)
84.92m (278' 7")	Charles Clover (UK)
84.84m (278' 4")	Fred Luke (USA)
84.76m (278' 1")	Raimo Pihl (Swe)
84.44m (277' 0")	Aleksey Chupiliko (Sov)
84.08m (275' 10")	Janis Lusis (Sov)
83.80m (274' 11")	Ivan Morgul (Sov)

DECATHLON

8308pts	Bruce Jenner (USA)
8229pts	Yves Le Roy (Fra)
8207pts	Ryszard Skowronek (Pol)
8132pts	Guido Kratschmer (WG)
8122pts	Leonid Litvinyenko (Sov)
8033pts	Fred Dixon (USA)
7994pts	Anatoliy Gratschov (Sov)
7988pts	Fred Samara (USA)
7969pts	John Warkentin (USA)
7945pts	Kurt Bendlin (WG)
7939pts	Jeff Bennett (USA)
7939pts	Raimo Pihl (Swe)
7938pts	Ron Evans (USA)
7934pts	Philipp Andres (Swi)
7930pts	Steve Gough (USA
7914pts	Viktor Chelnokov (Sov)
7903pts	Rudolf Sigert (Sov)
7890pts	Ludek Pernica (Cze)
7884pts	Aleksandr Grebenyuk (Sov)
7874pts	Runald Backman (Swe)

WOMEN

w = wind assisted.   i = indoor mark

100 METRES

10.9	Irena Szewinska (Pol)
11.0	Renate Stecher (EG)
11.1	Andrea Lynch (UK)
11.1	Barbel Eckert (EG)
11.1	Monika Meyer (EG)
11.2	Raelene Boyle (Aus)
11.2	Annegret Richter (EG)
11.2	Jelica Pavlicic (Yug)

100 metres (cont)

11.2	Ellen Streidt (EG)
11.2	Aniela Szubert (Pol)
11.2	Wilma Van Gool (Hol)
11.2	Helen Golden (UK)
11.2	Christina Heinich (EG)
11.3	19 girls

200 METRES

22.0	Irena Szewinska (Pol)
22.4	Renate Stecher (EG)
22.5	Raelene Boyle (Aus)
22.7	Denise Robertson (Aus)
22.8	Doris Maletzki (EG)
22.8	Riitta Salin (Fin)
22.9	Alice Annum (Gha)
22.9	Ellen Streidt (EG)
22.9	Petra Kandarr (EG)
22.9	Karla Bodendorf (EG)
22.9	Mona-Lisa Pursiainen (Fin)
22.9	Jennifer Lamy (Aus)
23.0	Helen Golden (UK)
23.0	Claudie van Straaten (SA)
23.0	Christina Heinich (EG)
23.1	Jelica Pavlicic (Yug)
23.1	Marjorie Bailey (Can)
23.1	Margaret Sargent (Aus)
23.2	Marina Sidorova (Sov)
23.2	Andrea Lynch (UK)
23.2	Fran Sichting (USA)

400 METRES
(*440 yards time less 0.3)

49.9	Irena Szewinska (Pol)
50.1	Riitta Salin (Fin)
50.7	Ellen Streidt (EG)
50.9	Rita Wilden (WG)
51.0	Jelica Pavlicic (Yug)
51.2	Mariana Suman (Rom)
51.2	Nadyezhda Ilyina (Sov)
51.2	Angelika Handt (EG)
51.6	Yvonne Saunders (Can)
51.8	Donna Murray (UK)
51.8	Karoline Kafer (Aut)
51.9	Verona Bernard (UK)
51.9★	Debra Sapenter (USA)
52.0	Jozefina Cerchlanova (Cze)
52.0	Krystyna Kacperczyk (Pol)
52.1	Charlene Rendina (Aus)
52.2	Claudie van Straaten (SA)

400 metres (cont)

52.2	Waltraud Dietsch (EG)
52.3	Aurelia Penton (Cub)
52.4	Brigitte Rohde (EG)

800 METRES
(*880 yards time less 0.8)

1:58.1	Lilyana Tomova (Bul)
1:58.6	Mariana Suman (Rom)
1:58.8	Gunhild Hoffmeister (EG)
1:59.9	Marie-Francoise Dubois (Fra)
2:00.1	Valentina Gerasimova (Sov)
2:00.4	Elzbieta Katolik (Pol)
2:00.5	Nikolina Schtereva (Bul)
2:00.6	Waltraud Pohland (EG)
2:00.8	Nina Morgunova (Sov)
2:00.9	Ulrike Klapezynski (EG)
2:01.0	Maritta Cierpinski (EG)
2:01.1	Charlene Rendina (Aus)
2:01.5	Gisela Klein (WG)
2:01.6★i	Mary Decker (USA) (& 2:02.3)
2:01.7	Krystyna Kacperczyk (Pol)
2:02.0	Sue Haden (NZ)
2:02.3	Gunilla Lindh (Swe)
2:02.3	Julia Sofyina (Sov)
2:02.5	Elfi Zinn (EG)
2:02.5	Robin Campbell (USA)

1500 METRES

4:02.3	Gunhild Hoffmeister (EG)
4:05.0	Lilyana Tomova (Bul)
4:05.2	Grete Andersen (Nor)
4:05.9	Tatyana Kazankina (Sov)
4:07.8	Glenda Reiser (Can)
4:08.9	Tamara Pangelova (Sov)
4:09.8	Lyudmila Bragina (Sov)
4:09.9	Ulrike Klapezynski (EG)
4:09.9	Gunilla Lindh (Swe)
4:10.3	Francie Larrieu (USA)
4:10.5	Natalia Andrei (Rom)
4:10.5	Thelma Wright (Can)
4:10.7	Joan Allison (UK)
4:10.7	Karin Krebs (EG)
4:11.0i	Tonka Petrova (Bul) (& 4:12.0)
4:11.5	Ellen Wellmann (WG)
4:11.6	Nina Holmen (Fin)
4:11.6	Carmen Valero (Spa)
4:11.7	Tamara Kazachkova (Sov)
4:12.0	Marie-Francoise Dubois (Fra)

ATHLETICS 75

3000 METRES

8:52.8	Lyudmila Bragina (Sov)
8:55.2	Nina Holmen (Fin)
8:55.6	Joyce Smith (UK)
8:59.0	Natalia Andrei (Rom)
9:01.4	Paola Cacchi (Ita)
9:03.2	Francie Larrieu (USA)
9:03.4	Thelma Wright (Can)
9:04.4	Tamara Pangelova (Sov)
9:05.2	Bronislawa Ludwichowska (Pol)
9:07.0	Ann Yeoman (UK)
9:07.6	Tonka Petrova (Bul)
9:09.4	Bronislawa Doborzynska (Pol)
9:09.6	Jadwiga Drazek (Pol)
9:09.6	Renate Pentlinowska (Pol)
9:11.8	Irina Bondarchuk (Sov)
9:12.2	Eva Gustafsson (Swe)
9:13.6	Aja Veissa (Sov)
9:14.0	Urszula Prasek (Pol)
9:14.6	Lyudmila Korchagina (Sov)
9:14.8	Marijke Moser (Hol)

100 METRES HURDLES

12.4	Annelie Ehrhardt (EG)
12.5	Teresa Nowak (Pol)
12.7	Annerose Fiedler (EG)
12.9	Valeria Stefanescu (Rom)
13.0	Judy Vernon (UK)
13.0	Blondelle Thompson (UK)
13.0	Meta Antenen (Swi)
13.0	Natalia Lebedyeva (Sov)
13.1	Roswitha Walden (EG)
13.1	Gudrun Berend (EG)
13.1	Ilona Bruzsenyak (Hun)
13.1	Penka Sokolova (Bul)
13.2	Grazyna Rabsztyn (Pol)
13.2	Marlies Koschinski (WG)
13.2	Johanna Schaller (EG)
13.2	Barbel Eckert (EG)
13.2	Mamie Rallins (USA)
13.2	Hybre de Lange (SA)
13.2	Tatiana Anisimova (Sov)
13.2	Zoya Spasovkhodskaya (Sov)
13.2	Ina Van Rensburg (SA)
13.2	Pat Johnson (USA)
13.2	Nadezhda Tkachenko (Sov)

HIGH JUMP

1.95m (6' 4¾")	Rosemarie Witschas (EG)
1.92m (6' 3½")	Virginia Ioan (Rom)

High Jump (cont)

1.92m (6' 3½")i	Rita Kirst (EG) (& 1.90)
1.91m (6' 3¼")	Milada Karbanova (Cze)
1.90m (6' 2¾")	Sara Simeoni (Ita)
1.87m (6' 1½")	Maria Mracnova (Cze)
1.87m (6' 1½")	Debbie Brill (Can)
1.87m (6' 1½")	Miloslava Hubnerova (Cze)
1.87m (6' 1½")i	Erika Rudolf (Hun) (& 1.84)
1.86m (6' 1¼")	Vera Bradacova (Cze)
1.86m (6' 1¼")	Barbara Lawton (UK)
1.86m (6' 1¼")	Karin Wagner (WG)
1.86m (6' 1¼")	Galina Filatova (Sov)
1.86m (6' 1¼")	Erica Teodorescu (Rom)
1.86m (6' 1¼")i	Cornelia Popa (Rom)
1.86m (6' 1¼")i	Tamara Galka (Sov) (& 1.85)
1.85m (6' 0¾")	Ulrike Meyfarth (WG)
1.85m (6' 0¾")	Joni Huntley (USA)
1.84m (6' 0½")	Gabriela Krause (EG)
1.84m (6' 0½")	Annemieke Bouma (Hol)
1.84m (6' 0½")	Marie-Christine Debourse (Fra)

LONG JUMP

6.77m (22' 2½")	Angela Schmalfeld (EG)
6.77m (22' 2½")	Marianne Voelzke (EG)
6.69m (21' 11½")i	Meta Antenen (Swi)
6.67m (21' 10¾")	Eva Suranova (Cze)
6.66m (21' 10¼")	Lidia Alfeyeva (Sov)
6.65m (21' 10")	Ilona Bruzsenyak (Hun)
6.62m (21' 8¾")	Maroula Lambrou (Gre)
6.59m (21' 7½")	Ildiko Szabo (Hun)
6.59m (21' 7½")	Pirkko Helenius (Fin)
6.59m (21' 7½")	Martha Watson (USA)
6.58m (21' 7¼")	Tatyana Timokhova (Sov)
6.58m (21' 7¼")	Valeria Stefanescu (Rom)
6.56m (21' 6¼")	Margarita Treinite (Sov)
6.56m (21' 6¼")	Jarmila Nygrynova (Cze)
6.56m (21' 6¼")	Nadyezhda Tkachenko (Sov)
6.55m (21' 6")	Tuula Rautanen (Fin)
6.55m (21' 6")	Kristina Albertus (EG)
6.54m (21' 5½")	Birgit Wilkes (WG)
6.50m (21' 4")	Dorina Catineanu (Rom)
6.50m (21' 4")	Modupe Oshikoya (Nig)
6.50m (21' 4")	Willye White (USA)

SHOT

21.57m (70' 9¼")	Helena Fibingerova (Cze)
21.22m (69' 7½")	Nadyezhda Chizhova (Sov)
20.61m (67' 7½")	Marianne Adam (EG)
19.93m (65' 4¾")	Ivanka Khristova (Bul)
19.68m (64' 6¾")	Elena Stoyanova (Bul)
19.40m (63' 7¾")	Marita Lange (EG)

Above left: *Ainsley Bennett (3) – Britain's No. 1 at 200 metres and a character of the team.* **Above right:** *Bronislaw Malinowski, iron man of middle-distance running, competes as European 3000m steeplechase champion at the Coca-Cola International.* **Below:** *Bill Hartley (right) – his strength at 400m hurdling became Britain's strength in the 4 × 400m relay.*

Above: Mighty Val Harrison at 5ft 4½in clears 1.82 metres (5' 11½") in the WAAA Championship – just short of her personal best of 1.84 metres (6' 0¼").
Left and below: One of the attractions of the 1974 British season was the presence at some meetings of shot-putter Al Feuerbach and high jumper Dwight Stones, surrounded by autograph hunters and talking to Britain's former mile world recordholder, Derek Ibbotson.
Opposite page: 'Big Bren' achieved a lifetime ambition when creating a world record for the 3000 metres in front of his home crowd at Gateshead.

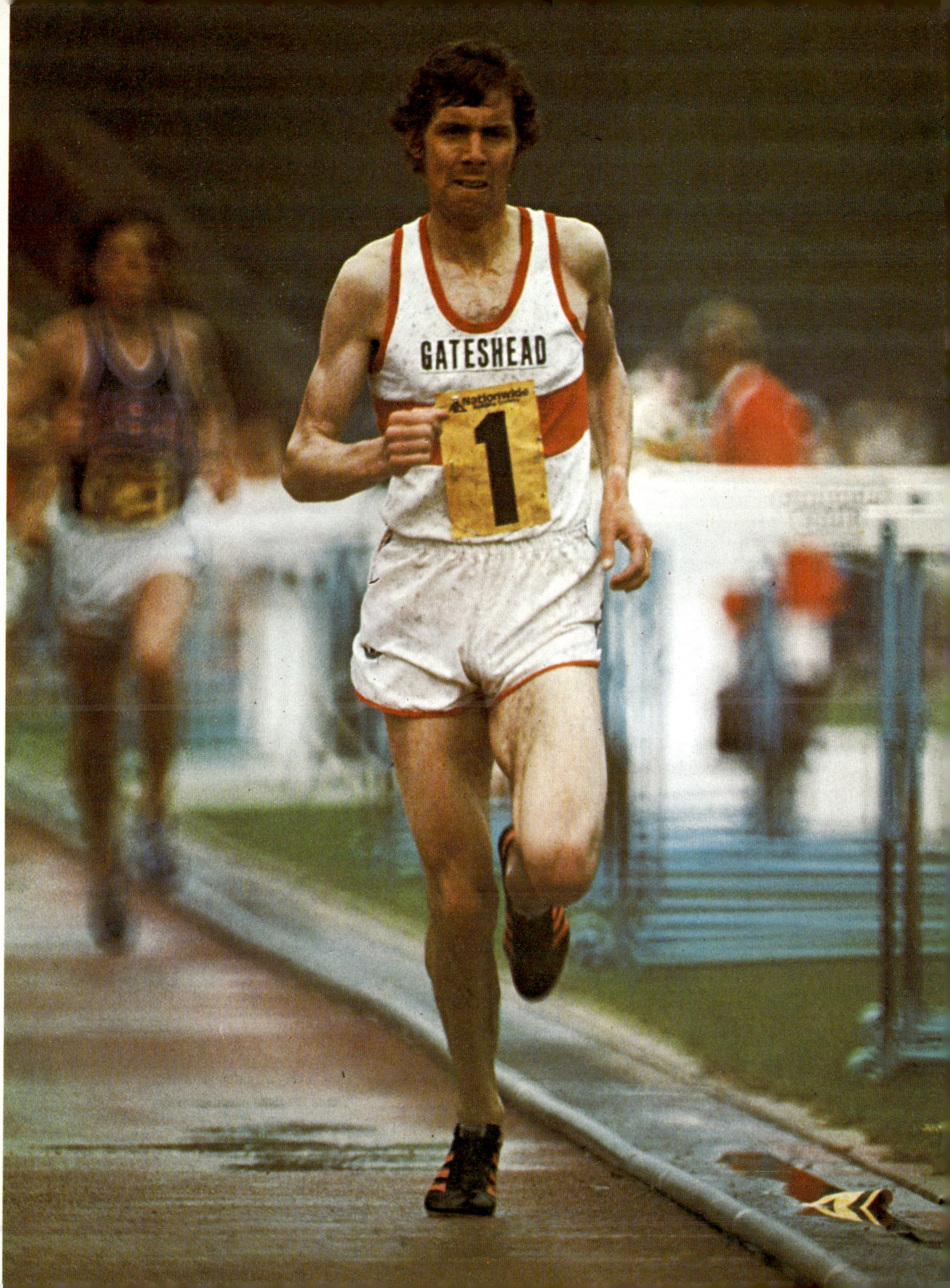
GATESHEAD
1

Above: *Donna Murray (white shorts) – because her move up from 200 to 400 metres caught the full glare of the publicity spotlight, her European performance may have disappointed; but her potential at the longer distance remains untarnished.*
Left: *Leslie Kiernan, 17, and Joyce Smith, more than twice her age – two of Britain's golden girls.*

WORLD ALL-TIME LIST

Shot (cont)
19.39m (63' 7½") Faina Melnik (Sov)
19.23m (63' 1¼") Ilona Schoknecht (EG)
19.16m (62' 10¼")i Antonia Ivanova (Sov) (& 18.78)
19.12m (62' 8¾") Yelena Korablyeva (Sov)
19.07m (62' 6¾") Esfir Kravchevska (Sov)
18.98m (62' 3¼") Ludwika Chewinska (Pol)
18.45m (60' 6¼") Radostina Bakhtschevanova (Bul)
18.43m (60' 5¾") Raisa Taranda (Sov)
18.40m (60' 4½") Rimma Makauskaite (Sov)
18.36m (60' 3") Tamara Bufyetova (Sov)
18.19m (59' 8½")i Gabriele Greiner-Engwicht (EG)
18.18m (59' 7¾") Brigitte Griessing (EG)
18.02m (59' 1½") Valentina Cioltan (Rom)
17.98m (59' 0") Brunhilde Loewe (EG)

DISCUS
69.90m (229' 4") Faina Melnik (Sov)
68.48m (224' 8") Maria Vergova (Bul)
66.22m (217' 3") Gabriele Hinzmann (EG)
65.84m (216' 0") Argentina Menis (Rom)
63.26m (207' 6") Evelyn Schlaak (EG)
61.84m (202' 11") Karin Holdke (EG)
61.38m (201' 4") Barbara Regel (EG)
61.24m (200' 11") Annelie Braun (EG)
61.14m (200' 7") Helena Vyhnalova (Cze)
60.90m (199' 10") Nadezhda Jerocha (Sov)
60.80m (199' 6") Olga Andrianova (Sov)
60.62m (198' 11") Olimpia Catarama (Rom)
60.52m (198' 7") Nadezhda Khrolenkova (Sov)
60.44m (198' 3") Nelli Sivopliassova (Sov)
60.40m (198' 2") Vasilka Stoyeva (Bul)
60.20m (197' 6") Liesel Westermann (WG)
60.14m (197' 4") Helgi Parts (Sov)
60.02m (196' 11") Sabine Engel (EG)
59.92m (196' 7") Natalia Gorbacheva (Sov)
59.78m (196' 1") Galina Savyenkova (Sov)

JAVELIN
67.22m (220' 6") Ruth Fuchs (EG)
64.34m (211' 1") Jacqueline Todten (EG)

Javelin (cont)
63.08m (206' 11") Felicja Kinder (Pol)
62.60m (205' 4") Lutvjan Mollova (Bul)
61.92m (203' 2") Kathy Schmidt (USA)
61.66m (202' 3") Nastasa Bezjak (Yug)
61.56m (202' 0") Eva Janko (Aut)
61.18m (200' 9") Svyetlana Babitsch (Sov)
61.14m (200' 7") Maria Vago (Hun)
60.40m (198' 2") Marion Becker (WG)
60.26m (197' 8") Tatyana Zhigalova (Sov)
59.20m (194' 3") Sabine Kargel (EG)
58.76m (192' 9") Daniela Jaworska (Pol)
58.62m (192' 4") Ioanna Pecec-Stancu (Rom)
58.60m (192' 3") Ute Hommola (EG)
58.54m (192' 1") Lynn Cannon (USA)
58.50m (191' 11") Eve Zorgo (Rom)
58.22m (191' 0") Ameli Koloska (WG)
57.76m (189' 6") Renate Sliwinska (Pol)
57.32m (188' 1") Zsuzsa Zheliaskova (Sov)
57.32m (188' 1") Regina Stange (EG)

PENTATHLON
4776pts Nadyezhda Tkachenko (Sov)
4684pts Burglinde Pollak (EG)
4628pts Zoya Spasovkhodskaya (Sov)
4562pts Christel Voss (WG)
4561pts Snezhana Yurukova (Bul)
4561pts Ilona Bruzsenyak (Hun)
4557pts Lyudmila Popovskaya (Sov)
4548pts Sigrun Thon (EG)
4543pts Tatyana Vorokhobko (Sov)
4538pts Margit Olfert (EG)
4538pts Barbel Muller (EG)
4531pts Margot Eppinger (WG)
4502pts Djurdica Focic (Yug)
4472pts Olga Rukavishnikova (Sov)
4455pts Mary Peters (UK)
4445pts Liese Prokop (Aut)
4435pts Margit Papp (Hun)
4434pts Larisa Beliakova (Sov)
4431pts Ulrica Jacob (WG)
4423pts Modupe Oshikoya (Nig)

World All-Time List (as at 31 December 1974)

MEN   w = wind assisted. i = indoor mark

100 METRES
(y = 100 yards time)
                                9.9 Charlie Greene (USA); 1968
                                9.9 Eddie Hart (USA); 1972
                                9.9 Rey Robinson (USA); 1972
9.0y Ivory Crockett (USA); 1974   9.9 Steve Williams (USA); 1974
9.9 Jim Hines (USA); 1968   9.1y Bob Hayes (USA); 1963

241

100 metres (cont)

9.1y		Harry Jerome (Can); 1966
9.1y		John Carlos (USA); 1969
9.1y		Willie McGee (USA); 1970
10.0		Armin Hary (WG); 1960
		and 32 other athletes

200 METRES
(*220 yards time less 0.1)

19.7	John Carlos (USA); 1968
19.8	Tommie Smith (USA); 1968
19.8	Don Quarrie (Jam); 1971
20.0	Peter Norman (Aus); 1968
20.0	Larry Black (USA); 1972
20.0	Valeriy Borzov (Sov); 1972
20.1*	Henry Carr (USA); 1964
20.1*	Willie Turner (USA); 1967
20.1*	Mike Fray (Jam); 1968
20.1	Paul Nash (SA); 1968
20.1	Clyde Glosson (USA); 1968
20.1	Larry Questad (USA); 1968
20.1	Jerry Bright (USA); 1968
20.1	Tom Randolph (USA); 1968
20.1	Willie Deckard (USA); 1971
20.1*	Marshall Dill (USA); 1971
20.1*	Carl Lawson (Jam); 1973
20.2	11 athletes

400 METRES
(*440 yards time less 0.3)

43.8	Lee Evans (USA); 1968
43.9	Larry James (USA); 1968
44.1	Wayne Collett (USA); 1972
44.2*	John Smith (USA); 1971
44.2	Fred Newhouse (USA); 1972
44.4	Vince Matthews (USA); 1968
44.4	Ron Freeman (USA); 1968
44.4*	Curtis Mills (USA); 1969
44.5	Tommie Smith (USA); 1967
44.6*	Adolph Plummer (USA); 1963
44.7	Karl Honz (WG); 1972
44.7*	Benny Brown (USA); 1973
44.7*	Maurice Peoples (USA); 1973
44.7	Alberto Juantorena (Cub); 1974
44.9	10 athletes

800 METRES
(*880 yards time less 0.7)

1:43.4*	Rick Wohlhuter (USA); 1974
1:43.7	Marcello Fiasconaro (Ita); 1973
1:43.9*	John Kipkurgat (Ken); 1974
1:44.1	Luciano Susanj (Yug); 1974
1:44.2*	Jim Ryun (USA); 1966

800 metres (cont)

1:44.2	Mike Boit (Ken); 1974
1:44.3	Peter Snell (NZ); 1962
1:44.3	Ralph Doubell (Aus); 1968
1:44.3	David Wottle (USA); 1972
1:44.4*	Danie Malan (SA); 1973
1:44.5	Wilson Kiprugut (Ken); 1968
1:44.5	Pekka Vasala (Fin); 1972
1:44.7	Dicky Broberg (SA); 1971
1:44.8	Ken Swenson (USA); 1970
1:44.9	Franz Josef Kemper (WG); 1966
1:44.9	Walter Adams (WG); 1970
1:44.9	John Walker (NZ); 1974
1:45.0	Wade Bell (USA); 1967
1:45.1	Andrew Carter (UK); 1973
1:45.2*	Byron Dyce (Jam); 1969
1:45.2	Juris Luzins (USA); 1971

1500 METRES

3:32.2	Filbert Bayi (Tan); 1974
3:32.5	John Walker (NZ); 1974
3:33.1	Jim Ryun (USA); 1967
3:33.2	Ben Jipcho (Ken); 1974
3:33.9	Rod Dixon (NZ); 1974
3:34.0	Jean Wadoux (Fra); 1970
3:34.2	Graham Crouch (Aus); 1974
3:34.9	Kipchoge Keino (Ken); 1968
3:35.6	Herb Elliott (Aus); 1960
3:36.0	Marty Liquori (USA); 1971
3:36.2	David Wottle (USA); 1973
3:36.3	Michel Jazy (Fra); 1966
3:36.3	Francesco Arese (Ita); 1971
3:36.3	Pekka Vasala (Fin); 1972
3:36.4	Jurgen May (EG – later WG); 1965
3:36.4	Len Hilton (USA); 1974
3:36.5	Bodo Tummler (WG); 1968
3:36.6	Ulf Hogberg (Swe); 1974
3:36.7	Anders Garderud (Swe); 1974
3:36.8	Tom Hansen (Den); 1973
3:36.8	Jacques Boxberger (Fra); 1973
3:36.8	Mike Boit (Ken); 1974

1 MILE

3:51.1	Jim Ryun (USA); 1967
3:52.0	Ben Jipcho (Ken); 1973
3:52.6	Filbert Bayi (Tan); 1973
3:53.1	Kipchoge Keino (Ken); 1967
3:53.2	Tony Waldrop (USA); 1974
3:53.3	David Wottle (USA); 1973
3:53.6	Michel Jazy (Fra); 1965
3:53.8	Jurgen May (EG – later WG); 1965
3:53.8	Bodo Tummler (WG); 1968

WORLD ALL-TIME LIST

1 mile (cont)

3:54.1	Peter Snell (NZ); 1964
3:54.4	Rick Wohlhuter (USA); 1974
3:54.5	Herb Elliott (Aus); 1958
3:54.5	Ulf Hogberg (Swe); 1974
3:54.6	Marty Liquori (USA); 1971
3:54.6	Steve Prefontaine (USA); 1973
3:54.7	John Hartnett (Eir); 1973
3:54.9	Rod Dixon (NZ); 1974
3:54.9	John Walker (NZ); 1974
3:55.0	Denis Fikes (USA); 1974
3:55.3	Peter Stewart (UK); 1972
3:55.4	Jim Grelle (USA); 1965
3:55.4	Mike Boit (Ken); 1974

5000 METRES
(*3 miles time plus 28.0)

13:13.0	Emiel Puttemans (Bel); 1972
13:14.4	Ben Jipcho (Ken); 1974
13:14.6	Brendan Foster (UK); 1974
13:16.4	Lasse Viren (Fin); 1972
13:16.6	Ron Clarke (Aus); 1966
13:17.2	Dave Bedford (UK); 1972
13:18.4	Dick Quax (NZ); 1973
13:19.4*	Steve Prefontaine (USA); 1974 (& 13:22.2); 1974
13:19.8	Ian McCafferty (UK); 1972
13:20.0*	Frank Shorter (USA); 1974
13:20.4	Knut Kvalheim (Nor); 1974
13:20.6	Harald Norpoth (WG); 1973
13:21.0*	Gerry Lindgren (USA); 1966
13:22.4	Gianni Del Buono (Ita); 1972
13:22.8	Ian Stewart (UK); 1970
13:23.2	Paul Mose (Ken); 1973
13:23.4	Dick Buerkle (USA); 1974
13:23.6	Dave Black (UK); 1973
13:23.6	Paul Geis (USA) 1974
13:24.0	Manfred Kuschmann (EG); 1974

10,000 METRES

27:30.8	Dave Bedford (UK); 1973
27:38.4	Lasse Viren (Fin); 1972
27:39.4	Ron Clarke (Aus); 1965
27:39.6	Emiel Puttemans (Bel); 1972
27:41.0	Miruts Yifter (Eth); 1972
27:43.6	Steve Prefontaine (USA); 1974
27:46.4	Dick Tayler (NZ); 1974
27:48.2	Mariano Haro (Spa); 1972
27:48.6	Dave Black (UK); 1974
27:51.4	Frank Shorter (USA); 1972

10,000 metres (cont)

27:52.8	Juha Vaatainen (Fin); 1971
27:53.4	Jurgen Haase (EG); 1971
27:54.8	Mohamed Gammoudi (Tun); 1972
27:56.4	Rashid Sharafetdinov (Sov); 1971
27:57.0	Richard Juma (Ken); 1974
27:58.4	Dane Korica (Yug); 1971
27:58.6	Nikolay Sviridov (Sov); 1973
27:59.8	Pavel Andreyev (Sov); 1973
28:01.0	Vadim Mochalov (Sov); 1973
28:01.4	Javier Alvarez (Spa); 1971

MARATHON

2:08:33.6	Derek Clayton (Aus); 1969
2:09:12.0	Ian Thompson (UK); 1974
2:09:28.0	Ron Hill (UK); 1970
2:10:30.0	Frank Shorter (USA); 1972
2:10:37.8	Akio Usami (Jap); 1970
2:10:47.8	Bill Adcocks (UK); 1968
2:11:12.0	Eamon O'Reilly (USA); 1970
2:11:12.6	John Farrington (Aus); 1973
2:11:12.8	Jerome Drayton (Can); 1969
2:11:13.0	Karel Lismont (Bel); 1974
2:11:17.0	Seiichiro Sasaki (Jap); 1967
2:11:18.6	Jack Foster (NZ); 1974
2:11:35.8	Ken Moore (USA); 1970
2:12:00.0	Morio Shigematsu (Jap); 1965
2:12:02.4	Eckhard Lesse (EG); 1974
2:12:03.4	Hayami Tanimura (Jap); 1969
2:12:04.0	Jim Alder (UK); 1970
2:12:10.6	Pekka Paivarinta (Fin); 1974
2:12:11.2	Abebe Bikila (Eth); 1964
2:12:12.0	Yoshiaki Unetani (Jap); 1970

3000 METRES STEEPLECHASE

8:14.0	Ben Jipcho (Ken); 1973
8:14.2	Anders Garderud (Swe); 1974
8:15.0	Bronislaw Malinowski (Pol); 1974
8:18.0	Michael Karst (WG); 1974
8:19.0	Franco Fava (Ita); 1974
8:19.6	Tapio Kantanen (Fin); 1974
8:21.6	Takaharu Koyama (Jap); 1974
8:22.0	Kerry O'Brien (Aus); 1970
8:22.2	Vladimir Dudin (Sov); 1969
8:22.6	John Davies (UK); 1974
8:23.0	Willi Maier (WG); 1973
8:23.2	Doug Brown (USA); 1974
8:23.4	Aleksandr Morozov (Sov); 1969
8:23.6	Kazimierz Maranda (Pol); 1972
8:23.6	Kipchoge Keino (Ken); 1972
8:23.6	Gerard Buchheit (Fra); 1973

3000 metres Steeplechase (cont)

8:23.8	Amos Biwott (Ken); 1972
8:23.8	Dusan Moravcik (Cze); 1972
8:24.0	Evans Mogaka (Ken); 1973
8:24.0	Dans Glans (Swe); 1974

110 METRES HURDLES

(y = 120 yards time)

13.0y	Rod Milburn (USA); 1971
13.2	Martin Lauer (WG); 1959
13.2	Lee Calhoun (USA); 1960
13.2	Earl McCullouch (USA); 1967
13.2y	Erv Hall (USA); 1969
13.2	Willie Davenport (USA); 1969
13.2y	Thomas Hill (USA); 1970
13.2	Guy Drut (Fra); 1974
13.3y	Jerry Tarr (USA); 1962
13.3y	Richmond Flowers (USA); 1968
13.3	Leon Coleman (USA); 1969
13.3	Marcus Walker (USA); 1970
13.3	Frank Siebeck (EG); 1972
13.3	Alejandro Casanas (Cub); 1972
13.3	Leszek Wodzynski (Pol); 1974
13.3	Miroslaw Wodzynski (Pol); 1974
13.3	Charles Foster (USA); 1974
13.3y	Charles Rich (USA); 1974
13.4	22 athletes

400 METRES HURDLES

(*440 yards time less 0.3)

47.8	John Akii-Bua (Uga); 1972
48.1	David Hemery (UK); 1968
48.1	Jim Bolding (USA); 1974
48.4	Ralph Mann (USA); 1972
48.6	Jean-Claude Nallet (Fra); 1970
48.6	Dick Bruggeman (USA); 1972
48.6	Jim Seymour (USA); 1972
48.8	Geoff Vanderstock (USA); 1968
48.8	Alan Pascoe (UK); 1974
48.9*	Wayne Collett (USA); 1970
49.0*	Gert Potgieter (SA); 1960
49.0	Ron Whitney (USA); 1968
49.0	Gerhard Hennige (WG); 1968
49.0	John Sherwood (UK); 1968
49.0*	Wes Williams (USA); 1971
49.0	William Koskei (Ken); 1972
49.1	6 athletes

HIGH JUMP

2.30m (7′ 6½″)	Dwight Stones (USA); 1973
2.29m (7′ 6¼″)	Ni Chih Chin (Chi); 1970
2.29m (7′ 6¼″)	Pat Matzdorf (USA); 1971
2.28m (7′ 5¾″)	Valeriy Brumel (Sov); 1963
2.25m (7′ 4½″)	Juri Tarmak (Sov); 1972
2.25m (7′ 4½″)	Tom Woods (USA); 1973
2.25m (7′ 4½″)	Jesper Torring (Den); 1974
2.25m (7′ 4½″)	Kestutis Sapka (Sov); 1974
2.24m (7′ 4¼″)	Dick Fosbury (USA); 1968
2.24m (7′ 4¼″)	Hermann Magerl (WG); 1972
2.24m (7′ 4¼″)	John Beers (Can); 1973
2.24m (7′ 4¼″)	Istvan Major (Hun); 1973
2.24m (7′ 4¼″)	Vladimir Abramov (Sov); 1974
2.23m (7′ 4″)	Reynaldo Brown (USA); 1973
2.23m (7′ 3¾″)	John Thomas (USA); 1960
2.23m (7′ 3¾″)	Rustam Akhmetov (Sov); 1971
2.23m (7′ 3¾″)	Stefan Junge (EG); 1972
2.23m (7′ 3¾″)i	Sergey Budalov (Sov); 1974
2.23m (7′ 3¾″)	Imants Karlsons (Sov); 1974
2.23m (7′ 3¾″)	Rune Almen (Swe); 1974

POLE VAULT

5.63m (18′ 5½″)	Bob Seagren (USA); 1972
5.59m (18′ 4″)	Kjell Isaksson (Swe); 1972
5.59m (18′ 4″)	Steve Smith (USA), 1974
5.50m (18′ 0½″)	Jan Johnson (USA); 1972
5.50m (18′ 0½″)	Wolfgang Nordwig (EG); 1972
5.49m (18′ 0¼″)	Christos Papanicolaou (Gre); 1970
5.49m (18′ 0¼″)	Dave Roberts (USA); 1972
5.47m (17′ 11½″)	Antti Kalliomaki (Fin); 1973
5.45m (17′ 10½″)	Renato Dionisi (Ita); 1972
5.44m (17′ 10¼″)	John Pennel (USA); 1969
5.42m (17′ 9½″)	Francois Tracanelli (Fra); 1973
5.42m (17′ 9½″)	Tadeusz Slusarski (Pol); 1974
5.41m (17′ 9″)	Yuriy Isakov (Sov); 1973
5.40m (17′ 8½″)	Dick Railsback (USA); 1969
5.40m (17′ 8½″)	Claus Schiprowski (WG); 1968
5.40m (17′ 8½″)	Wojciech Buciarski (Pol); 1974
5.40m (17′ 8½″)	Casey Carrigan (USA); 1974
5.40m (17′ 8½″)	Vladimir Kishkun (Sov); 1974
5.38m (17′ 8″)i	Vic Dias (USA); 1974
5.38m (17′ 8″)i	Buddy Williamson (USA); 1974
5.38m (17′ 7¾″)	Paul Wilson (USA); 1967

LONG JUMP

8.90m (29′ 2½″)	Bob Beamon (USA); 1968
8.35m (27′ 5″)	Ralph Boston (USA); 1965
8.35m (27′ 4¾″)	Igor Ter-Ovanesyan (Sov); 1967
8.35m (27′ 4¾″)	Josef Schwarz (WG); 1970

WORLD ALL-TIME LIST

Long Jump (cont)

8.34m (27' 4½")	Randy Williams (USA); 1972
8.30m (27' 2¾")	Arnie Robinson (USA); 1974
8.25m (27' 0¾")	Ron Coleman (USA); 1971
8.24m (27' 0½")	James McAlister (USA); 1973
8.24m (27' 0½")	Nedo Stekic (Yug); 1974
8.23m (27' 0¼")	Norm Tate (USA); 1971
8.23m (27' 0")	Lynn Davies (UK); 1968
8.22m (26' 11¾")	Preston Carrington (USA); 1972
8.21m (26' 11¼")	Waldemar Stepien (Pol); 1969
8.20m (26' 10¾")	Bouncy Moore (USA); 1974
8.19m (26' 10½")	Klaus Beer (EG); 1968
8.19m (26' 10½")	Henry Hines (USA); 1972
8.18m (26' 10")	Hans Baumgartner (WG); 1972
8.17m (26' 9¾")i	Jean-Francois Bonheme (Fra); 1974
8.16m (26' 9½")	Rainer Stenius (Fin); 1966
8.16m (26' 9½")	Phil Shinnick (USA); 1968

TRIPLE JUMP

17.44m (57' 2¾")	Viktor Saneyev (Sov); 1972
17.40m (57' 1")	Pedro Perez (Cub); 1971
17.31m (56' 9½")	Jorg Drehmel (EG); 1972
17.27m (56' 8")	Nelson Prudencio (Bra); 1968
17.22m (56' 6")	Giuseppe Gentile (Ita); 1968
17.20m (56' 5¼")	Mikhail Bariban (Sov); 1973
17.12m (56' 2")	Carol Corbu (Rom); 1971
17.07m (56' 0")	Dave Smith (USA); 1972
17.06m (55' 11¾")	Michal Joachimowski (Pol); 1973
17.03m (55' 10½")	Josef Szmidt (Pol); 1960
17.02m (55' 10")	Phil May (Aus); 1968
17.01m (55' 9¾")	Nikolay Dudkin (Sov); 1970
17.00m (55' 9¼")	Pertti Pousi (Fin); 1968
17.00m (55' 9¼")	Gustavo Platt (Cuba); 1973
16.98m (55' 8½")	John Craft (USA); 1973
16.94m (55' 7")	Heinz-Gunter Schenk (EG); 1972
16.92m (55' 6¼")	Aleksandr Zolotaryev (Sov); 1967
16.84m (55' 3")	Andrzej Sonntag (Pol); 1973
16.83m (55' 2½")	Nikolay Sinichkin (Sov); 1974
16.82m (55' 2¼")	Klaus Neumann (EG); 1968
16.82m (55' 2¼")	Gennadiy Byessonov (Sov); 1972
16.82m (55' 2¼")	Charlton Ehizuelen (Nig); 1974

SHOT

22.02m (72' 2¾")i	George Woods (USA); 1974 (& 21.42m (70' 3½"); 1974)
21.82m (71' 7¼")	Al Feuerbach (USA); 1973
21.78m (71' 5½")	Randy Matson (USA); 1967
21.70m (71' 2½")	Aleksandr Barishnikov (Sov); 1974
21.67m (71' 1¼")	Hartmut Briesenick (EG); 1973
21.60m (70' 10½")i	Brian Oldfield (USA); 1973

Shot (cont)

21.42m (70' 3½")i	Fred DeBernardi (USA); 1974 (& 21.41m (70' 3"); 1974)
21.37m (70' 1½")	Geoff Capes (UK); 1974
21.35m (70' 0½")	Ron Semkiw (USA); 1974
21.32m (69' 11½")	Heinz-Joachim Rothenburg (EG); 1972
21.31m (69' 11")	Hans-Peter Gies (EG); 1972
21.26m (69' 9")	Reijo Stahlberg (Fin); 1974
21.19m (69' 6¼")	Wladyslaw Komar (Pol); 1974
21.05m (69' 0¾")	Terry Albritton (USA); 1974
21.04m (69' 0½")	Jaroslav Brabec (Cze); 1973
21.01m (68' 11½")	Neil Steinhauer (USA); 1967
20.97m (68' 9¾")i	Karl Salb (USA); 1973
20.80m (68' 3")	Ralf Reichenbach (WG); 1974
20.71m (67' 11½")	Nagui Assad (Egy); 1972
20.69m (67' 10¾")	Valeriy Voikin (Sov); 1974
20.68m (67' 10")	Dallas Long (USA); 1964

DISCUS

70.38m (230' 11")	Jay Silvester (USA); 1971
68.40m (224' 5")	Ricky Bruch (Swe); 1972
68.08m (223' 4")	John Powell (USA); 1974
68.04m (223' 3")	John Van Reenan (SA); 1974
67.38m (221' 1")	Tim Vollmer (USA); 1971
67.18m (220' 5")	Ludvik Danek (Cze); 1974
66.92m (219' 7")	Geza Fejer (Hun); 1971
66.52m (218' 3")	Pentti Kahma (Fin); 1974
66.38m (217' 9")	Janos Muranyi (Hun); 1971
66.38m (217' 9")	Siegfried Pachale (EG); 1973
65.90m (216' 2")	Jon Cole (USA); 1972
65.88m (216' 2")	Dirk Wippermann (WG); 1971
65.84m (216' 0")	Mike Hoffman (USA); 1971
65.60m (215' 3")	Markku Tuokko (Fin); 1973
65.44m (214' 8")	Ferenc Tegla (Hun); 1971
65.22m (214' 0")	Viktor Penzikov (Sov); 1974
65.16m (213' 9")	Randy Matson (USA); 1967
65.14m (213' 8")	Mac Wilkins (USA); 1974
64.94m (213' 1")	Gunnar Muller (EG); 1974
64.94m (213' 0")	Bill Tancred (UK); 1974

HAMMER

76.66m (251' 6")	Aleksey Spiridonov (Sov); 1974
76.60m (251' 4")	Reinhard Theimer (EG); 1974
76.40m (250' 8")	Walter Schmidt (WG); 1971
75.88m (248' 11")	Anatoliy Bondarchuk (Sov); 1972
75.78m (248' 7")	Iosif Gamskiy (Sov); 1971
75.52m (247' 9")	Valentin Dmitryenko (Sov); 1974
74.96m (245' 11")	Jochen Sachse (EG); 1972
74.90m (245' 9")	Uwe Beyer (WG); 1971
74.52m (244' 6")	Romuald Klim (Sov); 1969

ATHLETICS 75

Hammer (cont)
74.44m (244' 3")	Dzhumbyer Pkhakadze (Sov); 1974
74.36m (243' 11")	Mario Vecchiatto (Ita); 1972
74.04m (242' 11")	Vasiliy Khmelevskiy (Sov); 1972
73.98m (242' 8")	Karl Hans Riehm (WG); 1973
73.76m (242' 0")	Gyula Zsivotzky (Hun); 1968
73.72m (241' 10")	Anatoliy Shuplyakov (Sov); 1969
73.70m (241' 9")	Klaus Dieter Beilig (EG); 1974
73.44m (240' 11")	Erwin Klein (WG); 1974
73.36m (240' 8")	Manfred Huning (WG); 1974
73.28m (240' 5")	Istvan Encsi (Hun); 1971
73.08m (239' 9")	Lutz Caspers (WG); 1972

JAVELIN

94.08m (308' 8")	Klaus Wolfermann (WG); 1973
93.90m (308' 1")	Hannu Siitonen (Fin); 1973
93.80m (307' 9")	Janis Lusis (Sov); 1972
92.70m (304' 1")	Jorma Kinnunen (Fin); 1969
92.64m (303' 11")	Pauli Nevala (Fin); 1970
91.72m (300' 11")	Terje Pedersen (Nor); 1964
91.44m (300' 0")	Mark Murro (USA); 1970
90.92m (298' 3")	Cary Feldman (USA); 1973
90.68m (297' 6")	Manfred Stolle (EG); 1971
89.32m (293' 0")	Janis Donins (Sov); 1971
88.94m (291' 9")	Bill Skinner (USA); 1970
88.64m (290' 10")	Sam Colson (USA); 1973
88.52m (290' 5")	Seppo Hovinen (Fin); 1973
87.76m (287' 11")	Ake Nilsson (Swe); 1968
87.44m (286' 10")	Miklos Nemeth (Hun); 1974

Javelin (cont)
87.06m (285' 7")	Gergely Kulcsar (Hun); 1968
86.76m (284' 8")	Frank Covelli (USA); 1968
86.74m (284' 7")	Carlo Lievore (Ita); 1961
86.70m (284' 5")	Aleksandr Makarov (Sov); 1974
86.58m (284' 0")	John Tushaus (USA); 1966

DECATHLON

8454pts	Nikolay Avilov (Sov); 1972
8417pts	Bill Toomey (USA); 1969
8319pts	Kurt Bendlin (WG); 1967
8308pts	Bruce Jenner (USA); 1974
8279pts	Joachim Kirst (EG); 1969
8237pts	Boris Ivanov (Sov); 1971
8230pts	Russ Hodge (USA); 1966
8229pts	Yves Le Roy (Fra); 1974
8207pts	Ryszard Skowronek (Pol); 1974
8188pts	Lennart Hedmark (Swe); 1973
8155pts	Phil Mulkey (USA); 1961
8136pts	Josef Zeilbauer (Aut); 1973
8134pts	Rudolf Sigert (Sov); 1973
8132pts	Guido Kratschmer (WG); 1974
8130pts	Rudiger Demmig (EG); 1970
8122pts	Hans-Joachim Walde (WG); 1971
8122pts	Leonid Litvinyenko (Sov); 1974
8121pts	Jeff Bennett (USA); 1973
8120pts	Jeff Bannister (USA); 1971
8100pts	Aleksandr Blinyayev (Sov); 1973

WOMEN

w = wind assisted.   i = indoor mark

100 METRES

10.8	Renate Stecher (EG); 1973
10.9	Irena Szewinska (Pol); 1974
11.0	Wyomia Tyus (USA); 1968
11.0	Chi Cheng (Tai); 1970
11.0	Ellen Streidt (EG); 1972
11.0	Eva Gleskova (Cze); 1972
11.0	Doris Selmigkeit (EG); 1973
11.0	Petra Kandarr (EG); 1973
11.0	Mona-Lisa Pursiainen (Fin); 1973
11.1	Barbara Ferrell (USA); 1967
11.1	Lyudmila Samotyesova (Sov); 1968
11.1	Margaret Bailes (USA); 1968
11.1	Raelene Boyle (Aus); 1968
11.1	Inge Helten (WG); 1971
11.1	Alice Annum (Gha); 1971
11.1	Sylvianne Telliez (Fra); 1972
11.1	Wilma Van Gool (Hol); 1972
11.1	Barbel Struppert (EG); 1972
11.1	Silvia Chivas (Cub); 1972
11.1	Christina Heinich (EG); 1973
11.1	Monika Meyer (EG); 1973
11.1	Doris Maletzki (EG); 1973
11.1	Barbel Eckert (EG); 1974

200 METRES
(*220 yards time less 0.1)

22.0	Irena Szewinska (Pol); 1974
22.1	Renate Stecher (EG); 1973
22.4	Chi Cheng (Tai); 1970
22.4	Petra Kandarr (EG); 1973
22.4	Mona-Lisa Pursiainen (Fin); 1973
22.5	Raelene Boyle (Aus); 1972

200 metres (cont)

22.7	Marina Sidorova (Sov); 1973
22.7	Ellen Streidt (EG); 1973
22.7	Denise Robertson (Aus); 1974
22.8*	Margaret Burvill (Aus); 1964
22.8	Barbara Ferrell (USA); 1968
22.8	Jennifer Lamy (Aus); 1968
22.8	Gyorgyi Balogh (Hun); 1971
22.8	Monika Zehrt (EG); 1972
22.8	Nadyezhda Besfamilnaya (Sov); 1972
22.8	Doris Maletzki (EG); 1974
22.8	Riitta Salin (Fin); 1974
22.9	Barbel Eckert (EG); 1973
22.9	Wilma Rudolph (USA); 1960
22.9	Margaret Bailes (USA); 1968
22.9	Christina Heinich (EG); 1972
22.9	Annegret Kroniger (WG); 1972

400 METRES

49.9	Irena Szewinska (Pol); 1974
50.1	Riitta Salin (Fin); 1974
50.7	Ellen Streidt (EG); 1974
50.9	Rita Wilden (WG); 1974
51.0	Marilyn Neufville (Jam); 1970
51.0	Monika Zehrt (EG); 1972
51.0	Jelica Pavlicic (Yug); 1974
51.1	Rita Kuhne (EG); 1973
51.2	Sin Kim Dan (NK); 1964
51.2	Mariana Suman (Rom); 1974
51.2	Nadyezhda Ilyina (Sov); 1974
51.2	Angelika Handt (EG); 1974
51.3	Mona-Lisa Pursiainen (Fin); 1973
51.5	Helga Seidler (EG); 1972
51.5	Dagmar Kasling (EG); 1972
51.6	Kathy Hammond (USA); 1972
51.6	Yvonne Saunders (Can); 1974
51.7	Nicole Duclos (Fra); 1969
51.7	Colette Besson (Fra); 1969
51.7	Gyorgyi Balogh (Hun); 1972

800 METRES

1:57.5	Svetla Slateva (Bul); 1973
1:58.0	Sin Kim Dan (NK); 1964
1:58.1	Lilyana Tomova (Bul); 1974
1:58.5	Hildegard Falck (WG); 1971
1:58.6	Mariana Suman (Rom); 1974
1:58.7	Nijole Sabaite (Sov); 1972
1:58.8	Gunhild Hoffmeister (EG); 1974
1:59.6	Vera Nikolic (Yug); 1972
1:59.8	Elzbieta Katolik (Pol); 1973
1:59.9	Vasilina Amzina (Bul); 1972

800 metres (cont)

1:59.9	Maritta Politz (EG); 1973
1:59.9	Marie-Francoise Dubois (Fra); 1974
2:00.0	Ileana Silai (Rom); 1972
2:00.1	Karin Krebs (EG); 1973
2:00.1	Valentina Gerasimova (Sov); 1974
2:00.2	Rosemary Wright (UK); 1972
2:00.2	Abigail Hoffman (Can); 1972
2:00.5	Nikolina Schtereva (Bul); 1974
2:00.6	Waltraud Pohland (EG); 1974
2:00.8	Nina Morgunova (Sov); 1974

1500 METRES

4:01.4	Lyudmila Bragina (Sov); 1972
4:02.3	Gunhild Hoffmeister (EG); 1974
4:02.9	Paola Cacchi (Ita); 1972
4:04.1	Karin Krebs (EG); 1972
4:04.8	Sheila Carey (UK); 1972
4:05.0	Lilyana Tomova (Bul); 1974
4:05.1	Ilja Keizer (Hol); 1972
4:05.2	Grete Andersen (Nor); 1974
4:05.9	Tatyana Kazankina (Sov); 1974
4:06.5	Tamara Pangelova (Sov); 1972
4:06.7	Glenda Reiser (Can); 1972
4:06.7	Ellen Tittel (WG); 1972
4:07.5	Inger Knutsson (Swe); 1973
4:07.6	Regina Kleinau (EG); 1972
4:08.1	Jenny Orr (Aus); 1972
4:08.4	Jaroslava Jehlickova (Cze); 1972
4:08.8	Bernie Boxem (Hol); 1972
4:09.0	Tonka Petrova (Bul); 1973
4:09.1	Vassilene Amzina (Bul); 1972
4:09.4	Joyce Smith (UK); 1972

3000 METRES

8:52.8	Lyudmila Bragina (Sov); 1974
8:55.2	Nina Holmen (Fin); 1974
8:55.6	Joyce Smith (UK); 1974
8:56.6	Paola Cacchi (Ita); 1973
8:58.4	Inger Knutsson (Swe); 1973
8:59.0	Natalia Andrei (Rom); 1974
9:03.0	Pirjo Vihonen (Fin); 1973
9:03.2	Francie Larrieu (USA); 1974
9:03.4	Thelma Wright (Can); 1974
9:04.4	Tamara Pangelova (Sov); 1974
9:05.2	Bronislawa Ludwichowska (Pol); 1974
9:07.0	Ann Yeoman (UK); 1974
9:07.6	Tonka Petrova (Bul); 1974
9:09.4	Bronislawa Doborzynska (Pol); 1974
9:09.6	Maria Istomina (Sov); 1973

3000 metres (cont)

9:09.6	Jadwiga Drazek (Pol); 1974
9:09.6	Renata Pentlinowska (Pol); 1974
9:11.8	Irina Bondarchuk (Sov); 1974
9:12.2	Zsuzsa Volgyi (Hun); 1973
9:12.2	Eva Gustafsson (Swe); 1974

100 METRES HURDLES

12.3	Annelie Ehrhardt (EG); 1973
12.5	Pamela Ryan (Aus); 1972
12.5	Teresa Nowak (Pol); 1974
12.6	Karin Balzer (EG); 1971
12.7	Teresa Sukniewicz (Pol); 1970
12.7	Valeria Stefanescu (Rom); 1972
12.7	Danuta Straszynska (Pol); 1972
12.7	Grazyna Rabsztyn (Pol); 1972
12.7	Annerose Fiedler (EG); 1974
12.8	Chi Cheng (Tai); 1970
12.8	Barbel Podeswa (EG); 1972
13.0	Pat Johnson (USA); 1972
13.0	Johanna Schaller (EG); 1973
13.0	Judy Vernon (UK); 1974
13.0	Blondelle Thompson (UK); 1974
13.0	Meta Antenen (Swi); 1974
13.0	Natalia Lebedyeva (Sov); 1974
13.1	15 girls

HIGH JUMP

1.95m (6′ 4¾″)	Rosemarie Witschas (EG); 1974
1.94m (6′ 4½″)	Yordanka Blagoyeva (Bul); 1972
1.93m (6′ 4″)	Ilona Gusenbauer (Aut); 1972
1.92m (6′ 3½″)	Ulrike Meyfarth (WG); 1972
1.92m (6′ 3½″)	Virginia Ioan (Rom); 1974
1.92m (6′ 3½″)i	Rita Kirst (EG) (& 1.90m); 1974
1.91m (6′ 3¼″)	Iolanda Balas (Rom); 1961
1.91m (6′ 3¼″)	Milada Karbanova (Cze); 1974
1.90m (6′ 2¾″)	Sara Simeoni (Ita); 1974
1.88m (6′ 2″)	Antonia Lazaryeva (Sov); 1971
1.88m (6′ 2″)	Cornelia Popescu (Rom); 1973
1.87m (6′ 1½″)	Valentina Chulkova (Sov); 1971
1.87m (6′ 1½″)	Rita Gildemeister (EG); 1973
1.87m (6′ 1½″)	Miloslava Hubnerova (Cze); 1972
1.87m (6′ 1½″)	Barbara Lawton (UK); 1973
1.87m (6′ 1½″)	Maria Mracnova (Cze); 1974
1.87m (6′ 1½″)	Debbie Brill (Can); 1974
1.87m (6′ 1½″)i	Erika Rudolf (Hun); 1974
1.86m (6′ 1¼″)	6 girls

LONG JUMP

6.84m (22′ 5¼″)	Heide Rosendahl (WG); 1970
6.82m (22′ 4½″)	Viorica Viscopoleanu (Rom); 1968
6.81m (22′ 4¼″)	Margrit Herbst (EG); 1971
6.77m (22′ 2½″)	Diana Yorgova (Bul); 1972
6.77m (22′ 2½″)	Angela Schmalfeld (EG); 1974
6.77m (22′ 2½″)	Marianne Voelzke (EG); 1974
6.76m (22′ 2¼″)	Mary Rand (UK); 1964
6.76m (22′ 2¼″)	Ingrid Mickler (WG); 1971
6.73m (22′ 1″)	Tatyana Shchelkanova (Sov); 1966
6.73m (22′ 1″)	Sheila Sherwood (UK); 1970
6.73m (22′ 1″)	Meta Antenen (Swi); 1971
6.69m (21′ 11½″)	Angelika Liebsch (EG); 1972
6.67m (21′ 10½″)	Irena Szewinska (Pol); 1968
6.67m (21′ 10½″)	Eva Suranova (Cze); 1972
6.66m (21′ 10¼″)	Tatyana Talisheva (Sov); 1968
6.66m (21′ 10¼″)	Lidia Alfeyeva (Sov); 1974
6.65m (21′ 10″)	Ilona Bruzsenyak (Hun); 1974
6.64m (21′ 9½″)	Sieglinde Ammann (Swi); 1969
6.62m (21′ 8¾″)	Margarite Treinite (Sov); 1973
6.62m (21′ 8¾″)	Maroula Lambrou (Gre); 1974

SHOT

21.57m (70′ 9¼″)	Helena Fibingerova (Cze); 1974
21.45m (70′ 4½″)	Nadyezhda Chizhova (Sov); 1973
20.61m (67′ 7½″)	Marianne Adam (EG); 1974
20.22m (66′ 4″)	Margitta Gummel (EG); 1972
19.93m (65′ 4¾″)	Ivanka Khristova (Bul); 1974
19.68m (64′ 6¾″)	Elena Stoyanova (Bul); 1974
19.52m (64′ 0½″)	Esfir Kravchevska (Sov); 1973
19.40m (63′ 7¾″)	Marita Lange (EG); 1974
19.39m (63′ 7½″)	Antonina Ivanova (Sov); 1971
19.39m (63′ 7½″)	Faina Melnik (Sov); 1974
19.23m (63′ 1¼″)	Ilona Schoknecht (EG); 1974
19.12m (62′ 8¾″)	Yelena Korablyeva (Sov); 1974
19.06m (62′ 6½″)	Ludwika Chewinska (Pol); 1972
18.91m (62′ 0½″)	Raissa Taranda (Sov); 1972
18.90m (62′ 0¼″)	Hannelore Friedel (EG); 1971
18.81m (61′ 8½″)	Ingeborg Friedrich (EG); 1972
18.64m (61′ 1¾″)	Gabrielle Greiner (EG); 1973
18.59m (61′ 0″)	Tamara Press (Sov); 1965
18.57m (60′ 11″)	Galina Nyekrasova (Sov); 1972
18.45m (60′ 6½″)	Radostina Bakhtschevanova (Bul); 1974

DISCUS

69.90m (229′ 4″)	Faina Melnik (Sov); 1974
68.48m (224′ 8″)	Maria Vergova (Bul); 1974
67.32m (220′ 10″)	Argentina Menis (Rom); 1972
67.02m (219′ 10″)	Gabriele Hinzmann (EG); 1973
64.96m (213′ 1″)	Liesel Westermann (WG); 1972

1974 WORLD RANKINGS

Discus (cont)
64.34m (211' 1")	Vassilka Stoyeva (Bul); 1972
63.66m (208' 10")	Karin Illgen (EG); 1970
63.26m (207' 6")	Evelyn Schlaak (EG); 1974
62.86m (206' 3")	Tamara Danilova (Sov); 1972
62.78m (206' 0")	Carmen Ionescu (Rom); 1972
62.06m (203' 7")	Lia Manoliu (Rom); 1972
61.98m (203' 4")	Svyetla Bozhkova (Bul); 1973
61.88m (203' 0")	Lyudmila Muravyeva (Sov); 1971
61.84m (202' 11")	Karin Holdke (EG); 1974
61.64m (202' 3")	Christine Spielberg (EG); 1968
61.38m (201' 4")	Barbara Regel (EG); 1974
61.24m (200' 11")	Annelie Braun (EG); 1974
61.14m (200' 7")	Helena Vyhnalova (Cze); 1974
61.10m (200' 5")	Olimpia Catarama (Rom); 1972
60.98m (200' 1")	Sabine Engel (EG); 1973

JAVELIN

67.22m (220' 6")	Ruth Fuchs (EG); 1974
64.34m (211' 1")	Jacqueline Todten (EG); 1974
63.96m (209' 10")	Elvira Ozolina (Sov); 1973
63.42m (208' 1")	Kathy Schmidt (USA); 1973
63.08m (206' 11")	Felicja Kinder (Pol); 1974
62.70m (205' 8")	Ewa Gryziecka (Pol); 1972
62.60m (205' 4")	Lutcjan Mollova (Bul); 1974
62.40m (204' 9")	Yelena Gorchakova (Sov); 1964
62.30m (204' 5")	Daniela Jaworska (Pol); 1973
62.24m (204' 2")	Petra Rivers (Aus); 1972
62.12m (203' 10")	Nastasa Urbancic (Yug); 1973
62.04m (203' 6")	Nina Marakina (Sov); 1971
62.00m (203' 5")	Svyetlana Babitsch (Sov); 1973

Javelin (cont)
61.80m (202' 9")	Eva Janko (Aut); 1973
61.42m (201' 6")	Marion Becker (Rom–WG); 1972
61.14m (200' 7")	Maria Vago (Hun); 1974
61.02m (200' 2")	Ameli Koloska (WG); 1972
60.68m (199' 1")	Mihaela Penes (Rom); 1967
60.58m (198' 9")	Angela Ranky (Hun); 1969
60.56m (198' 8")	Barbara Friedrich (USA); 1967

PENTATHLON

4932pts	Burglinde Pollak (EG); 1973
4801pts	Mary Peters (UK); 1972
4791pts	Heide Rosendahl (WG); 1972
4776pts	Nadyezhda Tkachenko (Sov); 1974
4754pts	Valentina Tikhomirova (Sov); 1973
4727pts	Liese Prokop (Aut); 1969
4693pts	Christine Bodner (EG); 1972
4680pts	Margit Herbst (EG); 1971
4666pts	Ingrid Mickler (WG); 1970
4647pts	Angela Schmalfeld (EG); 1973
4628pts	Zoya Spasovkhodskaya (Sov); 1974
4617pts	Ilona Bruzsenyak (Hun); 1973
4562pts	Christel Voss (WG); 1974
4561pts	Snezhana Yurukova (Bul); 1974
4557pts	Lyudmila Popovskaya (Sov); 1974
4548pts	Sigrun Thon (EG); 1974
4543pts	Tatyana Vorokhobko (Sov); 1974
4538pts	Barbel Muller (EG); 1974
4531pts	Margot Eppinger (WG); 1974
4528pts	Margit Papp (Hun); 1973

UK Top 20 1974

MEN w = wind assisted. i = indoor mark

100 METRES

10.3	Don Halliday		10.6	Scott Brodie
10.3	Les Piggot		10.6	Ron Griffiths
10.4	Derek Cole		10.6	C.J. Kirkpatrick
10.5	Steve Green		10.6	Ian Matthews
10.5	Chris Monk		10.7	Malcolm Kelly
10.5	Roger Jenkins		10.7	Jack Paterson
10.5	Brian Green		10.7	Ian Saunders
10.5	David Roberts		10.7	Andrew Cornaby
10.6	Gareth Edwards		10.7	Chris Lodge
10.6	Roy Turkington		10.7	Peter Blackburn
10.6	Ainsley Bennett		10.7	Richard Meredith
10.6	Tim Bonsor		10.7	Barrie Kelly
			10.7	Terry Collins

ATHLETICS 75

200 METRES

20.5	David Jenkins
20.8	Ainsley Bennett
20.9	Chris Monk
21.1	Steve Green
21.3	Terry Collins
21.4	Ian Matthews
21.5	Derek Cole
21.5	Graham Malcolm
21.5	Roger Jenkins
21.5	Andrew Harley
21.5	Steve Hall
21.6	Steve White
21.6	Ian Saunders
21.6	Stuart Bell
21.6	Les Hoyte
21.6	Robert Kislingbury
21.7	Don Halliday
21.7	Bill Hartley
21.7	David Roberts
21.7	Glen Cohen
21.7	David Artley
21.7	Gordon Wood
21.7	Colin O'Neill
21.7	Andrew McMaster

400 METRES

45.2	David Jenkins
46.6	Jim Aukett
46.7	Steve Marlow
46.7	Roger Jenkins
46.8	Glen Cohen
46.9	John Wilson
47.0	Ainsley Bennett
47.3	Mick Delaney
47.3	Ian Saunders
47.4	Bill Hartley
47.5	Steve Ovett
47.6	Danny Laing
47.6	Bob Benn
47.8	Joe Chivers
47.8	Chris Van Rees
47.8	Alan Pascoe
48.0	Wynford Leyshon
48.0	Mark Clark
48.1	Brian Jones
48.2	Colin Campbell

800 METRES
(*880 yards time less 0.7)

1:45.6	Andy Carter
1:45.8	Steve Ovett
1:46.3	Phil Lewis
1:46.8	David McMeekin
1:47.7	Tony Settle
1:47.8	Peter Browne
1:47.8	Colin Campbell
1:48.4	Frank Clement
1:48.9	John Greatrex
1:49.4	Norman Gregor
1:49.8	John Kirkbride
1:50.1	Tony Dyke
1:50.1	Alan Mottershead
1:50.2	Alan Gibson
1:50.4	Brian Gordon
1:50.4	John Glover
1:50.4	Ray Weatherburn
1:50.5	Jim Douglas
1:50.5	Eddie Coffey
1:50.6*	Ray Smedley

1500 METRES

3:37.4	Frank Clement
3:37.6	Brendan Foster
3:39.6	Ray Smedley
3:39.8	John Kirkbride
3:41.4	Phil Banning
3:42.3	Jim Douglas
3:42.6	David Gibbon
3:43.1	Paul Lawther
3:43.1	David McMeekin
3:43.1	Ron MacDonald
3:43.4	Adrian Weatherhead
3:43.5	Julian Goater
3:43.6	Clive Thomas
3:43.7	Peter Ratcliffe
3:44.4	Richard Newble
3:44.5	John Greatrex
3:44.5	David Moorcroft
3:45.0	Bob Maplestone
3:45.1	Roy Young
3:45.8	Stewart Easton

1 MILE

3:57.4	Frank Clement
3:57.7	Ray Smedley
3:58.4	Brendan Foster
3:58.9	Ron Martin

250

1974 UK RANKINGS

1 mile (cont)

3:59.4	Steve Ovett
4:00.2	David Black
4:00.9	Chris Barber
4:01.0	Chris Stewart
4:01.0	Clive Thomas
4:01.3	David Gibbon
4:02.3	Peter Ratcliffe
4:02.3	David Nicholl
4:02.6	Jim Douglas
4:02.6	Nick Rose
4:03.3	Ron MacDonald
4:03.4	David Wright
4:03.5	Bob Maplestone
4:03.7	Tony Settle
4:04.0	David Lowes
4:04.3	Julian Goater

5000 METRES
(*3 miles time plus 28.0)

13:14.6	Brendan Foster
13:23.6	David Black
13:28.8	David Bedford
13:28.8	Tony Simmons
13:35.2	Bernie Ford
13:38.4	Chris Stewart
13:39.0	Tony Staynings
13:40.4	Ian Stewart
13:40.4	Mike Baxter
13:42.6	Ricky Wilde
13:44.0	Nick Rose
13:45.6	Gordon Minty
13:45.8	Richard Newble
13:48.0	Adrian Weatherhead
13:48.2	Frank Briscoe
13:49.6	John Davies
13:51.2	Jim Brown
13:52.2	Keith Penny
13:52.8	Julian Goater
13:53.0	Barry Smith
13:53.0	Steve Walker

10,000 METRES

27:48.6	David Black
28:14.8	David Bedford
28:15.8	Bernie Ford
28:16.0	Mike Baxter
28:17.2	Ian Stewart
28:19.4	Tony Simmons
28:20.8	Jim Brown
28:25.8	Grenville Tuck
28:37.4	Keith Penny

10,000 metres (cont)

28:40.8	Bernie Plain
28:41.2	Frank Briscoe
28:43.0	John Brown
28:44.4	Gordon Minty
28:49.8	Steve Walker
28:54.0	Chris Stewart
28:54.8	Richard Newble
28:59.6	Jon Wigley
28:59.8	Peter Standing
29:04.2	Bob Holt
29:10.4	John Bednarski

MARATHON

2:09:12	Ian Thompson
2:13:12	Chris Stewart
2:14:15	Don Macgregor
2:14:56	Bernie Plain
2:16:07	Colin Kirkham
2:16:28	Jim Wight
2:16:39	Don Faircloth
2:16:47	Malcolm Thomas
2:17:02	Bernie Allen
2:17:23	Ron Hill
2:17:36	Bob Lunnon
2:18:33	Dic Evans
2:18:49	Max Coleby
2:19:01	Jim Dingwall
2:19:18	Rob Heron
2:19:25	Eric Austin
2:19:32	Harry Leeming
2:19:37	John Norman
2:19:52	Bob Sercombe
2:20:04	Colin Moxsom

3000 METRES STEEPLECHASE

8:22.6	John Davies
8:29.6	John Bicourt
8:32.2	David Camp
8:34.2	Steve Hollings
8:36.2	Bernard Hayward
8:38.2	Clive Thomas
8:38.8	Roger Bean
8:40.2	Dennis Coates
8:40.2	Tony Staynings
8:45.0	Ian Gilmour
8:45.0	Andy Holden
8:50.6	Adrian Weatherhead
8:50.6	Ron McAndrew
8:53.4	Nick Jeffrey

3000 metres (cont)

8:53.6	Steve Mitchell
8:54.2	Dic Evans
8:55.2	Gareth Bryan-Jones
8:57.2	Roger Cytlau
8:58.0	Gerry Stevens
8:58.2	Colin Moxsom

110 METRES HURDLES

13.7	C. J. Kirkpatrick
13.8	Berwyn Price
13.9	David Wilson
14.1	Alan Pascoe
14.3	Graham Gower
14.5	Stewart McCallum
14.5	Peter Kelly
14.7	Alan Cronin
14.8	Richard Palmer
14.8	Alan Davis
14.8	Graham Shaw
14.9	Angus McKenzie
14.9	Robert Davidson
14.9	Paul Hambley
14.9	David Kidner
15.0	Neil Gerrard
15.0	Malcolm Kindon
15.0	Keith Purves
15.0	Tony James
15.0	Michael Jackson
15.0	Robert Danville

400 METRES HURDLES

48.8	Alan Pascoe
49.9	Bill Hartley
50.6	Colin O'Neill
50.7	Steve Black
51.5	Steve James
51.6	Norman Gregor
52.3	Alun James
52.6	Wynford Leyshon
52.7	Stewart McCallum
52.8	Berwyn Price
52.9	John Sherwood
53.3	C. J. Kirkpatrick
53.5	Mike Whittingham
53.6	Orrie Fenn
53.7	Harry Robinson
53.7	Wilbert Greaves
53.8	Paul Hambley
53.8	Paul Young
53.9	Paul Beattie
53.9	Steve Johnson

HIGH JUMP

2.11m (6′ 11″)	Colin Boreham
2.06m (6′ 9″)	Alan Lerwill
2.05m (6′ 8¾″)	Mike Butterfield
2.03m (6′ 8″)	Gary Vose
2.03m (6′ 8″)	Angus McKenzie
2.03m (6′ 8″)	Brian Burgess
2.02m (6′ 7½″)	Milton Palmer
2.02m (6′ 7½″)	Roy Mitchell
2.01m (6′ 7″)	Chris Wilson
2.00m (6′ 6¾″)	Mike Campbell
2.00m (6′ 6¾″)	Martyn Shorten
2.00m (6′ 6¾″)	Innes Murray
2.00m (6′ 6¾″)	Tony Brewster
1.98m (6′ 6″)	Geraint Griffiths
1.98m (6′ 6″)	David Kidner
1.97m (6′ 5½″)	Alan Dainton
1.96m (6′ 5″)	Danny Coyle
1.96m (6′ 5″)	Ron Fullelove
1.96m (6′ 5″)	Nigel Edge
1.96m (6′ 5″)	John Hills
1.96m (6′ 5″)	Chris Richards

POLE VAULT

5.20m (17′ 0¾″)	Mike Bull
5.20m (17′ 0¾″)	Brian Hooper
4.90m (16′ 0¾″)	Allan Williams
4.71m (15′ 5½″)	Jeff Fenge
4.70m (15′ 5″)	David Lease
4.67m (15′ 3¾″)	Keith Stock
4.60m (15′ 1″)	Chris Boreham
4.50m (14′ 9″)	Steve Chappell
4.50m (14′ 9″)	Nick Phipps
4.50m (14′ 9″)	Chris Kidd
4.49m (14′ 8¾″)	Islwyn Rees
4.49m (14′ 8¾″)	Jeff Gutteridge
4.30m (14′ 1¼″)	David Kidner
4.30m (14′ 1¼″)	Willoughby Best
4.27m (14′ 0″)	Dick Williamson
4.26m (13′ 11¾″)	Phil Goulding
4.25m (13′ 11¼″)	Alan Drayton
4.20m (13′ 9¼″)	Steve Clark
4.20m (13′ 9¼″)	Robin Griffiths
4.20m (13′ 9¼″)	Tim Gardner

LONG JUMP

7.98m (26′ 2¼″)	Alan Lerwill
7.63m (25′ 0½″)	Geoff Hignett
7.56m (24′ 9¾″)	Don Porter
7.48m (24′ 6½″)	Roy Mitchell

Long Jump (cont)

7.47m (24′ 6¼″)	Phil Scott
7.47m (24′ 6¼″)	Stewart Atkins
7.45m (24′ 5½″)	Peter Templeton
7.41m (24′ 3¾″)	Trevor Paice
7.35m (24′ 1½″)	Billie Kirkpatrick
7.34m (24′ 1″)	Roy Turkington
7.32m (24′ 0¼″)	Derek Cole
7.31m (23′ 11¾″)	Peter Blackburn
7.27m (23′ 10¼″)	Bob Johnson
7.27m (23′ 10¼″)	Colin Wright
7.24m (23′ 9″)	Willie Clark
7.22m (23′ 8¼″)	Steve Wright
7.20m (23′ 7½″)	Jack Morgan
7.20m (23′ 7½″)	Graham Byham
7.20m (23′ 7½″)	Alan Wells
7.19m (23′ 7¼″)	Steve White

TRIPLE JUMP

15.78m (51′ 9¼″)	Willie Clark
15.76m (51′ 8½″)	David Johnson
15.73m (51′ 7¼″)i	Peter Blackburn
15.65m (51′ 4¼″)	Aston Moore
15.59m (51′ 1¾″)	Rodney Heward-Mills
15.50m (50′ 10¼″)	Tony Wadhams
15.44m (50′ 8″)	Frank Attoh
15.40m (50′ 6¼″)	Bob Johnson
15.35m (50′ 4½″)	John Vernon
15.31m (50′ 2¾″)	Alan Lerwill
15.27m (50′ 1¼″)	Peter Knowles
15.21m (49′ 11″)	Garry Doerr
15.18m (49′ 9¾″)	John Phillips
15.13m (49′ 7¾″)	Andy Vincent
15.10m (49′ 6½″)	Reynold Edwards
15.01m (49′ 3″)	Peter Davies
14.97m (49′ 1½″)	George Riley
14.95m (49′ 0¾″)	George Owens
14.94m (49′ 0¼″)	Matthew Cannavan
14.93m (48′ 11¾″)	Chris Kidd

SHOT

21.37m (70′ 1½″)	Geoff Capes
20.43m (67′ 0½″)	Mike Winch
19.43m (63′ 9″)	Bill Tancred
18.35m (60′ 2½″)	Peter Tancred
17.79m (58′ 4½″)	John Alderson
17.44m (57′ 2¾″)	Bill Fuller
16.59m (54′ 5¼″)	Bob Dale
16.47m (54′ 0½″)	Sid Clark
16.38m (53′ 9″)	Andy Drzewiecki
16.30m (53′ 5¾″)	Andy Kerr

Shot (cont)

16.29m (53′ 5½″)	Tony Satchwell
16.27m (53′ 4½″)	Paul Rees
16.25m (53′ 3¾″)	John Watts
15.99m (52′ 5½″)	Mike Cushion
15.94m (52′ 3¾″)	Nick Parry
15.91m (52′ 2½″)	Erol Palsay
15.82m (51′ 11″)	John Hillier
15.76m (51′ 8½″)	Neil Griffin
15.72m (51′ 7″)	Allan Seatory
15.61m (51′ 2¾″)	Ted Kelland

DISCUS

64.94m (213′ 1″)	Bill Tancred
61.00m (200′ 0″)	Allan Seatory
60.16m (197′ 4″)	Peter Tancred
59.76m (196′ 1″)	John Hillier
58.78m (192′ 10″)	John Watts
57.84m (189′ 9″)	Mike Cushion
56.48m (185′ 4″)	Mike Winch
54.36m (178′ 4″)	Guy Dirkin
54.10m (177′ 6″)	Geoff Capes
54.02m (177′ 3″)	Denis Roscoe
53.20m (174′ 6″)	Andy Drzewiecki
52.14m (171′ 1″)	Ted Kelland
52.06m (170′ 9″)	Danny Maloney
51.88m (170′ 2″)	Geoff Tyler
51.32m (168′ 4″)	Neil Griffin
50.26m (164′ 11″)	Paul Rees
50.22m (164′ 9″)	Arthur McKenzie
49.48m (162′ 4″)	John Turton
49.00m (160′ 9″)	Bill Fuller
48.92m (160′ 6″)	Peter Gordon

HAMMER

71.00m (232′ 11″)	Ian Chipchase
70.88m (232′ 6″)	Howard Payne
69.48m (227′ 11″)	Chris Black
68.80m (225′ 9″)	Barry Williams
67.66m (222′ 0″)	Paul Dickenson
64.48m (211′ 6″)	James Whitehead
62.10m (203′ 9″)	Peter Aston
62.10m (203′ 9″)	Chris Melluish
62.00m (203′ 5″)	Eric Berry
60.66m (199′ 0″)	Bruce Fraser
60.50m (198′ 6″)	Peter Gordon
59.52m (195′ 3″)	Lawrence Bryce
59.10m (193′ 11″)	Philip Scott
58.40m (191′ 7″)	Arthur McKenzie
57.48m (188′ 7″)	Thomas Campbell
57.30m (188′ 0″)	Willie Robertson

ATHLETICS 75

Hammer (cont)
55.70m (182' 9")	Eric Johnston
55.36m (181' 7")	Chris Davison
55.28m (181' 4")	Michael Emens
55.14m (180' 11")	David Bayes

JAVELIN

84.92m (278' 7")	Charles Clover
82.38m (270' 3")	David Travis
80.20m (263' 1")	Kevin Sheppard
79.48m (260' 9")	Brian Roberts
75.98m (249' 3")	Ronald Silvester
72.48m (237' 9")	Kenneth Holmes
72.20m (236' 10")	Phillip Hollywood
72.10m (236' 6")	David Ottley
71.68m (235' 2")	David Heath
70.38m (230' 11")	Keith Turnbull
69.76m (228' 10")	Pawlo Ostapowycz
69.62m (228' 5")	Chris Harrison
69.54m (228' 2")	David Birkmyre
68.54m (224' 10")	Barry Sanderson
68.10m (223' 5")	Paul Stewart
68.06m (223' 3")	Nicholas Aplin
67.98m (223' 0")	Colin Taylor
67.96m (222' 11")	Peter Yates
67.26m (220' 8")	Neville Thompson
66.80m (219' 2")	Graham Daws

DECATHLON

7417pts	Mike Bull
7277pts	Barry King
7188pts	David Kidner
7127pts	Alan Drayton
7088pts	Roy Mitchell
7035pts	Mike Corden
6712pts	Nick Phipps
6707pts	Clifford Brooks
6694pts	Chris Youngs
6472pts	Roy Snow
6400pts	Panaytios Zeniou
6314pts	Mike Lomas
6228pts	Linbert Spencer
6192pts	Wayne Dubose
6088pts	Bruce McEwan
6074pts	Alan Shaw
6073pts	John Howell
6038pts	Godfrey Ward
6003pts	Graham Walker
5973pts	John Crotty

20 KILOMETRES WALK

88:50	Amos Seddon
89:04	Roger Mills
89:26	Olly Flynn
89:49	Peter Marlow
90:02	Bob Dobson
90:07	Paul Nihill
92:36	Ron Wallwork
93:01	Carl Lawton
93:18	Tony Taylor
93:26	Brian Adams
93:28	Stuart Maidment
93:45	Eric Taylor
93:58	Mike Holmes
93:59	Ken Carter
94:06	Roy Thorpe
94:11	Lou Mockett
94:21	John Warhurst
95:07	Jacky Lord
95:55	Dennis Holly
96:04	Peter Selby

50 KILOMETRES WALK

4:11:22	Bob Dobson
4:18:58	John Warhurst
4:24:08	Roy Thorpe
4:27:21	Alec Banyard
4:30:16	Mel McCann
4:30:40	Peter Hodkinson
4:31:44	Carl Lawton
4:31:51	Brian Adams
4:32:15	Ray Middleton
4:35:19	John Nye
4:36:30	John Lees
4:37:59	Ken Harding
4:39:03	Charly Fogg
4:40:08	Mike Holmes
4:40:14	Roy Posner
4:44:08	Peter Selby
4:46:55	Geoff Hunwicks
4:47:00	Shaun Lightman
4:47:40	Barry Ingarfield
4:48:22	Stuart Ashton

1974 UK RANKINGS

WOMEN

w = wind assisted.   i = indoor mark

100 METRES

11.1	Andrea Lynch
11.2	Helen Golden
11.3	Sonia Lannaman
11.5	Linda Barratt
11.6	Margaret Williams
11.6	Denise Ramsden
11.7	Donna Murray
11.8	Sandra Pengilley
11.8	Sharon Colyear
11.8	Wendy Hill
11.8	Judy Vernon
11.8	Janis Walsh
11.9	Karen Walker
11.9	Blondelle Thompson
11.9	Wendy Clarke
11.9	Elaine Douglas
11.9	Jenny Pawsey
11.9	Val Peat
11.9	Jannette Roscoe
11.9	Myra Nimmo
11.9	Gladys Taylor
11.9	Ruth Morris

200 METRES

23.0	Helen Golden
23.2	Andrea Lynch
23.3	Donna Murray
23.3	Sharon Colyear
23.5	Margaret Williams
23.6	Verona Bernard
23.7	Ruth Kennedy
23.8	Wendy Hill
23.8	Sonia Lannaman
23.9	Judy Vernon
23.9	Gladys Taylor
23.9	Jannette Roscoe
24.0	Diane Heath
24.1	Sandra Pengilley
24.2	Linda Barratt
24.2	Barbara Martin
24.3	Averil McClelland
24.3	Blondelle Thompson
24.3	Elaine Douglas
24.4	Hazel Oakes
24.4	Lorna Drysdale
24.4	Janis Walsh
24.4	Alison MacRitchie
24.4	Denise Ramsden

400 METRES

51.8	Donna Murray
51.9	Verona Bernard/Elder
52.9	Jannette Roscoe
53.5	Ruth Kennedy
53.8	Christine Warden
53.9	Liz Barnes
54.1	Wendy Hill
54.6	Anne Littlejohn
54.9	Linda Taylor
54.9	Paula Lloyd
55.0	Evelyn McMeekin
55.0	Adrienne Smyth
55.3	Jane Colebrook
55.4	Averil Halliday
55.4	Dawn Webster
55.4	Anne Clarkson
55.4	Sandra Pengilley
55.5	Diane Heath
55.6	Ann Robertson
55.8	Gloria Dourass
55.8	Gladys Taylor

800 METRES

2:02.8	Lesley Kiernan
2:03.1	Joan Allison
2:03.9	Rosemary Wright
2:05.9	Margaret Coomber
2:06.2	Gloria Dourass
2:07.1	Mary Sonner
2:07.2	Norine Braithwaite
2:07.5	Hilary Tanner/Hollick
2:07.8	Christine McMeekin
2:08.5	Jane Colebrook
2:08.6	Susan Howell
2:08.7	Pat Cropper
2:08.8	Jean Lochhead
2:08.8	Ann Clarkson
2:09.1	Sheila Carey
2:09.3	Christine Tranter
2:09.7	Pam Reece
2:09.8	Christine Haskett
2:09.9	Paula Yeoman
2:10.0	Annette Roberts

1500 METRES

4:10.7	Joan Allison
4:12.0	Joyce Smith

255

ATHLETICS 75

1500 metres (cont)

4:14.7	Mary Stewart
4:18.5	Ann Yeoman
4:18.8	Christine Haskett
4:19.0	Paula Yeoman
4:21.0	Norine Braithwaite
4:22.8	Christine Tranter
4:24.2	Carol Gould
4:24.5	Margaret Coomber
4:24.7	Rosemary Wright
4:25.7	Glynis Goodburn/Penny
4:26.4	Jean Lochhead
4:26.9	Sheila Carey
4:28.0	Ruth Morrish
4:28.0	Annette Roberts
4:28.5	Margaret Beacham
4:28.5	Penelope Yule
4:28.7	Christine Curthoys
4:29.0	Carol McLoughlin

3000 METRES

8:55.6	Joyce Smith
9:07.0	Ann Yeoman
9:19.8	Paula Yeoman
9:20.2	Carol Gould
9:31.8	Christine Haskett
9:33.0	Glynis Goodburn/Penny
9:33.8	Alison Blake
9:36.4	Christine Readdy
9:36.8	Rita Ridley
9:37.6	Val Howe
9:39.6	Kay Barnett
9:44.8	Carol McLoughlin
9:49.2	Christine Curthoys
9:56.0	Margaret Ashcroft
9:56.4	Ruth Morrish
9:57.2	Annette Roberts
9:58.2	Moira O'Boyle
9:58.8	Jean Lochhead
9:59.8	Angela Briscoe
10:00.0	Betty Price

100 METRES HURDLES

13.0	Judy Vernon
13.0	Blondelle Thompson
13.5	Lorna Drysdale
13.7	Susan Holmstrom
13.8	Myra Nimmo
13.8	Lynne Ilott
13.8	Pat Pryce
13.9	Mary Peters

100 metres Hurdles (cont)

13.9	Ann Wilson
14.1	Diana Stewart
14.2	Sue Mapstone
14.2	Pat Chapman
14.2	Janet Honour
14.2	Lorna Boothe
14.2	Bridget Ruttledge
14.2	Sharon Colyear
14.3	Elizabeth Eddy
14.4	Sue Wright
14.4	Barbara Corbett
14.4	Helen Alderton
14.4	Jane Long

400 METRES HURDLES

58.0	Christine Warden
59.5	Susan Howell
61.1	Lorna Boothe
62.4	Janis Farry
62.4	Linda Robinson
62.4	Sharon Colyear
62.9	Lynne Davies
63.4	Gillian Howell
63.9	Margaret Cope
64.3	Audrey Pedro

HIGH JUMP

1.86m (6' 1¼")	Barbara Lawton
1.83m (6' 0")	Val Harrison
1.80m (5' 10¾")	Sue Wright
1.80m (5' 10¾")	Ruth Watt
1.77m (5' 9¾")	Fiona Stacey
1.77m (5' 9¾")	Anne Gilson
1.76m (5' 9¼")	Penny Dimmock
1.76m (5' 9¼")	Ann Wilson
1.76m (5' 9¼")	Teresa Dainton
1.76m (5' 9¼")	Rosaline Few
1.75m (5' 8¾")	Sue Vickers
1.75m (5' 8¾")	Carol Mathers
1.75m (5' 8¾")	Gillian Smith
1.75m (5' 8¾")	Joy Crouchley
1.75m (5' 8¾")	Valerie Mullin
1.75m (5' 8¾")	Denise Bird
1.75m (5' 8¾")	Karen Allinson
1.74m (5' 8½")	Mary Peters
1.74m (5' 8½")	Denise Cooper
1.73m (5' 8")	3 athletes

1974 UK RANKINGS

LONG JUMP

6.51m (21' 4½")	Ruth Martin-Jones
6.34m (20' 9¾")	Myra Nimmo
6.26m (20' 6½")	Ann Wilson
6.24m (20' 5¾")	Maureen Chitty
6.21m (20' 4½")	Sheila Sherwood
6.18m (20' 3½")	Sue Wright
6.08m (19' 11½")	Janet Honour
6.04m (19' 9¾")	Sue Mapstone
6.03m (19' 9½")	Pamela Williams
6.00m (19' 8¼")	Julie Jay
5.94m (19' 5¾")	Pat Chapman
5.91m (19' 4¾")	Bridget Ruttledge
5.88m (19' 3½")	Anita Neil
5.85m (19' 2¼")	Sue Reeve
5.84m (19' 2")	Lorna Boothe
5.84m (19' 2")	Barbara Clark
5.81m (19' 0¾")	Mary Peters
5.81m (19' 0¾")	Kathryn Warren
5.80m (19' 0½")	Nnenna Njoku
5.80m (19' 0½")	Joy Bowerman

SHOT

15.40m (50' 6¼")	Mary Peters
15.40m (50' 6¼")	Brenda Bedford
14.70m (48' 2¾")	Janis Kerr
14.67m (48' 1¾")	Rosemary Payne
13.68m (44' 10¾")	Heather Stuart
13.48m (44' 2¾")	Dorothy Howarth
13.32m (43' 8½")	Elizabeth Elliott
13.30m (43' 7¾")	Margaret Ritchie
13.28m (43' 6¾")	Vanessa Redford
13.01m (42' 8¼")	Venissa Head
12.97m (42' 6½")	Janet Thompson
12.96m (42' 6¼")	Dorothy Swinyard
12.94m (42' 5½")	Jose Frampton
12.93m (42' 5¼")	Jean Atack
12.76m (41' 10½")	Anne Goodlad
12.76m (41' 10½")	Sue Reeve
12.51m (41' 0½")	Nnenna Njoku
12.50m (41' 0")	Judith Oakes
12.47m (40' 11")	Janet Beese
12.25m (40' 2¼")	Gwen Bird

DISCUS

55.44m (181' 11")	Rosemary Payne
52.18m (171' 2")	Margaret Ritchie
51.30m (168' 3")	Dorothy Swinyard
49.94m (163' 10")	Janet Thompson
49.12m (161' 2")	Jean Fielding

Discus (cont)

48.82m (160' 2")	Lesley Mallin
48.06m (157' 8")	Brenda Bedford
47.18m (154' 9")	Janis Kerr
47.02m (154' 3")	Jackie Elsmore
46.24m (151' 8")	Gwen Bird
45.42m (149' 0")	Jose Frampton
43.88m (144' 0")	Lynne Irish
43.22m (141' 9")	Heather Stuart
43.18m (141' 8")	Karen Mallard
43.14m (141' 6")	Delyth Prothero
41.66m (136' 8")	Janet Beese
41.62m (136' 7")	Linda King
41.56m (136' 4")	Vivienne Head
41.36m (135' 8")	Mary Fuller
41.00m (134' 6")	Valerie Watson

JAVELIN

55.04m (180' 7")	Theresa Sanderson
51.98m (170' 6")	Sharon Corbett
51.32m (168' 4")	Yvonne Fountain
50.00m (164' 0")	Pru Carter
49.78m (163' 4")	Anne Goodlad
48.44m (158' 11")	Anne Farquhar
47.24m (155' 0")	Sylvia Brodie
45.86m (150' 5")	Angela King
45.42m (149' 0")	Judith Barnes
44.80m (147' 0")	Julie King
44.08m (144' 7")	Kim Skuse
44.08m (144' 7")	Averil Williams
43.52m (142' 9")	Susan James
43.18m (141' 8")	Carol Johnson
42.68m (140' 0")	Lesley Rice
42.56m (139' 7")	Linda Stratford
42.50m (139' 5")	Shara Spragg
42.40m (139' 2")	Janeen Williams
42.22m (138' 6")	Christine Green
41.72m (136' 10")	Brenda Gill

PENTATHLON

4455pts	Mary Peters
4248pts	Ann Wilson
4192pts	Sue Wright
4112pts	Sue Mapstone
4061pts	Gillian Smith
4043pts	Janet Honour
4022pts	Pat Chapman

257

Pentathlon (cont)

4021pts	Gladys Taylor	3687pts	Bridget Ruttledge
3877pts	Theresa Sanderson	3625pts	Joy Crouchley
3817pts	Myra Nimmo	3614pts	Sylvie Brodie
3808pts	Susan Hodgson	3591pts	Diana Stewart
3770pts	Valerie Mullin	3579pts	Jackie Philp
3697pts	Barbara Corbett	3554pts	Carol Mathers
		3550pts	Allison Manley

UK All-Time Top 20 (as at 31 December 1974)

MEN w = wind assisted. i = indoor mark

100 METRES
(★ 100 yards time plus 0.9sec)

10.1	David Jenkins; 1972
10.1	Brian Green; 1972
10.2	McDonald Bailey; 1951
10.2	Menzies Campbell; 1967
10.2★w	Peter Radford; 1960
10.2w	Ian Green; 1970
10.2w	Les Piggot; 1972
10.3	Roy Sandstrom; 1956
10.3	David Jones; 1961
10.3	Berwyn Jones; 1963
10.3	Ron Jones; 1968
10.3	Martin Reynolds; 1968
10.3	Barrie Kelly; 1968
10.3	Don Halliday; 1972
10.3★w	Dave Segal; 1961
10.3★w	Alf Meakin; 1961
10.3★w	Alistair McIlroy; 1962
10.3w	Roger Walters; 1969
10.3w	Ian Turnbull; 1970

200 METRES
(★ 220 yards time less 0.1sec)

20.3	David Jenkins; 1972
20.4★	Peter Radford; 1960
20.6	Dick Steane; 1968
20.6w	Martin Reynolds; 1970
20.6w	Ainsley Bennett; 1974
20.7★	Menzies Campbell; 1967
20.7	Ralph Banthorpe; 1968
20.7	Brian Green; 1972
20.7	Chris Monk; 1973
20.7★w	David Jones; 1961
20.8	Howard Davies; 1968
20.8	Don Halliday; 1972
20.9	McDonald Bailey; 1950
20.9	Robbie Brightwell; 1962

200 metres (cont)

20.9	Alan Pascoe; 1972
20.9★w	Adrian Metcalfe; 1961
20.9w	Ian Matthews; 1972

400 METRES
(★ 440 yards time less 0.3sec)

45.2	David Jenkins; 1973
45.6★	Robbie Brightwell; 1962
45.7	Adrian Metcalfe; 1961
45.9	Colin Campbell; 1968
45.9	Martin Winbolt Lewis; 1968
46.0	Tim Graham; 1964
46.1	Martin Reynolds; 1972
46.1	Peter Gabbett; 1972
46.2	Gary Armstrong; 1972
46.3	John Wrighton; 1958
46.3	John Wilson; 1973
46.5★	Ted Sampson; 1958
46.5	John Salisbury; 1958
46.5	Barry Jackson; 1962
46.6	Malcolm Yardley; 1960
46.6	John Robertson; 1968
46.6	Martin Bilham; 1970
46.6	Jim Aukett; 1974

800 METRES
(★ 880 yards time less 0.7sec)

1:45.1	Andy Carter; 1973
1:45.8	Steve Ovett; 1974
1:46.0	Frank Clement; 1973
1:46.1	Colin Campbell; 1972
1:46.2	Pete Browne; 1973
1:46.3	Chris Carter; 1966
1:46.3	Phil Lewis; 1974
1:46.5	John Boulter; 1966
1:46.6	Derek Johnson; 1957
1:46.7★	John Davies; 1968

UK ALL-TIME LIST

800 metres (cont)
1:46.8	Bob Adams; 1969
1:46.8	Dave Cropper; 1973
1:46.8	David McMeekin; 1974
1:47.0	Brian Hewson; 1958
1:47.0	Mike Rawson; 1958
1:47.4*	Bill Cornell; 1963
1:47.4*	Robbie Brightwell; 1964
1:47.5	Jim Paterson; 1957
1:47.5*	Mike Varah; 1967
1:47.5	Martin Winbolt Lewis; 1970

1500 METRES
(* Time converted from 1 mile)

3:37.4	Frank Clement; 1974
3:37.6	Brendan Foster; 1974
3:38.0* (3:55.3)	Peter Stewart; 1972
3:38.4* (3:55.7)	Alan Simpson; 1965
3:38.5	Ray Smedley; 1972
3:38.6* (3:56.0)	Jim Douglas; 1972
3:38.7* (3:56.1)	Neill Duggan; 1966
3:38.7	John Kirkbride; 1972
3:39.1	Ian Stewart; 1969
3:39.2* (3:56.6)	Walter Wilkinson; 1971
3:39.4* (3:56.8)	Ian McCafferty; 1969
3:39.4	John Whetton; 1969
3:39.7* (3:57.2)	Derek Ibbotson; 1957
3:39.7	Bob Maplestone; 1972
3:39.9	Phil Banning; 1973
3:40.0* (3:57.5)	Mike Wiggs; 1965
3:40.2* (3:57.7)	Andy Green; 1965
3:40.4	John Boulter; 1964
3:40.5* (3:58.0)	Stan Taylor; 1962
3:40.5	Jim McGuinness; 1973

5000 METRES

13:14.6	Brendan Foster; 1974
13:17.2	Dave Bedford; 1972
13:19.8	Ian McCafferty; 1972
13:22.8	Ian Stewart; 1970
13:23.6	David Black; 1974
13:26.2	Dick Taylor; 1970
13:28.8	Tony Simmons; 1974
13:29.8	Allan Rushmer; 1970
13:30.8	Ricky Wilde; 1972
13:33.0	Mike Wiggs; 1965
13:35.2	Mike Baxter; 1970
13:35.4	Bernard Ford; 1974
13:36.8	Gordon Pirie; 1956
13:37.8	Roger Clark; 1973
13:38.0	Gordon Minty; 1972

5000 metres (cont)
13:38.2	Jack Lane; 1972
13:38.4	Chris Stewart; 1974
13:38.6	Bernard Plain; 1973
13:38.8	Julian Goater; 1973
13:39.0	Henk Altmann; 1966
13:39.0	Tony Staynings; 1974

10,000 METRES
(* Time converted from 6 miles)

27:30.8	Dave Bedford; 1973
27:48.6	David Black; 1974
28:01.6	Tony Simmons; 1973
28:06.6	Dick Taylor; 1969
28:10.0	Bernard Ford; 1973
28:11.8	Lachie Stewart; 1970
28:14.8	Mike Tagg; 1971
28:16.0	Mike Baxter; 1974
28:17.2	Ian Stewart; 1974
28:19.6* (27:20.8)	Gordon Minty; 1973
28:20.6	Bernard Plain; 1973
28:20.8	Jim Brown; 1974
28:21.0* (27:22.2)	Tim Johnston; 1968
28:21.4	Roger Matthews; 1970
28:22.6* (27:23.8)	Bruce Tulloh; 1966
28:23.6* (27:24.8)	Roy Fowler; 1966
28:24.0	Jack Lane; 1971
28:25.0* (27:26.0)	Ron Hill; 1966
28:25.4* (27:26.4)	Mike Bullivant; 1964
28:25.8	Grenville Tuck; 1974

MARATHON

2:09:12	Ian Thompson; 1974
2:09:28	Ron Hill; 1970
2:10:48	Bill Adcocks; 1968
2:12:04	Jim Alder; 1970
2:12:19	Don Faircloth; 1970
2:13:12	Chris Stewart; 1974
2:13:27	Trevor Wright; 1971
2:13:45	Alastair Wood; 1966
2:13:55	Basil Heatley; 1964
2:14:15	Don Macgregor; 1974
2:14:43	Brian Kilby; 1963
2:14:56	Bernard Plain; 1974
2:15:17	Colin Kirkham; 1972
2:15:26	Tim Johnston; 1968
2:15:27	Alex Wight; 1971
2:15:32	Fergus Murray; 1970
2:15:37	Juan Taylor; 1964

259

ATHLETICS 75

Marathon (cont)
2:15:43	Jim Wight; 1971
2:15:44	Steve Badgery; 1971
2:15:59	Eric Austin; 1972
2:15:59	Mal Thomas; 1973

3000 METRES STEEPLECHASE
8:22.6	John Davies; 1974
8:26.4	Andy Holden; 1972
8:26.6	John Bicourt; 1973
8:27.8	Steve Hollings; 1973
8:28.6	Dave Bedford; 1971
8:30.8	Gerry Stevens; 1969
8:32.2	David Camp; 1974
8:32.4	Maurice Herriott; 1964
8:33.0	John Jackson; 1969
8:33.8	Gareth Bryan-Jones; 1970
8:33.8	Peter Morris; 1973
8:35.6	Ron McAndrew; 1971
8:36.2	Bernard Hayward; 1974
8:37.0	Ernie Pomfret; 1967
8:38.2	Clive Thomas; 1974
8:38.8	Roger Bean; 1974
8:40.2	Dennis Coates; 1974
8:40.2	Tony Staynings; 1974
8:40.8	Bill Mullett; 1969
8:41.2	Chris Brasher; 1956

110 METRES HURDLES
(★ 120 yards time)
13.5	Berwyn Price; 1973
13.6	David Hemery; 1969
13.7	Alan Pascoe; 1969
13.7	C. J. Kirkpatrick; 1974
13.9	Mike Parker; 1963
13.9	David Wilson; 1974
14.0★w	Bob Birrell; 1961
14.1★	Lawrie Taitt; 1963
14.1	Mike Hogan; 1963
14.1	Stuart Storey; 1967
14.1	Graham Gower; 1972
14.1w	Don Finlay; 1937
14.2★	Rodney Morrod; 1964
14.2	Andy Todd; 1967
14.2★w	Peter Hildreth; 1959
14.2★w	Desmond Price; 1959
14.2★w	Tony Hogarth; 1968
14.2★w	Rupert Legge; 1968
14.3★	Jack Parker; 1955
14.3	Peter Kelly; 1973
14.3★w	Vic Matthews; 1959

400 METRES HURDLES
(★ 440 yards time less 0.3sec)
48.1	David Hemery; 1968
48.8	Alan Pascoe; 1974
49.0	John Sherwood; 1968
49.9	Andy Todd; 1969
49.9	Bill Hartley; 1974
50.1	John Cooper; 1964
50.6	Colin O'Neill; 1974
50.7	Peter Warden; 1966
50.7	Steve Black; 1974
50.8	David Scharer; 1971
51.0	Tom Farrell; 1960
51.0	Chris Surety; 1961
51.3★	Chris Goudge; 1958
51.3	Mike Hogan; 1964
51.3	Robin Woodland; 1966
51.5★	Harry Kane; 1954
51.5	Bob Roberts; 1969
51.5	Steve James; 1974
51.6	Norman Gregor; 1974
51.7	Bob Shaw; 1956
51.7	John Cook; 1964
51.7	Tony Collins; 1969

HIGH JUMP
2.11m (6' 11")	Colin Boreham; 1974
2.10m (6' 10¾")	Alan Lerwill; 1973
2.09m (6' 10¼")	David Livesey; 1971
2.08m (6' 10")	Gordon Miller; 1964
2.08m (6' 9¾")	Mike Campbell; 1971
2.07m (6' 9½")	Crawford Fairbrother; 1964
2.06m (6' 9")	Phil Taylor; 1970
2.06m (6' 9")	Mike Butterfield; 1973
2.05m (6' 9")	David Wilson; 1971
2.03m (6' 8")	Angus McKenzie; 1972
2.03m (6' 8")	Garry Vose; 1974
2.03m (6' 8")	Brian Burgess; 1974
2.02m (6' 7½")	Alan Paterson; 1947
2.02m (6' 7½")	Peter Wells; 1954
2.02m (6' 7½")	John Ellicock; 1971
2.02m (6' 7½")	Dave Kidner; 1972
2.02m (6' 7½")	Milton Palmer; 1974
2.02m (6' 7½")	Roy Mitchell; 1974
2.01m (6' 7")	Leon Hall; 1969
2.01m (6' 7")	Chris Wilson; 1974

POLE VAULT
5.25m (17' 2¾")	Mike Bull; 1973
5.20m (17' 0¾")	Brian Hooper; 1974

Pole Vault (cont)

4.90m (16′ 0¾″)	Stuart Tufton; 1972
4.90m (16′ 0¾″)	Allan Williams; 1974
4.87m (16′ 0″)	Mike Bryant; 1971
4.80m (15′ 9″)	Dave Lease; 1972
4.71m (15′ 5½″)	Steve Chappell; 1970
4.71m (15′ 5½″)	Jeff Fenge; 1974
4.68m (15′ 4½″)	David Stevenson; 1968
4.67m (15′ 4″)	Keith Stock; 1974
4.62m (15′ 2″)	Martin Higdon; 1970
4.60m (15′ 1¼″)	Gordon Rule; 1968
4.60m (15′ 1″)	Peter Gabbett; 1972
4.60m (15′ 1″)	Chris Boreham; 1974
4.57m (15′ 0″)	Trevor Burton; 1964
4.50m (14′ 9″)	Girish Patel; 1973
4.50m (14′ 9″)	Chris Kidd; 1974
4.50m (14′ 9″)	Nick Phipps; 1974
4.49m (14′ 8¾″)	Iswlyn Rees; 1974
4.49m (14′ 8¾″)	Jeffrey Gutteridge; 1974

LONG JUMP

8.23m (27′ 0″)	Lynn Davies; 1968
8.15m (26′ 9″)w	Alan Lerwill; 1972
7.89m (25′ 10¾″)	John Morbey; 1966
7.82m (25′ 7¾″)	Peter Reed; 1968
7.79m (25′ 6¾″)	Geoff Hignett; 1971
7.74m (25′ 4¾″)	Fred Alsop; 1964
7.74m (25′ 4¾″)i	Phil Scott; 1973
7.70m (25′ 3¼″)w	Derek Cole; 1972
7.67m (25′ 2″)	David Walker; 1968
7.65m (25′ 1¾″)w	Calvin Greenaway; 1973
7.63m (25′ 0½″)w	John Howell; 1961
7.61m (24′ 11¾″)w	Stewart Atkins; 1972
7.59m (24′ 10¾″)	Roy Cruttenden; 1956
7.56m (24′ 9¾″)	Don Porter; 1974
7.55m (24′ 9½″)	Gwyn Williams; 1968
7.54m (24′ 8¾″)	Ken Wilmshurst; 1954
7.51m (24′ 7¾″)i	Peter Templeton; 1971
7.51m (24′ 7¾″)w	Peter Gabbett; 1970
7.49m (24′ 7″)	Jerry Gangadeen; 1973
7.47m (24′ 6″)	John Elias; 1968

TRIPLE JUMP

16.65m (54′ 7½″)w	Fred Alsop; 1965
16.49m (54′ 1¼″)w	Tony Wadhams; 1969
16.22m (53′ 2½″)	Derek Boosey; 1968
16.21m (53′ 2¼″)w	Alan Lerwill; 1971
15.97m (52′ 4¾″)	Mike Ralph; 1964
15.82m (51′ 11″)	Graham Hamlyn; 1968
15.80m (51′ 10″)	David Johnson; 1972
15.78m (51′ 9¼″)	Willie Clark; 1974

Triple Jump (cont)

15.77m (51′ 9″)	Peter Blackburn; 1973
15.77m (51′ 9″)	Chris Colman; 1973
15.77m (51′ 8¾″)	John Vernon; 1968
15.71m (51′ 6½″)	John Crotty; 1970
15.65m (51′ 4¼″)	Aston Moore; 1974
15.64m (51′ 4″)	Graham Webb; 1969
15.60m (51′ 2¼″)	Ken Wilmshurst; 1956
15.53m (50′ 11½″)	Peter Drew; 1968
15.51m (50′ 10¾″)w	Roy Spinks; 1970
15.47m (50′ 9¼″)w	Bob Johnson; 1970
15.47m (50′ 9″)	David Macbeth; 1967
15.46m (50′ 8¾″)w	Peter Knowles; 1974

SHOT

21.37m (70′ 1½″)	Geoff Capes; 1974
20.43m (67′ 0½″)	Mike Winch; 1974
19.56m (64′ 2″)	Arthur Rowe; 1961
19.43m (63′ 9″)	Bill Tancred; 1974
19.18m (62′ 11″)	Jeff Teale; 1968
18.62m (61′ 1¼″)	Martyn Lucking; 1962
18.59m (61′ 0″)	Alan Carter; 1965
18.50m (60′ 8½″)	Mike Lindsay; 1963
18.35m (60′ 2½″)	Peter Tancred; 1974
18.05m (59′ 2¾″)	John Watts; 1972
17.87m (58′ 7½″)	Bill Fuller; 1972
17.79m (58′ 4½″)	John Alderson; 1974
17.40m (57′ 1″)	Barry King; 1970
17.17m (56′ 4″)	Allan Seatory; 1972
16.95m (55′ 7½″)	Nick Morgan; 1961
16.94m (55′ 7″)	Tony Elvin; 1966
16.91m (55′ 6″)	Barclay Palmer; 1956
16.83m (55′ 2¾″)	John Savidge; 1954
16.68m (54′ 8¾″)	Andy Kerr; 1973
16.63m (54′ 6¾″)	David Harrison; 1961

DISCUS

64.94m (213′ 1″)	Bill Tancred; 1974
61.00m (200′ 1″)	Allan Seatory; 1974
60.16m (197′ 4″)	Peter Tancred; 1974
59.76m (196′ 1″)	John Hillier; 1974
59.70m (195′ 10″)	John Watts; 1972
58.34m (191′ 5″)	Geoff Capes; 1973
57.84m (189′ 9″)	Mike Cushion; 1974
57.58m (188′ 11″)	Arthur McKenzie; 1969
57.42m (188′ 5″)	Mike Winch; 1973
57.00m (187′ 0″)	Gerry Carr; 1965
56.70m (186′ 0″)	Roy Hollingsworth; 1963
55.44m (181′ 11″)	Dennis Roscoe; 1971
55.32m (181′ 6″)	Mike Lindsay; 1960
54.36m (178′ 4″)	Guy Dirkin; 1974

Discus (cont)
54.26m (178' 0")	Mark Pharaoh; 1956
54.00m (177' 2")	Eric Cleaver; 1962
53.66m (176' 0")	Barry King; 1966
53.54m (175' 8")	Tony Satchwell; 1973
53.20m (174' 6")	Andy Drzewiecki; 1974
52.80m (173' 3")	Peter Nimmo; 1965

HAMMER
71.26m (233' 9")	Barry Williams; 1973
71.00m (232' 11")	Ian Chipchase; 1974
70.88m (232' 6")	Howard Payne; 1974
69.48m (227' 11")	Chris Black; 1974
67.66m (222' 0")	Paul Dickenson; 1974
64.94m (213' 1")	Mike Ellis; 1959
64.80m (212' 7")	Bruce Fraser; 1973
64.48m (211' 6")	Jim Whitehead; 1974
62.54m (205' 2")	Tony Elvin; 1970
62.28m (204' 4")	Lawrie Bryce; 1973
62.10m (203' 9")	Peter Aston; 1974
62.10m (203' 9")	Chris Melluish; 1974
62.00m (203' 5")	Eric Berry; 1974
61.72m (202' 6")	Peter Seddon; 1967
60.54m (198' 7")	Niall McDonald; 1970
60.50m (198' 6")	Peter Gordon; 1974
59.62m (195' 7")	Peter Allday; 1956
59.10m (193' 11")	Phil Scott; 1974
58.94m (193' 4")	David Bayes; 1968
58.68m (192' 6")	Ewan Douglas; 1955

JAVELIN
84.92m (278' 7")	Charles Clover; 1974
83.44m (273' 9")	Dave Travis; 1970
81.92m (268' 9")	John Fitzsimons; 1969
80.20m (263' 1")	Kevin Sheppard; 1974
79.48m (260' 9")	Brian Roberts; 1974
79.24m (260' 0")	John McSorley; 1962
79.24m (260' 0")	John Greasley; 1963
77.94m (255' 8")	Colin Smith; 1962
77.38m (253' 10")	Dave Sorrell; 1972
76.42m (250' 9")	Mike Wootton; 1972
75.98m (249' 3")	Ron Silvester; 1974
75.88m (248' 11")	David Birkmyre; 1971
75.48m (247' 8")	Nigel Sherlock; 1969
75.12m (246' 5")	Mladen Gavrilovic; 1970
74.90m (245' 9")	Neville Hart-Ives; 1971
74.76m (245' 3")	Dick Perkins; 1967
74.56m (244' 7")	John Kitching; 1960
74.52m (244' 6")	Barry Sanderson; 1966
74.32m (243' 10")	Roger Lane; 1960
74.30m (243' 9")	Richard Miller; 1963

DECATHLON
8040pts	Peter Gabbett; 1972
7676pts	Barry King; 1972
7451pts	Clive Longe; 1969
7417pts	Mike Bull; 1974
7401pts	Stewart McCallum; 1973
7336pts	Dave Kidner; 1973
7127pts	Alan Drayton; 1974
7119pts	Ray Knox; 1973
7088pts	Roy Mitchell; 1974
7066pts	Dave Travis; 1968
7035pts	Mike Corden; 1974
7033pts	Jim Smith; 1970
7002pts	Derek Clarke; 1965
6894pts	Stuart Scott; 1971
6893pts	David Hemery; 1969
6887pts	Nick Phipps; 1973
6866pts	David Gaskin; 1966
6840pts	Norman Foster; 1965
6739pts	Barry Sanderson; 1970
6731pts	David Wilson; 1971

20 KILOMETRES WALK (road)
84:50	Paul Nihill; 1972
87:59	Phil Embleton; 1971
88:15	Ken Matthews; 1960
88:50	Amos Seddon; 1974
89:04	Roger Mills; 1974
89:26	Olly Flynn; 1974
89:37	John Warhurst; 1973
89:49	Peter Marlow; 1974
89:59	John Webb; 1968
90:02	Bob Dobson; 1974
90:16	Roy Thorpe; 1973
90:35	Peter Fullager; 1970
91:01	Ron Wallwork; 1970
91:10	Shaun Lightman; 1969
91:10	Bill Sutherland; 1969
91:10	Steve Gower; 1973
91:43	Stan Vickers; 1960
91:53	Bryan Eley; 1969
91:59	Peter Marlow; 1973
92:30	Bob Clark; 1961

50 KILOMETRES WALK (road)
(t = track race)
4:11:22t	Bob Dobson; 1974
4:11:31	Paul Nihill; 1964
4:12:19	Don Thompson; 1959
4:12:37	John Warhurst; 1972
4:14:03	Tom Misson; 1959

UK ALL-TIME LIST

50 kilometres Walk (cont)

4:15:13	Shaun Lightman; 1973	4:22:45	Charley Fogg; 1965
4:15:51	Ray Middleton; 1972	4:24:02	Howard Timms; 1972
4:19:00	Carl Lawton; 1971	4:24:08	Roy Thorpe; 1974
4:19:13	Bryan Eley; 1969	4:24:54	John Hedgethorne; 1971
4:19:55	Mike Holmes; 1973	4:25:50	John Paddick; 1965
4:20:05	George Chaplin; 1972	4:26:40	Albert Johnson; 1958
4:21:02	Ron Wallwork; 1971	4:27:00	David Watts; 1965
		4:27:21	Alec Banyard; 1974

WOMEN

w = wind assisted.   i = indoor mark

100 METRES
(★ 100 yards time plus 1.0sec)

11.1	Andrea Lynch; 1974
11.2	Helen Golden; 1974
11.3	Dorothy Hyman; 1963
11.3	Della James; 1968
11.3	Val Peat; 1968
11.3	Anita Neil; 1971
11.3	Sonia Lannaman; 1974
11.3w	Margaret Critchley; 1972
11.4★w	Jill Hall; 1966
11.4★w	Denise Ramsden; 1967
11.4	Liz Sutherland; 1973
11.5★w	Daphne Arden; 1966
11.5	Jenny Smart; 1961
11.5	Madeleine Cobb; 1972
11.5	Linda Barratt; 1974
11.5w	June Paul; 1956
11.5w	Heather Armitage; 1956
11.5w	Liz Gill; 1965
11.5w	Liz Johns; 1971
11.5w	Donna Murray; 1972
11.5w	Sandra Belt; 1972
11.5w	Jannette Roscoe; 1973
11.5w	Sharon Colyear; 1973

200 METRES
(★ 220 yards time less 0.1sec)

22.9w	Donna Murray; 1974
23.0	Helen Golden; 1974
23.1w	Margaret Critchley; 1970
23.2	Dorothy Hyman; 1963
23.2	Andrea Lynch; 1974
23.3	Val Peat; 1969
23.4	Lillian Board; 1968
23.4w	Maureen Tranter; 1970
23.5★	Daphne Arden; 1964

200 metres (cont)

23.5	Della Pascoe; 1972
23.5	Verona Bernard; 1973
23.5	Sharon Colyear; 1974
23.6	Jenny Smart; 1961
23.6★	Janet Simpson; 1964
23.6	Marilyn Neufville; 1970
23.6	Anita Neil; 1970
23.6	Judy Vernon; 1973
23.6w	Mary Rand; 1967
23.6w	Madeleine Cobb; 1969

400 METRES
(★ 440 yards time less 0.3sec)

51.8	Donna Murray; 1974
51.9	Verona Bernard; 1974
52.1	Lillian Board; 1968
52.2	Ann Packer; 1964
52.3†	Marilyn Neufville; 1970
52.5	Janet Simpson; 1968
52.9	Jannette Roscoe; 1974
53.2	Joy Grieveson; 1963
53.2	Rosemary Stirling; 1971
53.6	Mary Green; 1968
53.8★	Deirdre Watkinson; 1966
53.8	Christine Warden; 1974
53.8	Ruth Kennedy; 1974
53.9	Liz Barnes; 1974
54.0	Molly Hiscox; 1959
54.0	Avril Bowring; 1970
54.1	Barbara Lyall; 1970
54.1	Dawn Webster; 1971
54.1	Maureen Tranter; 1972
54.1	Wendy Hill; 1974

† Ratified as UK Junior record but achieved after competing for Jamaica.

263

ATHLETICS 75

800 METRES

2:00.2	Rosemary Stirling; 1972
2:01.1	Ann Packer; 1964
2:01.2	Joan Allison; 1973
2:01.4	Lillian Board; 1969
2:01.7	Pat Lowe; 1971
2:02.0	Margaret Coomber; 1973
2:02.8	Lesley Kiernan; 1974
2:02.9	Sheila Carey; 1971
2:03.2	Anne Smith; 1966
2:04.1	Pam Piercy; 1966
2:04.4	Thelwyn Bateman; 1971
2:04.6	Shirley Somervell; 1974
2:05.0	Joy Jordan; 1962
2:05.3	Mary Hodson; 1964
2:05.3	Norine Braithwaite; 1973
2:05.5	Rita Ridley; 1971
2:05.5	Sandra Sutherland; 1971
2:05.6	Gloria O'Leary; 1973
2:05.8	Iris Lincoln; 1968
2:05.8	Georgena Craig; 1970

1500 METRES
(★ Time converted from 1 mile)

4:04.8	Sheila Carey; 1972
4:09.4	Joyce Smith; 1972
4:10.7	Joan Allison; 1974
4:12.7	Rita Ridley; 1971
4:14.7	Mary Stewart; 1974
4:15.8	Norine Braithwaite; 1973
4:16.3★ (4:37.0)	Anne Smith; 1967
4:17.2	Margaret Beacham; 1971
4:18.5	Ann Yeoman; 1974
4:18.6	Jean Lochhead; 1972
4:18.8	Christine Haskett; 1974
4:19.0	Paula Yeoman; 1974
4:20.0	Shirley Somervell; 1973
4:20.7	Thelwyn Bateman; 1973
4:21.0	Gillian Tivey; 1970
4:21.7	Christine Curthoys; 1973
4:22.3	Jane Perry; 1970
4:22.4	Margaret Coomber; 1970
4:22.5	Penelope Yule; 1973
4:22.8	Christine Tranter; 1974

3000 METRES

8:55.6	Joyce Smith; 1974
9:07.0	Ann Yeoman; 1974
9:13.6	Rita Ridley; 1973
9:19.8	Paula Yeoman; 1974
9:20.1	Carol Gould; 1974

3000 metres (cont)

9:31.8	Christine Haskett; 1974
9:33.0	Ann Barrass; 1973
9:33.0	Glynis Goodburn; 1974
9:33.8	Alison Blake; 1974
9:36.0	Liz Connors; 1973
9:36.4	Joan Allison; 1972
9:36.4	Christine Readdy; 1974
9:37.4	Wanda Sosinka; 1972
9:37.6	Val Howe; 1974
9:38.8	Jean Lochhead; 1972
9:39.6	Kay Barnett; 1974
9:39.8	Pat Winter; 1972
9:39.8	Thelwyn Bateman; 1973
9:40.4	Bronwen Cardy; 1971
9:40.6	Penelope Yule; 1973

100 METRES HURDLES

13.0	Judy Vernon; 1974
13.0	Blondelle Thompson; 1974
13.1w	Mary Peters; 1972
13.2w	Ann Wilson; 1972
13.4	Chris Bell; 1970
13.5	Pat Pryce; 1972
13.5	Lorna Drysdale; 1974
13.5w	Myra Nimmo; 1974
13.6w	Lynne Ilott; 1974
13.7	Sue Scott; 1970
13.7	Susan Holmstrom; 1974
13.7w	Sue Hayward; 1969
13.8	Pat Jones; 1967
13.8	Sheila Garnett; 1970
13.8w	Janet Honour; 1972
14.0w	Moira Walls; 1970
14.0w	Moira Niccol; 1972
14.0w	Sue Mapstone; 1974
14.0w	Pat Chapman; 1974

400 METRES HURDLES

58.9	Christine Warden; 1974
59.9	Judy Vernon; 1973
61.1	Sandra Dyson; 1971
61.1	Susan Howell; 1974
62.2	Lorna Boothe; 1974
62.3	Barbara Corbett; 1973
62.4	Janice Farry; 1974
62.4	Linda Robinson; 1974
62.4	Sharon Colyear; 1974
62.9	Lynne Davies; 1974

UK ALL-TIME LIST

HIGH JUMP

1.87m (6' 1½")	Barbara Inkpen; 1973
1.83m (6' 0")	Linda Hedmark; 1971
1.83m (6' 0")	Valerie Harrison; 1974
1.82m (5' 11½")	Mary Peters; 1972
1.80m (5' 10¾")	Carol Mathers; 1973
1.80m (5' 10¾")	Sue Wright; 1974
1.80m (5' 10¾")	Ruth Watt; 1974
1.78m (5' 10")	Sue Vickers; 1973
1.77m (5' 9¾")	Ann Wilson; 1973
1.77m (5' 9¾")	Fiona Stacey; 1974
1.77m (5' 9¾")	Anne Gilson; 1974
1.76m (5' 9¼")	Frances Slaap; 1964
1.76m (5' 9¼")	Penny Dimmock; 1972
1.76m (5' 9¼")	Rosaline Few; 1972
1.76m (5' 9¼")	Denise Brown; 1973
1.76m (5' 9¼")	Teresa Dainton; 1974
1.75m (5' 8¾")	Sue Hutchinson; 1973
1.75m (5' 8¾")	Gillian Smith; 1974
1.75m (5' 8¾")	Joy Crouchley; 1974
1.75m (5' 8¾")	Valerie Mullin; 1974

LONG JUMP

6.76m (22' 2¼")	Mary Rand; 1964
6.73m (22' 1")	Sheila Sherwood; 1970
6.57m (21' 6¾")w	Ann Wilson; 1970
6.54m (21' 5½")w	Ruth Martin-Jones; 1972
6.48m (21' 3¼")w	Moira Walls; 1970
6.43m (21' 1¼")	Myra Nimmo; 1973
6.40m (21' 0")w	Barbara-Anne Barrett; 1971
6.39m (20' 11¾")	Maureen Chitty; 1972
6.39m (20' 11¾")w	Alix Stevenson; 1970
6.33m (20' 9¼")	Barbara Inkpen; 1970
6.33m (20' 9¼")w	Sue Scott; 1968
6.27m (20' 7")	Anita Neil; 1970
6.26m (20' 6½")w	Sheila Hoskin; 1956
6.23m (20' 5¼")	Jackie Caswell; 1968
6.20m (20' 4¼")w	Julie Jay; 1974
6.18m (20' 3½")	Judy Vernon; 1971
6.18m (20' 3½")	Sue Wright; 1974
6.17m (20' 3")w	Anne M. Wilson; 1966
6.15m (20' 2¼")w	Shirley Clelland; 1970
6.15m (20' 2¼")w	Sue Mapstone; 1972

SHOT

16.40m (53' 9¾")	Mary Peters; 1970
16.15m (53' 0")	Brenda Bedford; 1973
15.18m (49' 9¾")	Suzanne Allday; 1964
14.77m (48' 5½")	Gay Porter; 1970
14.70m (48' 2¾")	Janis Kerr; 1974

Shot (cont)

14.67m (48' 1¾")	Rosemary Payne; 1974
14.46m (47' 5¼")	Heather Stuart; 1973
14.05m (46' 1¼")	Sue Barrett; 1971
14.03m (46' 0½")	Jenny Bloss; 1968
13.96m (45' 9¾")	Dorothy Swinyard; 1973
13.96m (45' 9¼")	Josephine Cook; 1958
13.92m (45' 8")	Kathryn Duckett; 1966
13.75m (45' 1¼")	Brenda Gill; 1964
13.64m (44' 9¼")	Moira Kerr; 1966
13.57m (44' 6½")	Deborah Kerr; 1970
13.43m (44' 0¾")	Dorothy Howarth; 1973
13.31m (43' 8")	Vanessa Redford; 1973
13.30m (43' 7¾")	Margaret Ritchie; 1974
13.30m (43' 7½")	Margaret Pulman; 1970
13.28m (43' 7")	Linda Haldane; 1971

DISCUS

58.02m (190' 4")	Rosemary Payne; 1972
52.18m (171' 2")	Margaret Ritchie; 1974
51.60m (169' 3")	Dorothy Swinyard; 1973
50.58m (165' 11")	Brenda Bedford; 1968
49.94m (163' 10")	Janet Thompson; 1974
49.66m (162' 11")	Gay Porter; 1970
49.12m (161' 2")	Jean Fielding; 1974
48.82m (160' 2")	Lesley Mallin; 1974
48.20m (158' 2")	Jackie Elsmore; 1973
47.70m (156' 6")	Suzanne Allday; 1958
47.18m (154' 9")	Janis Kerr; 1974
46.68m (153' 2")	Jose Frampton; 1972
46.24m (151' 8")	Gwen Bird; 1974
45.80m (150' 3")	Maya Giri; 1958
45.74m (150' 1")	Barbara James; 1969
45.46m (149' 2")	Heather Stuart; 1973
45.02m (147' 8")	Maureen Arnold; 1966
44.80m (147' 0")	Jenny Bloss; 1968
44.76m (146' 10")	Wendy Thomas; 1964
44.76m (146' 10")	Jill Lucas; 1969

JAVELIN

55.60m (182' 5")	Sue Platt; 1968
55.04m (180' 7")	Theresa Sanderson; 1974
54.18m (177' 9")	Rosemary Morgan; 1964
53.88m (176' 9")	Sharon Corbett; 1973
52.10m (170' 11")	Anne Goodlad; 1973
51.56m (169' 2")	Jean Randall; 1972
51.50m (168' 11")	Pru French; 1972
51.32m (168' 4")	Yvonne Fountain; 1974
50.82m (166' 9")	Anne Farquhar; 1970
49.58m (162' 8")	Shara Spragg; 1969
49.50m (162' 5")	Averil Williams; 1960

265

Javelin (cont)
49.18m (161' 4")	Angela King; 1973
47.70m (156' 6")	Janet Baker; 1971
47.60m (156' 2")	Barbara Nicholls; 1963
47.48m (155' 9")	Barbara Thomas; 1970
47.48m (155' 9")	Judith St Ange; 1971
46.70m (153' 2")	Susan James; 1973
46.30m (151' 11")	Brenda Gill; 1969
45.72m (150' 0")	Mary Tadd; 1959
45.56m (149' 6")	Monica Podmore; 1960

PENTATHLON
(* with 80 metres hurdles)

4801pts	Mary Peters; 1972
4435pts* (5035)	Mary Rand; 1964
4433pts	Ann Wilson; 1972
4294pts	Ruth Martin-Jones; 1972
4193pts* (4786)	Sue Scott; 1968
4192pts	Sue Wright; 1974
4161pts	Janet Honour; 1972
4123pts* (4704)	Moira Walls; 1970
4112pts	Sue Mapstone; 1974
4088pts	Gladys Taylor; 1973
4079pts (4655)	Judy Vernon; 1971
4061pts	Gillian Smith; 1974
4022pts	Pat Chapman; 1974
3890pts (4473)	Sue Hayward; 1969
3883pts (4458)	Shirley Clelland; 1970
3877pts	Theresa Sanderson; 1974
3859pts* (4441)	Pat Jones; 1967
3817pts	Myra Nimmo; 1974
3810pts* (4379)	Thelma Hopkins; 1961
3808pts	Susan Hodgson; 1974

Scores in brackets are from the 1954 tables.

2500 METRES WALK

12:17.8	Brenda Cook; 1972
12:26.8	Sally Wish; 1974
12:28.0	Margaret Lewis; 1971
12:28.8	Betty Jenkins; 1972

3000 METRES WALK

14:33.6	Marion Fawkes; 1974
14:58.0	Christine Coleman; 1973
14:59.4	Betty Jenkins; 1973
15:00.6	Sally Wish; 1972
15:01.2	Judy Farr; 1971
15:03.0	Barbara Cook; 1973

5000 METRES WALK

25:02.0	Marion Fawkes; 1974
25:09.2	Betty Jenkins; 1972
25:34.0	Sally Wish; 1973
25:38.4	Pamela Branson; 1974
25:46.8	Sylvia Saunders; 1974
25:53.0	Christine Coleman; 1973

Learning from the Stars

Discus – Pentti Kahma
Javelin – Hannu Siitonen
Shot – Hartmut Briesenick

DISCUS

Pentti Kahma (Fin). *Born* Alavieska, 3.12.1943; *Height:* 1.88m (6' 2"); *Weight:* 110kg (243lb); *Best marks:* Discus 66.52m (218' 3"), Shot 17.98m (59' 0"), Long jump 7.21m (23' 8" in 1969, the same year he first reached 200ft with the discus!) Decathlon 6551 points.

Big, strong, and rangey, Pentti Kahma has never lost that all-round athleticism that made him a good decathlete, and his consistency over the past few seasons brought its just reward in Rome with a winning throw of 63.62 (208' 9") in the last round. Like all throws, optimum distance is achieved by having maximum speed at the moment of release and the right angle of release. What often determines both is balance, and the 'key' to good discus throwing is the careful transfer of bodyweight from right to left leg at the back of the circle before commencing the turn.

Kahma uses a wide stance (Fig 1) but while the arm is still pulled back with the discus he moves his weight solidly on to the left leg in Fig 2. Only then is he in a balanced position to pivot on the left foot and drive across the circle, leading with his

LEARNING FROM THE STARS

right knee (Fig 4). This running rotation keeps him wound up like a spring, with his feet pointing 180° away from the discus, which is carried behind his back but at shoulder height (Figs 5 & 6).

Now the weight firmly returns over the right foot, which has landed halfway across the 8ft 2in circle. Before there is time for the body to unwind, the left foot must come to ground quickly to provide a wide, strong throwing base. As the unwinding occurs at speed, so leg and trunk extension add to the pulling force on the discus and give the right angle of release. Throughout the turn and pull, the arm is kept as long as possible to increase angular momentum as shown in Figs 7–10.

The moment just prior to release is epitomised in Fig 11, but no series of pictures can demonstrate the sheer speed at which all this happens. It is the harmony of speed, strength, and good technique that produces consistently good results and this in turn stems from practising the right things rather than developing bad habits. It is a rare athlete indeed who can clearly picture for himself all that he is doing while spinning at speed in a discus circle. This is the job for a trained observer or coach.

4

5

6

10

11

12

269

JAVELIN

Hannu Siitonen (Fin). *Born* Parikkala 18.3.1949; *Height:* 1.83m (6′ 0″); *Weight:* 84kg (185lb). *Best mark:* 93.90m (308′ 1″).

The man who brought an end to the incredible reign of Janis Lusis (USSR), who had won the four previous European titles, stretching as far back as 1962. In fact, Lusis is the man observing Siitonen so closely in Fig 1 as he demonstrates the form that won the title and recaptured for Finland some of her former glory at this event.

Although Siitonen has won no previous medals at Olympic or European Championships, his breakthrough was anticipated because of his remarkably consistent throwing of around 290ft for several seasons. The sequence shows him coming out of his penultimate stride and into his throwing position. Following quite a fast approach run, the javelin is held nicely aligned parallel to the shoulders as he begins to lean back prior to driving the

LEARNING FROM THE STARS

right heel down fast in Fig 2. The javelin rests on the heel of the hand with palm upwards. The hips have turned sideways to the direction of throw and are in effect 'cocked' ready to strike as the left leg reaches out for the long throwing stride in Fig 4. As his weight moves forward beyond the supporting leg (his right), so begins the drive from the right foot. The 'cocked' hips are then released as the leg extends, but as the chest moves square to the direction of the throw the javelin is delayed as far back as possible until the left leg is down on the ground to act as a brace. This achieves the magnificent bow-like action in Figs 6 & 7 which is paramount to all good throwing. The pictures also demonstrate graphically the tremendous strength combined with mobility necessary for top class javelin throwing, even though at 6 feet tall and just over 13 stones Siitonen is no giant, especially in the company of other throwers.

Note: The sequence runs from right to left.

271

SHOT

Hartmut Briesenick (EG)
Born Luckenwalde 17.3.1949; *Height:* 1.91m (6' 3¼"); *Weight:* 116kg (256lb). *Best marks:* Shot 21.67m (71' 1¼"), Discus 57.56m (188' 10"). First European to reach 21 metres (1971) and 70 feet (1972).

The two greatest contributory factors in achieving distance with the shot are the speed of its release and the angle of release, and any technique employed must be directed to this end. Since the shot is a weighty projectile, enormous strength is needed to achieve optimum release speed, and only sound technique will ensure that the right degree of elevation has been reached and that the rules are adhered to, especially in terms of staying in the circle after release so that a controlled exit can be made. In a lack-lustre competition in Rome, Briesenick had to dig deep into his competitive resources to find the form that made him reigning champion. Only in the fifth round did he overtake Reichenbach of West Germany.

His form shown here is solid and dependable. Balanced over his right foot in Fig 1, he passes quickly through the T position of Fig 2 to sink over the right

LEARNING FROM THE STARS

knee ready for a powerful drive across the circle (Figs 3 & 4). As the right leg extends to achieve the drive, Briesenick demonstrates how well he keeps his shoulders square to the rear of the circle with the shot cradled in a position outside the line of the right knee. Even as the right leg extends and lifts vertically, starting the upward drive of his powerful trunk, he maintains the discipline of delaying his rotation towards the front until his left leg is down firm against the stopboard in Fig 7. As the drive from the right leg becomes a spent force in Fig 8, so the powerful turning movement of the trunk continues the acceleration (Fig 9). The left leg has become an effective brace against which to drive and only a massively strong right arm can extend fast enough to drive the shot even faster before the moment of release. Having established the right line of drive he can achieve the right angle of release, and having provided his own brake with the left foot just slightly left of centre of the stopboard, he can safely remain in the circle by quickly reversing his feet as in Fig 12.

The European Cup
Cliff Temple *The Sunday Times*

From time to time athletics, a sport primarily for the individual, is moulded into a team competition. Whether rightly or wrongly is a matter of constant debate, but among those competitions that have their foundations in the number of points a group of athletes can accumulate between them, the European Cup, which reaches its fifth edition in 1975, is the most prestigious.

Europe is now recognised as the liveliest athletics continent, with hordes of American stars pouring across the Atlantic every summer, when their own domestic season has ended, to 'learn from the Europeans'. So naturally, as each country within Europe strives to prove that it can produce the best athletes through its own specific coaching and living standards, the European Cup has become a competition which, if it had not been inaugurated in 1965, would certainly have to be invented now.

The competition calls for one athlete in each event per country, and six countries take part in each of the three semi-finals with the top two progressing to the final; scoring is on an uncomplicated 6–5–4–3–2–1 points basis. So is the strongest athletic nation, therefore, always the winner of the Cup? That is another story. The winners would say yes, the losers would say no.

In many ways, the normal dual international match, with two or three athletes per side, gives a fairer indication of the merit of country A compared to country B because the performance of the second or third best athlete in, say, the shot putt makes a difference to the overall score. In the European Cup the champion of a country finds the loneliness that his title can bring. To give an example: if the Cup had been held last summer, in 1974, Britain's points score in the shot putt would have rested very much on Geoff Capes, who would have been capable of winning the event. If he had been injured, our number two, Mike Winch, could probably have held his own. But if he too had been injured, we would have plummeted to an almost certain last place in that event. So a victory by Capes would not really have reflected the true standing of British shot putting in Europe in the same way as, say, a 5000 or 10,000 metres win by Brendan Foster, Dave Black, Tony Simmons, or Dave Bedford would have reflected our distance running strength.

The European Cup, or the Bruno Zauli European Cup to use its proper title as it was named after the late president of the IAAF's European Committee, was not the happiest of hunting grounds for British athletes in its formative years, when it was titled the Europa Cup. In the inaugural Cup final at Stuttgart in 1965, Britain's men finished a distant sixth and last with 48 points, 12 points behind fifth-placed

France. In the eight field events, only triple jumper Fred Alsop (fourth) could finish higher than fifth or sixth place for the British team, and the performances prompted our controversial former track world record holder Gordon Pirie to fume about the field eventers: '. . . it is time that they – and the 110 metres hurdlers – were left out of international competition until they reach respectable standards. As it is, they go round on athletics tours on nothing – like a famous hurdler who smugly confessed that he did not bother to train because he could make the team with no effort.'

While there was some sympathy for Pirie's views, that attitude, if acted on, would have halted progress rather than allowed even small headway to be made. And on this occasion it was not just the field events that spelt disaster. In the 100 metres, David Jones was left on the line, still in his starting blocks, as his rivals raced off; he did not even score a point for finishing as he walked off the track in disgust. The sprint relay squad was also disqualified, while our 4×400 metres team was a distant last. And though it was largely a different team to the one that took so many Olympic medals in Tokyo less than a year before, there was obviously a lot of rebuilding to do in British athletics.

Britain's women, in fact, had not even reached their final, which was held separately in the early days of the competition, unexpectedly failing by a point to catch Hungary and the Netherlands in the semi-final at Fontainebleau – after having dropped the baton in their sprint relay too!

Both men's and women's finals were eventually won by the USSR, with the Soviet men defeating their West German hosts by just one point. The Cup was here to stay, but it could scarcely have been a worse start for Britain.

More disappointment was to follow in 1967, the second edition, when our men failed even to survive the semi-final at Duisburg. With just the result of the triple jump to come, Britain were lying third, one point behind Hungary, but eventual defeat for Fred Alsop by Hungary's Kalocsai meant the slight chance of saving a qualifying place had vanished. Significantly, on the track Britain had scored 59 points to Hungary's 43, but in the field they lagged 22–41.

Apart from Britain's track and field imbalance, another aspect of European Cup athletics to have become firmly established was the odd tactics that often came into play in the longer races. In the 5000 metres at Duisburg, for instance, the world class trio of Ian McCafferty (GB), Lajos Mecser (Hungary), and Harald Norpoth (West Germany), all Olympic men, were so busy watching each other like cyclists, anxious not to make the first move, that they let a totally unknown Swiss runner named Walter Huss build up a 100 metres lead on them in the first five laps. Sad to record, the fame of Herr Huss was shortlived for the trio's gamble paid off and they gradually closed the gap, ending up with a frantic 400-metre sprint, covered in around 54 seconds, as Norpoth beat McCafferty to the line. But one of the ironies was that they would probably not have minded much even if Huss *had* won, because Switzerland were already too far back to challenge the team situation. The big names just had to beat each other.

One brighter note for Britain in 1967 was that the women did manage to get through their semi-final in Oslo, despite the fact that Della James was disqualified for two false starts in the 100 metres, scoring no points. The position finally rested on the sprint relay, and this time Della made up for her earlier lapse by anchoring Britain to victory and a place in the final.

At the final itself, held in Kiev, the British girls almost passed all expectations. Although they were fifth overall with 34 points, they were only just behind Poland (35) and West Germany (36). But for the three throwing events, which yielded one fifth and two sixth places, they could easily have finished third overall behind the winners, USSR.

If 1965 had been a trough of despair for our women athletes, then the sun was beginning to shine through now, and we even had what was to be our only European Cup final victory until 1973 through Lillian Board, who had made her mark as an international star that summer and won the 400 metres in Kiev in 53.7, the second fastest of her career up to that point.

Any doubt about the excitement of such a team competition was swept away in the men's final. After the last track event, the 4 × 400 metres relay, the USSR had retained the Cup by just one single point, with 81, ahead of West Germany and East Germany, who both had 80, though the West Germans were awarded second place on the grounds of more individual victories. Not only did this result prove tense in itself; it also silenced cynics who had predicted long before the inauguration of the Cup that the Soviet Union would always win it. The increasing strength of the two Germanys was very real, and in the three years before the next European Cup, in 1970, they were to nose their way ahead of the Russians.

In 1970 the East German women won the final in Budapest with 70 points, ahead of West Germany (63) and the dethroned Russians, who were able to gather together only a paltry 43 points for third place. The Soviet men fared slightly better in their final at Stockholm, beating the West Germans narrowly, but still losing their crown to the East Germans by nearly 10 points.

Once again the British men failed to make the final, but this time there was a more legitimate excuse and one that did not affect any other entry in the European Cup: the Commonwealth Games. The dual participation in Commonwealth and European athletics may have some advantages to British athletes, but an awkward clash can play havoc. So it was that just a week after the end of the Commonwealth Games in Edinburgh, essentially low-key among major Games, the British men found themselves, mentally and physically weary, in Zurich for a European Cup semi-final against five countries that had been preparing all year for this competition.

Zurich was definitely the low point of 1970. Britain had only one winner, and he, paradoxically, was a field events man – and a thrower into the bargain. Dave Travis, just crowned Commonwealth champion, produced a Commonwealth record of 273ft 9in to win and defeat the Soviet Olympic champion, Janis Lusis. But that was the only joy. As a team, Britain was not within 30 points of reaching the final, finishing third and out of the competition for another three years.

The British girls, meanwhile, were coping better with post-Edinburgh blues

Right: *Lillian Board gave British fans something to cheer about when she won Britain's first European Cup final victory – in the 400 metres at Kiev in 1967.*

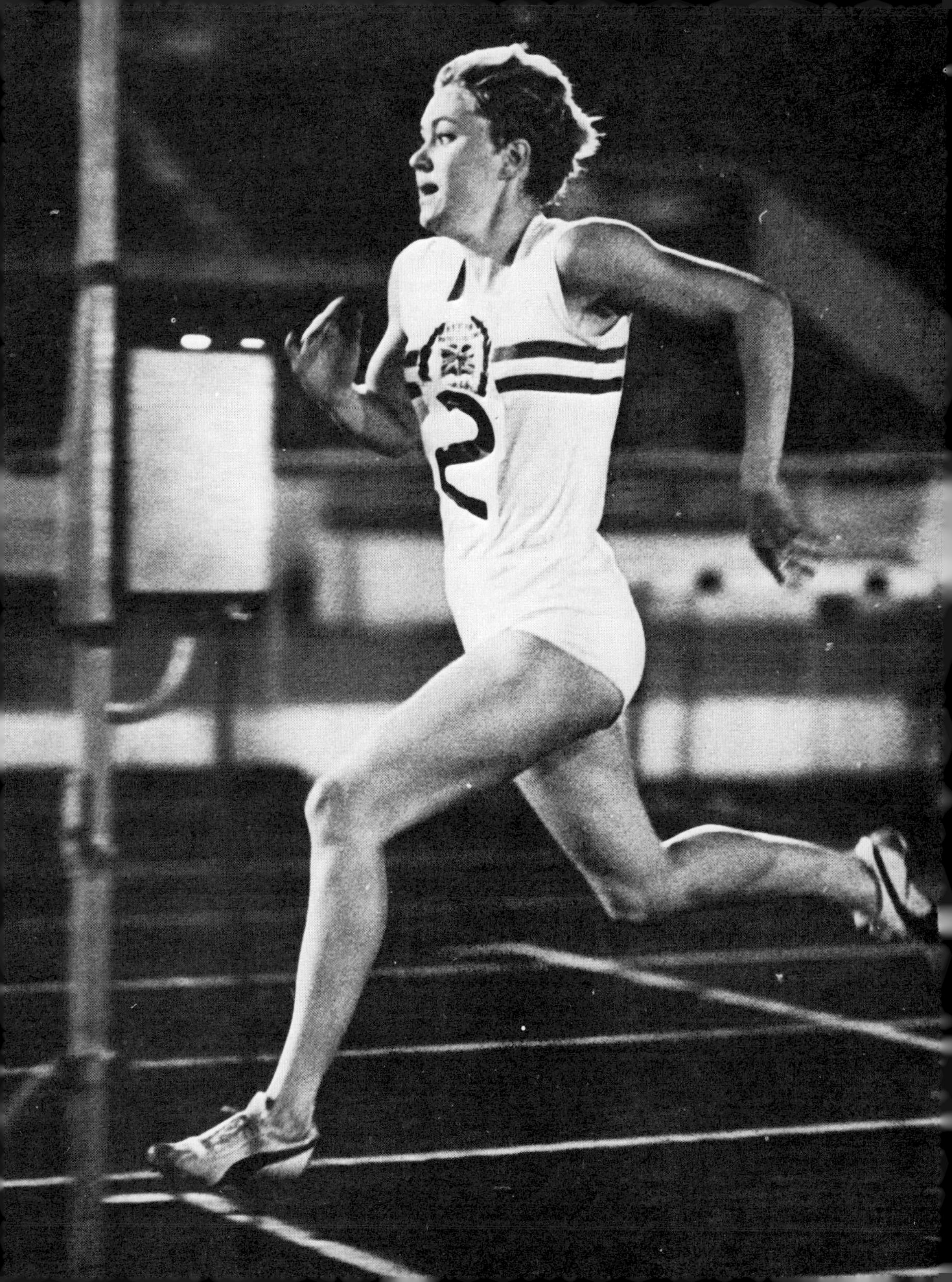

ATHLETICS 75

Frank Clement wins the 1500 metres at Edinburgh.

in their semi-final and qualified comfortably, helped by UK records from Margaret Critchley (23.2 200m) and Christine Bell (13.4 100m hurdles). But the final in Budapest was something of a disappointment as Britain finished one point behind fourth-placed Poland (33), only just avoiding sharing the wooden spoon with Hungary.

So, three British attempts in the European Cup had not been overwhelmingly successful, and when the 1973 celebration was awarded to Edinburgh there was much speculation about how we would cope: would it be humiliation or inspiration?

The opening day, the women's final saw a crushing display of superiority by the East Germans, who piled up 72 out of a possible maximum of 78 points – with a world record in the javelin (216ft 10in) by Ruth Fuchs thrown in for good measure. It left their old rivals, the USSR, with their hands full trying to ward off the attack of a newcomer to the European Cup scene, Bulgaria, who had made dramatic strides in the previous seasons and only just failed to wrest second place from the Soviets. Britain, without an individual winner, finished fifth.

But it was the men's track performances that will long stay in the British fans' memories. After such a chequered history in European Cup competition, which some felt must have been designed to hold up our national athletic deficiencies for all to see, it was glorious to savour some British success at last. On the Saturday, Frank Clement ran away from the 1500 metres field to become (after Lillian Board) Britain's second ever European Cup final winner. And then on Sunday, Alan Pascoe (400 metres hurdles), Andy Carter

(800 metres), Chris Monk (200 metres), and Brendan Foster (5000 metres) became our third, fourth, fifth, and sixth such winners. We had waited six years for our second European Cup winner – and then five came in just over 24 hours!

Britain's score on the track (50 points) was higher than any other nation, but once again the field events tempered that score. Finally Britain finished fourth with 71½, while the USSR regained their men's title from East Germany, despite having been disqualified in the sprint relay. For the first time, however, British fans were able to say; well, perhaps it isn't such a bad event after all.

In 1975 it may be more difficult. It would be too much to hope for such track success again, and although the throwers have improved, the jumping events in Britain are still of a lamentable standard by world class. The event begins with preliminary rounds among the smaller nations in May and June, and then the semi-finals proper are staged on the weekend of 12, 13 July. The British men are drawn at home, on the Crystal Palace track, while other men's semi-finals are being held at Leipzig and Turin. The women's semi-finals are held the same weekend at Budapest, Ludenscheid (W. Germany), and Sofia, with both men's and women's finals being held in Nice on 16, 17 August.

EUROPEAN CUP RESULTS

1965
Men (Stuttgart): **1** USSR 86; **2** West Germany 85; **3** Poland 69; **4** East Germany 69; **5** France 60; **6** Great Britain 48.
Women (Kassel): **1** USSR 56; **2** East Germany 42; **3** Poland 38; **4** West Germany 37; **5** Hungary 32; **6** Netherlands 25.
1967
Men (Kiev): **1** USSR 81; **2** West Germany 80; **3** East Germany 80; **4** Poland 68; **5** France 57; **6** Hungary 53.
Women (Kiev): **1** USSR 51; **2** East Germany 43; **3** West Germany 36; **4** Poland 35; **5** Great Britain 34; **6** Hungary 32.
1970
Men (Stockholm): **1** East Germany 102; **2** USSR 92½; **3** West Germany 91; **4** Poland 82; **5** France 77½; **6** Sweden 68; **7** Italy 47.
Women (Budapest): **1** East Germany 70; **2** West Germany 63; **3** USSR 43; **4** Poland 33; **5** Great Britain 32; **6** Hungary 32.
1973
Men (Edinburgh): **1** USSR 82½; **2** East Germany 78½; **3** West Germany 76; **4** Great Britain 71½; **5** Finland 64½; **6** France 45.
Women (Edinburgh): **1** East Germany 72; **2** USSR 52; **3** Bulgaria 50; **4** West Germany 36; **5** Great Britain 36; **6** Romania 27.

1975 European Cup

MEN
Qualifying Round (14–15 June)
At Athens: Austria, Bulgaria, Denmark, Greece, Luxembourg, Norway, Romania.
At Lisbon: Belgium, Iceland, Irish Republic, Netherlands, Portugal, Spain, Switzerland.
(First three teams in each tie qualify for semi-final round)

Semi-Final Round (12–13 July)
At Leipzig: East Germany, Finland, France, Yugoslavia, plus second-placed teams from Athens and Lisbon ties.
(France, as hosts, qualify automatically for final; plus the other two best teams)
At London: Poland, Soviet Union, Sweden, United Kingdom, plus winner of Lisbon tie and third-placed team from Athens.
(Soviet Union, as holders, qualify automatically for final; plus the other two best teams)
At Turin: Czechoslovakia, Hungary, Italy, West Germany, plus winner of Athens tie and third-placed team from Lisbon.
(First two teams qualify for final)

WOMEN
Qualifying Round (14–15 June)
At Madrid: Belgium, Czechoslovakia, Portugal, Spain, Sweden, Switzerland.
At Osijek: Austria, Denmark, Iceland, Irish Republic, Norway, Yugoslavia.
(First three teams in each tie qualify for semi-final round)

Semi-Final Round (12–13 July)
At Budapest: France, Hungary, Romania, Soviet Union, plus winner of Osijek tie and third-placed team from Madrid.
(France, as hosts, qualify automatically for final; plus the other two best teams)
At Ludenscheid: Finland, Italy, Poland, West Germany, plus winner of Madrid tie and third-placed team from Osijek.
(First two teams qualify for final)
At Sofia: Bulgaria, East Germany, Netherlands, United Kingdom, plus second-placed teams from Madrid and Osijek ties.
(East Germany, as holders, qualify automatically for final; plus the other two best teams)

EUROPEAN CUP FORM CHART

As a guide to the prospects for the 1975 European Cup finals, to be staged in Nice on 16–17 August, we present here the leading 1974 performer in each event from the nations most likely to reach the finals. The countries are placed in the order of finish that would occur in a hypothetical contest based on those figures, with East Germany emerging as favourites for both the men's and women's competitions.

MEN

Event	*East Germany*	*Soviet Union*	*West Germany*	*United Kingdom*	*Finland*	*Poland*	*France*	*Czechoslovakia*
100m	10.2 Zenk	10.1 Silovs	10.0 Ommer	10.3 Halliday	10.3 Vilen	10.2 Nowosz	10.2 Metz	10.3 Matousek
200m	20.2 Zenk	20.5 Zhidkikh	20.5 Hofmeister	20.5 Jenkins	20.5 Rajamaki	20.6 Werner	20.6 Cherrier	20.8 Matousek
400m	45.8 Scheibe	46.4 Nossenko	45.0 Honz	45.2 Jenkins	45.5 Kukkoaho	46.2 Wasik	46.0 Demarthon	46.4 Kodejs
800m	1:46.0 Fromm	1:46.0 Ponomaryov	1:46.3 Schmid	1:45.6 Carter	1:45.9 Taskinen	1:46.7 Wasilewski	1:46.8 Philippe	1:47.1 Plachy
1500m	3:39.0 Justus	3:40.0 Anissim	3:39.0 Wessinghage	3:37.4 Clement	3:39.4 Vasala	3:39.3 Malinowski	3:37.9 Philippe	3:39.4 Kovac
5000m	13:24.0 Kuschmann	13:29.8 Kuznyetsov	13:32.0 Hildenbrand	13:14.6 Foster	13:24.6 Viren	13:28.0 Malinowski	13:43.4 Cairoche	13:28.2 Hoffman
10,000m	28:09.6 Kuschmann	28:24.0 Motschalov	28:20.8 Kruger	27:48.6 Black	28:18.4 Paivarinta	28:25.2 Malinowski	28:37.6 Liardet	28:21.8 Hoffman
3000m Steeplechase	8:30.0 Straub	8:26.6 Skripka	8:18.0 Karst	8:22.6 Davies	8:19.6 Kantanen	8:15.0 Malinowski	8:24.6 Buchheit	8:28.0 Moravcik
110m Hurdles	13.3 Siebeck	13.7 Perevertsev	13.6 Schumann	13.7 Kirkpatrick	14.2 Salin	13.3 Wodzynski	13.2 Drut	13.5 Cech
400m Hurdles	49.2 Schonberger	49.3 Gavrilenko	49.8 Ziegler	48.8 Pascoe	51.1 Koivu	49.8 Hewelt	48.9 Nallet	49.1 Kodejs
High Jump	2.20m (7′2½″) Beilschmidt	2.25m (7′4½″) Sapka	2.18m (7′1¾″) Boller	2.11m (6′11″) Boreham	2.19m (7′2¼″) Sundell	2.20m (7′2½″) Wszola	2.18m (7′1¾″) Sainte-Rose	2.22m (7′3¼″) Maly
Pole Vault	5.25m (17′2¾″) Reinhardt	5.40m (17′8½″) Kishkun	5.33m (17′5¾″) Kuretzky	5.20m (17′0¾″) Bull	5.30m (17′4½″) Kalliomaki	5.42m (17′9¼″) Slusarski	5.20m (17′0¾″) Abada	5.00m (16′4¾″) Hadinger
Long Jump	8.18m (26′10″) Klauss	8.17m (26′9¾″) Podluzhny	8.00m (26′3″) Baumgartner	7.98m (26′2¼″) Lerwill	7.79m (25′6¾″) Suvitie	8.15m (26′9″) Cybulski	8.00m (26′3″) Bonheme	7.78m (25′6¼″) Broz
Triple Jump	17.06m (55′11¾″) Drehmel	17.23m (56′6½″) Saneyev	16.44m (53′11¼″) Franz	15.78m (51′9¼″) Clark	16.39m (53′9¼″) Kuukasjarvi	16.87m (55′4¼″) Joachimowski	16.40m (53′9¾″) Lamitie	16.68m (54′8¾″) Vycichlo
Shot	20.91m (68′7¼″) Rothenburg	21.70m (71′2½″) Baryshnikov	20.80m (68′3″) Reichenbach	21.37m (70′1½″) Capes	21.26m (69′9″) Stahlberg	21.19m (69′6¼″) Komar	19.00m (62′4″) Beer	20.47m (67′2″) Vlk
Discus	65.64m (215′4″) Pachale	65.22m (214′0″) Penzikov	64.26m (210′10″) Neu	64.94m (213′1″) Tancred	66.52m (218′3″) Kahma	63.52m (208′5″) Gajdzinski	59.76m (196′1″) Piette	67.18m (220′5″) Danek
Hammer	76·60m (251′4″) Theimer	76.66m (251′6″) Spiridonov	73.44m (240′11″) Klein	71.00m (232′11″) Chipchase	71.74m (235′4″) Kangas	71.00m (232′11″) Rys	70.30m (230′8″) Prikhodko	72.14m (236′8″) Hajek
Javelin	85.46m (280′4″) Hanisch	86.70m (284′5″) Makarov	88.26m (289′7″) Wolfermann	84.92m (278′7″) Clover	89.58m (293′11″) Siitonen	80.36m (263′8″) Damszel	80.90m (265′5″) Leroy	80.58m (264′4″) Badiak
4×100m	39.0	39.0	39.0	39.7	39.5	39.4	38.7	39.3
4×400m	3:04.0	3:05.3	3:03.5	3:03.3	3:03.6	3:05.4	3:04.6	3:06.3

WOMEN

Event	*East Germany*	*Soviet Union*	*Poland*	*West Germany*	*Romania*	*Bulgaria*	*United Kingdom*	*France*
100m	11.0 Stecher	11.1 Maslakova	10.9 Szewinska	11.2 Richter	11.5 Stefanescu	11.5 Panayatova	11.1 Lynch	11.4 Telliez
200m	22.4 Stecher	23.2 Sidorova	22.0 Szewinska	23.2 Richter	23.5 Stefanescu	23.6 Panayatova	23.0 Golden	23.4 Telliez
400m	50.7 Streidt	51.2 Ilyina	49.9 Szewinska	50.9 Wilden	51.2 Suman	53.7 Shtereva	51.8 Murray	52.9 Leclerc
800m	1:58.8 Hoffmeister	2:00.1 Gerasimova	2:00.4 Katolik	2:01.5 Klein	1:58.6 Suman	1:58.1 Tomova	2:02.8 Kiernan	1:59.9 Dubois
1500m	4:02.3 Hoffmeister	4:05.9 Kazankina	4:14.2 Katolik	4:11.5 Wellmann	4:10.5 Andrei	4:05.0 Tomova	4:10.7 Allison	4:12.0 Dubois
100m Hurdles	12.4 Ehrhardt	13.0 Lebedyeva	12.5 Nowak	13.2 Koschinski	12.9 Stefanescu	13.3 Sokolova	13.0 Vernon	13.3 Rega
High Jump	1.95m (6′4¾″) Witschas	1.86m (6′1¼″) Filatova	1.78m (5′10″) Holowinska	1.86m (6′1¼″) Wagner	1.92m (6′3½″) Ioan	1.80m (5′10¾″) Valkanova	1.86m (6′1¼″) Lawton	1.84m (6′0½″) Debourse
Long Jump	6.77m (22′2½″) Schmalfeld	6.66m (21′10¼″) Alfeyeva	6.40m (21′0″) Wlodarczyk	6.54m (21′5½″) Wilkes	6.58m (21′7¼″) Stefanescu	6.34m (20′9¾″) Sokolova	6.38m (20′11¼″) Martin-Jones	6.28m (20′7¼″) Curtet
Shot	20.61m (67′7½″) Adam	21.22m (69′7½″) Chizhova	18.98m (62′3¼″) Chewinska	17.30m (56′9¼″) Wilms	18.02m (59′1½″) Cioltan	19.93m (65′4¾″) Khristova	15.40m (50′6¼″) Bedford	16.01m (52′6½″) Bertimon
Discus	66.22m (217′3″) Hinzmann	69.90m (229′4″) Melnik	57.14m (187′5″) Rosani	60.20m (197′6″) Westermann	65.84m (216′0″) Menis	68.48m (224′8″) Vergova	55.44m (181′11″) Payne	52.00m (170′7″) Jarry
Javelin	67.22m (220′6″) Fuchs	61.18m (200′9″) Babitsch	63.08m (206′11″) Kinder	60.40m (198′2″) Becker	58.62m (192′4″) Pecec	62.60m (205′4″) Mollova	55.04m (180′7″) Sanderson	50.22m (164′9″) Cretel
4×100m	42.5	43.7	43.1	42.8	45.7	45.6	43.9	44.2
4×400m	3:25.2	3:26.1	3:26.4	3:27.9	3:30.8	3:37.3	3:29.2	3:36.9

Directory of Current Polyurethane All-Weather Athletic Tracks in Great Britain

Parliament Hill
Nassington Road
Hampstead Heath
London
8-lane 400-metre circuit with full field events facilities

Kirkby Sports Stadium
Whitefield Drive
Kirkby
Nr Liverpool
8-lane 400-metre circuit with full field events facilities

Ashton Playing Fields
Woodford Green
Essex
6-lane 400-metre circuit with 8-lane sprint straight and full field events facilities

Vansittart Road
Recreation Ground
Windsor
Berkshire
6-lane 400-metre circuit with field events facilities

Wards Langloan
Coatbridge
Scotland
8-lane 400-metre circuit with field events facilities

'TARTAN' TRACK INSTALLATIONS

Military Stadium
Queens Avenue
Aldershot
Hampshire

Cwmbran Stadium
Torfaen District County
Henllys Way
Cwmbran
Gwent NP4 7XL

Harvey Hadden Stadium
Wigman Road
Bilborough
Nottingham

Clairville Stadium
Park Road South
Middlesbrough
Cleveland

Gateshead Sports Stadium
Neilson Road
Gateshead
Co Durham

New River Sports Centre
White Hart Lane
Haringey
London N22

West London Stadium
Du Cane Road
Wormwood Scrubs
London W12

Whitchurch Athletics Centre
Banfield
Whitchurch
Bristol BS14 0XA

Aldersley Stadium
Aldersley Road
Tettenhall
Wolverhampton

Hadley Stadium
Waterloo Road
Smethwick
Warley
West Midlands

Crystal Palace National
Sports Centre
Norwood
London SE19

Meadowbank Sports Centre
London Road
Edinburgh

Princess Mary Playing Fields
Bradford Road
Rawfold
Cleckheaton
Yorkshire

Grangemouth Stadium
Kersiebank Avenue
Grangemouth
Scotland

Edinburgh Corporation

Meadowbank Sports Centre

**Badminton · Athletics · Cycling · Golf · Judo
Basketball · Keep Fit · Table Tennis
Weight Training · Rock Climbing**

Facilities for viewing or participating in these and many other activities
Open 7 days a week 9a.m. to 11p.m.
Cafeteria for meals and snacks
Car Park adjacent
For further information about events
Telephone 031·661·5351

POLYURETHANE ALL-WEATHER TRACKS IN GREAT BRITAIN

The new electronic scoreboard at Crystal Palace, in South East London, welcomes the athletes of the world to the capital stadium of the United Kingdom. photo Tony Duffy.

Mary Peters Track
Queen's University
Upper Malone Road
Belfast
Northern Ireland

Stretford Stadium
Longford Park
Stretford
Trafford
Manchester

285

Official Bodies, Officers, and Addresses

BRITISH AMATEUR ATHLETIC BOARD

President: HRH The Prince Philip, Duke of Edinburgh KG, KT, OM, GBE
Chairman: H.M. Abrahams CBE
Hon Sec: A.A. Gold CBE
Hon Treasurer: Miss M. Hartman MBE
Asst Hon Treasurer: H.R.H. Stinson
Clerk to the Board: Miss M. Tupholme
Offices of the Board: 70 Brompton Road, London SW3 1EE. Tel: 01–584 7715.

AMATEUR ATHLETIC ASSOCIATION

Patron: Her Majesty The Queen
President: The Most Hon The Marquess of Exeter KCMG, LLD
Hon Sec: B.E. Willis
Hon Treasurer: R.L. Stroud ACIS, AIB
National Administrator: F.J. Martell JP
Clerk to the AAA: Miss K.M. Gabb
Offices of the AAA: 70 Brompton Road, London SW3 1EE. Tel: 01–584 7715.

MIDLAND COUNTIES AAA

Hon Sec: M.A. Farrell
Offices: Devonshire House, High Street, Deritend, Birmingham B12 0LP. Tel: 021–773 1631.

NORTHERN COUNTIES AA

Hon Sec: J.C. Rice
Offices: Rooms 288–290 Corn Exchange Building, Fennell Street, Manchester M4 3HF. Tel: 061–834 2603.

SOUTHERN COUNTIES AAA

Hon Sec: A.J.C. Kendall BEM
Offices: 70 Brompton Road, London SW3 1EE. Tel: 01–584 7715.

WELSH AAA

Hon Sec: B.L. Baldwin MBE, 9 Campbell Terrace, Mountain Ash, Glamorgan.

NORTHERN IRELAND AAA

Hon Sec: G.E. Wilson, 72 Woodview Crescent, Lisburn, Co. Antrim, Northern Ireland.

SCOTTISH AAA

Hon Sec: E.S. Murray, 25 Bearsden Road, Glasgow G13 1YL. Tel: 041–959 4436.

WOMEN'S AMATEUR ATHLETIC ASSOCIATION

President: Lady Luke
Chairman: Mrs V. Searle
Hon Sec: Miss M. Hartman MBE
Hon Treasurer: Miss E.M. Holland
Offices: 70 Brompton Road, London SW3 1EE. Tel: 01–584 6876.

MIDLAND COUNTIES WAAA

Hon Sec: Mrs D. Nelson Neal, 22 Wrekin Road, Perry Barr, Birmingham 22C.

NORTHERN COUNTIES WAAA

Hon Sec: Mrs M. Oakley, 10 Byemoor Close, Easby Lane, Great Ayton, County Cleveland.

SOUTHERN COUNTIES WAAA

Hon Sec: Mrs J. Lindsay, 28 Wykeham Hill, Wembley HA9 9RZ, Middlesex.

WELSH WAAA

Hon Sec: Miss R.M. Courtney, 135 Rhyd-y-Penan Road, Cyncoed, Cardiff CF2 6PZ.

NORTHERN IRELAND WAAA

Hon Sec: Mrs M. Kyle, 'Tir-Na-Nog', Old Galgorm Road, Ballymena, Co. Antrim, Northern Ireland.

SCOTTISH WAAA

Hon Sec: Mrs I.M. Brown, 11 Rutland Street, Edinburgh 1.

UNITED KINGDOM COACHING SCHEME

The Coaching Scheme is administered by a coaching committee. General enquiries should be made to: The Coaching Office, BAAB, 63 Woodfield Lane, Lower Ashtead, Surrey. Tel: Ashtead (Surrey) 77169.
Hon Coaching Secretary: S/Ldr C.N. Cobb MBE, RAF (Retd).

BAAB NATIONAL COACHES IN ATHLETICS

Principal National Coaches: D.C.V. Watts & J. Le Masurier.
National Coaches: W.E. Marlow (Midlands), T. McNab, D.R. Kay (South), W.H.C. Paish, C.T. Johnson (North), F. Dick (Scotland), M. Arnold (Wales).

Principal National Coaches work from Headquarters and are responsible for technical direction. National Coaches are attached to an area or region. Six joint coaching committees have been set up and applications for the services of the appropriate coach should be made to the Hon Secretary of the joint coaching committee as follows:
Midlands: Miss M. Lingen, 23 Brentnall Drive, Four Oaks, Sutton Coldfield, Warwickshire.
North: Mr G.K. Thompson, 'Gorey', 23 Pannatt Hill, Millom, Cumbria.
N. Ireland: Mr N. Morton, 24 Beechgrove Gardens, Belfast BT6 0NP.
Scotland: c/o Whitehall, Shore Road, Aberdour KY3 0TX, Fife.
South: Mrs A. Swallow, c/o 4 Southfields, Roxton, Beds MK44 3EX.
Wales: Mr J.A. Clemo, 10 Church Street, Cardiff, Glamorgan, Wales.

Further information on the British Amateur Athletic Board and the Coaching Scheme can be found in *British Athletics Handbook 1975*. This Handbook also contains results of all international matches and championships of the eight bodies who constitute the BAAB, and a complete list of records – world, European, Commonwealth, and UK all-comers and national. *British Athletics Handbook 1975* is obtainable from the AAA/BAAB Sales Centre, 5 Church Road, Great Bookham, Surrey. Price 75p.